WILEY

Interpretation and Application of International Standards on Auditing

D1388478

WILEY

Interpretation and Application of International Standards on Auditing

Steven Collings
Leavitt Walmsley Associates Ltd

A John Wiley and Sons, Ltd., Publication

Extracts from Final IFAC Publications or Exposure Drafts of Proposed IFAC Publications

All extracts from the 2010 Handbook of International Quality Control, Auditing, Review, Other Assurance,
and Related Services Pronouncements (April 2010) of the International Auditing and Assurance Board,
published by the International Federation of Accountants (IFAC) in April 2010 are used with permission of
IFAC.

Library of Congress Cataloging-in-Publication Data

Collings, Steven
Interpretation and application of international standards on auditing / Steven Collings.
    p. cm.
  ISBN 978-0-470-66112-3 (paperback)
  1. Auditing – Standards.   2. Financial Statements – Standards.   I. Title.
  HF5626.C653 2011
  657′.450218–dc22

A catalogue record for this book is available from the British Library.

ISBN 978-0-470-66112-3 (paperback); ISBN 978-0-470-97970-9 (ebk);
ISBN 978-1-119-97378-2 (epub); ISBN 978-1-119-97379-9 (emobi)

Typeset in 10/11pt Times by Aptara Inc., New Delhi, India
Printed and bound in the United Kingdom by TJ International, Padstow, Cornwall

CONTENTS

Chapter	Title	Page No.
	Preface	ix
	Acknowledgements	xi
	About the Author	xiii
1	The History of Auditing	1
2	The Clarity Project	7
3	The Code of Ethics for Professional Accountants	15
4	ISA 200 (revised and redrafted) Overall Objectives of the Independent Auditor and the Conduct of an Audit in Accordance with International Standards on Auditing	25
5	ISA 210 (redrafted) Agreeing the Terms of Audit Engagements	35
6	ISA 220 (redrafted) Quality Control for an Audit of Financial Statements	39
7	ISA 230 (revised) Audit Documentation	45
8	ISA 240 (redrafted) The Auditor's Responsibilities Relating to Fraud in an Audit of Financial Statements	49
9	ISA 250 (redrafted) Consideration of Laws and Regulations in an Audit of Financial Statements	63
10	ISA 260 (revised and redrafted) Communication with Those Charged with Governance	69
11	ISA 265 Communicating Deficiencies in Internal Control to Those Charged with Governance and Management	79
12	ISA 300 (redrafted) Planning an Audit of Financial Statements	85
13	ISA 315 (redrafted) Identifying and Assessing the Risks of Material Misstatement Through Understanding the Entity and its Environment	91
14	ISA 320 (revised and redrafted) Materiality in Planning and Performing an Audit	121
15	ISA 330 (redrafted) The Auditor's Responses to Assessed Risks	127
16	ISA 402 (revised and redrafted) Audit Considerations Relating to an Entity Using a Service Organisation	135
17	ISA 450 (revised and redrafted) Evaluation of Misstatements Identified during the Audit	141
18	ISA 500 (redrafted) Audit Evidence	145
19	ISA 501 (redrafted) Audit Evidence — Specific Considerations for Selected Items	157

Chapter	Title	Page No.
20	ISA 505 (revised and redrafted) External Confirmations	165
21	ISA 510 (redrafted) Initial Audit Engagements — Opening Balances	169
22	ISA 520 (redrafted) Analytical Procedures	173
23	ISA 530 (redrafted) Audit Sampling	181
24	ISA 540 (revised and redrafted) Auditing Accounting Estimates, Including Fair Value Accounting Estimates, and Related Disclosures	191
25	ISA 550 (revised and redrafted) Related Parties	203
26	ISA 560 (redrafted) Subsequent Events	213
27	ISA 570 (redrafted) Going Concern	221
28	ISA 580 (revised and redrafted) Management Representations	231
29	ISA 600 (revised and redrafted) Special Considerations — Audits of Group Financial Statements (Including the Work of Component Auditors)	239
30	ISA 610 (redrafted) Using the Work of Internal Auditors	249
31	ISA 620 (revised and redrafted) Using the Work of an Auditor's Expert	253
32	ISA 700 (revised) Forming an Opinion on the Financial Statements	257
33	ISA 705 (revised and redrafted) Modifications to the Opinion in the Independent Auditor's Report	265
34	ISA 706 (revised and redrafted) Emphasis of Matter Paragraphs and Other Matter(s) Paragraphs in the Independent Auditors' Report	269
35	ISA 710 (redrafted) Comparative Information — Corresponding Figures and Comparative Financial Statements	273
36	ISA 720 (redrafted) The Auditor's Responsibilities Relating to Other Information in Documents Containing Audited Financial Statements	279
37	ISA 800 (revised and redrafted) Special Considerations — Audits of Financial Statements Prepared in Accordance with Special Purpose Frameworks	283
38	ISA 805 (revised and redrafted) Special Considerations — Audits of Single Financial Statements and Specific Elements, Accounts or Items of a Financial Statement	287
39	ISA 810 (revised and redrafted) Engagements to Report on Summary Financial Statements	291
40	The Framework for the Preparation and Presentation of Financial Statements	299

Chapter	Title	Page No.
41	IFRS for Small and Medium Entities (SMEs)	307
42	ISQC 1 'Quality Control for Firms that Perform Audits and Reviews of Financial Statements, and Other Assurance and Related Services Engagements'	321
	Appendix 1: Overview of IFRS and IAS	335
	Appendix 2: Illustrative Audit Tests	433
	Appendix 3: Illustrative Financial Statements	445
	Appendix 4: Illustrative Auditor Report (UK and Ireland)	607
	Index	617

PREFACE

Auditing throughout the world has undergone a substantial amount of change in recent years. The well-publicised corporate disasters that rocked the profession over the last few years have largely contributed to these changes. In many countries domestic standards were replaced with International Standards on Auditing (ISAs) in an attempt to ensure that auditors throughout the world were applying the same level of standards throughout an audit assignment and, thus, ensuring that audit quality remained consistent on a country by country basis.

Standards, whether they are International Financial Reporting Standards (IFRS) or ISAs, frequently change in an attempt to improve and clarify their application throughout the audit and accounting profession. This publication aims to assist auditors in the interpretation and application of auditing standards as it is often the case that many ISAs can be extremely complex and difficult to apply in real life situations. Throughout the profession, audit firms are often criticised for failing to apply auditing standards sufficiently enough to enable an efficient audit to take place. In today's modern profession the correct application of auditing standards is pivotal — not only to demonstrate to professional regulators that auditing standards have been applied throughout an audit assignment — but also to ensure the audit client receives a service that is both beneficial and cost effective to them, and undertaken in accordance with a prescribed framework.

This publication looks at the full ISAs. Most jurisdictions have adopted ISAs but have tailored them to their specific requirements, for example the UK has adopted ISAs but they are termed ISA (UK and Ireland). This publication has been written following the IAASB 'Clarity Project' which is discussed in Chapter 2. The final versions of the Clarified standards were issued in October 2009. The new standards, on which this publication is based, come into effect for audits for periods commencing on or after 15 December 2009, thus, in many cases, auditors will not be affected by this deadline until audits of December 2010 year ends.

Notwithstanding that the Clarified standards may not affect some auditors until December 2010 year ends, it is imperative that auditors are in the process of considering how they will be ready to implement the Clarified standards and this publication aims to assist accountants and auditors in understanding the requirements of each Clarified standard together with the Ethical standards by which professional accountants are bound.

Packed with illustrations, this publication illustrates the practicalities in applying the Clarified ISAs, providing a summary of the main technical content of the IFRS/IAS and providing illustrative financial statements and auditors' reports.

ACKNOWLEDGEMENTS

Writing a book, whether a professional title or a work of fiction, is a project which brings with it a whole host of challenges and is certainly not a one-person project. This book would not have seen the light of day had it not been for certain individuals who have contributed significantly to its production. Every individual who knows me has, in one way or another, influenced my career and my writing and it is to all those that do know me that I express my heartfelt thanks and gratitude.

I would like to place on record my sincere thanks and gratitude to the publishing team at John Wiley & Sons. In particular I would like to thank the Executive Commissioning Editor at John Wiley & Sons, Jenny McCall, for her support during the writing and publishing stages as well as her colleague Gemma Valler for her support during the production of this book. Without the support and input of these individuals, this book would not have been possible.

I would like to thank Francesca Warren for all her help in the copyediting process.

I would like to thank Mr Les Leavitt, Managing Director of Leavitt Walmsley Associates Ltd for his support over the years. Les has been extremely supportive of this project and has been closely involved with its production.

I would like to express my sincere thanks to my technical reviewers: the lecturer and author, Mr Roger Bryant MSc BSc (Econ) FCA FCCA of Small Company Reporting Ltd, Caroline Fox BA ACA, Chartered Accountant and Mrs Annette Smyth MAAT ACCA of Bob Collyer & Co Accountants, for their input into this book and whose opinions and comments have been invaluable during the writing of this book.

I would also like to thank the team at IRIS Software for their permission to use some aspects of their audit methodologies contained in their AUDITOR Programme.

Last, but certainly not least, I would like to thank all my family and friends, all of whom feature in this book at some point, for their support during the course of this project.

All errors are my own and come with apologies.

ABOUT THE AUTHOR

Steven Collings FMAAT FCCA is the Audit and Technical Director at Leavitt Walmsley Associates Limited, who are based in Manchester in the United Kingdom. Steven qualified as a Member of the Association of Accounting Technicians (AAT) in 2000 and then went on to qualify as an Associate Chartered Certified Accountant (ACCA) in 2005. Steven also holds the ACCA Diploma in International Financial Reporting Standards (DipIFRS) and the Certificates in IFRS and International Auditing Standards from ACCA. Steven also holds Statutory Auditor status in the United Kingdom.

Steven has specialised in auditing and financial reporting issues and has been writing professionally for several years. He has written several articles which have been published in the various accounting media concerning auditing and financial reporting. Steven writes extensively for AccountingWEB.co.uk on financial reporting and auditing issues, and has also had several articles published in various professional journals.

Steven lectures on all aspects of financial reporting and auditing issues and regularly speaks at events held for accountants in practice.

Some examples of Steven's articles can be found on the book's companion website at www.wiley.com/go/collings

1 THE HISTORY OF AUDITING

In order to appreciate the significance of correct interpretation and application of International Standards on Auditing (ISAs), one needs to first set the historical context.

Auditing has been a worldwide profession for hundreds of years. Historically, auditing was concerned with accounting for government activities and reviewing the work done by tax collectors. In the early years of auditing, the keeping and maintaining of accounting records was done primarily to detect fraudulent activity. The industrial revolution in the mid 1700s to the mid 1800s was responsible for the increased demand in auditors because this period saw an increase in responsibility being passed from owners to managers. This led to an increased requirement for auditors who were independent of management and who were engaged not only to be alert for errors within financial records but also errors within the records. In simple terms, deliberate errors in order to achieve personal financial gain were deemed to be fraudulent activity (as is still the case today) whilst error was (and still is) unintentional.

During the early 1700s the concept of 'sampling' was introduced. Sampling is where auditors select a sample of items that make up various balances and was used where it is not economically viable to physically examine all the transactions that have taken place. This practice is still pivotal today. This is one of the main areas which this publication looks at in respect of the redrafted ISAs.

During the 1940s it was clear that the auditor's role had developed into that of providing an opinion on the financial statements and that the detection of fraud and error had taken a very much subordinate role in the objective of an audit. It developed that management were responsible for the prevention and detection of fraud and that the auditor's work should not be concerned primarily with detecting fraud but should be planned in such a way that they will detect a material fraud. This view was formalised much earlier in the United Kingdom (UK) than the 1940s, as Lord Justice Lopez in the Kingston Cotton Mill,1896, said that the auditor's role in an entity should be that of a 'watchdog' rather than a 'bloodhound'. Lord Justice Lopez said:

> *It is the duty of an auditor to bring to bear on the work he has to perform that skill, care and caution which a reasonably careful, cautious auditor would use. What is reasonable skill, care and caution must depend on the particular circumstances of each case. An auditor is not bound to be a detective, or, as was said to approach his work with suspicion, or with a foregone conclusion that there is something wrong. He is a watchdog not a bloodhound. He is justified in believing tried servants of the company in whom confidence is placed by the company. He is entitled to assume that they are honest and rely upon their representations, provided he takes reasonable care.*
>
> Lord Justice Lopez – Kingston Cotton Mill 1896.

The view here was that the auditor should act with such reasonable care and skill in order that their work will have a reasonable chance of detecting a material fraud and other errors. This view is still the same today with auditing standards now requiring auditors to adopt and maintain a degree of professional scepticism by assuming that the financial statements will contain a material misstatement due to fraud. This issue is discussed in Chapter 8.

RISK-BASED AUDITING

Since the early 1980s audit fees have increased to reflect the fact that audits need to be undertaken effectively and efficiently. Audit firms have developed a technique known as 'risk-based' auditing which involves the auditor determining the nature, timing and extent of various audit procedures. This method of auditing is based on the auditor's assessment of the risk that the financial statements of an entity contain a material misstatement.

REGULATION

In the vast majority of countries who practice audit, the auditing profession is regulated under legislation. For example, in the UK auditing is a regulated profession under the Companies Act. It is for this reason that not all professional accountants can practice audit-related work, unless they have obtained statutory auditor status.

The objective of the audit exercise is to enable the auditor to express an opinion on whether the financial statements present fairly in all material respects the entity's affairs at the reporting date as well as form an opinion on whether they have been properly prepared in accordance with the applicable reporting framework.

INTERNAL AND EXTERNAL AUDITING

Auditing predominantly takes two forms: internal and external audit. An internal audit function is usually a department that is set up within an entity which is staffed by employees of that entity who will provide internal audit functions which benefit the entity as a whole. In many cases, the role of internal audit is often outsourced. Internal audit departments will have their roles dictated by management of that organisation. Internal auditors will comply with their own set of auditing standards which are largely independent of the ISAs. Internal auditing functions by, amongst other things, examining, evaluating and reporting to management on the adequacy and effectiveness of components of the accounting and internal control systems. In other words, internal auditing exists to add value and improve an organisation's operations.

External audit, which this publication is concerned with, is usually a statutory requirement imposed on an entity. For example, in the UK, companies are required by statute to have their financial statements audited if, under the Companies Act 2006, any one of the thresholds shown in table 1.1 are breached.

Where reference to 'net' and 'gross' are made, this is in relation to intra-group trading. Gross means intra-group sales have not been eliminated, net means that elimination has occurred in accordance with the requirement of IAS 27 'Consolidated and Separate Financial Statements'.

Other jurisdictions may have their own eligibility criteria for audit and audit exemption. The auditor's opinion on the financial statements is not an opinion of absolute correctness because of the inherent limitations associated with an audit. The limitations inherent in an audit of general purpose financial statements are discussed in Chapter 4. There is often a concept

Table 1.1   Auditing thresholds

	Turnover	*Balance Sheet (Gross Assets)*	*No. of Employees*
Small company	£6.5 million	£3.26 million	50
Small group	£6.5 million net	£3.26 million net	50
	£7.8 million gross	£3.9 million gross	50
Medium-sized company	£25.9 million	£12.9 million net	250
Medium-sized group	£25.9 million net	£12.9 million net	250
	£31.1 million gross	£15.5 million gross	250

Note: The table relates to accounting periods which commence on or after 6 April 2008, following the amendment by statutory instrument 393.

of perception gap because some third parties often assume that an audited set of financial statements can give absolute assurance. It is for this very reason that reference to 'reasonable assurance' is made within the auditor's report.

It could also be the case that an entity is required to have a statutory audit because the members chose to have an audit when the company was incorporated. This is often the case when a company has such a condition in their Articles of Association.

External stakeholders, such as banks and financiers can also impose a requirement for audit on an entity even if they are not required by statute to have an audit undertaken on their financial statements. In an increasing number of cases, financiers do require a certain level of assurance. In today's modern profession, there are an increasing number of assurance engagements being carried out.

ASSURANCE ENGAGEMENT

An assurance engagement is one where a professional accountant evaluates, or measures, a subject matter that is the responsibility of another party against suitable criteria, and expresses an opinion which provides the intended user with a level of assurance about that subject matter. In other words, it is an engagement to express an opinion giving assurance to a set of people on information which is the responsibility of others.

An audit can be distinguished from other assurance engagements in the following ways:

Audit engagement: the auditor provides a high, but not absolute, level of assurance that the information audited is free from material misstatement. This is expressed positively in the audit report as 'reasonable assurance'.

Review engagement: the auditor provides a moderate level of assurance that the information subject to review is free of material misstatement. This is expressed in the form of 'negative assurance'.

Negative assurance is where an auditor gives an assurance that nothing has come to his/her attention which indicates that the financial statements have not been prepared according to the framework. In other words, the auditor gives his/her assurance in the absence of any evidence to the contrary.

FEATURES OF AN AUDIT

In general terms, an audit will involve the examination of an entity's financial statements and of the disclosures contained therein. As a rule, the auditor is not responsible for preparing the financial statements, though in some cases the auditors may be involved provided adequate safeguards have been implemented to maintain independence. The end result of the audit is the auditor's opinion on the financial statements as to whether the financial statements give a true and fair view, or present fairly in all material respects, the state of the entity's affairs.

In order to arrive at their opinion, the auditor must be seen to be *independent* of the entity that is being subject to audit. For the purposes of audit, 'independent' means not having any significant personal interest in the entity. Ensuring the auditor is independent also guarantees that the objective of the audit is achieved and a professional and unbiased view is taken.

Because it is highly unlikely that two audit assignments will be identical, it is important that audit assignments are undertaken in a logical and structured manner. The objective of the audit is to ensure that the financial statements of an entity give a true and fair view, or present fairly in all material aspects, the state of the company's affairs at its reporting date. It would therefore be irresponsible for the auditor to undertake an audit in a sporadic and unplanned manner.

Before any detailed audit work takes place on an audit assignment, the auditor is required to undertake a thorough programme of planning. Planning is a significant area impacted by the redrafting process of the Clarity project and is looked at in more detail in Chapter 13. Without sufficient planning, the auditor is unable to document that they have gained a sufficient understanding of the entity in order to enable an efficient audit to take place. The planning will take various forms and includes the following programme of documentation:

- the entity's background and history;
- its policies and procedures;
- key management and staff;
- significant accounting policies;
- the environment in which the entity operates;
- accounting systems;
- any problems encountered in previous audits;
- a timetable for key events;
- the audit budget;
- the audit strategy;
- meetings held with the client prior to the audit; and
- meetings of the audit team prior to the client.

A full risk assessment is also required at the planning stage and the audit strategy is then developed as a result of this risk assessment to ensure that the audit procedures adopted during the course of the audit are responsive to the risks identified at the planning stage.

A review of the entire audit process is summarised in table 1.2.

Table 1.2 shows that the initial step in the audit process is the planning of the audit. Two fundamental standards must be complied with in this respect: ISA 300 (redrafted) 'Planning an Audit of Financial Statements' and ISA 315 (redrafted) 'Obtaining an Understanding of the Entity and its Environment and Assessing the Risk of Material Misstatement'.

Table 1.2   The Audit Process

	New Audit	*Recurring Audit*
Legal and ethical matters	Consider	Review
Acceptance and letter of engagement	Prepare and issue	Review and update where necessary
Obtain an understanding of the entity and its environment	Obtain and prepare	Review and update where necessary

The auditor will document their understanding of the accounting and internal control systems present at the audit client. This will also involve the auditor undertaking a risk assessment in order that the procedures the auditor adopts during the course of the detailed audit work are responsive to those risks.

The next step is for the auditor to consider the various ways in which they will generate sufficient and appropriate audit evidence (audit evidence is discussed in Chapter 18). Audit evidence can be obtained from a variety of means, but usually from either tests of controls or substantive procedures, or a mix of both. In determining whether the evidence can be gathered from tests of controls (and, therefore, reduced detailed substantive testing) the auditor must assess whether the internal controls operate effectively; in other words, ensuring that the controls will prevent, detect and correct a material misstatement within the accounting systems in a timely manner. Tests of controls are often referred to as 'compliance tests'. Any significant deficiencies in internal controls will be notified to those charged with governance in accordance with the provisions of ISA 265 'Communicating Deficiencies in Internal Control to those Charged with Governance and Management' (see Chapter 11).

The above summary highlights the primary objective of the external audit. The objective of the audit looks at the primary needs of external stakeholders of an entity, as opposed to the requirements of an entity's management. External stakeholders usually include, amongst others, an entity's bankers, trade payables and receivables, employees, potential investors and employees. The audit is therefore concerned with ensuring that the general purpose financial statements are objective, free from bias and manipulation and relevant to the needs of the users of those financial statements.

INDEPENDENCE

Auditors are expected to be independent of the reporting entity. The Conceptual Framework Approach to Independence identifies two aspects of independence:

- independence of mind; and
- independence in appearance.

Independence of Mind

Independence of mind enables the auditor to form an opinion without being affected by influences that would compromise the auditor's professional judgement. Independence of mind will allow the auditor to act with integrity and exercise objectivity at all times during the course of the audit. Independence of mind will also allow the auditor to act with professional scepticism.

[IESBA Code]

Independence in Appearance

Independence in appearance is achieved when the auditor avoids facts and circumstances that are so significant that a reasonable and informed third party would conclude that the auditor's integrity, objectivity and professional scepticism has been compromised.

[IESBA Code]

Threats to Independence

Any threats to the auditor's independence must be eradicated in totality or mitigated to an acceptable level. The auditor also has an obligation to ensure that where they identify threats to independence adequate safeguards are applied. Where the auditor concludes that adequate safeguards cannot be applied to eradicate the threat in totality or mitigate it to an acceptable level, the auditor must resign from the audit engagement or decline the audit engagement. Threats to independence could arise in the following circumstances:

- Auditor's personal interest. The auditor may fear losing the audit fee.
- Intimidation. The auditor may be intimidated by dominant or aggressive management.
- Long association. If the auditor has had a long association with the client, they may be too sympathetic to the client.
- Performing non-audit work and subsequently auditing that work (referred to as a 'self-review' threat).

Chapter Roundup

The primary objective of the audit is for the auditor to express an opinion about the truth and fairness (or whether the financial statements present fairly, in all material respects) the state of the entity's financial affairs at the end of the reporting period.

Acceptance procedures include: consideration of legal and ethical issues, preparing the letter of engagement and obtaining an understanding of the entity.

The auditor should undertake a sufficient programme of planning before the detailed audit work commences to identify key areas of the audit and to devise the audit strategy. The auditor should also review the legal and ethical issues surrounding their engagement, review and update the letter of engagement, review and update their understanding of the entity and the environment in which it operates.

The auditor must be independent in order to maintain the objectivity of the audit. Any threats to this independence should be minimised to an acceptable level. Where such threats cannot be minimised to an acceptable level, then the auditor should consider their ability to continue as auditor.

The auditor does not have a direct responsibility to look for fraud during the course of an audit, as the responsibility for the prevention and detection of fraud rests with management. However, the auditor should plan their work and their procedures with an expectation that the financial statements might be materially misstated due to fraud.

2 THE CLARITY PROJECT

In 2004, the International Auditing and Assurance Standards Board (IAASB) undertook a programme in which the objective was to enhance the clarity of its ISAs. The IAASB said that the overall aim of its clarity project was to enhance the understandability of the ISAs which would then enable consistent application of the standards and improve audit quality on a worldwide level.

All of the ISAs have been rewritten as part of the Clarity project. Each standard is now structured in a new way, with clear objectives, definitions and requirements, together with application and other explanatory material. The structure of the new standards makes it easier to understand what is required and what is purely guidance. In addition, ISQC 1 'Quality Control for Firms that Perform Audits and Reviews of Financial Statements, and Other Assurance and Related Services Engagements' has been rewritten and the revised guidance on quality control procedures will also become effective at the same time as the Clarified ISAs.

A summary of the clarity project is as follows:

- 19 ISAs and ISQC 1 'Quality Control for Firms that Perform Audits and Reviews of Financial Statements, and Other Assurance and Related Service Engagements' have been redrafted. You will see '(redrafted)' contained after the ISA/ISQC 1 number.
- 16 ISAs have been both revised and redrafted to reflect the new Clarity conventions and format. You will see '(revised and redrafted)' contained after the ISA number.
- Two new standards have been issued: one relating to communication — ISA 265 'Communicating Deficiencies in Internal Controls to Those Charged with Governance and Management' and another relating to the evaluation of misstatements: ISA 450 'Evaluation of Misstatements Identified During the Audit'.
- ISA 540 'Audit of Accounting Estimates' and 545 'Auditing Fair Value Measurements and Disclosures' have been combined in ISA 540 (revised and redrafted) 'Auditing Accounting Estimates and, Including Fair Value Accounting Estimates, and Related Disclosures'.

Whilst all the ISAs have been rewritten, there are main areas of audit work that are affected by the changes to Clarified ISAs.

ISA 600 (revised and redrafted) The Audit of Group Financial Statements

The revised ISA is far more wide-ranging than the previous standard and sets out new requirements in respect of the relationship between the group engagement team and the component auditors. It is therefore expected that this will have the most impact on group audits where you are not the auditor for the whole group.

The Clarity project in this area will result in auditors having to give more thought to this area of their work, the following areas are likely to require additional thought and documentation:

- Consideration of whether the engagement is a group audit within the scope of ISA 600 (revised and redrafted).
- Scoping the group audit, including determining significant components in the group.
- Gaining an understanding of the group-wide internal control environment and the consolidation process.
- Determining materiality and performance materiality for the group and its components.
- Obtaining an understanding of the component auditors involved in the work.

ISA 550 (revised and redrafted) Related Parties

The revised ISA includes a number of specific new requirements to ensure that auditors place a greater emphasis on a risk-based approach in this area and improve the identification of related party relationships and transactions which have not already been disclosed by management.

This revised and redrafted standard recognises that risks of material misstatement are higher when related parties are involved. This clarified standard requires related party relationships and transactions to be considered explicitly in the engagement team's fraud discussion and an understanding of controls relevant to related parties to be obtained.

The standard requires that where controls are not present in this area, the auditor may be required to report the fact to those charged with governance. In addition, the updated standard requires the auditor to challenge any management assertion that transactions with related parties are on an arm's length basis.

ISA 540 (revised and redrafted) Auditing Accounting Estimates, Including Fair Value Accounting Estimates and Related Disclosures

This ISA introduces requirements for greater rigour and scepticism into the audit of accounting estimates, including the auditor's consideration of indicators of possible management bias. The ISA now also includes new requirements in respect of:

- Specific matters for the auditor to gain an understanding of in order to assess risk.
- Evaluation of estimation uncertainty and determining any significant risks.
- Requirement to perform substantive procedures to respond to significant risks.

The scope of this standard has been updated to be extended to fair values. The extension of this standard to be applicable to fair values was hardly surprising during the Clarity project given the ongoing debate concerning the use of fair values in financial reporting frameworks.

ISA 265 Communicating Deficiencies in Internal Control to Those Charged with Governance and Management

This is a new ISA which is designed to address the way in which auditors report control deficiencies to those charged with governance. The main objective is to increase the quality of the communication to management and also to focus on the definition of a significant deficiency in internal control and/or a missing control which requires formal reporting.

It is important that auditors' risk assessments include consideration of the types of control they would expect to find at an audit client taking into consideration its size, complexity and nature. If relevant controls are missing, their absence should be reported to the appropriate level of management or to those charged with governance even if they do not directly impact on the planned audit procedures.

ISA 450 Evaluation of Misstatements Identified During the Audit

This is another new standard and is derived from the revisions to ISA 320 on audit materiality. Among other things, it requires accumulating misstatements, reassessment of materiality and specific documentation.

ISA 530 Audit Sampling

The clarified ISAs provide a foundation for risk-based auditing which means that the auditors will plan their procedures using a risk assessment which is in turn built on an understanding of the entity and the environment in which it operates.

The clarified ISA emphasises the point that it would be extremely rare for any deviation or misstatement identified in a sample to be considered an anomalous error and not representative of the whole population. Where auditors wish to make a decision as to whether a deviation or misstatement is anomalous, then they should obtain sufficient appropriate evidence to support the position.

ISA 260 Significant Difficulties

ISA 260 has been revised to emphasise the importance of effective two-way communication between the auditor and those charged with governance of the audit client. Where the auditor encounters significant difficulties during the course of an audit (for example, the unavailability of expected information), then the auditor is required to notify such significant difficulties to the appropriate level of management or those charged with governance. Where auditors feel that the two-way communication has not been effective, then they should consider their ability to accept re-appointment if the conclusion is that the level of two-way communication has been inadequate for their purposes.

ISA 570 Going Concern

ISA 570 has not been revised, but it has been redrafted in a way which has now given rise to a significant number of elevations — in particular, where events or conditions cast significant doubt on the entity's ability to continue as a going concern. Auditors should obtain evidence concerning management's assertion where they conclude that the going concern basis is appropriate in their particular circumstances by evaluating management's plans for future actions and considering whether those plans are feasible.

Auditor's Reports

ISAs 700, 705 and 706 deal with reporting matters. Different jurisdictions will have different formats of auditors' reports. Where auditors consider a modification of an auditor's report, or where an emphasis of matter paragraph is deemed to be appropriate, care should be taken over the form and content of the report. ISA 705 'Modifications to the Opinion in the Independent Auditor's Report' (Chapter 33) and ISA 706 'Emphasis of Matter Paragraphs and Other Matter Paragraphs in the Auditors' Report' (Chapter 34) should be consulted.

A list of the revised and/or redrafted standards in the clarity project is given below:

- ISA 200 (revised and redrafted) 'Overall Objective of the Independent Auditor, and the Conduct of an Audit in Accordance with ISAs'.
- ISA 210 (redrafted) 'Agreeing the Terms of Audit Engagements'.
- ISA 220 (redrafted) 'Quality Control for an Audit of Financial Statements'.
- ISA 230 (redrafted) 'Audit Documentation'.
- ISA 240 (redrafted) 'The Auditor's Responsibility to Consider Fraud in an Audit of Financial Statements'.
- ISA 250 (redrafted) 'The Auditor's Responsibilities Related to Laws and Regulations in an Audit of Financial Statements'.
- ISA 260 (revised and redrafted) 'Communication with Those Charged with Governance'.
- ISA 265 'Communicating Deficiencies in Internal Control' (this is a new standard borne out of the Clarity Project).
- ISA 300 (redrafted) 'Planning an Audit of Financial Statements'.
- ISA 315 (redrafted) 'Obtaining an Understanding of the Entity and its Environment and Assessing the Risks of Material Misstatement'.
- ISA 320 and ISA 450 (revised and redrafted) 'Materiality and Evaluation of Misstatements' (ISA 450 is a new standard borne out of the Clarity Project).
- ISA 330 (redrafted) 'The Auditor's Procedures in Response to Assessed Risks'.
- ISA 402 (revised and redrafted) 'Audit Considerations Relating to an Entity Using a Third Party Service Organisation'.
- ISA 500 (redrafted) 'Considering the Relevance and Reliability of Audit Evidence'.
- ISA 501 (redrafted) 'Audit Evidence Regarding Specific Financial Statement Account Balances and Disclosures'.
- ISA 505 (revised and redrafted) 'External Confirmations'.
- ISA 510 (redrafted) 'Initial Audit Engagements — Opening Balances'.
- ISA 520 (redrafted) 'Analytical Procedures'.
- ISA 530 (redrafted) 'Audit Sampling'.
- ISA 540 (revised and redrafted) 'Auditing Accounting Estimates, Including Fair Value Accounting Estimates, and Related Disclosures'.
- ISA 550 (revised and redrafted) 'Related Parties'.
- ISA 560 (redrafted) 'Subsequent Events'.
- ISA 570 (redrafted) 'Going Concern'.
- ISA 580 (revised and redrafted) 'Written Representations'.
- ISA 600 (revised and redrafted) 'The Audit of Group Financial Statements'.
- ISA 610 (redrafted) 'The Auditor's Consideration of the Internal Audit Function'.
- ISA 620 (revised and redrafted) 'Using the Work of an Auditor's Expert'.

- ISA 700 (redrafted) 'The Independent Auditor's Report on General Purpose Financial Statements'.
- ISA 705 (revised and redrafted) 'Modifications to the Opinion in the Independent Auditor's Report'.
- ISA 706 (revised and redrafted) 'Emphasis of Matter Paragraphs and Other Matter(s) Paragraphs in the Independent Auditor's Report'.
- ISA 710 (redrafted) 'Comparative Information, Corresponding Figures and Comparative Financial Statements'.
- ISA 720 (redrafted) 'The Auditor's Responsibility in Relation to Other Financial Information in Documents Containing Audited Financial Statements'.
- ISA 800 (revised and redrafted) 'Special Considerations — Audits of Financial Statements Prepared in Accordance with Special Purpose Frameworks'.
- ISA 805 (revised and redrafted) 'Special Considerations — Audits of Single Financial Statements and Specific Elements, Accounts or Items of a Financial Statement'.
- ISA 810 — 'Engagements to Report on Summary Financial Statements'.
- ISQC 1 (redrafted) 'Quality Control for Firms that Perform Audits and Reviews of Financial Statements, and Other Assurance and Related Service Engagements'.

The IAASB clarity project was primarily undertaken in order to improve the standards to achieve the following:

- Identifying the auditor's overall objectives when conducting an audit in accordance with the ISAs.
- Setting an objective in each ISA and establishing the auditor's obligation in relation to that objective.
- Clarifying the obligations imposed on the auditor by the ISAs and improving the language used to convey such requirements to the auditor.
- Improving the readability and understandability of the ISAs by restructuring and redrafting the ISAs.

The IAASB has redrafted several of the ISAs. Where an ISA has been redrafted it essentially means that the standard has a new structure to it. Each redrafted standard will contain a new structure as follows:

- Introduction.
- Objective.
- Definitions.
- Requirements.
- Application.
- Other Explanatory Material.

Introduction This paragraph contains information concerning the standard including the purpose, scope and subject matter of the ISA. It also contains information regarding the responsibilities of the auditor and others in the context of which the ISA is set.

Objective Each ISA contains a statement of the auditor's objective in the audit area which the ISA is set.

Definitions   The Clarity Project included adding an element for greater understanding of the ISAs and as such, applicable terms contained within the ISAs have now been defined.

Requirements   Each ISA is supported by clearly stated requirements. Phrases such as 'the auditor should' have now been replaced by phrases such as 'the auditor shall'. This improvement was welcomed by the profession because it clears any ambiguity because the word 'shall' indicates that the standard expects something of the auditor rather than 'should' which indicates that the standard 'may' expect something of the auditor in certain circumstances.

Application   Each ISA clearly explains more precisely what the auditor is required to do in order to achieve the objective of the ISA in question. Where applicable, the ISA may also contain illustrative examples of procedures that may be applicable in certain circumstances.

Other Explanatory Material   Other explanatory material may be contained within an ISA in order to help the auditor understand the ISAs overall objective and application.

The impact of the IAASB's Clarity Project is one which will contribute significantly to the enhancement and uniformity of audit quality on a worldwide level. The IAASB set out to undertake its clarity project in the hope that it will also encourage international convergence and assist audit firms that operate internationally by harmonising auditing standards.

The revised and redrafted ISAs are more rules based which is accentuated further by the removal of the word 'should' and replacing it with the word 'shall'. The auditing profession has long since been based on professional judgement and there are arguments that a more rules-based approach to auditing removes this judgement by imposing mandatory requirements on auditors in areas that might not, necessarily, be appropriate to certain entities. For example, there are lots of entities in the small-medium sector that have relatively simple internal controls and the rules-based ISAs might result in a company having such simple internal controls being over-audited. Conversely, entities who have relatively complex issues attached to their financial and reporting systems might be under-audited.

To combat these issues, auditors should ensure that they tailor the requirements of each ISA to their specific needs but keeping in mind that use of the word 'shall' in the context of an ISA means that the requirement is mandatory and must be carried out regardless of any other circumstances such as complexity, size or cost. The IAASB view such an approach to the application of auditing standards as one which will lead to consistent application of the ISAs and result in enhanced audit quality worldwide.

Chapter Roundup

The Clarity Project was completed in 2009 and has resulted in rewrites of the International Standards on Auditing (ISAs).

19 ISAs and ISQC 1 have been redrafted.

16 ISAs have been both revised and redrafted.

Two new standards have been issued: ISA 265 'Communicating Deficiencies in Internal Control to Those Charged with Governance and Management' and ISA 450 'Evaluation of Misstatements Identified During the Audit'.

The Clarified ISAs are effective for audits of financial statements commencing on or after 15 December 2009.

A notable feature of the Clarified ISAs is removal of the word 'should' in the context of performing an audit procedure and replacing it with the word 'shall'.

3 THE CODE OF ETHICS FOR PROFESSIONAL ACCOUNTANTS

Professional accountants are governed by ethical standards by which they must comply. It is generally accepted that auditors have a direct responsibility to the shareholders of the entity in which they are auditing, however, professional accountants, whether they work in audit practice or not, are also required to act in the public interest. The Code of Ethics for Professional Accountants has been prescribed by the International Ethics Standards Board of Accountants (IESBA).

The Code of Ethics for Professional Accountants prescribes the requirements for professional accountants, whether they work in audit practice or not. Member bodies of IFAC must not apply any less stringent standards than those stated in their Code. In some jurisdictions, there could be Ethical requirements which differ from the IESBA Code. Professional accountants must be aware of the differences and must comply with the more stringent requirements and guidance unless a law or regulation prohibits such compliance.

The Code of Ethics for Professional Accountants is split into three parts:

- Part A establishes the fundamental principles of professional ethics for accountants, which provides a professional framework for applying those principles.
- Part B applies to professional accountants who work in practice.
- Part C applies to professional accountants who work in business and those professional accountants who work in practice may find Part C relevant to their needs.

FUNDAMENTAL PRINCIPLES

A professional accountant is required to observe compliance with five fundamental principles:

- Integrity.
- Objectivity.
- Professional Competence and Due Care.
- Confidentiality.
- Professional Behaviour.

Integrity

At all times during the course of their work, a professional accountant must be honest and straightforward in all professional and business relationships. In order for a professional accountant to observe the fundamental principle of integrity the professional accountant should not allow their name to be associated with reports, returns or other forms of communication where the professional accountant believes that the information:

(a) contains a materially false or misleading statement;
(b) contains statements or information obtained recklessly; or
(c) omits or obscures information required to be included where such omission or obscurity would be misleading.

In terms of auditing, it could be the case that an auditor's opinion is modified because the financial statements which have been subject to audit do not give a true and fair view, or present fairly in all material aspects. In these circumstances, where the auditor's opinion is modified then the professional accountant will not be considered to be in breach of the circumstances detailed in (a) to (c) above.

Objectivity

A professional accountant should not allow bias, conflict of interest or undue influence of others to override professional or business judgements.

In some cases, the auditor may be exposed to situations that may impair objectivity. The auditor should, in all cases, ensure that objectivity is not impaired by implementing safeguards to maintain independence and objectivity.

Professional Competence and Due Care

A professional accountant has a duty to maintain professional knowledge and skill at the level required to ensure that their client receives a competent and professional service. Audit firms must not, therefore, accept appointment as auditor unless they are competent and have sufficient resources available to undertake the work.

Professional accountants also have an obligation to act diligently in accordance with appropriate technical and professional standards when providing professional services. Professional competence can also be sub-divided into two phrases:

• Attainment of professional competence.
• Maintenance of professional competence.

In order to maintain professional competence, professional accountants must be up to date with technical developments. Continuing Professional Development will guarantee maintenance of professional competence and ensure that the professional accountant performs work competently within professional environments.

Confidentiality

Confidentiality is of paramount importance and section 140 of the IESBA Code of Ethics contains the obligations of a professional accountant to maintain confidentiality as well as establishing the circumstances where the professional accountant can depart from this fundamental principle.

Professional accountants have a duty to ensure that confidentiality is observed at all times. This means that the professional accountant should refrain from:

- Disclosing outside the audit firm confidential information acquired as a result of professional and business relationships without proper and specific authority or unless there is a legal or professional right or duty to disclose.
- Using confidential information acquired as a result of professional and business relationships to their personal advantage or to the advantage of third parties.

Even outside of the business or practice environment, a professional accountant has an obligation to preserve confidentiality. Professional accountants, therefore, must ensure that they do not, inadvertently or otherwise, disclose information in a social environment.

A professional accountant is also required to maintain confidentiality of information disclosed by a prospective client or employer.

A professional accountant should also consider the need to maintain confidentiality of information within a firm or employing organisation.

A professional accountant should take all reasonable steps to ensure that staff under the professional accountant's control and persons from whom advice and assistance is sought also respect the professional accountant's duty of confidentiality.

Professional Behaviour

At all times, professional accountants must comply with relevant laws and regulations and avoid all action which would discredit the profession. Accountants need to be seen to behave in a professional manner at all times, and this behaviour extends to the professional accountant's marketing or advertising.

The professional accountant must not mislead clients or employers by stating that they have professional qualifications, when they have not. Nor should they offer themselves available for work which they are not professionally competent to undertake. Professional accountants also have an obligation to ensure that they do not make disparaging references or unsubstantiated comparisons to the work of others.

THREATS AND SAFEGUARDS

At all times during the auditing process, the auditor must remain independent to ensure the audit objective is maintained. Varying degrees of circumstances or relationships can create threats which in turn may affect more than one fundamental ethical principle. Where the auditor identifies a threat then they are required to employ safeguards to ensure the threat is reduced to an acceptable level.

Auditing categorises threats into one or more of the following categories:

- Self-interest threat.
- Self-review threat.
- Advocacy threat.

- Familiarity threat.
- Intimidation threat.

A self-interest threat occurs when a financial or other interest will inappropriately influence the professional accountant's judgement or behaviour. This could occur, for example, where the professional accountant holds shares in a reporting entity or where the audit firm has undue dependence on the fees from an audit client.

A self-review threat occurs when the professional accountant relies on information prepared by the professional accountant or another individual in the professional accountant's firm. An example of a self-review threat is where the professional accountant prepares a set of financial statements for a reporting entity and then audits the same financial statements. In addition, where a member of the audit or assurance team has joined the audit firm from the audit client, then this will also give rise to a self-review threat if that person is engaged on the audit of his/her previous employer.

An advocacy threat occurs when the professional accountant promotes a client's or employer's position to the point that the professional accountant's objectivity is compromised. An example of an advocacy threat is the professional accountant representing a client in legal proceedings.

A familiarity threat arises when a professional accountant becomes disproportionately close or familiar with the client to the extent that they may be too sympathetic to their interests.

An intimidation threat occurs when the professional accountant is put under pressure by a client or employer to the extent that the professional accountant may be deterred from acting objectively.

SAFEGUARDS

Safeguards are actions by the professional accountant in an attempt to either eradicate the threats in totality or reduce those threats to an acceptable level and can fall into two categories:

- safeguards created by the profession, legislation or regulation; and
- safeguards in the actual working environment.

Safeguards created by the profession include compliance with professional standards, including those laid down by the professional accountant's professional body. There are also other safeguards which include:

- training and development;
- corporate governance regulations;
- regulatory monitoring by professional bodies; and
- external reviews.

Training and development includes training and experience requirements for entry into the profession and maintenance of these skills by undertaking Continuing Professional Development (CPD).

Regulatory monitoring includes reviews of professional accountants work by professional bodies (for example ACCA) to ensure that professional standards, independence and objectivity are maintained at all times.

External reviews can take various forms, but in terms of auditing are usually split into two types of review:

- hot file review; and
- cold file review.

A 'hot' file review is undertaken by an external file reviewer prior to the auditor's report being issued. Such reviews look at the audit work undertaken and whether the audit evidence is sufficient and appropriate enough to support the proposed opinion in the auditor's report.

A 'cold' file review is undertaken by an external file reviewer after the auditor's report has been issued. Such reviews can be mandatorily required by various professional bodies, or they can be undertaken as part of a regulatory monitoring visit. In addition, a cold file review can be undertaken on a periodic basis by the firm as part of their quality assurance procedures.

An audit firm should make sure that they have firm-wide safeguards which guarantee that the firm complies, in all respects, with the fundamental principles and ensure that their staff act, at all times, in the interests of the public.

There are varying procedures which firms can adopt to ensure that the firm has adequate safeguards in place to deal with threats, such as:

- Published policies to identify various threats and the procedures to be adopted in evaluating the significance of those threats. In instances where the threats cannot be eradicated or mitigated to an acceptable level, then the firm should resign or decline the engagement.
- Engaging different partners on audit and non-audit engagements.
- Engaging different staff on audit engagements where non-audit services have been provided to an audit client.
- Discussing difficult or contentious issues arising during the course of an audit with specifically trained staff, for example, complicated taxation matters should be referred to a firm's tax department or tax partner.
- Ensuring staff are kept technically up to date through the use of CPD.
- Formulating a disciplinary mechanism to promote a firm's policies and procedures.
- Ensuring regular, independent, file reviews are undertaken to make sure the firm's audit work is in compliance with auditing standards.
- Rotating senior personnel.

The above list is not exhaustive, but it provides examples of the issues which audit firms need to consider in order to ensure that adequate safeguards are put in place.

ACCEPTING AN AUDIT CLIENT

A key principle which professional accountants need to comply with is ensuring that they do not undertake work which they are not professionally competent to perform. This principle is of paramount importance to all professional accountants, including auditors. Where a potential client enquires about employing the services of a professional accountant, the professional accountant must ensure that they are technically, and professionally, competent to undertake the work on behalf of the client and that they also have the necessary resources available to service the client.

Prior to accepting an engagement, the professional accountant must also consider whether acceptance of a particular client would give rise to any threats to compliance with fundamental principles. For example, the professional accountant should consider whether the client is involved in illegal or immoral activities or whether the potential client has questionable financial reporting practices.

Where the professional accountant identifies such threats to the fundamental principles, then the professional accountant should consider whether these threats can be reduced to an acceptable level. Where these threats cannot be reduced to an acceptable level, or eradicated in totality, the professional accountant must decline the engagement.

In the absence of such threats, or where threats to the fundamental principles have been mitigated to an acceptable level, then the professional accountant must ensure that the services they have been asked to perform by the client can be performed competently by the professional accountant. Where the practice is a firm, the engagement partner should ensure that the firm has appropriate staff to deal with the client's affairs competently.

The firm should also ensure that they develop an appropriate level of understanding of the nature of the client's business and evaluate issues such as the complexity of the entity's operations and develop an understanding of the nature and scope of the work to be performed.

Clients in specialized industries may require the audit firm to ensure that they have the staff able to deal with such specialism competently. This may involve the use of experts (for example, where the audit client has complex financial instruments which require annual valuations). The audit firm must ensure that they have the necessary resources available to deal with such issues.

Where the professional accountant has been asked to act on behalf of a client in respect of their accounting requirements, the professional accountant needs to ensure that both accountant and client have a realistic timeframe to undertake the relevant work. The professional accountant should consider any deadlines imposed on its audit client. For example, a Solicitor may have to have the Accountants' Report submitted to their regulatory body (in the UK, the regulatory body for Solicitors is the Solicitors Regulation Authority, previously the Law Society) six months after the end of the reporting date. The professional accountant should ensure they are able to meet these deadlines at the same time as ensuring that the work they undertake for the client is undertaken competently and sufficiently.

On accepting an engagement, the incoming accountant will generally be required to initiate discussion with the client's previous accountant in order to obtain professional clearance. The incoming accountant will usually ask the outgoing accountant whether there is anything, professional or otherwise, that needs to be brought to the attention of the incoming accountant in order to help them decide whether or not to accept the engagement. Various jurisdictions may have other relevant legal, and other, regulations which govern such requests.

The outgoing accountant has a professional duty to ensure that the information they supply to the incoming accountant is provided to them honestly and free from any ambiguity.

CONFLICTS OF INTERESTS

A professional accountant has a duty, at all times, to identify any circumstances which might give rise to a conflict of interest. The firm should also ensure that they have procedures in place which will deal with any such conflicts of interest, which will generally entail notifying the client of a conflict of interest and seeking their consent to act in such circumstances. Where the professional accountant has been refused consent then the professional accountant has a duty not to act, or continue to act, for the party or parties giving rise to the conflict of interest.

Where a conflict of interest arises, then safeguards must be employed. Such safeguards could be the use of separate engagement teams (also known as 'Chinese walls'). Where the use of separate engagement teams are employed, then each team must observe confidentiality. The firm should also ensure that they undertake a regular review of the safeguards employed at firm level. The review of such safeguards should be undertaken by a senior official who is not involved with the relevant client engagements.

In some cases, conflicts of interests may create a threat to one or more of the fundamental principles. Where these threats cannot be eradicated in totality, or mitigated to an acceptable level, then the professional accountant has a duty not to accept the engagement.

FEES

Professional accountants have the freedom to quote whatever fee is deemed appropriate for the level of work involved. However, professional accountants need to be careful to avoid 'lowballing' — that is, where a professional accountant quotes a fee that is so low that it may become difficult to perform the required work in accordance with the technical and professional standards. This creates a self-interest threat.

Professional accountants have a duty to ensure that the fees they quote to a client are appropriate having regard to the level and skill of the staff required to perform the engagement. Professional accountants should also ensure that their clients are made aware of both the terms of the engagement and the fees agreed. This is usually achieved by way of a letter of engagement which the client is required to sign to confirm they understand the terms on which the professional accountant is engaged and also the nature and scope of the work which they will perform.

In the event that the client requires other services, for example, where the client requires taxation services to be completed by the firm, in addition to audit work, then a separate letter of engagement may be required.

There are instances where professional accountants may receive a referral fee or commission in relation to a client. Typically, this could occur where the client requires a specialist service which is not provided by the professional accountant so a referral fee may be received by the professional accountant in referring the client to another professional accountant who specialises in the area of work the client requires. This creates a self-interest threat to objectivity and professional competence and due care and the professional accountant referring the client to another professional accountant should ensure that they have relevant safeguards in place to deal with such a threat. This could involve:

- Disclosure of the commission or referral fee to another professional accountant for the work referred to them.
- Disclosure of the commission or referral fee to the client concerned and obtaining their permission to receive such a fee.

GIFTS AND HOSPITALITY

Some clients may offer gifts and/or hospitality to professional accountants and professional accountants need to ensure that acceptance of such gifts and hospitality does not breach the fundamental principles.

Whether or not this warrants a threat would depend on the nature, value and overall intent by the client of the offer of gifts and hospitality. For example, a client treating a professional accountant to lunch after completion of a long and difficult assignment might be construed by the professional accountant to be trivial and inconsequential after the professional accountant weighs up all the specific facts and circumstances. However, where the professional accountant concludes that threats to fundamental principles cannot be eradicated in totality or reduced to an acceptable level, then the professional accountant must not accept the gift or hospitality.

CLIENT ASSETS

A professional accountant has a duty to ensure that any threats to the fundamental principles by holding of client assets is eradicated in totality or reduced to an acceptable level. Professional accountants also have a duty to evaluate the source of such assets in order to comply with relevant laws and regulations, for example Money Laundering Regulations.

Where the professional accountant has custody of client assets, for example, by holding client money, then they should ensure that the self-interest threat that arises in such circumstances is reduced to an acceptable level. This can be achieved by:

- Holding client assets separately from the firm's assets.
- Using such assets for the purposes intended.
- Being able to readily account for such assets.
- Complying with all relevant laws and regulations in respect of holding such assets.

FAMILY AND CLOSE RELATIONSHIPS

Where family or close relationships exist between a member of the audit team and a director, officer or certain employee of the audit client, then this will create a self-interest, familiarity or intimidation threat, depending on a number of factors.

When an immediate family member or a member of the audit team is (a) a director or officer of the audit client, or (b) an employee that is able to exert influence over the preparation of the client's accounting records or the financial statements on which the firm will express an opinion, the individual concerned must be removed from the audit team. There are no other safeguards which can be implemented because the closeness of such a relationship will not reduce the threat to an acceptable level if the individual concerned is not removed from the audit team.

There are also situations whereby a former member of the audit team may have taken up employment with the audit client. In such circumstances, independence is likely to be threatened to such an extent that it would be unlikely to be able to reduce the threat to an acceptable level. Independence would, therefore, be deemed to be compromised if a former member of the audit team or the audit partner joins the audit client as a director or officer; or as an employee with the ability to exert influence over the accounting records and financial statements to which the audit firm will express an opinion. Exceptions to this threat are where the individual is not entitled to any benefits or payments from the firm, unless made in accordance with fixed pre-determined arrangements, and any amount owed to the individual is not material to the firm: in addition, where the individual does not participate in the firm's business or professional activities.

Examples of safeguards which can be implemented to minimise the threat to acceptable could be to modify the audit plan and assign individuals to the audit who have sufficient experience in relation to the individual who has joined the client. The audit firm may also have the work of the former member of the audit client reviewed by another professional accountant.

NON-AUDIT SERVICES PROVIDED TO THE CLIENT

It is extremely common for audit firms to undertake non audit services on behalf of an audit client. For example, audit firms may provide taxation related services to an audit client. The threat here is in relation to a 'self-review' threat. In terms of auditing, the self-review threat must be reduced to an acceptable level, for example, by having a 'hot' file review or employing the use of 'Chinese walls'. If the threat to independence cannot be mitigated to an acceptable level, the audit firm should either cease to act in the capacity of auditors, or decline the engagement.

Chapter Roundup

Professional ethics are pivotal to the accountancy and auditing profession and professional accountants must ensure they comply, at all times, with professional ethics.

The fundamental principles include: integrity, objectivity and independence, professional competence and due care, confidentiality and compliance with technical standards.

Where threats to independence are identified, these must be reduced to an acceptable level.

---

4 ISA 200 (REVISED AND REDRAFTED) OVERALL OBJECTIVES OF THE INDEPENDENT AUDITOR AND THE CONDUCT OF AN AUDIT IN ACCORDANCE WITH INTERNATIONAL STANDARDS ON AUDITING

ISA 200 (revised and redrafted) deals with the independent auditor's responsibilities when conducting an audit of financial statements in accordance with the International Standards on Auditing (ISAs). ISA 200 sets out the objectives of the independent auditor and also explains the nature and scope of an audit which will enable the independent auditor to meet the objectives. This ISA is considered such a fundamental ISA that all the other ISAs refer to them being read in conjunction with this ISA.

In all respects, the auditor is required to comply with the ISAs and ISA 200 explains the auditor's responsibility to ensure that an audit of financial statements must be undertaken in accordance with the ISAs. The ISAs do not address issues that the auditor is required to comply with that may exist in various legislations (for example, Companies Acts) and the auditor should ensure that they comply with all relevant legal, regulatory or professional obligations.

Illustration

The year-end financial statements of Parsonova Enterprises Limited, a company based in the UK, have been prepared but no disclosure has been made in the financial statements showing the total amount of directors' remuneration that has been paid to the directors in the year. The directors do not wish to include such disclosure because they believe such information to be sensitive.

The requirement to disclose directors' remuneration and other benefits is a Companies Act requirement and, therefore, disclosure of such transactions is a statutory requirement.

THE AUDIT OF FINANCIAL STATEMENTS

The general purpose of an audit is to enhance the credibility of the financial statements, thus ensuring the user of the financial statements can make reasonable, informed decisions about an entity. The opinion the auditor arrives at is that of whether the information contained within the financial statements is presented fairly, in all material respects. In addition, the auditor will also form an opinion as to whether the financial statements have been properly prepared in accordance with the relevant financial reporting framework, for example, International Financial Reporting Standards (IFRS). Auditors who follow the ISAs and the ethical guidelines will be able to form an opinion provided evidence is available to support their opinion [ISA200.3]. If evidence is lacking the auditor will not be able to form an opinion and should modify their report accordingly.

It is widely known that an external audit has inherent limitations which results in the auditor's opinion being persuasive rather than conclusive. However, the ISAs do require the auditor to obtain reasonable assurance that the financial statements are free from material misstatement, whether caused by fraud or error. Such reasonable assurance is obtained when the auditor has obtained sufficient and appropriate audit evidence to reduce audit risk. Audit risk is the risk that the auditor will express an inappropriate audit opinion and audit risk must be reduced to an acceptably low level. For the purposes of this ISA 'reasonable assurance' is considered a high level of assurance [ISA200.5].

Materiality

During the planning and the detailed audit work the auditor will assess materiality. Materiality is discussed in more detail in Chapter 14. Materiality is a concept which is applied by the auditor in assessing whether the effect of identified misstatements, or omissions of information, would reasonably be expected to influence the economic decisions of users of the financial statements.

Materiality is defined as:

> *A difference between the amount, classification, presentation or disclosure of a reported financial statement item and the amount, classification, presentation or disclosure that is required for the item to be in accordance with the applicable financial reporting framework. Misstatements can arise from fraud or error.*
>
> [ISA 200.13(i)]

Illustration

The financial statements of Ogroboria Inc for the year ended 31 December 2009 show the following:

Revenue	$120 million
Profit before taxation	$25 million
Gross assets	$460 million

Immediately after the year end, Ogroboria Inc was successfully sued for damages in respect of a serious breach of Health and Safety legislation. Legal proceedings were instigated in July 2009 amounting to $10 million. The directors of Ogroboria Inc have not included the provision as the damages were not paid until after the year end. During the course of the audit, the auditors have become aware of this issue.

Under the provisions of IAS 37 'Provisions, Contingent Liabilities and Contingent Assets' the directors had sufficient information available in order to make a provision. The requirements of IAS 37 state that in order to recognise a provision, the following three criteria must be met:

1. The entity has a present obligation (legal or constructive) as a result of a past event. Ogroboria has a legal obligation as a result of the legal judgement.
2. It is probable that an outflow of resources embodying economic benefits will be required to settle the obligation. Monetary amounts will have to be paid to settle the legal obligation.
3. A reliable estimate can be made of the amount of the obligation. The amount of damages has been confirmed at $10 million.

In addition, IAS 10 'Events After the Reporting Period' would confirm that this is an 'adjusting' event which would require the financial statements to be restated to take account of the claim for damages.

The damages amount to $10 million, which equates to 40% of profit before taxation so would be regarded as highly material. Such an omission would clearly influence the economic decisions of the users of the financial statements, for example, a potential investor. In this example, if the directors fail to adjust the financial statements to take account of the damages, then the auditor must modify their report accordingly.

Judgements about materiality are made by the auditor having reference to the surrounding circumstances and the needs of the users of the financial statements. In this respect, the auditor would not be concerned with the detection of immaterial misstatements in the financial statements.

In the illustration above, if Ogroboria Inc had misstated a prepayment by $200 then this would not be material in its entirety, though it could become material when this misstatement is aggregated with other misstatements in the financial statements.

Audit Evidence

Auditors gather audit evidence to support the amounts and disclosures contained within a set of general purpose financial statements. Audit evidence, therefore, needs to support the opinion given in the auditor's report. For example, if an audit opinion is unmodified then the audit evidence must be both sufficient and appropriate enough to be able to support this opinion. Audit evidence is looked at in detail in Chapter 18.

Audit evidence can take many forms such as recalculating amounts contained within the financial statements, obtaining evidence from an entity's accounting records, discussions with the audit client and external confirmations, such as circularisation or bank confirmations. The sufficiency and appropriateness of audit evidence is interrelated. *Sufficiency* is the measure of the quantity of evidence, whereas *appropriateness* is the measure of the quality of that audit evidence.

In order for an auditor to place reliance on audit evidence, the auditor needs to consider the source and nature of the evidence gathered.

Audit evidence is governed by the provisions in ISA 500 and sufficient and appropriate audit evidence will allow the auditor to draw reasonable conclusions on which to base the audit opinion. A large degree of professional judgement is required by the auditor in ensuring that the audit evidence gathered by them is sufficient and appropriate enough and the auditor must have regard to ISA 500 and other ISAs in establishing whether additional requirements are needed to ensure that the audit evidence gathered is sufficient and appropriate.

For audit evidence to be appropriate, auditors need to ensure that the evidence supports and corroborates management's assertions. For example, auditors would need to establish whether the going concern basis of preparing the financial statements is appropriate given the circumstances. In adopting their procedures, the auditors may discover facts and circumstances which may contradict management's assertion that the entity is able to continue as a going concern (see ISA 570, Chapter 27). Conversely, the evidence the auditors gather may well substantiate the assertion that the entity is a going concern.

Case Study — Vantis PLC

In their audit of Vantis PLC interim financial statements, Ernst and Young issued a going concern warning about the group. Higher costs and a slower than expected start to Quarter 2 trading was cited as the main reason for the group's reduced profitability and weakening liquidity.

Vantis PLC were also the Insolvency Practitioners of Stanford International Bank and fees in respect of the work undertaken on this insolvency had not been recovered. The result of this going concern warning was a reduction in the group's share price to 17p as opposed to 29p the previous Friday before the going concern warning was issued.

Risk

Risk is prevalent in every audit and every client will have a degree of risk attached to them. Auditors assess the levels of risk attached to their audit client and tailor their audit procedures accordingly to address these risks.

Illustration

Entity A Inc operates in the food industry. The principal activity of the entity involves the distribution of foodstuffs to local shopkeepers and franchises. Delivery drivers collect cash from the local shopkeepers and franchises, which is recorded in a receipt book and in turn passed to the accounts department for reconciling and subsequent banking.

In this illustration, the auditors should deem the cash-based nature of the business as high risk as the risk of material misstatement due to fraud is considered higher in cash-based entities.

The auditor's assessment of risk is again a matter of professional judgement and in this respect the auditor needs to ensure they comply with the provisions laid down in ISA 315 'Identifying and Assessing the Risks of Material Misstatement through Understanding the Entity and its Environment'. ISA 315 is considered in more detail in Chapter 13.

The risk of material misstatement can exist at two levels:

- the financial statement level; and
- the assertion level. [ISA 200.A34]

The risk of material misstatement at financial statement level means that the financial statements as a whole may contain material misstatement. The risk of material misstatement at the assertion levels relates to classes of transactions, account balances and disclosures. Risks at the assertion level are assessed by the auditor to identify the nature, timing and extent of further audit procedures which are necessary in order to enable the auditor to gather sufficient and appropriate audit evidence.

When assessing the risk of material misstatement at the assertion level, the auditor should address two components of risk: inherent risk and control risk.

Inherent risk represents the auditor's assessment that there might be a material misstatement relating to an assertion within the financial statements without taking into consideration the effect of any related internal controls. Inherent risk might be higher for some assertions and related classes of transactions, account balances and disclosures than for others — particularly if there are complex calculations involved, such as determining the fair value of a complex financial instrument. In addition, there could also be some external factors which would affect inherent risk such as technical obsolescence which could impact on assets being more susceptible to overstatement. [ISA200.A38]

Control risk represents the auditor's assessment of the likelihood that a material misstatement in relation to a financial statement assertion will not be detected or corrected on a timely basis by the clients internal control system. It is widely understood that no matter how well designed or robust an internal control system is, it can only reduce, not eliminate in totality, risks of material misstatement. Internal controls can be overridden by management, if they so desire (for example, overriding internal controls for personal financial gain). In addition, weaknesses in internal controls can be exploited so some control risk will always exist. The standards require an auditor to test the operating effectiveness of internal controls if the auditor takes them into account in assessing risk. If the auditor does not take the operating effectiveness of the controls into account when assessing risk, then there would be no need to test the operating effectiveness of the controls but the audit will be wholly substantive. However, with control tests the substantive work can be less rigorous.

FINANCIAL STATEMENT RISK AND DETECTION RISK

Financial statement risk is not defined in the Glossary to the ISAs, but it does state that audit risk is a function of material misstatement and detection risk. It is the risk that the financial statements contain a material misstatement. Detection risk is the risk that a material misstatement within a financial statement assertion will not be detected by the auditor's substantive testing, and there is an inverse relationship between the two.

The auditor could deem financial statement risk as low which means that the auditor's assessment that the financial statements contain a material misstatement is low. In turn, this also means that the auditor is seeking to place reliance on an entity's internal control systems. If financial statement risk is deemed low, then detection risk becomes high due to the fact that the auditor is seeking to place more reliance on an entity's internal control systems and undertake less detailed substantive testing. In some situations, the auditor could assess financial statement risk as low but not rely on the control system, thus undertaking the audit using substantive procedures.

Conversely, if the auditor concludes that an entity's internal control systems cannot be relied on and, thus, deems financial statement risk to be high, then detection risk becomes low because the auditor will undertake more detailed substantive procedures. Detection risk is largely under the control of the auditor. If the auditor strengthens their procedures they will lower detection risk and, thus, overall risk. If inherent risk or control risk increase they must strengthen their procedures in order to keep audit risk at an acceptable level.

Inherent Limitations of Auditing

Due to the inherent limitations of auditing, detection risk can only ever be reduced, not eliminated in totality so some detection risk will always exist. Inherent limitations of an audit arise because of deadlines, the audit work to be undertaken, financial reporting issues and the general nature of auditing procedures.

Inherent limitations arising from financial reporting issues refer to the way financial statements, in general, are prepared. Financial statements will always contain some degree of judgement on the part of the directors or subjective decisions and, consequently, financial statements are subject to an inherent level of variability which cannot be eliminated by the application of auditing procedures. Accounting estimates and judgements are often incorporated within the financial statements such as inventory provisions, bad debt provisions and accruals. However, the mere concept of including such accounting estimates as a means of being 'prudent' does not relieve the auditor of the requirement to give specific consideration to issues such as accounting estimates and the ISAs recognise this by virtue of ISA 540 'Auditing Accounting Estimates, Including Fair Value Accounting Estimates and Related Disclosures' (see Chapter 24).

The general nature of auditing procedures gives rise to certain limitations. The fact that management could override an entity's internal control system could mean that the information obtained during the course is also incomplete even though the auditor has performed the audit procedures necessary to obtain assurance that all the relevant information has been obtained.

Fraud issues are often very difficult to detect simply because of the nature of fraud. Fraud, by its nature, is designed to be concealed and as such, fraud could be sophistically and carefully organised. The auditor may well not pick up on a fraud, though with a degree of professional scepticism and sufficiently designed auditing procedures, the auditor should pick up on a material fraud. In recent years, the auditor's methodology of dealing with fraud has seen changes by more emphasis being placed on maintaining a degree of professional scepticism.

Because of the inherent limitations of an audit the auditor needs to plan the audit so that it will be performed in an effective manner and ensure the auditor pays particular attention to those areas of the financial statements which are most expected to contain material misstatement, whether due to fraud or error. Those areas the auditor has concluded are low risk areas will have less effort devoted to them.

In some cases the auditor could have planned and properly performed the audit in accordance with ISAs but still fail to detect a material misstatement. This is an unavoidable risk and may not in itself indicate a failure to conduct the audit in accordance with the ISAs. The auditor, however, cannot use this as an excuse for not performing adequate audit procedures to generate sufficient and appropriate audit evidence.

AUDITING IN ACCORDANCE WITH ISAs

The auditors have an obligation to ensure that the audit they undertake is performed in accordance with the ISAs. Conforming with the ISAs will allow the auditor to express an opinion on the financial statements.

Each ISA has its scope, effective date and any specific limitation of the applicability of a specific ISA made clear in them. The auditor can adopt an ISA before its effective date unless it is otherwise stated in the ISA. [ISA200.A54]

Different jurisdictions will have different obligations for auditors and they may be required to comply with legal or regulatory requirements. In these circumstances, the auditor should comply with each ISA relevant to the audit client as well as complying with the relevant standards of that jurisdiction or country. [ISA200.A56]

ISA CONTENT

The ISAs have been clarified in accordance with the 'Clarity Project' and will be applicable for audits commencing on or after 15 December 2009. The Clarity Project was undertaken to make each ISA more understandable for their users and to clear up ambiguous content, such as replacing the word 'should' with 'shall' [ISA200.A58]. This ensures that where a standard says the auditor *shall* undertake an audit procedure, then there is no doubt in the mind of the auditor whether they should or should not undertake a procedure. There are some critics which say that the use of the word shall detracts the auditor from using their professional judgement in cases where an auditing standard is deemed applicable to a particular audit client. However, the main objective of the Clarity Project was to increase understanding of the ISAs and, therefore, where an ISA is deemed applicable to a specific audit client, the whole of that ISA becomes applicable. Certain parts of the ISAs cannot be 'cherry picked'.

Illustration

Entity A Inc is a single entity and has prepared its financial statements to 31 December 2010. The audit firm is using the Clarified ISAs in order to undertake this audit assignment.

As Entity A is not part of a group (i.e. it is a simple 'stand-alone' company) then ISA 600 (revised and redrafted) 'The Audit of Group Financial Statements' will not be deemed applicable and, therefore, none of the provisions in ISA 600 will be consulted.

Had Entity A been part of a group, then all of the provisions in ISA 600 would then become applicable.

Each clarified ISA contains introductory material, where applicable which addresses issues such as:

- the purpose of the ISA and any other ISAs which the ISA relates to;
- the subject matter of the ISA;
- the responsibilities of the auditor in respect of the subject matter of the ISA; and
- the context in which the ISA is set.

In addition to the above, each clarified ISA may contain, where applicable, a separate section which includes definitions and a description of the meanings of certain terms used in the ISA which will enable auditors to apply and interpret each ISA consistently.

All clarified ISAs contain their objective which will enable the auditor to understand the outcome of a particular ISA, which will be specific enough to enable the auditor to understand what needs to be achieved and the methods that need to be adopted by the auditor to achieve the objective of the ISA.

Where an ISA interrelates to another ISA this will also be indicated within the ISA. For example, when planning an audit in accordance with ISA 315 and assessing the risk profile of the audit client in accordance with ISA 330. Where standards interrelate with each other, then the auditor should ensure that they have regard to the objectives and requirements of the other relevant ISAs in order that all objectives of the relevant ISAs can be achieved.

Audit clients will vary and not all of the ISAs may be relevant to every audit assignment. For example, where use of the auditor's experts is not required then the provisions in ISA 620 will not be relevant (see also the illustration above). However, in some circumstances, this ISA will become relevant — for example, if the client has a complicated financial instrument which is required to be carried at fair value, the auditor may employ an expert to evaluate the work of another valuer.

In addition to ensuring that the auditor complies with relevant ISAs, they should also make sure that they comply with the conditional requirements of each ISA. For example, where the auditor discovers material weaknesses in internal controls then they have a duty under ISA 265 to communicate these deficiencies to those charged with governance. This represents an implicit conditional requirement. An explicit conditional requirement could be, for example, where the auditor is required to issue a modified audit opinion if they have not attended the inventory count where inventory is a material audit area (this would cause a limitation of scope).

Whether the auditor has achieved the objective stated in the ISA is a matter of professional judgement on the part of the auditor and circumstances can arise where the auditor cannot achieve the objective of an ISA. Such circumstances can occur, for instance, due to a limitation of scope.

Chapter Roundup

ISA 200 outlines the overall objective of the auditor and explains the nature and scope of an audit to assist the auditor in meeting those objectives.

The auditor should also comply with other relevant legal, regulatory or professional obligations.

The overall objective of the auditor is to express an opinion as to whether the financial statements present fairly, in all material respects, the state of the entity's affairs at the reporting date. Sufficient and appropriate audit evidence must be obtained to support this opinion. Where evidence is lacking, the auditor considers the impact on their report.

The concept of materiality is applied by the auditor both in planning and performing the audit. ISA 450 also requires the auditor to evaluate the effect of identified misstatements on the audit, together with the effect of any uncorrected misstatements.

Auditors must assess levels of risk and tailor audit procedures to address these risks. Risk of material misstatement can exist at both the financial statement and assertion level.

Detection risk is largely under the control of the auditor. If the auditor strengthens audit procedures, this will lower detection risk and, thus, overall risk.

The audit is designed to give reasonable, but not absolute, assurance that the financial statements are free from material misstatement. There are inherent limitations associated with an audit.

The Clarified ISAs contain introductory material, where applicable, which addresses issues such as: the purpose of the ISA, any other relevant ISAs, subject matter of the ISA, responsibilities of the auditor in respect of the subject matter and the context in which the ISA is set.

5 ISA 210 (REDRAFTED) AGREEING THE TERMS OF AUDIT ENGAGEMENTS

ISA 210 deals with the auditor's responsibilities in agreeing the terms of the audit engagement with management and, where appropriate, those charged with governance. In agreeing these terms, the auditor will ensure that certain preconditions for an audit are present [ISA210.1]. Management[1] and, where appropriate, those charged with governance, are responsible for those preconditions. It follows that the objective of this standard is to enable the auditor to:

- establish whether the preconditions for an audit are present; [ISA210.3(a)] and
- confirm that there is a common understanding between the auditor and management of the terms of the audit engagement. [ISA210.3(b)]

It is only if these criteria can be agreed that the auditor should accept or continue an audit engagement. It is extremely important, therefore, that a clear understanding of the rules and ISA content is obtained to avoid any doubt as to whether to accept or continue an audit engagement.

For the purposes of this ISA, preconditions are the use of an acceptable financial reporting framework by management in the preparation of the entity's financial statements and the agreement by management and, where applicable, those charged with governance on the premise of the audit to be conducted. [ISA210.4]

In determining whether the preconditions are met, the auditor must conclude whether the financial reporting framework used by management in the preparation of the entity's financial statements is acceptable [ISA210.6(a)] and obtaining confirmation from management that they acknowledge their responsibilities for the preparation of the financial statements in accordance with the relevant reporting framework including, where applicable, their fair presentation [ISA210.6(b)(i)]. Management must also acknowledge their responsibilities for internal controls insofar as ensuring that such controls will enable the financial statements to be free from material misstatement, whether due to fraud or error. [ISA210.6(b)(ii)]

Under this ISA, management must also ensure that they provide the auditor with:

- access to all information that management is aware of which is relevant to the preparation of the financial statements; [ISA210.6(b)(iii)(a)]
- any other information which the auditor may request for the purposes of the audit; [ISA210.6(b)(iii)(b)] and
- unrestricted access to persons within the entity who will provide the auditor with relevant audit evidence. [ISA210.6(b)(iii)(c)]

---

[1] Where 'management' is stated, going forward that should be taken to mean 'or those charged with governance', where appropriate.

Limitation on Scope Prior to Audit Engagement Acceptance

In circumstances where management imposes a limitation on the auditor's work in terms of the proposed engagement, and the auditor concludes that such a limitation on scope will result in the audit opinion being disclaimed, then the auditor must not accept such an engagement unless the auditor is specifically required to do so, for example, because of laws or regulations. [ISA210.7]

Where other conditions prohibit the preconditions of an audit being met, then the auditor must discuss the issues with management and, where applicable, those charged with governance. The auditor shall not accept such an engagement where the auditor concludes that the financial reporting framework which is to be applied in the preparation of the financial statements is unacceptable or if the auditor is not in possession of management's agreement to their responsibilities. [ISA210.8]

In many cases the preconditions of an audit can be met and in such cases then the auditor must agree the terms of the audit engagement with management and, where applicable, those charged with governance. This agreement is usually outlined by way of a letter of engagement and will normally comprise:

- the objective and the scope of the audit;
- the auditor's responsibilities;
- the responsibilities of management;
- identification of the financial reporting framework for the preparation of the financial statements (for example, International Financial Reporting Standards); and
- reference to the expected form and content of any reports to be issued by the auditor and a statement that there might be circumstances in which a report may differ from its expected form and content. [ISA210.10(a) to (e)]

It is in the interests of both the auditor and the client that the auditor sends an audit engagement letter before the commencement of the audit to avoid misunderstandings with regard to the audit. Some jurisdictions may have the objective and scope of an audit, together with the responsibilities of management and auditor established in law. As a result, the form and content of the audit engagement letter may vary for each entity.

In many cases audits will be recurring. Where recurring audits are concerned revisions to the existing letter of engagement may be required and/or reminders to management.

Illustration — Audit Letter of Engagement — ISA (UK and Ireland)

The Directors of Lakeside Engineering Inc

Dear Sirs,

You have requested that we audit the financial statements of Lakeside Engineering Inc, which comprise the statement of financial position as at 31 December 20XX, and the statement of comprehensive income, statement of changes in equity and the statement of cash flows for the year then ended, and a summary of significant accounting policies and other explanatory information. We are pleased to confirm our acceptance and our understanding of this audit engagement by means of this letter of engagement. Our audit will be conducted with the objective of our expressing an opinion on the financial statements.

Responsibilities of the auditor

We will conduct our audit in accordance with International Standards on Auditing (ISAs). Those standards require that we comply with ethical requirements and plan and perform the audit to obtain reasonable assurance about whether the financial statements are free from material misstatement. An audit involves performing procedures to obtain audit evidence about the amounts and disclosures in the financial statements. The procedures selected depend on the auditor's judgement, including the assessment of the risks of material misstatement of the financial statements, whether due to fraud or error. An audit also includes evaluating the appropriateness of accounting policies used and the reasonableness of accounting estimates made by management, as well as evaluating the overall presentation of the financial statements.

Because of the inherent limitations of an audit, together with the inherent limitations of internal control, there is an unavoidable risk that some material misstatements may not be detected, even though the audit is properly planned and performed in accordance with ISAs.

In making our risk assessments, we consider internal control relevant to the entity's preparation of the financial statements in order to design audit procedures that are appropriate in the circumstances, but not for the purpose of expressing an opinion on the effectiveness of the entity's internal control. However, we will communicate to you in writing any significant deficiencies in internal control relevant to the audit of the financial statements that we have identified during the audit.

Our audit will be conducted on the basis that management and, where applicable, those charged with governance, acknowledge and understand that they have responsibility:

(a) For the preparation and fair presentation of the financial statements in accordance with International Financial Reporting Standards.
(b) For such internal control as management determines is necessary to enable the preparation of financial statements that are free from material misstatement, whether due to fraud or error.
(c) To provide us with:

    (i)   Access to all information management is aware of that is relevant to the preparation of the financial statements such as records, documentation and other matters.
    (ii) Additional information that we may request from management for the purpose of the audit.
    (iii) Unrestricted access to persons within the entity from whom we determine it necessary to obtain audit evidence.

As part of our audit procedures, we will request from management and, where applicable, those charged with governance, written confirmation concerning representations made to us in connection with the audit.

We look forward to full co-operation with your staff and we trust that they will make available to us whatever records, documentation and other information are requested in connection with our audit.

Our fees, which are billed as work progresses, are based on the time required by the individuals assigned to the audit engagement plus out-of-pocket expenses. Individual hourly rates vary according to the degree of responsibility involved and the experience and skill required.

This letter will be effective for future years until it is terminated, amended or superseded. We would be grateful if you could please sign and return the attached copy of this letter to indicate that it is in accordance with your understanding of the arrangements for our audit of the financial statements.

Yours faithfully,

Collier & Co

Acknowledged and agreed on behalf of Lakeside Engineering Inc by

. . . .

Director   Date

The auditor should not agree to a change in the engagement terms if there is no reasonable justification for doing so. [ISA210.14]

If the terms of the engagement are changed, then the auditor and management must agree on and record the revised terms of the engagement in a subsequent engagement letter or other suitable form of written agreement.

Chapter Roundup

The auditor shall only accept or continue an audit engagement if the preconditions for an audit are present and there is a confirmed common understanding between the auditor and management of the terms of the audit engagement.

Preconditions are the use of an acceptable financial reporting framework and agreement by management and, where applicable, those charged with governance on the premise of the audit to be conducted.

Where management impose a scope limitation on the auditor's work in terms of the proposed engagement which will result in a disclaimer of opinion, the auditor must not accept the engagement unless required by law or regulation.

Agreement to the terms of the audit engagement is usually outlined in a letter of engagement.

The letter of engagement for recurring audits should be reviewed annually and updated where necessary.

The auditor should not agree to a change in the terms of the engagement if there is no reasonable justification for doing so.

If changes are agreed between management and the auditor, a subsequent letter of engagement or other suitable form of written agreement should be issued.

6 ISA 220 (REDRAFTED) QUALITY CONTROL FOR AN AUDIT OF FINANCIAL STATEMENTS

This ISA deals with the responsibilities the auditor has in connection with quality control procedures for an audit of financial statements.

Quality control is a pivotal aspect of an audit. Without certain quality control procedures, an audit may fail to be effective. ISQC 1 'Quality Control for Firms that Perform Audits and Reviews of Financial Statements, and Other Assurance and Related Services Engagements' stipulates that a firm has an obligation to establish and maintain a system of quality control to provide it with reasonable assurance that:

(a) The firm and its personnel comply with professional standards and applicable legal and regulatory requirements. [ISA220.2(a)]
(b) The reports issued by the firm or engagement partners are appropriate to the circumstances. [ISA220.2(b)]

It follows, therefore, that engagement teams have a responsibility to implement quality control procedures that are applicable to an audit assignment and provide the firm with relevant information to enable implementation of the firm's systems and quality control procedures.

Audits must comply with professional standards and also applicable legal and regulatory frameworks. For example, in the UK, audits must be conducted in accordance with ISAs (UK and Ireland) and the Companies Act.

The engagement partner must take full responsibility for the audit and the overall quality control. During the course of the audit, the engagement partner must also be alert for any evidence of non-compliance with applicable ethical requirements by any member of the audit engagement team. ISA220.7(a) defines the engagement partner as:

> *the partner or other person in the firm who is responsible for the audit engagement and its performance and for the auditor's report that is issued on behalf of the firm and who, where required, has the appropriate authority from a professional, legal, or regulatory body.*
> [ISA220.7(a)]

If any matters come to the engagement partner's attention by way of the firm's system of quality control, or by any other route, that members of the engagement team have not been complying with applicable ethical requirements, the engagement partner must then take appropriate action.

For the purposes of this standard, the relevant ethical requirements are the fundamental principles of professional ethics laid down in the IFAC code, which are:

- integrity;
- objectivity;
- professional competence and due care;
- confidentiality; and
- professional behaviour.

These principles are further discussed in Chapter 3.

CONTINUING AUDITS

For recurring audits, the engagement partner must be satisfied that appropriate procedures regarding the acceptance and continuance of audit client relationships have been met. The engagement partner must also consider any information that would have caused the firm to decline the audit engagement had that information been available at the time. [ISA220.13]

The audit engagement partner must also consider:

- The integrity of the principal owners, key management and those charged with governance of the entity.
- Whether the audit engagement team has the necessary skill set in order to undertake the audit in accordance with professional standards and applicable legal and regulatory frameworks, as well as determining whether the firm has the time to undertake the audit and the resources needed.
- Whether the audit firm can comply with relevant ethical requirements.
- Review the significant matters that have arisen out of the current or previous audits and the implication of these significant matters on the continuing relationship. [ISA220.A8]

THE ENGAGEMENT TEAM

The engagement partner is responsible for assigning a team to a particular audit assignment. In assigning a team to an audit, the engagement partner has a responsibility to ensure that the team is competent to perform the work required and that the team has the relevant skills and capabilities in order to perform the audit engagement in accordance with professional standards and the applicable legal and regulatory framework.

The engagement partner must ensure that the engagement team is aware of their responsibilities, including the need to comply with relevant ethical requirements and must ensure that the engagement team understands the objectives of the work required.

Engagement partners must ensure that appropriate personnel are selected by considering the complexity of the audit and the nature of the entity's business. For example, in the audit of a pension scheme, it would be inappropriate to have audit team members assigned to such an audit who have no experience of auditing a pension scheme.

Engagement partners must also consider any risk related issues and any problems that may arise during the course of the audit.

Less experienced members of the audit engagement team must be encouraged to ask questions of other senior and more experienced members of the engagement team. Audit engagement partners must also ensure that tasks are assigned to members of the audit engagement team that they are competent to undertake.

More experienced team members must undertake regular reviews of work of those less experienced team members, ensuring that the work complies with professional standards and applicable laws and regulatory frameworks. More experienced team members must also consider whether there is a need to revise the timing, nature and extent of audit procedures and whether the work performed supports the conclusions reached. In addition, more experienced members of the engagement team must also review whether or not the audit evidence obtained is sufficient and appropriate.

REVIEW

The audit engagement partner has a responsibility to ensure that the audit team have generated sufficient and appropriate audit evidence to support the opinion that the engagement partner will form on an entity's financial statements. In doing so, the engagement partner must ensure that the audit is directed, supervised and performed in compliance with all professional standards and applicable legal and regulatory frameworks.

The engagement partner must also be responsible for performing a review of the audit documentation and hold discussions with the engagement teams concerning the audit documentation. The discussion should address whether sufficient appropriate audit evidence has been obtained to support the conclusions reached and for the auditor's report to be issued. This review and discussion must take place before the date of the auditor's report.

The engagement partner must ensure that they undertake a timely review of the audit work, in particular those areas that require critical judgement or those areas that are particularly difficult or contentious. The engagement partner should also review the critical risks and other areas that the audit engagement partner considers important. [ISA220.A18]

In undertaking the review of the audit documentation, the audit engagement partner need not review every single document pertaining to the audit, though they may choose to do so. However, it is important that the engagement partner documents the extent and timing of their review to comply with the requirements laid down in ISA 230. [ISA220.A19]

The engagement partner also has a responsibility to ensure that the auditor's report is appropriate in the circumstances. For example, if the financial statements contain material misstatements, then the audit engagement partner must consider the material misstatements in issuing an appropriate opinion.

Use of an Auditor's Expert

There could be cases where an audit requires someone with specialist knowledge of a certain area. For example, agreeing the valuations placed on a complex financial instrument. In such cases the engagement partner is responsible for agreeing with that team member the nature, scope and objectives of the member's work; and the respective roles of, and the nature, timing and extent of communication between, that member and other members of the audit team.

In addition, the engagement partner must also review the adequacy of that member's work including the relevance and reasonableness of that member's findings or conclusions and their consistency with other audit evidence obtained during the course of the audit. [ISA220.A20]

DIFFICULT AND CONTENTIOUS MATTERS

The audit engagement partner must ensure that the engagement team has consulted appropriately where difficult and contentious matters have been encountered. For example, in the case of a difficult taxation issue, the engagement partner should ensure that an appropriate tax expert has been consulted in this respect.

Where consultation with others on difficult or contentious matters is deemed appropriate, the engagement partner must ensure that those consulted have the appropriate knowledge, seniority and experience in order to be effective. In some cases it may be appropriate to consult outside the firm, for example, on difficult taxation matters.

QUALITY CONTROL REVIEW

The audit engagement partner must ensure that where he/she has concluded that a quality control review is required, then an engagement quality control reviewer has been appointed. The engagement partner has a responsibility to ensure that he/she discusses significant matters arising during the audit with the quality control reviewer.

Practical Insight

It is often the case that some firms of auditors will perform non-audit services for their client, for example, payroll or taxation services. In such cases, the audit engagement partner must consider whether a quality control review is required by reference to the threats imposed by virtue of the non-audit work the firm performs for the audit client.

The quality control reviewer must perform an objective evaluation of the significant judgements made by the engagement team and the conclusions reached. The quality control reviewer must discuss significant matters with the engagement partner as well as undertake a review of the financial statements subject to audit and the proposed auditor's report. Quality control reviewers must also undertake a review of the audit documentation in respect of the significant judgements made, evaluate the conclusions reached by the engagement team and determine the appropriateness of these conclusions.

Where the audit client is a listed entity, then the quality control reviewer must also consider:

- The engagement team's independence in relation to the audit assignment.
- Whether the engagement team has consulted appropriate personnel in respect of difficult or contentious issues.
- Whether the audit documentation reflects the work performed in relation to the significant judgements as well as supporting the conclusions reached by the engagement team.

In some cases, the quality control reviewer may not agree with the opinions of the engagement team. Where such differences arise, then the audit engagement team will follow the firm's policies and procedures for dealing with and resolving differences of opinion.

'HOT' AND 'COLD' REVIEWS

'Hot' and 'Cold' file reviews are often undertaken to guarantee compliance with quality control and ensure that audits are conducted in accordance with the ISAs. 'Hot' reviews are undertaken prior to the audit report being signed in order to identify any issues which should be resolved, or additional audit procedures which should be undertaken, prior to the audit report being issued. In contrast, 'cold' file reviews are undertaken after the auditor's report has been signed.

Chapter Roundup

ISA 220 runs in collaboration with ISQC 1 'Quality Control for Firms that Perform Audits and Reviews of Financial Statements, and Other Assurance and Related Services Engagements'.

ISA 220 requires the firm to establish and maintain a system of quality control to provide it with reasonable assurance that:

(a) the firm and personnel comply with professional standards and applicable legal and regu-latory requirements; and

(b) the reports issued by the firm or engagement partners are appropriate in the circumstances.

The engagement partner takes full responsibility for the audit and overall quality control.

Engagement partners must take appropriate action where there is evidence that members of the engagement team have not been complying with applicable ethical requirements.

In recurring audits, the engagement partner must consider any information that would have caused the firm to decline the audit engagement had that information been available at the time.

Engagement partners are responsible for assigning a team to a particular audit assignment.

More experienced team members must undertake regular reviews of the work of less experienced team members.

The engagement partner must undertake a review of the evidence which the engagement team have generated to support the audit opinion.

The engagement partner need not review every single document, but does need to document the extent and timing of their review.

The engagement partner must ensure adequate consultation has occurred by the engagement team in respect of difficult and contentious issues.

Quality control reviews must be undertaken where required. These primarily take the form of 'hot' and 'cold' file reviews.

---

7 ISA 230 (REVISED) AUDIT DOCUMENTATION

This standard deals with the responsibilities of the auditor in terms of preparing audit documentation for an audit of financial statements. Although the title of this ISA may sound fairly innocuous, the concept of audit *evidence*; *enabling* effective *review*, including *quality control* are vital and necessary features of any audit. This has been demonstrated in a recent well-publicised court case involving auditors.

Audit documentation that meets the requirements of this ISA provides the evidence of the basis of the auditor's conclusions and evidence that the work performed was planned and performed in accordance with the ISAs. [ISA230.2]

Audit documents must record the audit procedures performed and are commonly referred to as 'working papers'. Audit documentation must be prepared on a timely basis and in such a way that allows an experienced auditor, with no previous connection to the audit assignment, to understand the nature, timing and extent of audit procedures performed. In addition, the documentation must also ensure that an experienced auditor, with no previous connection to the audit assignment, is able to understand the results of the audit procedures and the audit evidence obtained as a result of those procedures, together with being able to understand the significant matters arising during the course of the audit and the conclusions reached therefrom.

Preparing sufficient and appropriate audit documentation on a timely basis will enhance the quality of the audit and facilitate the effective review and evaluation of the audit evidence obtained and the conclusions drawn therefrom.

Audit documentation should record:

- The identifying characteristics of the specific items or matters tested.
- Who performed the audit work and the date the audit work was completed.
- Who reviewed the audit work and the date the audit work was reviewed. [ISA230.9]

Where the auditor identifies information that is inconsistent with the auditor's final conclusions, then the auditor needs to document how the inconsistencies have been addressed. [ISA230.11]

There may be exceptional circumstances when an auditor needs to depart from a relevant requirement in the ISAs. In such circumstances then the auditor needs to document how the alternative audit procedures adopted achieve the requirement and the reasons for the departure. [ISA230.12]

ASSEMBLY

The auditor should assemble and complete the administrative tasks pertinent to the audit in a timely manner. When the audit file has been assembled then the auditor must not delete or discard any of the audit documentation before the end of its retention period. [ISA230.14.15]

In exceptional circumstances, the auditor may perform additional or new procedures which result in new conclusions being drawn from the additional or new procedures. Where this occurs, the audit shall document:

- The circumstances encountered.
- The new or additional audit procedures performed, audit evidence obtained and conclusions reached, as well as their effect on the auditor's report.
- When and by whom the resulting changes to audit documentation were made and reviewed. [ISA230.16]

Illustration of an Audit Working Paper

Client: Cardello Enterprises Inc
Subject: Health and Safety
File Ref: C4
Year End: 31 December 20X8

Prepared by: AJP
Date: 02.03.20X9
Reviewed by: TFR
Date: 20.03.20X9

Objective

The objective of this meeting was to confirm whether or not the company has complied with its obligations under Health and Safety legislation. Health and Safety legislation has been deemed a central law and regulation for Cardello Enterprises Inc and any breach of such may have going concern issues.

Work Performed

We held a discussion with Lucas Stevens, Managing Director, on 2 March 20XX to discuss the company's compliance with Health and Safety legislation. Lucas Stevens provided me with a copy of the latest Health and Safety inspection which was undertaken on 1 February 20XX (refer to schedule C5). This report confirms that the company's Health and Safety procedures are sufficient and that they have complied with Health and Safety legislation. Lucas Stevens confirmed that they have three internal Health and Safety specialists as well as an external Health and Safety specialist who monitors, on a regular basis, the company's compliance with Health and Safety issues.

Lucas Stevens confirmed that the entity takes Health and Safety extremely seriously and any employees who breach Health and Safety are taken through the entity's disciplinary procedures.

Results and Evaluation

See schedule C5 for the results of the Health and Safety inspection undertaken by the Health and Safety Directorate. I have also obtained copies of the internal Health and Safety Review which was undertaken on 21 March 20XX (refer to schedule C6). There was no indication of any breach of Health and Safety legislation.

Conclusion

Based on the evidence obtained, I am satisfied that no breaches of Health and Safety legislation have occurred.

ISA 230 allows audit documentation to be recorded on paper or recorded in an electronic format. More audit firms are switching to electronic audit documentation in their attempts to contribute to environmentally friendly issues.

Auditors need to document any discussions held with the client on a timely basis as discussion is an audit procedure. For example, in the illustration above, the auditor had documented their discussions with the client in connection with health and safety issues. ISA 500 recognises that such discussions, in their entirety, do not constitute an adequate basis for the auditor to form a conclusion, but it does help explain or clarify information contained within audit documentation.

Illustration

In identifying related parties, the auditor will discuss such issues with management and, where applicable, those charged with governance. ISA 500 recognises that 'inquiry' complements additional audit procedures and the auditor will undertake additional procedures to generate sufficient appropriate audit evidence that all related parties have been identified and adequately disclosed within the financial statements. Such procedures may include review of correspondence, review of the entries held by the Registrar of Companies (Companies House in the UK), review of the bank audit letter(s), review of legal correspondence and review of accounting records.

Audit documentation will also confirm compliance with other ISAs, for example:

- Planning documentation will confirm compliance with ISA 315.
- The auditor's report will confirm compliance with ISA 700.
- A signed letter of engagement prior to commencement of the audit confirms management have agreed to the terms of the audit engagement.

Without such documentation on file, it is not possible to demonstrate compliance with this, or indeed other, ISAs.

SIGNIFICANT MATTERS

In a lot of cases there are instances when significant matters require significant judgements by the auditor. In such cases, the auditor needs to document the matters that have given rise to the significant risks, which are usually addressed at the planning stage. The auditor also needs to document the results of all the audit procedures performed during the audit together with any circumstances that cause the auditor significant difficulty in applying audit procedures. As the audit file must also support the audit opinion, the auditor also needs to document any findings that could result in the modification to an audit opinion. For example, if the company has refused to prepare a statement of cash flows, this needs to be documented.

Auditors also need to document the basis for their conclusions in subjective areas, such as related parties (see the illustration above). In addition, where it is deemed necessary to utilise the services of an expert, the auditor needs to document the basis for these conclusions.

All audit procedures need to be documented. For example, where the auditor is testing payables for understatement, they would ordinarily look at a sample of goods received notes. Identification of specific items or matters tested need to be documented to show compliance with ISAs. For areas that require observance procedures, for example, attendance at the inventory count, then the auditor may record the process or matter being observed, the relevant individuals and their respective responsibilities as well as the items of inventory that were subject to sampling.

DEPARTURES FROM THE REQUIREMENTS OF ISAs

Certain audits will require compliance with certain ISAs. For example, if the entity being audited is not a member of a group or the parent of a group, then nothing in ISA 600 will be relevant. Where ISAs are relevant to an audit of financial statements, then all requirements contained with the ISA become a requirement.

Audit documentation should only be applied to ISAs that are relevant in the circumstances.

ISA 230 (revised) should be applied having regard to the provisions in ISQC 1 'Quality Control for Firms that Perform Audits and Reviews of Financial Statements, and Other Assurance and Related Services Engagements' insofar as issues such as:

- timely completion;
- enabling of quality control; and
- retention of documentation.

Chapter Roundup

Audit documentation facilitates effective reviews of audit work which also confirms quality control compliance.

Audit documentation is commonly referred to as 'working papers' or 'workpapers'.

Audit documentation should be prepared in such a way that allows an experienced auditor, with no previous connection to the audit, to understand the nature, timing and extent of audit procedures performed, the results thereof, the evidence obtained as a result of those procedures and gain an understanding of significant matters arising during the course of the audit together with the conclusions reached.

Documentation should record:

(a)   the identifying characteristics of the specific items or matters tested;
(b)   who performed the audit work and the date it was completed; and
(c)   who reviewed the audit work and the date it was reviewed.

Where departure from a relevant requirement in the ISAs is necessary, the auditor shall document how the alternative procedures adopted achieved the requirement together with reasons for the departure.

Audit files shall be assembled in a timely manner. ISQC 1 suggests full file assembly within 60 days of the auditor's report being signed.

Where additional and/or new procedures result in new conclusions being drawn, the auditor shall document:

(a)   the circumstances encountered;
(b)   the new and/or additional procedures performed, the evidence obtained and the conclusions reached together with the effect on the auditor's report; and
(c)   when, and by whom, the resulting changes to the audit documentation were made and reviewed.

8 ISA 240 (REDRAFTED) THE AUDITOR'S RESPONSIBILITIES RELATING TO FRAUD IN AN AUDIT OF FINANCIAL STATEMENTS

The objective of this ISA is to outline the responsibilities the auditor has in connection with fraud issues. Fraud can be extremely difficult to detect due to the fact that most frauds are designed to be concealed. Fraud has become a major issue within the accountancy profession over recent years, which has been accentuated by well-publicised corporate disasters.

It is widely understood that misstatements within a set of general purpose financial statements can arise from either fraud or error. Misstatements within a set of financial statements are classified as fraud or error depending on whether they are intentional or unintentional.

ISA 240 (redrafted) differentiates fraud from error and defines fraud as:

> *an intentional act by one or more individuals among management, those charged with govern-ance, employees, or third parties, involving the use of deception to obtain an unjust or illegal advantage.*
>
> [ISA240.11(a)]

Error, on the other hand, is defined as:

> *an unintentional misstatement in the financial statements including the omission of an amount or disclosure.*
>
> [ISA240.11(b)]

Fraud can also be sub-divided into two further categories:

- management fraud; and
- employee fraud.

Management fraud refers to fraud involving one or more members of management or those charged with governance whilst employee fraud refers to the level of fraud committed by non-management. In addition, the term 'manipulation of financial statements' refers to the financial statements being deliberately amended to achieve a higher or lower earnings level than has actually occurred — this is also referred to as 'earnings management'.

Primarily, management fraud involves management overriding the internal controls within an entity. The actual amounts involved can be substantial and the auditors need to consider this carefully. ISA 240 (redrafted) requires the auditor to maintain an attitude of professional scepticism, thus allowing the auditor to recognise that a material misstatement due to fraud could potentially exist. Regardless of the auditor's past history with the audit client and integrity of management or those charged with governance, the auditor must maintain a degree of professional scepticism throughout the course of the audit.

Employee fraud, on the other hand, is concerned with employees exploiting weaknesses in the internal control environment for personal financial gain. These instances of fraud could occur at both ends of the spectrum in that they may be very small to substantial.

ISA 240 (redrafted) requires the auditor to consider fraud and error at the planning stage with the expectation that the financial statements may contain a material misstatement which has been caused by fraud or error. The auditors should:

- Discuss fraud risk and incidence with management and those charged with governance and document this discussion.
- Discuss with the engagement team how the financial statements may be susceptible to material misstatement whether caused by fraud or error.
- Consider whether one or more fraud risk factors are present.
- Perform audit procedures to test the appropriateness of journal entries, test the risk of management override of internal controls, review accounting estimates and their appropriateness and understand the business rationale for transactions outside the normal course of business.
- Obtain specific representations from management and those charged with governance including its assessment of the risk of fraud.
- Consider the implications under the auditor's legal and regulatory obligations.

Fraud, by its very nature, can be extremely difficult to detect and in some cases even a material fraud can remain unnoticed by the auditor despite the audit work being satisfactory. This is accentuated by the inherent limitations in an audit and the fact that the risk of not detecting a material misstatement resulting from fraud is higher than the risk of not detecting a material misstatement due to error. It follows, therefore, that the audit opinion may be unmodified but that is not to say that the financial statements are absolutely free from material misstatement or error.

RESPONSIBILITIES

The overall responsibility to prevent and detect fraud or error lies with management and those charged with governance. Management and those charged with governance should establish a control environment and have policies and procedures in place to safeguard the entity's assets and ensure efficient conduct of the entity's business. Management and those charged with governance also have a responsibility to ensure that the internal controls adopted by them and the policies and procedures put in place by them also allow the entity to prepare financial statements that present fairly, in all material respects, in accordance with their specific financial reporting framework.

Even the most robust internal controls will not prevent the risk of misstatements within the financial statements. At best they will reduce, but certainly not eliminate, the risk of misstatement.

As part of the audit planning, the auditor may be able to identify potential opportunities for fraud to be committed and they will obtain reasonable assurance that the financial statements taken, as a whole, are free from material misstatement whether caused by fraud or error. Again, it is impossible for the auditor to obtain absolute assurance that material misstatements within the financial statements will be detected because of the inherent limitations of an audit, such as the use of judgement, limited sampling techniques and the fact that the audit evidence obtained by the auditor is persuasive rather than conclusive in nature.

DISCUSSION AMONGST THE ENGAGEMENT TEAM

ISA 240 (redrafted) requires the engagement team to discuss the susceptibility of the entity's financial statements to material misstatements due to fraud. The engagement partner must also be involved in this discussion and allows the engagement team the opportunity for more experienced members to share their insights about how and where the financial statements may contain a material misstatement due to fraud. Such a discussion should ordinarily cover:

- How management could override the entity's internal controls and how the financial statements could potentially be misstated due to fraud.
- How the entity could manipulate the financial statements for the purposes of 'earnings management'.
- Whether there are incentives or pressures for management or others to commit fraud — for example, a breach in loan covenants.
- How management and those charged with governance implement sufficient controls and oversee employees who have access to cash or other assets of the entity.
- Whether management or other key employees have had an unusual change of lifestyle or demonstrate unexplained behaviour.
- Ensuring that all members of the engagement team maintain a degree of professional scepticism throughout the assignment.
- Whether there are any circumstances present that may give rise to a presence of fraudulent activity.
- Discussions about how unpredictable audit testing can be undertaken and the nature, timing and extent of that testing.
- How audit procedures are selected to respond to the risk that the financial statements contain a material misstatement due to fraud.
- Discussions concerning any allegations of fraudulent activity. [ISA240.A11]

This discussion is a vital aspect of the audit planning as it allows the engagement team to develop an audit strategy that is directly responsive to the risk that the financial statements contain a material misstatement due to fraud.

Where a small audit is being carried out, it may be the case that the auditor is a sole practitioner, therefore without an engagement team available. Where this is the case, then the sole practitioner will consider the susceptibility of the financial statements to material misstatement due to fraud.

RISK ASSESSMENT

The provisions in ISA 315 (redrafted) require the auditor to obtain an understanding of the entity and the environment in which it operates. This also includes a requirement for the auditor to consider the risk that the financial statements contain a material misstatement due to fraud. In undertaking their risk assessment, the auditor must ensure they discuss with management and those charged with governance how they exercise oversight of the management's internal controls and how these mitigate the risk of fraud.

Discussions with management and those charged with governance are not absolute. Indeed, the mere fact that the auditor has discussed the risk of fraud with management and those charged with governance, who may confirm that no fraud has been committed during the year, or that they are not aware of any allegations of fraud, is simply not enough to reduce the risk of material misstatement due to fraud to an acceptable level. In recognition of this, the auditor should also ensure that they:

- Consider whether one or more fraud risk factors are present.
- Perform analytical procedures to identify whether any unusual or unexpected trends have occurred in the financial statements.
- Refer to other information that has come to light that may indicate whether the financial statements contain a material misstatement due to fraud.

Discussions with management and those charged with governance should identify the likely levels of risk that the financial statements contain a material misstatement due to fraud. In many cases, it is appropriate to discuss with management and those charged with governance how they ensure that they communicate ethical issues to their employees as well as identify the processes involved and adopted by management and those charged with governance in terms of mitigating the risk of material misstatement due to fraud.

CHARACTERISTICS OF FRAUD

Fraud is essentially categorised into:

- fraudulent financial reporting; and
- misappropriation of assets.

Each category of fraud generally involves incentives or pressures to commit fraud. For example, if financiers have imposed covenants on loans and the entity is in breach of those covenants which then pose a risk that the financier will 'call in' their debt this may present an opportunity for fraudulent financial reporting.

Misappropriation of Assets

Misappropriation of assets can occur when an individual exploits a weakness in the entity's internal control environment. Consider the following illustration.

Illustration

Facts

Stopford Interiors Inc operates in the 'Do-it-Yourself' industry and is largely cash-based. It employs ten till operatives and one clerical assistant in the cash office. The store opens seven days a week and the clerical assistant works Monday to Friday. Each weekend's takings are kept in the store safe and are banked when the clerical assistant returns to work on the Monday.

The clerical assistant is responsible for ensuring that each till 'balances' and daily reconciliations are performed by the clerical assistant. Any discrepancies over $20 are investigated with any discrepancies under this threshold being written off.

The audit for the year ended 31 December 2010 is being planned and this is the first year the audit firm has audited the entity. The audit senior has been reviewing the bank reconciliation relating to the previous year's audit, which had been obtained by the previous firm of auditors. The bank reconciliation has an outstanding lodgement of $7,000 relating to cash banked on 31 December 2009 which is expected to clear the bank statements immediately in January 2010.

The audit senior has noted that the $7,000 has not, in fact, cleared when expected and has approached the clerical assistant in an attempt to resolve why this money has not cleared the bank when expected. The clerical assistant stated that the cash balances as at 31 December 2009 had been 'double-counted' in error and as a result the bank reconciliation was over-stated by $7,000.

The audit senior approached the audit manager with this explanation and the audit manager confirmed that more substantive detailed testing should be undertaken on the takings in an attempt to confirm whether or not this was an anomalous error or whether there was, in fact, a problem with the internal controls.

Result

It was found that the clerical assistant had committed a fraud resulting in a financial loss to the company of some $25,000 over a two-year period. The clerical assistant had exploited a weakness in the company's internal control environment being that of a complete lack of segregation of duties. It was found that management were divorced from the day-to-day overseeing of the cash bankings.

The above illustration demonstrates how a financial fraud can be committed by an employee who exploits a weakness in the internal control environment and how misappropriation of assets can occur by management, and those charged with governance, failing to implement a satisfactory level of internal controls.

Other examples of asset misappropriation could include inventing fictitious employees or suppliers and then allowing the company to pay for goods or services not received or stealing the entity's inventory for personal use or sale. In such rare cases, the entity's assets could be used to secure personal finance (i.e. by allowing financiers to place a charge on the entity's assets).

Fraudulent Financial Reporting

Fraudulent financial reporting, however, is where management and those charged with governance deceive the users of financial statements by manipulating the financial statements in such a way to achieve a certain outcome. For example, financial statements could be manipulated to reduce tax liabilities by reducing revenues or increasing expenses. Conversely, financial statements could be manipulated in the opposite way by inflating profitability in an attempt to secure bank finance, avoid breaching loan covenants or deceive potential investors.

Fraudulent financial reporting can be engineered in a number of ways. Primarily, fraudulent financial reporting is achieved by altering the accounting records or supporting documentation from which the financial statements are prepared. In addition, fraudulent financial reporting may be engineered by the misapplication of accounting principles. Other techniques to achieve fraudulent financial reporting are:

- Recording fictitious journal entries, particularly close to the year end.
- Inappropriately adjusting assumptions and changing judgements used to estimate account balances.
- Omitting, advancing or delaying recognition in the financial statements of events and transactions that have occurred during the reporting period.
- Concealing, or not disclosing, facts that could affect the amounts recorded in the financial statements.
- Engaging in complex transactions that are structured to deliberately misrepresent the financial position or financial performance of the entity.
- Altering records and terms related to significant and unusual transactions.

Practical Insight

Accounting for leases has always posed a problem for the accountancy profession because of the way certain leases are accounted for in an entity's income statement and/or statement of financial position (balance sheet). The main problem is incorrectly classifying a 'finance' lease as an 'operating lease' resulting in 'off-balance sheet finance'. There are proposals between the International Accounting Standards Board (IASB) and the American Financial Accounting Standards Board (FASB) to overhaul lease accounting so that all leases appear as finance leases within an entity's statement of financial position (balance sheet). Current requirements for a finance lease to be recognised in an entity's statement of financial position (balance sheet) are where the risks and rewards of ownership of the leased asset have substantially passed to the lessee. However, the IASB and FASB have concluded that regardless of whether a lease is classified as an operating lease, lease contracts will always create rights and obligations that meet the definition of an asset and a liability.

AUDIT TESTING

In dealing with fraud issues, the auditor should, at all times, maintain a degree of professional scepticism and expect that the financial statements may contain a material misstatement due to fraud. The following audit tests cover a broad range of situations, though the following may not be appropriate or necessary in each circumstance.

- Unannounced visits by the auditor to conduct inventory counts at locations not previously visited by the auditors.
- Developing an element of unpredictability in audit procedures.
- Reviews of management information for periods other than at the reporting date and investigating any unusual transactions or amendments.
- Performing substantive analytical procedures using disaggregated data. For example looking at the gross profit margins by location, line of business or month and comparing the results of these procedures to the auditor's expectations.
- Seeking additional audit evidence from sources outside of the entity.
- Where other firms of auditors are used, for example at one or more subsidiaries, divisions or branches, discussing with them the extent of the work necessary to address the risk of material misstatement due to fraud.

- Performing 'computer assisted audit techniques' (CAATs) such as data mining to test for anomalies in a population.
- Where an act of fraud has been committed discuss with the entity's staff the controls in place and how they address the risk.
- Performing procedures on account reconciliations for periods other than the reporting date.
- Testing the integrity of computer-produced records and transactions.

FRAUD IN RELATION TO REVENUE RECOGNITION

Revenue recognition has been a fraud 'hot spot' in the profession for many years. The recognition of revenue in the correct reporting period is critical if fraudulent financial reporting is to be avoided and it is important that the auditor performs procedures that are responsive to the risk of material misstatement due to revenue recognition. A prime example of fraudulent financial reporting due to revenue recognition is where an entity deliberately recognises revenue in a later period principally to reduce its tax liabilities.

The concept of revenue recognition can be a complex issue and in recent years has been the subject of some high profile accounting restatements, particularly in the US. Undeniably, there can be a temptation to manipulate revenue for various reasons and it is for this reason that standard setters are particularly keen on the principles of revenue recognition. In addition, there can sometimes be considerable taxation implications if revenue is inappropriately recognised or if it is deferred inappropriately.

Revenue recognition is dealt with in IAS 18 'Revenue'. In the UK, Application Note G (ANG) to FRS 5 'Reporting the Substance of Transactions' deals with such issues. Both standards, however, take a similar stance.

ANG does not define the term 'revenue'. The basic principle to be applied when considering revenue is to decipher whether there is an increase in an asset (i.e. receivables/debtors) or a reduction in a liability (for example, where a customer has made an advance payment and the reporting entity has fulfilled some of its obligations). ANG does, in fact, define 'turnover' as:

The revenue resulting from exchange transactions under which a seller supplies to customers the goods or services that it is in business to provide.

Example 1

A motor dealer is in the business of selling new and used vehicles. It has a fleet of demonstration vehicles which it allows customers to test drive before they decide to purchase. The dealer adopts a policy of using the demonstration vehicles for one year and then selling the vehicles on. The question is, does the sale of one of the used vehicles constitute revenue or is it a disposal of non-current (fixed) assets?

As the motor dealer is in the business of selling new and used vehicles, the sale of one of the demonstration vehicles would constitute revenue.

Example 2

Company A Limited is a distributor of construction equipment and has recently expanded its operations to the extent that it has had a purpose-built distribution centre built and has sold its old building for $500,000.

The sale of the company's premises would not give rise to revenue because such a sale of company premises would be a disposal of a non-current (fixed) asset and as such the gain or loss on disposal of the company premises would be reported separately after operating profit within the income statement.

Long-Term Contractual Performance

Long-term contracts are also covered in the provisions in IAS 11 'Construction Contracts' and UK SSAP 9 'Stocks and Work-in-Progress'. Again, both standards take a similar stance.

Long-term contracts need to be assessed on a contract-by-contract basis. Turnover and related costs are accounted for in the income statement as contract activity progresses. A typical calculation is as follows:

Total contract revenue $\times$ % of completion = revenue to be recognised

---

Example 3

A contractor has a fixed price contract for $12,000. The total estimated costs amount to $7,500 resulting in an expected profit of $4,500. At the end of year one, the contract is estimated to be 40% complete.

As the contract is deemed to make a profit, the entity should record ($12,000 $\times$ 40%) $4,800 in revenue. It should also recognise ($7,500 $\times$ 40%) $3,000 in costs resulting in a profit being recognised of $1,800 in year one.

If the contract was estimated to make a loss of $1,000, for example, then the entity should still recognise $4,800 in revenue, but then $5,800 of costs to result in the loss being recognised of $1,000. IAS 11 states that losses should be recognised as soon as they are foreseen.

UITF Abstract 40 (UK Only)

The Urgent Issues Task Force issued Abstract 40 on 10 March 2005. This gave rise to considerably controversy in the profession; because prior to the issuance of UITF 40, entities such as professional partnerships (firms of solicitors and accountants etc.) recognised revenue in their financial statements when fee notes were raised. Any work-in-progress was carried forward to the next accounting period. UITF 40 says that revenue should be recognised when the entity obtains a 'right to consideration'.

Of course it can sometimes be difficult to establish when a right to consideration has been obtained. Most accountants' view is that no right to consideration exists until the work is complete (a half-completed tax return is often cited). On the basis that no right to consideration exists, no revenue or profit is recognised and work-in-progress is carried forward to the next accounting period. This defers profit and, thus, the associated tax liability.

Where the view is that a right to consideration exists throughout an assignment, all such activity must be accounted for as revenue and no work-in-progress is carried forward in the statement of financial position (balance sheet). This then accelerates revenue and profit and, thus, tax liabilities will also be accelerated. In the UK, HM Revenue and Customs did introduce 'spreading provisions' but in order for the spreading provisions to be granted the reporting entity's accounting policy must be GAAP compliant.

Payments in Advance

Where an entity receives payments in advance, these payments do not represent revenue because they have not been earned by the entity. The entity receiving the payment has to fulfil its obligations to its customer. Until the seller fulfils its obligations, the increase in cash is matched by an increase in liabilities which represents the entity's obligations owed to its customer.

Payments in advance can also relate to invoices issued to customers which span two accounting periods. For example, if an entity's year end is 31 March 2010 and it invoices its customers on 31 March 2010 for services for the period 1 April 2010 to 30 September 2010, the entity should recognise the sale in the next accounting period (the year to 31 March 2011).

Bill and Hold Arrangements

Under these types of arrangements, legal title to goods passes before the goods have been delivered.

Under normal circumstances, revenue on the sale of such goods will only ever be recognised when the performance conditions have been satisfied (for example, delivery of the goods to the buyer). Normally, customers may place an order for goods and then take delivery and the seller would recognise revenue upon delivery of the goods to the customer. However, in order for sales to be recognised as 'bill and hold' arrangements, there have to be some specific conditions met in order to distinguish bill and hold arrangements from executor contracts, such conditions are:

- The goods should be complete and ready for immediate delivery.
- The seller does not retain any significant performance obligations other than simply storing the goods safely and arranging for their delivery at the customer's request.
- The seller should have the right to be paid regardless of whether the goods are shipped (subject to any rights of return).
- The goods are capable of being separately identified and not capable of being used to fulfil other orders.
- The terms of the bill and hold sale should be in accordance with the customer's commercial objectives and not those of the seller.

Rights of Return

It is very common for entities, particularly those in the retail industry, to have a policy of giving refunds on returned goods, regardless of whether the goods are defective or not. Rights of return can be explicit or implicit in contractual arrangements and can also arise through statutory requirements. Revenue should exclude the sales value of expected returns. The retailer should be able to estimate reliably the sales value of the returns by looking at historical trends, for example, looking at the amount of similar goods that have been returned in the past as a proportion of total sales of that particular product.

However, where the seller cannot reliably estimate the value of future returns, it should calculate the maximum amount possible that it could be required to pay back to customers.

Example 4

A retailer sells a range of jumpers for $20 each. The cost to the retailer is $10 and the retailer's returns policy allows customers to return goods within 28 days of purchase if the jumpers are unworn and undamaged. Historical trends have shown that approximately 10% of these jumpers will be returned by customers with half of them being resold.

The retailer should recognise $20 – (10% × $20 = $2) = $18 as turnover with the remaining $2 being recognised as a provision for returned goods. Cost of sales on each sale is the cost of the jumpers at $10 less ($10/$20 × 50% = $0.25c), therefore $9/75. The 25c reduction in stock will partially offset the provision for returns.

Warranties

Manufacturers of goods will often include a warranty. In addition, customers can also purchase an extended warranty.

Example 5

A manufacturer of hairdryers places a one-year warranty on its products. Customers can also purchase warranties to cover years two and three.

Where customers take up the extended warranty, the revenue should be deferred and recognised in revenue on a straight-line basis over the period for which the extended warranty is provided.

Presentation of Revenue as Principal or Agent

In order to recognise revenue as principal, all risks and rewards should be retained by the principal. Usually this will be evident by the ability to set the price of the goods and have exposure to the risks of technical obsolescence of the goods.

Where the seller acts as principal turnover, the gross amount is received or receivable in return for the principal's performance under the contract.

Where the seller acts as an agent, the commission the agent receives is reported as revenue. The commission is calculated as the amount billed to the customer less the amount paid to the principal.

Example 6

Company A (the agent) arranges to ship goods to Company B on behalf of Company C (the principal). The terms of the arrangement are that Company B will pay Company A, who will then pay Company C. Company A will take a 20% commission.

In the above illustration, Company A is acting as agent. It will receive payment from Company B which it will then pass on to Company C, less 20% commission. Company A should recognise the amount billed to the customer (Company B) less the amount paid to the principal (Company C) as revenue. It should not recognise any amounts in its turnover as agent that have to be paid to the principal.

PROCEDURES ON REVENUE RECOGNITION

Some typical procedures are as follows:

- Performing substantive analytical procedures on disaggregated data such as the comparison of revenue reporting on a month-by-month basis and comparing this to the auditor's expectations.
- Performing procedures on an entity's sales or shipment of goods near the end of the reporting period and making enquiries of an entity's sales personnel concerning any unusual terms or conditions associated with these transactions.
- Obtaining confirmations from customers concerning certain terms and conditions relative to a sale. Certain goods may be subject to conditions such as 'sale or return' or cancellation or refund provisions. Such revenue recognition is often influenced by such terms and conditions.
- Perform observance procedures at one or more locations at the reporting date to observe goods being shipped or prepared for shipment and performing cut-off procedures.

The risk of fraud in relation to revenue recognition may be greater in some entities than in others. For example, the risk of fraud in relation to revenue recognition is greater in a largely cash-based business.

The presumption that there is a risk of fraud relating to revenue recognition can be rebutted because the auditor may conclude that the risk of material misstatement due to revenue recognition is not applicable to the entity under audit. Where this presumption is rebutted, it is important that the auditor clearly documents the reasons for rebutting this presumption as required by the ISA.

Illustration

Entity A's principal activity is that of online auction of real estate. It was set up on 1 January 2010 with a reporting date of 31 December 2010. Unfortunately, Entity A has so far been unable to secure any sales because of legal formalities which have not yet been resolved. Therefore, no sales have been reported in the financial statement of Entity A. Entity A is part of a large group based in the UK which is required to be audited under the Companies Act. The auditors have obtained sufficient appropriate audit evidence concerning the fact that Entity A has not undertaken any sales during the year.

The risk of fraud relating to revenue recognition can be rebutted in the case of Entity A because no revenue has been recognised in the financial statements and sufficient appropriate audit evidence has been obtained by the auditor in this respect. However, it is a requirement of the ISA that the auditor documents the reasons for rebutting this presumption.

COMMUNICATION OF FRAUD MATTERS

Where the auditor has obtained evidence that fraud exists, or may exist, the auditor must bring the matter to the attention of the appropriate level of management as soon as is practicable. There is no *de minimis* level in this respect and regardless of how inconsequential the fraud is the auditor must bring it to the attention of the appropriate level of management as soon as is reasonably practicable. In determining the appropriate level of management, the auditor uses their professional judgement and ordinarily the appropriate level of management is at least one level above the person(s) who appears to be involved with the (suspected) fraud.

In communicating matters of fraud to those charged with governance the auditor can choose between oral communication and written communication. In cases where fraud involves senior management or a fraud that results in material misstatement within the financial statements, the auditor has a responsibility to report such in a timely manner and also report such matters in writing.

There may be circumstances when the integrity or honesty of management or those charged with governance is brought into doubt. Where such circumstances arise then the auditor must obtain legal advice to assist in determining the most appropriate course of action.

In certain jurisdictions, the auditor may have a responsibility to communicate matters of fraud to external regulatory bodies and in such cases the auditor's duty of confidentiality may be overridden by statute and the auditor may also consider it appropriate to obtain legal advice to determine the most appropriate course of action in the circumstances. This is particularly relevant in jurisdictions that apply Money Laundering Regulations.

Chapter Roundup

Fraud and error are separately identified in ISA 240. Fraud is 'an intentional act by one or more individuals among management, those charged with governance, employees, or third parties, involving the use of deception to obtain an unjust or illegal advantage.'

Error is 'an unintentional misstatement in the financial statements including the omission of an amount or disclosure.'

Fraud can be sub-divided into 'management fraud' and 'employee fraud'.

Auditors must adopt an attitude of professional scepticism at all stages of the audit.

Discussions about fraud must take place amongst the engagement team and engagement partner.

The responsibility to prevent and detect fraud or error lies with management and those charged with governance.

Discussions with management and those charged with governance should identify the likely risks that the financial statements contain a material misstatement due to fraud.

Fraud can be categorised as fraudulent financial reporting and asset misappropriation.

If the presumption that fraud in relation to revenue recognition is rebutted, the auditor must clearly document the reasons for rebutting this presumption.

Communication of instances of fraud should be made to the appropriate level of management. Where the integrity or honesty of management is brought into question the auditor must seek legal advice.

9 ISA 250 (REDRAFTED) CONSIDERATION OF LAWS AND REGULATIONS IN AN AUDIT OF FINANCIAL STATEMENTS

ISA 250 (redrafted) stipulates the auditor's responsibility to consider laws and regulations pertinent to an audit client in an audit of their financial statements.

Some laws and regulations have a direct effect on the financial statements (for example, in the UK, the Companies Act 2006 has a direct effect on the financial statements). Other laws and regulations do not have a direct effect on the financial statements but may instead have a direct effect on how the entity conducts its business. An example of such a law could be the Health and Safety at Work Act in the UK. Other industries may operate in heavily regulated industries such as banks. [ISA250.2]

The auditor needs to consider laws and regulations pertinent to the client because a breach in such may result in fines or other consequences which may have a material effect on the financial statements.

Responsibility for ensuring that the entity complies with all laws and regulations applicable to it rests with management and those charged with governance. The auditor's responsibility is to identify any non-compliance of laws and regulations which may result in material misstatement within the financial statements. The auditor does not have a responsibility to detect non-compliance with laws and regulations, and whether an act constitutes non-compliance is a matter for a court of law to determine. [ISA250.3]

In recognition that there are laws and regulations that have a direct effect on the financial statements and other laws and regulations that do not then ISA 250 (redrafted) deals with these two instances as follows:

- The provisions of those laws which have a direct effect on the financial statement of a reporting entity such as tax laws. [ISA250.6(a)]
- The provisions of those laws which do not have a direct effect on the financial statements of a reporting entity but compliance with which may have a fundamental effect on the operating aspects of the business and any non-compliance of such may result in material penalties being levied by the appropriate regulatory authorities. [ISA250.6(b)]

ISA 250 (redrafted) defines non-compliance as:

Acts of omission or commission by the entity, either intentional or unintentional, which are contrary to the prevailing laws or regulations. Such acts include transactions entered into by, or in the name of, the entity, or on its behalf, by those charged with governance, management or employees. Non-compliance does not include personal misconduct (unrelated to the business activities of the entity) by those charged with governance, management or employees of the entity.

[ISA250.11]

THE AUDITOR'S CONSIDERATIONS

ISA 315 requires the auditor to obtain an understanding of the entity and the environment in which it operates. The auditor shall also gain an understanding of the entity's legal and regulatory framework and how the entity is complying with that framework.

The auditor needs to gather sufficient evidence to obtain reasonable assurance that the entity is complying with laws and regulations applicable to it. In gathering that evidence the auditor shall perform audit procedures to help identify any acts of non-compliance with the entity's laws and regulations by:

- Making inquiries of management and, where appropriate, those charged with governance to identify whether the entity is complying with such laws and regulations. [ISA250.14(a)]
- Inspect correspondence, where applicable, with relevant licensing or regulatory authorities. [ISA250.14(b)]

The auditor shall ensure that they have written representations from management and, where applicable, those charged with governance, in confirming that all known or suspected non-compliance with laws and regulations have been brought to the auditor's attention. Where the auditor does not identify, or suspect, any act of non-compliance then there is no requirement for the auditor to perform audit tests concerning the entity's compliance with laws and regulations applicable to it.

The auditor shall document the laws and regulations pertinent to the entity and the controls in place to mitigate the risk of non-compliance. In documenting laws and regulations, auditors may find it helpful to use a tabular format which can be headed up as follows:

Law or Regulation	Impact of Breach of Law/Regulation	Controls to Mitigate	Audit Work

---

Illustration

The audit of Lakeside Chemicals Inc is being planned for the year ended 31 December 2010. During the initial assessment the auditor has identified three laws and regulations which are central to the entity's ability to continue as a going concern, namely:

1. Health and Safety legislation.
2. Fire Regulations.
3. Environment Pollution.

Client: Lakeside Chemicals Inc
Subject: Central Laws and Regulations
File Ref: 3.2 (17)
Year End: 31 December 2010

Prepared by: ABC
Date: 5 January 2011
Reviewed by: DEF
Date:

The following laws and regulations are central to the entity's ability to continue as a going concern.

Law or Regulation	Impact of Breach of Law/Regulation	Controls to Mitigate	Audit Work
Health and Safety	Potential litigation — could be sizeable and impact on going concern.	Basic training. Insistence on obtaining basic certificates. Health and safety reviews. Health and safety manual.	Discussions with directors. Review any H&S reports undertaken by a third party. Representation letter. Spot checks. Review correspondence.
Fire Regulations	Risk of substantial loss due to fire. Sizeable fines from the fire authority which could impact on going concern.	Regular assessment in conjunction with Health and Safety. Regular inspection by fire authorities.	Discussions with directors. Check fire extinguishers for evidence of dates of last check. Review correspondence.
Environment Pollution	Sizeable fines which could have an impact on going concern.	Regular assessment by utility companies. Less chemical waste is beneficial to the client as effluent charges will reduce. Regular monitoring of waste.	Review effluent bills during the year. Discuss with directors. Review correspondence.

NON-COMPLIANCE WITH LAWS AND REGULATIONS

Where an act of non-compliance has been identified by the auditor the auditor shall gain an understanding of the nature of the act of non-compliance and the reasons behind its occurrence. In addition, the auditor must also evaluate the possible effect on the financial statements. [ISA250.18]

Where the auditor suspects that there may be an act of non-compliance the auditor shall discuss the matter with management and, where applicable, those charged with governance. Where the outcome of these discussions is insufficient and the effect of non-compliance may be material to the financial statements, legal advice must be sought. The auditor shall also consider the lack of sufficient information about suspected non-compliance and the effect this will have on the auditor's opinion. [ISA250.19]

Where the act of non-compliance occurs between management and those charged with governance, any communication by the auditor concerning non-compliance shall be made to the next higher level of authority of the entity. Again, if the next higher level of authority of the entity does not exist the auditor must obtain legal advice concerning the act of non-compliance. [ISA250.24]

AUDIT OPINION ON THE FINANCIAL STATEMENTS CONCERNING NON-COMPLIANCE

If the auditor concludes that an act of non-compliance has a material effect on the financial statements and has not been reflected in the financial statements the auditor must express a qualified or adverse opinion. [ISA250.25]

Where the auditor is unable to obtain sufficient and appropriate audit evidence to evaluate whether non-compliance that may be material has in fact occurred, the auditor must express a qualified opinion or disclaim an opinion on the grounds of a limitation of scope. [ISA250.26]

If circumstances surrounding potential non-compliance give rise to a limitation of scope the auditor must evaluate the effect on the auditor's opinion. [ISA250.27]

The auditor also has an obligation to report an act of non-compliance to regulatory and enforcement authorities. This may also apply to suspected acts of non-compliance in cases where there is a statutory duty or it is in the general public interest.

Illustration

Placebo Chemicals Inc manufactures chemicals for use in various cleaning products for both household and industrial users. The company's reporting date is 31 December 2009 and on 23 November 2009 the company received a fine from a regulatory authority amounting to $500,000 for failing to dispose of potentially lethal chemicals in a responsible manner and in accordance with legislation governing such disposal. This fine was paid on 5 January 2010. The company's financial statements, which have been prepared under IFRS, for the year end 31 December 2009 have failed to correctly reflect the impact of the fine in them. The board are particularly keen to report a profit this year as they are seeking to make an Initial Public Offering (IPO) on a recognised stock exchange and in their general meeting, it was decided that it was appropriate for them to recognise the impact of the fine in the succeeding year's financial statements as recognising the fine in the current year would turn a reported profit into a loss, which would have a detrimental impact on the company's ability to secure flotation on the stock exchange. In their annual general meeting, the board concluded that it would also be in the company's best interest to 'keep quiet' about the non-compliance issue in front of the auditors.

Clearly by not properly reflecting the impact of the fine in the financial statements for the year ended 31 December 2009, the management team are guilty of fraudulent financial reporting. Not only have they failed to comply with legislation during the year under audit, the impact of which certainly has a material impact on the financial statements, but management may also be committing a further act of non-compliance with legislation by failing to disclose all relevant audit information to its auditors.

The auditors would undoubtedly pick up on the fact that there has been a material breach of legislation resulting in a material fine — if not before certainly during their review of events after the reporting date given the fact that management are deliberately trying to conceal information from the auditors in connection with this fine. The auditors must discuss the implications of failing to recognise a material payable and an associated reduction in profit and must also discuss with them the fact that regardless of the fact that the fine had been paid after the reporting date, a liability did exist at the reporting date. If management of Placebo Chemicals Inc refuse to properly reflect the fine in the 31 December 2009 financial statements, the auditor shall express a qualified or adverse opinion.

Companies are encouraged to adopt policies and procedures to ensure that they comply with all their laws and regulations. In larger entities these may be overseen by an audit committee or an internal audit function. In smaller entities compliance with laws and regulations can be achieved by having a monitoring system and ensuring that procedures meet legal and regulatory requirements. In addition, smaller entities may find it appropriate to maintain a register of laws and regulations which are applicable to them and appoint external agencies or other third parties to regularly check they are complying with them. A classic example of such a case would be a Health and Safety inspector visiting an entity to ensure they are complying in all respects with Health and Safety legislation. It is also fairly common for entities of all sizes to have a 'code of conduct' for their employees and third parties which they must conform to or face disciplinary action.

Where entities have such policies and procedures in place, the auditor must ensure they review these policies and procedures and any correspondence in order to gather evidence that the entity has complied with its laws and regulations. The auditor shall review the entity's policies and procedures and any correspondence and compare these to their knowledge and understanding of the entity's operations. The auditor shall also ensure that they are aware of any technical updates or new legislation which has been introduced which directly affects the entity and confirm whether management and, where applicable, those charged with governance are also aware of updates or new legislation which will affect them.

CHARACTERISTICS OF NON-COMPLIANCE WITH LAWS AND REGULATIONS

In many cases the auditor can identify an act of non-compliance with laws and regulations from sources other than word of mouth from management or those charged with governance. For example:

- Investigations by regulatory or professional bodies could be indicative of an act of non-compliance.
- Adverse media comment.
- Unusual group structures, particularly where subsidiaries/branches/divisions are situated in 'tax havens'.
- Unusual related party transactions.
- Payments for goods and services to countries other than those from where the goods and services have been received.
- Unauthorised transactions.
- Purchasing goods and/or services at prices inordinately above or below fair value.
- Lack of sufficient audit trails for certain transactions.
- Unusual payments or receipts.

RIGHTS AND DUTIES TO REPORT TO REGULATORS IN THE FINANCIAL SECTOR

The auditor's rights and duties to report instances of non-compliance with laws and regulations vary depending on the jurisdiction. In some cases the duty of confidentiality is overridden by a requirement to report non-compliance with laws and regulations to regulatory bodies by law.

Where the auditor is an auditor of a financial institution they may have a statutory duty to report any act of non-compliance or any suspected act of non-compliance to regulatory bodies. In such cases, the auditor must consider whether it is appropriate to obtain legal advice in order to determine the most appropriate course of action.

Suggested Tests for Establishing Compliance with Laws and Regulations

Based on our understanding of the entity's industry, regulatory environment and other external factors and following discussions with management, identify the laws and regulations which have a fundamental effect on the operations of the entity.

Review the extent to which the entity is in compliance with relevant laws and regulations; consider systems in place to ensure compliance and action taken in the event of non-compliance.

Identify any instances of non-compliance, review correspondence or other relevant documentation with the regulatory authorities and consider the impact on the financial statements.

Chapter Roundup

Some laws and regulations have a direct effect on the financial statements, for example, the Companies Act 2006 in the UK. Others may not have a direct effect on the financial statements but may directly affect the conduct of the entity's business, for example Health and Safety at Work legislation.

Laws and regulations need to be considered because a breach in such could result in fines or other consequences which may have a material effect on the financial statements.

Responsibility for compliance with laws and regulations rests with management and those charged with governance.

The auditor shall discuss with management and, where applicable, those charged with governance any suspected acts of non-compliance with laws and regulations.

Any acts of non-compliance between management and those charged with governance must be notified to the next higher level of authority. Where no higher level of authority exists legal advice must be sought.

A qualified or adverse opinion is expressed if the act of non-compliance with laws and regulations has a material effect on the financial statements which has not been reflected within those financial statements.

A qualified, or disclaimer of, opinion will be expressed by the auditor if the auditor is unable to obtain sufficient and appropriate audit evidence to evaluate whether non-compliance that may be material to the financial statement has occurred.

If the auditor encounters situations giving rise to a limitation on the scope of the audit work, the auditor shall evaluate the effect of such a scope limitation on the audit opinion.

10 ISA 260 (REVISED AND REDRAFTED) COMMUNICATION WITH THOSE CHARGED WITH GOVERNANCE

ISA 260 (revised and redrafted) deals with the auditor's responsibility to communicate audit related matters to those charged with governance. The revised and redrafted ISA gives particular focus to two-way communication. The close analysis of the standard that follows helps us have greater understanding on what matters should be significant for those charged with governance; and in particular what the follow-on impact is when there are difficulties.

It is important to understand that this particular standard does not deal with the auditor's requirements to communicate with an entity's management or owners unless they have been specifically charged with a governance role. ISA 260 (revised and redrafted) defines 'those charged with governance' as:

> *The person(s) or organisation(s) (for example, a corporate trustee) with responsibility for overseeing the strategic direction of the entity and obligations related to the accountability of the entity. This includes overseeing the financial reporting process. For some entities in some jurisdictions, those charged with governance may include management personnel, for example, executive members of a governance board of a private or public sector entity, or an owner-manager.*
>
> [ISA260.10(a)]

ISA 260 then goes on to define 'management' as:

> *The person(s) with executive responsibility for the conduct of the entity's operations. For some entities in some jurisdictions, management includes some or all of those charged with governance, for example, executive members of a governance board, or an owner-manager.*
> [ISA260.10(b)]

Effective Two-Way Communication

Effective two-way communication is a key aspect of this standard and this standard recognises the importance of this requirement. It is essential for two-way communication to be achieved during the course of an audit in order to develop a constructive working relationship. A typical example would be to consider the requirements of the auditor to gain an understanding of the entity and the environment in which it operates. Without effective two-way communication, the requirements to gain an understanding of the entity and the environment in which it operates would not be achieved. In respect of effective two-way communication, the auditor needs to determine whether the two-way communication process has been effective in order for an efficient audit to be carried out. Where the two-way communication process has not been effective, then the auditor needs to evaluate the effect that the financial statements might contain a material misstatement and also consider whether the ineffective two-way communication has resulted in a failure to obtain sufficient and appropriate audit evidence and in these respects, the auditor will take appropriate action.

ISA 260 (revised and redrafted) applies in a two-way direction, that is, auditor to client and client to auditor. Management of an entity have a responsibility to communicate matters of governance to those charged with governance. The primary objective of this standard is to communicate matters to those charged with governance in relation to the financial statement audit and to communicate an overview of the planned scope and timing of the audit. In addition, the standard also requires the auditor to obtain governance information from those charged with governance relevant to the audit as well as ensuring that the auditor provides timely results of the audit to the client.

Forms of Communication

The auditor's communication of audit related matters to those charged with governance can be made orally or in writing. The auditor needs to use professional judgement in deciphering which form of communication is appropriate in the circumstances and typical influential factors on the auditor's decision are:

- The size, operating structure, legal structure and communications processes of the entity being subject to audit.
- The nature, sensitivity and significance of the audit matters of governance interest to be communicated.
- The arrangements made with respect to periodic meetings or reporting of audit matters of governance interest.
- The amount of on-going contact and dialogue the auditor has with those charged with governance.
- The obligations imposed by statutory and legal requirements.

In some cases the auditor may decide that oral communication of audit matters to those charged with governance is appropriate. Where oral communications are judged appropriate then the auditor documents in the working papers the matters communicated and any responses to those matters. There may be circumstances where the auditor judges oral communication to be appropriate in the circumstances, but must also take into consideration the nature, sensitivity and significance of the matter(s) and also consider whether it is appropriate to confirm the discussions in respect of the matter(s) discussed in writing.

Significant Findings

ISA 260 (revised and redrafted) requires the auditor to communicate in writing to those charged with governance any significant findings from the audit where the auditor's professional judgement suggests that oral communication would not be adequate. [ISA260.19]

SUBGROUPS

Consider the following structure:

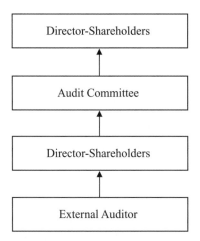

In this structure, the audit committee has been charged with a governance role and, thus, the auditor will report into the audit committee who then report into the director-shareholders. The audit committee is referred to as a 'subgroup' which has been charged with governance. However, the auditor shall also consider whether the auditor needs to communicate with the subgroup's governing body which in this structure would be the director-shareholders. The auditor needs to consider the respective responsibilities of the subgroup and the governing body as well as the nature of the matter(s) to be communicated to those charged with governance. In addition, the auditor also needs to consider whether the subgroup has the authority to take action in relation to the information being communicated and also consider any legal or regulatory matters.

On the other hand, if we were to consider a small entity that does not have an audit committee, the structure will simply be:

In this simple structure (one which is commonly seen in small, owner-managed businesses) the external auditors report directly to the director-shareholders. The director-shareholders could have management responsibilities in their capacity as directors and governance responsibilities in their capacity as shareholders; then the auditor does not need to communicate audit related matters twice to the same director-shareholders.

COMMUNICATION OF MATTERS PRIOR TO THE AUDIT

Prior to the detailed audit of the financial statements, it is a requirement that the auditor communicates to those charged with governance the responsibilities of the auditor, which is to form and express an opinion on the financial statements which management have prepared and which have been overseen by those charged with governance. The auditor shall also ensure that they make those charged with governance aware that the audit of the financial statements does not relieve those charged with governance of their responsibilities.

It is also a requirement that the auditor informs those charged with governance of the general overview of the planned scope and timing of the audit. This is a particularly important issue to discuss with those charged with governance as it will enable them governance to gain a much better understanding of the auditor's work in terms of their risk assessment and by enabling those charged with governance to understand the inherent limitations of an audit. From the auditor's perspective, communicating the planned scope and timing of the audit will also enable the auditor to achieve a better understanding of the entity and the environment in which it operates.

When discussing the planned scope of the audit, it is important that the auditor does not discuss in too much detail the detailed tests to be performed as this may result in the audit becoming too predictable. An element of unpredictability in audit procedures will ensure that audit procedures are responsive to the assessed levels of risk in each audit area.

Illustration — Excerpt of Typical Scope of Service in a Letter of Engagement

Scope of Our Services

Our audit will be carried out with the objective of expressing an opinion on the financial statements.

During the initial discussions, the auditor should also discuss with those charged with governance the reporting structure and to whom the auditor reports ensuring that the auditor is reporting to a body, or individual, who has been charged with a governance role.

COMMUNICATION OF AUDIT FINDINGS

The auditor must also communicate to those charged with governance the findings from the audit. In particular, the auditor must communicate to those charged with governance:

- The auditor's views about the qualitative aspects of the entity's accounting practices and financial reporting. This includes accounting policies, accounting estimates and financial statement disclosures. [ISA260.16(a)]
- Significant difficulties, if any, encountered during the audit. [ISA260.16(b)]
- Where any of those charged with governance are not involved in managing the entity, the auditor should communicate significant matters, if any, arising from the audit that were discussed, or subject to correspondence with management. [ISA260.16(c)(i)]
- Written representations that the auditor is requesting. [ISA260.16(c)(ii)]
- Any other significant matters arising from the audit. [ISA260.16(d)]

Qualitative Aspects of Accounting Practices

The auditor should communicate to those charged with governance issues relating to the qualitative aspects of the entity's accounting practices. This involves the entity's use and application of its accounting policies relative to its particular circumstances. Some examples of qualitative aspects of accounting practices communicated to those charged with governance are as follows:

- In some jurisdictions, it is permissible to adopt the use of what are referred to as the 'alternative accounting rules'. For example, it is common for entities in some jurisdictions to adopt the use of the revaluation model of recognising non-current assets as opposed to the depreciated historic cost model. The auditor may identify which classes of asset have been subjected to the alternative accounting rules and offer information concerning the accounting policies of such similar entities.
- Where the entity changes an accounting policy or legislation requires the entity to make a mandatory change to an accounting policy, the auditor may refer to such a change in their communication.
- Where there is transaction or event within the financial statements which is not covered by a particular accounting standard and management have had to develop an accounting policy accordingly, the auditor may communicate such matters.
- The use of accounting estimates by management and the risk of material misstatement relating to these estimates.
- The issues identified in financial statement disclosures, particularly sensitive disclosures such as related party transactions or contingent liabilities.
- The extent to which the financial statements are affected by unusual transactions, such as a non-recurring fine or substantial write off of asset values.
- Details of any uncorrected misstatements within the financial statements. For example, the entity may decide not to correct trifling errors on the basis of their immateriality.

Significant Difficulties Encountered During the Audit

The auditor should communicate to those charged with governance any significant difficulties encountered during the audit. This could involve a multitude of instances but typically:

- Any significant delays in obtaining information or explanations from management.
- Any inordinate time restrictions imposed which resulted in audit procedures not being carried out thoroughly enough.
- Any imposed limitations placed by the auditor or the entity.
- A lack of co-operation by management.
- Unavailability of information or a lack of information to support amounts and disclosures within the financial statements.

Separate Roles of Governance and Management

In some entities, management are not charged with governance and the auditor may need to discuss certain significant audit-related matters with management which they then must communicate to those charged with governance. Typically discussions with management concerning significant issues may include the way that management are managing the day to day running of the business as well as any material accounting policies that may need to be revised as they are no longer appropriate to the company's circumstances. It may be that the company is planning expansion and the auditor may need to discuss with management how they are proposing to ensure the expansion programme is a success.

Written Representations

The auditor may need to obtain written representations concerning some transactions or events contained within a set of general purpose financial statements. These representations are often referred to as 'letters of representation' or 'management representation' and are obtained as a form of audit evidence, but are not a substitute for other audit evidence. The auditor needs to communicate to those charged with governance the written representations it wishes to obtain and an example letter of representation is shown in Chapter 28.

Other Significant Matters

Other significant matters arising from an audit will all depend on the entity and the audit itself. Typically other significant matters may relate to uncorrected misstatements or the fact that the entity has inadequate internal controls procedures to prevent, detect and correct a material misstatement within the financial statements. The provisions in ISA 265 shall be considered where deficiencies in internal controls have been evidenced.

An illustrative example of a letter covering the above aspects is shown below:

Billingham & Co
Chartered Certified Accountants and Registered Auditors
123 High Street
Anytown
AH14 8UU

The Directors
Cordisan Enterprises Inc
456 Low Street
Any Country
HG76 8UU

Dear Directors,

Following the completion of the audit for the year ended 31 December 2010, we are obliged under International Standard on Auditing 260 to communicate in writing to yourselves the findings from our audit as follows:

Qualitative Aspects of the Entity's Accounting Practices and Financial Reporting

The entity has prepared its financial statements under the International Financial Reporting Standards. We have not become aware of any material departure from the relevant reporting standards and we did not come across any areas of the financial statements which departed from the entity's adopted accounting policies.

Management Representation Letter

We have submitted, under separate cover, a management representation letter which confirms that the directors have made available all the relevant accounting records and other related information including the minutes of all directors' and shareholders' meetings and you have acknowledged on the management representation letter your responsibility for the financial statements which you have prepared for the entity.

In addition, you have also confirmed your responsibilities under [insert relevant legislation] and acknowledged that you have made available all relevant audit information to ourselves.

You have also confirmed in the management representation letter that there are directors' loans made by the company amounting to $430,000.

You have confirmed that you have identified and approved all related party transactions and provided the information for disclosure of all transactions relevant to the entity in the financial statements for the year ended 31 December 2010. You have confirmed that the directors' are regarded as ultimate controlling parties by virtue of their ability to act in concert in respect of the operations of the company. You have also confirmed that you are not aware of any other matters which are required to be disclosed under IAS 24 'Related Party Disclosures' in respect of related parties.

You have confirmed that the inventory valuation is a fair reflection of the true cost which has been stated in the entity's financial statements at an amount of $324,000.

You have also confirmed to us that there have been no events since the reporting date which necessitates revision of any figures included in the financial statements or any additional notes thereto.

You have also confirmed that you have reviewed any events occurring in subsidiary undertakings since the date of their respective statements of financial position in order that the financial statements present fairly, in all material respects, the state of the affairs of the entity.

You have prepared the financial statements on a going concern basis and have assessed all aspects of the appropriateness of the going concern basis and have taken account of all information covering the period of at least twelve months' from the date of approval of the entity's financial statements.

You have also confirmed to us that you have complied with all laws and regulations of which you as directors are aware and you have also confirmed that in your opinion, there are no material contingencies which have not been provided for in the entity's financial statements and which could have an effect on the entity as a going concern.

You have confirmed to us that there are no instances of fraudulent activities which the management are aware, or should be aware of which would give rise to the financial statements being materially misstated.

Uncorrected Misstatements

During the course of our audit of the financial statements, we have become aware of immaterial, uncorrected misstatements and you have informed us that you do not wish for them to be corrected on the basis of their immateriality.

Expected Modifications to Our Audit Report

We do not expect to modify our auditors' opinion on the financial statements as at 31 December 2010 and our opinion will be unqualified.

Material Weaknesses in the Internal Control Environment

During the course of the audit of the financial statements for the year ended 31 December 2010, we have undertaken a review of the entity's internal control environment and assessed the appropriateness of the internal controls and the effectiveness of the internal controls.

We confirm that our audit has revealed no material weaknesses in the internal control environment which would adversely affect the entity's ability to record, process and summarise and report financial and other relevant data which would result in a material misstatement in the financial statements.

Planning Information

During the course of our audit we planned and performed our audit procedures in such a way that would enable us to obtain all necessary information to satisfy ourselves that the financial statements comply with International Financial Reporting Standards and to satisfy ourselves that the financial statements for the year ended 31 December 2010 are free from material misstatement whether caused by fraud or error.

We assess the entity's internal control environment and consider whether or not reliance can be placed on the internal controls present. We also consider the entity's use of service entities and assess the extent of how much reliance can be placed on the internal controls present in the service entity.

Confidentiality

This letter has been prepared for the sole use of Cordisan Enterprises Inc and its auditors. It must not be disclosed to any third party or quoted or referred to without the written consent of ourselves and no responsibility is assumed by ourselves to any other person or corporate entity.

We would be grateful if each director could sign the acknowledgement of the contents of this letter and return a copy of the signed letter to us.

Yours faithfully

Billingham & Co

Additional Requirements for Listed Clients

Where the audit firm is auditing a listed client, then the auditor should communicate to those charged with governance:

- That the engagement team and others within the audit firm and network firms, where applicable, have complied with all relevant ethical requirements relating to independence. [ISA260.17(a)]
- All relationships and other matters between the firm, network firms and the entity, that in the auditor's professional judgement may reasonably be thought to bear on independence. In this respect the auditor should also communicate total

fees levied by the audit firm for audit and non-audit services including those fees levied by network firms to the entity and components' controlled by the entity. These fees must be allocated to categories that are appropriate to assist those charged with governance in assessing the effect of services on the auditor's independence. [ISA260.17(b)(i)]

- The auditor also needs to communicate to those charged with governance the related safeguards that have been implemented by the audit firm to eliminate threats to independence or to reduce them to an acceptable level. [ISA260.17(b)(ii)]

The auditor shall communicate such matters in writing to those charged with governance if the auditor concludes that oral communication of such matters is insufficient. However, in the case of listed entities, the auditor needs to communicate the requirements for listed entities in writing. The auditor shall also ensure that they communicate audit related matters to those charged with governance on a timely basis.

ISA 260 contains an Appendix (Appendix 1) which identifies paragraphs in other ISAs that require communication of specific matters with those charged with governance. The Appendix states that the list is not a substitute for considering the requirements and related application and other explanatory material in ISAs.

Appendix 1 of ISA 260 identifies the following paragraphs referring to communication with those charged with governance and with management:

> *ISQC 1 'Quality Control for Firms that Perform Audits and Reviews of Financial Statements, and Other Assurance and Related Services Engagements' — paragraph 30(a).*
>
> *ISA 240 'The Auditor's Responsibilities Related to Fraud in an Audit of Financial Statements' — paragraphs 21, 38(c)(i) and 40–42.*
>
> *ISA 250 'Consideration of Laws and Regulations in an Audit of Financial Statements' — paragraphs 14, 19 and 22–24.*
>
> *ISA 265 'Communicating Deficiencies in Internal Control to Those Charged with Governance and Management' — paragraph 9.*
>
> *ISA 450 'Evaluation of Misstatements Identified During the Audit' — paragraphs 12–13.*
>
> *ISA 505 'External Confirmations' — paragraph 9.*
>
> *ISA 510 'Initial Audit Engagements — Opening Balances' — paragraph 7.*
>
> *ISA 550 'Related Parties' — paragraph 27.*
>
> *ISA 560 'Subsequent Events' — paragraphs 7(b)—(c), 10(a), 13(b), 14(a) and 17.*
>
> *ISA 570 'Going Concern' — paragraph 23.*
>
> *ISA 600 'Special Considerations – Audits of Group Financial Statements (Including the Work of Component Auditors)' — paragraph 49.*
>
> *ISA 705 'Modifications to the Opinion in the Independent Auditor's Report' — paragraphs 12, 14, 19(a) and 28.*
>
> *ISA 706 'Emphasis of Matter Paragraphs and Other Matter Paragraphs in the Independent Auditor's Report' — paragraph 9.*
>
> *ISA 710 'Comparative Information — Corresponding Figures and Comparative Financial Statements' — paragraph 18.*
>
> *ISA 720 'The Auditor's Responsibilities Relating to Other Information in Documents Containing Audited Financial Statements' — paragraphs 10, 13 and 16.*

[Appendix 1 to ISA 260]

Chapter Roundup

The auditor must consider whether the two-way communication process has been adequate to enable an efficient audit.

Laws and regulations may prevent communication of specific matters by the auditor. In such cases the auditor may consider legal advice.

The auditor shall communicate their responsibilities in relation to the audit of the financial statements.

The auditor shall communicate the planned scope and timing of the audit.

Significant findings from the audit must be communicated to those charged with governance, including any significant difficulties or any other significant matters.

Additional matters are required to be communicated to those charged with governance in respect of listed clients.

Communication can be made orally or in writing, but must be made on a timely basis.

The auditor shall communicate to those charged with governance:

(a) Qualitative aspects of the entity's accounting practices and financial reporting.
(b) Significant difficulties, if any, encountered during the audit.
(c) Significant matters, if any, discussed, or subject to correspondence with management.
(d) Written representations the auditor is requesting.
(e) Other significant matters.

11 ISA 265 COMMUNICATING DEFICIENCIES IN INTERNAL CONTROL TO THOSE CHARGED WITH GOVERNANCE AND MANAGEMENT

ISA 265 is a new standard which was born out of the IAASB Clarity Project and its primary objective is to deal with the auditor's responsibility to communicate deficiencies in internal control appropriately to those charged with governance and management of the entity. It distinguishes what communication is necessary to each of these two parties.

ISA 265 recognises that the objective of the auditor is to communicate appropriately to those charged with governance and management any deficiencies in internal control that the auditor has identified during the course of the audit and which are of significant importance to warrant their respective attention.

DEFICIENCIES IN INTERNAL CONTROLS

Deficiencies in internal controls can occur in any control environment, regardless of how robustly the system has been designed. Even the best internal control systems devised by the best management cannot eliminate the risk of material misstatement within the financial statements. At best, a robust internal control system can only reduce the risk of material misstatement within the financial statements, not eliminate it entirely.

Deficiencies in internal control exist when a control is designed and implemented in such a way that it is unable to prevent, detect and correct misstatements in the financial statements on a timely basis or a control which is required to prevent, detect and correct misstatements is not present at all [ISA265.6(a)]. Significant deficiencies are those deficiencies, or a combination of deficiencies, which the auditor judges to be of sufficient importance to be brought to the attention of those charged with governance [ISA265.6(b)].

Significant Deficiencies
- Examples of matters that should be considered in determining whether a deficiency is significant are: Deficiencies which will result in a material misstatement in the financial statements.
- Susceptibility to loss or fraud of the entity's assets or liabilities.
- The financial statement amounts exposed to the deficiencies.
- General monitoring of controls.
- The volume of activity that has occurred or could occur in the account balance or class of transactions exposed to the deficiency or deficiencies.

- The cause and frequency of the exceptions detected as a result of the deficiencies in the controls.
- A lack of control over transactions such as non-recurring journal entries, particularly at period end.
- A lack of control over related party transactions.
- A lack of control over significant transactions outside the entity's normal course of business.

The above is merely a broad range of examples of significant deficiencies and auditors may come across other such deficiencies particular to their clients own circumstances.

Indicators of Significant Deficiencies

Entities, large and small, will have differing levels of internal controls. Small audit clients may have relatively simple internal controls which are as effective and robust as those present in a large multi-million turnover audit client and the auditor should keep in mind the appropriateness of the internal controls present in relation to the size and complexity of the audit client. However, typical indicators of significant deficiencies are:

- A lack of internal controls and a lack of interest on the part of management to ensure that significant transactions are properly scrutinised (particularly those in which management are financially interested).
- Fraudulent activity on behalf of management regardless of materiality or a willingness to accept trivial discrepancies.
- A lack of co-operation by management in improving previously identified deficiencies in internal control by the auditors.
- Identification by the auditor of misstatements within the financial statements not detected by the internal controls present.
- Lack of management integrity.
- An inability on the part of management to properly oversee the preparation of the financial statements.
- Restatement of previously issued financial statements to reflect the correction of a material misstatement due to fraud or error.

AUDITOR RESPONSIBILITIES

Auditors are not responsible for designing and implementing an entity's internal control system. This responsibility lies with the entity's management and those charged with governance. Auditors are responsible for reporting deficiencies and recommending improvements to those deficiencies to those charged with governance.

In an audit of financial statements, the auditor will gain an understanding of the entity and the environment in which it operates in accordance with the provisions in ISA315. Gaining an understanding of the entity and the environment in which it operates enables the auditor to identify the areas susceptible to material misstatement and allows the auditor the opportunity to assess the internal controls present in the entity.

Upon discovery of one or more deficiencies then the auditor must decipher, on the basis of the audit work performed, whether the identified deficiencies both individually and combined, constitute significant deficiencies as defined in ISA265.6(b). Where the auditor concludes that the deficiencies are significant deficiencies then the auditor shall communicate these deficiencies in internal control to those charged with governance on a timely basis.

In addition, the auditor shall also communicate significant deficiencies in internal controls to an appropriate level of management. The auditor shall also ensure that this communication informs management:

- About the deficiencies in the internal controls that the auditor intends to communicate to those charged with governance. However, it is particularly important that the auditor considers whether it would, in fact, be inappropriate to communicate with management directly given the particular circumstances so judgement should be used in this area.
- Any other deficiencies identified during the course of the audit which have not been communicated to management by any other individuals or parties and that, in the professional judgement of the auditor, are of sufficient importance to warrant management's attention.

The auditor may wish to include additional information in their communication such as an indication that if the auditor had performed more extensive procedures on the internal control they may have identified more deficiencies to be reported. Conversely, in some cases some previously reported deficiencies may not, in fact, need to have been reported following further audit procedures.

In some cases the auditor may hold a discussion with management to determine whether deficiencies in internal control have been identified. Where the auditor judges this action appropriate, the auditor shall ensure that the level of management they discuss identified deficiencies with is the level of management who are familiar with the internal control area concerned. However, it may be the case that the auditor considers it appropriate not to discuss with management any identified deficiencies in internal control, particularly when the findings appear to call management's integrity or competence into question [ISA265.A1].

Where significant deficiencies in internal control have been identified by the auditor, the auditor must include in the written communication of significant internal control deficiencies:

- A description of the deficiencies identified by the auditors in internal controls and an explanation of their potential effects [ISA265.11(a)].
- Sufficient information to allow those charged with governance and management to understand the context of the communication. The auditor must ensure that they explain that:
  - (i) The purpose of the audit was for the auditor to express an opinion on the financial statements [ISA265.11(b)(i)].
  - (ii) The audit included consideration of internal controls relevant to the preparation of the financial statements in order to design audit procedures that are appropriate in the circumstances, but not for the purpose of expressing an opinion on the effectiveness of internal control [ISA265.11(b)(ii)].
  - (iii) The matters being reported are limited to those deficiencies that the auditor has identified during the audit and that the auditor has concluded are of sufficient importance to merit being reported to those charged with governance [ISA265.11(b)(iii)].

The auditor may initially discuss significant deficiencies in internal control with management and, when appropriate, with those charged with governance, which will allow management the sufficient time to remedy the deficiencies in internal control to minimise the risk of material misstatement within the financial statements. Determining the level of detail to which the auditor should communicate significant deficiencies to those charged with governance is a matter of professional judgement for the auditor but ISA 265 at paragraph A15 states that the auditor shall consider:

- The nature of the entity. Is it a public interest entity? If so, communication of significant deficiencies in internal control may be different to that relating to a non-public interest entity.
- The size and complexity of the business. The communication required for a small owner-managed non-publicly accountable business may be much less than that of a multi-million turnover business.
- The nature of the significant deficiencies which the auditor has identified.
- Legal and regulatory requirements.
- The governance composition. [ISA265.A15]

Insignificant Deficiencies

During the course of an audit, the auditor may identify other deficiencies in the internal controls which are not considered to be significant. Where such deficiencies are identified then the auditor needs to use professional judgement in the circumstances, taking into account the likelihood and potential magnitude of misstatements that may arise in the financial statements as a result of those deficiencies. The communication of other deficiencies in internal control that warrant management's attention may be made orally and not necessarily in writing, though the auditor shall document details of the oral discussion made with management.

Consider the following illustration.

Illustration

You are an audit manager responsible for the audit of Bramlow Clothing Inc for the year ended 31 December 2009, a retail clothing outlet that operates simply from one store. The company is an owner-managed business and has relatively simple but effective internal controls in place. During your review of the previous year's audit file you note that you had communicated deficiencies in respect of the authorisation procedures of invoices which you had judged not to be significant. The notes of the discussion revealed that the management of Bramlow Clothing Inc considered the need to authorise every supplier invoice that came into the entity, by virtue of a signature on the invoice, impractical because the managing director opens the post on a daily basis, thus seeing every invoice that comes into the entity and all invoices are attached to the back of payments when they are presented to the managing director to sign.

In the scenario above the audit manager had previously communicated other deficiencies in internal control to those charged with governance, that is, the managing director. The managing director had chosen not to remedy the deficiency on the grounds that it was unnecessary to do so and other procedures, which those charged with governance deemed acceptable, were implemented.

If the auditor has previously communicated deficiencies in internal control, other than significant deficiencies, to those charged with governance, but they have chosen not to remedy them for cost or other reasons, the auditor need not repeat the communication in the current period. In addition, if Bramlow Clothing Inc had an internal audit function which had previously communicated the deficiency to those charged with governance, the auditor also need not repeat the communication. However, if there had been a change of management in Bramlow Clothing Inc, then it may be appropriate to communicate the other deficiencies again as the new management may wish to implement changes to ensure that the deficiencies are addressed.

The auditor may have previously communicated a significant deficiency to management and those charged with governance. If the significant deficiency has not been remedied the auditor may repeat the description of the deficiency from the previous communication or make reference to that previous communication. The auditor may also ask management or, where applicable, those charged with governance, why such a significant deficiency has not been remedied, as such a failure to act, in itself, may be a significant deficiency [ISA265.A17].

The auditor should also consider whether the other deficiencies previously communicated to management have now become a significant deficiency requiring communication with those charged with governance. For example, if management had been recommended to authorise all purchase invoices, but had not chosen to do so on the grounds of its impracticality but then this weakness had resulted in a fraud being committed.

In some cases those charged with governance may wish to be made aware of any other deficiencies in internal control or the auditor may wish to inform those charged with governance of other deficiencies. In such cases the auditor may report orally or in writing to those charged with governance as they deem appropriate.

Communication with Regulatory or Other Relevant Parties

In some jurisdictions the auditor has an obligation to report significant deficiencies in internal controls to regulatory bodies or other relevant parties. This is particularly the case with listed entities. The auditor must follow the correct protocol and notify regulatory and other relevant parties as prescribed in law or regulation under the specific terms and definitions for those types of deficiency. Where the jurisdiction has not defined terms, then the auditor is to use professional judgement to determine the matters to be communicated further to the legal or regulatory requirement.

In some jurisdictions, legal or regulatory requirements may require the auditor to furnish copies of the auditor's written communication to such regulators. Where this is the case then the communication may identify such regulatory authorities.

Chapter Roundup

ISA 265 is a new standard born out of the IAASB Clarity Project.

Its objective is to ensure the auditor communicates deficiencies in internal control appropriate to management and those charged with governance.

Significant deficiencies are deficiencies which the auditor judges to be of sufficient importance to be brought to the attention of those charged with governance.

Upon discovery of one or more deficiencies, the auditor must evaluate whether, on the basis of the audit work performed, the identified deficiencies (individually and combined) constitute significant deficiencies.

Significant deficiencies must be communicated to those charged with governance on a timely basis, as well as to the appropriate levels of management.

Where the auditor considers the integrity or competence of management is brought into question, the auditor may not consider it appropriate to discuss such deficiencies with management.

Insignificant deficiencies that have been previously notified, which have not been remedied, need not be repeated.

Previously identified insignificant deficiencies may become significant deficiencies in the current period audit.

Failure to act in respect of a previously notified significant deficiency may, in itself, constitute a significant deficiency.

12 ISA 300 (REDRAFTED) PLANNING AN AUDIT OF FINANCIAL STATEMENTS

Audits of financial statements need to be planned in such a way to allow an effective audit to be performed. An efficient and effective audit can only be undertaken if adequate planning has taken place which involves establishing the overall audit strategy and developing the actual audit plan.

The objective of ISA 300 is to establish the overall audit strategy and to develop an audit plan to reduce audit risk to an acceptably low level. The planning of the audit shall involve the engagement partner and other key members of the audit team who shall all be involved in both the audit planning and discussions amongst the engagement team [ISA300.5].

PRELIMINARY ENGAGEMENT ACTIVITIES

When the auditor engages a new audit client, ISA 300 stipulates certain procedures which are to be carried out:

- Perform procedures required by ISA 220 regarding the continuance of the client relationship and the specific audit engagement [ISA300.6(a)].
- Evaluating compliance with relevant ethical requirements, including independence, in accordance with ISA 220 [ISA300.6(b)].
- Establishing an understanding of the terms of the engagement, as required by ISA 210 [ISA300.6(c)].

By performing the above procedures, the auditor is ensuring that independence is maintained to perform the audit, as well as that there are adequate resources and technical competences available to perform an efficient audit. Undertaking the above procedures also allows the auditor to ensure that there are no issues with management integrity which will affect the auditor's willingness to continue the engagement and also that there is no misunderstanding with the audit client as to the terms of the engagement.

The auditor shall also communicate with the entity's previous auditors where there has been a change of auditors in accordance with the relevant ethical requirements. Reviews of the predecessor auditor's working papers can help establish the overall audit strategy unless this is prohibited by law or regulation. Europe-wide requirements now require a predecessor auditor to supply information to a successor and this requirement has now been incorporated in the audit regulations.

PLANNING ACTIVITIES

Planning activities for initial engagements will often be in more depth than for a recurring audit because the auditor will not have previous experience of the audit engagement and, therefore, the auditor needs to obtain a thorough understanding of the entity and the environment in which it operates in accordance with ISA 315. Initial engagements will also include additional audit procedures to be carried out regarding opening balances in accordance with the provisions of ISA 510.

At the planning stage, the auditor will develop the overall audit strategy which sets the scope, timing and direction of the audit which in turn assists in the development of the detailed audit plan and identifies problem areas as well as important audit areas. The audit strategy involves:

- Identifying the characteristics of the engagement that define its scope.
- Ascertaining the reporting objectives of the engagement to plan the timing of the audit and the nature of the communications required.
- Considering the factors that, in the auditor's professional judgement, are significant in directing the engagement team's efforts.
- Considering the results of the preliminary engagement activities and, where applicable, whether knowledge gained on other engagements performed by the engagement partner for the entity is relevant.
- Ascertaining the nature, extent and timing of resources necessary to perform the engagement. [ISA300.8(a) to (e)]

AUDIT STRATEGY

The overall audit strategy is concerned with the scope, timing and direction of the audit which then guides the detailed audit plan. The establishment of the overall audit strategy involves:

- Determining the characteristics of the engagement that define its scope, such as the financial reporting framework used by the entity, industry-specific reporting requirements and the locations and components of the entity. Auditors should also consider the need for any reconciliation to another financial reporting framework, such as US GAAP.
- Ascertaining the reporting objectives of the engagement to plan the timing of the audit and the nature of the communications required, such as deadlines for interim and final reporting, and key dates for expected communications with management and those charged with governance.
- Considering the important factors that will determine the focus of the engagement team's efforts, such as determination of appropriate materiality levels, preliminary identification of areas where there may be higher risks of material misstatement, preliminary identification of material components and account balances, evaluation of whether the auditor may plan to obtain evidence regarding the effectiveness of internal control, and identification of recent significant entity-specific, industry, financial reporting or other relevant developments.
- The extent to which components are audited by other auditors.
- The nature of the business segments to be audited, including the need for specialised knowledge.

- The need for a statutory audit of standalone financial statements in addition to an audit for consolidation purposes.
- The availability of the work of internal auditors and the extent of the auditor's potential reliance on such work.
- The expected use of audit evidence obtained in previous audits, such as tests of controls.
- The effect of information technology on the audit procedures and the use of computer-assisted audit techniques.
- The co-ordination of the expected coverage and timing of the audit work with any reviews of interim financial information and the effect on the audit of the information obtained during such reviews.

The audit strategy also allows the auditor the opportunity to consider:

- The resources it will deploy for certain high risk areas or whether to deploy the use of experts.
- The amount of resources to devote to specific audit areas. For example, the number of team members to engage on observing the inventory count.
- When resources are deployed, that is, at interim periods or at the end of the reporting period.
- How the resources are managed, directed and supervised, such as when team briefing and debriefing meetings are expected to be held, how engagement partner and manager reviews are expected to take place and whether engagement quality control reviews are required. [ISA300.A8]

Once the audit strategy has been established, the detailed audit plan can be developed to address the various matters identified in the overall audit strategy. The audit strategy and audit plan are closely interrelated as changes in one may result in changes to the other.

THE AUDIT PLAN

The audit plan is more detailed than the audit strategy. The audit plan should document the nature, timing and extent of the audit procedures which are to be performed by the engagement team members in order to obtain sufficient appropriate audit evidence to reduce audit risk to an acceptably low level.

The detailed audit plan should also contain a description of the nature, timing and extent of planned further audit procedures at the assertion level for each material class of transactions, account balances and disclosures. The audit plan should also contain details of other audit procedures to be adopted such as whether the use of experts are required for certain high risk areas to ensure that the audit is carried out in accordance with the ISAs. Throughout, the auditor must ensure that the audit plan is developed with its prime objective in mind which is to reduce audit risk to an acceptably low level.

The audit plan includes:

- A description of the nature, timing and extent of planned risk assessment procedures to address the risk of material misstatement, as determined under ISA 315.
- A description of the nature, timing and extent of planned further audit procedures at the assertion level for each material class of transactions, account balances and disclosures

as required under ISA 330. The plan for further procedures reflects the auditor's decision whether to test the operating effectiveness of controls, and the nature, timing and extent of planned substantive procedures.

- Such other audit procedures required to be carried out on the assignment in order to comply with the ISAs. For example, whether the use of an expert is required for complex transactions such as the valuation of financial instruments at fair value.

Changes to the Plan

Planning is a continual and iterative process throughout the audit engagement. Unexpected changes, conditions or the audit evidence gathered from the results of other audit procedures may require the audit plan to be changed or updated where necessary. In performing substantive testing on certain audit areas, the results of this testing may contradict the evidence gathered when testing the operating effectiveness of internal controls in the same audit area. Where such changes to the audit plan are required, the auditor must re-evaluate the audit procedures based on the revised consideration of assessed risks at the assertion level for all or some of the classes of transactions, account balances or disclosures.

DIRECTION, SUPERVISION AND REVIEW

The auditor will plan the nature, timing and extent of direction and supervision of the engagement team members and review their work. This is a particularly important issue when it comes to less experienced members of the engagement team. The auditor should ensure that only the more experienced members of the engagement team undertake more complex work in key audit areas. For example, it would be inappropriate to have an audit junior undertaking audit procedures on complex financial instruments such as derivatives. Such work needs to be undertaken by a more senior member of the engagement team who has suitable experience and knowledge. In most cases, such areas may need the use of experts, which is discussed in ISA 620 (Chapter 31).

When planning the nature, timing and extent of direction and supervision of the engagement team, the auditor needs to consider various factors, including:

- The size and complexity of the entity.
- The area of the audit.
- The assessed risks of material misstatement. Where the assessed risk of material misstatement increases the auditor will ordinarily increase the extent and timeliness of direction and supervision of engagement team members which will involve the auditor performing a more detailed review of their work.
- The capabilities and competence of the individual team members performing the audit work.

In some cases, the audit being carried out may be undertaken by a sole practitioner. Where this is the case the issue concerning the direction, supervision and review will not apply because the sole practitioner will already be aware of the material issues. However, the sole practitioner needs to keep in mind the requirement for the audit to be undertaken in accordance with the ISAs and, as a result, the auditor should consider the need to consult with other suitably-experienced auditors or the auditor's professional body. In some cases, the sole practitioner may also determine that an external 'hot' or 'cold' file review should take place.

DOCUMENTATION

In terms of documentation, it is important that the overall audit strategy contains a record of the key decisions considered necessary to properly plan the audit. Any significant changes made during the audit engagement, and the reasons for the significant changes, shall also be documented accordingly.

It is very common in today's audit profession for standard audit programmes to be used to document the overall audit strategy which can include checklists to ensure compliance. Such audit programmes must be tailored to the client's requirements rather than simply be completed as a 'tick box' exercise. As an alternative, the auditor might consider the use of a memorandum that contains key decisions regarding the overall scope, timing and conduct of the audit. In determining the appropriate form of documentation, the auditor needs to consider:

- The size and complexity of the audit client.
- Materiality.
- Extent of other documentation.
- Circumstances of the specific audit engagement.

COMMUNICATION WITH THOSE CHARGED WITH GOVERNANCE AND MANAGEMENT

Discussions with those charged with governance usually include the overall audit strategy and timing of the audit together with any potential limitations or additional requirements. Discussions with management usually occur to facilitate the conduct and management of the audit engagement. Auditors should keep in mind that the overall audit strategy and audit plan are their responsibility. Auditors should also ensure that discussions with those charged with governance and management concerning the audit strategy and audit plan are not too in-depth to make the audit procedures too predictable.

Chapter Roundup

The planning of the audit involves establishing the overall audit strategy and developing the audit plan.

Planning must involve the engagement partner and other key members of the audit engagement team.

Preliminary engagements will involve more in-depth work as the auditor will not have any previous experience of the audit.

The audit plan may require revision, or updating, due to unexpected changes, conditions or the audit evidence gathered from the results of audit procedures.

Changes to the plan require the auditor to reassess the audit procedures based on the revised consideration of assessed risks at the assertion level.

The auditor will plan the nature, timing and extent of direction and supervision of engagement team members and review their work.

Overall audit strategy must contain a record of the key decisions considered necessary to properly plan the audit. Any significant changes during the audit engagement are also documented together with the reasons for the significant change.

13 ISA 315 (REDRAFTED) IDENTIFYING AND ASSESSING THE RISKS OF MATERIAL MISSTATEMENT THROUGH UNDERSTANDING THE ENTITY AND ITS ENVIRONMENT

ISA 315 (redrafted) is a particularly important standard and is a companion standard to ISA 300 (redrafted). ISA 315 is concerned with the auditor gaining an understanding of the entity and the environment in which it operates to identify and assess the risk of material misstatement within the financial statements together with assessing the entity's internal control environment. Its primary objective is to ensure that the auditor identifies and assesses the risk of material misstatement, whether due to fraud or error, at both the financial statement and assertion level. When the auditor has sufficient understanding of the entity and the environment in which it operates, the auditor then has a basis for designing and implementing audit procedures to respond to the assessed risks of material misstatement.

RISK ASSESSMENT

The auditor must undertake risk assessment procedures which involve inquiries of management and others in the entity, analytical procedures and additional procedures such as observance and inspection [ISA315.6(a)]. It is important to understand that risk assessment procedures alone do not provide sufficient appropriate audit evidence on which to base the auditor's opinion.

The auditor shall also consider whether it is appropriate to undertake additional procedures relative to the circumstances. For example, if the audit client has an item of property stated at valuation, then it may be appropriate for the auditor to consider making inquiries concerning the valuation expert that the entity has used.

Inquiry

Ordinarily, the vast majority of information which the auditor obtains is that from management. However, it may be useful for the auditor to discuss relevant and appropriate issues with other staff members, for example, warehouse managers during the course of observing the inventory count. The auditor must consider what information may be obtained from holding such discussions. For example:

- Discussions with the sales order processing staff may allow the auditor a more detailed insight into the way sales orders are processed.
- Discussions with in-house legal advisers may help to understand the nature and materiality of ongoing litigation or defence claims and gain an understanding of the levels of provisions or contingencies that may be required in the financial statements.

- Marketing personnel may be able to give the auditor an insight into future marketing strategies.
- Production staff may be able to give the auditor an insight into future technological advances concerning their products or new products which have influenced rises in revenues.

ISA 315 is principally concerned with identifying risks of material misstatement within the financial statements and it follows, therefore, that the auditor may find it appropriate to obtain information through inquiries of others within the entity.

Analytical Procedures

The use of analytical procedures will help the auditor in identifying any aspects which the auditor was not aware of. This will also assist the auditor in designing specific audit procedures to address those issues and the procedures devised by the auditor must be responsive to the assessed levels of risk.

Analytical review will also enable the auditor to identify any unusual trends or characteristics within the financial statements. This is particularly useful as this will enable the auditor to identify risks of material misstatement, especially in relation to fraud.

Illustration

The auditor of Entity A is planning the audit of the financial statements for the year ended 31 December 2010. The gross profit margin in 2010 is 40% and in 2009 was 52%. The reduction is beyond the expectations of the auditor.

Analytical procedures will highlight the unexpected reduction in gross margins and the auditor will plan their audit procedures accordingly to ascertain the reasoning behind the reduction.

Observation and Inspection

Observation and inspection procedures will enable the auditor to gather evidence concerning the assertions made by management and others which will then provide information concerning the entity and its environment. Ordinarily, observation and inspection procedures will include:

- Observation of the entity's activities and operations.
- Inspection of documents, such as internal control procedures, manuals and such like.
- Reviews of reports prepared by management such as interim management accounts and board minutes.
- Performing walk-through tests on various controls.

Illustration

Where the inventory valuation is material to the financial statements, the auditor will attend the inventory counting in order to form an opinion as to whether the procedures adopted by management insofar as the inventory counting is concerned would reduce the risk of material misstatement in relation to the inventory figure. It will also enable the auditor to verify the existence and valuation of inventory as well as evaluating the valuations placed on damaged, obsolete or slow-moving items of inventory.

In recurring audits, information obtained in prior periods may provide the auditor with information concerning the entity. For example, the nature of the entity and the environment in which it operates will have been documented in the prior year working papers together with information concerning significant changes expected in the current year. In using this information, the auditor needs to consider whether changes have occurred to that information which may affect the relevance of that information in the current audit.

Illustration

Gabriella Inc has a 31 December year end. You were the auditor for the year ended 31 December 2008 and during your discussions with Lucas Stevens, the Managing Director, he informed you that during the course of 2009 the company was looking to change its computerised accounting system to a bespoke system. This change was felt necessary because the company wished to expand its operations organically and more detailed management reports were required.

This discussion was fully documented on the prior year audit working paper file in the 'points forward' section.

During the planning of the 31 December 2009 financial statements, the above point has been brought forward onto the current year's planning memorandum as a key audit area. Subsequent discussions with Lucas Stevens have confirmed that the company has not, in fact, implemented the new computerised accounting package due to technical issues which has rendered the new package inappropriate for the purposes of the entity.

In the above illustration, the auditor has revisited the prior year audit file and has identified a significant change that Gabriella Inc was planning to make. However, subsequent discussions have confirmed that this change in the financial reporting mechanism has not materialised and as a consequence this information is not relevant to the current year's audit. Notwithstanding the fact that this information is no longer relevant, this does not preclude the auditor from further gaining a sufficient understanding of the entity in order to identify and assess the risk of material misstatement.

Discussion Amongst the Engagement Team

Discussion amongst the engagement team is mandatory under ISA 315. Part of the planning will involve the engagement team, including the engagement partner, discussing the entity being audited and will allow those experienced team members to share their knowledge and experience of the entity. In particular the engagement team must discuss the areas in which the financial statements of the entity may be susceptible to material misstatement whether due to fraud or error [ISA315.A14]. ISA 240 gives guidance on the discussions that should be held amongst the engagement team in relation to fraud.

Holding discussions amongst the engagement team will allow the team to gain a better understanding of the entity and the environment in which it operates, because all members of the team, together with the engagement partner, will share their knowledge. This is particularly important where junior members of staff are assisting on the audit. It is also an opportunity to discuss the audit procedures that may be performed on certain audit areas, particularly high risk areas, and allow decisions to be made concerning the nature, timing and extent of any additional audit procedures which may be deemed necessary.

In some audit firms, the engagement team may be located in different offices, or even different countries. This is more prominent in large accountancy practices. Professional judgement is used to determine which members of the engagement team are included in the discussion but must certainly involve key members of the engagement team. Not all members of the engagement team have to have extensive and detailed knowledge of the audit client (e.g. junior members), and communication plans which are agreed by the engagement partner may be useful in such situations. [ISA315.A15]

Smaller audits often just involve a sole practitioner undertaking the audit of an entity's financial statements and clearly an engagement team discussion will not occur. In these situations, it is the responsibility of the sole practitioner to consider the susceptibility of misstatement within the financial statements due to fraud or error. [ISA315.A16]

Understanding the Entity and its Environment and its Internal Control

The auditor must understand the entity, the environment in which it operates and its internal control structure in order that an efficient audit can be carried out. Failing to gain an understanding of the entity means that the auditor will go into the audit 'blind' which will lead to all sorts of problems during the audit. Auditing is about much more than simply whether bank reconciliation statements add up or the statement of financial position (balance sheet) is in agreement with the underlying accounting records. It is about how the processes in an entity work and how amounts and disclosures start their journey from their inception to their ultimate destination within the financial statements, and about whether these processes (internal controls) are sufficient to prevent, detect and correct misstatements on a timely basis.

The auditor needs to understand the entity's external factors such as industrial and regulatory factors including its applicable financial reporting framework.

Illustration

Whitaker Enterprises Ltd is a UK-based entity with a December year end which is quoted on the Alternative Investment Market (i.e. 'AIM' listed). The auditors are planning the audit of the entity's financial statements for the year ended 31 December 2010.

The company is publicly-traded with it being AIM-listed. Since January 2007, such entities in the UK are compelled to prepare their financial statements under International Financial Reporting Standards (IFRS).

Other factors which the auditor needs to consider when gaining an understanding of the entity and the environment in which it operates are:

- The entity's selection and application of its accounting policies.
- Objectives of the entity and its strategies.
- External factors affecting the business.
- Cyclical or seasonal activity which may help when applying analytical procedures.
- The market in which the entity operates.
- Technological advances or obsolescence of the entity's products.
- Legislation and environment related factors.

- Taxation issues.
- Financing issues.
- Economic conditions such as recession, inflation, currency and interest rate issues.

Illustration

Construction contracts can be complex and the appropriate revenue recognition will vary depending on the substance of the arrangements. A specific accounting standard exists in this area (IAS 11 'Construction Contracts'). The auditor should obtain an understanding of the entity's accounting policy in relation to construction contracts and decipher whether such a policy is appropriate in the circumstances. The auditor should also consider revenue recognition in relation to 'milestone arrangements' and ensure any estimates used are reasonable in the circumstances.

Specific Factors to Consider

A large part of gaining an understanding of the entity and the environment in which it operates is looking at specifics attached to an entity. Examples of 'specific' factors which the auditor should consider when gaining an understanding of the entity and the environment in which it operates are given as follows:

- The entity's business operations such as:
  - revenue streams;
  - it's products and services;
  - geographic dispersion;
  - key customers and suppliers;
  - legal and regulatory issues;
  - related party issues; and
  - research and development activities and expenditure.
- Investments and investment activities including any planned or recently executed acquisitions, investments in securities, capital investment activities and joint ventures and special-purpose entities.
- Financing and financing activities such as major subsidiaries and associated entities, including consolidated and non-consolidated structures, debt structure and related terms, beneficial owners and any use of derivative financial instruments.
- Financial reporting issues such as the use of accounting policies and any industry-specific requirements, revenue recognition practices, fair value accounting, foreign currencies and consideration of complex transactions such as those which give rise to 'substance over form' issues.

NATURE OF THE ENTITY

It is vital that the auditor gains a thorough understanding as to the nature of the entity, particularly if the entity has a complex structure attached to it. Simple, owner-managed businesses that have a relatively straightforward and less-complex internal structure will require a lot less consideration as to their nature than a large, multi-location, listed 'blue-chip' entity. Consider the following illustration.

Illustration

Roche Inc is a successful manufacturer of power-coated roller shutters which are fixed to the exterior of domestic and commercial properties to enhance security issues. It has recently acquired 100% of the net assets of Antley Inc who operates in the same industry.

Whilst the above illustration does not necessarily give rise to Roche Inc having a 'complex' structure, it does give rise to additional considerations which the auditor must take into account when planning their audit of Roche's financial statements such as:

- Has any goodwill been accounted for in accordance with relevant accounting standards (such as IFRS 3) or has the acquisition been made under a 'bargain purchase' resulting in any negative goodwill?
- Does Roche Inc need to prepare consolidated financial statements? Certain jurisdictions allow 'small' groups exemption from preparing consolidated financial statements.
- How has Roche Inc financed the acquisition of Antley Inc? Are there any contingent consideration issues which need to be considered? If so, have assets and liabilities subject to the contingencies been valued at fair value at the acquisition date in accordance with IFRS 3 'Business Combinations'?

The auditor should also gain an understanding of the entity's owners, other individuals and entities which the entity is involved with. This is particularly useful as it helps the auditor to understand whether there have been, or if there potentially are, any related party transactions which need to be considered. ISA 550 gives additional guidance in this area.

Gaining an understanding of the entity and the environment in which it operates can be a long-winded process depending on the size and complexity of the audit engagement being planned. However, in some cases it can be a relatively simple process, particularly if the audit engagement is a small audit with a relatively simple internal control structure and no complex transactions.

ACCOUNTING POLICIES

Auditors are required to obtain an understanding of the entity's selection and application of accounting policies and consider whether they are appropriate for its business and consistent with the applicable financial reporting framework and accounting policies used in the relevant industry.

IAS 8 'Accounting Policies, Estimates and Errors' defines accounting policies as:

> *the specific principles, bases, conventions, rules, and practices applied by an entity in preparing and presenting financial statements.*

It is, therefore, imperative that the auditor gains an understanding of an entity's accounting policies, not only to ensure that the financial statements are prepared under the prescribed policies, but also that the accounting policies selected by an entity are appropriate in the circumstances.

Auditors need to consider whether the entity has any complicated transactions and review the accounting policies to ensure the transactions are accounted for appropriately as well as that the accounting policy is also appropriate in the circumstances. Under the IFRS regime, if a transaction or event is not dealt with by IFRS, management are to devise their own policies having regard to the provisions in the International Accounting Standard Board (IASB) 'Framework for the Preparation and Presentation of Financial Statements'. In this respect, the auditor needs to evaluate the effect of accounting policies adopted and applied by management for which there is a lack of authoritative guidance or consensus to ensure it is appropriate.

It is fairly common for entities to change their accounting policies because revisions will ensure the financial statements present more relevant and reliable information. Auditors must review changes to an entity's accounting policies to ensure they have been correctly accounted for and that they do, in fact, present a more relevant and reliable view, as well as ensuring any relevant disclosures have been made. This is also particularly important where new financial reporting standards or legislation are introduced.

Illustration

In 2008, an entity decided to revalue its land and buildings using the revaluation model as management felt this model would present more relevant and reliable information within the financial statements. In 2009 management decided that they no longer wished to use the revaluation model and wanted to switch back to depreciated historic cost.

Management will change such a policy because they deem the revised policy to present more relevant and reliable information within the financial statements. It is generally accepted that fair value is more relevant and reliable than depreciated historic cost and, therefore, to switch back to depreciated historic cost would be inappropriate.

OBJECTIVES AND STRATEGIES AND RELATED BUSINESS RISKS

The auditor must obtain an understanding of the entity's objectives and strategies, and the related business risks that may result in material misstatement within the financial statements. 'Business risk' is primarily concerned with external factors that could affect the entity which may result in material misstatement within the financial statements. It arises as a result of significant conditions, events, circumstances, actions or inactions that could adversely affect the entity's ability to achieve its objectives and execute its strategies. Conversely, management's objectives and strategies could be inappropriate. Auditors may find the use of a 'SWAT' and 'PEST' analysis particularly useful when gaining an understanding of business risks.

Practical Insight

Internet companies saw a huge growth in the 1990s until 2000 when such companies (known as 'dot com' companies) were failing at massive rates. Various reasons have been cited for the failing of such; for example, the 'year 2000' switchover. Auditors of such companies may not have predicted that such a collapse would occur, though this is an illustration of how business risk can arise from change. Conversely, a failure to recognise the need for change may also give rise to business risk.

Not all business risks will give rise to material misstatements within the financial statements and it follows, therefore, that the auditor does not have a direct responsibility to identify or assess all business risks. The auditor must, however, gain a sufficient understanding of the business risks facing the entity to allow the auditor to understand the likelihood of material misstatement within the financial statements. Management are also responsible for ensuring that they identify business risks and develop approaches to address those risks. Examples of matters that the auditor should consider are given below:

- Industry developments — does the entity possess the required level of personnel or expertise to deal with changes in the industry?
- New products and services.
- Business expansion — has demand been accurately estimated to warrant the expansion?
- Regulatory requirements — is there increased legal exposure?
- Current and prospective financing requirements.
- IT issues — are systems compatible?
- Effects of implementing a strategy, particularly any effects that will lead to new accounting requirements.
- New accounting legislation. [ISA315.A32]

MEASUREMENT AND REVIEW OF FINANCIAL PERFORMANCE

It is widely understood that internal and external pressures can be placed on the management of an entity. For example, pressure can be placed on management by the shareholders to ensure that the entity generates sufficient profits so that a particular level of dividend can be paid to the shareholders. Banks and financiers can also put financial performance pressure on management by imposing loan covenants which, if breached, will warrant a withdrawal of financial support. These pressures can motivate management to deal with the pressures by improving business, or motivate management to misstate the financial statements (fraudulent financial reporting).

Case Study — Daniels Inc

Daniels Inc has entered into a Factoring agreement with an external financier. The terms of the agreement are that the Financier will fund 80% of sales invoices issued to its customers immediately upon submission to the Financier, with the final 20% being paid to Daniels Inc when the customer eventually settles the invoice.

During the recent recession, Daniels Inc has suffered increasing levels of cash flow difficulties due to customers 'tightening their belts' and the loss of a key account. Shareholders are also putting pressure on management to ensure that dividends are paid to them.

In this case study, pressure is being put on the entity by the shareholders to ensure that they receive a prescribed level of dividend. Clearly there is a risk that material misstatement could occur in the financial statements by the raising of fictitious sales invoices in order to release cash flow. External business risks are the recent recession and the fact that the entity has entered into a 'factoring' agreement with an external financier. The auditor should be prompted to address this risk by devising audit procedures which are responsive to the risk identified.

Measurement and Review of Financial Performance

Measurement and review of financial performance is not the same as the monitoring of controls. The measurement and review of performance is directed at whether business performance is meeting the objectives set by management whereas monitoring of controls is specifically concerned with the effective operation of an entity's internal control system. [ISA315.A37]

Reviews of financial performance are primarily undertaken by looking at key performance indicators (financial and non-financial) and undertaking exercises such as ratio analysis to help identify any unusual trends or characteristics within the financial statements.

In gaining an understanding of the entity and the environment in which it operates, the auditor ordinarily looks at internal information such as budgets, forecasts, management accounts and reports and can compare these to that of competitors. The auditor must also compare the results of the review of internal information to their understanding of the entity which may indicate areas which need additional attention. For example, if payroll costs have increased more significantly than expected, the auditor should devise additional audit procedures to ascertain the reasons for such an increase, as this could be indicative of fraud or error. Discussion with management or those charged with governance may indicate (bona fide) reasons for such an increase, though discussion in its entirety would not normally generate sufficient and appropriate audit evidence to support a higher than expected increase. The auditor should undertake additional substantive procedures to address the risk of material misstatement in this respect.

Auditors could also review external reports such as reports from credit rating agencies. These reports can offer a lot of information to auditors to help them understand the entity. For example, a low-rated entity may have considerable cash flow difficulties or be involved in litigation.

INTERNAL CONTROLS

The auditor shall obtain an understanding of internal control relevant to the audit. This allows the auditor to identify factors that affect the risk of material misstatement within the financial statements. An ineffective internal control environment is much more likely to give rise to material misstatement than an effective internal control environment. It is also widely understood that even the most robust of internal control systems will not eliminate the risk of material misstatement; it merely reduces the risk of material misstatement.

In considering the internal controls, the auditor needs to give regard to:

- The nature and complexity of the audit client.
- Materiality.
- The diversity and complexity of the entity's operations.
- Legal and regulatory requirements.
- Whether, and how, a specific control, individually or in combination with others prevents, or detects and corrects, material misstatements.
- The significance of the related risk.
- The circumstances and the applicable component of internal control.

Internal control is the process designed and implemented by those charged with governance, management and other personnel to provide reasonable assurance about the achievement of the entity's objectives. Internal controls are primarily designed and implemented to address business risks identified by management and the ways in which internal controls are designed depend on the nature and complexity of the entity. A small owner-managed business will have less complicated internal controls in place than a multi-million turnover 'blue-chip' listed entity. However, by having less complicated internal controls, a small owner-managed business is no less efficient than a 'blue-chip' entity and can still achieve its objectives.

Limitations of Internal Control

Internal controls can be manipulated and even overridden. Usually employee fraud is committed by the exploitation of a weakness in the internal control environment (for example, a lack of segregation of duties). Management fraud is usually achieved by the overriding of internal controls. Auditors should appreciate that internal controls may not be effective or even understood by those personnel operating the control which may result in a material misstatement occurring.

For the purposes of the ISAs, internal controls can be split into five components which provide a useful framework for auditors to consider how different aspects of an entity's internal control may affect the audit:

- The control environment.
- The entity's risk assessment process.
- The information system, including the related business processes, relevant to financial reporting and communication.
- Control activities.

Monitoring of controls. [ISA315.A51(a) to (e)]

The Control Environment

The control environment is a crucial aspect in any entity. It is also an issue that should be communicated to all staff and management in order to ensure that effective controls are complied with. It is widely understood that the effectiveness of controls cannot rise above the integrity and ethical values of the people who create, administer and monitor them. Management need to ensure that they adopt procedures to deter personnel in engaging in dishonest, illegal or unethical acts. For example, an entity could have a 'Code of Conduct' which stipulates the standards of behaviour expected of personnel in their work. Equally an employee handbook may communicate the integrity and ethical values effectively. Personnel also need to be technically competent and possess the required skills and knowledge in order for them to carry out their duties efficiently and for the benefit of the entity.

Management are pivotal in ensuring that personnel participate in an entity's control environment and those charged with governance are responsible for overseeing the control environment and the process of reviewing the entity's effectiveness of internal controls.

The organisational structure is also vital in ensuring compliance with the control environment. In a small, owner-managed business, the organisational structure may be as simple as personnel reporting to the managing director. However, more complex entities will involve considering key areas of authority and responsibility and appropriate lines of reporting. Developing key areas of authority and responsibility also extends to the assignment of authority and responsibility so that personnel understand the entity's objectives and know how their individual duties inter-relate and contribute to those objectives.

Human Resources

Human resources play a vital role in the entity's controls. For example, the selection of appropriately qualified individuals for various roles and having procedures in place to check the individuals background (Criminal Record Bureau checks). Entities may have policies and procedures in place in respect of training and continued professional development which allow for promotion of individuals to higher levels of responsibility.

Audit evidence relating to an entity's control environment can be obtained via inquiries and other risk assessment procedures such as the inspection of documents — for example, a 'code of conduct'.

The existence of a reliable control environment is a positive factor but auditors should appreciate that such a reliable control environment will deter fraud but not prevent it; and it is in recognition of this that professional scepticism is required during the course of an audit of financial statements. Conversely, deficiencies in the internal control environment may impact heavily on the audit as more detailed substantive testing will be required on key audit areas. ISA 330 recognises that the control environment influences the nature, timing and extent of the auditor's further procedures.

Case Study — Aidan Inc

Aidan Inc operates in the shipping industry. The company has not computerised its financial reporting function and most of its operations are manual including the raising of sales invoices to its customers. Aidan Inc's managing director is Ian Stuarts and he is assisted by Michelle Stevens who is also his domestic partner. They employ a finance administrator, Les Bury, who is assisted by Lisa Pauls. The sales office administrator is Leah Lucas.

Supplier payments are made when the suppliers issue reminders because Les Bury is often dealing with other daily tasks such as the allocation of cash and the authorising of credit notes due to erroneous sales invoices being raised by the sales office administrator. These instances are very frequent and have resulted in the loss of customers. Lisa Pauls assists in processing invoices through the manual bookkeeping system, which is often done incorrectly due to Lisa Paul's lack of double-entry bookkeeping knowledge.

The credit control function is relatively poor as Ian Stuarts and Michelle Stevens are away from the company, often for long periods, as Ian has other business interests worldwide. This also contributes to the poor administration of supplier payments because Ian Stuarts and Michelle Stevens are the only signatories on the bank account.

Case Study — Charlotte Inc

Charlotte Inc's principal activity is that of the sale of disposable clothing. It is headed up by four directors who are as follows:

1.   Norah Hall — Managing Director
2.   Janet Heaton — Sales Director
3.   Stella Whitaker — Marketing Director
4.   Paul Bury — Finance Director

The company has a dedicated sales and purchasing function which is overseen by departmental managers. Purchasing is authorised by the purchasing manager and any major purchases, such as property, plant and equipment are authorised by Paul Bury prior to the purchase. All purchases have requisitions and authorisations attached to them which are then subsequently attached to the supplier invoice.

Sales are raised using the company's information system which is a bespoke system and integrates all sales, purchasing, finance and other ad-hoc reporting features. The company has a dedicated sales ledger clerk who is also responsible for credit control procedures. The company's finance department is sufficiently structured and there is a strong segregation of duties within all departments.

Recent years have seen the company's financial performance go from strength to strength and the company has recently invested in a new distribution centre and offices to house their continued expansion. The company prepares monthly management accounts, which are discussed in monthly board meetings and compared to the budgeted information which is set at the start of the financial year.

In the Aidan Inc case study above there are practically no controls in place to prevent, detect and correct misstatements in a timely manner. Indeed, this is accentuated by the fact that those charged with governance (Ian Stuarts and Michelle Stevens) are essentially divorced from the day to day operations. Les Bury is involved in the authorisation of credit notes which, from the scenario, we can see are quite frequent has and have resulted in the loss of customers. Indeed, Aidan Inc has already seen a downturn in sales which is mainly due to its lack of internal controls. Management's failure to commit sufficient resources to internal controls will undoubtedly have an effect on the auditor's strategy. As the controls in place are clearly weak, the auditor may depart from testing them and will have to undertake a mainly substantive audit which could result in extra costs and time.

In the Charlotte Inc case study this entity clearly has a strong control environment which is evidenced by its expansion plans and strong management team. This control environment, whilst being strong, will not eliminate the risk of material misstatement, but merely reduce it. It will, however, influence the auditor's evaluation of the effectiveness of other controls and the auditor's assessment of the risks of material misstatement. The risk of material misstatement could well be judged low in contrast to that of Aidan Inc.

Entity's Risk Assessment Process

The entity should have risk assessment processes in place to deal with the business risks identified relevant to the preparation of the financial statements. For financial reporting purposes, this should estimate the level of business risks and their significance as well as identifying the likelihood of their occurrence. Risks can arise or change due to circumstances, examples of which are:

- Changes in the regulatory or operating environment can result in changes in competitive pressures and significantly different risks.
- New personnel may have a different focus or understanding of internal control.
- Significant and rapid changes in information systems can change the risk relating to internal control.
- Significant and rapid expansion of operations can strain controls and increase the risk of a breakdown in controls.
- Incorporating new technologies into production processes or information systems may change the risk associated with internal control.
- Entering into business areas with which an entity has little experience may introduce new risks associated with internal control.
- Restructurings may be accompanied by staff reductions, changes in supervision and segregation of duties that may alter the risk associated with internal control.
- The expansion or acquisition of foreign operations carries new and often unique risks that may affect internal control, for example, additional or changed risks from foreign currency transactions.
- Adoption of new accounting principles or changing accounting principles may affect risks in preparing financial statements.

Information Systems, Including the Related Business Processes, Relevant to Financial Reporting and Communication

In today's age most entity's deal with reporting and communicating financial issues through the use of information technology (IT). The related processes involve procedures that:

- Identify and record all valid transactions.
- Describe on a timely basis the transactions in sufficient detail to permit proper classification of transactions for financial reporting.
- Measure the value of transactions in a manner that permits recording their proper monetary value in the financial statements.
- Determine the time period in which transactions occurred to permit recording of transactions in the proper accounting period.
- Present properly the transactions and related disclosures in the financial statements.

The quality of the system-generated information affects management's ability to make appropriate decisions in managing and controlling the entity's activities and to prepare reliable financial reports.

Control Activities

Control activities can encompass a whole host of processes and can entail:

- Authorisation procedures.
- Performance reviews.

- Information processing.
- Physical controls.
- Segregation of duties. [ISA315.A88]

The auditor must obtain a sufficient understanding of the control activities to assess all risks of material misstatement at the assertion level and to design further audit procedures responsive to the levels of assessed risk.

Authorisation Procedures

Authorisation procedures can involve the authorisation of:

- Capital expenditure and disposal of non-current assets.
- Human resources requirements.
- Supplier invoices.
- Payments and bank transfers.
- Personnel expenses and payroll.
- Finance and charges over company assets.

Performance Reviews

Performance reviews can take the form of:

- Reviewing actual financial results against budget information and cash flow forecasts.
- Comparison of sales on a month-by-month basis.
- Comparing one year's financial information with another.
- Comparison of entities within similar industries.

Information Processing

Information processing concerns the application controls which apply to the processing of individual applications and the general IT controls which are policies and procedures that relate to many applications and support the effective functioning of application controls by helping to ensure the continued proper operation of IT systems.

Physical Controls

Physical controls concern the safeguarding of the entity's assets such as locked warehouses and preserving confidential records. It also concerns the security of IT related systems such as password-protected applications as well as dealing with the periodic counting and comparison with amounts shown on the control records (for example, a count of inventory and comparison with inventory records). Auditors need to consider the extent to which physical controls mitigate the threat of theft of company assets.

Illustration

Entity A undertakes monthly inventory counts to ensure there are no large disparities between inventories on hand and the inventory recorded in the information systems. Entity B operates in the same industry and performs an inventory count once a year.

The controls in place to mitigate theft of company assets in Entity A are more efficient than those in Entity B as Entity A undertakes more periodic counting of inventory than Entity B.

Segregation of Duties

Segregation of duties is intended to reduce the opportunity to allow any one person to be in a position to perpetrate and conceal errors or fraud. The concept works by assigning different people the responsibility to authorise and account for transactions and different people to safeguard company assets.

Illustration

The purchase ledger function of an entity is primarily operated by one individual. However, other various functions of the purchase ledger function are dealt with by other individuals. For example:

1. The purchase ledger clerk will run the due payments report.
2. The finance director authorises which payables are to be paid.
3. The purchase ledger clerk prepares the payments and provides backing documentation to the payments (purchase invoices).
4. Two signatures sign the payment.

INFORMATION TECHNOLOGY

The auditor must obtain an understanding of how the entity has responded to any risks arising from IT. These are sub-divided into two further categories:

- application controls, and
- general controls.

Application Controls

Application controls are manual or automated procedures that typically operate at a business process level [ISA315.A97]. Application controls help to ensure that transactions that have occurred are authorised and completely and accurately recorded. They are a subset of an entity's internal control, and include edit checks of input data and numerical sequence checks with manual follow-up of exception reports or correction at the point of entry [ISA315.A97].

General Controls

General controls are policies and procedures that relate to many applications and support the effective functioning of application controls by helping to ensure the continued proper operations of information systems. General IT controls that maintain the integrity of information and security of data commonly include controls over the following:

- Data centre and network operations.
- System software acquisition, change and maintenance.
- Program change.
- Access security.
- Application system acquisition, development and maintenance. [ISA315.A96]

Monitoring of Controls

Management are responsible for the monitoring of an entity's control environment. The auditor is required to obtain an understanding of the major types of activities that the entity uses to monitor internal control over financial reporting, including those related to control activities relevant to the audit, and how the entity initiates corrective actions to its controls.

Various methods exist to monitor internal controls, such as preparing bank reconciliation statements on a monthly basis and ensuring the entity complies with its legal and regulatory obligations. If management do not monitor controls then the effect could be personnel failing to comply with the controls or the controls becoming obsolete as management will fail to consider whether the controls are operating as they should be. For example, if management do not ensure that the finance department is reconciling the bank reconciliation on a regular basis, then it may be forgotten about, which could then result in misstatements failing to be prevented, detected and corrected in a timely manner, which in turn may result in a material misstatement.

External regulators may monitor controls such as tax authorities ensuring that correct levels of tax are being paid by an entity. Other regulators may include the audit of controls by auditors employed by financiers who will not necessarily conduct their audit in accordance with ISAs. Accreditation agencies may assess an entity's internal controls before being awarded accreditation (such as ISO Accreditation). Entity's that employ the use of internal audit functions may also have their internal controls monitored by the internal audit department.

ASSESSING THE RISKS OF MATERIAL MISSTATEMENT

For the purposes of assessing the risks of material misstatement, the auditor shall identify and assess the risks of material misstatement at the financial statement level, and at the assertion level for classes of transactions, account balances and disclosures.

There are generally four fundamental audit approaches to responding to levels of risk in each audit:

1. Substantive approach.
2. Statement of financial position (balance sheet) approach.
3. Systems-based approach.
4. Risk-based approach.

Substantive Approach

The substantive approach targets large volumes of transactions and account balances without any particular focus on specified areas of the financial statements.

Statement of Financial Position (Balance Sheet) Approach

In the statement of financial position (balance sheet) approach, substantive procedures are focussed on statement of financial position (balance sheet) accounts with limited procedures being carried out on the income statement/profit and loss account items. These procedures are justified on the basis that if all management assertions for all the statement of financial position (balance sheet) accounts are tested and verified, then the profit/loss figure for the reporting period will not be materially misstated.

Systems-Based Approach

The systems-based approach looks at the effectiveness of the entity's internal control environment, often referred to as 'control tests' or 'tests of control'. The auditor will then perform substantive procedures in those areas where it is considered that the systems objectives will not be met. Conversely, the auditor will reduce detailed substantive testing in those areas that the auditor considers the objectives will be met.

Risk-Based Approach

The risk-based approach looks at the risks faced by the business and resources will be directed to those areas of the audit where it is considered a material misstatement will arise.

ISA 315 compels auditors to adopt a risk-based approach to audits. The auditor is required to adopt a 'top-down' approach to auditing where the word 'top' refers to the day-to-day operations of the entity and 'down' refers to the financial statements of the entity. This approach enables the auditor to identify the key risks faced by the business on a day-to-day basis and the impact these risks could have on the financial statements and, thus, allow the auditor to plan their work accordingly. Risks can be categorised as follows:

- Financial risks such as cash flow risks.
- Compliance risks such as breaching of laws and regulations.
- Operational risks such as loss of key employees and loss of data risk.

There are four fundamental risk factors involved in dealing with risk assessment procedures:

Financial Statement Risk

This is the risk that the financial statements of an entity contain a material misstatement. (Note that the glossary to the ISAs does not define 'financial statement risk' but does say that audit risk is a function of material misstatement and detection risk.)

Detection Risk

This is the risk that the auditor will fail to detect material misstatement(s).

Inherent Risk

Inherent risk is the susceptibility of an assertion to a misstatement which could be material, individually or when aggregated with other misstatements, assuming that there were no related internal controls. It is limited to either the nature of the item in the financial statements under review or the nature of the entity.

Control Risk

Control risk is the risk that a misstatement could occur in an assertion and that could be material individually or when aggregated with other misstatements, which is not detected and corrected on a timely basis by the internal controls. As discussed in Chapter 4, detection risk and financial statement risk have an inverse relationship which means that the lower the financial statement risk (because of reliance on internal controls) the higher the detection risk.

In gaining an understanding of the entity and the internal control environment, the auditor's understanding may raise doubts as to the effectiveness of the internal control environment and its ability to prevent, detect and correct misstatements on a timely basis. These concerns could be due to the integrity of management and the concerns could be so extreme that the audit cannot be conducted. It may also be the case that the entity's records are so poor that such limitations on audit scope may warrant a qualified or even a disclaimed opinion.

Assertions

Management may, implicitly or explicitly, make assertions regarding the recognition, measurement, presentation and disclosure of the various elements of financial statements and related disclosures. Assertions can be split into the following three categories:

- Classes of transactions.
- Account balances.
- Presentation and disclosure.

Classes of Transactions

Occurrence — transactions and events that have been recorded have occurred and pertain to the entity.

Completeness — all transactions and events that should have been recorded have been recorded.

Accuracy — amounts and other data relating to recorded transactions and events have been recorded appropriately.

Cut-offs — transactions and events have been recorded in the correct accounting period.

Classification — transactions and events have been recorded in the proper accounts.

Account Balances

Existence — assets, liabilities and equity interests exist.

Rights and obligations — the entity holds or controls the rights to assets, and liabilities are the obligations of the entity.

Completeness — all assets, liabilities and equity interest that should have been recorded have been recorded.

Valuation and allocation — assets, liabilities and equity interests are included in the financial statements at appropriate amounts and any resulting valuation or allocation adjustments are appropriately recorded.

Presentation and Disclosure

Occurrence and rights and obligations — disclosed events, transactions and other matters have occurred and pertain to the entity.

Completeness — all disclosures that should have been included in the financial statements have been included.

Classification and understandability — financial information is appropriately presented and described, and disclosures are clearly expressed.

Accuracy and valuation — financial and other information are disclosed fairly and at appropriate amounts.

When the auditor completes risk assessment procedures, these procedures will determine the nature, timing and extent of further audit procedures to be performed and must be responsive to the levels of risk assessed. The overall purpose of ISA 315 is to reduce the risk of material misstatement to an acceptable level, but what circumstances are indicative of material misstatements within the financial statements?

There are a whole host of differing circumstances which may give rise to a risk of material misstatement within the financial statements and the auditor gains an understanding of the entity and the environment in which it operates in order to assess the levels of risk and devise audit procedures accordingly. No two audits will be the same and, thus, it follows that every audit will carry differing levels of risk. Conditions and events that may indicate risks of material misstatement are as follows:

- Entities operating in hyperinflationary economies.
- Lack of management integrity.
- Complex structures.
- Significant transactions with related parties.
- Complex financing arrangements and off-balance sheet finance.
- Poor accounting records and lack of internal controls.
- Installation of new IT systems.
- A history of past misstatements.
- Pending litigation and contingent liabilities.
- Introduction of new legislation and accounting standards.
- Accounting estimates which require a high degree of judgement.
- Complex financial instruments.
- Industrial changes.
- Going concern and liquidity issues.
- Complicated accounting policies.

The above is a broad range of conditions and events which may indicate a risk of material misstatement within the financial statements and it is accepted that auditors will be faced with other circumstances which may indicate a risk of material misstatement within the financial statements.

Significant Risks

Where a risk is deemed 'significant' by the auditor, then they shall perform audit procedures which are specifically responsive to the risk(s) in accordance with the provisions laid down in ISA 330. In addition, the auditor is also required to identify and assess the risk of material misstatement due to fraud and, therefore, the auditor is compelled to comply with the provisions and refer to the guidance in ISA 240, and maintain a degree of professional scepticism throughout the course of the audit.

Risks for Which Substantive Procedures Alone do not Provide Sufficient Appropriate Audit Evidence

In some circumstances, risks for which substantive procedures alone do not provide sufficient appropriate audit evidence may arise particularly where processes are highly automated with little or no manual intervention. Where these situations arise, then the auditor will undertake additional procedures, for example, control tests.

Revisions of Risk Assessment

Planning and risk assessment is an ongoing activity during an audit. In recognition of this, information may come to the auditor's attention during the course of an audit which differs significantly from the information available when the risk assessment was carried out. The result may mean that the risk assessment may not properly reflect the true circumstances of the entity and further audit procedures may not be effective in detecting material misstatements. ISA 330 gives further guidance in this area.

Illustration

The previous year's audit showed an entity's internal control environment to be operating effectively. However, issues have come to the auditor's attention during the course of the current year's audit which suggest that the internal controls have not been operating as effectively in the current year.

In such situations, the auditor will reassess risk and revise their audit procedures accordingly to take account of the revised risk assessment.

Documentation

Professional judgement is to be used on the part of the auditor in determining the form and extent of documentation in respect of:

- Discussion amongst the engagement team.
- The understanding of the entity and the environment in which it operates, as well as sources from which this evidence is obtained and the risk assessment procedures performed.
- Identified and assessed risks of material misstatement both at the financial statement level and at the assertion level.
- The risks and related controls identified.

The auditor should also ensure that documentation complies with the provisions in ISA 230.

Smaller and less complex audits may require a lot less documentation than audits of much larger and more complex entities. Documentation for smaller entities may be incorporated within the overall strategy and audit plan and the risk assessment may also be documented separately or as part of the auditor's documentation of further audit procedures in deciding the content of documentation. The auditor shall have regard to the size, nature and complexity of the entity and its internal control.

As a general rule, the auditor must document:

- The discussion amongst the engagement team regarding the susceptibility of the entity's financial statements to material misstatements due to fraud or error and the significant decisions reached.
- Key elements of the understanding regarding each of the aspects of the entity and its environment identified. This includes each of the internal control components identified to assess the risks of material misstatements of the financial statements; the sources of information from which the understanding was obtained; and the risk assessment procedures.
- The identified and assessed risks of material misstatement at the financial statement level and the assertion level.
- The risks identified and related controls evaluated. [ISA315.32]

Communication

ISA 315 requires the auditor to make those charged with governance or management at an appropriate level of responsibility aware, as soon as is practicable, of material weaknesses in the design or implementation of internal control which have come to the auditor's attention.

The auditor should also have regard to the provisions laid down in ISA 260 and ISA 265.

The appendix to this chapter contains some typical planning notes to illustrate the provisions in ISA 315.

Chapter Roundup

The auditor must obtain an understanding of the entity and its environment, including its internal control to identify and assess the risks of material misstatement in the financial statements whether due to fraud or error.

Risk assessment procedures involve inquiries of management and others within the entity, analytical procedures and other appropriate procedures such as observation and inspection.

The engagement team must discuss the entity and the areas in which the financial statements are susceptible to material misstatement. This discussion provides an opportunity for all team members to share knowledge and discuss the audit procedures to be performed in certain areas.

The auditor must obtain an understanding of the entity's accounting policies, objectives, strategies and related business risks.

The auditor must obtain an understanding of the entity's internal control environment and the inherent limitations of internal controls.

The auditor must obtain an understanding of the entity's control activities to assess all risks of material misstatement at the assertion level.

The auditor shall obtain an understanding of how the entity has responded to risks arising from IT.

The four fundamental audit approaches to responding to levels of risk are:

1. Substantive approach.
2. Statement of financial position (balance sheet) approach.
3. Systems-based approach.
4. Risk-based approach.

The four fundamental risk factors involved in dealing with risk assessment procedures are:

1. Financial statement risk.
2. Detection risk.
3. Inherent risk.
4. Control risk.

Planning and risk assessment is an ongoing activity during the audit.

Planning and risk assessment shall be documented.

Material weaknesses in the design or implementation of internal control must be communicated to management and those charged with governance as soon as is reasonably practicable.

APPENDIX TO ISA 315 ILLUSTRATIVE PLANNING NOTES

The following illustrative planning notes are based on a fictitious company, Arbold Enterprises Limited.

Client: Arbold Enterprises Limited	**Prepared by:** MN
Subject: Audit Planning	**Date:** 03.04.XX
File Ref: 3.2	**Reviewed by:** OP
Year End: 31 July 2010	**Date:** 04.04.XX

Objective

To document our understanding of the client and to plan an overall audit strategy.

3.2 (1) General   Arbold Enterprises Limited was established in 1982 to meet a growing demand for specialised tools in the North West of England. The company is based in the North West. On 15 June 2007, the company acquired 100% of the shares in Brown Enterprises Limited, which is based in the North East of England, for a consideration of £20,000. The outlet in the North East is still in operation.

The company supplies specialised tools to its various customer base in the UK. In 2008 the company merged with Blue Enterprises Limited. Blue Enterprises Limited was formerly a sole trader entity owned by the current managing director, Lucas Stevens.

3.2 (2) Risks

General Business Risks   The company is in a dominant position within the sector it operates in. The company has remained competitive and this is backed up by its recent acquisition of Brown Enterprises Limited to further its planned expansion.

The main business risk faced by the company is in relation to increases in tool prices. The well publicised recession which has hit the world has had an effect on the company. Initial discussions with the client suggest that the increase in tool prices which they suffer is passed on to the customer in order to remain profitable.

The company does not export goods and, therefore, does not suffer any kind of currency risks or fluctuations in exchange rates.

The company supplies major suppliers to the high street tool stores as well as to local outlets. The risk faced here is in relation to the fact that small tool stores are in competition with the larger companies and such larger stores are responsible for the demise of the much smaller stores. Whilst the company does aim to maintain an even spread of customers, the risk is present that the loss of a large proportion of smaller retail operations may have an impact on the company's going concern.

The company operates a confidential invoice discounting arrangement which was primarily entered into as a source of finance, especially during the initial stages of its planned expansion programme. As the expansion plans have progressed, the actual need for the invoice discounting arrangement is diminishing and the directors are now considering moving away from this arrangement.

The general risk here is that there may be fees payable to rescind the confidential invoice discounting arrangement and this could have an impact on the company's short-term cash flow.

Financial Statement Risks

The company has a dedicated finance department, which comprises:

> Sales Ledger and Credit Control
> Sales and Purchase Order Processing
> Purchase Ledger and General Ledger
> Accounts Manager
> External Company Accountant

The company also has an administrative function at its branch in the North East.

Adequate internal controls appear to be in place with regards to safeguarding the assets of the company and other sensitive information. This is not a first year audit and our experience of the internal control systems is that they are fairly strong and management are not divorced from day to day operations.

The company's financial statements are prepared by the external accountants, Byrne & Co. The external accountancy firm is not regulated by a professional institute and the external accountant is not qualified. There is a risk that the financial statements may be misstated due to lack of technical expertise on behalf of the external accountants.

Due to the unregulated status of the external accountant, there is a risk of complacency on the part of the accountant and the director to manipulate the result to achieve a desired outcome (especially as the company is undergoing expansion plans). There is the possibility of the company acquiring the premises it operates in the North West from the current landlord, so finance will have to be arranged, and so the risk here is that the financial statements may be boosted for the purposes of securing additional finance that may be required.

The company supplies tools to its customers and other services which are all standard rates for the purposes of value added tax. The tax authorities have not undertaken a compliance inspection in the last few years and the risk here is that returns to the taxation authorities may contain misstatements.

The company utilises the services of delivery drivers, on both a self-employed and an employed basis to deliver goods to customers. These drivers are also responsible for collecting payments from customers, usually in the form of cash. Each driver is given a jar which contains the cash and these jars are subsequently passed to the accounts department on a daily basis when the driver returns from delivering. There is a substantial financial statement risk here due to fraud, so additional work on the sales and income completeness will have to be undertaken.

The company is subjected to quarterly audits by its invoice discounting company and these audits are primarily concerned with the validity and completeness of its sales as the company is able to draw down approximately 80% of the value of the sales invoices submitted to the invoice discounting company on an immediate basis. These quarterly audits by the invoice discounting company appear not to have yielded any problems, however, the external audit firm should communicate with the invoice discounting company or review correspondence from the invoice discounting company to confirm that there have been no problems encountered which may affect our audit work.

During our initial discussions with the client it appears that there is a lack of segregation of duties in connection with the company's payroll function. Lisa Howard in the accounts department is responsible for preparing, finalising and paying the company payroll. There does not appear to be any interim checks done on the payroll at any intervening period, nor does it appear that anyone authorises the payroll. This also poses a significant financial statement risk in terms of fraud.

Management's Attitude to Risk

The management are aware of the risks faced in their business both externally and internally. The managing director is very much 'hands on' and keeps a close eye on the overall sector. Price increases suffered by the company are immediately passed on to the customer. Where customers are dissatisfied with the price increases, the company endeavours to work with the customer to reach an amicable solution. The director confirmed that customers are satisfied with the services they receive and only the minority of customers (very few, in fact) will complain about suffering price increases.

The company is keen to grow organically to minimise the exposure of its business risk and is currently seeking additional acquisitions.

3.2 (3) Control Environment   The company appears to have a strong internal control environment in place to:

1. Safeguard the assets of the company.
2. Prevent and detect fraud.
3. Restrict access to sensitive information.
4. Control the personnel access to computerised information.
5. Control document flow and processing.

Section 4.1 of the permanent audit file details the internal controls present that prevent fraud and/or error. Such processes include the checking of invoices by the order processing department and the finance manager. These are then finally checked by the managing director when the invoice is eventually paid (all invoices are given to the managing director with the cheque). All invoices are then stamped as 'paid' when they have been paid to prevent duplication. All supplier statements are reconciled as and when they come in.

The company's cheque book is kept with the finance manager in a locked office. There are no pre-signed blank cheques kept on the premises. All cash is banked daily.

The bank account is maintained by the finance manager and reconciled on a daily basis. The bank reconciliations are also reviewed by the external accountant. The managing director also has access to the bank accounts and regularly reviews these. The directors are very much 'hands on' and are not divorced from the day to day running of the company.

The company uses a well known accounting package as its financial reporting tool and payroll processing.

In terms of the payroll function, an initial discussion with the client suggests a weakness within this area. The person doing the payroll (Lynn Howard in the accounts department) has overall control for every aspect of the payroll function. Lynn prepares and finalises the payroll and then subsequently generates the payments within the company's BACS programme (BACS is only used to pay employees — not suppliers). There does not appear to be any segregation of duties in respect of the payroll function and this has been noted in the financial statement risks above. It is planned that a letter of weakness be sent to the client in this regard if our audit testing reveals that this is still the case.

3.2 (4) Financing   The company does not have any convertible debt. The company does utilise the services of an invoice discounting arrangement and we will review the terms of this arrangement and consider whether the invoice discounting account is nearing its limits or whether there have been any breaches in the past. The company purchases its vehicles on hire purchase contracts and operates a bank overdraft.

The company is looking to purchase the premises it operates from in the North West and finance may be required to secure this purchase.

The company also has operating leases and in accordance with the prescribed accounting standards, where the company enters into a lease which essentially passes all the risk and rewards of ownership of the asset, this lease is treated as finance lease and capitalised with a corresponding payable being recognised. Leases which are not finance leases (where the risk and rewards of ownership essentially remain with the lessor) are accounted for as operating leases and rentals charged to the statement of comprehensive income as incurred.

3.2 (5) External Environment and Further Business Risks   The company is reliant on its key supplier, Ellis Tools Ltd. This is an extremely well-known supplier based in the North West whose financial statements are shown on schedule 3.2(a). The financial statements suggest that there are no apparent problems with its going concern, which can minimise the risk of over dependence on one key supplier.

In terms of over reliance on key customers, the client appears to have an even spread of customers.

3.2 (6) Summary of Main Risks   The cash-based nature of the company and the fact that it raises in excess of 1,000 invoices per week mean that income completeness contains significant risks at the planning stage of the audit. This area will require considerable audit work undertaken by the senior rather than the assistant.

More detailed audit work on the payroll will have to be undertaken in light of the lack of segregation of duties.

A review of the going concern of the company will have to be undertaken.

A review of the invoice discounting arrangement, in particular to ensure that no breaches have occurred, will have to be undertaken. Correspondence with the invoice discounting company may also have to be entered into to gain an understanding of how the overall arrangement is being complied with.

3.2 (7) The Regulatory Environment   The company has to comply with the main legislation such as Health and Safety at Work Act 1974, National Minimum Wages Act and Disability Discrimination Act, etc. In addition, the Companies Acts are also applicable to this client.

Money laundering regulations are also applicable and the auditor will also keep this in mind during the course of the audit. The audit team are fully aware of their responsibilities under the money laundering regulations.

3.2 (8) Significant Accounting Policies   Detailed below are the significant accounting policies applicable to this audit client:

Basis of Financial Statement Preparation   The financial statements are going to be prepared in accordance with the historical cost convention. Initial reviews of the financial statements confirm that the company is not eligible for reduced disclosures under the Financial Reporting Standard for Smaller Entities.

Non-Current Assets   Non-current assets are initially recorded at their cost price and written off over their economic useful lives at the following rates:

Property, plant and equipment:	5 years straight line.
Fixtures and fittings:	10 years straight line.
Motor vehicles:	25% reducing balance.

Revenue   Revenue represents the despatch and sales of goods, excluding value added tax (where applicable) net of trade discounts and in accordance with IAS 18 'Revenue'.

Inventory   Initially, inventory is immaterial to the financial statements of the entity, however, it is accounted for in accordance with the provisions in IAS 2 'Inventory' on the basis of lower of cost or net realisable value.

Deferred Taxation   Deferred tax is recognised in respect of temporary differences that have originated but not reversed at the reporting date. Deferred tax is accounted for on an undiscounted basis in accordance with IAS 12 'Income Taxes'. Deferred tax assets are only recognised when the company has available tax losses which it can carry forward against profits in the next financial year. For the year ended 31 July 2010, the company has not got any deferred tax assets.

Pensions   The company operates a defined contribution pension scheme. The assets of the scheme are held separately from those of the company in an independently administered fund. All contributions to the defined contribution scheme are charged to the statement of comprehensive income and any unpaid contributions at the reporting date are accrued for. Any contributions paid over and above the annual requirement are subsequently prepaid and are released to the statement of comprehensive income in the period(s) to which they relate. As at the 31 July 2010, the company did not have any prepaid contributions, nor were any contributions in arrears.

Complex Transactions   The company does not have any complex transactions such as consignment inventory.

3.2 (9) Management Overview   The directors of the company are:

Mr Alex Smith — Managing Director
Mrs Jenny Smith — Director

Key personnel are:

Mr S Hoyle — External Accountant
Ms Annette Smyth — Accounts Manager
Mr Mark Ellis — Transport Manager

Both directors are involved in the day to day running of the company and aim to keep the company at its competitive advantage.

Management meet on a regular basis to discuss issues affecting the business and to review the management information to keep an eye on the cash flow of the business, the profitability, the aged receivables, the invoice discounting account and to see how they can improve/exceed expectations.

3.2 (1) Audit Plan — Initial Matters Arising   Discussions took place with the client on 3 March 2010 at the clients premises in the North West (see file reference 3.2(b)). The planning meeting (see 3.2 (c)) took place on Monday 10 March 2010 and the initial matters arising were as follows:

Fraud   Professional scepticism will have to be adopted during the course of the audit. An expectation of incomplete revenue to either reduce corporate tax liabilities or value added tax returns will be present during the course of the audit. Money laundering regulations will also have to be considered if we are unable to conclude that revenue is complete.

Due to the nature of the cash side of the entity, more detailed audit work will have to be undertaken by the senior to confirm the director's assertion that all bankings are intact and complete and that no instance of fraudulent activity has taken place during the year.

Fraud for personal financial gain is not expected, however, we will have to assume it is present at a factor of 100% and reduce it accordingly by virtue of our audit testing.

Gross Profit Margins

Our initial analytical review (see schedule 5.1) suggests that gross profit margins have remained consistent with the prior year, which is in line with our expectations.

Overrider Provisions

A growing feature within industries these days is an overrider provision where a company will give rebates if suppliers purchase a pre-determined amount on a periodic basis. There is no overrider provision within the financial statements and we will have to confirm that there are not, in fact, any overrider provisions offered to suppliers or customers which have not been accounted for in the financial statements.

Motor Expenses – Vehicle Leasing

A review of the vehicle leases will have to be undertaken to confirm if these are operating or finance leases and the subsequent recoverability of value added taxes if they are leasing (i.e. check that the value added tax reclaimed is restricted to 50%).

Invoice Discounting Agreement

We will need to obtain confirmation through the audit to confirm that the terms of the invoice discounting agreement are being adhered to and that there have been no breaches. We will also need to confirm the director's assertion that the company is well below the limit on the invoice discounting account.

Merger with Blue Enterprises

We will need to obtain details of the merger of the company during the year to confirm it is correctly accounted for within the financial statements.

Going Concern

We will need to confirm that the directors are happy that the company is still a going concern for the foreseeable future and obtain details of how they have arrived at their conclusion that it is or it is not a going concern. Reviews of the invoice discounting agreement, the financial statements of key suppliers and customers and the financial statements of the client should give an indication in this regard.

Depreciation

Depreciation charges appear to have significantly increased on the previous year — work will have to be done on these to confirm they have been correctly calculated in accordance with the company's prescribed accounting policies.

Inventory

Initial thoughts are that inventory is immaterial to the financial statements. However, it may become material when aggregated with other immaterial misstatements. We will need to check the calculation of the inventory, review inventory counting sheets and check the figure is appropriate as it is similar to the previous year.

Supplier Disputes

The company has one major supplier, and we will need to confirm that there are no disputes with this supplier which may restrict goods being delivered, which could have an impact on the day to day running of the business (deliveries of goods are made on a daily basis).

Internal Controls

Work will have to be done on the internal controls of the company, i.e. 'walk through' tests and checks on control account reconciliations for periods other than the reporting date, to confirm the internal controls we understand to be operable do in fact operate.

Recoverability of Loans

Loans are outstanding to the company. The loans do not appear to have reduced on the previous year so recoverability of these loans will have to be addressed.

3.2 (11) High Risk and Problem Areas   Initial planning would suggest that the key problem areas are going to be:

1.   Sales – i.e. 'cash based'.
2.   Value Added Tax.
3.   Recoverability of loans.
4.   Leasing – high risk of 'off balance sheet' finance.

3.2 (12) Related Party Issues   The company directors have interests with other companies. Transactions and events relating to these companies will have to be disclosed as related parties in accordance with IAS 24 'Related Party Disclosures'. We will also have to review correspondence for evidence of any other related parties and review the bank audit letter for any related parties, for example, directors' personal guarantees.

Other audit testing such as invoice reviews and generally being alert to transactions that may be related parties should be undertaken.

Initial discussions with the client confirm that Mr and Mrs Smith (director-shareholders) are both married and have children. Mr Smith has confirmed that neither of his children (or any other family members) are in the employment of the company or have any influence over the running of the company.

14 ISA 320 (REVISED AND REDRAFTED) MATERIALITY IN PLANNING AND PERFORMING AN AUDIT

ISA 320 outlines the auditor's responsibility in relation to the concept of materiality. It also interrelates with the provisions laid down in ISA 450 'Evaluation of Misstatements Identified During the Audit' to which auditors must also refer as this provides guidance on how materiality is applied in evaluating the effect of identified misstatements on the audit and of uncorrected misstatements.

Audit materiality is wholly judgemental and judgements concerning materiality are made in relation to the specific circumstances surrounding the entity. In addition, judgements are also made having regard to the size, complexity and objectives of the entity.

Materiality is set at the planning stage of the audit and auditors are aware that certain transactions or events may be material both in nature as well as in value. Consider the following simple case study:

Case Study

On 1 January 2010 the managing director of ABC Inc transferred his entire holding in the entity's issued share capital to the newly-formed holding company, XYZ Group Inc. The audit for the year end 31 December 2010 is being planned of the financial statements which show the following net assets:

Issued share capital	$100 (made up of 100 $1 shares)
Retained earnings	$590,000

We can see from the above that the issued share capital is made up of 100 $1 shares which were previously owned by the managing director and which have been transferred to the newly-formed parent company during the period under review. This is a transaction which is material in nature.

It is widely understood that an item is material if its omission or misstatement could influence the economic decisions of users taken on the basis of the financial statements. The objective of the audit is to enable the auditor to express an opinion to give reasonable assurance that the financial statements are free from all *material* misstatement and whether they conform to an acceptable financial reporting framework. There are several quantitative guidelines in practice to determine materiality but the general rule is that professional judgement is to be exercised by the auditor in determining the levels of materiality.

Performance Materiality

ISA 320.9 defines performance materiality as:

> *the amount or amounts set by the auditor at less than materiality for the financial statements as a whole to reduce to an appropriately low level the probability that the aggregate of uncorrected and undetected misstatements exceeds materiality for the financial statements as a whole. If applicable, performance materiality also refers to the amount or amounts set by the auditor at less than the materiality level or levels for particular classes of transactions, account balances or disclosures.*

[ISA320.9]

In general, materiality is often calculated as:

- Percentage of revenue.
- Percentage of gross profit.
- Percentage of gross assets.
- Percentage of equity.
- Blended methods combining the above and finding an average.
- Sliding scale methods which vary with the size of the entity.

Qualitative factors must be taken into consideration when assessing materiality which can be viewed as nature of the item involved and impact of the item involved.

Nature of the Item Involved

Many items in financial statements are, by their nature, subject to a high degree of subjectivity, such as depreciation charges applied to non-current assets. In respect of these items the auditor will have to accept a reasonable margin of error.

By contrast, other items leave very little scope for judgement, such as issued share capital or bank balances. On these types of items, the auditor will typically take a tighter view on the question of materiality. It is likely that auditors will typically expect this type of item to be correct.

Impact of the Item Involved

This principle relates back to the definition of materiality — the impact of the item on the view presented to the user of the financial statements. The suggestion is that errors which may not be great in numerical terms may have a major impact on the picture presented by the financial statements.

A common method of calculating materiality is to use a numerical approach. A typical method is shown in the following illustration.

Illustration

The audit of Candora Inc is being planned for the year ended 31 March 2010. Extracts from the entity's financial statements are as follows:

Revenue	$10 million
Pre-tax profit	$4 million
Non-current assets (NBV)	$17 million
Current assets	$5 million

We can use the above figures to calculate materiality using the following percentages and then striking an average:

1% of revenue	$10m × 1% = $100,000
2% of gross assets	$22m × 2% = $440,000
10% of profit before taxation	$4m × 10% = $400,000
	$940,000
As an approximate average	$313,333
Materiality assessed at (say)	$313,000

Reasonable Assurance

The wording of the standard auditor's report refers to the fact that the auditor must obtain 'reasonable assurance' that the financial statements are free from material misstatement.

ISA 200 examines the concept of reasonable assurance. It is explained that it means a high, but not absolute, level of assurance is being given. An auditor cannot give absolute assurance that the financial statements are completely free from errors because there will always be inherent limitations in an audit that affect the auditor's ability to detect material misstatements, such as:

- The use of testing and sampling during the audit.
- The inherent limitations of internal control.
- The possibility of misrepresentation for fraudulent purposes.

It follows, therefore, that while an unmodified audit opinion is not a guarantee the financial statements are free from material misstatement, and it does offer a high level of assurance from an independent professionally-qualified accountant, so adding to the perceived reliability of the financial statements.

The concept of materiality is applied by the auditor both in planning and performing the audit and assessing the effect of identified misstatements on the audit and of uncorrected misstatements, if any, on the financial statement when forming the opinion in the auditor's report. In some cases, misstatements may cause the auditor to assess them as material even if they are below the materiality threshold both individually and when aggregated with other misstatements.

Illustration

An entity makes small losses year on year, then it produces a $15,000 profit. Materiality has been assessed at $50,000.

In the above the auditor would usually accept errors below $50,000 in isolation provided they don't become material when aggregated with other (potential) misstatements. However, consider that the auditor discovered a $30,000 unprovided accrual and this was the only error discovered.

$30,000 on the face of it would seem immaterial when compared to the assessed materiality level of $50,000. However, an unprovided accrual of $30,000 would turn the $15,000 profit into a $15,000 loss.

Consideration must be given to how such an omission would influence the user of the financial statements. In this illustration, potential investors would almost think twice if a $15,000 profit turned into a $15,000 loss.

Revision of Materiality

When the auditor becomes aware of information that would have caused the auditor to determine a different level of materiality previously, the auditor must revise materiality for the financial statements as a whole. The auditor should also consider this revision in the context of the audit procedures already performed and determine whether the nature, timing and extent of such procedures still remains appropriate.

Documentation

In respect of materiality, the auditor must ensure that documentation includes the following:

(a) Materiality for the financial statements as a whole.
(b) If applicable, the materiality level or levels for particular classes of transactions, account balances or disclosures.
(c) Performance materiality.
(d) Any revisions of (a)–(c) as the audit progressed. [ISA320.14]

Evaluating the Effect of Misstatements and Communication

The IAASB Clarity project introduced a companion ISA to ISA 320; that of ISA 450 *'Evaluation of Misstatements Identified During the Audit'* which is discussed further in Chapter 17.

In assessing whether the financial statements are materially misstated, the auditor will evaluate the effect of misstatements individually and when aggregated with other misstatements. The aggregate of uncorrected misstatements comprises:

• Specific misstatements identified by the auditor, for example, a misstatement in closing inventories at the end of the period.
• Projected misstatements which are the auditor's best estimate of other misstatements which cannot be specifically identified.

Illustration

Error Projection

An auditor undertakes tests on sales invoices. The value of the invoices tested was $35,000 out of total sales of $100,000.

The auditor divided their population as follows:

    (a)   The auditor tests **all** material items. These amounted to $20,000 and included an error of $1,000.

Since the auditor has tested all material items, these errors will not be reproduced in the population which has not been tested and the likely error from this source is, therefore, limited to $1,000.

    (b)   The auditor tests a number of other invoices amounting to $15,000 and found an error of $500.

The error in the sample could be reproduced in the population. In this case the population and sample are limited to the non-material items. The projected error by extrapolation will be the error discovered ($500) × the population ($80,000) ÷ the sample ($15,000), that is, $2,667.

The total projected error is, therefore, $1,000 + $2,667 = $3,667.

Since the actual errors discovered will probably be adjusted, the likely error in the financial statements is projected error ($3,667) less adjustments of $1,500 = $2,167.

If the auditor had not split the population and sample into two distinct elements, the projected error would be found by extrapolating over the total population and would have been error discovered ($1,500) × population ($100,000) ÷ sample ($35,000), that is, $4,286.

Material Misstatements

If the auditor considers the misstatements result in the financial statements being materially misstated, the auditor must consider whether reducing audit risk by extending audit procedures or requesting management to adjust the financial statements is necessary.

In situations where management refuse to correct the misstatements and the results of extending audit procedures do not enable the auditor to conclude that the aggregate of uncorrected misstatements is not material, the auditor will consider the impact of these misstatements in forming their opinion to be communicated in the auditor's report. This will involve modifying the audit opinion accordingly and the auditor shall ensure they comply with the provisions laid down in ISA 700 'The Independent Auditor's Report on General Purpose Financial Statements'.

There may be situations where misstatements, both individually and in aggregate, may fall below the materiality level but may be approaching the materiality level. In such situations, the auditor must consider reducing audit risk by performing additional audit procedures or requesting that management adjust the financial statements for the identified misstatements.

Communication

Where the auditor discovers material misstatements within the financial statements, the auditor must communicate these misstatements to an appropriate level of management on a timely basis and consider the need to report the misstatement(s) to those charged with governance in accordance with ISA 260.

Chapter Roundup

An item is material if its error or omission is likely to influence the decisions taken by the user of the financial statements.

ISA 450 is a companion standard to ISA 320.

Materiality is wholly judgemental and such judgements are made having regard to the specific circumstances surrounding the entity as well as to the size, complexity and objectives of the entity.

Materiality is set at the planning stage of the audit.

It is mandatory for materiality to be assessed where an audit opinion is given.

There are several quantitative guidelines in assessing materiality but qualitative factors must also be considered.

Performance materiality is the amount set by the auditor which is less than the materiality level for the financial statements as a whole.

Auditors must revise materiality when they become aware of information that would have caused a different materiality level to be previously determined.

Documentation should include:

1. Materiality levels for the financial statements as a whole.
2. Where applicable, materiality for particular classes of transactions, account balances or disclosures.
3. Performance materiality.
4. Any revisions of (1)–(3) as the audit progresses.

---

15 ISA 330 (REDRAFTED) THE AUDITOR'S RESPONSES TO ASSESSED RISKS

Risk features extremely heavily in auditing and one of the primary functions involved in auditing is identifying the risks faced by an entity, both business and financial, and reducing these risks to an acceptable level. ISA 330 deals with the responsibilities faced by the auditor in designing and implementing audit procedures which specifically respond to the risk of material misstatement. ISA 330 interrelates to that of ISA 315 in identifying and assessing the risks of material misstatement by gaining an understanding of the entity and the environment in which it operates.

Auditors have a responsibility to gather sufficient appropriate audit evidence to support the overall audit opinion and this audit evidence is gathered, primarily, through two fundamental processes:

- Substantive testing.
- Tests of controls.

ISA 330 defines substantive testing and tests of controls as follows:

Substantive procedures — an audit procedure designed to detect material misstatements at the assertion level. Substantive procedures comprise:

(a) Tests of details (of classes of transactions, account balances, and disclosures); and
(b) Substantive analytical procedures.

Tests of controls — an audit procedure designed to evaluate the operating effectiveness of controls in preventing, or detecting and correcting, material misstatements at the assertion level.

[ISA330.4 (a) and (b)]

The phrase 'responsive to the assessed risk of material misstatement' relates to the auditor's approach for designing and performing further audit procedures. The procedures the auditor adopts must respond to the assessed level of risk of material misstatement. The auditor may consider that tests of controls would not be appropriate and, thus, gather sufficient appropriate audit evidence from a wholly substantive approach. Where the auditor considers a wholly substantive approach appropriate, the auditor shall be satisfied that performing only substantive procedures would reduce the risk of material misstatement to an acceptably low level.

It follows, therefore, that the audit procedures must be responsive to the assessed level of risk of material misstatement at both the assertion level and at the financial statement level.

At the Assertion Level

Audit procedures to address the risk of material misstatement at the assertion level need to be responsive to the assessed levels of risk. The auditor shall consider the reasons for the assessment given to the risk of material misstatement at the assertion level for each class of transactions, account balance and disclosure. The auditor shall consider both inherent risk and control risk. Inherent risk in auditing terms is the risk that the account or section being audited is materially misstated without considering the related internal controls due to fraud or error. In assessing inherent risk the auditor needs to consider various factors including the complexity of determining the account amount (particularly if it is an estimate), past history including whether there have been any past errors, the circumstances of the entity's business and the environment in which it operates and management's overall risk awareness.

Control risk is the risk that the internal controls present in a certain area of the accounting system will not prevent, detect and correct a material misstatement in a timely manner.

The auditor takes the above risks into consideration at the assertion level and considers the likelihood of material misstatement. The auditor may also consider it appropriate to obtain more persuasive audit evidence in areas where the assessed level of risk of material misstatement is considered high.

Tests of Control

Tests of controls at the assertion level are required in order that the auditor can gain sufficient appropriate audit evidence concerning the operating effectiveness of the internal control environment. The auditor may also test the operating effectiveness of the internal control environment where the auditor concludes that substantive procedures alone will not provide sufficient appropriate audit evidence at the assertion level. [ISA330.8]

In recognition of the inverse relationship between financial statement risk and detection risk, the auditor is required to obtain more persuasive audit evidence to address the risk of material misstatement where the auditor places greater reliance on the internal control environment.

When the auditor is designing tests of controls the auditor needs to take into consideration how the controls have been applied during the period under review and how consistently those controls have been applied as well as looking at how, or by what means, they have been applied. In some cases, audits can be undertaken at interim periods during the year and the auditor may have undertaken tests of controls during the financial period. Where changes to those internal controls have been implemented subsequent to the interim audits, the auditor needs to obtain audit evidence about the significant changes to the internal controls subsequent to the interim period and also consider the additional audit evidence that needs to be obtained for the remaining period. [ISA330.12]

Ordinarily, the auditor will perform other audit procedures in combination with inquiry to test the operating effectiveness of controls. Inquiry alone is not enough to generate sufficient appropriate audit evidence and this is why it is necessary to combine inquiry with other audit procedures.

Recurring Audits and Test of Controls

It is widely recognised that for continuing engagements, tests of controls will have been undertaken in previous audits and evidence will be on file concerning the operating effectiveness of those internal controls. In some jurisdictions, detailed testing of internal controls is only required in every third audit and indeed ISA 330 recommends detailed testing of internal controls every third audit. Other jurisdictions may recommend shorter or longer intervening periods to undertake more rigorous tests of internal controls. There are various factors which need to be taken into consideration concerning the time period that should elapse before further detailed testing of the controls. The factors to consider are generally:

- The risk of material misstatement.
- The general operating effectiveness of the internal controls.
- The extent of reliance on the internal control.
- The effectiveness of general IT related internal controls.
- The application of the internal control by the entity.

Auditors may feel additional factors need to be taken into account when considering the time period that should elapse before further detailed testing of controls takes place, but the above are a broad range of factors. Regardless of the time period that should elapse before further detailed testing of controls, the auditor shall test the operating effectiveness of some controls during each audit.

If the auditor is going to place reliance on evidence from previous audits, the auditor should consider the relevance of the evidence being relied on. For example, if an entity makes significant changes to an internal control subsequent to the previous audit, that evidence is essentially redundant for the current audit even though the evidence may have confirmed the operating effectiveness of the previous controls. Where changes to internal controls have been implemented by the entity in the current year, the auditor shall obtain audit evidence concerning the operating effectiveness of the revised controls in the current audit.

Illustration

Tests of Control on a Sales Order Cycle

Lakeside Clothing Inc operates in the disposal clothing sector. It has a fully computerised accounting and financial reporting system which also operates a sales and purchase ordering facility which is administered by the sales and purchasing departments respectively. During the course of the audit of Lakeside Clothing's financial statements for the year ended 31 December 2010 the auditors have reviewed the prior year's working papers and held discussions with management concerning the sales order cycle. Management have confirmed to the auditors that there have been no changes to the internal controls pertaining to the sales order cycle since the previous audit. The audit manager has concluded that internal controls in this area need to be tested because this is the third successive audit performed by the audit firm.

The auditor will watch sales orders being placed and witness the initiation of the transaction from initial order through to the actual raising of the sales invoice. The purpose of this test is to ensure that the internal controls present in this area reduce the risk of material misstatement within the financial statements. Material misstatement could occur if the internal controls do not prevent, detect and correct, on a timely basis, misstatements. For example, if the system 'forgets' to invoice a customer for goods supplied, and this failing is not picked up by the system on a timely basis, there is a risk that goods could leave Lakeside Clothing and not be invoiced, resulting in possible financial loss to the company.

Evaluating the Operating Effectiveness of Internal Controls

Controls can be made up of two component parts: direct controls and indirect controls.

Direct controls directly relate to the assertions, but could also contain indirect controls which they rely on. For example, in a sales control the information system may generate an exception report when a customer exceeds agreed credit limits. In such cases the auditor will consider how such exception reports are dealt with.

When evaluating the operational effectiveness of the internal controls, the auditor needs to assess whether misstatements that have been detected by way of substantive procedures are indicative that the internal controls are not operating as effectively as they should be. Where the auditor identifies that misstatements have been made they should consider whether the tests of controls are reliable enough to provide appropriate audit evidence or whether additional tests of controls are appropriate. In some cases, the auditor may depart from tests of controls, particularly where the auditor renders them ineffective and, thus, undertake substantive procedures.

Extent of Tests of Controls

The extent of control tests will vary depending on the size and complexity of the audit assignment. The auditor designs tests of controls in order to gain sufficient and appropriate audit evidence that the controls have operated effectively throughout the reporting period. There are factors which the auditor needs to consider when deciphering the extent of tests of controls, such as:

- The frequency of the performance of the control by the entity during the period.
- The length of time during the audit period that the auditor is relying on the operating effectiveness of the control.
- The relevance and reliability of the audit evidence to be obtained in supporting that the control prevents, or detects and corrects, material misstatements at the assertion level.
- The extent to which audit evidence is obtained from tests of other controls related to the assertion.
- The extent to which the auditor plans to rely on the operating effectiveness of the control in the assessment of risk.
- The expected deviation from the control.

Substantive Procedures

Substantive procedures are the detailed procedures used by auditors to collect audit evidence that the assertions made by management in the financial statements (both figures and disclosures) are reliable and are in accordance with the applicable financial reporting framework and relevant legislation. Where internal controls are deemed ineffective, the auditor will ordinarily rely more on substantive analytical procedures to see if the numbers 'make sense' and to obtain explanations for any unexpected fluctuations in the financial statements. Where internal controls are deemed ineffective, the auditor will rely more on substantive test of detail to gather sufficient and appropriate audit evidence.

Regardless of the assessed levels of risk, the auditor must design and perform substantive procedures for each material class of transaction, account balance and disclosure.

Substantive procedures or substantive tests are those activities performed by the auditor that gather evidence as to the validity and/or accuracy of account balances and underlying transactions. Management may implicitly assert that account balances and underlying classes of transactions are complete and valid, and the auditor will gather evidence to support this assertion by agreeing amounts in the financial statements to their underlying records. For example, substantive testing for income completeness will involve the auditor:

- Starting from initiation of the sale, that is, from receipt of a customer order.
- Tracing the order through to the goods despatch note.
- From the despatch note, tracing the transaction to the sales invoice.
- From the sales invoice, tracing the transaction through the sales ledger.
- From the sales ledger, tracing the transaction through to the receivables control account.
- From the receivables control account, tracing the transaction to its ultimate destination: revenue in the financial statements.

There are generally two categories of substantive procedures: analytical procedures and tests of detail. Analytical procedures, which are applied at several stages of the audit, generally provide less reliable evidence than tests of detail, whereas tests of detail are applied in the substantive testing stage.

Timing of Tests

Some auditors will attend audit clients and perform substantive procedures during interim periods — for example, on a quarterly basis. Where these situations arise, the auditor should perform substantive procedures and tests of control for the remaining period or, where the auditor deems it appropriate, perform substantive procedures only [ISA330.22 (b)]. In instances where the auditor detects misstatements which they were not expecting, the auditor shall evaluate the effect of these misstatements and whether the risk assessment and the nature, timing and extent of substantive procedures need to be amended. In considering when to perform audit procedures, the auditor also considers:

- The control environment.
- When relevant information will be available.
- The period to which the audit evidence relates.
- The nature of the risk.

Certain audit procedures can only be performed after the reporting date has passed, such as agreeing the financial statements to underlying records and examining adjustments made to the financial statements during the course of their preparation. There could also be risks that the entity has incomplete sales revenue or items of costs have not been included within the financial statements. The auditor will perform procedures to respond to those risks, such as testing cut-offs.

Audit Evidence versus Audit Procedure

The ultimate objective of ISA 330 is to ensure that the procedures the auditor adopts respond to the assessed levels of risk of material misstatement. Audit evidence and audit procedure are not the same things.

Audit Evidence   *Audit evidence* is independent, third party confirmation which substantiates the information contained in the financial statements. For example, a bank audit letter is audit evidence in that it is independent, is in writing and confirms the balances on the bank account(s) at the period end and will also disclose the nature of any securities pledged by the company which should be disclosed within the financial statements.

Audit evidence is collated by the auditor as a result of the audit procedures they adopt.

Illustration

Let us consider the receivables circularisation procedure. A list of aged receivables is obtained from the client as at the reporting date. The auditor will devise specific sampling methods to decipher which receivables are going to be included in the circularisation. Letters are then sent to the customers in the sample confirming the balance on their payables ledger at the reporting date. Ordinarily, these letters are sent to the customers by the audit firm, not the client. Non-replies are subsequently followed up. Where follow-ups still do not generate any replies, alternative audit procedures are adopted by the auditor, for example, checking after date cash receipts to verify the existence of the receivable at the reporting date.

From the above scenario, we can distinguish the audit procedures from the audit evidence. The procedures include determining the receivables which will be included in the sample, preparing the letters, verifying whether or not the balance agrees with the customer's payable ledger and chasing up non-replies or devising alternative audit procedures. Audit evidence is the letter back from the customer confirming whether or not they are in agreement with the balance owed to the entity at the reporting date or documentation detailing alternative audit procedures adopted to verify the balance on the customer's ledger in the event of non-replies. This is just one independent procedure on the receivables in the statement of financial position (balance sheet) at the reporting date.

Audit Procedures   *Audit procedures* are procedures which the auditor adopts to obtain evidence. In themselves, they are not evidence. For example, counting petty cash is a procedure, attending inventory count at the reporting date is a procedure, inspecting non-current assets is a procedure. Procedures are, therefore, not evidence, they generate the audit evidence.

Audit procedures are determined at the planning stage and effective audit planning will ensure sufficient appropriate audit evidence is gathered to support the audit opinion. Consider the following illustration.

Illustration

Alpha Limited operates in the UK. The audit of the financial statements is nearing completion ready for the audit manager to undertake his review of the file prior to submission to the engagement partner.

Within the financial statements is a provision for restructuring costs which is material to the financial statements of Alpha Limited.

Clearly the issue is whether the evidence supporting the provision allows the provision to be viable in accordance with FRS 12 or IAS 37 'Provisions, Contingent Liabilities and Contingent Assets'. In order for provisions to be viable, they have to conform to three criteria laid down in FRS 12 or IAS 37:

1. Alpha has to have a present obligation (either legal or constructive) arising as a result of past events.
2. It is probable that a transfer of economic benefits will be required to settle the obligation.
3. The obligation can be measured reliably.

The auditors should gather evidence to satisfy the above criteria as well as ensure that the accounting standards have been correctly applied. The audit evidence may be:

1. Board minutes detailing management's plans to restructure.
2. A copy of the announcement of the restructuring which should be before the reporting date in order to recognise the provision at the reporting date.
3. Schedules detailing the redundancy payments and evidence to show that these are being made in accordance with Contracts of Employment and any relevant domestic legislation.
4. A schedule detailing the amounts to be paid to each redundant employee. The schedule would be annotated to show that all relevant employees have been included and that calculations have been checked for a relevant sample of employees affected.
5. Copies of legal correspondence and copies of any relevant board minutes detailing the management representations in connection with any additional costs that would be incurred on restructuring, for example, any provisions in onerous contracts.
6. Evidence to prove that the accounting standards have been complied with, for example, date of redundancy announcements, carrying value of any associated assets which have been stated at recoverable amounts and correct calculation of redundancy payments.

Evaluation of the Sufficiency and Appropriateness of Audit Evidence

The auditor has a responsibility to ensure that the risks of material misstatement at the assertion level remains appropriate and this is achieved by evaluating whether the audit evidence obtained is sufficient and appropriate. The audit of financial statements is a cumulative process and auditor's will frequently change their risk assessments and planning to respond to varying degrees of factors encountered during the course of an audit.

During the course of an audit, information may come to the auditor's attention of which the auditor was not previously aware and which may cause the auditor to modify the initial risk assessment. Such factors which the auditor may not have expected when undertaking their initial risk assessments are:

- Significant weaknesses encountered in internal control during the reporting period.
- Deviations from controls.
- Fraudulent activity.
- Changes to controls which have been ineffective.
- Significant misstatements within the financial statements.

The auditor considers factors which have been identified and must then determine whether the tests on the controls performed provide an appropriate basis for reliance on those controls or whether additional tests of controls are necessary. In some situations, the auditor may consider that reliance on internal controls cannot be made and as such adopt more substantive procedures.

In evaluating audit evidence, the auditor shall consider whether sufficient appropriate audit evidence has been obtained to reduce the risk of material misstatement to an acceptably low level. The auditor will consider the audit evidence as a whole, regardless of whether it corroborates or contradicts the assertions in the financial statements.

Audit evidence should be gathered which supports the opinion by the auditor on the financial statements. Where the auditor concludes the audit evidence obtained is not sufficient and appropriate, then the auditor should attempt to obtain further audit evidence. In situations where the auditor is not able to obtain further audit evidence, then the auditor's report should be qualified or disclaimed.

Documentation

It is a requirement for the auditor to document the overall responses in order to address the assessed risk of material misstatement at the financial statement level and the nature, timing and extent of the further audit procedures, the linkage of those procedures with the assessed risks at the assertion level and the results of the audit procedures. In addition, if the auditor plans to use audit evidence about the operating effectiveness of controls obtained in prior audits, he/she should document the conclusions reached with regard to relying on those controls that were tested in a previous audit. Such documentation should also accord with the provisions laid down in ISA 230.

Chapter Roundup

Risk features heavily in auditing and one of the primary functions of audit is to reduce risk to an acceptable level.

Auditors can gather sufficient and appropriate audit evidence through substantive procedures and control tests.

All audit procedures must be responsive to the assessed levels of risk.

Detailed tests of control in recurring audits should be undertaken at least every third audit, but auditors shall consider other relevant factors when considering the time period that should elapse before further detailed testing.

Substantive procedures include analytical procedures and tests of detail.

Audit procedures generate the audit evidence, audit procedures in themselves are not audit evidence.

The risk assessment must be modified if information comes to the auditor's attention which the auditor was not previously aware of.

Audit evidence must be evaluated for sufficiency and appropriateness to determine if the evidence reduces the risk of material misstatement to an acceptably low level.

---

16 ISA 402 (REVISED AND REDRAFTED) AUDIT CONSIDERATIONS RELATING TO AN ENTITY USING A SERVICE ORGANISATION

ISA 402 deals with the responsibility the auditor has to obtain sufficient appropriate audit evidence when an entity uses a service organisation. For the purposes of ISA 402, the definition of a 'service organisation' is:

> *A third-party organisation (or segment of a third-party organisation) that provides services to user entities that are part of those entities' information systems relevant to financial reporting.*
>
> [ISA402.8 (e)]

Today it is becoming increasingly common for businesses to outsource certain functions of their business. For example, payroll is often outsourced to a dedicated payroll agency in order to ease the administrative burdens for the entity. Where an entity outsources certain aspects of its business, the auditor needs to obtain an understanding of the nature and significance of the services provided by the service organisation together with the effect on the user-entity's internal controls. The objective here is to consider the risk of material misstatement and design audit procedures which are specifically responsive to those risks.

Obtaining an Understanding of the Services Provided by a Service Organisation, Including Internal Control

Auditors have a duty to gain an understanding of the entity which they are auditing together with an understanding of the environment in which the entity operates in accordance with provisions laid down in ISA 315. This extends to the requirement to understand the nature of the services provided to a user-entity by a service organisation and the effect the use of the service organisation has on the user-entity's internal control environment.

Examples of service organisations which an entity may use are:

- Payroll agencies.
- Asset management entities.
- Receivables management entities (such as factoring/invoice discounting entities).
- Tax compliance entities.

Illustration

Consider a user-entity that utilises the services of a payroll agency which prepares and administers the payroll for the user-entity's 200 staff members. Clearly the transactions processed by the payroll agency will be material to the user-entity's financial statements and it follows that the auditor should evaluate the design and implementation of relevant controls at the user-entity that relate to the services provided by the payroll agency. The auditor should also evaluate the controls present at the payroll agency, especially as the payroll charges in the financial statements will be material to the financial statements.

Gaining an Understanding of the Entity and its Environment

In many cases, the auditor can gain a sufficient understanding of the nature and significance of the services provided by the service organisation from the user-entity. However, there could be occasions where the auditor is unable to gain a sufficient understanding of the nature and significance of the services provided and, in such situations, the auditor shall obtain that understanding from other sources, which could include:

- Visiting the service organisation to obtain an understanding of the relevant controls.
- Obtaining a type 1 or type 2 report, where available (see below).
- Using another auditor to perform procedures to obtain the relevant information about the controls at the service organisation. Contacting the service organisation through the user-entity to obtain information. [ISA402.12]

It is important that the auditor obtains an understanding of the entity and its environment in order to determine the significance of the service organisation to the entity itself and the significance the service organisation has on the actual audit.

Matters the auditor needs to consider relating to the service organisation are:

- The nature of the services provided by the service organisation.
- Contractual terms and the relationship between the entity and the service organisation.
- The extent to which the internal controls of the entity interact with those controls at the service organisation.
- The service organisation's strengths and capabilities together with the technical competence of the service organisation.
- Information available on the internal controls relevant to the service organisation's information systems such as IT processes.
- The types of transactions processed by the service organisation.

Information can be gathered from a wide variety of sources concerning the nature of the services provided by a service organisation and the user entity will undoubtedly possess varying degrees of information which the auditor can use to obtain an understanding of the services provided by the service organisation such as:

- Technical and user manuals.
- Contracts between the service organisation and the user entity.

- Prior year audit working papers where the use of service organisations by the user entity is recurring.
- Management letters and reports by the service auditor.

Types of Reports

If the auditor is unable to obtain a sufficient understanding of the service organisation from the user entity, then it can obtain a report, where available, on the service organisation.

ISA 402 specifies and defines two types of reports:

- type 1; and
- type 2.

A type 1 report is a report on the design and description of controls present at a service organisation and should comprise:

(a)   a description, prepared by management of the service organisation, of the service organisation's system, control objectives and related controls that have been designed and implemented as at a specified date; and

(b)   a report by the service auditor with the objective of conveying reasonable assurance that includes the service auditor's opinion on the description of the service organisation's system, control objectives and related controls and the suitability of the design of the controls to achieve the specified control objectives. [ISA402.8 (b)]

A type 2 report is a report on the description, design and operating effectiveness of controls at a service organisation which comprises:

(a)   a description, prepared by management of the service organisation, of the service organisation's system, control objectives and related controls, their design and implementation as at a specified date or throughout a specified period and, in some cases, their operating effectiveness throughout a specified period; and

(b)   A report by the service auditor with the objective of conveying reasonable assurance including:

    (i)   the service auditor's opinion on the description of the service organisation's system, control objectives and related controls, the suitability of the design of the controls to achieve the specified control objectives and the operating effectiveness of the controls; and

    (ii)   A description of the service auditor's test of the controls and the results thereof. [ISA402.8(c)]

In situations where the auditor plans to use a type 1 or type 2 report as audit evidence to support the auditor's understanding concerning the design and implementation of controls present at the service organisation, the auditor needs to firstly determine whether the description and design of controls present at the service organisation is relevant to the audit in terms of dates. For example, it would be inappropriate to use a type 1 or a type 2 report for controls relevant to a 31 December 2010 year end when the audit concerns the financial statements as at 31 December

2009. In addition, the auditor should also evaluate the sufficiency and appropriateness of the evidence provided by the report for the understanding of the user entity's internal control.

Responding to the Risk of Material Misstatement

The auditor's responses to the risks of material misstatement are covered primarily in ISA 330. However, for the purposes of ISA 402, if the auditor concludes that the activities of the service organisation are significant to the entity and relevant to the audit, the auditor shall obtain a sufficient understanding of the entity and its environment, including its internal control, to identify the risks of material misstatement and design further audit procedures in response to the assessed risks.

The auditor will normally determine whether sufficient appropriate audit evidence can be gathered from information held at the user-entity. In the event that sufficient appropriate audit evidence cannot be gathered from information held at the user-entity, the auditor must perform further procedures to obtain sufficient appropriate audit evidence. This can include the use of another auditor to perform those procedures. However, if the auditor uses the report of a service organisation auditor, the auditor shall consider making inquiries concerning that auditor's professional competence in the context of the specific assignment undertaken by the service organisation auditor.

Tests of Control

The auditor may conclude that the controls present at a service organisation operate effectively but audit evidence will need to be obtained to support this conclusion. In obtaining sufficient appropriate audit evidence the auditor may perform tests of controls at the service organisation or they may use another auditor to perform tests of controls. Sufficient appropriate audit evidence may also be gathered by obtaining a type 2 report where available.

Where the auditor uses a type 2 report as audit evidence, the auditor needs to consider whether this report will provide sufficient appropriate audit evidence concerning the operating effectiveness of the controls to support the user auditor's risk assessment. In determining whether the type 2 report will provide sufficient appropriate audit evidence, the auditor should determine whether the description, design and operating effectiveness of controls at the service organisation are at a date relevant to the audit. The auditor should also determine whether complementary user-entity controls are relevant to the user-entity. For the purposes of ISA 402, the definition of 'complementary user-entity controls' is:

> *Controls that the service organisation assumes, in the design of its service, will be implemented by user entities, and which, if necessary to achieve control objectives, are identified in the description of its system.*

[ISA402.8 (a)]

In addition, the auditor will consider the time period covered by the tests of controls and consider the time that has elapsed since the last detailed tests of controls. Finally, the auditor shall also consider whether tests of controls performed by the service auditor are appropriate to the assertions in the user-entity's financial statements and ensure that they provide sufficient appropriate audit evidence to support the user auditor's risk assessment.

Accounting Records

In some instances, service organisations may retain accounting records on behalf of a user-entity. In these circumstances, the auditor shall assess whether the arrangements affect the auditor's reporting responsibilities in relation to accounting records arising from law or regulation. Such a consideration is necessary because in some jurisdictions there is a requirement in legislation to maintain accounting records which are sufficient to disclose with reasonable accuracy, at any time, the financial position of the entity and which enable management to ensure that the company's financial statements meet regulatory requirements, as well as safeguarding against falsification and providing the management and the entity's auditors with access to its accounting records at any time. This is particularly the case in the UK under the Companies Act 2006.

In some jurisdictions, auditors have obligations relating to entities complying with requirements to maintain proper accounting records. Where doubt exists about the entity's compliance with such legislation, the auditor may advise those charged with governance to seek legal advice in connection with the matter(s) giving rise to the doubt.

Inability to Obtain Sufficient Appropriate Audit Evidence

In situations where the auditor, despite all best efforts, has failed to obtain sufficient appropriate audit evidence regarding the services provided by the service organisation the auditor should modify the opinion in the user auditor's report in accordance with the provisions in ISA 705 'Modifications to the Opinion in the Independent Auditor's Report'. Matters which would ordinarily give rise to such an opinion being issued are:

- A lack of controls adopted by the entity or a lack of records maintained by the entity.
- The service organisation has not made available a report from the service auditors concerning the operating effectiveness of its controls which the auditor considers sufficient for the audit.
- The auditor is unable to carry out sufficient tests on the operating effectiveness of the controls at the service organisation, and it has not been possible for those tests to be undertaken by the service organisation's auditor. [ISA402.A42]

A disclaimed opinion is to be given in the auditor's report where the possible effects of the resulting limitation on the scope of their work is so material or pervasive that the auditor is unable to express an opinion [ISA402.A42]. A qualified opinion is given if the effect of the limitation is not so material or pervasive but there could be possible adjustments to the financial statements had the limitations not existed.

Fraud and Non-Compliance with Laws and Regulations

The auditor should make inquiries of the user entity's management as to whether the service organisation has reported any matters concerning fraud or non-compliance with laws and regulations. Where the service-user has made reports concerning fraud or non-compliance with laws and regulations the auditor is required to consider the effects of such reports on the nature, timing and extent of further audit procedures. In some cases it may be appropriate to contact the service organisation that has made the report to consider the effect on the nature, timing and extent of further audit procedures.

Chapter Roundup

It is becoming increasingly common for businesses to outsource various functions of their business.

The auditor shall obtain an understanding of the nature and significance of the services provided to the audit client by the service organisation, together with the effect on the user-entity's internal controls.

Type 1 or type 2 reports, where available, can enable an understanding of the nature and significance of the services provided by the service organisation.

Where evidence concerning the nature of the services provided by a service organisation and its internal is lacking, the auditor must perform other procedures to obtain sufficient appropriate audit evidence.

Where further procedures confirm evidence is lacking, modifications to the auditor's report will be required. Where the possible effects of the limitation are so material and pervasive, a disclaimer of opinion will be given.

Some service organisations may retain accounting records on behalf of a user-entity. In such instances, the auditor shall assess whether such an arrangement affects their reporting responsibilities in relation to accounting records arising from laws or regulations.

---

17 ISA 450 (REVISED AND REDRAFTED) EVALUATION OF MISSTATEMENTS IDENTIFIED DURING THE AUDIT

During the course of an audit, the auditor may discover misstatements within the financial statements. ISA 450 requires the auditor to evaluate the effect of identified misstatements on the audit and also to evaluate the effect of any uncorrected misstatements when forming an opinion on the financial statements. This is important, particularly in terms of reconsidering materiality (ISA 320).

ISA 450 defines a misstatement as:

> *A difference between the amount, classification, presentation, or disclosure of a reported financial statement item and the amount, classification, presentation, or disclosure that is required for the item to be in accordance with the applicable financial reporting framework. Misstatements can arise from error or fraud.*
>
> *When the auditor expresses an opinion on whether the financial statements are presented fairly, in all material respects, or give a true and fair view, misstatements also include those adjustments of amounts classifications, presentation, or disclosures that, in the auditor's judgement, are necessary for the financial statements to be presented fairly, in all material respects, or to give a true and fair view.*

[ISA450.4 (a)]

Uncorrected misstatements are those misstatements which have been identified by the auditor during the course of their audit which have not been corrected.

Misstatements arise from inaccurate gathering and processing of information as well as weaknesses in the internal control functions. Incorrect interpretation of facts or oversights can also result in misstatements arising in the financial statements. It is widely recognised that financial statements often contain estimates and judgements, such as accrued expenses, bad debt provisions, inventory provisions and other accounting estimates which may be an incorrect estimate giving rise to misstatements within the financial statements. Fraud can also result in misstatement within the financial statements, and auditors need to consider the provisions in ISA 240.

In evaluating misstatements, the auditor considers the materiality of the misstatements. Any misstatements which are clearly trivial need not be accumulated because the auditor will expect such amounts not to have a material effect on the financial statements [ISA450.A2]. In some situations, the auditor may have doubt on whether one or more misstatements are clearly trivial and where this doubt exists, the matter is considered not to be clearly trivial. It is important to understand that 'clearly trivial' is not the same as 'not material'.

ISA 450 refers to three types of misstatements:

- Factual misstatements.
- Judgemental misstatements.
- Projected misstatements.

FACTUAL MISSTATEMENTS

Factual misstatements are simply misstatements about which there is no doubt. For example, if a bank balance is incorrectly stated within the financial statements.

JUDGEMENTAL MISSTATEMENTS

Judgemental misstatements are misstatements by management regarding accounting estimates, or the selection of accounting policies, which the auditor considers unreasonable or inappropriate.

PROJECTED MISSTATEMENTS

Projected misstatements are the auditor's 'best estimate' of misstatements in populations, which involves the auditor projecting errors in audit samples to the entire population from which the sample was drawn.

ANOMALOUS ERROR

Some misstatements can be isolated, which are referred to as an 'anomalous' error. An example of an anomalous error is where an incorrect formula has been included in a spreadsheet cell which calculates the cost of inventory but which has not occurred anywhere else. Conversely, some misstatements might not be isolated and can arise through inappropriate accounting policies, or a failing in internal controls, the effect of which is widespread throughout the financial statements.

ISA 530 emphasises that it would be extremely rare for any deviation or misstatement identified in a sample to be considered an anomalous error and not representative of the whole population; and so sufficient appropriate audit evidence shall be obtained by the auditor where the auditor concludes a misstatement is anomalous.

EVALUATING THE EFFECT OF UNCORRECTED MISSTATEMENTS

Materiality levels must be set where audit opinions are given on an entity's financial statements and ISA 320 deals with materiality issues. Therefore, as the audit progresses and misstatements are identified, it may be necessary to revise the materiality level accordingly depending on the nature of the misstatements and the circumstances in which they have arisen. In addition, facts may arise which the auditor was not previously aware of which would have caused the auditor to have determined a different level of materiality. Where revisions are made to a previously assessed materiality level during the course of an audit, because of situations which the auditor was not previously aware of, the auditor shall also consider the nature, timing and extent of further audit procedures so as to ensure that the audit evidence obtain is sufficient and appropriate. Performance materiality shall also be reconsidered in the event that the materiality level is subsequently lowered.

An item is material if its omission or misstatement could influence the economic decisions of users taken on the basis of the financial statements. If an individual misstatement is judged to be material, then it is unlikely that it can be offset by other misstatements within the financial statements [ISA450.A14]. There may be occasions when it is considered appropriate to offset immaterial misstatements within the same account balance or class of transaction, but the auditor shall consider the risk of further undetected misstatements before deciding that offsetting immaterial misstatement is appropriate.

Illustration

During the course of the audit, the auditor discovered a material overstatement of revenue which had been offset by a material overstatement of expenses, therefore resulting in no effect on profit before taxation.

The financial statements as a whole will be materially misstated because offsetting a material over-statement in revenue against a material overstatement in expenses is not appropriate.

PRIOR PERIOD UNCORRECTED MISSTATEMENTS

Auditors shall consider the possibility that uncorrected misstatements discovered in the previous audit, which were judged to be immaterial, may well become material misstatements in the current period when aggregated with other misstatements and auditor's use of a consistent evaluation approach will ensure that such an approach provides consistency from one period to the next.

COMMUNICATION

The auditor has a duty to report misstatements to an appropriate level of management on a timely basis. However, the auditor must also consider the circumstances in which the misstatement(s) have arisen, because law or regulation might prohibit the auditor from communicating such matters; and in some cases the auditor may conclude that it is appropriate to seek legal advice on such matters. An example of situations where regulation prohibits the auditor from communicating such matters would be in respect of Money Laundering Regulations and the 'tipping off' provisions.

In cases where it is not prohibitive to discuss misstatements with management, then the auditor should discuss the misstatements with them on a timely basis. This allows the management the opportunity to confirm whether the misstatements are, in fact, misstatements and if they are it gives management the opportunity to correct the misstatements. Management may even wish trivial misstatements to be corrected in order to maintain accurate accounting records.

In some audits, immaterial misstatements may be made up of a large number of immaterial misstatements which, even when aggregated, still remain immaterial. Where this is the case the auditor can simply communicate the number of misstatements and overall monetary effect of the misstatements rather than go through every single misstatement.

In terms of communicating to management and those charged with governance; if management and those charged with governance are the same individuals (as is often found in small, owner-managed businesses) then only one communication would be necessary.

WRITTEN REPRESENTATIONS

Where the auditor is also requesting written representations from those charged with governance, he or she needs to communicate the written representations being requested. The auditor shall also ensure that they obtain written representations concerning uncorrected misstatements. The implications of a failure to correct misstatements will also be communicated to those charged with governance.

DOCUMENTATION

ISA 450 requires auditor's documentation to take into account the aggregate effect of uncorrected misstatements and whether the materiality level(s) for particular classes of transactions, account balances or disclosures has been exceeded. The auditor shall also ensure that they document the effect of uncorrected misstatements on key ratios or trends as well as compliance with legal, regulatory and contractual requirements.

Chapter Roundup

The auditor must evaluate the effect of any uncorrected misstatements when forming an opinion on the financial statements.

Misstatements can arise from inaccurate gathering and processing of information as well as internal control weaknesses.

'Clearly trivial' is not the same as 'not material'.

Clearly trivial misstatements need not be accumulated because the auditor will expect such amounts not to have a material effect on the financial statements.

Any doubts as to whether one or more misstatements are 'clearly trivial' are considered to mean they are not clearly trivial.

The ISA identifies three types of material misstatement:

1. Factual misstatement.
2. Judgemental misstatement.
3. Projected misstatement.

Auditors must obtain sufficient appropriate audit evidence to corroborate an anomalous error.

Auditors must discuss misstatements with management on a timely basis, where it is not prohibitive to discuss such misstatements with them.

Performance materiality should also be reconsidered if situations arise during the course of the audit which result in the materiality level being subsequently lowered.

Consideration will be given by the auditor to uncorrected misstatements in the previous audit which have become material in the current audit.

Written representations shall be obtained concerning uncorrected misstatements.

---

18 ISA 500 (REDRAFTED) AUDIT EVIDENCE

ISA 500 stipulates what constitutes audit evidence and lays down the guidance that auditors are required to follow in the design and performance of audit procedures which will allow sufficient appropriate audit evidence to be gathered to give reasonable assurance that the financial statements do not contain material misstatement. The phrase 'reasonable assurance' is a crucial aspect of the auditor's report because this refers to the fact that the financial statements are not correct in absolute terms, simply because of the limitations inherent in an audit. Such limitations are:

- Judgements made on behalf of auditors including risk assessments and materiality as well as judging which tests are appropriate and which tests are not.
- It is not practical to test 100% of every item within the financial statements.
- Inherent limitations in accounting and internal controls.
- Possibilities that client staff and management may not be entirely honest.
- Estimates used in the financial statements.

It is for the above reasons that auditors 'express an opinion' rather than 'certify' the accounts are completely accurate.

Auditors cannot use the inherent limitations as an excuse for not performing a full, thorough and efficient audit. Throughout this book I have referred to audit evidence being 'sufficient' and 'appropriate'.

Sufficient refers to the quantity, as well as the quality, of the audit evidence which needs to be gathered.

Appropriate refers to the quality of the audit evidence gathered as well as to the relevance and the reliability of the audit evidence gathered. Audit evidence should also be documented sufficiently for quality control reasons in order that it can be referred to at a later date, as well as for evaluation purposes prior to the issuance of the auditor's report.

Audit evidence essentially needs to support the opinion given in the auditor's report and, thus, it follows that the audit file needs to 'tell the story' behind how the auditor has arrived at their audit opinion. Auditors have been criticised in the past by regulatory bodies because the audit evidence that they have obtained has not been sufficient or appropriate enough to warrant the audit opinion. Auditors should, therefore, ensure that when audit procedures are designed and performed that consideration is given to whether those procedures are adequate enough to generate sufficient appropriate audit evidence. This involves auditors considering the relevance and reliability of the information to be used as audit evidence.

Sometimes the evidence that the auditor will require is beyond the expertise of the auditor and the auditor will need to rely on the work of an expert. The relevant procedures to be adopted by the auditor, where there is reliance on the work of an expert, are discussed further in this chapter and are covered in Chapter 31.

Audit evidence can be obtained from other sources outside of the entity being subject to audit. For example, bank confirmations can offer audit evidence concerning the existence of bank accounts at the reporting date and can also offer audit evidence concerning the disclosures made in the financial statements relating to secured debts and the nature of the security pledged. Audit evidence can be positive and negative in nature. For example, audit evidence can serve to corroborate the assertions made by management; conversely, audit evidence can also contradict such assertions.

METHODS OF OBTAINING AUDIT EVIDENCE

Auditors can gather audit evidence from a variety of sources including:

- Inspection.
- Observance.
- External confirmation.
- Recalculation.
- Reperformance.
- Analytical procedures.
- Inquiry.

Inspection of assets that are recorded in the accounting records confirms existence and gives evidence of valuation but does not confirm rights and obligations [ISA500.A16]. Confirmation that assets seen are recorded in accounting records gives evidence of completeness.

Inspection of documentation confirms that an asset exists or a transaction has occurred.

Confirmation that items recorded in supporting documentation are recorded in accounting records tests completeness. Cut-offs can be verified by inspection of reverse population; that is, checking transactions recorded after the reporting date against supporting documentation to confirm that they occurred after the reporting date. Inspection also provides evidence of valuation/measurement, rights and obligations and the nature of items (presentation and disclosure). It can also be used to compare documents and confirm authorisation.

Observation involves watching a procedure being performed (for example, an inventory count). This procedure has inherent limitations as it only confirms procedure took place when the auditor was watching.

External confirmations involve seeking information from external sources such as bank audit letters or circularisation of receivables.

Recalculation involves checking the arithmetic accuracy of client's records.

Reperformance involves reperforming various reconciliations as at the reporting date or at interim periods to check controls have been operating effectively, for example, reperforming a bank reconciliation statement.

Analytical procedures consist of comparing items, for example, current year financial information with prior year financial information, and analysing predictable relationships such as the relationship of trade receivables with revenue. It can also be used to help identify any unusual trends or characteristics within the financial statements.

Inquiry involves seeking information from client staff or management.

AUDIT PROCEDURES AND THE FINANCIAL STATEMENT ASSERTIONS

The above audit procedures identified for the purposes of obtaining audit evidence can be linked into the financial statement assertions as shown below. Financial statement assertions are the representations of management that are embodied in the financial statements. By approving the financial statements, management are making representations about the information therein. These representations or assertions may be described as:

- Existence.
- Rights and obligations.
- Occurrence.
- Completeness.
- Valuation.
- Measurement.
- Presentation and disclosure.

In any audit, it is important that the auditor evaluates whether the audit evidence obtained is sufficiently appropriate. 'Sufficiency' and 'appropriateness' are interrelated and apply to both tests of controls and substantive testing.

The determination as to whether audit evidence is sufficient and appropriate will depend on a number of factors, such as:

- The risk assessment.
- The nature of the accounting and internal control systems.
- Materiality.
- The auditor's experience of previous audits including the auditor's knowledge of the business and the environment in which it operates.
- The results of audit procedures.
- The source and reliability of the information available.

Illustration

Audit Evidence

Post date events (sometimes referred to as 'subsequent events') are those events which occur between the reporting date (period/year end) and the date of the auditor's report. The auditor's objective when undertaking a review of post date events is to obtain sufficient appropriate audit evidence to give reasonable assurance that all material post date events have been accounted for, and the necessary adjustment or note made in the entity's financial statements. Audit evidence in this area can be gathered by:

(1) Reviewing the following records for details of any post date events:

    (a)   cash book;
    (b)   sales day book;
    (c)   purchase day book; and
    (d)   journal.

(2) Examining minutes of meetings and other correspondence for information relating to subsequent events.
(3) Examining management accounts, budgets and cash flow forecasts prepared for a date after the reporting date.
(4) Reviewing likely risk areas which could give rise to post date events.
(5) Reviewing the register of charges.
(6) Inquiring with management.
(7) Reviewing the bank audit letter for details of any potential post date events.
(8) Considering the need to consult with the entity's legal advisers regarding possible claims or contingent liabilities which may affect the entity's financial position at the balance sheet date.

The auditor will review the evidence gathered and consider those events which have given rise to, or suggest evidence of, post date events and ensure that the post date events have been correctly classified between 'adjusting' and 'non-adjusting' events as per the provisions in IAS 10 'Events After the Reporting Date'.

RECURRING AUDITS

It is widely understood that in many cases auditors perform audits for the same audit client from one year to the next. Evidence can sometimes be used from prior year audits, such as where the auditor has undertaken a detailed test of controls in the previous year and, thus, concludes that reliance can be placed on the operating effectiveness of the controls. Where the auditor places reliance on evidence gained in previous audits, the auditor must ensure that the audit evidence to which they are relying is both relevant and reliable for the purposes of the current year audit. It would be inappropriate for the auditor to rely on audit evidence which is irrelevant for the current year's audit if it was out of date, for example, if the client had undertaken significant changes in various internal controls.

USE OF MANAGEMENT REPRESENTATIONS AS AUDIT EVIDENCE

Management representations are a common source of audit evidence in the auditing profession. The auditor needs to discuss with management, and those charged with governance, the issues to which they are seeking representation in order to ensure that management and those charged with governance know what they are signing. The management representation (frequently referred to as the 'letter of representation') should only refer to matters which are material to the financial statements.

Management representations are not to be used as an alternative to gathering sufficient appropriate audit evidence. This is an important concept because where the auditor cannot obtain sufficient appropriate audit evidence in certain areas this may constitute a limitation on the scope of an audit for which it may be necessary to consider the implications for the auditor's report.

The management letter itself should:

- Be addressed to the auditor.
- Contain specified information.
- Be appropriately dated — usually the same date as the auditor's report.
- Only be approved by those with specific knowledge of the relevant matters.

A typical management representation is shown in the following illustration.

Illustration

Management Representation Letter

Sanvayan Enterprises Inc
15 January 20X9

> Thomson, Rooms, Bishop & Co
> Chartered Certified Accountants and
> Registered Auditors
> 8 Westway Street
> Anytown
> Any Country

Dear Sirs,

Financial Statements for the year ended 31 December 2010.

The financial statements for the year ended 31 December 2010 have been considered and approved at a duly convened meeting of the board of directors. The undersigned were authorised to sign the statement of position on behalf of the board of directors and give you the following assurances.

To the best of our knowledge and belief and having made appropriate enquiries:

(a)   **Availability of Information**
All the accounting records have been made available to you for the purpose of your audit and all transactions undertaken by the company have been properly reflected and recorded in the accounting records. All other records and related information have been made available to you including the minutes of all directors' and shareholders' meetings, which are a complete and authentic record of the proceedings at those meetings.
        We acknowledge as directors our responsibilities for preparing the financial statements in accordance with the applicable law and International Financial Reporting Standards.

(b)   **Transactions with the Directors (or persons connected with them)**
At no time during the year has the company had any arrangement, transactions or agreement to provide credit facilities (including advances credit and guarantees) for directors. The directors have not made any personal guarantees on behalf of the company.

(c) **Related Party Transactions**

During the year the directors have identified and approved related party transactions and provided the information for disclosure of all transactions relevant to the company in the consolidated financial statements. They are not aware of any other matters which are required to be disclosed under IAS 24 'Related Party Disclosures' in respect of related party disclosures.

The directors have identified the ultimate controlling party has made sufficient disclosure within the consolidated financial statements to accord with the required related party disclosures.

(d) **Inventories**

The inventories figure of $466,980 is a fair reflection of the true cost of inventory to the company within the financial statements.

(e) **Events after the Reporting Date**

The company acquired a 99% holding in Bartholomew Inc on 14 February 20X0. The directors confirm that sufficient disclosure of this material transaction has been included in the report of the directors for prominence.

(f) **Going Concern**

The financial statements have been prepared on the going concern basis. In assessing the appropriateness of the going concern basis, the directors have taken account of all relevant information covering a period of at least twelve months from the date of the approval of the financial statements.

(g) **Compliance with Laws and/or Regulations**

All those events which involve possible non-compliance with Laws or Regulations of which the directors are aware together with the actual or contingent consequences which may arise therefrom have been disclosed to you.

(h) **Contingent Liabilities**

The Directors confirm that all contingent liabilities relating to the company have been disclosed within the financial statements and all relevant provisions have been accounted for with IAS 37 requirements.

(i) **Fraud**

The directors confirm that they acknowledge their responsibilities to safeguard the company's assets and confirm that the directors are not aware of any allegations of fraud, or suspected fraud, affecting the entity's financial statements communicated by employees, former employees, analysts, regulators or others.

The directors acknowledge their responsibilities for the design and the implementation of internal control systems to prevent and detect fraud and confirm that they have disclosed to you the results of their risk assessment that the financial statements maybe misstated as a result of fraud.

Yours faithfully,

Mr S Jones — Chief Executive

Sanvayan Enterprises Inc

THE USE OF EXPERTS AS AUDIT EVIDENCE

In many cases, the auditor's expertise will be limited and, therefore, it will be necessary to employ someone with different expert knowledge to enable the auditor to gain sufficient appropriate audit evidence. It is important that, where the auditor's experience is limited, the auditor employs the work of an expert to ensure that the risk of material misstatement can be reduced to an acceptable level. For example, if an entity operates a defined benefit pension scheme, actuarial information will be required from the actuaries, which the auditor may not have any experience of reperforming. Experts can be used to:

- Provide specialist advice on a particular matter which affects the financial statements, for example, the valuations placed on complex financial instruments, such as derivatives, or actuarial assumptions; and
- Enable the auditors to obtain sufficient appropriate audit evidence concerning certain financial statement assertions.

ISA 620 (see Chapter 31) deals with the specific issues concerning the use of an auditor's expert, but ISA 500 requires the auditor to evaluate the technical competencies of the expert as well as the objectivity of the expert (it is particularly important that the expert is 'independent' of the entity). In recognition of this requirement, the auditor shall gain an understanding of the specific matters the expert will undertake and evaluate the appropriateness of the expert's work to determine whether it is sufficiently reliable. The auditor shall also have regard to whether the expert has any financial interest in the entity or whether he/she has any business or personal relationships, or if there are any other circumstances which may affect the independence and objectivity of the expert.

In determining whether the work undertaken by the expert is sufficient and appropriate the auditor shall consider the following matters:

- The nature and complexity of the matter which requires the expert.
- The expert's experience and reputation in the field in which the auditor is seeking audit evidence.
- The independency and objectivity of the expert — for example, is the expert employed by the entity?
- The professional qualifications of the expert.
- Whether any alternative sources of audit evidence are available.
- Whether management have any influence over the performance of the work by the expert or whether management wholly rely on the expert.
- The auditor's previous experience with the work of the expert.

Illustration

Consider an entity that operates a defined benefit pension scheme in the UK. Defined benefit pension schemes are very difficult to account for because the entity is making promises to employees to pay a certain level of pension, which will usually be based on their final salary, the number of years they work for the employer and a pre-determined fraction. The entity employs a qualified actuary to deal with the defined benefit pension scheme. The defined benefit pension scheme is considered material to the entity's financial statements.

Such pension schemes in the UK require the use of actuaries who will model the expected liabilities taking into account variables such as the time value of money. Accountants and auditors in the UK generally do not have the relevant skills and expertise needed to model the expected liabilities in respect of defined benefit pension schemes to be incorporated within an entity's financial statements.

> In this situation, the actuary is employed by the entity, therefore, the auditor will need to engage an expert (an independent actuary) to verify the actuarial information so that the auditor can gain reasonable assurance that pension fund assets and liabilities and the accounting input have been correctly made.

In respect of defined benefit pension schemes, it is often the case that 'actuarial gains and losses' arise. Actuarial gains and losses are changes in actuarial deficits or surpluses that have arisen because actuarial assumptions have changed (or events have not coincided with actuarial assumptions made for the previous valuation).

Auditors do not have the expertise to judge the assumptions and methods used by the expert; these are the responsibility of the expert. However, the auditors should seek to obtain an understanding of these assumptions to consider their reasonableness based on other audit evidence.

EVALUATING THE EXPERT'S WORK FOR AUDIT EVIDENCE

The auditors need to evaluate whether the work of the expert and the evidence gained is sufficient and appropriate. Where the audit evidence from the expert is insufficient and there are no satisfactory alternative sources of evidence, the auditors should consider the implications for their audit report.

In arriving at their conclusion as to whether the expert's work is sufficient and appropriate, the auditor needs to take into consideration various factors such as:

- Whether the findings and conclusions reached by the expert are consistent with other sources of audit evidence gained.
- Where judgements and assumptions are used (as in the defined benefit pension scheme scenario above), whether these judgements and assumptions are reasonable.
- Where source data is used, the relevance and completeness of that source data.

SELECTION AND SAMPLING TECHNIQUES

A significant method used in gaining sufficient appropriate audit evidence is the use of selection and sampling techniques. ISA 500 at paragraph A52 suggests three methods of obtaining audit evidence:

- selecting all items (100% sampling);
- selecting specific items; and
- audit sampling. [ISA500.A52]

Selection of All Items

Selection of all items is only appropriate for certain items. For example, it would be impossible to select 100% testing on sales invoices for a large, multi-national listed entity, as clearly this would be uneconomical. Selection of 100% of items can be used when there are only a few items which would warrant 100% testing. Other audit procedures such as 'proof in total' calculations can also achieve 100% testing such as the recalculation of depreciation charges in the period.

Illustration

'Proof in Total'

An entity's depreciation policy for depreciating their motor vehicles is 25% on a reducing balance basis. The financial statements for the year ended 31 December 2010 show the following information: Motor Vehicles

Cost	$12,000
Accumulated depreciation	($5,250)

The depreciation charge for the year in respect of motor vehicles amounts to $1,688.

The auditor can use 'proof in total' calculations to verify the depreciation charge for the year by essentially reperforming the calculation as follows: Expected Charge

(Cost $12,000 less accumulated depreciation $5,250) = $6,750 × 25% = $1,688

Actual charge ($1,688)

Difference $nil

Selection of Specific Items

The selection of specific items is generally more common in auditing. This involves testing specific items such as high value or key items. Auditors often select high risk items or items material in nature when devising which specific items to test.

It is important to understand that the selection of specific items is not the same as audit *sampling*, hence the reason why ISA 500 distinguishes audit sampling separately.

Audit Sampling

Sampling is where the auditor applies audit procedures to less than 100% of the population. For example, the auditor may obtain the aged list of receivables at the reporting date. The total amount of receivables shown in the financial statements as 'trade receivables' is known as the 'population'. The auditor may only sample 70% of this population.

If sampling is used and errors are discovered in samples, it will be necessary to 'project' these errors, so as to form an opinion on the number of errors likely to exist in the total population. The results from the selection of specific items cannot be projected to the entire population. Audit sampling is considered further in Chapter 23.

When devising sample sizes, the auditor needs to ensure that they reflect the assessment of materiality and risk. Auditors also need to consider that when designing tests to generate sufficient appropriate audit evidence they understand that no two audits will be the same, even if the entity being audited is in the similar industry to another audit client which the auditor has had dealings with. Tests therefore need to be tailored to specifics.

DOCUMENTATION AND WORKING PAPERS

All audit work must be documented because this provides evidence of the audit work done to support the audit opinion, as well as enabling effective review for quality control purposes. In certain areas of the audit, audit evidence may be difficult to obtain, such as that relating to related parties and the auditor may have made inquiries of management to help towards generating sufficient appropriate audit evidence. Remember, inquiry alone is often complementary to other audit tests; on its own inquiry does not provide sufficient appropriate audit evidence. Where discussions with management, or other client staff, are held then it is important that notes are made of the conversations and any representations are made in writing (see letter of representation above). Audit working papers should be prepared in accordance with the provisions in ISA 230, and should ordinarily contain the following information:

- The name of the client.
- The accounting period.
- The title of the schedule.
- The source of the data being tested.
- A key or legend explaining any 'ticks' or audit symbols used.
- The initial of the person preparing the schedule and the date the schedule was prepared.
- The initial of the person reviewing the schedule and the date the scheduled was reviewed.
- Details of the work carried out.

Audit documentation needs to be reviewed by an appropriate level of personnel at the audit firm to ensure that:

- The work has been performed in accordance with the audit programme.
- The work performed and the results obtained have been adequately documented.
- Any significant matters or difficulties encountered have been resolved or are reflected in audit conclusions.
- The conclusions expressed are consistent with the results of the work performed and support the audit opinion.

Auditing is an accumulative process and it is important that the audit plan and risk assessment are reviewed on a timely basis to ensure that they remain appropriate.

REVIEW

There are occasions, either because of threats to independence or obligations to comply with professional bodies, when audit firms are required to have the audit work they perform reviewed for quality assurance purposes. This is particularly the case where professional bodies inspect their member firm's audit work. There are generally two types of audit file review which can be done:

- hot file review; and
- cold file review.

A hot file review is undertaken prior to the audit report being signed to identify whether the audit evidence is sufficient and appropriate or whether further additional procedures are required. Hot file reviews are mainly undertaken where a threat to independence has been identified, such as the audit firm being involved in the accounts preparation, or where professional bodies mandatorily impose such reviews on audit firms for quality assurance purposes.

Cold file reviews are reviews of audit files after the auditor's report has been signed. These are the most common type undertaken during inspections by professional bodies and will entail the reviewer reviewing the audit work to ensure that it is sufficient and appropriate and that the audit evidence supports the audit opinion.

Chapter Roundup

Audit evidence must be 'sufficient' and 'appropriate'.

The audit evidence obtained must support the opinion in the auditor's report.

Evidence can be obtained from: inspection, observance, external confirmation, recalculation, reperformance, analytical procedures and inquiry.

Whether audit evidence is sufficient and appropriate depends on a number of factors.

Evidence can be used from the previous year's audit but it must be both relevant and reliable for the current year's audit.

The use of management representations as evidence cannot be an alternative to obtaining sufficient and appropriate audit evidence.

Auditors may utilise the services of experts to provide audit evidence on certain specialist areas, and this work, together with the evidence obtained, should be evaluated by the auditor to confirm it is sufficient and appropriate.

Selection and sampling techniques identify three methods of obtaining evidence: 100% sampling, selection of specific items and audit sampling.

All audit work must be documented in accordance with ISA 230 provisions as this provides evidence of the audit work undertaken.

---

19 ISA 501 (REDRAFTED) AUDIT EVIDENCE — SPECIFIC CONSIDERATIONS FOR SELECTED ITEMS

ISA 501 deals with three specific items that may be contained within a set of general purpose financial statements and for which the auditor may need to obtain sufficient appropriate audit evidence. It deals with specific considerations for:

- inventory;
- litigation and claims; and
- segment information.

In terms of financial statement assertions, ISA 501 looks to address whether, at the reporting date, inventory actually exists and whether the values placed on the inventory are appropriate with regard to the condition of the inventory. Litigation and claims pertaining to the entity need to be complete and segment information needs to be correctly presented and disclosed within the financial statements.

INVENTORY

In a lot of cases, inventory is material to the financial statements of a reporting entity and, where inventory is material to the financial statements, it is important that the auditor obtains sufficient appropriate audit evidence to confirm its existence and valuation. Inventory is an audit area that is open to manipulation and is often subject to varying degrees of estimation.

The Use of Directional Testing and Inventory

Widely recognised, but less-used in today's modern audit practice, is the use of directional testing. Directional testing is a concept which was developed in the early 1980s and is conceptually straight forward because it is based on the principles of double-entry. Debit items are tested for overstatement, whilst credit items are tested for understatement. By testing debits directly for overstatements, the corresponding credit entries are indirectly being tested for understatement. Directional testing is important for two reasons:

- It helps ensure that there is neither overstatement nor understatement in the accounts in relation to assets, liabilities, income or expenditure.
- It is cost effective, as by testing one nominal ledger account there will automatically be a test carried out on another nominal ledger account.

The problem with inventory is that it appears both in the statement of financial position (balance sheet) and the statement of comprehensive income (income statement). Therefore, a common procedure to address the fact that inventory is easy to manipulate because it appears in both primary financial statements is to attend the inventory count.

Attendance at Inventory Count

Attendance at the inventory count is primarily an observance procedure. It allows the auditor the opportunity to review the procedures and instructions that management have put in place to oversee the results of the inventory count. It also allows the auditor to see the inventory count being undertaken. In planning the attendance at the physical inventory count, the auditor will need to consider factors such as:

- The risk of material misstatement due to inventory valuation.
- The entity's control environment and management's attitude to controls.
- The timing of the count — for example, if counting is to take place on 31 December then this may cause issues for the auditor in terms of resources available.
- Locations of the audit client (particularly overseas or long distance branches).
- Whether the inventory is so specialised in nature that the use of an auditor's expert is necessary (ISA 620).

Ordinarily the auditor will attend the audit client's inventory count when it is being undertaken rather than when the procedure has been completed because the auditor needs to evaluate whether the procedures put in place by management will reduce the risk of material misstatement within the financial statements insofar as the inventory valuation is concerned. By attending the inventory count during the counting process, the auditor will be able to perform inspections of the inventory, primarily to check the condition of the inventory, as well as to identify any obsolete or slow-moving items and check the valuations placed on these.

During attendance at the inventory count, the auditor will perform test counts by test checking counts of inventory in a two-way direction — from the counts recorded on the inventory sheets to the actual inventory and from the inventory to the inventory sheets. This test allows the auditor to identify any discrepancies between inventory counts and those recorded on the inventory sheets.

The auditor's responsibility in terms of inventory valuation does not end once they are satisfied that the procedures put in place by management in respect of the inventory would reduce the risk of material misstatement within the financial statements. Indeed, it is widely understood that observance procedures have their limitations as procedures will undoubtedly be applied correctly if the auditor is watching the procedure being undertaken. The auditor, therefore, has to perform audit procedures on the entity's final inventory records to ascertain whether they correctly reflect actual inventory results.

Auditor Unable to Attend Inventory Counting

Unforeseen circumstances happen and in instances where the auditor is unable to attend the inventory count, the auditor can attend physical inventory counting on an alternative date and undertake audit procedures on intervening transactions. [ISA501.6]

Where the auditor is unable to attend the inventory count because it is not practical to do so, for example, due to geographical restrictions, the auditor shall adopt additional audit procedures to obtain sufficient appropriate audit evidence concerning the existence and condition of inventory [ISA501.7]. This is more practical when the audit client maintains a perpetual inventory, though consideration has to be given to how reliable these perpetual inventory records actually are and whether they will allow the audit to gather sufficient appropriate audit evidence concerning the existence and condition of the inventory at the reporting date.

Practical Insight

Cordonisos Inc is an American-based entity with a subsidiary in China. The year-end inventory count is being undertaken and the auditors consider the inventory to be highly material to the financial statements. In addition, a material sum of inventory is held at the subsidiary in China; however, the auditors consider that it is impracticable to perform inventory counts on the inventory held in China.

An alternative procedure to obtain sufficient appropriate audit evidence concerning the existence and condition of the inventory held in China is to approach an audit firm in China to request they attend the subsidiary and perform the audit procedures. When undertaking such a request, the auditor should also have regard to the experience and technical competence of the audit firm being commissioned to undertake the inventory count in China.

The above practical insight demonstrates a situation where the auditor is not able to attend a subsidiary of its audit client but where there are alternative procedures that can be put in place to obtain sufficient appropriate audit evidence. The auditor may find that the provisions in ISA 600 'Special Considerations — Audits of Group Financial Statements (Including the Work of Component Auditors)' may be relevant in these circumstances.

Where there are no alternative procedures and attendance at physical counting is impracticable, the auditor will modify their audit opinion in accordance with the provisions in ISA 705.

Inventory Held by Third Parties

Inventory belonging to an audit client may be held by third parties. For example, it is quite common for inventory to be held in specially designed and separately managed warehouses that provide facilities for the storage of such inventory.

Where inventory is held by third parties, the auditor needs to obtain sufficient appropriate audit evidence concerning the existence and condition of that inventory. Sufficient appropriate audit evidence can be obtained by requesting confirmation from the third party about the quantities held and the condition of the inventory as well as arranging for inspection procedures to be carried out to confirm the quantities and condition of the inventory.

Again, where the auditor is unable to obtain sufficient appropriate audit evidence concerning the inventory held by third parties and the inventory held by third parties is considered material, the auditor shall modify the opinion in their report.

Practical Insight

Bury Enterprises Inc operates in the chemical industry. Due to the nature of the chemicals involved, it stores such chemicals in a specialised warehouse which is located twenty miles from the base location and twenty six miles from the auditor's premises. The year end is 31 March 2010. The warehouse has no other connections to the audit client other than storing their inventories and performing inventory counts on their behalf.

In this situation, the auditor could obtain sufficient appropriate audit evidence concerning the existence and condition of the inventory by requesting confirmation from the warehouse as to the quantities held by them and the condition of the inventory. In addition, it would also not be impracticable for the auditor to attend the warehouse to physically count and inspect the inventory given that it is only twenty six miles from their premises.

Tests Performed at Inventory Attendance

Examples of procedures the auditor will undertake during physical counting of inventory are as follows:

1. Tour the areas to be covered and ascertain the nature, locations and size of inventory to be counted.
2. Check all instructions are adhered to.
3. Ensure that inventory is neither counted, nor recorded twice.
4. Ensure that no inventory is omitted from the count, or that it is not recorded.
5. Note all damaged or obsolete inventory separately.
6. Check that third party inventory are identified and noted.
7. Enquire whether any client inventory is held by third parties and discuss with the manager whether confirmation is required.
8. Ensure that inventory sheets are controlled and signed.
9. Carry out tests counts of the inventory and agree to the inventory sheets.
10. Select a sample of items from the inventory sheets and check the count.
11. Mark the inventory sheets tested and check enough details have been recorded to enable us to follow the items counted into the final inventory sheets.
12. Record the number of sheets used and initial the sheets to ensure that all and only valid sheets are included in the final summaries.
13. Check that cut-off procedures are adequate to ensure that inventory includes only those items purchased at the year end and excludes those items sold at the year end.
14. Record the last numbers prior to counting evidencing: (a) goods inwards and (b) goods despatched.
15. Carry out any other tests specific to the entity.

LITIGATION AND CLAIMS

Litigation and claims can be a contentious issue in terms of auditing. In some cases, the client may be reluctant to disclose or account for such litigation and claims because of adverse publicity this may bring or the effect it may have on the entity's ability to secure finance. The auditor needs to be aware of such issues to address the risk of material misstatement.

During the risk assessment phase, the auditor may use their knowledge of the audit client and past history as a basis for identifying the risk of material misstatement due to litigation and claims. For example, an entity that has frequent disputes with its suppliers or customers or other external entities may be more susceptible to litigation and claims than one that does not. Indeed, even the most efficiently run and highly ethical entities may have instances of litigation and claims being brought against them.

The auditor must devise procedures to ensure that the risk of material misstatement due to litigation and claims is reduced to an acceptable level.

A good source of sufficient audit evidence is direct communication with the entity's legal advisers. Direct communication with the entity's legal advisers provides the auditor with evidence concerning financial estimates made within the entity's financial statements (this links in with ISA 540 'Auditing Accounting Estimates, Including Fair Value Accounting Estimates, and Related Disclosures'.) This is particularly useful if the litigation or claim spans more than one reporting period. Consider the following illustration.

Illustration

Dodgy Inc has had a claim brought against them in respect of the failure to adhere to contractual terms in respect of a construction contract between them and its customer. The customer is claiming that Dodgy Inc failed to undertake timely remedial work in accordance with the contractual terms resulting in the loss of a key customer and considerable income. The claim is for $200,000 which is considered material to the financial statements. The financial statements for the year ended 30 April 2010 are being audited and contain a provision for damages and costs amounting to $75,000. Materiality has been set at $54,000.

The claim has been long-winded and arduous. Dodgy Inc have been actively defending the claim and management have informed the auditor that the claim is still ongoing. In enquiring as to how the $75,000 provision has been calculated, management inform the auditors that this is their 'best estimate' given the fact that they are of the opinion that they will actively settle on that amount. The auditor's have requested authority from management to liaise directly with the legal advisers, to which management have agreed.

The legal advisers have advised the auditor that it is unlikely that Dodgy Inc will successfully defend the case. The legal advisers have also stated that damages and costs, in favour of the plaintiff, have been estimated to be in the region of $375,000, being made up of the $200,000 claim plus costs of $175,000.

Dodgy Inc reports under the IFRS framework.

The provisions laid down in IAS 37 'Provisions, Contingent Liabilities and Contingent Assets' say that a provision should only be made if the following criteria are met:

1. The entity has a present obligation (legal or constructive) as a result of a past event.
2. It is probable that an outflow of resources embodying economic benefits will be required to settle the obligation.
3. A reliable estimate can be made of the amount of the obligation.

In this scenario, Dodgy Inc quite clearly meet all three criteria, and are correct in recognising a provision. The problem is the amount of the provision that they have recognised.

Management of Dodgy Inc have clearly misjudged the likelihood of successfully defending the case and their legal advisers have confirmed to the auditors that they are unlikely to successfully defend the claim. Costs have been estimated at $375,000, which is 500% more than Dodgy Inc have provided for.

The claim has been in existence for a considerable period of time and, therefore, the conditions resulting in the claim clearly existed at the reporting date. In light of the evidence obtained from Dodgy Inc's legal advisers, it is clear that the financial statements contain a material misstatement amounting to $300,000. In this situation, the auditor needs to advise management to correct the financial statements in order that the financial statements can present fairly, in all material respects, the state of the entity's affairs as at 30 April 2010, or modify their auditor's opinion accordingly.

The above scenario demonstrates how the provisions in ISA 501 work in terms of litigation and claims. In the scenario, the auditors have liaised directly with the legal advisers but it may be the case that the professional body the legal advisers belong to prohibit direct communication with auditors.

Where professional bodies prohibit legal advisers from entering into direct communication with auditors, then alternative audit evidence can be sought. This can include a letter prepared by the audit firm and transcribed onto the entity's notepaper requesting a list of litigation and claims, their likely outcomes and an estimate, where available, of likely costs involved. It is also common for audit firms to seek authorisation from management to attend meetings with management and legal counsel to discuss litigation and claims brought against the entity together, the likely outcome of such litigation and claims and an estimate, where available, of likely costs involved. Some entities may have in-house legal advisers who may be able to provide the auditor with sufficient appropriate audit evidence concerning litigation and claims, but as such litigation and claims may move at a fast pace, or be at a critical point, this information may not be relevant or reliable. As such, the auditor may require confirmation from the entity's external legal advisers.

Where the auditor is not able to obtain sufficient appropriate audit evidence concerning litigation and claims pertaining to the entity, the auditor shall modify the opinion in their report in accordance with the provisions in ISA 705.

Examples of procedures which can be adopted in gathering sufficient audit evidence are as follows:

- Review correspondence with legal advisers, bankers, customers, insurance providers and suppliers both before and after the reporting date.
- Correspond with the entity's legal advisers, where this is possible.
- Consider the likelihood of reimbursement.
- Discuss with management.
- Recalculate any provisions made.
- Compare the amount provided with any post date payments.
- In the event that it is not possible to estimate the amount for litigation or claim provisions, check that this is disclosed as a contingent liability in the financial statements.

SEGMENT INFORMATION

Segment information (also referred to as 'operating segments') is split into two component parts under IFRS 8:

- Reportable segments.
- Operating segments.

A reportable segment is an operating segment or aggregation of operating segments that meet specified criteria, whilst operating segments is a component of an entity about which separate financial information is available that is evaluated regularly by the chief operating decision maker in deciding how to allocate resources and in assessing performance.

In terms of the auditor's responsibility where segment information is concerned, the auditor does not have to form an opinion on the segment information on a standalone basis, but instead their responsibility is to obtain sufficient appropriate audit evidence concerning the segment information presented and disclosed within the financial statements in relation to the financial statements taken as a whole. [ISA501.A26]

Management are responsible for ensuring segment information is presented and disclosed correctly in the financial statements and the auditor will gauge an understanding of methods used by management in determining segment information. Such factors could include:

- Inter-segment trading and sales, transfers and charges between segments.
- Past experience with the audit client in respect of presentation and disclosure of segment information and whether there have been any inconsistencies experienced in past audits and in the current audit with respect to the adequacy of the disclosures.
- Comparing segment information to internal reports such as management accounts, budgets or forecasts, or using analytical procedures such as comparing operating profits as a percentage of sales.

Possible procedures for obtaining sufficient appropriate audit evidence concerning the presentation and disclosure of segment information are as follows:

- Obtain a schedule of revenue workings.
- Hold discussions with management concerning their basis for segmentation.
- Verify a sample of items to supporting documentation to ensure disclosure is appropriate.

Chapter Roundup

ISA 501 deals with the specific considerations relating to: inventory, litigation and claims and segment information.

The auditor must attend the inventory count where inventory is material to the financial statements.

Attendance at inventory count is an observance procedure and must be carried out in order to evaluate the procedures management have put in place and to assess whether these procedures will reduce the risk of material misstatement in relation to the inventory valuation.

Where there are no alternative procedures and attendance at the inventory count is considered impracticable, the auditor must modify their audit opinion accordingly.

The auditor must devise procedures to ensure the risk of material misstatements due to litigation and claims is reduced to an acceptable level.

Alternative evidence shall be sought where legal counsel's professional body prohibits direct communication with the auditors. Where sufficient appropriate audit evidence cannot be obtained, the auditor shall modify their opinion.

Auditors shall ensure that segmental information is presented and disclosed within the financial statements in relation to the financial statements taken as a whole.

20 ISA 505 (REVISED AND REDRAFTED) EXTERNAL CONFIRMATIONS

External confirmations are frequently used by the auditor to confirm that balances are correctly stated in the financial statements. For example, the auditor could request external confirmation from an entity's bankers to confirm the balances on the respective bank accounts agree with the reconciliations performed by the entity at the reporting date. External bank confirmation can also confirm the nature of any security which is required to be disclosed within the financial statements together with any related party issues that require disclosure such as directors' guarantees. Another common external confirmation is that of customer (receivable) circularisation to confirm the balance outstanding at the reporting date. Such external confirmations are not absolute and other confirmations may be necessary depending on the risk assessment and the nature and complexity of the client being subject to audit.

When selecting the appropriate confirmation, the auditor will take into consideration various factors such as the assertion being addressed, the likelihood of the response rate, whether management will allow such external confirmation to be made and past experience of the audit.

Practical Insight

A common audit procedure used by auditors is the circularisation of receivables. In this procedure, certain balances are selected using sampling methods and a letter is sent to the receivable, on the entity's notepaper by the audit firm (note the audit firm must send the request, not the entity). This letter will state the balance outstanding on the receivable's ledger as at the reporting date and the customer is required to agree or disagree with the amount claimed to be owing to the entity at the reporting date. Ordinarily the letter will request that the customer details any reconciling differences between the amount claimed to be owed on the entity's receivables ledger and that on the customer's payables ledger.

Such requests are quite common and go towards providing audit evidence concerning the existence of the receivable at the reporting date. However, such evidence cannot always be deemed 'sufficient' in its entirety because there is a risk that the letter may give a positive confirmation of the balance outstanding without verifying that the amount is, in fact, correct.

In the above practical insight, we have looked at a common external confirmation request which can serve as audit evidence but which is not deemed to be totally reliable in its entirety. An alternative procedure could be to omit the balance outstanding in the letter and ask the customer to confirm how much is outstanding on their payables ledger, and then compare this to the amount outstanding on the entity's receivables ledger. The problem here is that the response rate might be much lower because of the extra effort required by the entity's customer in providing such information.

In some instances, external confirmations may be sent out but replies not received. The auditor must follow up the non-replies and if non-replies are still not forthcoming, they shall adopt further audit procedures to gather sufficient appropriate audit evidence. In respect of receivables, the additional audit procedures adopted could be testing after date cash receipts. Conversely, payables could also be tested using after date cash techniques. The extent to which these are tested will depend on the risk assessment and the nature and complexity of the audit client as well as the account and assertion in question.

In considering whether the external confirmation request received goes to contribute to sufficient appropriate audit evidence, the auditor needs to consider various risk factors which could affect the request's reliability. For example, external confirmation requests are usually requested to be sent direct to the auditor. Where such requests are sent direct to the audit client, this may indicate a problem.

Electronic communication has become an increasingly popular way of correspondence, but such correspondence contains inherent issues. For example, it may be difficult to verify the sender of such correspondence, but the auditor may reduce such risks by having a secure electronic communication environment.

REFUSAL

If management refuse to allow the auditor to send an external confirmation request then this essentially gives rise to a limitation on audit scope and the auditor is required to discuss the reasons for the refusal with management in order to ascertain the reasons. The auditor shall also corroborate the reasons, because it may be the case that management are refusing the auditor permission to send an external confirmation request in an attempt to conceal fraud or error. Where the auditor considers such refusal indicates a fraud risk factor then they will revise the assessment of risk of material misstatement and consult the provisions in ISA 240.

OVERALL EVALUATION

The auditor needs to evaluate the results of external confirmations, in order to determine whether sufficient appropriate audit evidence has been obtained, by looking at all surrounding circumstances such as:

- Non-responses.
- Responses received which disagree with information contained in the entity's accounting records.
- Unreliable responses.

External confirmations may not necessarily contribute to sufficient appropriate audit evidence and the auditor needs to evaluate whether they have gathered sufficient appropriate audit evidence taking into account other audit procedures adopted or whether additional audit procedures need to be undertaken.

Illustration

Receivables Circularisation Letter

07 July 2010

> A Customer Inc
> Customer Address 1
> Customer Address 2
> County 1
> Post Code

Dear Sir(s)

For audit purposes, would you please confirm to our Auditors, [insert name of audit firm], of [insert auditor's address], your indebtedness to us as at 30 April 2010 which, according to our records, amounted to $12,000.

If the above is in agreement with your records, please sign in the space provided below and return this letter direct to our Auditors in the enclosed envelope.

If the amount is not in agreement with your records, please notify our Auditors direct of the amount shown by your records and, if possible, send them full particulars of the difference.

Please note that this is not a request for payment.

We should be grateful if you could give this request your early attention.

Yours faithfully,

Director

The amount shown above *is/is not in agreement with our records as at 30 April 2010.

Signed . . . .   Date . . . .

Title or position . . . .

* delete as appropriate

Chapter Roundup

External confirmations can provide audit evidence which is more reliable as it is obtained from outside sources.

Auditors shall consider factors such as the assertion being addressed, response rates, management permission and past experience of the audit.

For non-replies, alternative audit procedures should be applied.

If management refuse the auditor permission to send an external confirmation, the auditor shall discuss the reasons for such refusal. If the auditor considers the refusal gives rise to a fraud risk factor, the auditor must revise the assessment of risk and consult with the provisions in ISA 240.

21 ISA 510 (REDRAFTED) INITIAL AUDIT ENGAGEMENTS — OPENING BALANCES

The objective of ISA 510 is to outline the auditor's responsibilities in terms of whether the opening balances in initial engagements contain material misstatements which may affect the current period's financial statements and whether the entity's accounting policies have been consistently applied in the current period or whether any changes in accounting policy have been properly accounted for.

ISA 510 defines opening balances as:

> *Those balances that exist at the beginning of the period. Opening balances are based upon the closing balances of the prior period and reflect the effects of transactions and events of prior periods and accounting policies applied in the prior period. Opening balances also include matters requiring disclosure that existed at the beginning of the period, such as contingencies and commitments.*

[ISA510.4 (b)]

Initial engagements primarily arise for two reasons:

- The audit client changes auditor.
- The audit client is no longer eligible to apply audit exemption in accordance with legislative or other regulatory requirements — for example, banks and financiers may impose a mandatory requirement for audit despite the entity being eligible for audit exemption.

Instances such as the above require the auditor to evaluate the risk of material misstatement in relation to the opening balances and to adopt audit procedures to reduce this risk to an acceptably low level.

RECURRING AUDITS

In audits where the financial statements have been audited by the same auditor in both the current and preceding year the extent of the audit work required may only be limited to ensuring that the opening balances have been correctly brought forward, depending on the risk assessment and the nature, size and complexity of the entity and the accounting controls in operation.

INITIAL ENGAGEMENTS

Where the audit is an initial engagement the situation is more difficult. Sufficient appropriate audit evidence is required on the opening balances which may depend on factors such as:

- The entity's accounting policies.
- Whether the preceding period's financial statements were audited and, if so, whether the auditor's report was qualified.

- The nature of the opening balances, including the risk of their misstatement.
- The materiality of the opening balances relative to the current period's financial statements.

Ethical standards require incoming auditors to liaise with outgoing auditors and in some jurisdictions, legislation allows for incoming auditors to have access to the previous auditor's working papers. Such access to predecessor auditor's working papers can allow the incoming auditor to obtain sufficient appropriate audit evidence.

Additional procedures may also be undertaken by the incoming auditor concerning opening balances. For example, non-current assets and liabilities can be verified by inspection of accounting records and obtaining documentary evidence such as invoices for non-current assets, agreements/contracts for non-current liabilities and share certificates or other documentary evidence for items such as investments.

Current assets such as receivables can be verified by using techniques such as after date cash receipts in the current year to verify the existence of the assets at the end of the previous reporting period. Inventories pose a particular problem because whilst supporting evidence may be available for the current period's inventory valuation, there may be little in the way of evidence concerning the opening inventory in the financial statements.

Where this is the case and inventory is deemed material (both opening and closing inventory) to the financial statements, it may not necessarily be appropriate to issue a qualified auditor's report on the financial statements simply because of the opening inventory. Additional procedures can be used to provide sufficient appropriate audit evidence concerning opening inventories such as:

- Verifying the valuation of the opening inventory.
- Undertaking procedures such as cut-offs and analytical procedures on items such as gross profit.
- Reviewing predecessor auditor's working papers (where necessary) to obtain sufficient appropriate audit evidence concerning the closing inventory in the prior period.

Where sufficient appropriate audit evidence cannot be obtained to support the opening inventories valuation, the auditor should consider the impact of such a scope limitation on their audit opinion. This is usually a qualified opinion arising from a limitation on audit scope (see illustration).

LACK OF AUDIT EVIDENCE TO SUPPORT OPENING BALANCES

Auditors need to ensure they have undertaken all such procedures in an attempt to obtain sufficient appropriate audit evidence to confirm that the opening balances are free from material misstatement. However, in situations where auditors cannot obtain sufficient appropriate audit evidence they must consider the implications for such a limitation on audit scope for their opinion. Such implications could be the issuance of:

- A qualified audit opinion due to a limitation on audit scope — for example, if the auditors have been unable to obtain sufficient appropriate audit evidence to support the opening inventories valuation.

- A disclaimer of opinion where the possible effect of misstatement in the opening balances is so material or pervasive to the financial statements, as a whole, that they may be misleading.

ISA 510 recognises that opening inventory does pose problems with incoming auditors and allows a combination of qualified/disclaimed opinion to be issued with regard to the results of operations and cash flows, where relevant, but it may be the case that the auditors will express an unqualified opinion on the financial position (balance sheet) of an entity.

Illustration

Auditor Report — Appointment as Auditor after the Inventory Count

Independent Auditor's Report

[Insert appropriate addressee]

We have audited the accompanying financial statements of Entity A Inc, which comprise the statement of financial position as at 31 December 2010, and the statement of comprehensive income, statement of changes in equity and statement of cash flows for the year then ended, and a summary of significant accounting policies and other explanatory information.

Management's Responsibility for the Financial Statements   Management is responsible for the preparation and fair presentation of these financial statements in accordance with International Financial Reporting Standards, and for such internal control as management determines is necessary to enable the preparation of financial statements that are free from material misstatement, whether due to fraud or error.

Auditor's Responsibility   Our responsibility is to express an opinion on these financial statements based on our audit. We conducted our audit in accordance with International Standards on Auditing. Those standards require that we comply with ethical requirements and plan and perform the audit to obtain reasonable assurance about whether the financial statements are free from material misstatement.

An audit involves performing procedures to obtain audit evidence about the amounts and disclosures in the financial statements. The procedures selected depend on the auditor's judgement, including the assessment of the risks of material misstatement of the financial statements, whether due to fraud or error. In making those risk assessments, the auditor considers internal control relevant to the entity's preparation and fair presentation of the financial statements in order to design audit procedures that are appropriate in the circumstances, but not for the purpose of expressing an opinion on the effectiveness of the entity's internal control. An audit also includes evaluating the appropriateness of accounting policies used and the reasonableness of accounting estimates made by management, as well as evaluating the overall presentation of the financial statements.

We believe that the audit evidence we have obtained is sufficient and appropriate to provide a basis for our qualified audit opinion.

Basis for Qualified Opinion   We were appointed as auditors of the company on 30 June 2011 and, thus, did not observe the counting of the physical inventories at the beginning of the year. We were unable to satisfy ourselves by alternative means concerning inventory quantities held at 31 December 2010. Since opening inventories enter into the determination of the financial performance and cash flows, we were unable to determine whether adjustments might have been necessary in respect of the profit for the year reported in the statement of comprehensive income and the net cash flows from operating activities reported in the statement of cash flows.

Qualified Opinion   In our opinion, except for the possible effects of the matter described in the Basis for Qualified Opinion paragraph, the financial statements present fairly, in all material respect [or give a true and fair view of] the financial position of Entity A Inc as at 31 December 2010, and of its financial performance and its cash flows for the year then ended in accordance with International Financial Reporting Standards.

Other Matter   The financial statements of Entity A Inc for the year ended 31 December 2009 were audited by another auditor who expressed an unmodified opinion on those financial statements on 31 March 2010.

Auditor's signature

Date of the auditor's report

Auditor's address

Chapter Roundup

Initial engagements will require more attention is devoted to opening balances to evaluate the risk that the opening balances are materially misstated and procedures should be adopted to reduce this risk.

Opening inventory poses particular difficulties, but a modified opinion may not necessarily be appropriate if sufficient and appropriate audit evidence can be obtained concerning opening inventories.

A lack of evidence concerning opening balances will give rise to a modified or disclaimer of opinion.

22 ISA 520 (REDRAFTED) ANALYTICAL PROCEDURES

ISA 520 deals with the auditors' responsibilities in terms of the use of analytical procedures, which are also referred to as substantive analytical procedures. Analytical procedures are an essential tool in analysing the relationships between items of financial data, or between items of financial and non-financial data, deriving from the same period. In addition, analytical procedures also help to compare financial information deriving from different periods to identify inconsistencies and predicted patterns or significant fluctuations and unexpected relationships, and the results of investigations thereof.

ANALYTICAL PROCEDURES AT THE PLANNING STAGE

Analytical procedures are a particularly useful audit procedure at the planning stage of an audit because they allow the auditor to consider whether reliance can be placed on analytical review to reduce risk or whether the auditor needs to increase work in any area.

Analytical procedures used at the planning stage of the audit can identify those audit areas which might be considered 'key' audit areas. For example, if the gross profit margins have reduced disproportionately from one year to the next, the auditor may focus on understanding why this reduction has occurred and ask questions such as 'has inventory been valued correctly?' 'Are cut-offs correct?' 'Is revenue complete?'

Analytical procedures used in planning have to be seen in conjunction with the auditor's risk analysis and materiality. Possible sources of information pertaining to the client could include:

- Interim management accounts.
- Budgets.
- Interim financial information.
- VAT returns.
- Board minutes.
- Correspondence.
- Reviews of audit related correspondence files.
- Non-financial information.

As well as determining the nature, extent and timing of various audit procedures, analytical procedures can also indicate aspects of the entity to which the auditor was not previously aware or if fluctuations have occurred within the financial statement information which was not in accordance with the auditor's expectations. Analytical procedures are not used just in the planning stage of the audit; indeed, they can be used throughout the detailed audit work and can also be used at the final stage of the audit as an overview of the financial statements to ensure that the information contained in the financial statements is in accordance with the auditor's understanding of the entity and that adequate explanations as well as sufficient appropriate audit evidence has been obtained in respect of unexpected fluctuations within financial statement amounts.

The use of substantive analytical procedures requires an element of judgement on behalf of the auditor, and the auditor needs to take factors into account such as the nature of the assertion as well as the risk of material misstatement. This is particularly the case where the auditor determines that the internal control environment in a certain audit area is weak, thus not relying on the internal controls but instead undertaking more substantive analytical procedures.

RELIANCE ON ANALYTICAL PROCEDURES

Analytical procedures are more reliable in terms of audit evidence if they come from sources independent from, rather than internal to, the client. The auditor determines the reliability of the data to be used in designing substantive analytical procedures by referring to:

1.   The source of the information made available.
2.   The comparability of the information made available.
3.   The nature and relevance of the information made available.
4.   The controls in place over the preparation of the information made available.

The auditor will have more confidence in the information made available to be used in designing substantive analytical procedures if the controls over the information are operating effectively. In this respect, the auditor may consider testing the operating effectiveness of the controls.

INVESTIGATING THE RESULTS OF ANALYTICAL PROCEDURES

Where analytical procedures produce results which indicate fluctuations or relationships that are not consistent with the auditor's expectations, the auditor must discuss the inconsistencies with management to determine whether the responses received from management can go towards obtaining additional sufficient appropriate audit evidence. The auditor needs to use professional judgement in determining whether the results of the analytical procedures, together with the inquiries of management, require additional audit procedures to be adopted to obtain sufficient appropriate audit evidence.

ANALYTICAL PROCEDURES AS AN OVERVIEW
AT THE END OF THE AUDIT

Analytical procedures must be applied by the auditor at, or near, the end of the audit when forming an opinion as to whether the financial statements as a whole are consistent with the auditor's expectations.

Applying analytical procedure at the end or near the end of the audit is intended to allow the auditor to consider whether their conclusions, which have been drawn as a result of the procedures applied during the audit, corroborate those conclusions in relation to individual components or elements of the financial statements. It will also assist the auditor in forming an overall conclusion as to the reasonableness of the financial statements.

Illustration

The audit of Entity A Inc is nearing completion and the auditor has applied analytical procedures in order to form a conclusion as to whether the financial statements, as a whole, are consistent with his understanding of the entity. In applying these procedures, the auditor has identified a further unrecognised risk of material misstatement within the financial statements.

In situations where the auditor identifies further unrecognised risks of material misstatement, the auditor shall re-evaluate the planned audit procedures in light of the revised risk assessment for all (or some) of the classes of transactions, account balances or disclosures and related assertions.

PRACTICAL TECHNIQUES

Analytical procedures are an extremely useful and significant tool, not only at the planning stage of the audit, but also during the audit and at the final review stage. Typical techniques which can be adopted during audit work are as follows:

- Ratio analysis.
- Review of prior period financial information.
- Reasonableness tests.
- Income statement expenditure review.
- Other techniques.

Ratio Analysis

Ratio analysis is often (if not always) used during the course of an audit and can be indicative of a wide variety of situations including fraud and error. Ratios mean very little when used in isolation and should be compared to prior-period financial information, financial information used for a comparable entity, budgets, cash flows and other such relevant and available information.

Review of Prior Period Financial Information

A review of the current and prior period financial statements is often undertaken to identify fluctuations in the trends. Often revenue and expense accounts are related to the statement of financial position (balance sheet) accounts and comparisons should be made to ensure relationships are reasonable.

Reasonableness Tests

Usually referred to as 'proof in total' tests, these can offer confirmation that the amounts in the financial statements are fairly stated. The auditor will recalculate the expected value of an item and compare it to the actual amount in the financial statements. This can be illustrated using non-current assets and straight line depreciation. The auditor will perform the following calculation:

$$(\text{cost} + \text{additions} - \text{disposals}) \times \text{depreciation } \% = \text{charge per financial statements}$$

The auditor's expected charge per the financial statements will be compared with that of the charge in the financial statements to determine whether any misstatements have arisen.

Income Statement Expenditure Review

Reviews of the expense accounts in the statement of comprehensive income (income statement) are widely adopted because such reviews will allow the auditor to focus on any disproportionate increases/decreases in expense accounts, particularly when testing for inappropriate expensing of capital items.

Other Techniques

Other techniques which can be used during analytical review procedures are:

- Comparison of trends in production and sales.
- Consideration of inflation, industrial disputes, changes in production methods and changes in activity on the payroll charge in the financial statements.
- Comparison of rent charges to the annual rental agreement.
- Comparison of finance costs with loan/leasing/hire purchase agreements.
- Operating lease charges to the leasing agreement.
- Inquiry with management concerning major variances.
- Comparison of actual financial information with that of budgeted financial information.

Illustration

Analytical Review

The objective is to apply analytical procedures as risk assessment procedures to obtain an understanding of the entity and its environment at the planning stage and in overall review at the end of the audit. In addition, analytical procedures can also be applied as substantive procedures where applicable.

Examples of Analytical Procedures   Analytical procedures include the consideration of comparison of the entity's financial information with, for example:

1. Comparable information for prior periods.
2. Anticipated results for the entity, such as budgets or forecasts, or expectations of the auditor, such as estimation.
3. Similar industry information.
   Analytical procedures can also include consideration of relationships:
4. Among elements of financial information that would be expected to conform to a predictable pattern based on the entity's experience, such as gross margin percentages.
5. Between the financial information and relevant non-financial information, such as between payroll costs and the number of employees.

SUGGESTED TESTS

Planning Stage

At the planning stage apply analytical procedures as risk assessment procedures to obtain an understanding of the entity and its environment. This may indicate aspects of the entity of which the auditor was unaware and will assist in assessing the risks of material misstatement in order to determine the nature, timing and extent of further audit procedures. (Note that full financial statement information may not be available at this stage and alternative information could be in the form of tax returns, etc.)

At Completion Stage

At the completion stage, apply analytical procedures to form an overall conclusion as to whether the financial statements as a whole are consistent with the auditor's understanding.

Analytical Procedures as Substantive Procedures (optional)

The decision about which audit procedures to use to achieve a particular objective is based on the auditor's judgement. Specifically, it requires the auditor to consider the expected effectiveness and efficiency of the available audit procedures in order to reduce the assessed risk of material misstatement at the assertion level to an acceptably low level.

Detail the analytical procedures used as substantive procedures ensuring the following are considered:

    (a)   That the reliability of the data used is assessed.
    (b)   Whether the expectation is sufficiently precise.
    (c)   The acceptable difference of recorded amounts from expected values.

Illustration

Initial Analytical Review

Objective   To establish if the results of the review procedures are consistent with expectations and to seek to reduce the extent of detailed substantive testing.

Revenue   Revenue has seen an increase of 47% which is in line with our expectations and as per our discussions in the audit clearance meeting last year when the CEO made us aware that there would be a significant increase in contracts being awarded to the entity between 2009 and 2010. There are issues concerning 'discrepancies' which arise due to disagreements between the client and the contract provider. These discrepancies are beyond the control of the client and are reviewed by the contract provider at a later date; therefore, because the client cannot control the contract provider, nor sue the contract provider for recovery of these discrepancy amounts, these discrepancies are not recognised as income, nor is a corresponding receivable in the statement of financial position recognised. This is in accordance with the IASB 'Framework for the Preparation and Presentation of Financial Statements' in terms of asset recognition.

Cost of Sales   The increase in revenue due to the increased contracts has also seen cost of sales increase as a direct result. Margins are down on the previous year which is due to the way commissions are calculated as per a revised agreement.

Directors' Remuneration   Directors' remuneration has increased on the previous year due to a higher level of bonus being paid to the directors.

Rent   The increase in rent payments is due to the new premises. There have also been additional rental payments due to another property provider in respect of the property in the South West.

Insurance   Insurance has increased due to the increase in revenue.

Wages   Staff numbers have increased vastly to cope with the additional contracts. In addition, the national minimum wage has also been increased — this in turn has also had an effect on social security costs which have seen an increase.

Motor Expenses   The rise in motor expenses is mainly due to the leasing of the vehicles. Increases in fuel and insurance as well as repairs and maintenance have also contributed to the rise.

Training Costs   Training costs were down because the previous year saw a large amount spent on management training, which was a one-off expense.

Legal Fees   There have been significant increases in legal fees due to the disputes with a major supplier, which are currently ongoing.

Depreciation   Depreciation charges have increased due to the additional investment during the year in respect of computer equipment.

Illustration

Final Analytical Review

Objective   To document our findings during the course of the audit and to document the main changes between the expected and actual figures/ratios within the financial statements of the client for the year ended 31 December 2010.

Revenue   Revenue has increased considerably during the year because of additional contracts. This is in line with our expectations.

Gross Profit Margins   Gross margins have seen a reduction from the previous year because of the highly lucrative business, the original agreement of 4% commission based on the revenue of the entity was reinstated. This agreement is shown on section L of the permanent audit file. In addition, some contracts have seen reduced margins, but nothing too serious.

Receivable Days   The receivable days are in line with our expectations.

Overall Financial Statement Review   Generally all areas have seen growth which accords with the notes of our discussion with the directors in the previous year. Additional contracts, particularly in the Southern regions, have seen massive growth and activity which has had an impact on all areas of the financial statements. The statement of financial position continues to show a strong position, with net assets more than doubling.

Conclusion   We are satisfied that analytical review procedures, used as an overview of the financial statements, has helped us to identify the underlying reasons for any increases and decreases in the figures beyond our expectations. We have identified unusual trends and characteristics which have been adequately explained but in general most increases are because of the substantially higher levels of activity being undertaken by the client.

The review of our audit work has also confirmed that where unusual trends exist in the financial statements, that sufficient evidence is on file to support the assertions made by management.

Chapter Roundup

Analytical procedures (and substantive analytical procedures) should be applied throughout the audit, but particularly at the planning and conclusion stages.

Applying analytical procedures near the end of the audit will assist the auditor in forming an opinion as to whether the financial statements are consistent with the auditor's knowledge and understanding of the entity.

Analytical procedures can also serve to indicate aspects of the entity of which the auditor was not previously aware.

Information which comes from sources independent to the entity is more reliable than information internal to the entity.

Practical techniques can involve ratio analysis, review of comparable information and reasonableness tests.

	Audit Risk		Inherent Risk		Control Risk		*(Detection Risk)* Sampling Risk		Non-Sampling Risk
Risk levels	5%	=	80%	×	35%	×	18%	×	100%

23 ISA 530 (REDRAFTED) AUDIT SAMPLING

In Chapter 18, we looked at the subject of audit sampling and the way it can be applied in an audit of general purpose financial statements. ISA 530 deals with the responsibility the auditor has when using audit sampling and drawing conclusions about the population from which the sample is drawn. In Chapter 18 we discussed three methods of obtaining audit evidence:

- 100% sampling.
- Selecting specific items.
- Audit sampling.

It is worth pointing out that the selection of specific items is not the same as audit sampling because errors cannot be projected to an entire population in the same way as they can when applying audit sampling.

AUDIT SAMPLING

Audit sampling is a technique used by the auditor in applying audit procedures to less than 100% of an account balance or class of transaction. Its objective is to enable auditors to obtain and evaluate evidence about some of the characteristics of the items selected in order to form a conclusion about the population sampled.

Illustration

Population

An entity produces a list of receivables balances as at 31 December 2010, which is shown below:

Receivable	$
Adams J	178,000
Bury L	25,000
Bury P	15,000
Cahill A P	92,000
Heaton J	11,000
Scanlon L	176,000
Westhead L	28,000
Whatmough H	10,000
	535,000

This figure is shown in the financial statements as 'trade receivables'.
This figure is also known as the 'population'.

Where the auditor uses sampling in the above illustration, they will restrict the application of audit procedures to less than 100%, that is, possibly only test 70% of the population.

Some testing procedures do not involve audit sampling. Such procedures involve 100% testing of items and testing all items with a certain characteristic (a 'sub-population'), for example, items over a certain value.

Illustration

During the audit of trade receivables, the auditor applies audit procedures to receivables balances in excess of $20,000.

The auditor's testing of receivables balances in excess of $20,000 constitutes 100% testing of a sub-population, or in other words selective testing of high-value items. As a consequence, the results of such a test cannot be projected to the whole population.

SAMPLING RISK

Sampling risk can occur in both tests of controls and substantive procedures and is the risk that the auditor draws the wrong conclusion from audit sampling. Essentially, there are two types of sampling risk:

1. The risk that the auditor will conclude (in the case of tests of controls) that controls are more effective than they actually are, or in the case of tests of detail (substantive procedures), that a material error does not exist when in fact it does. This will more likely lead to an incorrect opinion being formed.
2. The risk that the auditor will conclude (in the case of tests of controls) that controls are less effective than they actually are, or in the case of tests of detail (substantive procedures), that a material error does exist when in fact it does not. This will more likely lead to additional work to establish that initial conclusions were incorrect. [ISA530.5]

Non-sampling risk causes the auditor to reach an incorrect conclusion for reasons other than the size of the sample. For example, the auditor may use inappropriate audit procedures or misinterpret audit evidence which would then result in the auditor failing to spot an error.

SETTING THE SAMPLE SIZE

In today's modern auditing profession, the use of computers is becoming much more common as we move faster into a 'paperless' age. Whichever way is adopted by the auditor in setting their sample sizes, it is crucial that items selected must be representative of the population. For example, a sample size of 10% of a population is less representative of a population than a sample size of 80%, so auditors need to ensure that when undertaking sampling the sample is representative of the population. The auditor should also ensure that results can also be projected to the entire population. This in turn serves to reduce sampling risk to an acceptably low level. Many audit firms (particularly large audit firms) will standardise their sampling sizes based on general and specific risk factors, for example see Figure 23.1.

		Audit Risk		Inherent Risk		Control Risk		*(Detection Risk)* Sampling Risk		Non-Sampling Risk
Risk levels	5%	=	80%	×	35%	×	18%	×	100%	

Figure 23.1   Detection risk

Sample sizes need to reflect the level of sampling risk which the auditor is willing to accept. Where sampling risk is considered high, then the sample size will be greater. When planning the audit procedures to be adopted, the decision to sample account balances and transactions is influenced by:

1. The materiality and number of items in the population.
2. Inherent risk.
3. Testing (i.e. performing the audit procedures).
4. Evaluation of audit procedures.

SAMPLE SELECTION

The design and selection of samples depend on the specific objectives which the test is to achieve as well as the auditors judgements in combining sampling with other audit procedures in order to achieve the overall objective.

Audit sampling can be applied using statistical and non-statistical methods and there are a number of methods which the auditor can use in selecting their sample, such as:

Statistical techniques:

- Random sampling.
- Systematic (interval) sampling.
- Stratified sampling.

Non-statistical techniques:

- Haphazard sampling.
- Block selection.
- Judgement selection.

Random sampling uses sampling without replacement; that is, once an item has been selected for testing it is removed from the population and is not subject to reselection. Auditors can use random number tables or random number generators when implementing this technique.

Systematic (interval) sampling is where the auditor will take the number of sampling units in the population and divide this into the sample size to give a sampling interval. For example, in a sales invoice sample, where the sampling interval is twenty, the auditor will determine a starting point for the sample and sample every twentieth invoice thereafter.

Illustration

Systematic (interval) Sampling

In their test for income completeness, the auditor will ensure that sales invoices are raised for all goods despatched. All despatch notes raised during the year are the population, and the sample size has been calculated as 100.

Method of selection: systematic sampling

Sampling interval calculation:

$$\frac{\text{Population}}{\text{Sample size}} \quad \frac{17{,}249 - 12{,}283 \ (\text{note 1})}{100} = 50 \ (\text{rounded up})$$

Random start: 28 (between 0 and 50)

Selection Procedure:

Despatch Note No.
12311   (12283 + 28)
12361   (12311 + 50)
12411   (12361 + 50)
12461   (12411 + 50)
And so on.

Note 1

12283 and 17249 are the first and last despatch notes in the year.

Stratified sampling means dividing the population into stratas.

Illustration

Stratified Sampling   In a payroll sample the auditor splits the sample between full-time males, part-time males, full-time females and part-time females, and works out the percentage of each stratum in the population. For example, if 30% of the population are full-time males, 40% full-time females, 20% part-time males and 10% part-time females, the sample will consist of 30% full-time males, 40% full-time females, 20% part-time males and 10% part-time females.

Haphazard sampling may be an acceptable alternative to random selection provided the auditors are satisfied that the sample is representative of the entire population. Auditors should take care to ensure that using such a technique does not involve 'doctoring' the sample in any way to deliberately avoid items which, for example, are difficult to locate. All items in the population should stand a chance of being sampled.

Block selection is a technique where the auditor applies procedures to such items that all occur in the same block of time or sequence. An example of block selection may be testing amounts received from customers in the month of September. Alternatively, a 'block' of remittance advices received in September may be tested in their entirety. Care should be taken when using block selection as a sampling technique because valid references cannot be made beyond the period or block examined. Where the auditor does use block selection, many blocks should be selected to help minimise sampling risk.

Judgement selection is where the auditor uses their own professional judgement in selecting items for sampling. There are 3 basic issues which determine which items should be selected for sampling:

- The value of the items.
- The relative risk (items prone to error should be given special attention).
- The representativeness (the sample should be representative of the population).

As mentioned previously, statistical sampling allows each sampling unit to stand a chance for selection. However, the use of non-statistical sampling essentially removes this probability and wholly depends on the auditor's judgement. Where such techniques are used it is important that the auditor keeps in mind the objective of sampling, which is to provide a reasonable basis for the auditor to draw valid conclusions. Therefore, when adopting non-statistical sampling as a method of sampling, the auditor should ensure that the sample is a representative sample which will avoid bias.

EVALUATION OF AUDIT SAMPLING

In tests of control, tolerable misstatement is the maximum rates of deviation from a prescribed control procedure that auditors are willing to accept in the population and still conclude that the preliminary risk assessment is still valid. In today's auditing profession, this rate is likely to be low because the auditor is likely to be concentrating on testing important controls. Where tests of controls reveal an unexpectedly high deviation rate, additional procedures will be necessary because this will be indicative of the financial statements containing a material misstatement.

In substantive procedures, tolerable misstatement is the maximum monetary error in an account balance or class of transaction that auditors are willing to accept so that, when the results of all audit procedures are considered, they are able to conclude, with reasonable assurance, that the financial statements do not contain a material misstatement. Sometimes tolerable misstatement for substantive tests will be the materiality rate. The auditor will consider both projected misstatements and anomalous errors and where the aggregate of these exceeds tolerable materiality the sample selected cannot provide a reasonable basis for conclusion about the population. In addition, where projected and anomalous misstatements approach tolerable materiality it is likely that the auditor will conclude that there is an unacceptably high sampling risk that the actual misstatement in the population will exceed the auditor's tolerable misstatement. Where these situations arise, the auditor considers whether performing additional audit procedures will reduce the risk to an acceptably low level.

If the auditor concludes that audit sampling has not provided a sound basis on which they can draw valid conclusions concerning the population, the auditor should request management investigate the misstatements which have been identified by the auditor during their sampling and consider the nature, timing and extent of further audit procedures.

In any event it is necessary for the auditor to analyse deviations and misstatements because they could all possess the same characteristics which may be indicative of fraud.

Illustration

In a cash-based retail business, it may be the case that till 'shorts' may occur on a certain day of the week when certain individuals are not present. This could be indicative of a fraud.

When evaluating misstatements in a sample, the auditor needs to be sure that the misstatements are in fact, misstatements. For example, the posting of a supplier invoice to an incorrect receivables ledger account will not affect the total payables.

When using audit sampling the auditors will project misstatements discovered in the sample on to the relevant population. When projecting errors, it is important the auditor uses a consistent projection method which is the same as the method used to select the sampling unit. Projecting errors involves the auditor extrapolating the errors found in the sample. Two methods of error projection can be used.

- The ratio method.
- The difference method.

Ratio Method

The ratio method is illustrated below and should be used when the amount of error in an item relates to the size of the item. As the monetary value of the item increases, so does the monetary value of the error.

Illustration

Audit Sampling and Error Projection   We are the auditors of Sampling Inc and we are testing the sales invoices. The population of sales invoices sampled amounted to $100,000 and the values of the invoices in our sample amounted to $35,000. The following are the results of our sampling:

1. We tested all material items in the sample which amounted to $20,000 and included an error of $1,000. As we have tested all material items in the sample the error will not be reproduced in the remainder of the population and in this respect the likely error from this sample is limited to $1,000.
2. We tested a number of other invoices amounting to $15,000 and found an error of $500. In contrast to the testing in (1), this error could be reproduced in the sample because both the population and the sample are limited to the remaining non-material items. The 'projected' error by extrapolation will be the error discovered ($500) × the remaining population of ($100,000−$20,000) $80,000 ÷ the sample $15,000, that is, $2,667.

The total projected error is $1,000 + $2,667, that is, $3,667. If management decide to correct the 'actual' adjustments which are $1,000 found in (1) and $500 in (2), that is, $1,500 then the projected error will be $2,167. This method is commonly referred to as the 'ratio method'.

If the above samples had not been split into two elements (i.e. material items and non-material items) then the projected error would be found by extrapolating over the total population. This would have increased the errors discovered because the errors would have been calculated as $1,500 × the population of $100,000 ÷ the sample of $35,000 = $4,286.

Difference Method

The difference method should be used where the error does not have a direct relationship to the monetary value of the item. It is relatively constant for all items, and so will increase in proportion to the number of items in the population. It is calculated by using the following formula:

$$\text{Error found in the sample} \times \frac{\text{Number of items in population}}{\text{Number of items in sample}} = \text{Most likely error in population}$$

Illustration

During the course of the control tests to ensure all goods despatched are invoiced, the auditor has noted the following deviations:

Summary of Deviations

Number of despatch notes not found	1
Number of despatch notes without invoices	3
Authorised cancellations	(1)
Actual deviations	3
Deviation rate = 3 ÷ 100 = 0.03	

Conclusion

Despatches are being invoiced satisfactorily as the error rate in the sample is acceptably low.

Note

For tests of control, the number of observed deviations divided by the sample size is the best estimate of the deviation rate in the population from which it was selected.

In evaluating misstatements, auditors also should consider whether misstatements can be classed as 'anomalous' errors, that is, 'one-off' errors which can be highlighted and that it is probable they have not been repeated. Where auditors conclude that such a misstatement is an anomalous error, then they can exclude such a misstatement from their projected misstatements. However, this does not preclude the anomalous error from being considered when evaluating all misstatements within the sample and auditors shall obtain sufficient appropriate audit evidence to corroborate the fact that an error or deviation is anomalous.

FACTORS THE AUDITORS SHOULD CONSIDER

Sample sizes can be affected by a wide range of factors and auditors need to consider these factors when calculating sample sizes. Some factors which affect the sample size for tests of controls are:

Sampling Risk   Where auditors rely on the results of tests of controls using audit sampling, the auditors will lower the sampling risk which in turns results in larger sample sizes. Where control risk is deemed low by the auditor, auditors are more likely to place reliance on audit evidence gained from tests of control. Conversely, where control risk is deemed high, then the auditor may not decide to perform tests of control, but instead may rely wholly on substantive testing.

Size of the Population   If the population is small, the auditor may decide that 100% sampling is appropriate, thus the size of the population in this respect has no impact on the sample size. However, where the population is large, the auditor needs to ensure a representative sample is obtained to gain sufficient appropriate audit evidence.

Materiality Level   Sample sizes will be lower where the materiality level has been assessed as high. Conversely, sample sizes will be higher when the materiality level is assessed as low.

Expected Error Rate   Where the auditor expects to encounter errors in their sampling, the sample size needs to be quite large so that the auditor can confirm that the actual error rate is less than the tolerable error rate. The auditor will ordinarily depart from tests of controls where the expected error rate is high.

Some factors which will affect the sample size in terms of substantive testing are:

- Inherent Risk
- Control Risk
- Detection Risk
- Population Value

Inherent Risk

Where inherent risk has been deemed high, the auditor will need to gather more evidence to support their conclusion.

Control Risk

Where control risk is deemed high, the auditor will need to obtain more evidence to support their conclusion by undertaking more substantive procedures.

Detection Risk

Sampling risk for substantive tests is one form of detection risk. The lower the sampling risk the auditors are willing to accept, the larger the sample size. Other substantive procedures may also provide audit evidence regarding the same financial statement assertions and, thus, reduce detection risk. This may reduce the extent of the auditors' reliance on the results of a substantive procedure using audit sampling.

The lower the reliance on the results of a substantive procedure using audit sampling, the higher the sampling risk the auditors are willing to accept and, thus, the smaller the sample size.

Population Value

The less material the monetary value of the population to the financial statements, the smaller the sample size that may be required.

Chapter Roundup

Three methods of obtaining audit evidence include 100% sampling, selection of specific items and audit sampling.

'Selection of specific items' is not the same as 'audit sampling'.

Audit sampling is a technique used to apply audit procedures to less than 100% of an account balance or class of transaction.

Two elements of risk include 'sampling risk' and 'non-sampling risk'.

Various methods are used to calculate sample sizes, but the items selected in the sample must be representative of the population.

Sample sizes need to reflect the level of sampling risk the auditor is willing to accept.

Audit sampling can be 'statistical' and 'non-statistical'.

Tolerable misstatement is the application of performance materiality and may be the same amount or an amount lower than performance materiality.

Deviations and misstatements identified by the auditor during their sampling must be investigated by the auditor to assess whether they contain the same characteristics which could be indicative of fraud.

Projection of errors can be undertaken using the ratio method or the difference method.

---

24 ISA 540 (REVISED AND REDRAFTED) AUDITING ACCOUNTING ESTIMATES, INCLUDING FAIR VALUE ACCOUNTING ESTIMATES, AND RELATED DISCLOSURES

ISA 540 (revised and redrafted) outlines the auditor's responsibility relating to auditing accounting estimates, including fair value accounting estimates and the related disclosures. The IAASB 'Clarity project' combined ISA 545 'Auditing Fair Value Measurements and Disclosures' with ISA 540 'Auditing of Accounting Estimates'.

It is widely understood that financial statements, generally, cannot be 100% correct merely because they contain estimations, such as:

- Depreciation provisions.
- Accrued expenses.
- Inventory provisions.
- Bad debt provisions.
- Warranty provisions.
- Deferred tax.
- Losses on construction contracts in progress.

The objective of this ISA is to ensure that the auditor obtains sufficient appropriate audit evidence to ensure that the accounting estimates and fair value accounting estimates are reasonable as well as ensuring that the related disclosure notes in the financial statements are adequate [ISA540.6].

Some accounting estimates are relatively easy to estimate, such as audit and accountancy accruals and accounting estimates that are frequently updated. Other accounting estimates may not be as straight forward and in some situations may require the use of an expert to determine their appropriateness, such as:

- Estimates for ongoing litigation cases.
- Estimates for complex financial instruments.
- Estimates used in the valuation of a defined benefit pension scheme.
- Share-based payments.
- Transactions involving the exchange of assets and/or liabilities with no monetary consideration.

In some cases, accounting estimates may be so uncertain that they may fail to meet the recognition criteria in the financial statements depending on the financial reporting framework that is being used by the entity. However, where accounting estimates do meet the recognition criteria, the judgements used by management involve using their best estimates in light of the information that is available to them, or could be obtained by them, when the financial statements are prepared by them.

ISA 540 defines an accounting estimate as:

> *An approximation of a monetary amount in the absence of a precise means of measurement. This term is used for an amount measured at fair value where there is estimation uncertainty, as well as for other amounts that require estimation. Where this ISA addresses only accounting estimates involving measurement at fair value, the term 'fair value accounting estimates' is used.*
>
> [ISA540.7 (a)]

It is the responsibility of directors and management to make accounting estimates which are included within the financial statements. Estimations of financial statement amounts increase the risk of material misstatement because of the uncertainty surrounding accounting estimates. The auditors should also use significant judgement when auditing accounting estimates because evidence relating to the accounting estimates is generally less than conclusive. ISA 315 requires the auditor to gain an understanding of the entity and the environment in which it operates together with obtaining an understanding of the internal controls present at the entity as well as the accounting controls, especially those which require the use of accounting estimates.

AT THE PLANNING STAGE

During the planning stage, the auditor will assess the financial reporting framework adopted by the entity (for example, IFRS) and determine how management identify transactions, events and conditions that may warrant estimation. The auditor must also obtain an understanding of how management estimates the amounts and the data that they have used in making their estimations. The auditor needs to understand the nature of the accounting estimate and assess its susceptibility for material misstatement. In assessing the susceptibility for material misstatement, the auditor will evaluate the degree of uncertainty associated with the estimation.

REVIEW AND TESTING PROCESS

In reviewing and testing accounting estimates, auditors can carry out a wide variety of testing and reviews, however, some of the most common review and testing procedures are listed below. Note, however, that each audit may require different processes to be used in reviewing and testing accounting estimates and some auditors may well have encountered different requirements, which need different levels of testing during an audit.

- Consider whether data is accurate, complete and reliable.
- Compare previous estimates with actual results.
- Test calculations involved in arriving at accounting estimates.
- Consider whether an expert is to be used where accounting estimates are required.

- Consider whether assumptions are consistent with those for other accounting estimates and with management's plans.
- Evaluate whether the bases used for assumptions are appropriate.
- Evaluate whether assumptions are reasonable in light of prior period results.
- Consider whether the formulae used remain appropriate in light of current circumstances.
- Consider management's approval procedures, confirming that they are performed by the appropriate level of management and evidenced.

During the audit of accounting estimates, the auditor needs to consider whether the financial reporting framework adopted by the audit client is relevant to the accounting estimate being used. Consider the following illustration:

Illustration

Palbarro Inc has a 31 December year end and reports under full IFRS for its financial reporting framework. The financial statements for 31 December 2010 have been prepared. On 1 January 2010, Palbarro Inc acquired 100% of the net assets of Braddigan Inc and the results of Braddigan Inc have been consolidated with Palbarro in accordance with IAS 27 'Consolidated and Separate Financial Statements'. The acquisition of Braddigan Inc on 1 January 2010 gave rise to an amount of $100,000 worth of purchased goodwill which has been accounted for in accordance with the provisions in IFRS 3 (revised) 'Business Combinations'. The management of Braddigan determined that this goodwill has an expected useful life of fifteen years and has, therefore, charged an amount of $6,667 worth of amortisation in the financial statements for the year ended 31 December 2010.

Entities adopting full IFRS as their reporting framework are not permitted to amortise goodwill under IFRS 3 — instead they must test the goodwill on an annual basis for impairment.

DEPRECIATION AND AMORTISATION

Depreciation and amortisation are accounting estimates, as it is management's best estimate of non-current assets' useful economic life and the writing off of their cost prices over their estimated useful lives. However, the illustration above shows how the auditor needs to consider the use of accounting estimates in light of the financial reporting framework adopted. Had Palbarro Inc reported under, say, UK GAAP, then it would be able to amortise goodwill over its estimate useful life under FRS 10 'Goodwill and Intangible Assets'.

The auditor needs to assess the risk of material misstatement by understanding how the accounting estimates have been arrived at and whether they have been applied consistently. The auditor shall also consider whether any changes to accounting estimates are appropriate and whether any changes in the methods used to arrive at the accounting estimates from the prior period are also appropriate. In assessing the levels of risk of material misstatement, the auditor needs to ensure that they consult the provisions in ISA 330. The auditor shall also devise tests of controls and undertake substantive procedures on management's estimation of accounting estimates. By gaining an understanding of the procedures adopted by management in the calculation and inclusion of accounting estimates in the financial statements is important for the auditor as this understanding will help them to design the nature, timing and extent of further audit procedures.

If the auditor considers an accounting estimate will give rise to a significant risk, the auditor shall obtain an understanding of the entity's controls. [ISA540.A50]

Auditors must assess the difference between the amount of an estimate supported by evidence and the estimate calculated by management. If the auditors believe that the difference is unreasonable an adjustment should be made. If management refuse to revise the estimate, the difference is considered a material misstatement and will be treated as such and the auditor should consider the impact this material misstatement has on the auditor's opinion, together with any other misstatements that they have identified during the course of the audit.

BIAS

Accounting estimates need to be used in light of the relevant information that may be available to management at the time the financial statements are prepared. However, management bias in terms of accounting estimates can be difficult to detect, especially in cases where a substantial amount of judgement is required in arriving at the accounting estimate. The intention of management insofar as the accounting estimate is concerned needs to be considered. This is an important consideration, because it could mean that if the management's intention is to report a certain level of profit, the accounting estimate(s) used could result in fraudulent financial reporting. However, not all accounting estimates give rise to fraudulent financial reporting; what does give rise to fraudulent financial reporting is management's intention to mislead the user(s) of the financial statements. ISA 540 at paragraph A125 gives examples of possible management bias including:

- Changes in accounting estimates, or the method for making the estimate where management have made a subjective assessment that there has been a change in circumstances.
- The use of an entity's own assumptions for fair value estimates which are inconsistent with observable marketplace assumptions.
- The selection or construction of significant assumptions that yield a point estimate favourable for management objectives.
- Selection of a point estimate that may indicate a pattern of optimism or pessimism. [ISA540.A125]

SUBSEQUENT EVENTS

A review of events that have arisen after the reporting date (often referred to as 'subsequent events' or 'post balance sheet events') may enable the auditor to obtain information concerning the reasonableness of accounting estimates. For example, the entity being subject to audit may be involved in a litigation claim at the reporting date. As audits are generally performed some time after the reporting date, evidence may be available (such as legal correspondence) which could help to support the accounting estimate included in the financial statements at the reporting date. Conversely, any evidence available after the reporting date may serve to contradict the accounting estimate made by management and in some cases; especially where the accounting estimate contains a material difference, the auditor could request that management revise the accounting estimate accordingly.

Independent and external audit evidence is generally considered more reliable audit evidence and the auditor may also seek audit evidence from sources outside the entity. For example, where accounting estimates have been used in relation to litigation cases, then the auditor could obtain external audit evidence by corresponding directly with the entity's legal advisers to ascertain whether any accounting estimates are reasonable. In some cases, external data can be obtained from industry-specific sources such as future inflation rates, interest rates, employment rates and anticipated market growth. However, it is generally accepted that, in most cases, accounting estimates are derived by use of internal data and where accounting estimates are generated by the use of internally-generated information the auditor should consider whether the accounting estimate is reasonable in light of the actual results in prior periods, consistent with those used for other accounting estimates and consistent with management's plans. Particular attention should be paid to accounting estimates that are sensitive to variation, subjective or susceptible to material misstatement.

EVALUATION OF AUDIT PROCEDURES

During the evaluation of audit procedures, the auditor shall assess the appropriateness of the accounting estimates in light of the audit evidence obtained. The auditor shall also ensure that the estimates are consistent and will document indicators of possible management bias identified during the course of the audit to assist in concluding whether the risk assessment and related responses remain appropriate, as well as evaluating whether the financial statements, as a whole, are free from material misstatement [ISA540.A128].

It is generally accepted that because of the inherent limitations used in estimates, such as judgement, it can be more difficult in evaluating whether accounting estimates are reasonable given the uncertainty surrounding them. Auditors often reperform the calculation of accounting estimates based on the evidence available to them at the time and based on previous estimates. Where there is a difference between the auditor's best estimate of the amount and the actual amount of the estimate that has been included within the financial statements, the auditor will ordinarily look to see if an adjustment is required.

AUDITING FAIR VALUE MEASUREMENTS AND DISCLOSURES

Fair Values

There have been ongoing debates within the profession concerning the use of fair values in financial reporting frameworks so the fact that the scope of this standard was extended to fair values during the IAASB Clarity Project was hardly surprising.

The purpose of ISA 540, insofar as fair values are concerned, is to provide guidance for auditors on their responsibilities in terms of auditing fair value measurements and their disclosure within the financial statements, in particular the measurement, presentation and disclosure of material assets and liabilities as well as specific components of equity which are presented, or disclosed, at fair value within the financial statements. The standard recognises that where estimates and fair values are concerned, there is an element of judgement required. Any area which requires judgement clearly has an inherent amount of imprecision attached to it. The risk is that the financial statements may contain a risk of material misstatement, particularly when fair values do not involve contractual cash flows, or where market information is unavailable. In addition, items carried at fair value within the financial statements will often fluctuate over time and may also be treated differently depending on the financial reporting framework that is used.

Illustration

Changes in the fair value of an item carried in an entity's statement of financial position (balance sheet) may need to be reflected directly in equity in one jurisdiction adopting a specific financial reporting framework, whilst another jurisdiction adopting an alternative financial reporting framework may require changes in the fair value of the same item carried in another entity's statement of financial position (balance sheet) to be reflected in income.

Responsibilities

Management are responsible for making the fair value measurements and disclosures within the financial statements. In terms of items carried at fair value, management's responsibilities extend to:

- Establishing an accounting and financial reporting process for determining fair value measurements and associated disclosures.
- Selecting appropriate valuation methods.
- Identifying and adequately supporting any significant assumptions which have been used in determining fair value.
- Ensuring that the presentation and disclosures of fair value measurements are in accordance with the entity's applicable financial reporting framework.

The auditor's primary objective in terms of fair values is to obtain sufficient appropriate audit evidence that the fair value measurements and disclosures within an entity's financial statements are in accordance with the entity's applicable financial reporting framework.

Auditor's Understanding and Risk

The auditor is required to obtain an understanding of the entity and the environment in which it operates. This understanding extends to an entity's internal control environment for the process of determining fair value measurements and disclosures. These internal control activities need to be assessed by the auditor to assess and identify the risks of material misstatement at the assertion level and for the auditor to design and perform further audit procedures to reduce the risk of material misstatement to an acceptable level.

Some items within the financial statements carried at fair value can be relatively simple to ascertain, particularly if there are published price quotations in which to determine fair value. Conversely, other items, particularly where published prices or contractual cash flows are unavailable, often pose considerable difficulties and require a large degree of judgement during the measurement process.

The auditor shall obtain an understanding of the entity and its process for determining fair value measurements and disclosures by considering such factors as:

- The experience and expertise of those who are determining the fair value.
- The independence of those who are determining the fair value (the auditor may consider engaging an expert where those determining fair value are not independent of the entity).

- The control activities over the process used to determine fair value measurements and the segregation of duties between those individuals who commit the entity to the underlying transactions and those who are responsible for undertaking the valuations of such.
- The extent to which the entity uses experts to determine fair value. This can also include the extent to which the entity uses service organisations to determine fair value. Where the entity uses service organisations, the provisions in ISA 402 shall apply.
- The significance of assumptions used in determining fair value, together with the methods used to monitor changes in those assumptions.
- The role of information technology.
- The controls that govern the reliability, consistency and timeliness of the data used in valuation techniques.

Once the auditor has gained an understanding of the entity's process for determining fair value measurements and disclosures, the auditor shall undertake a risk assessment and assess the risk of material misstatement, at the assertion level, related to the fair value measurements and disclosures in the financial statements. This will assist the auditor in determining the nature, timing and extent of further audit procedures.

Evaluating Fair Value

The auditor shall evaluate whether the fair value measurements and disclosures within the financial statements accord with the financial reporting framework adopted by the entity. This enables the auditor to confirm that the accounting and disclosure for assets and liabilities carried at fair value is appropriate in the circumstances.

Illustration

Westhead Enterprises Limited has a year end of 31 December 2010 and reports under UK GAPP. Included in the financial statements as at 31 December 2010 is a financial instrument which has been classified as 'held-to-maturity'. This financial instrument has been included within the financial statements at fair value.

Under the Companies Act 2006 (SI 2008/410 Sch.37), the following financial instruments may not be carried at fair value:

1. Financial instruments (other than derivatives) held-to-maturity.
2. Loans and receivables originated by the company and not held-for-trading purposes.
3. Interests in subsidiary undertakings, associated undertakings and joint ventures.
4. Equity instruments issued by the company.
5. Contracts for contingent consideration in a business combination.
6. Other financial instruments with such special characteristics that the instruments, according to Generally Accepted Accounting Principles or Practice, should be accounted for differently from other financial instruments.

Westhead Enterprises Limited should, therefore, not recognise the financial instrument at fair value, but should instead account for it under the historical cost accounting rules.

In the above illustration, Westhead Enterprises has incorrectly carried a financial instrument at fair value when legislation specifically prohibits such a valuation method being adopted in respect of the financial instrument concerned. This illustration demonstrates the requirement for an auditor to determine whether the method of measurement is appropriate in the circumstances.

Illustration

Vadher Inc reports under IFRS. Included within Vadher's statement of financial position (balance sheet) is a derivative financial instrument which is not publicly traded.

The problem here relates to the measurement criteria contained in IAS 39 'Financial Instruments: Recognition and Measurement'. Under IAS 39, derivative financial instruments must be carried at fair value. In cases where such instruments are publicly traded, it will be relatively simple to obtain a market price. However, Vadher has a derivative which is not publicly traded and, therefore, the problem lies within the fact that there will be a relatively high level of estimation uncertainty, particularly where such a valuation is based on significant assumptions.

In the above illustration, the auditor may deem it necessary to use the work of an auditor's expert particularly if the auditor determines that such work is adequate for the purposes of the audit and complies with the requirements laid down in ISA 620.

Audit Procedures

The auditor must design and perform further audit procedures which are responsive to the assessed levels of risk of material misstatement of assertions in relation to the entity's fair value measurements and disclosures.

Undoubtedly, where active market prices are available, these prices could well be the best audit evidence corroborating the fair value. The reality, however, is that some fair value measurements are more complex than others, particularly those without published prices and in some cases the auditor may consider it appropriate to engage an auditor's expert.

As the auditor is required to gain an understanding of the entity's process for determining fair value, this will guide the auditor in determining the nature, timing and extent of further audit procedures. Examples of such procedures could include:

- External Confirmation
- Fair Value Measurements
- Inspection
- Price Quotation
- Identification of Risk
- Significant Assumptions

External Confirmation   Where the auditor uses external confirmation as audit evidence, the auditor must consider the reliability of the confirmation and shall comply with the provisions laid down in ISA 505 'External Confirmations'. In considering the reliability of the confirmation, the auditor will assess the competence of the respondent as well as the respondent's independence, knowledge of the subject matter and the authority in which the respondent has replied.

Fair Value Measurements   Some entities may employ the use of experts to arrive at fair value measurements. In many cases, these valuations may be obtained at a date which does not coincide with the date at which the entity has measured and reported that information in its financial statements. Where these situations arise, the auditor must obtain sufficient appropriate audit evidence that management has taken into account the effect of transactions, events and subsequent changes in events occurring between the date of the fair value measurement and the reporting date.

Inspection   Certain assets may be carried at fair value, such as investment properties. In these instances, the auditor may consider it necessary to obtain information concerning the current physical condition of the property.

Price Quotation   If the auditor uses a price quotation in order to obtain audit evidence, the auditor will be required to obtain an understanding of the circumstances in which the quotation was developed. Such quotations may require adjustment under the entity's financial reporting framework.

Identification of Risk   The arrival at an accounting estimate or fair value measurement is based on a certain degree of assumption. In situations where the auditor determines there is a significant risk relating to fair value measurement, the auditor shall evaluate the significant assumptions used by management, taken individually and as a whole to assess whether they provide a reasonable basis for the fair value measurements and disclosures within the financial statements, paying particular attention to the significant assumptions underlying a particular valuation method with the objective here to determining whether such assumptions are reasonable in the circumstances.

It is important to appreciate that in the context of fair value measurements, the audit procedures performed by the auditor is not to provide an audit opinion on the assumptions themselves, but to provide sufficient appropriate audit evidence that the assumptions used in determining fair value are reasonable in the context of the audit of the financial statements as a whole.

Significant Assumptions   The auditor shall focus attention on those assumptions which are considered 'significant'. Significant assumptions are those assumptions which are sensitive to variation or uncertainty in terms of amount or nature. In addition, significant assumptions are those which are susceptible to misapplication or bias.

The auditor's consideration as to whether the assumptions provide a reasonable basis for the fair value measures relates to both the assumption on an individual level as well as the assumptions taken as a whole. This is particularly important because an assumption which is deemed to be reasonable in isolation, may not be considered reasonable when used in conjunction with other assumptions. In recognition of these issues, in order to be considered 'reasonable', such assumptions at an individual level, and taken as a whole, need to be both realistic and consistent with:

1. The economic circumstances of the entity.
2. Assumptions made in prior periods.

3.   The entity's plans.
4.   Cash flow risk and the potential variability of those cash flows, together with the related effects on the discount rates.
5.   Other relevant matters.

In some situations, management may place reliance on historical financial information. Where management place reliance on such historical financial information, the auditor shall assess whether such reliance is justified in the circumstances. The problem with using historical financial information is that such information may not be justified on the grounds that historical information may be out of date when taken in the context of future conditions or events. Information may also be freshly available which may give rise to the historical financial information used being out of date.

The use of models in arriving at fair value measurements is a common tool. The use of models does not provide a fair value which is precise because of the assumptions which are required. The auditor will assess whether the model used is appropriate in the circumstances as well as evaluating whether the assumptions used are reasonable. In addition the auditor will perform procedures on the data used to develop the fair value measurements to ascertain whether the fair value measurements have been properly determined from such data and assumptions.

SUBSEQUENT EVENTS

Subsequent events are dealt with in the provisions of ISA 5650 'Subsequent Events' and the auditor shall comply with all such provisions when considering the effects of subsequent events on the fair value measurements and disclosures within the financial statements.

FAIR VALUE DISCLOSURES

The financial reporting framework of an entity may require disclosure of fair value information within the financial statements. The auditor shall evaluate whether the disclosures about fair values made by the entity are in accordance with that financial reporting framework. In particular, the auditor will ensure that:

*   Valuation principles are appropriate under the entity's financial reporting framework.
*   The valuation principles have been consistently applied.
*   The method of estimation and significant assumptions used in arriving at fair value measurement has been adequately disclosed.
*   Any other disclosures required under the applicable financial reporting framework have been adequately disclosed.

RESULTS OF AUDIT PROCEDURES

The auditor shall evaluate the results of their audit procedures to assess whether the fair value measurements and related disclosures accord with the entity's financial reporting framework as well as evaluating that the audit evidence is sufficient and appropriate in light of other audit evidence obtained.

The auditor should also obtain representations from management concerning the reasonableness of significant assumptions used which shall also corroborate management's intention to carry out specific courses of action on behalf of the entity.

Chapter Roundup

Accounting estimates require judgement and ISA 540 requires the auditor to obtain sufficient appropriate audit evidence to ensure accounting estimates and fair value accounting estimates are reasonable and related disclosures are adequate.

Some accounting estimates may be so uncertain that they will fail to meet the recognition criteria in some financial reporting frameworks.

Management are responsible for making accounting estimates.

Auditors are required to obtain an understanding of the entity's controls over an accounting estimate where the auditor considers an estimate to give rise to a significant risk.

Fair values may require auditor's experts to provide sufficient appropriate audit evidence relating to the fair value measurement.

Fair value accounting policies must be assessed for appropriateness under the relevant financial reporting framework.

The auditor shall review events between the reporting date and the date of the auditor's report to ensure fair values and accounting estimates remain reasonable.

---

25 ISA 550 (REVISED AND REDRAFTED) RELATED PARTIES

ISA 550 outlines the responsibilities the auditor has in ensuring that management has correctly identified related party transactions and made sufficient disclosure of such transactions within the financial statements. IAS 24 'Related Party Disclosures' deals with the disclosure of such related party transactions. Under the provisions of IAS 24, a party is related to an entity if:

(a) Directly, or indirectly through intermediaries, the party

    (i) controls, or is controlled by, or is under common control with, the entity,
    (ii) has an interest in the entity that gives it significant influence over the entity,
    (iii) has joint control over the entity;

(b) the party is an associate;
(c) the party is a joint venture;
(d) the party is a member of the key management personnel of the entity or its parent;
(e) the party is a close member of the family and any individual referred to in (a) or (d);
(f) the party is an entity that is controlled, jointly controlled or significantly influenced by, or for which significant voting power in such entity resides with, directly or indirectly, any individual referred to in (d) or (e);
(g) the party is a post-employment benefit plan of the entity, or of any entity that is a related party of the entity.

It is widely understood that many transactions within an entity are entered into with related parties and may not necessarily carry any more risk of material misstatement than any other unrelated transaction. The overall objective of the auditor in respect of related parties is to perform audit procedures designed to obtain sufficient appropriate audit evidence regarding the identification and disclosure by management of related parties and the effect of related party transactions that are material to the financial statements.

Whilst it is accepted that related party transactions carry no more risk of material misstatement than any other unrelated transaction, the revised and redrafted standard recognises that the risk of material misstatement is higher when related parties are involved, particularly when related party transactions:

- Operate through complex structures.
- Are reliant on internal controls which are not sufficiently adequate to identify such transactions for disclosure within the financial statements.
- Have no monetary value or are entered into under abnormal terms.

In many jurisdictions, related party transactions are also subject to disclosure under domestic legislation. Such disclosure is often the minimum required disclosure and the financial reporting framework adopted by an entity will often require additional disclosures in the financial statements which are to be distributed to the shareholders. The main problem with related parties is their subjective nature, as well as the inherent limitations of an audit. For this reason, an audit cannot be expected to detect all material related party transactions, though this is not a reason for the auditor not to adopt appropriate audit procedures to gather sufficient appropriate audit evidence concerning related party transactions.

The auditor is required to gain an understanding of the entity and the environment in which it operates in accordance with the provisions laid down in ISA 315. In obtaining an understanding of the entity and the environment in which it operates, the auditor will also gain an understanding as to related party transactions. This understanding can be gained from past experience of the client and inquiry. Other audit evidence can be obtained from external sources such as bank confirmations, which will often disclose any guarantees which management have made on behalf of the company. The risk that undisclosed related party transactions will not be detected by the auditor is especially high when:

- Related party transactions have taken place without charge.
- Related party transactions are not evident to the auditor.
- Transactions are with a party that the auditors could not reasonably be expected to know is a related party.
- Active steps have been taken by management or those charged with governance to conceal either the full terms of a transaction, or that a transaction is, in substance, with a related party.
- Management may not be aware of all related party relationships.

Illustration

Concealment of a Related Party

Azure Inc is an extremely cash-rich entity which deals with the administration of a government contract. The entity's operations are highly confidential and they are responsible to the government for ensuring that confidentiality is maintained at all times. The entity has prepared their financial statements for the year ended 31 May 2010 and the financial reporting they have adopted in their preparation is International Financial Reporting Standards (IFRS).

The Chief Executive Officer (CEO) is Euan Brahm who has ultimate control over Azure Inc. Euan Brahm has a controlling interest in Brahm Enterprises; an entity which is located overseas in a country that is suffering from extreme hyperinflation. Because of high interest rates, Brahm Enterprises has been reluctant to approach its financiers for an additional working capital loan. However, Brahm Enterprises is experiencing huge restraints on its cash flow and the local government have confirmed that the hyperinflationary situation is not likely to ease in the foreseeable future. The board of Azure Inc have met at a duly convened meeting and a resolution was passed whereby it was agreed to lend Brahm Enterprises a sum of $5 million in order to ease the restraints on the entity's cash flow and allow for extra working capital requirements. The CEO considers this loan to be extremely sensitive information and has requested that the financial accountant does not disclose such a loan in the financial statements. Euan Brahm has been open and frank with the auditors concerning this disclosure issue and has also informed them about the transaction. Euan Brahm has said that the transaction is not a related party transaction because Azure Inc does not trade with Brahm Enterprises and both entities have extremely different principal activities. The auditors have concluded that the loan is material to the financial statements.

Euan Brahm is incorrect in his assumption that the transaction is not a related party transaction. Notwithstanding the fact that the two entities do not trade with each other, both entities are, in fact, under common control which deems them both related parties and as such disclosure of the loan to Brahm Enterprises will require disclosure. If management refuse to make appropriate disclosure in the financial statements, the auditor considers the impact on the auditor's report.

The above example illustrates a very common reason why disclosure of related party transactions may not occur in the financial statements. Often such transactions are sensitive and management may not necessarily want disclosure to be made. Under the IASB's *Framework for the Preparation and Presentation of Financial Statements,* the needs of users of the financial statements are considered, rather than the information that management and those charged with governance want to report in the financial statements.

Illustration

Insufficient Audit Procedures

Smyth Industries Inc operates in the retail clothing sector. Its reporting date is 31 March and its latest audited financial statements for the year ended 31 March 2010 show that the audit opinion on the financial statements was unqualified.

During the course of the audit of the financial statements, the auditor reviewed prior year working papers and obtained management representations concerning the identified related parties. The working papers show that there was one related party, which was a commercial entity and which the director of Smyth Industries had a controlling interest in. Sufficient disclosure of the transactions entered into between the two parties had been made in the financial statements and the auditors had received written representations from management concerning the identification of all related party transactions.

The entity operates in a jurisdiction where liability to corporation tax is affected by the number of entities under common control – these are referred to as 'associated entities' for tax purposes. The 'limits' for determining the rates of corporation tax chargeable are reduced depending on the number of associated entities. In other words, the limits eligible for tax at the small entities rate is divided by the number of associated entities. Smyth Industries Inc had included one associated entity in its tax computation for the year ended 31 March 2010 which had correctly appropriated the limits.

The company was subject to an investigation by the taxation authority and it was found that the director of the entity had, in fact, two other controlling interests in two separate entities. This meant that the entity had underpaid its tax liabilities for the year ended 31 March 2010. The tax authority was able to 'scale back' the underpaid tax liabilities six years, resulting in a significant payment to the tax authority in respect of the under-declared corporation tax. It was later found by the engagement partner that sufficient appropriate audit evidence could have been obtained by the auditors as the two other entities which the director had a controlling interest in were, in fact, on the public record.

The above illustration shows where audit procedures have not been sufficient in correctly identifying related parties and which, in certain tax jurisdictions, could result in the entity being presented with substantial tax liabilities where such related parties have not been identified in previous years.

Whilst it is management's responsibility to correctly disclose related parties within the financial statements, because of the subjective nature of related parties, such requirements are easily open to misinterpretation.

For auditors, the issues relating to related parties are not restricted to auditing the correct disclosure within the financial statements, though this is obviously a crucial aspect of the auditor's responsibilities. The auditors have responsibilities with regard to fraud and compliance with laws and regulations and in instances where the entity enters into related party transactions through complex structures, where there is no real need for complex structures, this could be indicative of fraud. It follows, therefore, that knowledge about the related parties of an entity and the transactions that are carried out with those parties are obtained by the auditor not only in seeking sufficient and appropriate audit evidence, but also ensuring that the application of accounting standards governing related party disclosures is correct.

EXAMPLES OF AUDIT PROCEDURES REGARDING RELATED PARTIES

- Review accounting records for, and note details of, transactions involving directors and those charged with governance and related parties. Obtain/prepare details of balances due to/from directors and related parties.
- Review receivables and payables for amounts due from and due to directors and related parties.
- Review minutes of meetings for details of transactions involving directors and related parties.
- Review correspondence and invoices from lawyers for existence of related parties.
- Review bank audit letters for existence of any personal guarantees or transactions involving related parties.
- Enquire of management and the directors as to whether transactions have taken place with related parties that are required to be disclosed.
- Obtain details of directorships with other entities by searching any available public records (in the UK, such searches can be done via Companies House).
- Review prior year working papers for names of known related parties.
- Enquire as to the names of all pension and other trusts established for the benefit of employees and the names of their management and trustees.
- Review the register of interests in shares to determine the name of the principal shareholders.
- Enquire of other auditors currently involved in the audit, or predecessor auditors, as to their knowledge of additional related parties.
- Review tax returns and any other documentation required under legislation for evidence as to the existence of related parties.

INDICATORS OF EVIDENCE OF RELATED PARTIES

- Transactions which have inordinate terms of trade or which have unusual prices, interest rates, guarantees and unusual payment terms.
- Transactions which appear to lack a logical business reason for their occurrence.
- Transactions where substance differs from form.
- Transactions processed or approved in a non-routine manner or by personnel who do not ordinarily deal with such transactions.
- Unusual transactions entered into shortly before or after the reporting date.

IDENTIFIED RELATED PARTY TRANSACTIONS

Where related party transactions have been identified and disclosed within the financial statements, the auditor will obtain sufficient appropriate audit evidence as to whether these transactions have been properly recorded and disclosed.

In a lot of cases, evidence concerning related party transactions can be extremely limited but the overall objective of ISA 550 is to ensure that the auditor obtains sufficient appropriate audit evidence concerning related party disclosures.

Where audit evidence concerning related party transactions is limited then the auditor can adopt further procedures, such as:

- Discuss the purpose of the transaction(s) with management or those charged with governance.
- Confirm the terms and amount of the transactions with the related party concerned.
- Corroborate with the related party the explanation of the purpose of the transaction and, if necessary, confirm that the transaction is genuine.
- Confirm or discuss information with persons associated with the transaction — for example, banks.

DISCLOSURE IN THE FINANCIAL STATEMENTS

The auditor needs to ensure that all identified related party transactions are appropriately disclosed within the financial statements. IAS 24 requires the following disclosures to be made in the financial statements:

- A description of the relationship.
- A description of the transactions.
- The amounts involved.
- Other elements of the transactions necessary for an understanding of the financial statements.
- Balances due to and from related parties at the reporting date.
- Amounts written off in the period on debts due to or from related parties.

Auditors also need to be aware that depending on the jurisdiction in which the entity operates, legislation may require additional disclosures to be made in the financial statements.

Practical Insight

Related Party Disclosure (Smyth Industries Inc)

During the year, the entity occupied premises owned by Shahinda Properties Inc. The directors have an interest in Shahinda Properties Inc. The value of the rents paid to Shahinda Properties Inc by Smyth Industries Inc amount to $55,000 (2009: $55,000). At the reporting date no amounts were owing to Shahinda Properties Inc.

During the period 1 August 2009–31 March 2010, the entity traded with H Smyth t/a Smyth & Smyth. The value of goods sold by Smyth Industries Inc to Smyth & Smyth amounted to $28,251 (2009: $36,054). The value of goods sold by Smyth and Smyth to Smyth Industries Inc amounted to $40,205 (2009: $52,225). All transactions entered into were under normal commercial terms.

As at 31 March 2010, an amount of $0 (2009: $6,572) was owed by Smyth Industries Inc to Smyth & Smyth and an amount of $0 (2009: $12,231) was owed to Smyth & Smyth by Smyth Industries Inc.

The entity paid an interim dividend of $77.6209 (2009: $90.75) per Ordinary $1 share to the directors of the entity. The total amount of dividends paid amounted to $77,000 (2009: $90,024).

MANAGEMENT REPRESENTATION

The auditor shall obtain written representations from management and those charged with governance concerning related party disclosures. In particular, the completeness of the information provided concerning the identification of related parties and the adequacy of the related party disclosures in the financial statements of the entity.

Management representations are not an alternative to undertaking other audit procedures to identify the risk of material misstatement within the financial statements concerning related party transactions. This concept is vital because if the auditor does not undertake relevant audit procedures to gather sufficient appropriate audit evidence concerning related party transactions, this may constitute a limitation on audit scope which may affect the opinion that is expressed by the auditor on the financial statements. The written representations obtained by the auditor include confirmation from management, key employees and those charged with governance that they have disclosed all transactions relevant to the entity and that they are not aware of any other such matters that require disclosure under domestic legislation or accounting standards. The auditor should discuss the matters they are seeking representation on with those responsible for giving the written confirmation, to ensure that they understand what it is they are confirming. Written confirmation concerning related parties should also be required of the appropriate level of management.

ULTIMATE CONTROLLING PARTY

In many jurisdictions, the ultimate controlling party is deemed to be a related party. However, the identification of the ultimate controlling party can be very difficult to identify, especially where the entity being audited is part of a multi-national group. Furthermore, if the entity is controlled by a trust, it could be extremely difficult to determine who, if anyone, has control over the trust.

Where the identity of the ultimate controlling party is determined, then disclosure within the financial statements is required, and sufficient audit evidence to corroborate the disclosure is needed. Consider the following illustrations.

Illustration

1 — Alicia Enterprises Inc

Alicia Enterprises Inc is an owner-managed entity with two directors, Alexander and Lucas. Each director has the following shareholding:

    Alexander: 60%
    Lucas: 40%

Under this setup, Alexander would be considered to have control over Alicia Enterprises because of his controlling shareholding. Ordinarily, shareholders with more than 50% of the issued equity share capital obtain control of the entity. The related party disclosure concerning the ultimate controlling party may be:

> *The ultimate controlling party is Alexander by virtue of his controlling shareholding in the entity.*

Illustration

2 — Cahill Chemicals Inc

Cahill Chemicals Inc has four directors who all have shares in the entity as follows:

A Cahill: 25%
B Cahill: 25%   100% shareholding which agrees to the financial statements
C Cahill: 25%
D Cahill: 25%

All the directors are actively involved in the running of the entity and all serve to ensure that the objectives of the entity are met.

In this illustration, no single director has control in terms of percentage. However, all the directors may be considered to be the ultimate controlling party because they act 'in concert' to ensure that the objectives of the entity are met. Where this situation applies, a typical related party disclosure in terms of ultimate control could be:

The Directors are considered to be the ultimate controlling party, by virtue of their ability to act in concert in respect of the operations of the entity.

Illustration

3 — Dormant Company has Control

Consider the following setup:

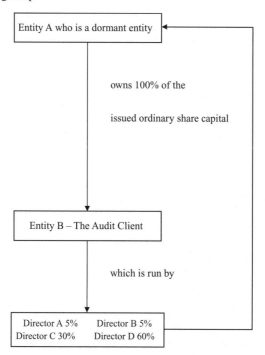

In this structure, Entity A (the parent) owns 100% of the issued share capital of Entity B (the trading entity which is the audit client). Entity B is run by four directors, all of whom own the equity share capital of the dormant, parent entity. Director D has the ultimate control of the parent entity by virtue of his controlling shareholding in that parent entity.

The related party disclosures should consider two issues:

1. The parent's control of the audit client.
2. The ultimate controlling party of the parent company.

Typical disclosures in the financial statements of Entity B would be:

Ultimate Parent Undertaking and Ultimate Controlling Party   The company is controlled by Entity A, an entity registered in [state country of residency] under entity number 123456 by virtue of its shareholding in the entity. Mr Director D is the ultimate controlling party of Entity A by virtue of his controlling shareholding in the parent entity.

AUDIT REPORTING

Where the auditor is unable to gather sufficient appropriate audit evidence concerning the related parties and transactions with such parties or concludes that their disclosure is not adequate, the auditor should modify their audit opinion.

Where disclosure of related party transactions has taken place within the financial statements, but the auditor concludes that the disclosures are inadequate, the auditor needs to issue either a qualified or adverse opinion depending on the circumstances surrounding the inadequacy. In addition, where the auditor is aware of an undisclosed related party transaction or an undisclosed controlling relationship, the auditor should disclose in the opinion section of the auditor's report the information that would have been included in the financial statements had the relevant requirements been followed.

COMMUNICATION WITH THOSE CHARGED WITH GOVERNANCE

Any significant matters which the auditor has encountered during the audit shall be communicated to those charged with governance to enable a common understanding of the nature and resolution of such matters. Such 'significant' issues may include:

- Non-disclosure, whether intentional or not, by management to the auditor of related parties or significant related party transactions which may alert those charged with governance to significant related party relationships which they were not previously aware of.
- Significant related party transactions that have not been appropriately authorised and/or approved which may give rise to suspected fraud.
- Disagreement with management regarding the accounting for and disclosure of significant related party transactions in accordance with the applicable financial reporting framework.
- Non-compliance with applicable law or regulation, prohibiting or restricting certain types of related party relationships.
- Difficulties in identifying the party who ultimately controls the entity. [ISA550.A50]

Chapter Roundup

Relevant financial reporting frameworks will often determine the definition of a related party, together with the relevant disclosures required in the financial statements.

The revised and redrafted ISA recognises that the risks of material misstatement are higher when related parties are involved.

The inherent problem concerning related party disclosures relates to their subjective nature.

The auditor's objective is to obtain an understanding of related party relationships and transactions sufficient to be able to reduce any fraud risk factors arising from related party relationships and conclude whether the financial statements achieve fair presentation and are not misleading.

Auditors must obtain sufficient appropriate audit evidence where related parties are concerned to ensure related party relationships and transactions have been properly identified, accounted for and disclosed in the financial statements.

26 ISA 560 (REDRAFTED) SUBSEQUENT EVENTS

ISA 560 (redrafted) outlines the auditor's responsibility in relation to subsequent events. For the purposes of ISA 560, subsequent events are those events that occur between the reporting date and the date of approval of the financial statements and signing of the auditors' report.

In summary, the auditor should perform audit procedures designed to obtain sufficient appropriate audit evidence that all events up to the date of the auditors' report that may require adjustment of, or disclosure in, the financial statements have been identified.

It is widely understood that an audit of an entity's financial statements often takes place sometime after the reporting date and during the intervening period, facts could arise that may affect the financial statements. There is also a relevant International Accounting Standard which deals with such events, IAS 10 'Events after the Reporting Period'.

The audit procedures to be adopted by the auditor where subsequent events are concerned may give rise to an adjustment to, or the inclusion of a note in, the financial statements. The auditor will adopt relevant procedures depending on the risk assessment of the client.

AUDIT PROCEDURES ON SUBSEQUENT EVENTS PRIOR TO THE DATE OF THE AUDITOR'S REPORT

Typical procedures the auditor may adopt when obtaining sufficient appropriate audit evidence in relation to subsequent events could include:

- Determining the extent to which management have established procedures adequate to identify relevant subsequent events.
- Review accounting records since the reporting date and note any material or unusual items.
- Review management information including minutes of meetings and note any material or unusual items.
- Hold discussions with management to discuss the effects of any material or unusual transactions or events since the reporting date to ascertain whether they qualify as subsequent events.
- Consider whether there is a need to consult the entity's legal advisers regarding possible claims and contingent liabilities which may affect the entity's financial position at the reporting date.
- Update review of accounting estimates, such as bad debt provisions, inventory provisions and so on, and confirm that there are no adjustments to be made.

Where the auditor becomes aware of events which materially affect the financial statements, the auditor shall consider whether such events have been properly accounted for and adequately disclosed within the financial statements.

Illustration

Recording of Work Done in Relation to Subsequent Events

Client: Folicent Manufacturing Inc	**Prepared by:** LLK
Subject: Subsequent Events Review	**Date:** 22 April 2009
File Ref: D3	**Reviewed by:** PLL
Accounting Period: 31 December 2008	**Date:** 5 May 2009

LLK attended Folicent Manufacturing Inc on 22 April 2009 to undertake the subsequent events review to determine whether there are any post date events which should be adjusted for or disclosed within the financial statements.

LLK held a discussion with Ethan Bury, the Chief Executive Officer, on 22 April 2009 with regards to subsequent events. LLK asked Ethan Bury about the situation relating to acquisitions after the reporting date. Ethan Bury said that no acquisitions had yet taken place, though talks were in progress about a possible purchase of a new building for their head office operations as they had outgrown their existing premises. Ethan Bury confirmed that the directors were looking to acquire entities in their market to strengthen their competitive advantage, though no potential acquire had been identified.

Identification of Subsequent Events

Ethan Bury said that neither the directors nor he were aware of any transactions or events which would give rise to a subsequent event. LLK reviewed the list of receivables at the current reporting date and all seemed in order. The bad debt provisions also appeared to remain appropriate.

LLK enquired as to any potential contingent liabilities. Ethan Bury confirmed there were no such transactions/events giving rise to a provision or contingency under the provisions in IAS 37 'Provisions, Contingent Liabilities and Contingent Assets'.

Additional Work   LLK reviewed the invoices during the succeeding financial year to identify any potential subsequent events. Particular attention was paid to any fee notes levied by legal advisers, though these did not give rise to a subsequent event.

LLK reviewed the management information and management accounts for the period up to 31 March 2009. Again, there was no indication of any adjusting event, or any contingencies.

LLK held a discussion on 22 April 2009 with Michelle Holmes, the entity's financial director. LLK enquired if she was aware of any transactions or events which would give rise to an adjusting event or additional disclosures within the financial statements. Michelle Holmes confirmed that there was nothing she was aware of which would necessitate revision of the financial statements or necessitate additional disclosure requirements being made within the financial statements.

Conclusion   Based on the above and my reviews of the entity's accounting records, management information and board minutes, I am satisfied that there are no events arising after the reporting date which require adjustment or disclosure in the financial statements.

SUBSEQUENT EVENTS DISCOVERED AFTER THE DATE OF THE AUDITOR'S REPORT BUT BEFORE THE FINANCIAL STATEMENTS ARE ISSUED

The auditor does not have any responsibility to perform audit procedures on the financial statements after they have been issued. Management have a responsibility to notify the auditors of any transactions or events that may affect the financial statements.

FINANCIAL STATEMENTS AMENDED BEFORE ISSUE BUT AFTER THE DATE OF THE AUDITOR'S REPORT

However, circumstances may arise when the auditor becomes aware of facts that may materially affect the financial statements. Where such situations arise, the auditor needs to consider whether the financial statements require amendment. The auditor shall also discuss the facts with management and, where appropriate, those charged with governance and ascertain whether the financial statements should be amended. The auditor shall also gain an understanding as to how management intends to deal with the matter giving rise to the amendment within the financial statements [ISA560.10].

In situations where management amend the financial statements, the auditor shall carry out the audit procedures necessary in light of the circumstances. The auditor shall also consider whether such a revision needs to be notified to any regulatory body, such as a recognised stock exchange on which an entity is listed. The auditor shall also ensure that they review the steps taken by management to make sure that anyone in receipt of the previously issued financial statements, together with the auditors' report is informed of the new situation.

When a new auditor's report is issued, the date of this report should not be dated any earlier than the date of the amended financial statements [ISA560.11].

In some jurisdictions, legislation allows management to amend previously approved financial statements. Where legislation allows for such amendment, the auditor needs to:

- amend the auditor's report to include an additional date that informs the user of the financial statements that their procedures on subsequent events have been limited to the amendment of the financial statements described in the notes to the financial statements; or
- issue a revised auditor's report which contains an emphasis of matter paragraph or other matter paragraph which clearly informs the user that the auditor's procedures on subsequent events have been limited to the amendment of the financial statements as described in the notes to the financial statements. [ISA560.12]

In jurisdictions which do not allow the financial statements to be amended after the date of the auditor's report, the auditor does not need to issue an amended or new report. However, in situations where the auditor's report has not yet been issued, the auditor should issue a modified audit opinion. Where the report of the auditor has been issued, then the auditor notifies management and, where applicable, those charged with governance, not to issue the financial statements to third parties before the necessary amendments to the financial statements are made. In circumstances where the financial statements have been issued to third parties, then the auditor will take the steps required to avoid reliance by third parties on the auditor's report [ISA560.13].

ADJUSTING AND NON-ADJUSTING EVENTS

The objective of a subsequent events review undertaken by the auditor is to enable the auditor to obtain reasonable assurance that all subsequent events have been properly reflected within the financial statements. Two types of adjustment to the financial statements may be applicable in certain situations:

- Adjusting subsequent events.
- Non-adjusting subsequent events.

Adjusting Events

Adjusting events are post date events which provide additional evidence of conditions existing at the reporting date. They are events which require adjustment within the financial statements.

Examples of 'Adjusting' Events

- The bankruptcy of a customer after the reporting date.
- Subsequent sales of inventory at prices significantly lower than cost which would confirm the net realisable value of the inventory.
- Items of property, plant and equipment sold subsequent to the reporting date at values significantly lower than the carrying amount which would indicate impairment.

Illustration

Adjusting Event

Over many years, Holandos Inc has made bonus payments to its operations director if the entity meets revenue and profitability targets. The financial statements for the year ended 31 December 2009 have been prepared which show that the entity's revenue and profitability have slowly declined over the last four years. Despite this decline in profitability, the directors have decided to give the operations director a bonus, based on previous formulae, which amounts to $70,000 and is material to the financial statements. The directors wish to include this bonus in the next year's financial statements in order to avoid reporting further reduced profitability.

Holandos Inc has a constructive obligation at the reporting date to pay the bonus because its past practice has always been to pay the bonus. In accordance with the provisions in IAS 37 'Provisions, Contingent Liabilities and Contingent Assets' the bonus should be provided within the financial statements because:

(1)   The entity has a constructive obligation, as described above.
(2)   It is probable that a transfer of economic benefits will be required to settle the obligation.
(3)   The bonus payment can be measured reliably.

Management should adjust the financial statements accordingly to properly reflect the bonus. If they refuse, the auditors should modify their opinion.

Illustration

Azlan Group PLC

Azlan Group PLC – Annual Report and Accounts – 5 April 1997
Chairman and Chief Executive's Statement (extract)

Overview   The financial year to 5 April 1997 has been one of major disappointment.

On 28 April 1997, Azlan announced that the anticipated pre-tax profits for the financial year ended 5 April 1997 would be broadly in line with market expectations at around £14.8 million and that cash flow from operating activities in the second half had improved significantly and was positive for that period. This announcement was based on the unaudited management accounts for that financial year, which showed a pre-tax profit of £15.1 million.

As a result of initial audit work by Azlan's auditors, KPMG Audit PLC., and inquiries by the new Group Finance Director, Peter Bertram, certain accounting issues were identified which required further investigation and which caused the board to conclude that the results for the financial year ended 5 April 1997 would be materially lower than previously indicated. Accordingly, the board requested the suspension of the listing of the company's ordinary shares on 13 June 1997. To assist the audit work, Azlan's Audit Committee appointed a specialist Forensic team from KPMG to investigate certain specific matters. Your board is now in a position to report on these matters and other issues which came to light during the course of the investigation carried out by the company and KPMG.

Your board regrets to inform you that, due principally to a serious failure of management and internal financial controls in the UK operations and at Group level during the financial year ended 5 April 1997, the management accounts which formed the basis of the 28 April 1997 announcement significantly overstated profits. The audited accounts for the financial year ended 5 April 1997, show a loss of £14.1 million before taxation. In addition, the audited accounts show a cash outflow from operating activities of £14.3 million during the financial year and a cash outflow, after financing of £4.1 million. There has also been a significant cash outflow since 5 April 1997, when the Group had net cash of £7.7 million, the reasons for which are described in more detail below.

In view of the deterioration in your company's financial position and in order to meet anticipated cash requirements, the Directors have had to seek revised bank facilities. The availability of the new bank facilities is conditional, *inter alia*, upon the receipt by the company of the net proceeds of the Rights Issue. The Rights Issue has been fully underwritten by SBC Warburg Dillon Read, which is also the broker to the Rights Issue.

The adjustments made as a result of the audit and forensic work is summarised below:

Financial Year Ended 5 April 1997	*Turnover £million*	*Pre-tax profit/(loss) £million*
Per unaudited management accounts	293.4	15.1
Adjustments		
Purchasing and inventory management		(16.6)
UK operations	(0.5)	(4.4)
Central costs		(3.6)
Overseas operations accounting adjustments		(1.7)
Consolidation adjustments		(1.1)
Additional costs and fees		(1.8)
Per audited financial statements	292.9	(14.1)

As the table above shows, the largest category of adjustments, totalling £16.6 million, relates to central purchasing and inventory management in the product business. These adjustments include balances which were incorrectly treated as recoverable from suppliers in respect of: returns of stock (£0.9 million); compensation for adverse product price movements (£2.7 million); and stock rotations, that is 'swapping' old stock for new (£3.4 million). Additional provisions of £3.3 million have been made for unreconciled balances on suppliers' statements, including £2.1 million in respect of one supplier alone. Further adjustments of £0.9 million were made to write off other unreconciled balances and £0.6 million to adjust for unrealised stock profits which had been incorrectly recognised in the profit and loss account. Finally, as a result of a thorough post year-end review, the stock provision (previously £0.5 million) was increased by £4.8 million to cover slow-moving, excess and obsolete stock.

The table above also shows adverse adjustments of £4.4 million in respect of the management accounts of the UK operations. Of this amount, £2.0 million was to increase provisions in respect of debtors no longer considered to be recoverable, £0.6 million to defer profit from services and training courses which had not been delivered at the year end, and £1.8 million of sundry adjustments.

Central costs were increased by a total of £3.6 million, which includes accruals of £0.9 million for overhead for the extra five days in the financial year, £0.8 million for general under accrual of expenses and the balance of £1.9 million in relation to sundry smaller adjustments, principally in respect of irrecoverable stock and debtor balances. Profits from overseas operations were reduced by £1.1 million reflecting adjustments to inter-company transactions in relation to pace protection and rebates on stock supplied by the Group and a further £0.6 million in respect of other sundry adjustments. Adjustments totalling £1.1 million were necessary principally to remove items which had been previously incorrectly charged against goodwill created on acquisitions. Additional costs and professional fees of £1.6 million have been incurred in respect of the audit and investigations.

Non-Adjusting Events

Non-adjusting events are post date events which concern conditions which did not exist at the reporting date.

Examples of 'Non-Adjusting Events'   The standard provides the definition of a 'non-adjusting' event as 'those which are indicative of conditions that arose after the reporting period', such as:

- An unusually large change in asset prices or foreign currency exchange rates.
- Commencement of legal proceeds borne out of events which occurred after the reporting date.
- A decline in market value of investments.
- Declaring a dividend to holders of equity instruments.
- A change in tax rates or the enactment or announcement of tax laws that significantly affect current and deferred tax assets and liabilities.
- Major ordinary share transactions or potential ordinary share transactions (though some transactions in ordinary shares are adjusting events for the purposes of disclosing earnings per share.)
- Destruction of a major production plant by a fire.
- The announcement, or commencement of, a major restructuring.

Chapter Roundup

All events, favourable and unfavourable, which occur between the reporting date and the date of the auditor's report, need to be taken into consideration.

There are two types of event: 'adjusting' and 'non-adjusting'.

Where the auditor becomes aware of events which materially affect the financial statements, the auditor shall consider whether they have been properly accounted for and/or disclosed within the financial statements.

Facts may become known to the auditor after the date of the auditor's report but before the date the financial statements are issued.

Facts may become known to the auditor after the financial statements have been issued.

27 ISA 570 (REDRAFTED) GOING CONCERN

ISA 570 (redrafted) outlines the auditor's responsibility in ascertaining whether management's use of the going concern assumption is appropriate in the preparation of the financial statements.

When an entity is considered to be a 'going concern', it means that the entity will continue in operational existence for the 'foreseeable future'.

GOING CONCERN PRESUMPTION

The going concern presumption is a fundamental concept in the preparation of financial statements. Under the going concern concept, an entity is considered to be a going concern if management do not have the intention, nor it is necessary, to liquidate, cease trading or seek protection from creditors pursuant to laws or regulation. Under the provisions in IAS 1 'Presentation of Financial Statements' management are required to make an assessment of the entity's ability to continue as a going concern. Some financial reporting frameworks may not make an explicit requirement for management to make an assessment of the entity's ability to continue as a going concern. However, since going concern is such a fundamental concept in the preparation of financial statements, management need to make such an assessment even if the financial reporting framework which they have adopted does not make any explicit requirements to do so [ISA570.4].

The assessment of going concern may be a simple and straight forward assessment in some entities, whereas other, more complex entities may be required to undertake a significant assessment to determine the appropriateness of the going concern concept. The assessment of going concern is undertaken by management and, where applicable, those charged with governance. It is a wholly judgemental exercise with obvious limitations and there are a wide range of factors which may affect the going concern assumption, such as:

- Financial issues.
- Managerial and operational issues.
- External factors.

Financial Issues

Factors which auditors need to consider in respect of an entity's financial issues are:

- Does the entity have net current liabilities?
- Does the entity have net liabilities?
- Is the entity able to pay its creditors on the due dates?
- Is the entity trading at, or in excess of, its agreed borrowing facilities?

- Are there any other indicators of serious liquidity or cash flow problems, either current or imminent, e.g. denial of trade credit?
- Does the entity have major debt repayments which are becoming due, for which funds are not likely to be readily available?
- Has the entity experienced significant trading or other losses which are likely to continue for the foreseeable future?

Managerial and Operational Issues

- Have management produced profit and cash flow projections which enable them to confirm their assessment of the entity's position for at least twelve months from the anticipated date of the auditor's report?
- Does the entity have adequate managerial resources?
- Is there indication of whether the entity's products are being sold into a rising/static/falling marketplace?
- Are there any significant problems associated with producing/delivering the entity's products/services to include raw materials or suitably skilled labour?
- Is the entity over-reliant on a small number of key suppliers?
- Is the entity over-reliant on a small number of key customers?

External Factors

- Are there any significant technical developments within the industry which may cause the entity's products to become obsolete in a short period of time?
- Is the entity at risk of losing particular skills or technical expertise which gives it an advantage over other competitors?
- Are there any legal or other regulatory issues affecting the entity's operations, or likely to affect its activities in the foreseeable future?
- Are there any political or global factors which may cause a significant adverse effect on the entity's ability to continue its operations?
- Is the entity subject to actual or potential litigation for which an adverse result would threaten its future viability?

During the planning stage, the auditor will obtain an understanding of the entity and the environment in which it operates and determine whether there are events or conditions which may cast doubt on the entity's ability to continue as a going concern.

Management are responsible for ascertaining whether the going concern assumption is appropriate in their given circumstances. Auditors need to obtain sufficient appropriate audit evidence to corroborate this assertion. Auditors shall also understand that the inherent limitations of deciphering whether the going concern assumption is appropriate may result in the inappropriate application of the going concern basis because any judgement about the future can only be made by using the evidence available at the time the financial statements are prepared. Auditors shall adopt the use of subsequent events review to ascertain whether the judgements made are reasonable in light of evidence that may become available subsequent to the financial statements being prepared and subsequent to management determining that the going concern basis is appropriate. Auditors also need to ascertain whether the going concern basis is appropriate even if the financial reporting framework used by the audit client does not explicitly require such an assessment to be made [ISA570.6].

PERIOD COVERED BY THE ASSESSMENT OF GOING CONCERN

Ordinarily management should make an assessment of going concern which covers a period of twelve months from the date of approval of the financial statements. In situations where management's assessment of going concern is less than twelve months from the date of the financial statements, the auditor should request that management extend its assessment period to twelve months from the date of the financial statements.

PRELIMINARY ASSESSMENT

During the course of developing the overall audit plan, the auditor carries out a risk assessment and part of this risk assessment is determining whether the entity may be unable to continue as a going concern. Factors that may affect whether the entity may be unable to continue as a going concern are:

- Whether the period to which management have assessed the entity's ability to continue as a going concern is reasonable in the circumstances.
- The controls in place for timely identification of warnings of future risk and uncertainties which the entity may face.
- Budgeted and/or forecasted information.
- Management accounts showing declining profitability or declining net assets.
- The key assumptions used in budgeted information are appropriate in the circumstances.
- The sensitivity of budgets and forecasts to variable factors both within the control of management and beyond the control of management.
- The adequacy of borrowing facilities.
- Indications of whether banks or financiers are reluctant to renew borrowing facilities.
- Management's future plans.

During the audit, the auditor must remain alert for any facts or circumstances which may cast significant doubt on the entity's ability to continue as a going concern. Where the auditor identifies circumstances which may affect the entity's ability to continue as a going concern, the auditor needs to evaluate those circumstances having regard to the risk assessment and whether the circumstances may give rise to a risk of material misstatement.

Some entities prepare preliminary assessments regarding the going concern basis. Where management have prepared such assessments, the auditor should review the assessment to identify whether management have properly included events or conditions pertinent to the entity to address the risks identified.

Where preliminary assessments have not been prepared by management the auditor should discuss with management how they have concluded that the going concern basis is appropriate in their particular circumstances. In situations where management have not undertaken a preliminary assessment of the entity's ability to continue as a going concern, and the auditor has identified events or conditions which cast doubt on the entity's ability to continue as a going concern, the auditor may request that management make their assessment. The auditor should also discuss with management what their future plans are for the business and consider their response in light of the events or conditions identified to ascertain whether the future plans are reasonable.

In lots of entities, management will use projections or budgeted information in assessing the use of the going concern presumption. The auditors must assess the reasonableness of the underlying assumptions used in such projections or budgeted information. The auditor may also consider it appropriate to obtain written representations from management concerning their assessment of the going concern basis.

Illustration

Loss-Making Entity Presumed to be a Going Concern

Southern Inc is a subsidiary undertaking of Northern Inc. In addition, there is also a fellow subsidiary entity, Eastern Inc. Northern Inc holds all the equity shares of both Southern Inc and Eastern Inc but does not trade itself — it is merely a 'holding' entity. Eastern Inc is a very cash-rich entity. The group is controlled by one individual who holds all the voting rights in Northern Inc, Damian Howarden. Northern Inc has been trading for one year and has sustained a heavy loss in the period. It appears that insufficient research was done into the planned principal activity of Southern Inc and the entity has failed to secure any sales in the year because of restrictions imposed by legislation which take a significant amount of time to overcome in order that the entity can obtain a licence to undertake its principal activity. During the year, Eastern Inc has been supporting Southern Inc by meeting its day to day expenses as well as the provision of a $200,000 loan to use once the entity begins to make sales.

In making their assessment of the going concern basis, Damian Howarden and his fellow board members have made a resolution that Eastern Inc will continue to support Southern Inc on the grounds that, once the entity begins trading, it is likely that there will be a high level of profitability and that Southern Inc will be able to make repayments of the debts owed to its fellow subsidiary. This resolution has been documented and a letter of support has been given to the auditors. Forecasts and correspondence suggest that Southern Inc will be able to satisfy all legal requirements and be issued with an appropriate licence in the next three months.

In the above scenario, we can see that Southern Inc is a member of a group structure which contains a highly cash-rich subsidiary, Eastern Inc. The board have made a resolution that Eastern Inc will continue to support Southern Inc for the foreseeable future. The auditor will look at the underlying information which supports the budgets as well as undertaking a review of correspondence concerning the issuance of a licence within the three month timescale notified to the auditors.

Assuming that sufficient appropriate audit evidence is obtained concerning the appropriateness of the going concern basis of Southern Inc, the auditor shall include an emphasis of matter paragraph in their report to highlight the fundamental uncertainty surrounding the going concern basis. Management should also ensure that a disclosure note in the financial statements is also included.

In contrast to the above, if we assume that Southern Inc was not part of a group structure and it was not receiving financial support from a fellow subsidiary, but management determine that the going concern basis is appropriate, whilst the auditors disagree and consider that the going concern basis is *not* appropriate, the auditor should express an adverse opinion.

If there is a material uncertainty as to whether the going concern basis is appropriate and no disclosure of such is made within the financial statements, the auditor should express a qualified or disclaimed opinion. This differs from the above paragraph, where the auditor has concluded that the going concern basis is not appropriate. In this paragraph, there is material uncertainty as to whether the going concern basis is appropriate.

EVALUATION OF MANAGEMENT'S ASSESSMENT OF GOING CONCERN

The overall objective that is required by ISA 570 is to ensure that management's assessment of going concern is appropriate in the circumstances. The auditor must evaluate management's assessment of going concern; in particular to ensure that it is appropriate for management to adopt the going concern basis in the preparation of the financial statements and that, where applicable, the financial statements contain adequate disclosure notes required for a better understanding of the going concern issues. In times of economic difficulty auditors need to pay particular attention to this area to ensure that the needs of the users of the financial statements are met.

In some jurisdictions those charged with governance may use a period of less than one year from the date of approval of the financial statements in assessing the going concern of the entity. It is sometimes the case that where domestic standards require disclosure of the fact that those charged with governance have used a period of less than one year from the date of approval of the financial statements, but have not disclosed that fact, the auditors should do so within their report.

Assessment of going concern takes account of a wide variety of information that those charged with governance are aware of at the time. In some cases the time period for assessing going concern may be limited due to circumstances beyond the control of those charged with governance, but such circumstances may well have been adequately disclosed within the financial statements. In order to obtain sufficient appropriate audit evidence, the auditor is required to assess the reasoning of those charged with governance in adopting a time period of less than one year based on the information, and this will form the basis of the auditor's procedures. The auditor must also assess whether the information available constitutes sufficient appropriate audit evidence. In some cases the auditor may conclude that additional disclosure is required.

SUFFICIENT AND APPROPRIATE AUDIT EVIDENCE

Whether audit evidence is sufficient and appropriate depends on the nature of the entity and factors such as the information available relating to future events and how far into the future those events lie. No two audit assignments are the same and some clients may produce cash flow forecasts and budgets to enable those charged with governance to assess the appropriateness of the going concern basis; in much smaller audits, such as audits of owner-managed entities, cash flow forecasts and budgets may not necessarily be available but alternative sources of audit evidence may well be available such as management accounts for future periods after the reporting date or discussions with management.

In evaluating management's assessment, the auditor is also required to consider a number of other factors such as:

- The operating effectiveness of the internal controls that are designed to identify future risks and uncertainties that the entity may face.
- How those charged with governance have addressed matters which may have given rise to concern about the appropriateness of the going concern basis.
- Whether the underlying information on which budgets and forecasts have been prepared are appropriate.

- The obligations on the entity that have been imposed by bankers and financiers.
- Whether overdraft facilities are due for renewal and consideration as to whether or not the banks will renew those facilities.

BORROWING FACILITIES

In terms of the auditor's examination of borrowing facilities, the auditor may consider that written confirmation be obtained concerning the existence and terms of borrowing facilities. Nowadays in times of economic difficulties, such as recession, it is becoming increasingly common for banks and financiers to restrict the availability of borrowing facilities and in some cases, banks and financiers may decline to renew borrowing facilities. This may have serious consequences on an entity which relies on bank overdrafts, and consequently on the entity's ability to continue trading as a going concern.

In obtaining sufficient appropriate audit evidence concerning the borrowing facilities, the auditor can obtain this through a variety of means. The bank audit letter will indicate the nature of borrowings and borrowing facilities and in many cases detail the dates of renewal — though will not necessarily indicate the bank's intentions to renew those facilities. In such cases, the auditor may attend meetings with those charged with governance and their bankers to ascertain the banks intention. However, where such meetings are held it is important that the banks understand why the auditor deems such an assessment of borrowing facilities necessary and that the relationships between the auditor, those charged with governance and the bankers are clarified at the outset and understood.

In situations where the auditor concludes they are unable to obtain sufficient appropriate audit evidence concerning the existence and terms of borrowing facilities and the intentions of the bankers/financiers, the auditor should consider whether such factors need to be disclosed as a note in the financial statements in order that the financial statements present fairly, in all material respects, the state of the entity's affairs and/or whether such circumstances need to be referred to in the report of the auditors.

AUDIT PROCEDURES WHEN EVENTS OR CONDITIONS ARE IDENTIFIED

In situations where the auditor identifies events or conditions which cast significant doubt on the entity's ability to continue as a going concern, the auditor shall review management's plans and obtain sufficient appropriate audit evidence in an attempt to mitigate material uncertainties. Where the auditor is unable to obtain sufficient appropriate audit evidence to mitigate the risks of material uncertainty to an acceptable level, the auditor shall consider the implications for the opinion to be formed. Auditors may also wish to obtain representation from management regarding their plans for future action.

Written confirmations of representation regarding the assessment by those charged with governance concerning the entity's ability to continue as a going concern are necessary in respect of matters which are judged material to the financial statements, especially where such representations are critical in obtaining sufficient appropriate audit evidence. For this reason, it is important that such representations are made by those charged with governance as opposed to management. A limitation on the scope of the auditor's work would result in a qualified opinion or disclaimer should the auditor be unable to obtain such written representations from those charged with governance.

In assessing the entity's ability to continue as a going concern, the auditor can adopt a number of procedures to obtain sufficient appropriate audit evidence to corroborate the assertions of those charged with governance where they deem the entity to continue as a going concern. Examples of such procedures are:

- Reviews of management accounts for periods after the reporting date.
- Analysing projections, budgets and cash flow forecasts and ascertaining the reasonableness of the assumptions and judgements used in their preparation.
- Discussions with those charged with governance as to how they have concluded that the entity has the ability to continue as a going concern.
- Reviewing legal correspondence to confirm the existence, and potential implications of, any ongoing litigation claims.
- Reviews of the bank confirmation letter to ascertain the length of time until borrowing facilities are renewed and obtaining confirmation from bankers as to their intentions.
- Confirmation of support from other subsidiaries in a group (often referred to as 'comfort letters').
- Reviewing the terms of borrowing facilities and any contracts in place with suppliers.

INFORMATION SYSTEMS

It is widely understood that assessing an entity's ability as a going concern requires a large degree of judgement on the part of management and those charged with governance. It follows, therefore, that the primary objective of the auditor is to consider the reliability of the entity's information systems to generate information that management and those charged with governance can base their judgements on.

REPORTING

Once the auditor has evaluated the audit evidence obtained in assessing the entity's ability to continue as a going concern, the auditor needs to determine whether a material uncertainty still exists, based on the audit procedures undertaken, on the entity's ability to continue as a going concern.

A material uncertainty exists when, in the auditor's judgement, the magnitude of the material uncertainty would require disclosure in the financial statements in order that the financial statements present fairly, in all material respects, the state of the entity's affairs at the reporting date. Where such disclosure is not made, and those charged with governance refuse to make such disclosure, the auditor shall express a qualified or adverse opinion. In view of the significant amount of judgement involved in assessing an entity's ability to continue as a going concern, the following situations may arise:

- The going concern basis is appropriate, but material uncertainty still exists.
- The going concern basis is deemed inappropriate.
- Management are unwilling to make or extend their assessment.

Going Concern Basis is Appropriate, but Material Uncertainty Still Exists

Consider the following illustration.

Illustration

Byrne Enterprises Inc is the parent of a group that has 3 subsidiaries; the group structure is as follows:

Byrne Enterprises Inc
Reece Enterprises
Hall Enterprises
Humphries Enterprises

Byrne Enterprises Inc owns the entire net assets of all three subsidiaries. Humphries Enterprises has had a significantly poor year resulting in no revenue being sustained and a heavy loss being incurred amounting to some $100,000. Hall Enterprises Inc has loaned Humphries Enterprises a sum of $200,000 in order to ensure that the entity has sufficient working capital in the event that revenue sources are able to be made. Management and those charged with governance of Byrne Enterprises Inc have made their assessment of Humphries Enterprises' ability to continue as a going concern and have made a resolution that Hall Enterprises will continue to support this entity until the entity starts to make profits, at which time Humphries Enterprises Inc will then start to repay the amounts loaned from Hall Enterprises. Hall Enterprises have not required Humphries Enterprises to pledge any assets as security for the amounts loaned on the grounds that these should be made available to any potential financiers in the future.

We can see from the above situation that a fellow subsidiary, Humphries Enterprises, has significant uncertainty inherent with its ability to continue as a going concern. As a 'stand-alone' entity, Humphries Enterprises would almost certainly not be a going concern. However, as a fellow-subsidiary entity, Hall Enterprises has offered its continued support to Humphries Enterprises, which should be in writing to the auditor (referred commonly to as a 'letter of support') then, provided other sufficient appropriate audit evidence has been obtained the going concern basis will be appropriate for Humphries Enterprises Inc, but clearly there is still material uncertainty concerning the entity's future ability. In this instance the auditor could express an unqualified opinion, but would modify their opinion to include an emphasis of matter paragraph which would highlight the existence of a material uncertainty relating to the events or conditions that cast significant doubt on the entity's ability to continue as a going concern. A typical emphasis of matter paragraph in Humphries Enterprises' financial statements, where the going concern basis is appropriate and adequate disclosure concerning the material uncertainty has been made is as follows:

Emphasis of Matter

Without qualifying our opinion, we draw attention to Note Y in the financial statements which indicates that the entity incurred a net loss of $X during the year ended 31 December 20X9 and, as of that date, the entity's current liabilities exceeded its total assets by $X. These conditions, along with other matters as set forth in Note Z, indicate the existence of a material uncertainty which may cast significant doubt about the entity's ability to continue as a going concern.

Going Concern Basis Deemed Inappropriate

Situations may arise during the course of an audit which result in the auditor concluding that the going concern basis which has been adopted by those charged with governance is inappropriate in light of the audit evidence obtained and the circumstances surrounding the entity. Consider the following illustration.

Illustration

Marchant Home Products Inc operates in the retail 'Do-it-Yourself' sector. Over recent years the entity's profitability and cash reserves have significantly declined due to economic difficulties and the fact that larger, more well-known entities have been able to offer similar products and services at higher discounted prices. Marchant Home Products Inc has been unable to compete with such stores. In 2008, Marchant Home Products Inc entered into a voluntary arrangement with its creditors. However, because of significant economic difficulties, Marchant Home Products Inc has failed to comply with terms of the voluntary arrangement and the entity has also been unsuccessful in its attempts to secure additional financing arrangements.

The financial statements for the year ended 31 January 2009 have been completed and those charged with governance have made an assessment of the entity's ability to continue as a going concern. Those charged with governance have concluded that the going concern basis is appropriate in their circumstances because the economic outlook is estimated to be quite good. However, because the entity has failed to comply with the terms of the voluntary arrangement, the entity's creditors are beginning a petition to wind up the entity.

Clearly in the situation above, Marchant Home Products Inc cannot be deemed to be a going concern because it has failed to comply with the terms of its voluntary arrangement with its creditors. In addition, the voluntary arrangement has failed because the entity's creditors are beginning proceedings to liquidate the entity.

The auditors should conclude that the going concern basis is not appropriate in the circumstances and, as such, should express either a qualified or an adverse opinion.

Management Unwilling to Make or Extend its Assessment

Management are responsible for making an assessment of the entity's ability to continue as a going concern. However, situations may arise where management are unwilling to make an assessment, possibly due to the fact that they do not have the resources available in order to make such an assessment, or refuse to extend their assessment where they have previously assessed the entity's ability to continue as a going concern.

Where management refuse to make an assessment, or extend their previous assessment, the auditor needs to consider the implications of such a refusal on their auditor's report because this will give rise to a limitation on the scope of the audit work. This is due to the fact that it is not the auditor's responsibility to rectify the lack of analysis of the going concern basis — this is the responsibility of management.

Given that all audits are different; in some situations a basic analysis of going concern may not preclude the auditor from concluding that the going concern basis is appropriate — particularly in smaller audits, such as those of owner-managed entities. However, in some situations, such a basic analysis may not be sufficient and may result in the auditor being unable to obtain sufficient appropriate audit evidence to corroborate management's and those charged with governance's assertion that the entity is deemed to be a going concern for the foreseeable future. In such situations, the auditor shall express a qualified or adverse opinion accordingly.

Illustration

Going Concern Procedures

1. Discuss with the directors the entity's position and record their plans and projections.
2. Review the forecasts, projections and any other information.
3. Establish whether the assumptions used in the preparation of the forecasts/projections are appropriate.
4. Consider whether the systems used for producing the information are adequate.
5. Consider how sensitive the information available is to changes in assumptions and the impact on the financial resources available.
6. If the directors have not prepared projections, or if they are for a period of less than twelve months from the date of approval of the financial statements, establish how they are going to form a view on the appropriateness of the going concern basis.
7. Review minutes of board/management meetings for indications of going concern issues.
8. Review terms of loan agreements and determine whether any may have been breached.
9. Confirm existence and terms of bank facilities.
10. Consider the adequacy of any disclosures in the financial statements in respect of going concern.

Chapter Roundup

The going concern concept is considered a fundamental concept in the preparation of financial statements. Some financial reporting frameworks make an explicit requirement for management to make an assessment of going concern, but as going concern is such a fundamental concept, management must make an assessment.

Auditors must consider: financial issues, managerial and operational issues and external factors.

Sufficient and appropriate audit evidence shall be obtained by the auditor to corroborate management's assertion that the going concern basis is appropriate.

The period covered by the assessment should be twelve months from the approval of the financial statements.

If preliminary assessments of going concern have been made, the auditor should discuss how they have concluded that the going concern basis is appropriate.

Written representations shall be obtained concerning an entity's ability to continue as a going concern. In the absence of such representations, this will cause a limitation of scope resulting in a qualified or disclaimer of opinion being expressed by the auditor.

28 ISA 580 (REVISED AND REDRAFTED) MANAGEMENT REPRESENTATIONS

ISA 580 (revised and redrafted) deals with the auditors' responsibilities in obtaining written representations from management on matters which are material to the financial statements when other sufficient appropriate audit evidence cannot reasonably be expected to exist.

Written representations can sometimes be necessary but on their own they cannot provide sufficient appropriate audit evidence. Written representations shall also not be used as an excuse for auditors not performing other audit procedures that could reasonably be expected to produce sufficient appropriate audit evidence concerning material items in the financial statements. Indeed, where alternative audit procedures cannot provide the auditor with sufficient appropriate audit evidence, this could well give rise to the auditor expressing a qualified opinion due to a limitation on the scope of their audit work. Written representations, therefore, are not a substitute for alternative audit procedures. Consider the following illustration.

Illustration

An entity uses the revaluation model for measuring its freehold buildings. In 2008 the building had a carrying amount of $75,000. In 2009, management have revalued the building to $175,000, resulting in a revaluation gain of $100,000. The auditors have sought representation from management concerning the revaluation and consider the representation by management as sufficient appropriate audit evidence.

Clearly the representation by management relating to the $100,000 uplift in the carrying amount of the freehold buildings is not sufficient appropriate audit evidence on its own and additional audit procedures can (and must) be adopted by the auditor to obtain further evidence concerning the revaluation. The building should have been valued by a qualified individual and, therefore, management should have in their possession a valuation provided by the valuer to corroborate the uplift. If the auditors are unable to corroborate the revaluation by obtaining the valuation, this will give rise to a limitation on the scope of the audit work and, therefore, the auditor should express a qualified opinion.

The above example illustrates the limitations with written representations because in many cases additional audit procedures can be adopted by the auditor to obtain alternative sufficient appropriate audit evidence.

The objectives of the auditor in terms of written representations are to confirm that those charged with governance have fulfilled their responsibilities in the preparation of the financial statements as well as ensuring that all relevant audit matters have been supplied to the auditor [ISA580.6]. This includes confirming that all books, records, minutes of meetings and other relevant documentation have been supplied to them and all relevant explanations have been given to enable the auditor to arrive at their opinion. In achieving this objective, the auditor will, therefore, seek representations from management and, where appropriate, those charged with governance on the specific assertions in the financial statements.

ISA 580 defines a written representation as:

> *A written statement by management provided to the auditor to confirm certain matters or to support other audit evidence. Written representations in this context do not include financial statements, the assertions therein, or supporting books and records.*
>
> [ISA580.7]

ISA 580 specifically deals with:

- Management responsibility for the financial statements.
- Representations by management used as audit evidence.
- Documentations of representations by management.
- Doubts Concerning the Reliability of Written Representations and Written Representations Not Provided.

MANAGEMENTS' RESPONSIBILITY FOR THE FINANCIAL STATEMENTS

Auditors shall seek representation from management and, where applicable, those charged with governance to confirm that they have fulfilled their responsibilities for the preparation of the financial statements in accordance with an applicable financial reporting framework [ISA580.10]. Audit evidence in this respect can usually be obtained by seeking representation in the form of a management representation; however, additional evidence can be obtained from resolutions in board meetings or by obtaining a signed copy of the financial statements.

REPRESENTATIONS BY MANAGEMENT TO BE USED AS AUDIT EVIDENCE

ISA 580 stipulates that the auditor shall obtain representations from management and, where applicable, those charged with governance, on matters which are material to the financial statements and on which no other evidence can be obtained. Such representations can include:

- Acknowledgement by management and, where applicable, those charged with governance, that they understand their responsibility for the design and implementation of internal controls to prevent and detect error.
- Immaterial misstatements which management and, where applicable, those charged with governance, do not wish to be corrected on the basis that they are immaterial both in isolation and when aggregated with other misstatements.

Auditors shall consider if there are any other sources that could be reasonably expected to provide sufficient appropriate audit evidence to corroborate management's assertions in their representations, such as external sources, as external audit evidence can sometimes be more reliable than internal audit evidence.

Auditors shall evaluate the responses made by management and, where applicable, those charged with governance, and consider whether the representations made by them appear reasonable and consistent with other audit evidence obtained during the course of the audit.

Representations by management which are to be used as audit evidence can sometimes be contradicted by other audit evidence obtained by the auditor. Where the auditor encounters such situations, the auditor shall investigate the contradiction as well as evaluate the reliability of other representations made by management. This is usually achieved by discussing the nature of the contradiction with the appropriate level of management and then seeking additional evidence concerning their explanations. Where management refuse to enter into discussions concerning the contradiction, the auditor should consider whether additional audit procedures can resolve the matter. If the auditor considers that additional audit procedures cannot resolve the matter they need to consider the impact of the contradicting evidence for their auditor's report.

Consider the following illustration.

Illustration

In the financial statements of Gabriella Industries Inc, reference is made to various related parties. Management have made representations that they have identified and disclosed all relevant related party transactions in accordance with the provisions laid down in IAS 24 'Related Parties'. As part of their normal audit procedures, the auditors have searched the public records for evidence of any unidentified related party transactions. The search has revealed that the controlling shareholder of Gabriella Industries Inc, who also acts in the capacity of Chief Executive Officer, holds a number of other directorships with entities based throughout Europe — one of the entities the director has a related party relationship with has not been disclosed in the financial statements and the auditor has discovered material transactions which have not been undertaken on an 'arms-length' basis.

This is an illustration of a subjective area of financial reporting — that of related parties. Auditors can sometimes be reliant on management and, where applicable, those charged with governance, in adequately disclosing transactions with related parties. In this situation, a material related party has not been disclosed which contradicts the assertions made by management in the letter of representation.

The auditor should investigate the reasons for the non-disclosure of the material related party transactions and evaluate the circumstances surrounding why disclosure has not been made in the financial statements as this could be indicative of fraud given the fact that the transactions entered into have not been entered into on an 'arms-length' basis.

If management refuse to make such a disclosure within the financial statements, then the auditor should express a qualified opinion.

DOCUMENTATIONS OF REPRESENTATIONS BY MANAGEMENT

Management representations should ideally be made in writing as such written representation is often more reliable audit evidence than oral audit evidence. However, in situations where the auditor considers oral audit evidence to be sufficient, the auditor should ensure that the discussion with management and, where applicable, those charged with governance is adequately documented.

Management representations are usually made in the form of a letter but additional representations such as signed financial statements and minutes of meetings can usually be deemed sufficient appropriate audit evidence. However, signed financial statements on their own are not sufficient appropriate audit evidence because they do not contain reference to specific representations.

Management representations letters are usually addressed to the auditor and contain specific information concerning the entity. The letter of representation should ordinarily be dated at the date the financial statements are approved. Letters of representations can be signed as near as practicable to the date of the auditors' report but not after.

Letters of representation are ordinarily signed by members of management who have direct responsibility for the entity and its financial operations. Other members of management, who do not have direct responsibility for the financial operations, may be requested to make representations concerning matters specific to their dealings within the entity.

Illustration

Management Representations

15 June 2010

Entity A Inc	Auditors LLP
Address 1	Address 1
Address 2	Address 2
Address 3	Address 3
Postcode	

Dear Sirs

Financial Statements as at 30 April 2010

The financial statements for the year ended 30 April 2010 have been considered and approved at a duly convened meeting of the board of directors. The undersigned were authorised to sign the statement of financial position (balance sheet) on behalf of the board and give you the following assurances.

To the best of our knowledge and belief, and having made appropriate enquiries:

Availability of Information

All the accounting records have been made available to you for the purpose of your audit and all transactions undertaken by the entity have been properly reflected and recorded in the accounting records. All other records and related information have been made available to you, including the minutes of all directors' and shareholders' meetings which are a complete and authentic record of the proceedings at those meetings.

We acknowledge as directors our responsibility for preparing the financial statements in accordance with applicable law and International Financial Reporting Standards.

Transactions with Directors (or persons connected with them)

The entity has provided advances to the directors which have been sufficiently disclosed within the financial statements. Mr and Mrs Smith have also provided Personal Guarantees to Bank PLC which is limited to the amount of $50,000 which has been disclosed within the financial statements.

Related Party Transactions

During the year the directors have identified and approved related party transactions and provided the information for disclosure of all transactions relevant to the entity in the financial statements. They are not aware of any other matters which are required to be disclosed under IAS 24 'Related Parties' or any other requirements.

Inventory

In our opinion the inventory valuation of $1,326,054 is a fair reflection of the true cost.

Events after the Reporting Date

There have been no events since the reporting date which necessitate revision of the figures included in the financial statements or the inclusion of a note thereto.

Going Concern

The financial statements have been prepared on a going concern basis. In assessing the appropriateness of the going concern basis, the directors have taken account of all relevant information covering a period of at least twelve months from the date of approval of the financial statements.

Compliance with Law and/or Regulations

All those events which involve possible non-compliance with law or regulations of which the directors are aware, together with the actual or contingent consequences which may arise therefrom, have been disclosed to you.

Contingent Liabilities

The directors confirm that there are no events which would give rise to a contingent liability disclosure as defined in IAS 37 'Provisions, Contingent Liabilities and Contingent Assets'.

Immaterial Misstatements

We confirm that, in the opinion of the directors, the uncorrected misstatements have not been adjusted for on the basis that they are immaterial, both individually and when aggregated with other misstatements.

Fraud

The directors confirm that we acknowledge our responsibilities to safeguard the entity's assets and we confirm that there are no fraudulent activities that we are aware of, or should be aware of, that have not been brought to your attention.

We acknowledge our responsibility for the design and implementation of internal control systems to prevent and detect fraud and we confirm that we have disclosed to you the results of our risk assessment that the financial statements maybe misstated as a result of fraud.

Yours faithfully,

For and On Behalf of:
Entity A Inc

DOUBTS CONCERNING THE RELIABILITY OF WRITTEN REPRESENTATIONS AND WRITTEN REPRESENTATIONS NOT PROVIDED

Where the auditor has doubts concerning the reliability of written representations the auditor shall perform other audit procedures which are designed to resolve the matter. Where additional procedures do not resolve the matter giving rise to the doubt, the auditor shall consider the impact the doubt has on the integrity, ethical values or diligence of management and consider the effect this may have on the reliability of representations, both oral and written, and consider the impact the doubt has on the audit evidence generally [ISA580.16].

The auditor may also wish to discuss the matters giving rise to the doubt and consider their responses and obtain sufficient appropriate audit evidence on their responses.

If management refuse to provide a representation that the auditor deems necessary, this will give rise to a limitation on the scope of the audit work and the auditor shall, therefore, express a qualified opinion. The auditor shall also consider the reasons why management have refused to make a representation and consider if the refusal has any other implications.

Fraud

Specific representation shall be sought from management concerning fraud. Ordinarily representations shall be sought that:

- Management acknowledges its responsibility for the design and implementation of internal control to prevent fraud.
- Management have disclosed to the auditor the results of its assessment of the risk that the financial statements may be materially misstated due to fraud.
- Management has disclosed to the auditor its knowledge of fraud or suspected fraud involving management, employees who have significant roles in internal control and others where fraud could have a material impact on the financial statements.
- Management has disclosed to the auditors its knowledge of any allegations of fraud, or suspected fraud, affecting the entity's financial statements communicated by employees, former employees, analysts, regulators or others.

Additional Specific Representations

No two audits are ever the same and auditors may request specific representations from one audit client, but not necessarily another audit client. Other 'specific' representations can be sought from management relating to:

- The entity's selection and use of accounting policies.
- Management's plans for the future.
- Actual and contingent liabilities.
- Inventory valuations.
- Ultimate controlling parties.
- Title to, or control over, assets.
- Specific laws and regulations.
- The valuations placed on fair value measurements and associated disclosures.
- Going concern.
- Related party transactions.

ISA 580 contains an appendix which identifies paragraphs in other ISAs which would require specific representations that are detailed below:

- ISA 240 'The Auditor's Responsibilities Relating to Fraud in an Audit of Financial Statements' — paragraph 39.
- ISA 250 'Consideration of Laws and Regulations in an Audit of Financial Statements' — paragraph 16.
- ISA 450 'Evaluation of Misstatements Identified During the Audit' — paragraph 12.
- ISA 501 'Audit Evidence — Specific Considerations for Selected Items' — paragraph 12.
- ISA 540 'Auditing Accounting Estimates, Including Fair Value Accounting Estimates, and Related Disclosures' — paragraph 22.
- ISA 550 'Related Parties' — paragraph 26.
- ISA 560 'Subsequent Events' — paragraph 9.
- ISA 570 'Going Concern' — paragraph 16(e).
- ISA 710 'Comparative Information — Corresponding Figures and Comparative Financial Statements' — paragraph 9.

Chapter Roundup

Written representations must be obtained concerning all material areas within the financial statements.

Written representations cannot be a substitute for alternative audit procedures.

The objectives of the auditor in terms of written representations are to confirm that those charged with governance have fulfilled their responsibilities in the preparation of the financial statements.

Auditors shall evaluate the responses made by management and, where applicable, those charged with governance and consider whether the representations appear reasonable and consistent with other audit evidence.

Where written representations contradict with other audit evidence, the auditor shall investigate the contradiction and evaluate the other representations made by management.

Representations can be made orally or in writing, but ideally in writing. Oral representations should be documented.

Written representations can be signed as near as practicable to the date of the auditor's report, but not after.

Specific representations shall be sought in relation to fraud matters.

---

29 ISA 600 (REVISED AND REDRAFTED) SPECIAL CONSIDERATIONS — AUDITS OF GROUP FINANCIAL STATEMENTS (INCLUDING THE WORK OF COMPONENT AUDITORS)

The objectives in ISA 600 (revised and redrafted) are twofold. First and foremost, the group auditor needs to establish that it is appropriate to act in the capacity of group auditor. Secondly, the group auditor also needs to ensure that sufficient appropriate audit evidence is gathered to support the opinion contained in the consolidated financial statements of the group. For the purposes of ISA 600:

'Principal auditor' means the auditor with responsibility for reporting on the financial statements of an entity when those financial statements include financial information of one or more component auditors audited by another auditor.

'Other auditor' means an auditor, other than the principal auditor, with responsibility for reporting on the financial information of a component which is included in the financial statements audited by the principal auditor. Other auditors include affiliated firms, whether using the same name or not, and correspondences, as well as unrelated auditors.

'Component' means a division, branch, subsidiary, joint venture, associated entity or other entity whose financial information is included in the financial statements audited by the principal auditor.

Consider the following illustration:

Illustration

AMG Inc is an entity who is registered in the UK. It has a wholly-owned subsidiary in China who carries a material amount of inventory. As inventory is material to the financial statements of AMG Inc, attendance at the inventory count is deemed necessary. It is impractical for the principal auditor to travel to AMG's subsidiary in China and they have, therefore, requested a Chinese firm of Auditors to attend their inventory count.

In the above illustration, the principal auditor is using the work of another auditor to observe the procedures adopted at the inventory count of the Chinese subsidiary. The principal auditor should, therefore, consider how the work of the other auditor will affect the audit. In particular to comply with the provisions in ISA 220, the principal auditor should ensure that component auditors have the specific levels of skills and competence to carry out the audit work effectively.

CONSOLIDATION PROCESS

Under ISA 600, the group auditor is required to obtain an understanding of the consolidation process, including the instructions issued by group management to component entities. A review of how the group financial statements are produced can be illustrated as follows.

Stage One

The first stage involves each component entity being audited for the purposes of forming an opinion on the individual entity's financial statements. These audits can either be done by the group auditor or a component auditor. Where component auditors are involved, the group auditor must consider how much additional work will need to be performed on the components for the purpose of expressing an opinion on the group financial statements.

Stage Two

The second stage involves the group's management consolidating the financial statements of each component entity. The group auditor needs to obtain an understanding of the consolidation process to ensure that the process has been followed correctly in accordance with the relevant financial reporting framework. For example, IAS 27 'Consolidated and Separate Financial Statements' governs the consolidation process for subsidiaries for those entities reporting under IFRS. The group auditor shall communicate clearly with component auditors about the scope and timing of their work on the financial information related to components and their findings [ISA600.8(b)(i)].

Stage Three

The third and final process involves the group auditor obtaining sufficient appropriate audit evidence regarding the financial information of the components as well as the consolidation process with the objective of forming and expressing an opinion on whether the group's financial statements are prepared, in all material respects, in accordance with the applicable reporting framework [ISA600.8(b)(ii)].

ACCEPTANCE AS GROUP ENGAGEMENT PARTNER

ISA 315 requires auditors to gain an understanding of an entity and the environment in which it operates. Group audits are no exception and invariably involve obtaining a greater depth of understanding because of the component parts of the group. ISA 220 is particularly relevant and should be applied by the group engagement partner in determining whether sufficient appropriate audit evidence can reasonably be expected to be obtained in relation to both the consolidation process and the financial information of the components on which to base the audit opinion [ISA600.12]. For these reasons, the group engagement team needs to obtain an understanding of the group, its components and the environment in which they operate. It follows, therefore, that it is vital the group auditor has a good understanding of the structure of the group and the materiality of each of its components.

If the group engagement partner concludes that sufficient appropriate audit evidence cannot be obtained due to the limitations imposed by group's management, which will result in a potential disclaimed opinion being expressed, then the group engagement partner must decline acceptance of the engagement. If the engagement is a continuing engagement then the auditor shall resign [ISA600.13].

In situations where domestic legislation or other regulation prohibits the auditor from resigning from a continuing engagement, the auditor shall express a disclaimed opinion on the group's financial statements [ISA600.13].

OBTAINING AN UNDERSTANDING OF THE GROUP, ITS COMPONENTS AND THE ENVIRONMENT IN WHICH THEY OPERATE

The group engagement team must gain a thorough understanding of the group, its component entities and the environment in which they operate in order to ensure that they can identify areas where material misstatement is likely to arise and undertake their risk assessment. Obtaining such an understanding involves the engagement team understanding the group-wide internal control systems which can be obtained either at the initial engagement stage or by reviewing prior year working papers. The engagement team is also required to understand the consolidation process and the instructions from group management to component entities.

An understanding of the consolidation process is a fundamental aspect of group financial statements and as such the group engagement team shall also obtain an understanding of the instructions issued by group management to its components. The auditor should undertake tests of group-wide controls to ensure their operating effectiveness where the auditor has concluded internal controls operate effectively, or where the auditor has concluded that substantive procedures alone would not provide sufficient appropriate audit evidence at the assertion level.

The group engagement team are compelled to approach and undertake the group audit assignment with a degree of professional scepticism. This is particularly the case when the group engagement team considers the consolidation adjustments and any associated reclassifications, which may give rise to material misstatement in the group financial statements due to fraud or error.

In obtaining an understanding of the group, its components and the environment in which they operate, the auditor needs to identify and assess the risks of material misstatement. Obtaining an understanding of such groups and their components will often be more in depth than with a 'stand-alone' audit client because the auditor needs to consider the controls in place across the whole of the group. The auditor shall also gain an understanding of the consolidation process and the instructions issued to management.

The group engagement team shall establish an overall group audit strategy and develop a group audit plan in accordance with ISA 300 [ISA600.15]. In addition, the group engagement partner shall review the overall group audit strategy and group audit plan [ISA600.16].

In a lot of cases, the principal auditor will use the work of other auditors in auditing the group. Where principal auditors use the work of other component auditors, the principal auditors shall consider the professional competence of the other auditor in the context of the specific assignment. Specifically the auditor will consider whether the component auditor has the necessary skills and technical competence in order to carry out the audit work effectively. Professional qualifications on their own may not necessarily mean that a component auditor has the necessary technical competences that are required to carry out the assignment. Moreover, a technically competent and qualified component auditor may also not possess the degree of skills and knowledge which the component entity requires, and in some instances the auditor may also require the use of experts.

Where principal auditors employ the services of other component auditors, the principal auditor shall perform procedures to enable the principal auditor to conclude whether, or not, the work of the other auditor is adequate for the principal auditor's purposes. Factors which the principal auditor needs to address with the other auditor are:

- Independence issues.
- Whether the other auditor will comply with ethical guidelines.
- How the work of the other auditor will be used.
- The accounting and auditing requirements of the component entity — in particular areas requiring special consideration (key risks, control environment).
- Timescales for performing and completing the work.
- Whether the other auditor has the resources available to enable an effective audit to be carried out.

Component auditors have sole responsibility for their audit opinion on the financial statements of the component they audit. They must not rely on the principal auditors informing them of matters which might have an impact on the financial statements of the component. If they wish to do so, they shall seek representations directly from management, or, where applicable, those charged with governance of the entity audited by the principal auditors.

The principal auditors have no obligation to provide information to other auditors. Where, during the course of their audit, they discover matters which they consider may be relevant to the other auditors' work; they shall discuss and agree on the appropriate course of action with those charged with governance. This may involve the principal auditors communicating directly with the other auditors, management or those charged with governance.

If the circumstances are such that the information cannot be passed to the other auditors, for example, due to sensitive commercial considerations, the principal auditors should take no further action. To divulge such information in these situations would be a breach of client confidentiality.

In situations where the component auditor is deemed not to be independent or where there are concerns about the component auditor's technical competence or understanding, the group engagement team will obtain sufficient appropriate audit evidence on the component's financial information without requesting the other auditor to perform work on the financial information of the component entity.

At all stages during the audit assignment, the component auditor must co-operate with the principal auditor and advise the principal auditor as soon as is reasonably practicable of any limitations on their work which they encounter. In addition, where the component auditor encounters issues which may require reporting to legal or regulatory bodies, they should communicate these matters to the principal auditor as soon as is reasonably practicable.

MATERIALITY

Materiality must be assessed where audit opinions are to be expressed and group audits will require materiality to be determined for the group financial statements as a whole at the time the audit strategy is being developed. In addition, component materiality shall also be determined by component auditors having regard to the risk assessment. In order to ensure the aggregate of uncorrected and undetected misstatements in the group's financial statements does not exceed the materiality level for the group financial statements as a whole, component materiality levels must be set lower than the materiality level for the group financial statements as a whole. In audits where components are deemed 'insignificant' the audit engagement partner shall undertake analytical procedures at group level [ISA600.21].

In situations where the engagement team conclude that sufficient appropriate audit evidence cannot be obtained from the work performed on the financial statements of components that are deemed 'insignificant' components, the work undertaken on the internal controls of insignificant components and the analytical procedures performed at group level, the auditor shall:

- Perform, or request a component auditor to perform, an audit on the component's financial information using component materiality.
- Perform an audit of one or more account balances, classes of transaction or disclosure.
- Undertake a review of the financial information of the component using component materiality.
- Devise specific procedures that will allow sufficient appropriate audit evidence to be obtained.

For all entities within the group, the group auditor shall review a report of the work done by the component auditor, regardless of materiality. After reviewing the work of the component auditor, the group auditor will then ascertain the extent of any further actions which need to be taken, or any further work which needs to be carried out, in order to ensure that the financial statements are free from material misstatement. Factors that the group auditor will ordinarily consider are:

- A review of the component auditor's working papers.
- Performing a risk assessment at component entity level.
- Participating in closing meetings with the component auditor and the management of the company.
- Reviews of the relevant parts of the component auditor's audit working papers.

Where the group auditor considers that additional work is necessary, the group auditor should determine the nature of the work necessary, and whether the work should be carried out by the group or component auditor.

SUBSEQUENT EVENTS

The group engagement team must consider any events that have occurred between the reporting date and the date of approval of the financial statements and the signing of the auditor's report, and as such the auditor is required to design and implement audit procedures that are designed to identify such events. In addition, where the principal auditor uses the services of component auditors, the principal auditor should request that the component auditor notifies the group engagement team if they become aware of any subsequent events that may require adjustment or disclosure within the financial statements.

Illustration

Group Audit with Going Concern Issue

Sarvonia Group owns three subsidiary entities all of which trade in the same industrial sector. One of the subsidiary's in the group has suffered a significant loss during the year and this is now the second year in which the same subsidiary has reported a heavy loss. The loss has been sustained due to the loss of two key customers. The subsidiary company in question has been deemed a going concern by management on the basis that the group will continue to support the subsidiary financially until such time as the entity returns to profit.

The above illustration would ordinarily require the auditor to obtain a 'support letter' from the group's management. It is sometimes the case that a subsidiary, when considered in isolation, does not appear to be a going concern. In the context of group financial statements, the parent and the subsidiary are seen to be a complete, single reporting entity, so if the group as a whole is a going concern, that is sufficient. However, the component auditor will need assurance that the subsidiary, in isolation, is a going concern. In such a case, the component auditor may request a support letter (also referred to as a 'comfort letter') from the management. This letter states that the intention of the parent is to continue to support the subsidiary, which makes it a going concern.

CONSOLIDATING SUBSIDIARIES REPORTING UNDER ALTERNATIVE GAAP

Consolidating a subsidiary from a developing country may be a problem for host countries as the basis of preparation of the subsidiary's financial statements may be so different to the parent's GAAP that the principal auditor will not be able to conclude that the financial statements present the entity's financial statements fairly. This is only a problem if the financial statements, or the differences caused by the basis of preparation are material to the group.

The problem can be averted by asking management and those charged with governance to restate the accounts under the parent's GAAP. The principal auditors might require that this restatement process is audited to ensure that it is accurate. However, the modern auditing profession is finding such difficulties easier to overcome with the increased internationalisation of accounting practices.

COMMUNICATION

Timely communication of the group engagement team's requirements to the component auditor shall take place. This communication must set out the work to be performed, the use to be made of that work and the form and content of the component auditor's communication with the group engagement team. It must include:

- A request that the component auditor will communicate with the group.
- The ethical and independence requirements relevant to the group.

- In the case of an audit or review of the financial information of the component, component materiality and, where applicable, materiality level(s) for particular classes of transactions, account balances or disclosures, together with the threshold above which misstatements cannot be regarded as 'clearly trivial'.
- Significant risks of material misstatement that have been identified in the group's financial statements due to fraud or error that is relevant to the work of the component auditor. It is also a requirement that the group engagement team will request the component auditor to communicate on a timely basis any other identified significant risks of material misstatement of the group financial statements, due to fraud or error, in the component, and the component auditor's responses to such risks.
- A list of related parties prepared by the group's management plus any related parties of which the group engagement team are aware. The group engagement team shall also request the component auditor to communicate to them, on a timely basis, related parties that have not previously been identified by the group engagement team. The group engagement team must also determine whether to identify such additional related parties to other component auditors. [ISA600.40]

At the conclusion of the group audit, the group engagement team will request the component auditor to communicate:

- Whether the component auditor has complied with all ethical and independence requirements as well as professional competences relevant to the group audit.
- Whether the component auditor has complied with the group engagement team's requests.
- Identification of the financial information of the component which the component auditor is reporting.
- Information on instances of non-compliance with laws and regulations that could give rise to material misstatement of the group's financial statements.
- A list of uncorrected misstatements of the financial information of the component which need not include misstatements which are below the threshold for clearly trivial misstatements.
- Indicators of possible management bias.
- A description of identified significant deficiencies in internal controls at component level.
- Other significant matters that the component auditor has communicated, or expects to communicate, to those charged with governance of the component, including fraud or suspected fraud involving component management employees who have significant roles in internal control at component level, or others where fraud resulted in material misstatement of the financial information of the component.
- Other matters which may be relevant to the group audit or that the component auditor wishes to draw to the attention of the group engagement team.
- The component auditor's overall findings, conclusions or opinion. [ISA600.41]

PROCEDURES FOR PLANNING AND UNDERTAKING GROUP AUDITS

- Establish if consolidated financial statements are required.
- Obtain and document an understanding of the group, its components and their activities.
- Ensure adequate documentation of the consolidation process is present.
- Agree the terms of the group audit engagement and issue a letter of engagement.

- Ensure the group engagement letter states that restrictions on:

  - the group auditor's access to component information, management or other auditors; or
  - the work to be performed which are imposed after the group auditor's acceptance of the engagement constitute a scope limitation that may affect the group audit opinion.

- Send out a group letter of instruction to each component auditor advising group auditors of all necessary requirements.
- Ensure letter of instruction to component auditors includes timetable for completing audit and details and dates for meeting with group auditors and management.
- Request confirmation from component auditors that they will:

  - Co-operate with the group engagement team.
  - Confirm their compliance with ethical and independence requirements.
  - Notify group auditor of any ethical or independence problems.
  - Advise the group auditor of materiality levels.
  - Advise on a timely basis of the risk of any fraud and error and its impact and also details of any fraud and error discovered.
  - Provide details of any related parties not previously identified.
  - Confirm the group engagement team's requirements will be complied with.
  - Provide information on instances of non-compliance with laws or regulations.
  - Provide a list of uncorrected misstatements and errors.
  - Provide indicators of possible management bias.
  - Provide indicators of going concern problems.
  - Provide a description of any identified material weaknesses in internal control.

- Ensure that an appropriate materiality level has been set for the group as a whole and for the individual components in the group.
- Ensure that there is adequate documentation of risk and the internal controls within the group.
- Establish and document which components within the group are significant and which are not.
- For non-significant components ensure that as a minimum, analytical procedures have been undertaken. Consider if further work is necessary.
- For significant components decide what further audit procedures are needed to be carried out including review of working papers if appropriate.
- Assess whether audit evidence obtained at components is adequate and document how this assessment has been carried out.
- If audit evidence is deemed insufficient, document and perform additional procedures necessary to provide sufficient and appropriate audit evidence.
- Agree figures in the financial statements to the consolidation workings.
- Check arithmetical accuracy of consolidation and workings.
- Consider if basis for prior year consolidation entries is still appropriate.
- Verify reconciliation of the movements in:

  - reserves;
  - non-controlling interests;
  - investments; and
  - deferred tax.

- Ensure that all intra-group balances and transactions have been eliminated during the consolidation process.

- Ensure that any unrealised profit in inventory and non-current assets has been eliminated.
- Ensure any investments in subsidiaries have been eliminated, including the provision for losses.
- Ensure that consistent accounting policies have been adopted throughout the group.
- Ensure that if dividends have been passed between entities within the group, that the pre-acquisition element has been correctly treated.

PROCEDURES FOR COMPLETION OF GROUP AUDITS

- Ensure appropriate work is carried out on the consolidation process. This should involve reviewing the instructions issued by group management to the components.
- Communicate any weaknesses identified in internal controls to group management.
- Ensure that there is communication with those charged with governance of the group. This should cover all the matters required by ISA 260 (revised and redrafted) and each of the following:
  - Overview of the type of work to be performed.
  - Overview of group auditors' planned involvement in work of component auditors.
  - Concerns over quality of any component auditor's work.
  - Any limitations on the group audit.
  - Any fraud or suspected fraud identified.
- Evaluate the adequacy of the work performed by the component auditor.
- Establish impact of any matters arising on the group audit report and group financial statements.
- Consider the effect of each component auditor's memorandum or report of work performed on the group audit.
- Ensure each component auditor's letter has been received and follow up non-replies.
- Ensure appropriate subsequent events work has been performed for all group components and the group as a whole.
- Ensure appropriate going concern work has been performed for all group components and the group as a whole.
- Ensure no evidence has come to light which would impact on the firm continuing as group auditors.

Chapter Roundup

The group auditor needs to establish that it is appropriate to act in the capacity of group auditor.

The group auditor also needs to ensure that sufficient appropriate audit evidence is gathered to support the opinion contained in the consolidated financial statements of the group.

Principal auditors should ensure other auditors comply with the provisions of ISA 220 as well as ethical and independence requirements, and that other auditors have the specific levels of skills and competence required to carry out the audit work effectively.

An understanding of the group and the environment in which it operates by the group engagement team, including group-wide controls, and the consolidation process is required.

In obtaining their understanding of the group, the group engagement team needs to identify and assess the risks of material misstatement.

Principal auditors have no obligation to provide information to other auditors. Where principal auditors discover matters relevant to other auditor's work, the principal auditors will discuss and agree on an appropriate course of action with those charged with governance.

Where component auditors are deemed not to be independent, or where concerns are present about the component auditor's technical competence, the group engagement team will obtain sufficient appropriate audit evidence on the component's financial statements.

Component materiality must be assessed by component auditors.

Where components are deemed 'insignificant', the audit engagement partner must undertake analytical procedures at group level.

For all entities within the group, the group auditor shall review a report of the work done by the component auditor, regardless of materiality.

The group engagement team must consider subsequent events and design and implement audit procedures which are designed to identify such events.

Various communications should take place between the group engagement team and the component auditor.

30 ISA 610 (REDRAFTED) USING THE WORK OF INTERNAL AUDITORS

ISA 610 deals with the auditor's responsibilities in relation to using the work of internal auditing. ISA 610 contains the following definitions which are relevant to this auditing standard:

Internal Audit Function

An appraisal activity established or provided as a service to the entity. Its functions include, amongst other things, examining, evaluating and monitoring the adequacy and effectiveness of internal control.

[ISA610.7 (a)]

Internal Auditors

Those individuals who perform the activities of the internal audit function. Internal auditors may belong to an internal audit department or equivalent function.

[ISA610.7 (b)]

The auditor will determine when, and to what extent, the work of internal auditing will be used. The primary reason that the auditor will want to use the work of internal auditing is if it will be adequate for the purposes of the external audit. Where the external auditors consider that the work will be adequate for the purposes of the external audit, the external auditors will determine the effect this work will have on the nature, timing and extent of their audit procedures.

The external auditors will consider various factors in determining whether the work of internal auditing will be adequate for the external audit. Such factors are:

- The objectivity of the internal audit function.
- The technical competence of the internal auditors.
- Whether the work has been performed with due care and skill.
- Whether there is likely to be effective communication between the internal auditors and the external auditors. [ISA610.9]

RELATIONSHIP BETWEEN INTERNAL AND EXTERNAL AUDITORS

The role of internal auditing is determined by management and is primarily concerned with:

- The monitoring of internal controls and recommending improvements thereto.
- Examination of financial and operating information.
- Review of the economy, efficiency and effectiveness of operations.
- Review of compliance with laws and regulations.

ROLE OF INTERNAL AND EXTERNAL AUDITORS

The roles and objectives of internal auditors differ from those of external auditors. Internal auditors are very much concerned with management's requirements and the internal control processes, and they play a key role in corporate governance, providing objective assurance on control and risk management. The external auditors' objectives are to form an independent opinion on the financial statements. Internal auditors, by definition, cannot, therefore, achieve the same degree of independence and objectivity, but that is not to say that the work of internal auditing cannot contribute to sufficient appropriate audit evidence being obtained by the external auditor.

The structure of an internal auditing function is often as follows:

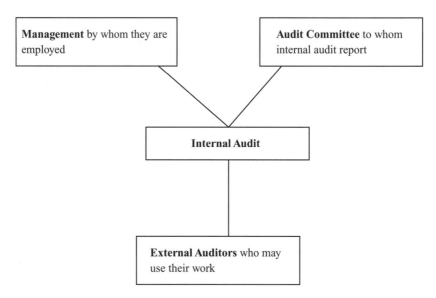

The differences between internal and external audit can be summarised as shown in Table 30.1.

Table 30.1   Differences between internal and external audit

	Internal Audit	*External Audit*
Reason	An activity designed to add value and improve an organisation's operations.	An exercise to enable auditors to express an opinion on the financial statements.
Reporting to	Internal auditors report to the board of directors, or other people charged with governance, such as the audit committee.	The external auditors report to the shareholders, or members, of a company on the stewardship of the directors.
Relating to	As demonstrated in the reason for their existence, internal audit's work relates to the operations of the organisation.	External audit's work relates to the financial statements. They are concerned with the financial records that underlie these.
Relationship with the entity	Internal auditors are very often employees of the organisation, although sometimes the internal audit function is outsourced.	External auditors are independent of the entity and its management. They are appointed by the shareholders.

OBTAINING AN UNDERSTANDING OF INTERNAL AUDITING

ISA 315 requires the auditor to obtain an understanding of the entity and the environment in which it operates. This is also the case where the entity has an internal audit function as the external auditor shall obtain a sufficient understanding of internal control activities to identify and assess the risks of material misstatement of the financial statements and design and perform further audit procedures.

In obtaining an understanding of the role of internal auditing, the auditor should consider:

- The organisational status and the reporting lines specific to internal auditing.
- Scope of the internal audit function.
- The technical competence of internal auditing staff.
- Whether internal auditing staff perform their work with due professional care.

It could possibly be the case that when the auditor has obtained an understanding of the role of internal audit they consider there to be no effect on their work. However, in cases where the auditor has used the work of internal auditing, the auditor needs to evaluate:

- Whether the work performed by internal auditing has been performed by persons having the relevant technical skills and competence.
- Whether sufficient appropriate audit evidence has been gathered to allow the external auditor to draw reasonable conclusions.
- Whether conclusions have been reached and are appropriate in the circumstances.
- Any exceptional or unusual matters which have been communicated to the external auditors by internal auditing have been resolved satisfactorily.
- The objectivity of internal auditing.
- Whether the work has been carried out with due professional care.

COMMUNICATION

It is more effective when internal auditing are free to communicate with external auditors as this allows the external auditor to have access to information which may allow external auditors to notify internal auditing of any significant matters which may affect them. It will also allow internal auditing to notify the external auditors of matters which may affect the external audit.

DOCUMENTATION

Where the external auditors use specific work of the internal auditors, the external auditor must document the conclusions reached concerning the evaluation of the adequacy of the work of the internal auditors.

Chapter Roundup

Internal auditors are concerned with the internal functions of the organisation. They exist to add value and improve an organisation's operations.

The role of internal audit may be outsourced.

The external auditors shall consider whether any reliance placed on the work of internal audit will be adequate for the purpose of the external audit, and determine the effect this work will have on the nature, timing and extent of the audit procedures.

Various factors must be considered by the external auditor in determining whether the work of internal audit will be adequate for the external audit.

Open communication between internal and external auditors will be more effective in identifying matters which may affect both internal and external auditors.

The auditor shall document the conclusions reached concerning the evaluation of the adequacy of the work of the internal auditors.

31 ISA 620 (REVISED AND REDRAFTED) USING THE WORK OF AN AUDITOR'S EXPERT

ISA 620 (revised and redrafted) outlines the auditor's responsibilities concerning the use of an auditor's expert in the context of auditing.

Auditors will often use auditor's experts in certain fields in an attempt to obtain sufficient appropriate audit evidence relating to a specific financial statement area. For example, where an entity has a defined benefit pension scheme, the auditor may need to consider appointing an auditor's expert to verify the actuarial information relating to the valuations placed on the pension scheme because the auditor will not be technically trained to undertake such valuations. Examples of other situations where the auditor may need to use the work of an auditor's expert are:

- Valuations of certain types of assets, for example land and buildings.
- Determination of quantities or physical condition of assets.
- The measurement of work completed and to be completed on construction contracts.
- Legal opinions.

When using the work performed by an expert, the auditor should obtain sufficient appropriate audit evidence that such work is adequate for the purposes of the audit. The auditor has a responsibility to form an opinion on the financial statements and simply by using experts in various areas of the audit does not eliminate any of this responsibility. An expert may be engaged by:

- A client to provide specialist advice on a particular matter which affects the financial statements.
- The auditor in order to obtain sufficient appropriate audit evidence regarding certain financial statement assertions.

ISA 620 contains the following definitions:

Auditor's Expert

An individual or organisation possessing expertise in a field other than accounting or auditing, whose work in that field is used by the auditor in obtaining sufficient appropriate audit evidence. An auditor's expert may be either an auditor's internal expert (who is a partner or staff, including temporary staff, of the auditor's firm or a network firm), or an auditor's external expert.

[ISA620.6(a)]

Expertise

Skills, knowledge and experience in a particular field.

[ISA620.6(b)]

Management's Expert

An individual or organisation possessing expertise in a field other than accounting or auditing, whose work in that field is used by the entity to assist the entity in preparing the financial statements.

[ISA620.6(c)]

APPOINTMENT OF AN EXPERT

Written instructions are normally issued which should outline the following (note, the list is not exhaustive and each particular audit may require additional instructions):

- The objective and scope of the expert's work.
- A general outline as to the specific matters the expert's report is to cover.
- The intended use of the expert's work; including the possible communication to third the parties of the expert's identity and extent of involvement.
- The extent of the expert's access to appropriate records and files.
- Information regarding the assumptions and methods intended to be used by the expert and their consistency with those used in prior periods.

In evaluating the work undertaken by an expert, the auditor shall consider various factors such as:

- The technical competence of the expert.
- The independence and objectivity of the expert.
- The professional qualifications of the expert.
- The experience and reputation in the field in which the auditor is seeking sufficient appropriate audit evidence.

When considering whether to use the work of an expert, the auditor should review:

- The importance of the matter being considered in the context of the financial statements.
- The risk of misstatement based on the nature and complexity of the matter.
- The quantity and quality of other available audit evidence.

EVALUATING THE WORK OF AN AUDITOR'S EXPERT

In evaluating the work of an auditor's expert, the auditor should assess whether the substance of the expert's findings is properly reflected in the financial statements or supports the financial statement assertions. In evaluating the work the auditor should pay specific attention to:

- The source data used.
- The assumptions and methods used.
- When the expert carried out the work.

- The reasons for any changes in assumptions and methods.
- The results of the expert's work in the light of the auditor's overall knowledge and understanding of the client and the results of other audit procedures.

Auditors do not have the expertise to judge the assumptions and methods used; these are the responsibility of the auditor's expert. However, the auditors shall seek to obtain an understanding of these assumptions, to consider their reasonableness based on other audit evidence, knowledge of the business and so on. In many instances, the auditor may test the source data. In cases where the source data are highly complex or technical, the auditor's expert may test the source data. The auditor can adopt alternative procedures such as inquiry or supervision or review of the expert's tests to evaluate the data's relevant, completeness and accuracy [ISA620.A39].

Where inconsistencies arise between the auditor's expert's work and other audit evidence, the auditors shall attempt to resolve them by discussion with both the entity and the expert. Additional audit procedures may also be necessary.

Where the auditor concludes that the audit evidence from the expert is insufficient and there are no other satisfactory alternative sources of evidence, the auditor shall express a modified opinion.

COMMUNICATION

ISA 620 discusses the issue of effective two-way communication and this concept is pivotal where the auditor uses the work of an auditor's expert. Effective two-way communication will enable proper integration of the nature, timing and extent of the auditor's expert's procedures. It is important to identify specific partners or staff who will liaise with the auditor's expert and deal with the communication matters between the auditor's expert and the entity.

Chapter Roundup

Auditors may use auditor's experts in attempts to obtain sufficient appropriate audit evidence relating to a specific financial statement area.

The auditor shall obtain sufficient appropriate audit evidence that such work is adequate for the purposes of the audit.

Using the work of an auditor's expert does not eliminate any of the auditor's other responsibilities in forming an opinion on the financial statements.

The auditor should consider various factors when evaluating the work of an auditor's expert.

Written instructions should be issued between the auditor and the auditor's expert regarding the work to be performed.

Where the auditor concludes the audit evidence from the auditor's expert is insufficient and there are no other satisfactory alternative sources of evidence, the auditor shall express a modified opinion.

32 ISA 700 (REVISED) FORMING AN OPINION ON THE FINANCIAL STATEMENTS

ISA 700 (revised) deals with the auditor's responsibilities to form an opinion on the financial statements of an entity as well as dealing with the form and content of the auditor's report. ISAs 705 and 706 deal specifically with the form and content of the auditor's report where the auditor expresses a modified opinion or includes an emphasis of matter paragraph.

The overall objective of an audit is to allow an external auditor to form an independent opinion on the financial statements and to conclude whether, or not, they present fairly, in all material respects, the state of the entity's affairs as at the reporting date. In forming their opinion, the auditor will evaluate the conclusions reached from the audit evidence obtained as well as forming an opinion as to whether the financial statements have been prepared in accordance with the applicable financial reporting framework (for example, under IFRS).

The principal matters which auditors consider in forming an opinion may be expressed in three questions:

- Have all procedures necessary to meet the International Standards on Auditing (ISAs) to obtain all the information and explanations necessary been completed?
- Have the financial statements been prepared in accordance with the applicable accounting requirements and under the appropriate financial reporting framework?
- Do the financial statements, as prepared by management, present fairly, in all material respects, the state of the entity's affairs at the reporting date?

The auditor's report should contain a clear written expression of opinion on the financial statements taken as a whole.

CONTENTS OF AN ISA STYLE AUDITOR'S REPORT

ISA 700 specifies the contents of an auditor's report which will ordinarily follow the following layout:

- Title.
- Addressee.
- Opening or introductory paragraph.
- Scope paragraph.
- Opinion paragraph.
- Date of the report.
- Auditor's address.
- Auditor's signature.

Some jurisdictions may also require the auditor's report to be signed in the auditor's own name. In the UK, section 503 of the Companies Act 2006 requires the auditor's report (where the auditor is an individual) to be signed by him or her.

Title

The auditor's report shall have an appropriate title. For example, the word 'independent' will often be required to be included so as to distinguish the auditor's report from other reports issued by the entity.

Addressee

The auditor's report should be appropriately addressed as required by the circumstances or by local guidelines. For example, in the UK, the auditor's report is usually addressed to the Shareholders (members) of an entity.

Opening or Introductory Paragraph

The auditor's report shall identify the financial statements being audited and contain a statement of the responsibility of the entity's management and the responsibility of the auditor.

Scope Paragraph

The auditor's report shall contain a reference to the ISAs, or relevant national standards or practices and a description of the work the auditor has performed.

Opinion Paragraph

This will contain reference to the financial reporting framework used to prepare the financial statements (for example, IFRS) and will also contain an expression of:

- an unqualified opinion;
- a qualified opinion;
- an adverse opinion; or
- a disclaimer of opinion.

We shall discuss these opinions later in the chapter.

Date of the Report

The auditor's report must be dated as this informs the user of the financial statements that the auditor has considered the effect of events and transactions of which the auditor has become aware that occurred up to that date.

Signature

The auditor's report must be signed by the auditor and can either be in the name of the audit firm, the personal name of the auditor or both. Different jurisdictions will have different rules in place for the signature.

In the UK it is mandatory for the auditor's report to be signed in the auditor's own name and they are referred to as the Senior Statutory Auditor.

Illustration

Unqualified Auditor's Report under ISA 700 (UK and Ireland)

Report of the Independent Auditors to the Shareholders of ABC Limited We have audited the financial statements of ABC Limited for the year ended 30 April 2009 on pages five to sixteen. These financial statements have been prepared under the accounting policies set out therein.

This report is made solely to the company's members, as a body, in accordance with Sections 495 and 496 of the Companies Act 2006. Our audit work has been undertaken so that we might state to the company's members those matters we are required to state to them in a Report of the Auditors and for no other purpose. To the fullest extent permitted by law, we do not accept or assume responsibility to anyone other than the company and the company's members as a body, for our audit work, for this report or for the opinions we have formed.

Respective Responsibilities of Director and Auditors The director's responsibilities for preparing the financial statements in accordance with applicable law and United Kingdom Accounting Standards (United Kingdom Generally Accepted Accounting Practice) are set out on pages two and three.

Our responsibility is to audit the financial statements in accordance with relevant legal and regulatory requirements and International Standards on Auditing (UK and Ireland).

We report to you our opinion as to whether the financial statements give a true and fair view and are properly prepared in accordance with the Companies Act 2006. We also report to you whether in our opinion the information given in the Report of the Directors is consistent with the financial statements.

In addition we report to you if, in our opinion, the company has not kept proper accounting records, if we have not received all the information and explanations we require for our audit, or if information specified by law regarding director's remuneration and other transactions is not disclosed.

We read the Report of the Director and consider the implications for our report if we become aware of any apparent misstatements within it.

Basis of Audit Opinion We conducted our audit in accordance with International Standards on Auditing (UK and Ireland) issued by the Auditing Practices Board. An audit includes examination, on a test basis, of evidence relevant to the amounts and disclosures in the financial statements. It also includes an assessment of the significant estimates and judgements made by the director in the preparation of the financial statements, and of whether the accounting policies are appropriate to the company's circumstances, consistently applied and adequately disclosed.

We planned and performed our audit so as to obtain all the information and explanations which we considered necessary in order to provide us with sufficient evidence to give reasonable assurance that the financial statements are free from material misstatement, whether caused by fraud or other irregularity or error. In forming our opinion we also evaluated the overall adequacy of the presentation of information in the financial statements.

Opinion   In our opinion:

the financial statements give a true and fair view, in accordance with United Kingdom Generally Accepted Accounting Practice, of the state of the company's affairs as at 30 April 2009 and of its profit for the year then ended;
the financial statements have been properly prepared in accordance with the Companies Act 2006; and
the information given in the Report of the Director is consistent with the financial statements.

John Smith (Senior Statutory Auditor)[1]
For and on behalf of
Smith & Co
Chartered Certified Accountants and
Registered Auditors
123 King Street
Any town
Any country

Date: 31 July 2009

[1]In some jurisdictions, for example, the UK, the auditor is required to sign the auditor's report in their own name.

UNQUALIFIED (UNMODIFIED) OPINION

An unqualified audit opinion should be expressed by the auditor when the auditor concludes that the financial statements present fairly, in all material respects, the state of the entity's affairs as at the reporting date. In the illustration above, reference has been made to an unqualified audit opinion based on ISAs (UK and Ireland). The term 'true and fair' is equivalent to the phrase 'present fairly, in all material respects'. Both indicate, amongst other things, that the auditor considers only those matters that are material to the financial statements.

MATTERS THAT DO NOT AFFECT THE AUDITOR'S OPINION

In certain situations, cases may arise when certain circumstances are present within an entity, but which do not affect the opinion formed by the auditor. Such instances commonly give rise to an 'emphasis of matter'.

Matters that do not affect the auditor's opinion may be included in an emphasis of matter paragraph. Such paragraphs are ordinarily included after the opinion paragraph and would refer to the fact that the auditor's opinion is not qualified in this respect. Emphasis of matter paragraphs are discussed in Chapter 33.

MATTERS THAT DO AFFECT THE AUDITOR'S OPINION

There are three instances that will affect the auditor's opinion, which are:

- Qualified opinion.
- Adverse opinion.
- Disclaimer of opinion.

Such opinions can arise in situations where the auditor has a limitation on the scope of their audit work or where there is a disagreement with management or those charged with governance over the accounting policies selected and their application.

QUALIFIED OPINION

A qualified opinion should be expressed when the auditor concludes that an unqualified opinion cannot be expressed but that the effect of any disagreement with management, or limitation on scope is not so material and pervasive as to require an adverse opinion or a disclaimer of opinion. A qualified opinion should be expressed as being 'except for' the effects of the matter to which the qualification relates.

ADVERSE OPINION

An adverse opinion should be expressed when the effect of a disagreement is so material and pervasive to the financial statements that the auditor concludes that a qualified opinion is not adequate to disclose the misleading or incomplete nature of the financial statements.

Where auditors express opinions, other than unqualified opinions, they should include a description of the reasons for the qualification and, unless impracticable, a quantification of the possible effect(s) on the financial statements.

Illustration

Adverse Opinion

Report of the Independent Auditors to the Shareholders of Entity A Ltd   We have audited the financial statements of Entity A Limited for the year ended 31 December 2010 on pages five to thirteen. The financial reporting framework that has been applied in their preparation is applicable by law and the International Financial Reporting Standards.

This report is made solely to the company's members, as a body, in accordance with Chapter 3 of Part 16 of Companies Act 2006. Our audit work has been undertaken so that we might state to the company's members those matters we are required to state to them in a Report of the Auditors and for no other purpose. To the fullest extent permitted by law, we do not accept or assume responsibility to anyone other than the company and the company's members as a body, for our audit work, for this report or for the opinions we have formed.

Respective Responsibilities of Directors and Auditors   As explained more fully in the Statement of Directors' Responsibilities set out on page two, the directors are responsible for the preparation of the financial statements and for being satisfied that they present fairly, in all material respects, the state of the entity's affairs. Our responsibility is to audit the financial statements in accordance with applicable law and International Standards on Auditing. Those standards require us to comply with the Ethical Standards for auditors.

Scope of the Audit of the Financial Statements   An audit involves obtaining evidence about the amounts and disclosures in the financial statements sufficient to give reasonable assurance that the financial statements are free from material misstatement, whether caused by fraud or error. This includes an assessment of: whether the accounting policies are appropriate to the company's circumstances and have been consistently applied and adequately disclosed; the reasonableness of significant accounting estimates made by the directors; and the overall presentation of the financial statements.

Adverse Opinion   As more fully explained in Note XX of the financial statements, the company has not complied with the requirements of IAS 19 'Retirement Benefits' as the directors consider that the costs involved in obtaining the actuarial information in relation to the company's defined benefit pension scheme cannot be justified. In our opinion, the company's accounting policy with respect to the pension scheme should comply with the requirements of IAS 19. If the company's accounting policy had complied with these requirements, the financial statements would reflect, at fair value, the assets and liabilities arising from the pension scheme, the changes in these fair values and other disclosures relating to the scheme as required under IAS 19. In view of the effect of the failure of the company to comply with the requirements of IAS 19, as referred to above, in our opinion the financial statements do not present fairly, in all material respects, the state of the company's affairs as at 31 December 2010 and of its profit (loss) for the year then ended. In all other respects, in our opinion the financial statements have been properly prepared in accordance with [relevant legislation].

Opinion on Other Matter   In our opinion the information given in the Report of the Directors for the financial year for which the financial statements are prepared is consistent with the financial statements.

Matters on which we are Required to Report by Exception   We have nothing to report in respect of the following matters where the [insert relevant legislation] requires us to report to you if, in our opinion:

- Adequate accounting records have not been kept, or returns adequate for our audit have not been received from branches not visited by us;
- the financial statements are not in agreement with the accounting records and returns;
- certain disclosures of directors' remuneration specified by law are not made; or
- we have not received all the information and explanations we require for our audit.

John Smith (Senior Statutory Auditor)
For and on behalf of
Audit Firm LLP
123 Any Street
Any town

Date:.............

DISCLAIMER OF OPINION

A disclaimer of opinion should be expressed when the possible effect of a limitation on the scope of the auditor's work is so material and pervasive that the auditor has not been able to obtain sufficient appropriate audit evidence and accordingly is unable to express an opinion on the financial statements.

Illustration

Opinion Paragraph

Because of the possible effect of the limitation in evidence available to us, we are unable to form an opinion as to whether the financial statements present fairly, in all material respects, the state of the entity's affairs as at 31 December 2010 or of its profit (loss) for the year then ended. In all other respects, in our opinion the financial statements have been properly prepared in accordance with [relevant legislation].

Where auditors express opinions, other than unqualified opinions, they should include a description of the reasons for the qualification and, unless impracticable, a quantification of the possible effect(s) on the financial statements.

Chapter Roundup

ISA 700 deals with the form and content of the auditor's report.

ISAs 705 and 706 deal with the form and content of the auditor's report where the auditor expresses a modified opinion or includes an emphasis of matter paragraph.

The report should contain a clear expression of an opinion on the financial statements taken as a whole.

There are eight elements in the auditor's report.

The report shall express an: unqualified (unmodified), qualified (modified), adverse or disclaimer of opinion.

Matters that do not affect the auditor's opinion but which the auditor may wish to bring to users attention will be highlighted in an emphasis of matter paragraph.

33 ISA 705 (REVISED AND REDRAFTED) MODIFICATIONS TO THE OPINION IN THE INDEPENDENT AUDITOR'S REPORT

Modifications to the opinion in the independent auditor's report include:

- Qualified opinion.
- Adverse opinion.
- Disclaimer of opinion.

ISA 705 (revised and redrafted) deals with the auditor's responsibilities when they conclude that a modification to their opinion is required. Professional judgement is often used on the part of the auditor, particularly in circumstances such as a limitation on the scope of the audit work, because it is often difficult to judge the overall effect such a scope limitation may have on the financial statements as a whole.

ISA 705 requires that where the auditor concludes that, based on the audit evidence in their possession, the financial statements are not free from material misstatement, or where the auditor is unable to obtain sufficient appropriate audit evidence, the opinion expressed by the auditor is to be modified [ISA705.4].

One source of uncertainty is limitation in the scope of an audit. A scope limitation will arise where the auditor is unable, for any reason, to obtain all the information and explanations which are considered necessary for the purpose of the audit, arising from:

- Absence of proper accounting records.
- An inability to carry out audit procedures considered necessary as, for example, where the auditor is unable to obtain satisfactory evidence concerning the existence or ownership of material assets.

When giving this type of opinion, the auditor shall assess:

- The quantity and type of evidence which may reasonably be expected to be available to support the figures or disclosures in the financial statements.
- The possible effect on the financial statements of the matter for which insufficient audit evidence is available.

QUALIFIED OPINION

A qualified opinion should be expressed by the auditor when the auditor concludes that an unqualified opinion cannot be expressed but the limitation on scope or disagreement giving rise to the qualified opinion is not so material and pervasive to warrant an adverse or disclaimer of opinion. Typically, the auditor will express a qualified opinion when, having concluded that the evidence obtained constitutes sufficient appropriate audit evidence, the misstatements identified by the auditor during the course of their audit, in isolation or when aggregated with other misstatements, are material, but not pervasive, to the financial statements. In addition, where the auditor is unable to obtain sufficient appropriate audit evidence to base their opinion, but the auditor concludes that the effect of the misstatements are material but not pervasive, then a qualified opinion should be expressed.

ISA 705 defines 'pervasive' as:

> *a term used, in the context of misstatements, to describe the effects on the financial statements of misstatements or the possible effects on the financial statements of misstatements, if any, that are undetected due to an inability to obtain sufficient appropriate audit evidence. Pervasive effects on the financial statements are those, that in the auditor's judgement:*
>
> 1. *Are not confined to specific elements, accounts or items of the financial statements.*
> 2. *If so confined, represent, or could represent, a substantial proportion of the financial statements.*
> 3. *In relation to disclosures are fundamental to users' understanding of the financial statements.*

[ISA 705.5(a)]

DISAGREEMENT

Disagreements can arise through a variety of circumstances, but typically over:

- Inappropriate accounting policies.
- The facts or amounts included in the financial statements.
- The manner or extent of disclosure of facts or amounts in the financial statements.
- Failure to comply with relevant legislation or other requirements.

Illustration

Qualified Opinion Expressed

Qualified Opinion Arising from Disagreement Concerning Accounting Treatment
Included in the receivables shown on the statement of financial position is an amount of $89,000 due from an entity which has ceased trading. ABC Inc has no security for this debit. In our opinion the entity is unlikely to receive any payment and full provision of $89,000 should have been made, reducing profit before taxation and net assets by that amount.

Except for the absence of this provision, in our opinion:

> *the financial statements present fairly, in all material respects, of the state of the entity's affairs as at 31 December 2009 and of its profit for the year then ended.*

ADVERSE OPINION

An adverse opinion should be expressed when the effect of a disagreement is so material and pervasive to the financial statements that the auditor considers that a qualified opinion would be inadequate to disclose the misleading or incomplete nature of the financial statements. Essentially, the auditors are concluding that the financial statements do not present fairly, in all material respects, the state of the entity's affairs at the reporting date.

Illustration

Adverse Opinion Expressed

As more fully explained in note X to the financial statements, no provision has been made for losses expected to arise on certain long-term contracts currently in progress, as the directors consider that such losses should be off-set against amounts recoverable on other long-term contracts. In our opinion, provision should be made for foreseeable losses on individual contracts as required by IAS 11 'Construction Contracts'. If losses had been so recognised the effect would have been to reduce profit before and after tax for the year and the contract work in progress as at 31 December 2009 by $98,000.

In view of the effect of the failure to provide for the losses referred to above, in our opinion the financial statements do not present fairly, in all material respects, the state of the entity's affairs as at 31 December 2009 and of its profit (loss) for the year then ended. In all other respects, in our opinion the financial statements have been properly prepared in accordance with [state domestic legislation].

DISCLAIMER OF OPINION

A disclaimer of opinion is expressed when the auditor is unable to obtain sufficient appropriate audit evidence on which to base the opinion. The auditor concludes that the potential effects on the financial statements may be both material and pervasive.

Illustration

Disclaimer of Opinion

Opinion: Disclaimer on view given by the financial statements.

Because of the possible effect of the limitation in evidence available to us, we are unable to form an opinion as to whether the financial statements present fairly, in all material respects, the state of the company's affairs as at 31 December 2010 or of its profit (loss) for the year then ended. In all other respects, in our opinion the financial statements have been properly prepared in accordance with [insert legislation].

COMMUNICATION

When the auditor expects to modify their opinion in the auditor's report, the auditor shall communicate with those charged with governance the circumstances that led to the expected modification and the proposed wording of the modification [ISA705.28].

Chapter Roundup

Modifications to the auditor's opinion include: qualified (modified) opinion, adverse opinion and disclaimer of opinion.

A qualified opinion is expressed when the limitation on scope or disagreement is not so material and pervasive to warrant an adverse or disclaimer of opinion.

An adverse opinion is expressed when the effect of a disagreement is so material and pervasive to the financial statements that the auditor considers a qualified opinion would be inadequate to disclose the misleading or incomplete nature of the financial statements.

A disclaimer of opinion is expressed when the auditor is unable to obtain sufficient appropriate audit evidence on which to base the opinion and the possible effects on the financial statements may be both material and pervasive.

34 ISA 706 (REVISED AND REDRAFTED) EMPHASIS OF MATTER PARAGRAPHS AND OTHER MATTER(S) PARAGRAPHS IN THE INDEPENDENT AUDITOR'S REPORT

In certain audits, situations may arise which do not affect the auditor's opinion on the financial statements, but which the auditor may wish to highlight in the independent auditor's report. ISA 706 (revised and redrafted) details the auditors' responsibilities for such issues.

EMPHASIS OF MATTER PARAGRAPHS

An 'emphasis of matter' paragraph is usually included in the financial statements when there is significant uncertainty about a situation(s), the outcome of which is dependent on future occurrences. A typical example of where there may be significant uncertainty is in respect of going concern. An entity may determine the going concern basis appropriate in the circumstances, and the auditors may well agree, but there could still well be uncertainty concerning the entity's ability to continue beyond the foreseeable future.

ISA 706 defines an emphasis of matter paragraph as:

> *A paragraph included in the auditor's report that refers to a matter appropriately presented or disclosed in the financial statements that, in the auditor's judgement, is of such importance that it is fundamental to users' understanding of the financial statements.*
>
> [ISA706.5 (a)]

Ordinarily, an emphasis of matter paragraph is included, after the opinion paragraph, in the report of the auditor. It will discuss in more detail the issue(s) surrounding the requirement for the emphasis of matter paragraph and will cross reference the issue to the matter, which may have also been disclosed as a note to the financial statements. The emphasis of matter paragraph will also refer to the fact that the auditor's opinion is not qualified in respect of the matter giving rise to the emphasis of matter paragraph.

The auditor will determine whether an uncertainty is significant by considering matters such as:

- The risk that the estimate included in the financial statements may be subject to change.
- The range of possible outcomes.
- The consequences of those outcomes on the view shown in the financial statements.

A common example of a situation where significant uncertainty is inherent is in relation to litigation matters.

Illustration

Emphasis of Matter Paragraph ISAs (UK and Ireland)

Opinion

In our opinion:

1. The financial statements give a true and fair view, in accordance with United Kingdom Generally Accepted Accounting Practice, of the state of the company's affairs as at 30 April 2009 and of its profit for the year then ended.
2. The financial statements have been properly prepared in accordance with the Companies Act 2006.
3. The information given in the Report of the Director is consistent with the financial statements.

Emphasis of Matter

Without qualifying our opinion, we draw attention to Note X to the financial statements. The company is the defendant in a legal case in respect of a breach of contract. The company has filed a counter action, and preliminary hearings and discovery proceedings on both actions are in progress. The ultimate outcome of the matter cannot presently be determined, and no provision for any liability that may result has been made in the financial statements.

There are other situations that may warrant an emphasis of matter paragraph being included in the auditor's report. Ordinarily, going concern problems or significant uncertainties may warrant an emphasis of matter paragraph. However, where the auditor encounters multiple uncertainties that are significant to the financial statements, they may consider it appropriate to express a disclaimer of opinion instead of including an emphasis of matter paragraph. Emphasis of matters paragraphs may also be required when there are additional statutory reporting responsibilities.

Where the auditor encounters multiple uncertainties, then depending on the magnitude of the multiple uncertainties, the auditor may conclude that an emphasis of matter paragraph is not appropriate and may conclude that it would be appropriate to express a disclaimer of opinion.

OTHER RELEVANT ISAs

ISA 706 contains an appendix which identifies paragraphs of other ISAs that require an auditor to include an 'other matter' paragraph within the auditor's report. It identifies the following paragraphs:

*   ISA 560 'Subsequent Events' — paragraphs 12(b) and 16.
*   ISA 710 'Comparative Information — Corresponding Figures and Comparative Financial Statements' — paragraphs 13–14, 16–17 and 19.
*   ISA 720 'The Auditor's Responsibilities Relating to Other Information in Documents Containing Audited Financial Statements' — paragraph 10(a).

Chapter Roundup

An emphasis of matter paragraph is a matter that does not affect the auditor's opinion.

An emphasis of matter paragraph is included in the auditor's report underneath the opinion paragraph.

Fundamental uncertainties ordinarily give rise to emphasis of matter paragraphs.

Where the auditor encounters multiple uncertainties, they may conclude an emphasis of matter paragraph is inadequate and a disclaimer of opinion is more appropriate in the circumstances.

35 ISA 710 (REDRAFTED) COMPARATIVE INFORMATION — CORRESPONDING FIGURES AND COMPARATIVE FINANCIAL STATEMENTS

Many jurisdictions have size limits that decipher whether or not an entity's financial statements must be subject to statutory audit, or whether the entity's management can take advantage of exemptions that may be available which enable the entity to become exempt from statutory audit. In many cases these size limits can be breached, resulting in the entity having to be mandatorily subjected to statutory audit.

ISA 710 (redrafted) outlines the auditor's responsibilities when dealing with comparative information of such entities.

Where the prior period's financial statements were not audited the auditor needs to obtain sufficient appropriate audit evidence concerning the prior period's financial statements.

ISA 710 contains the following definitions:

Comparative Information

The amounts and disclosures in the financial statements in respect of one or more prior periods in accordance with the applicable financial reporting framework.

[ISA710.6 (a)]

Corresponding Figures

Comparative information where amounts and other disclosures for the prior period are included as an integral part of the current period financial statements, and are included as an integral part of the current period financial statements, and are intended to be read only in relation to the amounts and other disclosures relating to the current period (referred to as 'current period figures'). The level of detail presented in the corresponding amounts and disclosures is dictated primarily by its relevance to the current period figures.

[ISA710.6 (b)]

Comparative Financial Statements

Comparative information where amounts and other disclosures for the prior period are included for comparison and with the financial statements of the current period but, if audited, are referred to in the auditor's opinion. The level of information included in those comparative financial statements is comparable with that of the financial statements of the current period.

[ISA710.6(c)]

OBTAINING AUDIT EVIDENCE CONCERNING OPENING BALANCES

Initial Engagements

Incoming auditors need to obtain sufficient appropriate audit evidence concerning the opening balances if those opening balances are considered material to the financial statements. Obtaining sufficient and appropriate audit evidence on the opening balances depends on a number of factors, such as:

- The accounting policies followed by the entity.
- Whether the preceding period's financial statements were audited and, if so, whether the auditor's report was modified.
- The nature of the opening balances, including the risk of their misstatement.
- The materiality of the opening balances relative to the current period's financial statements.

The auditors shall evaluate whether the accounting policies of the prior period are consistent with those of the current period, whether appropriate adjustments and/or disclosures have been made, and establish whether the prior period figures presented agree with the amounts and other disclosures presented in the prior period or whether appropriate adjustments and disclosures have been made.

In many cases, entities will have been subjected to audit in the prior period but have subsequently chosen to replace their auditors for whatever reason. In these circumstances, auditors shall also refer to the guidance in ISA 510 'Initial Engagements — Opening Balances'.

The overall objective of ISA 710 is to ensure that the opening balances and comparatives are reasonably stated and the suggested procedures may include:

- Using the previous year's financial statements, agree the current year's comparatives and confirm that current accounting policies have been consistently applied.
- Review main balance sheet opening balances and consider the risk of material misstatement in the current period's financial statements due to error in the brought forward figures. Where risks are identified, consider how these risks could be mitigated.
- Carry out sufficient audit procedures to confirm that the comparatives are reasonable. Where this is not possible, consider disclosure in the audit report.

Continuing Audits

The extent of audit procedures for comparatives may be significantly less than those for current year balances; in many cases they will be limited to a check that balances have been correctly brought forward into the current year. Materiality of any misstatements should be considered in relation to the current year figures.

Prior Period Modification

In audits where the previous year's report was modified the auditor needs to determine whether the matter giving rise to the qualification in the previous year has been satisfactorily resolved. If this is the case, the auditor's opinion in the current period need not refer to the previous modification. Where the matter giving rise to the qualification matter is still unresolved, two situations may apply:

- If the matter is material in the context of the current period's opening balances as well as comparatives, the report on the current period's financial statement should be qualified regarding opening balances and comparatives.
- If the matter does not affect the opening balances, but is material in the context of the current period's financial statements, the report on the current period's financial statements should refer to the comparatives. If comparatives are required by law or regulation, the reference will be in the form of a qualification on the grounds of non-compliance with that requirement. If comparatives are presented solely as good practice, the reference should be in the form of an explanatory paragraph.

In practice, the main reason for incoming auditors to express a qualified audit opinion on the opening balances is in relation to the inventories figure. Ordinarily, where inventory is considered material to a set of financial statements, the auditor will attend the inventory count in order to decipher whether the procedures adopted by management will reduce the risk of material misstatement in relation to the closing inventories figure. In the succeeding financial year, this figure will obviously form the opening inventories figure at the beginning of the next period.

Situations arise where the auditor is unable to obtain sufficient appropriate audit evidence concerning the opening inventories because the audit firm had not been appointed until after that date.

Illustration

Qualified Audit Report on the Grounds of Opening Inventory (UK Example)

We have audited the accompanying balance sheet of XYZ Limited as at 31 December 2009, and the related statements of income and cash flows for the year then ended. These financial statements are the responsibility of the company's management. Our responsibility is to express an opinion on these financial statements based on our audit.

We conducted our audit in accordance with International Standards on Auditing [or refer to applicable national standards or practice]. Those standards require that we plan and perform the audit to obtain reasonable assurance about whether the financial statements are free of material misstatement. An audit includes examining, on a test basis, evidence supporting the amounts and disclosures in the financial statements. An audit also includes assessing the accounting principles used and significant estimates made by management, as well as evaluating the overall financial statement presentation. We believe that our audit provides a reasonable basis for our opinion.

Because we were appointed auditors of the Company during 2009, we were not able to observe the counting of the physical inventories at the beginning of that (period) or satisfy ourselves concerning those inventory quantities by alternative means. Since opening inventories enter into the determination of the results of operations, we were unable to determine whether adjustments to the results of operations and opening retained earnings might be necessary for 2008. Our audit report on the financial statements for the (period) ended (balance sheet date) 2008 was modified accordingly.

In our opinion, except for the effect on the corresponding figures for 2008 of the adjustments, if any, to the results of operations for the (period) ended 2008, which might have been determined to be necessary had we been able to observe beginning inventory quantities as at . . . , the financial statements give a true and fair view of (or 'present fairly in all material respects') the financial position of the company as at 31 December 2009, and of the results of its operations and its cash flows for the year then ended in accordance with . . . (and comply with).

Prior Period Financial Statements Not Audited

In situations where the previous period's financial statements were not audited, the auditor states in an other matter paragraph in the auditor's report that the corresponding figures are unaudited [ISA710.14].

The fact that the previous period's figures were unaudited does not relieve the auditor of the requirement to obtain sufficient appropriate audit evidence that the opening balances do not contain misstatements that materially affect the current period's financial statements [ISA710.14].

Prior Period Financial Statements Audited by Predecessor Auditor

Where prior period financial statements have been audited by a predecessor auditor, the successor auditor, in addition to expressing an opinion on the current period's financial statements, shall state in an other matter paragraph:

(a) The financial statements of the prior period were audited by a predecessor auditor.
(b) The type of opinion expressed by the predecessor auditor and, if the opinion was modified, the reasons.
(c) The date of that report.

Unless the predecessor's auditor's report on the prior period's financial statements is re-issued [ISA710.17].

If, during the course of their audit, the successor auditors discover a material misstatement which affects the prior period, the successor auditor will communicate the misstatement to management and those charged with governance and request that the predecessor auditor be informed. In the event that the financial statements are amended and the predecessor auditor issues a new report on the revised financial statements, the auditor needs only to report on the current period [ISA710.18].

SUGGESTED TESTS FOR OBTAINING SUFFICIENT APPROPRIATE AUDIT EVIDENCE CONCERNING OPENING BALANCES

Non-current (Fixed) Assets

- Ensure that the accounting policies in respect of non-current (fixed) assets have been applied consistently and those depreciation policies are appropriate and the opening values have been correctly brought forward into the current year.
- Obtain confirmation of cost of a sample of non-current (fixed) assets.
- Where non-current (fixed) assets are stated at valuation, obtain confirmation of the carrying value as at the reporting date.

Current Assets

- Where available, obtain written procedures issued to employees concerning the inventory count.
- Where inventory counting has been undertaken at a date other than the reporting date, undertake appropriate procedures (such as 'roll-back' procedures) to verify the completeness of the closing inventory figure.
- Where available, obtain sufficient appropriate audit evidence concerning the opening inventories figure.
- For receivables, review after date cash receipts to obtain sufficient appropriate audit evidence concerning the existence of the debts at the previous year end.
- For bank and cash balances, obtain the prior year bank reconciliation statements and a copy of the bank letter from the outgoing auditors, where access to previous auditors' working papers is permitted.

Current Liabilities

- For payables, undertake after date cash payments to establish the completeness of closing payables at the previous year end.
- For loans and other finance obligations, obtain sufficient appropriate audit evidence concerning the completeness of the liabilities and the accuracy of the disclosures split between current and non-current liabilities. Bank loans can be verified by reference to the bank audit letter where access to previous auditors' working papers is permitted.

Equity

- Obtain details of shareholding by reference to share certificates and evidence available on any public records (for example, in the UK details held at Companies House will be available as audit evidence).

Chapter Roundup

The overall objective is to ensure that the opening balances and comparatives do not contain material misstatement.

Where prior period financial statements were not audited, the auditor shall obtain sufficient appropriate audit evidence concerning the prior period's financial statements.

The extent of audit procedures for comparatives of recurring audits may be significantly less than for initial engagements.

Where the prior period report was modified, the auditor shall determine whether the matter giving rise to the qualification has been satisfactorily resolved.

Where prior period financial statements were not audited, this fact is stated in an other matter paragraph in the auditor's report.

If successor auditors discover a material misstatement which affects the prior period, the successor auditor will communicate the misstatement to management and those charged with governance and request the predecessor auditor is informed.

36 ISA 720 (REDRAFTED) THE AUDITOR'S RESPONSIBILITIES RELATING TO OTHER INFORMATION IN DOCUMENTS CONTAINING AUDITED FINANCIAL STATEMENTS

ISA 720 (redrafted) deals with the auditor's responsibilities relating to other information in documents which contain audited financial statements. For the purposes of this standard, a document containing audited financial statements refers to annual reports (or similar documents), that are issued to owners and other similar stakeholders, which contain audited financial statements and the auditor's report.

ISA 720 contains definitions as follows:

OTHER INFORMATION

Financial and non-financial information (other than the financial statements and the auditor's report thereon) which is included either by law, regulation or custom, in a document containing audited financial statements and the auditor's report thereon.

[ISA720.5 (a)]

INCONSISTENCY

Other information that contradicts information contained in the audited financial statements. A material inconsistency may raise doubt about the audit conclusions drawn from the audit evidence previously obtained and, possibly, about the basis for the auditor's opinion on the financial statements.

[ISA720.5 (b)]

MISSTATEMENT OF FACT

Other information that is unrelated to matters appearing in the audited financial statements that is incorrectly stated or presented. A material misstatement of fact may undermine the credibility of the document containing audited financial statements.

[ISA720.5(c)]

In some jurisdictions, the auditor may have statutory responsibilities which are beyond the scope of ISA 720. In these instances, the auditor must comply with their statutory responsibilities.

'Other information' within a set of audited financial statements may include items such as reports by management or those charged with governance, key performance indicators, financial ratios, financial highlights and information contained on an entity's website. The auditor's responsibility is to read the other information and determine whether there are any inconsistencies (material or otherwise).

MATERIAL INCONSISTENCIES AND MATERIAL MISSTATEMENTS OF FACT

Where the auditor discovers material inconsistencies when reading other information, the auditor will discuss the inconsistencies with management and should seek to resolve them. For example, it may be that the report of the directors is not consistent with the financial statements. If management refuse to revise the other information the auditor shall seek legal advice in respect of the inconsistency [ISA720.A6].

AMENDMENTS

If an amendment is necessary in the audited financial statements and the entity refuses to make the amendment, the auditor should express a qualified or adverse opinion.

If an amendment is necessary in the other information and the entity refuses to make such an amendment, the auditor shall consider highlighting the matter giving rise to the inconsistency in the other information in the auditor's report by way of an emphasis of matter paragraph.

Illustration

Auditors Report Referring to Other Information (UK and Ireland)

Report of the Independent Auditors to the Shareholders of XYZ Limited   We have audited the financial statements of XYZ Limited for the year ended 31 July 2010 on pages five to nineteen. These financial statements have been prepared under the accounting policies set out therein.

This report is made solely to the company's members, as a body, in accordance with Sections 495 and 496 of the Companies Act 2006. Our audit work has been undertaken so that we might state to the company's members those matters we are required to state to them in a Report of the Auditors and for no other purpose. To the fullest extent permitted by law, we do not accept or assume responsibility to anyone other than the company and the company's members as a body, for our audit work, for this report, or for the opinions we have formed.

Respective Responsibilities of Director and Auditors   The director's responsibilities for preparing the financial statements in accordance with applicable law and United Kingdom Accounting Standards (United Kingdom Generally Accepted Accounting Practice) are set out on page three.

Our responsibility is to audit the financial statements in accordance with relevant legal and regulatory requirements and International Standards on Auditing (UK and Ireland).

We report to you our opinion as to whether the financial statements give a true and fair view and are properly prepared in accordance with the Companies Act 2006. We also report to you whether in our opinion the information given in the Report of the Director is consistent with the financial statements.

In addition we report to you if, in our opinion, the company has not kept proper accounting records, if we have not received all the information and explanations we require for our audit, or if information specified by law regarding director's remuneration and other transactions is not disclosed.

We read the Report of the Director and consider the implications for our report if we become aware of any apparent misstatements within it.

Basis of Audit Opinion   We conducted our audit in accordance with International Standards on Auditing (UK and Ireland) issued by the Auditing Practices Board. An audit includes examination, on a test basis, of evidence relevant to the amounts and disclosures in the financial statements. It also includes an assessment of the significant estimates and judgements made by the director in the preparation of the financial statements, and of whether the accounting policies are appropriate to the company's circumstances, consistently applied and adequately disclosed.

We planned and performed our audit so as to obtain all the information and explanations which we considered necessary in order to provide us with sufficient evidence to give reasonable assurance that the financial statements are free from material misstatement, whether caused by fraud or other irregularity or error. In forming our opinion we also evaluated the overall adequacy of the presentation of information in the financial statements.

Opinion   In our opinion:

- The financial statements give a true and fair view, in accordance with United Kingdom Generally Accepted Accounting Practice, of the state of the company's affairs as at 31 July 2010 and of its profit for the year then ended.

The financial statements have been properly prepared in accordance with the Companies Act 2006.

The information given in the Report of the Director is consistent with the financial statements.

Chapter Roundup

'Other information' refers to both financial and non-financial information (other than the audited financial statements and the auditor's report thereon).

Other information can be included in documents containing audited financial statements by way of law, regulation or custom.

Material misstatements of fact in other information can undermine the credibility of the financial statements.

Auditors shall comply with their statutory responsibilities where these are beyond the scope of ISA 720.

The auditor must read the other information and determine if there are any inconsistencies (material or otherwise).

Material inconsistencies shall be discussed with management.

If management refuse to revise the other information, legal advice shall be sought by the auditor.

If amendments are necessary in the audited financial statements and management refuse to make the amendments, a qualified or adverse opinion will be expressed.

If amendments are necessary to other information and management refuse to make the amendment, the auditor shall consider highlighting the matter(s) giving rise to the amendment in an emphasis of matter paragraph.

37 ISA 800 (REVISED AND REDRAFTED) SPECIAL CONSIDERATIONS — AUDITS OF FINANCIAL STATEMENTS PREPARED IN ACCORDANCE WITH SPECIAL PURPOSE FRAMEWORKS

The objective of ISA 800 (revised and redrafted) 'Special Considerations — Audits of Financial Statements Prepared in Accordance with Special Purpose Frameworks' is to outline the requirements of the auditor in respect of an audit of financial statements which have been prepared in accordance with a special purpose framework.

ISA 800 contains definitions as follows:

Special Purpose Financial Statements

Special purpose financial statements are financial statements prepared in accordance with a special purpose framework.

[ISA 800 paragraph 6a]

Special Purpose Framework

A Special Purpose Framework is a financial reporting framework designed to meet the financial information needs of specific users. The financial reporting framework may be a fair presentation framework or a compliance framework.

[ISA80.6b]

Examples of a special purpose framework could be the requirements by a third party regulatory body to prepare financial statements in a prescribed format to meet regulatory requirements or another framework which departs from a generally recognised financial reporting framework such as IFRS.

REPORTING

The auditor's report on a set of financial statements prepared in accordance with a special reporting framework will need to contain an emphasis of matter paragraph to alert the user of the financial statements that the financial statements have been prepared in accordance with a special purpose framework. This emphasis of matter paragraph is necessary because it will inform the user of the financial statements which have been prepared in accordance with a special purpose framework that they may not be suitable for another purpose, such as deciding whether to invest in the entity that has prepared the financial statements in accordance with a special purpose framework. [ISA800.14]

ACCEPTANCE OF THE ENGAGEMENT

The auditor is obliged under ISA 210 'Agreeing the Terms of Audit Engagements' to determine whether the financial statements of an entity which are being subject to statutory audit have been prepared under an acceptable financial reporting framework [ISA800.8]. ISA 800, at paragraph 8 establishes the factors which the auditor is required to gain an understanding of, these are:

- The purpose for which the financial statements are prepared [ISA800.8a].
- The intended users [ISA800.8b].
- The steps taken by management to determine that the applicable financial reporting framework is acceptable in the circumstances [ISA800.8c].

PLANNING AND UNDERTAKING THE AUDIT OF AN ENTITY THAT HAS PREPARED THEIR FINANCIAL STATEMENTS UNDER A SPECIAL PURPOSE FRAMEWORK

All audits must be carried out in accordance with the provisions in the ISAs and the auditor should assess whether application of the ISAs requires special attention in the circumstances of the engagement [ISA800.9].

In all audits, the planning of the audit requires the auditor to gain an understanding of the entity and the environment in which it operates as well as an understanding of how the entity selects and applies its accounting policies. Where an entity has prepared its financial statements in accordance with a special purpose framework, the auditor needs to obtain an understanding of any significant interpretations of the contract that management made in the preparation of the financial statements [ISA800.10].

ISA 800 at paragraph 10 recognises that management's interpretation may be significant when adoption of another 'reasonable' interpretation may have produced financial statements which are materially different in light of the information presented in the financial statements.

FORMING AN OPINION

ISA 700 should be applied when the auditor forms an opinion and reports on special purpose financial statements. The requirements in ISA 700 states that the auditor shall evaluate whether the financial statements adequately refer to, or describe, the financial reporting framework used in the preparation of the financial statements. In cases where the financial statements have been prepared in accordance with the provisions of a contract, the auditor shall evaluate whether the financial statements adequately describe any significant interpretations of the contract on which the financial statements are based [ISA800.12].

ISA 700 stipulates the form and content of the auditor's report, but in the case of special purpose financial statements the auditor's report shall also describe the purpose for which the financial statements are prepared, where appropriate, the intended users, or refer to a note in the special purpose financial statements which contains such information [ISA800.13(a)]. In addition, where management have a choice of financial reporting frameworks in the preparation of such financial statements, the explanation of management's responsibility for the financial statements shall also make reference to its responsibility for determining that applicable financial reporting framework and whether it is acceptable in the circumstances [ISA800.13(b)].

EMPHASIS OF MATTER PARAGRAPHS

Where financial statements are prepared using a special purpose framework, the auditor's report shall make reference to the fact that the financial statements may not be suitable for another purpose by way of an emphasis of matter paragraph [ISA800.14].

Chapter Roundup

ISA 800 deals with financial statements prepared under a special purpose framework.

A special purpose framework is a framework designed to meet the financial information needs of specific users. The framework can be a fair presentation or compliance framework.

The auditor's report will need to contain an emphasis of matter paragraph to alert the user to the fact that the financial statements have been prepared in accordance with a special purpose framework.

ISA 800 requires the auditor to determine:

1. The purpose for which the financial statements are prepared.
2. The intended users.
3. The steps management have taken to determine that the applicable financial reporting framework is acceptable.

The auditor forms an opinion on the special purpose financial statements prepared under a special purpose framework having regard to the provisions in ISA 700.

---

38 ISA 805 (REVISED AND REDRAFTED) SPECIAL CONSIDERATIONS — AUDITS OF SINGLE FINANCIAL STATEMENTS AND SPECIFIC ELEMENTS, ACCOUNTS OR ITEMS OF A FINANCIAL STATEMENT

The auditor's objective when applying ISAs in an audit of single financial statements or of specific element, account or item of a financial statement is to address the special considerations which are relevant to:

1. The acceptance of the engagement.
2. Planning and performance of that engagement.
3. Forming an opinion and reporting on the single financial statement or on the specific element, account or item of a financial statement. [ISA805.5]

ISA 805 contains definitions which are applicable to this standard:

> *'Element of a financial statement' or 'element' means an 'element, account or item of a financial statement'.*
>
> [ISA805.6(a)]

> *'International Financial Reporting Standards' means the International Financial Reporting Standards issued by the International Accounting Standards Board.*
>
> [ISA805.6(b)]

A single financial statement or reference to a specific element of a financial statement includes the related notes. The related notes ordinarily comprise a summary of significant accounting policies and other explanatory information relevant to the financial statement or to the element. [ISA805.6(c)]

AUDITING A SINGLE FINANCIAL STATEMENT OR SPECIFIC ELEMENT

The provisions in ISA 200 'Overall Objectives of the Independent Auditor and the Conduct of an Audit in Accordance with International Standards on Auditing' require the auditor to comply with all ISAs which are relevant to a particular audit. In some cases, the auditor may not be engaged to audit the entity's complete set of financial statements and in such situations; the auditor must consider whether the audit of a single financial statement or of a specific element of the financial statements in accordance with ISAs is practicable [ISA805.7].

In addition, the auditor must also consider whether the financial reporting framework used in the preparation of the financial statements is acceptable. Where the auditor is auditing a single financial statement or a specific element of a financial statement, the auditor must consider whether the financial reporting framework used in the preparation will result in the information presented together with the disclosures being understood by the user [ISA805.8].

PLANNING

During the planning stage, the auditor will consider which ISAs are relevant to the particular engagement.

Illustration

An entity is a single entity with no group structure which does not utilise the services of any form of internal audit function.

In this respect, the auditor can ignore all the provisions in ISA 600 'Special Considerations — Audits of Group Financial Statements (Including the Work of Component Auditors)' and ISA 610 'Using the Work of Internal Auditors'). All other ISAs pertinent to the entity will, however, be relevant in their entirety.

REPORTING

ISA 700 'Forming an Opinion and Reporting on Financial Statements' must be applied when forming an opinion and reporting. ISA 700 must also be adapted as necessary in the circumstances of the engagement [ISA805.11].

The auditor must express separate opinions where they are engaged to report on a single financial statement or on a specific element of a financial statement in conjunction with an engagement to audit the entity's complete set of financial statements [ISA805.12].

Where single financial statement or an audited specific element of a financial statement is concerned, these may be published with the entity's audited complete set of financial statements. The auditor will ask management to rectify a situation where the presentation of a single financial statement or of the specific element of a financial statement does not differentiate it sufficiently from the complete set of financial statements [ISA805.13].

Where the auditor modifies their opinion, or includes an emphasis of matter paragraph within their report, the auditor will determine the effect such a modification or inclusion of an emphasis of matter paragraph has on a single financial statement or on the specific element of a financial statement. An emphasis of matter paragraph should also be included in the single financial statement or on a specific element of those financial statements accordingly [ISA805.14].

ADVERSE OR DISCLAIMER OF OPINION

Situations may arise when the auditor expresses an adverse or disclaimer of opinion on an entity's complete set of financial statements as a whole. In such circumstances, the auditor cannot express an unmodified opinion on a single financial statement that forms part of the complete set of financial statements or on a specific element that forms part of those financial statements. To do so would mean the adverse or disclaimer of opinion on the complete set of financial statements is contradicted [ISA805.15].

ISA 805 at paragraph 16 outlines the requirements where the auditor considers it necessary to express an adverse or disclaimed opinion on an entity's complete set of financial statements as a whole, but nevertheless considers an unmodified opinion appropriate on the audit of a specific element, the auditor shall only express an unmodified opinion if:

1. The auditor is not prohibited by law or regulation from doing so [ISA805.16(a)].
2. That opinion is expressed in an auditor's report that is not published together with the auditor's report containing the adverse opinion or disclaimer of opinion [ISA805.16(b)].
3. The specific element does not constitute a major portion of the entity's complete set of financial statements [ISA805.16(c)].

Illustration

An auditor who expresses an adverse or disclaimer of opinion on the complete set of financial statements of an entity as a whole cannot express an unmodified opinion on a single financial statement of a complete set of financial statements because single financial statements are deemed to be a major portion of a complete set of financial statements.

Chapter Roundup

Auditors can be engaged to report on a single financial statement or a specific element of a financial statement.

An 'element' is defined in ISA 805 as an 'element, account or item of a financial statement'.

Where the auditor is engaged to report on a specific element or single financial statement, the auditor shall consider whether such an audit in accordance with the ISAs is practicable.

The auditor shall also consider whether the financial reporting framework used in the preparation of the financial statements is acceptable.

Auditors of a single financial statement or an element shall consider whether the financial reporting framework used in the preparation of the single financial statement or element thereof will result in the information presented, and the associated disclosures, being understood by the users.

All ISAs relevant to a particular assignment will be adopted in their entirety.

Single audited financial statements or specific audited elements of financial statements may be published with the entity's audited complete set of financial statements.

Where the presentation of single financial statements or the specific element of a financial statement does not differentiate it sufficiently from the complete set of financial statements, the auditor shall request management rectify the situation.

Auditors shall determine the effect of a modified opinion or an emphasis of matter paragraph on a single financial statement or specific element.

An emphasis of matter paragraph should also be included in the single financial statement or on a specific element of those financial statements accordingly.

Adverse or disclaimer of opinion in the entity's complete set of audited financial statements will mean the auditor cannot express an unmodified opinion on a single financial statement that forms part of the entity's complete set of financial statements.

39 ISA 810 (REVISED AND REDRAFTED) ENGAGEMENTS TO REPORT ON SUMMARY FINANCIAL STATEMENTS

The objective of ISA 810 is to outline the auditor's responsibility on determining:

(a) Whether it is acceptable to accept appointment to report on summary financial statements [ISA810.3(a)].

(b) Where the auditor accepts appointment to report on summary financial statements:

   (i)   to form an opinion on the summary financial statements based on the evaluation of conclusions drawn from the evidence obtained [ISA810.3(b)]; and

   (ii) to express clearly that opinion through a written report that also describes the basis for that opinion [ISA810.3(c)].

ISA810, at paragraph 4 contains the following definitions relevant to this ISA:

Applied Criteria

The criteria applied by management in the preparation of the summary financial statements.

[ISA810.4(a)]

Audited Financial Statements

Financial statements audited by the auditor in accordance with ISAs, and from which the summary financial statements are derived.

[ISA810.4(b)]

Summary Financial Statements

Historical financial information that is derived from financial statements but that contains less detail than the financial statements, while still providing a structured representation consistent with that provided by the financial statements of the entity's economic resources or obligations at a point in time or the changes therein for a period of time. Different jurisdictions may use different terminology to describe such historical financial information.

[ISA810.4(c)]

ACCEPTANCE

The ISA requires the auditor to accept appointment to report on summary financial statements only when the auditor has been engaged to audit the financial statements in accordance with ISAs from which the summary financial statements have been derived [ISA810.5].

If the auditor has been engaged to audit the financial statements in accordance with ISAs, then before accepting engagement to report on the summary financial statements, the auditor shall:

- Determine whether the applied criteria are acceptable [ISA810.6(a)].
- Obtain the agreement of management that it acknowledges and understands its responsibility:

    (i)   for the preparation of the summary financial statements in accordance with the applied criteria [ISA810.6(b)(i)];
    (ii)   to make the audited financial statements available to the intended users of the summary financial statements without undue difficulty (or, if law or regulation provides that the audited financial statements need not be made available to the intended users of the summary financial statements and establishes the criteria for the preparation of summary financial statements, to describe that law or regulation in the summary financial statements) [ISA810.6(b)(ii)]; and
    (iii) to include the auditor's report on the summary financial statements in any document that contains the summary financial statements and that indicates that the auditor has reported on them [ISA810.6(b)(iii)].

- Agree with management the form of opinion to be expressed on the summary financial statements [ISA810.6(c)].

UNACCEPTABLE APPLIED CRITERIA OR UNOBTAINABLE MANAGEMENT AGREEMENT

Where the auditor concludes that the applied criteria is unacceptable, or is unable to obtain the agreement of management as set out above, the auditor shall not accept appointment to report on the summary financial statements, unless a law or regulation requires the auditor to accept appointment to report on the summary financial statements. Where the auditor has to accept appointment because law or regulation compels the auditor to do so, the auditor's report on the summary financial statements must not indicate that the engagement was conducted in accordance with ISA 810 and such reference to this fact must be made in the terms of the engagement [ISA810.7].

AUDIT PROCEDURES

The auditor must perform the following procedures as required by ISA810. In addition, the auditor must also perform any additional audit procedures they consider necessary as the basis for the auditor's opinion on the summary financial statements [ISA810.8].

1. Evaluate whether the summary financial statements adequately disclose their summarised nature and identify the audited financial statements [ISA810.8(a)].
2. When summary financial statements are not accompanied by the audited financial statements, evaluate whether they clearly describe:

    (i)   From whom or where the audited financial statements are available [ISA 810.8(b)(i)]; or
    (ii)   The law or regulation that specifies that the audited financial statements need not be made available to the intended users of the summary financial statements and establishes the criteria for the preparation of the summary financial statements [ISA810.8(b)(ii)].

3.   Evaluate whether the summary financial statements adequately disclose the applied criteria [ISA810.8(c)].
4.   Compare the summary financial statements with the related information in the audited financial statements to determine whether the summary financial statements agree with or can be recalculated from the related information in the audited financial statements [ISA810.8(d)].
5.   Evaluate whether the summary financial statements are prepared in accordance with the applied criteria [ISA810.8(e)].
6.   Evaluate, in view of the purpose of the summary financial statements, whether the summary financial statements contain the information necessary, and are at an appropriate level of aggregation, so as not to be misleading in the circumstances [ISA810.8(f)].
7.   Evaluate whether the audited financial statements are available to the intended users of the summary financial statements without undue difficulty, unless law or regulation provides that they need not be made available and establishes the criteria for the preparation of the summary financial statements [ISA810.8(g)].

REPORTING

Where the auditor determines an unmodified opinion is appropriate, ISA 810 requires use of one of the following phrases (unless otherwise required by law or regulation):

(a)   *The summary financial statements are consistent, in all material respects, with the audited financial statements, in accordance with [the applied criteria]* [ISA810.9(a)];
(b)   *The summary financial statements are a fair summary of the audited financial statements, in accordance with [the applied criteria].* [ISA810.9(b)]

In some jurisdictions, law or regulation may prescribe different wording to that in (a) or (b) above. In such situations, the auditor is required to:

(a)   Apply the procedures described in 1–7 above and any further procedures necessary to enable the auditor to express the prescribed opinion [ISA810.10(a)]; and
(b)   Evaluate whether the users of the summary financial statements might understand the auditor's opinion on the summary financial statements and, if so, whether additional explanation in the auditor's report on the summary financial statements can mitigate possible misunderstanding [ISA810.10(b)].

In situations where the auditor concludes that any additional explanation could not mitigate possible misunderstanding, the auditor shall not accept appointment unless law or regulation requires the auditor to do so. Where the auditor is compelled by law or regulation to accept appointment, their report on the summary financial statements must not indicate that the engagement was carried out in accordance with this ISA [ISA810.11].

The auditor's report on the summary financial statements must include the following elements:

(a)   A title clearly indicating it as the report of an independent auditor [ISA810.14(a)].
(b)   An addressee [ISA810.14(b)].

(c) An introductory paragraph that:

    (i) identifies the summary financial statements on which the auditor is reporting, including the title of each statement included in the summary financial statements [ISA810.14(c)(i)];

    (ii) identifies the audited financial statements [ISA810.14(c)(ii)];

    (iii) refers to the auditor's report on the audited financial statements, the date of that report and, subject to any modifications to the opinion, emphasis of matter paragraph or other matter paragraph in the auditor's report, the fact that an unmodified opinion is expressed on the audited financial statements [ISA810.14(c)(iii)];

    (iv) if the date of the auditor's report on the summary financial statements is later than the date of the auditor's report on the audited financial statements, states that the summary financial statements and the audited financial statements do not reflect the effects of events that occurred subsequent to the date of the auditor's report on the audited financial statements [ISA810.14(c)(iv)]; and

    (v) a statement indicating that the summary financial statements do not contain all the disclosures required by the financial reporting framework applied in the preparation of the audited financial statements, and that reading the summary financial statements is not a substitute for reading the audited financial statements [ISA810.14(c)(v)].

(d) A description of management's responsibility for the summary financial statements, explaining that management is responsible for the preparation of the summary financial statements in accordance with the applied criteria [ISA810.14(d)].

(e) A statement that the auditor is responsible for expressing an opinion on the summary financial statements based on the procedures required in this ISA [ISA810.14(e)].

Illustration

Independent Auditor's Report to the Members of ABC Inc

The accompanying summary financial statements, which comprise the summary statement of comprehensive income as at 31 December 2010, the summary statement of comprehensive income and summary statement of cash flows for the year then ended, and related notes, are derived from the audited financial statements of ABC Inc for the year ended 31 December 2010. We expressed an unmodified audit opinion on those financial statements in our report dated 21 March 2011. Those financial statements, and the summary financial statements, do not reflect the effects of events that occurred subsequent to the date of our report on those financial statements.

The summary financial statements do not contain all the disclosures required by International Financial Reporting Standards. Reading the summary financial statements, therefore, is not a substitute for reading the audited financial statements of ABC Inc.

Management's Responsibility for the Summary Financial Statements Management is responsible for the preparation of a summary of the audited financial statements in accordance with [describe the established criteria].

Auditor's Responsibility Our responsibility is to express an opinion on the summary financial statements based on our procedures, which were conducted in accordance with International Standard on Auditing (ISA) 810 'Engagements to Report on Summary Financial Statements'.

Opinion   In our opinion, the summary financial statements derived from the audited financial statements of ABC Inc for the year ended 31 December 2010 are consistent, in all material respects with those financial statements, in accordance with [describe the established criteria].

Mr A Auditor

31 March 2011

123 Any Street

Any town

MODIFIED OPINIONS

Where the auditor has expressed a modified opinion or has included an emphasis of matter paragraph in the audited financial statements, but considers the summary financial statements to be consistent, in all material respects, with the audited financial statements, the auditor's report on the summary financial statements must state that the auditor's report on the audited financial statements contains a qualified opinion or an emphasis of matter paragraph or other matter paragraph [ISA810.17(a)]. The auditor's report on the summary financial statements must also describe the basis for the qualified opinion, emphasis of matter paragraph or other matter paragraph and the effect such a qualification or emphasis of matter paragraph or other matter paragraph has on the summary financial statements [ISA810.b(i)(ii)].

ADVERSE OR DISCLAIMER OF OPINIONS

Where the auditor has expressed an adverse or disclaimer of opinion on the audited financial statements, the auditor's report on the summary financial statements must:

- State that the auditor's report on the audited financial statements contains an adverse or disclaimer of opinion [ISA810.18(a)].
- Describe the basis for that adverse opinion or disclaimer of opinion [ISA810.18(b)].
- State that, as a result of the adverse opinion or disclaimer of opinion, it is inappropriate to express an opinion on the summary financial statements [ISA810.18(c)].

In situations where the auditor concludes that the summary financial statements are not consistent, in all material respects, or are not a fair summary of the audited financial statements, the auditor must express an adverse opinion [ISA810.19].

DISTRIBUTION

There may be occasions when the audited financial statements of an entity are prepared in accordance with a special purpose framework or where the use of the auditor's report on the audited financial statements is restricted. In such instances, the auditor must include a similar restriction or alert the user in the auditor's report on the summary financial statements that the audited financial statements have been prepared in accordance with a special purpose framework [ISA810.20].

COMPARATIVES

Where the audited financial statements of an entity contain comparative financial information but the summary financial statements do not, the auditor must determine the effect of the omission of the comparative financial information and whether the omission is reasonable in the circumstances. Where the auditor determines such an omission to be unreasonable, the auditor shall consider the effect of the omission on the auditor's report of the summary financial statements [ISA810.21].

Where the summary financial statements contain comparative information which was audited by another auditor, then the auditor shall have regard to the provisions in ISA 710 'Comparative Information — Corresponding Figures and Comparative Financial Statements' [ISA810.22].

UNAUDITED SUPPLEMENTARY INFORMATION

If management have included supplementary information within the summary financial statements which has not been audited, the auditor must ensure that this is clearly differentiated from the summary financial statements. If the auditor concludes that the unaudited supplementary information is not clearly differentiated from the summary financial statements, the auditor shall request management to change the presentation of the unaudited supplementary information. If management refuse to do so, the auditor must ensure that they include in their auditor's report on the summary financial statements that the unaudited supplementary information is not covered by the auditor's report [ISA810.23].

OTHER INFORMATION WITHIN SUMMARY FINANCIAL STATEMENTS

Where other information is included in the summary financial statements, the auditor must read this other information and related auditor's report to identify any material inconsistencies between the other information and the summary financial statements. Where the auditor identifies a material inconsistency the auditor must consider whether the summary financial statements or the other information need to be revised [ISA810.24].

Where the auditor discovers a material misstatement of fact, the auditor must discuss the situation with management [ISA810.24].

TIMING AND SUBSEQUENT EVENTS

The auditor's report on the summary financial statements may be dated later than the auditor's report on the audited financial statements. Where this is the case, the auditor's report on the summary financial statements must state that the summary financial statements do not reflect the effects of events that have occurred subsequent to the date of the auditor's report on the audited financial statements [ISA810.12].

Where the auditor becomes aware of conditions that existed at the date of the auditor's report on the audited financial statements of which the auditor was previously unaware, the auditor must not issue the auditor's report on the summary financial statements until the auditor has dealt with such matters in accordance with ISA 560 [ISA810.13].

AUDITOR ASSOCIATION

If an entity is not planning to include an auditor's report in a document which contains the summary financial statements which the auditor has expressed an opinion on, the auditor must request management include the report. If management refuse to include the auditor's report, the auditor must take appropriate action to prevent management from associating the auditor with the summary financial statements in that document [ISA810.25].

In addition, where the auditor has audited the financial statements of an entity but has not been engaged to report on the summary financial statements, and the auditor subsequently becomes aware that management of an entity are planning to make a statement in a document that contains summary financial statements which have been derived from the audited financial statements, the auditor must take steps to be satisfied that:

(a)   the reference to the auditor is made in the context of the auditor's report on the audited financial statements [ISA810.26(a)]; and

(b)   the statement does not give the impression that the auditor has reported on the summary financial statements [ISA810.26(b)].

If the above conditions are not met, the auditor will request that management change the statement to meet the above conditions. Alternatively, the auditor can be appointed to report on the summary financial statements. If management does not change the statement by deleting reference to the auditor, or appoint the auditor to report on the summary financial statements, the auditor must inform management that they disagree with references made to the auditor. In such cases, the auditor must carry out appropriate action to prevent management from inappropriately referring to the auditor [ISA810.26].

Chapter Roundup

Summary financial statements contain less detail than the full audited financial statements.

The auditor must determine whether the applied criteria applied by management in the preparation of the summary financial statements are acceptable.

The auditor must obtain management agreement that it acknowledges and understands its responsibility for the summary financial statements.

The auditor must perform the audit procedures required by ISA 810 as well as other procedures the auditor considers necessary to base their opinion on.

ISA 810 sets out the elements of the auditor's report on the summary financial statements.

If the full financial statements contain a modified opinion, or include an emphasis of matter paragraph, but the auditor considers the summary financial statements to be consistent, in all material respects, the auditor's report on the summary financial statements must state that the auditor's report on the audited financial statements contains a modified opinion or an emphasis of matter paragraph, and the basis for the modified opinion.

If the audited financial statements contains an adverse or disclaimer of opinion, the auditor's report on the summary financial statements must state that the auditor's report in the audited financial statements contains an adverse or disclaimer of opinion, state the basis for the adverse or disclaimer of opinion and the fact that as a result of the adverse or disclaimer of opinion it is inappropriate to express an opinion on the summary financial statements.

If the summary financial statements are not consistent, in all material respects, or are not a fair summary of the audited financial statements, the auditor must express an adverse opinion.

Unaudited supplementary information must be clearly differentiated from the summary financial statements. If such information is not clearly differentiated, the auditor must request management rectify the situation. If management refuse, the auditor must state in their report that the unaudited supplementary information is not covered by their report.

The auditor must read the other information contained in the summary financial statements to identify if there are any material inconsistencies between the other information and the summary financial statements.

The auditor's report on the summary financial statements must refer to the fact that the summary financial statements do not reflect the effects of events that occurred subsequent to the date of the auditor's report on the audited financial statements and the date of the auditor's report on the summary financial statements.

The auditor must ensure they request management to include an auditor's report in a document which contains the summary financial statements which the auditors have expressed an opinion on.

The auditor must ensure they are not associated with summary financial statements which they have not been engaged to report on.

40 THE FRAMEWORK FOR THE PREPARATION AND PRESENTATION OF FINANCIAL STATEMENTS

The International Accounting Standards Board (IASB) is responsible for the setting of International Financial Reporting Standards (IFRS) in accordance with their 'Framework for the Preparation and Presentation of Financial Statements' hereinafter referred to as the 'Framework Document'. The objective of the Framework Document is to set out the concepts that underlie the preparation and presentation of financial statements for external users as set out in the Framework. It is important at the outset to understand that the Framework Document itself does not have the force of an accounting standard — its primary purpose is to assist the IASB in developing new or revised accounting standards and to assist preparers of financial statements in applying accounting standards and dealing with the issues not covered by accounting standards. It is worth noting that where there is conflict between the Framework Document and an accounting standard, the standard will prevail. In addition the Framework Document:

- Assists the IASB in promoting global harmonisation and providing a basis for reducing the number of alternative accounting treatments permitted by international accounting standards.
- Assists national standard-setting bodies in developing national standards.
- Assists users of general purpose financial statements in interpreting the information contained in them.
- Assists auditors in forming an opinion as to whether the financial statements have been prepared with international accounting standards.
- Provides information to those who are interested in the work of the IASB about the approach adopted by the IASB in the development and revision of international accounting standards.

The Framework Document covers the following issues:

- The objectives.
- The underlying assumptions.
- The qualitative characteristics.
- The elements of the financial statements.
- The concepts of capital and capital maintenance.

THE OBJECTIVES

The objective of financial statements is to provide information about:

- The financial position of the entity.

- The financial performance of the entity.
- The changes in financial position of the entity.

The *financial position* of the entity is shown in the statement of financial position (previously the balance sheet).

The *financial performance* of the entity is shown in the statement of comprehensive income (previously the income statement).

The *change in financial position is* shown in the statement of cash flows (previously the cash flow statement).

The Financial Position

The financial position of an entity is affected by:

- (a)   the economic resources under its control;
- (b)   the way it is financially structured;
- (c)   the entity's liquidity and solvency; and
- (d)   the entity's capacity to adapt to change.

The Financial Performance

The financial performance (primarily profitability) can be assessed to:

- (a)   predict the opportunity to generate cash flows from the resources the entity controls; and
- (b)   form judgements about how the resources employed by the entity are effective.

Changes in Financial Position

These can be used to assess the investing, financing and operating activities as well as evaluate the entity's ability to generate cash and cash equivalents. In addition to evaluating the entity's ability to generate cash and cash equivalents, the changes in financial position can also be assessed to see how the entity uses those cash flows. The statement of cash flows is useful because it can convey information to the user of the financial statements which might not otherwise be conveyed in the statement of comprehensive income or the statement of financial position. A typical example is the amount of taxation *paid* during the year.

Illustration

The financial statements of Entity A Inc show a current liability in respect of taxation amounting to $100,000 in 2008. During the year to 31 December 2009, the entity experienced significant cash flow difficulties and entered into an arrangement to pay with the taxation authority. The provisions of the arrangement were:

$50,000 to be paid on 31 October 2009
$20,000 to be paid on 30 November 2009
$20,000 to be paid on 31 December 2009
$10,000 to be paid on 31 January 2010

The tax charge for the year ended 31 December 2009 (ignoring deferred taxation) amounted to $75,000.

The statement of financial position will show a current liability of $85,000 (being the $10,000 liability in respect of the prior year as at 31 December 2009 together with the current year's tax charge). The statement of comprehensive income will show a tax charge of $75,000 (being the current year tax charge on the profit). The statement of cash flows will show an amount of $90,000 being the tax paid to the authority during the year under the arrangement.

The above illustrates how one figure within a set of general purpose financial statements can be shown differently in each primary financial statement.

THE UNDERLYING ASSUMPTIONS

The Framework Document refers to two assumptions underlying the preparation of financial statements:

(a)   the accruals basis of accounting; and
(b)   the going concern basis.

The Accruals Basis

The accruals basis of accounting stipulates that an entity should recognise the effects of transactions and other events when they occur and not when they are paid or when cash is received in settlement.

In addition, an entity should also recognise transactions and events in the financial statements in the period to which they relate. By complying with the accruals concept, this ensures the financial statements inform users of obligations to pay cash in the future and also inform users of the entity's obligations to receive cash in the future.

The Going Concern Basis

If financial statements are prepared on a going concern basis, this assumes that the entity will continue in operation for the foreseeable future. This informs the user that the entity neither intends to liquidate or materially curtail the scale of operations. The Framework Document at paragraph 23 states the going concern basis is appropriate if the 'entity is a going concern and will continue in operation for the foreseeable future.'

THE QUALITATIVE CHARACTERISTICS

There are four qualitative characteristics which the IASB's Framework Document refers to:

(a)   Understandability.
(b)   Comparability.
(c)   Relevance.
(d)   Reliability.

Understandability and *comparability* are both 'presentation' issues within a set of financial statements. *Relevance* and *reliability* are both 'content' issues.

Understandability

Users of financial statements are assumed to have a good understanding of the business which the financial statements relate to as well as its activities. The users are expected to have knowledge of financial issues, and information about complicated matters should not be excluded on the basis that the entity considers the information to be too complicated for the users to understand.

Comparability

Users of financial statements must be able to compare financial statements of an entity to different entities in order to evaluate the financial position, performance and changes in financial position.

In addition, users should also be able to compare the financial statements of an entity through time; for example, from one year to the next. Therefore, financial statements must show corresponding information for preceding periods (these are often referred to as 'comparatives').

A prior year adjustment shall be undertaken if an entity changes an accounting policy in order to aid comparability. This ensures consistent measurement and display of the financial effect of like transactions and other events.

Relevance

Information must be relevant both in nature and materiality. Information is material if its omission or misstatement could influence the economic decisions of users taken on the basis of the financial statements. Relevance could also be determined by nature alone.

Illustration

Gabriella Inc sold Lucas Inc some goods amounting to $100,000. Gabriella Inc also has a controlling interest in Lucas Inc. The sale of goods from Gabriella to Lucas is one piece of information. The fact that Gabriella Inc has a controlling interest in Lucas Inc is dealt with in IAS 24 'Related Party Disclosures'.

Reliability

For financial statements to be reliable they need to be free from material error and bias. In addition, they should demonstrate faithful representation, prudence and completeness. Completeness should be within the margins of both cost and materiality but taking into consideration that an omission could cause information to be false or misleading resulting in unreliability. An item is material if its error or omission could affect the decisions made by the user of the financial statements.

Illustration

An entity has made small recurring losses over the past five years. In 2010 the entity makes a $15,000 profit. Materiality has been set at $40,000. During the audit of the financial statements, the auditor becomes aware of a provision that has not been made in the financial statements and which meets the criteria laid down in IAS 37 'Provisions, Contingent Liabilities and Contingent Assets'. This provision has been calculated at $30,000.

Whilst materiality has been set at $40,000, the provision will be material to the financial statements because it turns a $15,000 profit into a $15,000 loss. Clearly such a provision would influence the economic decisions made by the user of those financial statements.

Transactions within a set of financial statements should relate to their 'substance' rather than their legal form. This is particularly important when it comes to deciphering the accounting treatment of leases (IAS 17 'Leases'), goods on consignment (IAS 18 'Revenue') and financial instruments (IAS 39 'Financial Instruments: Recognition and Measurement'). The concept of prudence does still exist, though it is very much subordinate to that of substance.

THE ELEMENTS OF FINANCIAL STATEMENTS

Financial statements are made up of the following elements:

- (a) Assets.
- (b) Liabilities.
- (c) Equity.
- (d) Income.
- (e) Expenses.

Assets

An asset is a resource controlled by the entity as a result of past events from which future economic benefits are expected to flow [Framework paragraph 49(a)].

Illustration

The directors of an entity have invested an amount of $14,000 in respect of staff training. The directors wish to capitalise this expenditure on the basis that such training is required to ensure the staff are technically competent to be able to sell their products — the directors have also said that such expenditure meets the definition of an asset.

IAS 16 'Property, Plant and Equipment' specifically states at paragraph 19(c) that such costs are operating costs and as such capitalisation of the training costs is prohibited and should be expensed as and when they are incurred.

'Control' means the ability to restrict the use of an asset. For example, inventory could be stored in a locked warehouse. In contrast, if an entity has a highly skilled workforce then it cannot recognise them as an asset because the entity cannot control its workforce — they could leave at any time.

Liabilities

A liability is defined as 'a present obligation of the entity arising from past events, the settlement of which is expected to result in an outflow from the entity of resources embodying economic benefits' [Framework Document paragraph 49(b)].

Illustration

Byrne Enterprises Inc has an item of plant that requires a routine overhaul every five years. The directors of Byrne Enterprises wish to provide for one fifth of the cost of future overhauls.

The directors cannot provide for the future overhaul costs. These costs are merely an intention at the reporting date as opposed to an obligation. The directors could well sell the item of plant before the five years have expired.

Equity

Equity is the residual interest in the assets of an entity after deducting all its liabilities [Framework Document paragraph 70].

Income

Income is increases in economic benefits during the reporting period in the form of inflows (or enhancements) of assets or decreases of liabilities that result in increases in equity other than those relating to contributions from equity participants.

Income can include revenue and gains even though they may be included in equity rather than the statement of comprehensive income (income statement); for example, a revaluation surplus.

An example of a contribution from equity participants is the purchase of additional shares in the entity.

Expenses

Expenses are decreases in economic benefits during the reporting period in the form of outflows (or depletions) of assets or incurrences of liabilities that result in decreases in equity other than those relating to distributions to equity participants.

THE CONCEPTS OF CAPITAL AND CAPITAL MAINTENANCE

There are two concepts of capital. There is the 'financial' concept and there is the 'physical' concept.

Financial Concept of Capital Maintenance

The financial concept of capital is the same as net assets or equity of the entity.

It works on the basis that profit is earned only if the financial amount of the net assets at the end of the reporting period is more than the financial amount of net assets at the beginning of the period after excluding any distributions to, or contributions from, the owners during the period.

Physical Concept

The physical concept is regarded as the productive capacity of the entity based on operating capability.

It works on the basis that profit is earned only if the physical productive capacity of the entity at the end of the period is in excess of the physical productive capacity at the beginning of the period after excluding any distributions to, or contributions from, the owners during the period.

Chapter Roundup

The Framework Document assists the International Accounting Standards Board in the development of accounting standards and the review of existing standards.

In addition, the Framework Document assists the IASB in promoting global harmonisation and assists auditors in expressing an opinion as to whether the financial statements have been prepared in accordance with international accounting standards.

The Framework Document does not have the force of an accounting standard.

If there is conflict between the Framework Document and an accounting standard, the standard prevails.

The Framework Document deals with the objectives of financial statements.

The two fundamental principles in the Framework Document are the accruals basis of accounting and the concept of going concern.

The Framework Document recognises four qualitative characteristics: understandability, comparability, relevance and reliability.

Financial statements are made up of: assets, liabilities, equity, income and expenses.

The Framework Document also refers to the financial and physical concept of capital and capital maintenance.

---

41 IFRS FOR SMALL AND MEDIUM ENTITIES (SMEs)

The objective of the International Accounting Standards Board (IASB) is to produce accounting standards which result in financial statements giving relevant, reliable and useful information which are of high-quality and understandable.

In July 2009, the IASB issued the *International Financial Reporting Standards for Small and Medium-sized Entities* (IFRS for SMEs), which those entities who fall under the scope of 'small and medium' can adopt as their financial reporting framework. Offering reduced disclosure requirements from the mainstream IFRS, IFRS for SMEs provides an alternative framework that eligible entities can apply.

IFRS for SMEs is a standalone standard and was developed by incorporating the existing principles in full IFRS. However, due to its target audience, there are a number of accounting standards and practices which are not covered by the IFRS for SMEs, such as:

- Earnings per Share (IAS 33).
- Interim Financial Reporting (IAS 34).
- Segment Reporting (IFRS 8).
- Insurance Contracts (IFRS 4).
- Assets held for sale (IFRS 5).

SMALL–MEDIUM ENTERPRISE

There is currently no definition in IFRS as to what constitutes a 'small–medium' enterprise and the decision as to who qualifies as an SME currently lies with national regulatory authorities and standard-setters. Currently such regulatory authorities and standard-setters usually set eligibility criteria to qualify as an SME such as turnover tests, statement of financial position (balance sheet) tests and employee numbers. IFRS for SMEs states that small and medium-sized entities are those who:

(a) 'do not have public accountability' [IFRS for SMEs paragraph 1.2 (a)]; and
(b) 'publish general purpose financial statements for external users'. [IFRS for SMEs paragraph 1.2 (b)]

In contrast, the IFRS for SMEs describes the circumstances when an entity does have public accountability and, therefore, is not eligible to adopt IFRS for SMEs. Paragraphs 1.3 (a) and (b) of IFRS for SMEs state:

An entity has public accountability if:

    (a)   its debt or equity instruments are traded in a public market or it is in the process of issuing such instruments for trading in a public market (a domestic or foreign stock exchange or an over-the-counter market, including local and regional markets), or

> (b)   it holds assets in a fiduciary capacity for a broad group of outsiders as one of its primary businesses. This is typically the case for banks, credit unions, insurance companies, securities brokers/dealers, mutual funds and investment banks.

Currently users of IFRS are primarily the capital markets and, by definition, full IFRS would not necessarily be appropriate to those entities which fall under the scope of a small–medium entity simply because of the overwhelming disclosures that IFRS compels users to make in their financial statements.

In developing the IFRS for SMEs, the IASB considered the needs of small–medium entities, having particular regard to the users of their financial statements. It followed, therefore, that IFRS for SMEs, whilst based on the principles contained within full IFRS, should be simplified in order to encourage those who fall within its scope to adopt IFRS for SMEs. If an entity adopts IFRS for SMEs, it must follow the standard in its entirety. In other words an entity cannot 'mix and match' full IFRS with IFRS for SMEs, hence IFRS for SMEs being a standalone standard.

Examples of some of the simplifications IFRS for SMEs offers in contrast to full IFRS are:

> (a)   Goodwill and other intangibles with an indefinite life are amortised over their useful lives, but, if an intangible's useful life cannot be reliably estimated, the estimated useful life should be deemed as ten years. Full IFRS prohibits the amortisation of goodwill and instead requires entities to undertake annual impairment tests.
>
> (b)   Where the measurement of a defined benefit pension scheme would involve undue cost or effort on the part of the entity, then a simplified calculation is allowed.
>
> (c)   Entities who adopt IFRs for SMEs can adopt the cost model of measuring their investments in associates and joint ventures.

IFRS for SMEs prohibits the use of the revaluation model for property, plant and equipment as well as for intangible assets. In addition, IFRS for SMEs prohibits the use of proportionate consolidation for investments in jointly-controlled entities. Where financial instruments are concerned, entities who adopt the use of IAS 39 'Financial Instruments: Recognition and Measurement' should classify their financial instruments between:

- available-for-sale;
- held-to-maturity;
- financial assets/liabilities at fair value through profit or loss; and
- loans and receivables.

IFRS for SMEs eliminates the 'available-for-sale' and 'held-to-maturity' classifications.

Such simplifications were adopted by the IASB in view of the undue cost burden of financial reporting for SMEs under full IFRS. The IASB is currently encouraging all jurisdictions to adopt IFRS as its financial reporting framework in order to achieve global consistency.

FALL BACK TO FULL IFRS

In jurisdictions such as the UK, entities that are classed as 'small' entities cannot adopt the Financial Reporting Standard for Smaller Entities (FRSSE), which offers significantly reduced disclosure and simplified standards for those entities who qualify for its use. Where the FRSSE does not deal with a transaction or event, the user is required to default to the full accounting standards to decipher the correct accounting treatment. If the full UK accounting standards do not deal with such a transaction or event, then another GAAP is required to be consulted — for example, IFRS.

IFRS for SMEs is significantly different in its approach to dealing with such circumstances. IFRS for SMEs is a standalone standard and, therefore, where a transaction or event is not dealt with the user is not required to default to mainstream IFRS. Instead, the user is required to develop an accounting policy for the specific transaction or event in line with the principles laid down in the IASB 'Framework for the Preparation and Presentation of Financial Statements' (referred to as the 'Framework Document').

COMPLIANCE WITH IFRS FOR SMEs

Entities who adopt IFRS for SMEs can only make a 'one-way' switch. In other words, an entity cannot adopt IFRS for SMEs in one reporting period and then decide to switch back to domestic standards in the next.

Where financial statements are prepared using IFRS for SMEs, the basis of presentation note in the financial statements and the auditor's report must refer to compliance with IFRS for SMEs.

In developing the IFRS for SMEs, the IASB did not set an 'effective from' date because whether or not a specific jurisdiction adopts the standard as its financial reporting framework for SMEs is a matter for each jurisdiction to decide. However, an entity who chooses IFRS for SMEs as its financial reporting framework must prepare an opening statement of financial position (balance sheet) as at the date of transition to IFRS. The 'transition date' is the start of the earliest period for which comparative information is provided.

Illustration

Alex Inc has a year end of 31 December 2008 and has decided to report under IFRS.

The transition date is the start of the earliest period for which comparative information is provided. Therefore, as 2007 is the comparative year, the start of this period is 1 January 2007 (i.e. the closing 2006 trial balance).

In preparing its opening statement of financial position (balance sheet), a reporting entity adopting IFRS for SMEs must also:

(a) recognise all IFRS for SME assets and liabilities;
(b) not recognise assets and liabilities not permitted by IFRS for SMEs;
(c) classify assets and liabilities by IFRS for SMEs; and
(d) apply IFRS for SMEs in measuring all recognised assets and liabilities.

Paragraph 35.12 of IFRS for SMEs requires an entity to explain how the transition from its previous financial reporting framework to IFRS for SMEs has affected its reported financial position, financial performance and cash flows.

It should be noted that if a new IFRS is not yet mandatory, but early adoption is permitted, an entity who adopts IFRS for SMEs is permitted, but not required, to apply that IFRS in its first IFRS financial statements.

Paragraph 35.13 then goes on to state:

> *To comply with paragraph 35.12, an entity's first financial statements prepared under this IFRS shall include:*
>
> (a)   *a description of the nature of each change in accounting policy*
> (b)   *reconciliations of its equity determined in accordance with its previous financial reporting framework to its equity determined in accordance with this IFRS for both of the following dates:*
>
> > (i)   *the date of transition to this IFRS, and*
> > (ii) *the end of the latest period presented in the entity's most recent annual financial statements determined in accordance with its previous financial reporting framework*
>
> (c)   *a reconciliation of the profit or loss determined in accordance with its previous financial reporting framework for the latest period in the entity's most recent annual financial statements to its profit or loss determined in accordance with this IFRS for the same period.*

EXCEPTIONS TO THE RETROSPECTIVE APPLICATION OF OTHER IFRSs

IFRS for SMEs allows all of the exemptions in IFRS 1 'First-Time Adoption of International Financial Reporting Standards'. IFRS 1 was amended on 23 July 2009 and the amendments took effect from 1 January 2010 (further amendments are also planned to IFRS 1). The five exceptions, which are listed for completeness and not all necessarily applicable to SMEs, are as follows:

IAS 39 'Financial Instruments: Recognition and Measurement' — Derecognition of Financial Instruments   A first-time adopter shall apply the derecognition requirements in IAS 39 prospectively for transactions occurring on or after 1 January 2004. However, the entity may apply the derecognition requirements retrospectively provided that the needed information was obtained at the time of initially accounting for those transactions [IFRS1.B2–3].

IAS 39 'Financial Instruments: Recognition and Measurement' — Hedge Accounting
The general rule is that the entity shall not reflect in its opening IFRS statement of financial position (balance sheet) a hedging relationship of a type that does not qualify for hedge accounting in accordance with IAS 39. However, if an entity designated a net position as a hedged item in accordance with previous GAAP, it may designate an individual item within that net position as a hedged item in accordance with IFRS, provided that it does so no later than the date of transition to IFRSs [IFRS1.B5].

IAS 27 'Consolidated and Separate Financial Statements'— Non-Controlling Interest
IFRS1.B7 lists specific requirements and is only applicable for first-time adopters that apply

IAS 27R in their first IFRS reporting period. IFRS 1.B7 is applied for annual periods beginning on or after 1 July 2009 (IFRS 1.37), which is the same as the 2008 revisions to IAS 27R. Therefore:

(a)   An entity whose annual reporting period begins on 1 July applies IAS 27R and IFRS 1.B7 for the annual period ending 30 June 2010.

(b)   An entity whose annual reporting period begins on 1 January applies IAS 27R and IFRS 1.B7 for the annual period ending 31 December 2010.

IFRS 1.B7 and IAS 27R can be adopted earlier. However, where the revisions are adopted earlier, the provisions in IFRS 3R must then be applied at the same time. IFRS 3R and IAS 27R cannot be applied prior to the beginning of an annual period beginning on or after 30 June 2007. It follows, therefore, that an entity whose annual reporting period begins on 1 January may adopt early for the year beginning on 1 January 2008, but not the year beginning 1 January 2007.

The exceptions are:

- The amendment in paragraph 28 of IAS 27R requiring attribution of total comprehensive income to the owners of the parent and to the non-controlling interest even if this results in the non-controlling interests having a deficit balance.
- The requirement on accounting for changes in the parent's ownership interests in a subsidiary after control is obtained.

The requirements on accounting for a loss of control of a subsidiary and the related requirements of IFRS 5.8A (to classify assets and liabilities of that subsidiary as held for sale when the criteria are met, regardless of whether the first-time adopter will retain a non-controlling interest after the sale).

FULL-COST OIL AND GAS ASSETS

Entities using the full cost method may elect exemption from retrospective application of IFRSs for oil and gas assets. Entities electing this exemption will use the carrying amount under its old GAAP as the deemed cost of its oil and gas assets at the date of first-time adoption of IFRSs.

DETERMINING WHETHER AN ARRANGEMENT CONTAINS A LEASE

IFRIC 4 'Determining Whether an Arrangement Contains a Lease' is exempt from application where a first-time adopter with a leasing contract made the same type of determination of whether an arrangement contained a lease in accordance with its previous GAAP, albeit at a date other than that required by IFRIC 4.

OPTIONAL EXEMPTIONS FROM THE BASIC MEASUREMENT PRINCIPLES IN IFRS 1

IFRS 1 contains further optional exemptions to the general restatement and measurement principles which relate to:

- Business combinations.
- Share-based payment transactions.

- Insurance contracts.
- Fair value or revaluation as deemed cost.
- Leases.
- Employee benefits.
- Cumulative translation differences.
- Investments in subsidiaries, jointly-controlled entities, associates and joint ventures.
- Assets and liabilities of subsidiaries, associates and joint ventures.
- Compound financial instruments.
- Designation of previously recognised financial instruments.
- Fair value measurement of financial assets or financial liabilities at initial recognition.
- Decommissioning liabilities included in the cost of property, plant and equipment.
- Financial assets or intangible assets accounted for in accordance with IFRC 12 'Service Concession Arrangements'.
- Borrowing costs.

Detailed analysis of the above exceptions is outside the scope of this publication and users are encouraged to consult the mainstream IFRS 1 for details of the above exceptions.

IFRS FOR SMEs VERSUS UK GAAP

At the time of writing, IFRS for SMEs in the UK had not been adopted.

Looking at the proposed IFRS for SMEs, there are some notable differences which will affect practitioners who deal with those clients who could potentially fall under its scope.

INVESTMENT PROPERTIES

Current GAAP (SSAP 19 'Accounting for Investment Properties') requires investment properties to be carried in the balance sheet at their fair (market) value, with changes being recognised in the statement of total recognised gains and losses (STRGL) as opposed to the profit and loss account.

IFRS for SMEs at paragraph 16.7 requires fair values to be obtained where they can be obtained without undue cost or effort, with any changes in fair value being recognised directly through the profit and loss account (income statement). There would not be any effect on the tax liability as no gain or loss for tax purposes would arise until disposal of the asset.

FIXED ASSET REVALUATION

Current GAAP allows classes of fixed assets to be revalued to market value and FRS 15 'Tangible Fixed Assets' requires these valuations to be kept up to date where the revaluation model is adopted.

Under IFRS for SMEs at paragraph 17.15, revaluation of property, plant and equipment is not permitted.

BORROWING COSTS

If an entity constructs its own asset (for example, its own building), FRS 15 'Tangible Fixed Assets' permits borrowing costs to be capitalised as part of the cost of the asset.

IFRS for SMEs at paragraph 25.2 prohibits borrowing costs being capitalised and such costs must, therefore, be written off to the profit and loss account (income statement) as they are incurred.

INTANGIBLE ASSETS — DEVELOPMENT COSTS

SSAP 13 'Accounting for Research and Development' allows development costs to be capitalised if, and only if, certain criteria are met:

- There is a clearly defined project.
- The related expenditure is separately identifiable.
- The outcome of the project has been assessed with reasonable certainty as to both its technical feasibility and its ultimate commercial viability, considered in the light of factors such as likely market conditions (including competing products), public opinion and consumer and environmental legislation.
- The aggregate of the deferred development costs, any further development costs and related production, selling and administrative costs, is reasonably expected to be exceeded by related future sales or other revenues.
- Adequate resources exist, or are reasonably expected to be available, to enable the project to be completed, and to provide any consequential increases in working capital.

Where these conditions are satisfied, a company can defer development expenditure, but only until commercial production begins. SSAP 13 requires a company to amortise the expenditure it has capitalised from the time that commercial production of the product or service begins. Where a company is developing a product, commercial production begins when the company is manufacturing the product with a view to selling it commercially [SSAP 13.28].

Paragraph 18.14 of IFRS for SMEs requires internal development costs to be written off as they are incurred, unless they meet the recognition criteria at paragraph 18.4 which says an intangible asset can be recognised if, and only if:

- It is probable that the expected future economic benefits that are attributable to the asset will flow to the entity.
- The cost or value of the asset can be reliably measured.
- The asset does not result from expenditure incurred internally on an intangible item.

GOODWILL AND INTANGIBLE ASSETS

FRS 10 'Goodwill and Intangible Assets' allows an entity to amortise goodwill and intangible assets if the useful economic life of these assets are deemed to not exceed 20 years. Where the useful economic life is deemed to be longer than 20 years, non-amortisation must be supported by annual impairment reviews to ensure the assets are not carried in the balance sheet at any more than their recoverable amount.

IFRS for SMEs allows amortisation of goodwill at paragraph 19.23 (A) and other intangibles at paragraph 18.20 over a default period of 10 years where the entity is unable to make a reliable estimate of the asset(s) useful economic life.

REVALUATION OF INTANGIBLE ASSETS

FRS 10 'Goodwill and Intangible Assets' only permits the revaluation of intangible assets in circumstances where readily ascertainable market values can be obtained. In reality, hardly any intangible assets will have a readily ascertainable market value.

IFRS for SMEs does not allow intangible assets to be revalued. Paragraph 18.18 states that the entity will continue to measure intangible assets at cost less accumulated amortisation and any accumulated impairment losses. Section 27 of IFRS for SMEs deals with impairment of assets.

LEASES

SSAP 21 'Accounting for Leases and Hire Purchase Contracts' contains a 90% 'yardstick' test (amongst other principles) to determine whether the risks and rewards of ownership of the leased asset have passed to the lessee.

IFRS for SMEs follows the similar principles in IAS 17 'Leases' by saying capitalisation of the lease and recognition of a liability will occur when substantially all of the risks and rewards have been passed to the lessee (paragraph 20.4). IFRS for SMEs does not contain the 90% 'yardstick' test.

The International Accounting Standards Board (IASB) and the American Financial Accounting Standards Board (FASB) have been in collaboration to overhaul the area of lease accounting. The proposal is to make all 'operating leases' (those leases which are not on an entity's statement of financial position (balance sheet)) 'finance leases' (in other words, all leases will be on the statement of financial position (balance sheet)). An exposure draft was issued in August 2010 with a final standard due out in 2011.

BUSINESS COMBINATIONS

IFRS for SMEs requires the use of the purchase method for all business acquisitions at paragraph 19.6. FRS 6 'Acquisitions and Mergers' also considers the use of 'merger accounting'. FRS 6 defines a merger as:

> *A business combination that results in the creation of a new reporting entity formed from the combining parties, in which the shareholders of the combining entities come together in a partnership for the mutual sharing of the risks and benefits of the combined entity, and in which no party to the combination in substance obtains control over any other, or is otherwise seen to be dominant, whether by virtue of the proportion of its shareholders' rights in the combined entity, the influence of its directors or otherwise.*
>
> [FRS 6 paragraph 2]

The conditions in the United Kingdom's Companies Act and FRS 6 require certain tests to be satisfied:

- Offers to shareholders test.
- 90% holding test.
- Immaterial cash or non-equity consideration test.
- No identifiable acquirer or acquiree test.

- Joint participation in management test.
- Relative size test.
- Full participation in future performance test.

REVENUE RECOGNITION

UITF 40 requires revenue to be recognised when a 'critical event' has passed (usually referred to as a 'milestone'). These critical events generally mean when the right to consideration has passed.

IFRS for SMEs is worded slightly differently and does not specifically refer to a 'right to consideration' which suggests that revenue (particularly service revenue at paragraph 23.14) could be recognised at a later date than current GAAP requires. This, of course, would have a tax effect as the tax treatment would follow the accounting treatment.

DEFERRED TAXATION

FRS 19 'Deferred Taxation' and FRSSE refer to 'timing differences', which recognises the mismatch between the accounting periods in which gains and losses are reported in the financial statements compared to when the tax effects arise. IFRS for SMEs at paragraph 29.14 refers to 'temporary differences' which are concerned with the carrying amount of assets and liabilities in the financial statements compared to the effect on taxable profit if the associated assets or liabilities had been sold or settled at the balance sheet date. This approach is more complex than the FRS 19 approach and will give rise to many more deferred tax provisions being made.

FRS 19 also allows deferred tax balances to be discounted to present day values, whereas IFRS for SMEs prohibits such a practice (paragraph 29.23).

ASSOCIATES AND JOINT VENTURES
(CONSOLIDATED FINANCIAL STATEMENTS)

FRS 9 'Associates and Joint Ventures' requires joint ventures to be accounted for using the gross equity method whilst associates are accounted for under the equity method.

IFRS for SMEs (sections 14 and 15 respectively) allows three choices — the cost model, the equity method and the fair value model. However, where there is a quoted price (for example, on a recognised stock exchange) IFRS for SMEs requires the fair value model to be adopted.

DEFINED BENEFIT PENSION SCHEMES

IFRS for SMEs provides a number of simplifications where the valuation basis (the Projected Unit Credit Method) would require undue cost or effort. IFRS for SMEs also does not require the use of an independent actuary to provide a triennial valuation as current UK GAAP does, provided the entity is able to do so without undue cost or effort (paragraph 28.18).

STOCK (INVENTORY) VALUATION

SSAP 9 'Stocks and Long Term Contracts' allows stock to be valued using a 'last-in first-out' (LIFO) method.

Paragraph 13.18 of IFRS for SMEs follows the same treatment in IAS 2 'Inventories' and prohibits the use of LIFO as a basis for inventory valuation.

ACCOUNTING POLICIES

FRSSE runs in conjunction with full FRS and requires the preparer of the financial statements to default back to full FRS or another financial reporting framework (for example, IFRS or US GAAP) to decipher the accounting treatment (or best practice) of an issue which is not specifically addressed.

IFRS for SMEs is a standalone standard and would, therefore, require the directors to develop an accounting policy for an issue not addressed in IFRS for SMEs by having regard to the concepts and pervasive principles within IFRS for SMEs detailed at paragraph 10.4.

AGRICULTURE

IFRS for SMEs gives specific guidance on the accounting treatment of agricultural assets at section 34 'Specialised Activities'.

SUBSIDIARY UNDERTAKINGS

Under IFRS for SMEs, the consolidation boundary is determined by control, whereas in current UK GAAP there are other definitions of subsidiaries, including entities where there is the actual exercise of dominant influence or that are managed on a unified basis. The resulting difference here is that IFRS for SMEs may not necessarily require the consolidation of all the subsidiaries which are currently required in FRS 2 'Accounting for Subsidiary Undertakings', albeit such cases are not expected to occur on a frequent basis.

In terms of investments in subsidiaries, associates and joint ventures, IFRS for SMEs requires such combinations to be stated at fair value with changes in fair values being taken through profit or loss or, alternatively, measured at cost with annual impairment reviews being undertaken. FRS 9 'Associates and Joint Ventures' also allows such investments to be carried at fair value, but Companies Act 2006 (under the alternative accounting rules and subject to any amendments to the 4th Directive and the Companies Act) would not allow changes in the fair values of such investments to be taken straight to the profit and loss account.

FINANCIAL INSTRUMENTS

IFRS for SMEs requires investments in equities to be stated at fair value where these fair values can be reliably measured and changes in these fair values should be taken to profit or loss. IFRS for SMEs requires investments in equities to be stated at fair value where there are quoted market prices.

Current UK GAAP does not have a requirement for fair values and as such a historical cost approach is acceptable. Where the alternative accounting rules are adopted, Companies Act 2006 does not allow such changes in these fair values to be taken through profit or loss. The fair value rules would allow for this, but large and medium-sized entities using the alternative accounting rules would already have to comply with the provisions in FRS 26: 'Financial Instruments: Measurement' which also have the same requirements as IFRS for SMEs.

DERECOGNITION OF A FINANCIAL INSTRUMENT

IFRS for SMEs contain derecognition rules which are broadly based on the retention of the risks and rewards associated with the financial instrument. FRS 5 'Reporting the Substance of Transactions' contains various illustrations which determine when a financial instrument can be derecognised in the financial statements of an entity, though these illustrations are based on similar principles.

DERIVATIVES

Under IFRs for SMEs a derivative financial instrument would have to be carried in the statement of financial position at fair value. Under current UK GAAP, there is no requirement to do this and it is possible for such an instrument to be carried at amortised cost. Entities applying the alternative accounting rules under current UK GAAP would, however, have to state the derivative at fair value.

HEDGE ACCOUNTING

IFRS for SMEs permits hedge accounting only if certain strict criteria are met. Section 12.16 of IFRS for SMEs states:

To qualify for hedge accounting, an entity shall comply with all of the following conditions:

  (a)   The entity designates and documents the hedging relationship so that the risk being hedged, the hedged item and the hedging instrument are clearly identified and the risk in the hedged item is the risk being hedged with the hedging instrument.
  (b)   The hedged risk is one of the risks specified in paragraph 12.17. (See below)
  (c)   The hedging instrument is as specified in paragraph 12.18. (See below)
  *(d)   The entity expects the hedging instrument to be highly effective in offsetting the designated hedge risk. The **effectiveness of a hedge** is the degree to which changes in the fair value or cash flows of the hedged item that are attributable to the hedged risk are offset by changes in the fair value or cash flows of the hedging instrument.*
                                                        [IFRS for SMEs (paragraph 12.16)]

Paragraph 12.17 of IFRS for SMEs states:

This IFRS permits hedge accounting only for the following risks:

  (a)   Interest rate risk of a debt instrument measured at amortised cost.
  *(b)   Foreign exchange or interest rate risk in a firm commitment or a **highly probable forecast transaction.***
  (c)   Price risk of a commodity that it holds or in a firm commitment or highly probable forecast transaction to purchase or sell a commodity.
  (d)   Foreign exchange risk in a net investment in a foreign operation.
                                                        [Paragraph 12.17 IFRS for SME]

Paragraph 12.18 of IFRS for SMEs states:

This IFRS permits hedge accounting only if the hedging instrument has all of the following terms and conditions:

  (a)   It is an interest rate swap, a foreign currency swap, a foreign currency forward exchange contract or a commodity forward exchange contract that is expected to be

> *highly effective in offsetting a risk identified in paragraph 12.17 that is designated as the hedged risk.*
>
> (b) *It involves a party external to the reporting entity (i.e. external to the **group**, segment or individual entity being reported on).*
>
> (c) *Its **notional amount** is equal to the designated amount of the principal or notional amount of the hedged item.*
>
> (d) *It has a specified maturity date not later than:*
>
>> (i) *the maturity of the financial instrument being hedged.*
>>
>> (ii) *the expected settlement of the commodity purchase or sale commitment, or*
>>
>> (iii) *the occurrence of the highly probable forecast foreign currency or commodity transaction being hedged.*
>
> (e) *It has no prepayment, early termination or extension features.*
>
> [Paragraph 12.18 IFRS for SME]

The criteria to allow an entity to adopt hedge accounting are quite stringent. In contrast, there is nothing too definitive in UK GAAP except where the provisions in FRS 26 'Financial Instruments: Recognition and Measurement' are followed resulting in hedge accounting under UK GAAP being less strict than the principles in IFRS for SMEs.

DIVIDENDS FROM ASSOCIATES AND JOINT VENTURES

Under IFRS for SMEs, all dividends received from associates and joint ventures are to go to the income statement (profit and loss account) regardless of whether they come out of pre or post-acquisition reserves. The investment in the associate or joint venture is then subject to impairment.

The UK's Companies Act requires dividends from pre-acquisition profits and requires such dividends to be deducted from the cost of the investment.

PROPERTY, PLANT AND EQUIPMENT

Where the revaluation model is adopted by an entity, IFRS for SMEs allows residual values to be adjusted upwards as well as downwards in calculating depreciation. FRS 15 'Tangible Fixed Assets' restricts the uplift of residual values.

NEGATIVE GOODWILL

In some business combinations, a bargain purchase could occur which may result in negative goodwill. However, it has to be clear that a bargain purchase has, *de facto*, occurred.

Under IFRS for SMEs, the acquirer will:

- reassess the identification and measurement of the acquiree's assets, liabilities and provisions for contingent liabilities and the measurement of the cost of the combination; and
- recognise immediately in profit or loss any excess remaining after that reassessment. [IFRS for SMEs (paragraph 19.24)]

Under current UK GAAP, most cases would result in the gain being spread over several periods when assets and liabilities acquired would be realised/settled.

MEASUREMENT OF SHARES

IFRS for SMEs has a requirement at paragraph 22.8 to discount the amounts receivable for shares to their net present value. Current UK GAAP will not always allow this due to the provisions in the Companies Act 2006 and the amounts of interest recognised in the profit and loss account might have to be reclassified to the share premium account.

Chapter Roundup

IFRS for SMEs is based on mainstream International Financial Reporting Standards (IFRS) but has been simplified in view of its target audience.

The standard is a standalone standard, thus, if a transaction or event is not covered by IFRS for SMEs, an entity must develop a relevant accounting policy having regard to the concepts and pervasive principles outlined in the IASB's *Framework for the Preparation and Presentation of Financial Statements*.

There is currently no definition of an SME but the standard says IFRS for SMEs is relevant to entities which do not have public accountability and publish general purpose financial statements for external users.

Adoption of IFRS for SMEs is a 'one-way' switch.

There are some notable differences between IFRS for SMEs and current UK Generally Accepted Accounting Practice.

There are five exceptions for first-time adopters of IFRS for SMEs.

42 ISQC 1 'QUALITY CONTROL FOR FIRMS THAT PERFORM AUDITS AND REVIEWS OF FINANCIAL STATEMENTS, AND OTHER ASSURANCE AND RELATED SERVICES ENGAGEMENTS'

The purpose of ISQC 1 'Quality Control for Firms that Perform Audits and Reviews of Financial Statements, and Other Assurance and Related Services Engagements' is to outline the responsibilities of the practising firm of auditors in respect of its quality control procedures. Paragraph 11 of ISQC 1 states:

The objective of the firm is to establish and maintain a system of quality control to provide it with reasonable assurance that:

(a) The firm and its personnel comply with professional standards and applicable legal and regulatory requirements; and

(b) Reports issued by the firm or engagement partners are appropriate in the circumstances.

ISQC 1 covers the following issues relating to quality control:

- Leadership responsibilities for quality control within the audit firm.
- Relevant ethical requirements.
- Acceptance and continuance of client relationships and specific engagements.
- Human resources.
- Engagement performance.
- Monitoring.

The firm should have documented its quality control procedures in accordance with ISQC 1 requirements.

LEADERSHIP RESPONSIBILITIES FOR QUALITY CONTROL WITHIN THE AUDIT FIRM

It is imperative that a firm of practising auditors has a high standard of quality control to ensure compliance with International Standards on Auditing and to ensure that audit work is conducted to a high standard. The audit firm should appoint an appropriate person(s) to oversee the firm's system of quality control and to ensure compliance with ISQC 1 requirements.

RELEVANT ETHICAL REQUIREMENTS

Ethical standards have been discussed in Chapter 3 and ISQC 1 pays particular attention to independence requirements. It is important at all times that auditors remain independent and objective and where there are threats to an auditor's independence then sufficient safeguards should be implemented.

ACCEPTANCE AND CONTINUANCE OF CLIENT RELATIONSHIPS AND SPECIFIC ENGAGEMENTS

Audit firms should ensure that they have procedures in place for the acceptance of clients as well as reviewing continuing client relationships to ensure that the firm only undertakes work:

(a) It is competent to perform.
(b) Where it is able to comply with relevant ethical requirements.
(c) Where it has considered the integrity of the client and has confirmed that the client does not lack integrity.

HUMAN RESOURCES

The firm needs to ensure that it has procedures in place to allow only able and competent personnel to perform engagements in accordance with professional requirements. By ensuring this is complied with, the firm can be reasonably assured that the reports they issue are appropriate in the circumstances.

ENGAGEMENT PERFORMANCE

The firm needs to ensure that they have procedures in place to ensure that engagements are performed in accordance with professional standards as well as legal and regulatory requirements. Paragraph 32 of ISQC 1 states that such policies and procedures shall include:

(a) Matters relevant to promoting consistency in the quality of engagement performance.
(b) Supervision responsibilities.
(c) Review responsibilities. [ISQC1.32]

MONITORING

The firm should ensure that they have procedures in place to ensure that their ISQC 1 procedures are relevant and reliable in the circumstances. Where it is considered that ISQC 1 procedures are appropriate in the circumstances, the firm should ensure that they have procedures in place to ensure that they are operating effectively. Where deficiencies are noted the firm must have procedures in place to evaluate the effect of deficiencies noted.

Illustration

ISQC 1 Procedures

Audit Firm & Co

Quality Control for Audit Clients in Accordance with ISQC 1 *'Quality Control for Firms that Perform Audits and Reviews of Financial Statements, and Other Assurance and Related Services Engagements'*

Objective   The objective of the firm's quality control procedures are to ensure that all audits undertaken by the firm and the firm's staff are undertaken in a way that complies with all relevant auditing standards — namely International Standards on Auditing (ISAs) and comply with all ethical requirements. Achieving this objective will ensure each audit assignment is completed with due skill, care and attention and to a standard which will enable us to determine whether an audit client's financial statements represent a true and fair view, or present fairly in all material respects the state of the entity's affairs and, therefore, enable us to form an appropriate audit opinion.

Audit Staff and Responsibilities   The following staff members will assist, where appropriate, on audit assignments and be given work relevant to their professional qualifications and skills:

> M Holmes — Engagement Partner 1
> S Jones — Engagement Partner 2
> A Wilson — Audit Manager
> B Hynes — Audit Senior
> C Clough — Audit Senior
> D Farmers — Audit Assistant
> L Whiteley — Audit Assistant

The engagement partner will assess the staff's competence to undertake the required work and will also be responsible in ensuring that the audit staff (at all levels) are given the opportunity to keep their knowledge and skills up to date by (a) complying with Continuing Professional Development requirements of the professional body and (b) by attending courses which the engagement partner feels would be beneficial to keep the relevant staff up to date in order that they will be able to undertake audit work in accordance with the audit firm's requirements.

Leadership Responsibilities   The firm will adopt a hierarchical approach in leadership responsibilities for its audit work. Ultimately the engagement partner will have overall charge of the audit assignments and make final decisions on areas of contentious issues or differences of opinion, whether this is between staff members or staff and client or external reviewers of audit files. Where differences of opinion are encountered, they will firstly be addressed by the audit manager who will then, if necessary, address the issues with the engagement partner who will liaise with external sources, where appropriate, and whose opinion will be deemed as final.

All audit staff will report directly to the audit manager who will then report directly to the engagement partner on all audit assignments. All delegated audit work will be decided by the engagement partner and the audit manager and will be reviewed primarily by the audit manager and then passed for final review to the engagement partner.

The engagement partner will manage the firm's quality control policies and procedures and ensure that the audit firm:

(a)   Performs work that complies with professional standards and regulatory and legal requirements.

(b)   Issues reports that are appropriate in the circumstances.

At all times the firm must be seen to be producing high quality audit work commensurate with the skills and technical ability of its staff. In recognition of this requirement, regular reviews of all audit staff's work will be undertaken during and after the audit assignment. Where deficiencies in audit work are apparent, these will be discussed with the audit staff concerned with the engagement partner and, where applicable, the audit manager. Where it appears that training issues are required, then these will be addressed as appropriate.

It is the policy of this firm that all staff engaged on audit assignments maintains an appropriate degree of technical knowledge and competence. Where the engagement partner concludes a staff member is not technically competent to undertake an assignment, that staff member will not be permitted to have any dealings with that specific audit assignment. All members of staff are required to ensure that they maintain their technical knowledge by undertaking an appropriate amount of Continuing Professional Development, whether this is via training courses, obtaining professional qualifications or reading journals and attending seminars. The engagement partner will ensure that all staff maintains their Continuing Professional Development requirements accordingly.

For those staff members who belong to a recognised professional body, they will ensure that they comply with that professional body's Continuing Professional Development requirements. Where annual Continuing Professional Development returns are required to be submitted to that professional body, then that staff member concerned will ensure that they submit a copy of their completed Continuing Professional Development return to the engagement partner for placing in the staff member's personnel file.

Acceptance of a Client   The engagement partner will determine whether or not the audit firm has the required expertise and skills available within its resources in order to undertake the audit. The engagement partner will also assess whether, in accepting the audit appointment, the firm is able to comply with the ethical requirements in terms of:

(a)   Integrity.
(b)   Objectivity.
(c)   Professional competence and due care.
(d)   Confidentiality.
(e)   Professional behaviour.

The engagement partner will also 'vet' new audit clients to ensure that there are no issues which bring into question the integrity of the audit client, its management or its processes. Where the engagement partner discovers that there are issues which threaten the integrity of the audit client, the engagement partner will not accept the audit assignment.

In arriving at his conclusion to accept the audit engagement or not, the engagement partner will assess whether, in his opinion the client's integrity may be brought into question by considering:

(a)   The nature of the business.
(b)   Potential related party issues.
(c)   Whether there are frequent changes of advisers.
(d)   Previous audit opinions.
(e)   Any potential limitation on audit scope.
(f)   Money laundering issues and any past (or present) criminal activities.

Where the engagement partner concludes that there are no issues which do affect the integrity of the client, the normal policy of client identification for money laundering issues will take place and this will take place as soon as is reasonably practicable. The engagement partner will also follow the firm's policy for accepting a new client including completing the new client checklist and ensuring that the relevant processes are completed.

For audit clients who have approached this audit firm from another audit firm, the engagement partner will write to the former audit firm to ask for professional clearance in accordance with the ethical guidelines issued by our professional body.

Any non-replies for professional clearance will be followed up after a reasonable time has elapsed to give the former audit firm an opportunity to respond to the engagement partner's request and furnish us with the details requested in our clearance letter.

Continuing Audit Assignments   As part of the firm's policy for audit assignments, on completion of any audit assignment the audit team must meet and discuss whether there are any issues which came to light during the audit which would have prevented the firm from accepting the audit appointment if they knew about the issue(s) concerned.

In assessing continuing audit assignments, the firm will also consider whether there have been any issues which have given rise to conflicts of interest or whether the firm does not have sufficient resources for future audit assignments.

The engagement partner will also ensure that the firm's audit staff has adequate knowledge of the industry the audit client operates in and will ensure that, where appropriate, the audit staff engaged on the assignment has the specific skill and responsibility to carry out the assignment effectively. The engagement partner will also ensure that where experts are required, then the firm has access to those experts. The audit firm does have a portfolio of external experts (for example, taxation experts) who can be contacted when required.

Where experts are used, the engagement partner will ensure that they are independent and possess the necessary skills and capabilities and competence to enable the audit firm to complete the assignment effectively.

During any audit assignment, audit staff must ensure that they comply with the leadership responsibilities above. Any issue(s) that audit staff encounter in terms of money laundering must immediately be reported to the audit manager on discovery and under no circumstances must be communicated to the audit client. Where audit staff is unsure as to the course of action, they must discuss the issue with either the audit manager or the engagement partner as quickly as possible.

The audit manager will discuss the issue(s) with the engagement partner who will determine whether the issue(s) discovered give rise to a report being made to regulatory authorities in accordance with Money Laundering Regulations.

The engagement partner will assess the issue(s) discovered and determine whether it is necessary to withdraw from the engagement or the client relationship.

Where the engagement partner concludes that there is no alternative but to withdraw from the audit assignment and the client relationship, the engagement partner will discuss the issue(s) concerned with the appropriate level of client's management and the reasons for the withdrawal.

In determining whether there is a legal or professional requirement for the firm to report the person or persons who appointed the firm to regulatory authorities and discussing any reasons for the firm withdrawing from the assignment, the engagement partner will ensure that (s)he documents significant issues, consultations and conclusions as well as the basis for their conclusion.

Ethical Responsibilities   The engagement partner will review the firm's ethical responsibilities as the normal part of the audit planning. In particular, the engagement partner will consider its ethical responsibilities in terms of its:

(a)   Integrity.
(b)   Objectivity.
(c)   Professional competence and due care.
(d)   Confidentiality issues.
(e)   Professional behaviour.

In all audit assignments, the audit firm will ensure that at all times it remains independent and objective, and undertakes all audit work with professional competence. No audit work will be delegated to staff members who do not have the required expertise or experience to undertake such work. Audit staff should ensure they are familiar with the IFAC code in respect of ethical responsibilities and that they comply with those responsibilities at all times. Any breach of the above ethical responsibilities will result in the firm's disciplinary procedures being implemented.

During the course of the audit work, the information gathered by audit staff and the engagement partner will remain strictly confidential and any breaches of client confidentiality will result in the firm's disciplinary proceedings being implemented.

Where audit staff encounter issues that may cast doubt on that staff member's (or another staff member's) ethical responsibilities, then audit staff will have a responsibility to ensure such issues are immediately brought to the audit manager's attention who then has a responsibility to notify the engagement partner regardless of how small the issue.

In the event that an audit client makes a specific request or asks for information which may be in breach of ethical responsibilities, then that staff member must inform the audit manager as quickly as possible, who then has a duty to notify the engagement partner.

At all times during the course of the audit assignment, all audit staff of all seniorities, will ensure that they keep the objective of the audit in mind. They will demonstrate professional competence and maintain confidentiality. This includes ensuring that the audit client's information, paperwork and documentation is kept secure and that access is not gained to clients' information by unauthorised individuals.

Independence   The audit firm and its staff will remain independent of the client at all times and will form its audit opinion based on a wholly independent and objective approach.

It is the responsibility of the engagement partner to provide the audit staff with relevant information about the audit assignment and notify the audit staff as to the scope of the service to be provided to the client. In particular, the engagement partner and the audit staff need to take into account any provisions available to smaller entities in accordance with ethical standards. When considering these issues it is vital that the engagement partner and the audit manager consider the impact these provisions will have on the audit firm's report.

During the course of the audit, the audit manager will evaluate the independence adopted by both the firm and the audit staff and identify and evaluate circumstances whereby independence issues may be threatened. It is the responsibility of the audit manager and the engagement partner to ensure that all threats to independence are identified in a timely manner (a timely manner being defined by the audit firm as soon as is reasonably practicable). Once a threat to independence has been identified and it cannot be reduced to an acceptable level, then the engagement partner must decide whether or not to continue with the audit assignment or whether there is scope to reduce the threat to an acceptable level by engaging the use of outside reviewers (for example 'hot' file reviews). In the event that file reviews by external parties are required, the firm's appointed file reviewer is Mr A Reviewer of Reviewer & Co.

Before the commencement of any audit assignment, and as a matter of course during the audit planning, the engagement partner and the audit staff will determine whether they can satisfy the independence requirement shown in the audit independence checklist.

Where a staff member/engagement partner is unable to meet the independence requirements satisfactorily, then they will not be engaged on the audit assignment. In the event that the firm cannot demonstrate independence then the engagement partner will be withdrawn from the engagement.

Where the firm's engagement partner is unable to satisfy the independence requirements, then the firm will consider either resigning from the audit or re-appointing another engagement partner depending on the circumstances encountered.

Familiarity Threat   Inevitably, audit staff engaged on recurring audits will become familiar, with the client and the client's operations, which could result in a familiarity threat.

The engagement partner will review the staff's familiarity with the client and adopt procedures to ensure these threats are reduced to an acceptable level.

Such procedures will include the engagement partner reviewing staff's work and ensuring that the familiarity threats are reduced to an acceptable level. If the familiarity threat cannot be reduced to an acceptable level, then the firm will engage another staff member on the audit assignment.

Audit Planning   All audit assignments will be subjected to a rigorous audit plan. The plan will be overseen by the engagement partner and the audit manager. Such a plan will consist of the following:

(a)   A detailed planning meeting between the engagement partner and the audit staff to identify issues relevant to the audit assignment and consideration of key auditing and accounting standards which need to be addressed prior to the audit.

(b)   Consideration of fraud issues.

(c)   Consideration of any material change to the client's financial staff and/or operations during the year, and any impact this may have on detailed audit work.

(d)   A consideration of last year's audit and the findings therefrom.

(e)   A consideration of last year's audit opinion and whether we expect to issue a qualified/ unqualified audit opinion on the current year's audit and a consideration of any imposed limitation of scope.

(f)   A consideration of the client's internal control environment and whether detailed substantive audit testing is appropriate. (Note that the firm will adopt a policy where a client's internal controls are substantively tested as a matter of course at least every third audit).

(g)   Consideration as to the amount of detailed audit work that has to be undertaken and whether a wholly substantive approach is necessary in certain audit areas.

(h)   Consideration as to ethical issues such as independence, objectivity and Provisions Available to Smaller Entities.

(i)   Discussions with the audit staff as to any knowledge the engagement partner and/or other staff has of the client which will be pertinent to the current year's audit.

(j)   Consideration of information within the permanent audit file and whether or not this needs updating or is relevant.

The audit planning meeting will be held at least 2 weeks prior to the audit being undertaken and will be held during completion of the audit planning.

Audit Fieldwork   All on-site audit fieldwork will be undertaken in accordance with all the requirements of the audit programme and with consideration to those ISAs which are specifically relevant to the audit client in question. It should be noted that the clarified ISAs require all parts of an ISA to be complied with when a particular ISA is relevant.

Where sections of the audit programme are not relevant to the client then the audit manager will discuss with the engagement partner why, in the opinion of the audit staff, those requirements are not relevant. The engagement partner will then conclude whether or not those requirements are not relevant and these considerations will be documented on the current year's audit file.

Where those sections of the audit programme are relevant and are substantiated with audit work/evidence, then those sections of the audit programme will be cross-referenced to the relevant sections of the audit file showing the audit work performed and the audit evidence obtained.

All audit work undertaken on the audit assignment will be documented and summarised. A summarised schedule of all the audit work undertaken, procedures adopted and conclusions made will be documented at the front of each individual section of the current year's audit file. The summarised document will be cross-referenced to the relevant sections of the audit file showing the evidence and work performed.

All information obtained from the client during the course of the audit fieldwork will remain confidential between the audit client and the audit firm and any breaches of client confidentiality will be dealt with under the audit firm's disciplinary procedure.

All audit staff will act in a professional and courteous manner and any acts of unprofessional behaviour will be dealt with using the audit firm's disciplinary process.

During the course of the audit any contentious issues or matters requiring technical guidance will be raised primarily with the audit manager. The audit manager will then establish whether or not they are in a position to deal with the contentious issue/complex issue and if not the audit manager will raise the issue with the engagement partner who will decide on the best course of action. All correspondence relating to the contentious/complex issue will be placed on the current year's audit file and documented accordingly.

Audit Testing   All audit testing will be done in accordance with the audit plan being referred to. The nature, extent and timing of the audit testing will be documented within each individual section of the current year's audit file, summarised at the front of each audit section and cross-referenced accordingly.

Where audit testing fails, as a result of weaknesses or inappropriate testing, alternative testing will be considered. The audit staff will consult with the audit manager who will determine:

(a)   The appropriateness of the test that has failed.
(b)   Design further tests taking into consideration the audit area, the complexity of the area, the objective of the test to be performed and the knowledge of the client and the internal controls in place for that particular audit area.

Where tests of control, substantive testing or alternative tailored testing fails, the issue will be primarily raised with the audit manager who will then advise the engagement partner. The engagement partner will then consider the steps required to address the failures.

Discussions with management will take place as soon as is reasonably practicable to discuss the failings. At all times, these discussions will be documented and brought to the engagement partner's attention in order that they can consider the impact of the weaknesses and discussions on the audit opinion.

Audit Timescale The date of a client audit will be agreed with the client in writing. The audit manager will agree the dates and establish (based on their knowledge of the client and by reference to the previous audit file) as to how long will be deemed necessary to undertake the audit.

The audit firm will adopt a policy of requiring at least three months notice prior to undertaking an audit. Where audits are required on a lesser timescale, the engagement partner will decide on the best course of action.

Audit planning meetings will take place between the audit staff and the engagement partner at least two weeks prior to the detailed audit work being undertaken.

All extension to audit work due to technical issues or failings will be discussed with the audit manager who will then discuss the issues with the engagement partner. The engagement partner will then hold discussions with the client to address the issues and to determine the extent of the audit timescale required.

Material Weaknesses Where, during the course of an audit, a material weakness is found within the client's internal control environment which gives rise to a material misstatement within the client's financial statements, then the audit manager will report this issue to the engagement partner as soon as is reasonably practicable.

Where the engagement partner concludes that a material weakness exists, then the engagement partner will hold a discussion with the client to address the issue. The engagement partner will give the client ample opportunity to address the weakness. Where the weakness has given rise to a material error or misstatement within the financial statements, the engagement partner will give the client ample opportunity to correct the error.

Where the client refuses to correct any error(s) or weaknesses, the engagement partner will consider both the impact the error/weakness has on the audit report and, in certain circumstances, the appropriateness of continuing to act for the audit client and the relevance of seeking legal advice — particularly concerning material disputes between the audit firm and the audit client.

Audit Completion Upon completion of the detailed audit work, a review of the audit procedures, tests and conclusions will be undertaken by the audit manager pre-completion. The review will consider the following:

(a)   Whether the tests undertaken by the audit staff have achieved their objectives in accordance with ISAs.
(b)   Whether the outcomes of the tests have met our expectations, based on our knowledge of the client and our planning meetings.
(c)   Whether the information contained in the permanent audit file is still relevant or needs further updating.
(d)   Whether the tests of control/substantive testing or other tailored testing has revealed any significant weaknesses which cast doubt on the truth and fairness of the client's financial statements and whether the results of any further testing have reduced weaknesses to an acceptable level.
(e)   Whether any further audit work in relevant areas is required.

During the course of the review, the audit manager will refer to the materiality levels and determine whether or not the level is still appropriate bearing in mind the results of the audit work undertaken in each audit area, the complexity of the client and the nature of the client's business.

Where the materiality level is deemed inappropriate, the audit manager will discuss with the engagement partner the issues that have given rise to the inappropriateness and the engagement partner will then advise as to the relevant course of action with a view to adjusting the materiality level accordingly and agreeing with the audit manager the need for further appropriate audit work to be undertaken in those areas where the preliminary materiality level was inappropriate.

All audit files must be completed within the timescale defined during the audit planning meeting. Where an audit cannot be completed within this timescale, the engagement partner will consider the reasons and issue further instructions as to when the audit should be completed after consultation with the audit client.

Prior to commencement of the file completion and as soon as possible after the detailed audit work has been performed, a de-briefing meeting will be held between the audit manager and the engagement partner to discuss the findings of the audit and any issues which need to be brought to the attention of the engagement partner. The meeting will be held in the engagement partner's office as soon as the detailed audit work has been completed.

In the event that the engagement partner/audit manager is not available as soon as the detailed audit work has been completed, the meeting will take place as soon as is practicable but within no more than three weeks after the detailed audit work has been completed.

Upon completion of the detailed audit work and de-briefing meeting(s), the audit manager will have forty days to submit the file for review by the engagement partner and the engagement partner will have a further twenty days to review the file and the audit work undertaken and arrive at the audit opinion and issue the audit report. Upon completion of the audit report and submission of the financial statements to the client and appropriate authorities, the audit file will be considered for 'cold' review. The in-house timescales will be appropriately tailored for any requirements the audit client may have in terms of requiring the audited financial statements to be submitted by them.

In the event of independence threats, the audit report will not be signed until the independence threats have been reduced to an acceptable level and, if appropriate a 'hot' file review has taken place. The firm's appointed reviewer, Mr A Reviewer will be used for 'hot' and 'cold' file reviews on the basis of his independence.

All issues concerning material weaknesses or error will be documented within the firm's audit file.

Audit Report   Where an unqualified audit opinion is deemed appropriate, the audit firm will disclose such a conclusion in its letter to management as required by ISA 260 (revised). The letter to management will disclose all such information as required by ISA 260 (revised) and will be submitted to the client as soon as is reasonably practicable.

Where a qualified audit opinion is deemed appropriate or an emphasis of matter is to be included within the audit report then a meeting will be held with the audit manager the engagement partner to discuss the appropriateness of the opinion.

Where the engagement partner deems a qualified opinion appropriate, they will discuss the implications of such an opinion with the audit client with a view to obtaining the relevant audit information or being able to undertake the relevant audit testing in order to remedy the matter giving rise to the potential audit opinion.

Where there is no choice but to issue a qualified opinion, following discussions with the audit client, then the discussion will be documented on the current year's audit file and a letter informing the client of the reasons why a qualified audit opinion will be given and requesting a suitable response from the client.

In all circumstances, the audit opinion will be arrived at using the results of the audit, relevant auditing standards and guidance from our professional body, where appropriate.

All audit reports will be issued either on the day of or the day after approval of the financial statements.

Communication of Matters to the Audit Client The firm will communicate all matters to the audit client in accordance with ISA 260 (revised) and ISA 265.

In addition, the audit firm will also request management representations, where appropriate, and issue letters of comment where weaknesses are identified.

Where a weakness is identified, the audit firm will advise the audit client as to the impact the weakness has on the financial statements.

Where no weaknesses are identified and no material errors are found in relation to the audit client, a letter informing the audit client will be sent regardless to comply with ISA 260 (revised).

All finalised audited financial statements will be submitted to the audit client within three days of approval of the financial statements and signing of the auditor's report. The financial statements will be accompanied by a letter informing the management and, where applicable, those charged with governance, of the outcomes of any meetings held between the audit client and the audit firm and the end result of our auditor's report.

In all instances, a letter of engagement will be issued to the client to fulfil our obligations. This letter of engagement will be reviewed on an annual basis to determine its appropriateness. Monitoring The audit firm accepts its responsibility for ensuring that audit work is performed to the highest standards possible and in accordance with all legislative and regulatory requirements imposed on the audit firm.

To meet this requirement, the audit firm will submit, on an annual basis, (at least) one audit file for 'cold' file review. The decision as to which audit file(s) should be submitted for cold review will be made by the engagement partner and such a decision will be arrived at after considering:

(a)   The complexity of the audit client.
(b)   The work performed.
(c)   The audit report issued.
(d)   The points that arose during the course of the audit.
(e)   The number of contentious issues that arose during the course of the audit.

In selecting the file(s) for review, the engagement partner will take into consideration areas where (s)he feels the audit staff may be weak and, conversely, where (s)he feels the audit staff have significant strengths.

The results of the 'cold' file review will be taken into consideration by the engagement partner who will assist in the quality control of the audit firm. The quality control of the audit firm is reviewed on an annual basis.

Following a 'cold' file review, the results of such a review will be discussed with the staff engaged on the audit assignment. In particular any additional training which the engagement partner considers appropriate will also be taken into consideration and discussed with those members of staff.

Where any monitoring review stipulates deficiencies, the engagement partner will take an independent view on the deficiencies and consider whether these are valid given the circumstances in which the deficiency may have taken place. Where the engagement partner concludes the deficiency is a result of the firm's audit work, then the engagement partner will:

(a) Take appropriate action in relation to an individual engagement (for example, discuss with the audit client) or staff member(s).
(b) Communicate his/her findings to the client and/or personnel involved to aid the training and professional development.
(c) Review and/or change the audit firm's quality control policy or policies and procedures.
(d) Adopt the firm's disciplinary proceedings against staff member(s) who fails to comply with recommendations or the audit firm's quality control policies and procedures.

Following discussions with the staff members(s) following a monitoring procedure, the engagement partner will communicate the issues discussed to the staff member(s) in writing and a copy will be placed on the individual's personnel file. The discussions will include:

(a) A description of the monitoring procedures performed.
(b) The conclusions drawn from the monitoring procedure.
(c) Where relevant, a description of the deficiencies and recommended courses of action which should be taken to remedy the deficiency or deficiencies.

Where threats to independence are identified (for example, where the audit firm provides non-audit services to an audit client), the engagement partner will assess the threats and (if deemed appropriate) deploy the use of 'hot' reviews in order to minimise the risk to an acceptable level.

If the engagement partner cannot minimise the risk to an acceptable level by adhering to guidelines issued by the IAASB or via 'hot' review, the engagement partner will withdraw from the audit engagement.

Complaints Procedure In the unfortunate event of a complaint by a client about the audit firm or a member of the audit firm's staff, the letter of engagement provides the audit client with the procedures this firm has adopted to deal with complaints.

The audit client should approach the engagement partner with details of the complaint. The engagement partner will have sufficiently reasonable time to investigate the complaint and draw conclusions as to how the complaint arose, the nature of the complaint and the remedies available.

Where the audit client is not satisfied by the engagement partner's response, the engagement partner will discuss with the audit client the recommendations the audit client would like to be undertaken. If, in the opinion of the engagement partner, the audit client's recommendations cannot be implemented, then, in accordance with the engagement letter, the audit client has the right to take the matter up with our professional body.

All complaints are expected to be dealt with as swiftly as possible and at the satisfaction of both the audit firm and the audit client.

Where the complaint is in direct relation to a staff member, the staff member will have the opportunity to discuss the circumstances surrounding the complaint with the engagement partner to offer their input.

Where the complaint is in relation to the audit firm's system of quality control and/or technical issues, then all such complaints must be referred to the engagement partner for consideration and to third parties, for technical confirmation, if necessary.

The audit firm will deal with such complaints in as reasonable time as necessary.

General Summary

(a)   All audit files will contain the required documentation and evidence of appropriate testing to allow the reporting principal to form their opinion on whether the financial statements give a true and fair view, or present fairly in all material respects, the state of the entity's affairs.
(b)   All audit work from planning through to completion will be undertaken using technical guidance, relevant ISAs and guidance through our audit programme.
(c)   All material decisions will be discussed with the audit client as soon as is reasonably practicable by the audit manager and engagement partner.
(d)   All files will be completed satisfactorily and must be completed within a total of sixty days after the detailed audit work has been performed.
(e)   All meetings held with the client will be documented and confirmed with the client in writing.
(f)   All audit clients will be given a letter of engagement as soon as is reasonably practicable.
(g)   Management representations, management letters and communication of audit findings will be issued to the client as soon as is reasonably practicable.

I have read and understood the above policies in accordance with the firm's quality control procedures governed by ISQC 1.

Signed . . . .

Chapter Roundup

ISQC 1 deals with quality control issues and practising firms must ensure such issues are adequately documented in accordance with the standard.

ISQC 1 covers:

* Leadership responsibilities for quality control within the audit firm.
* Relevant ethical requirements.
* Acceptance and continuation of client relationships and specific engagements.
* Human resources.
* Engagement performance.
* Monitoring.

The firm should appoint an appropriately suitable person(s) to deal with and oversee ISQC 1 issues.

APPENDIX 1: OVERVIEW OF IFRS AND IAS

IFRS 1 'FIRST-TIME ADOPTION OF IFRS'

The objective of IFRS 1 is to make sure that a reporting entity that adopts IFRS as its financial reporting basis prepares financial statements that:

(a) Are clear for users and achieve 'comparability' over all the periods presented within the financial statements.
(b) Provide a suitable starting point for reporting under IFRS.
(c) Can be generated at a cost that does not exceed benefits to users.

An entity who chooses IFRS as its financial reporting basis must prepare an opening statement of financial position (balance sheet) at the date of transition to IFRS. In preparing its opening statement of financial position (balance sheet), a reporting entity must:

(a) Recognise all IFRS assets and liabilities.
(b) Not recognise assets and liabilities not permitted by IFRS.
(c) Classify assets and liabilities by IFRS.
(d) Apply IFRS in measuring all recognised assets and liabilities.

EXEMPTIONS

IFRS 1 grants limited exemptions in certain areas where the costs of complying with the requirements would outweigh the benefits to the users of financial statements detailed as follows:

Property, Plant and Equipment

IFRS 1 allows a 'frozen' revaluation derived from previous GAAP to be used as deemed cost.

Business Combinations

On adoption of IFRS, any positive goodwill in an entity's statement of financial position (balance sheet) is frozen and tested annually for impairment. Any negative goodwill must be written back to retained earnings.

Employee Benefits

Actuarial gains and losses on first-time adoption of IFRS can be recognised within the pension asset or liability. This is also the case where a spreading policy is adopted for actuarial gains and losses which arise after the date of transition to IFRS.

Exchange Difference Reserve

If an entity did not recognise an exchange difference reserve in its statement of financial position (balance sheet) under the previous GAAP, a separate exchange reserve does not have to be recognised under first-time adoption of IFRS. However, the exchange differences would not be recycled on disposal of the foreign subsidiary.

Financial Instruments

In the main, the provisions in IAS 32 'Financial Instruments: Presentation' and IAS 39 'Financial Instruments: Recognition and Measurement' relating to the comparative periods do not have to be followed in respect of first-time adoption of IFRS.

Current Developments

The International Accounting Standards Board (IASB) has put forward new proposals relating to organisations adopting IFRS for the first time.

The proposed amendments to *First Time Adoption of International Financial Reporting Standards* would see references to a fixed transition date of 1 January 2004 replaced with 'the date of transition to IFRSs'. This means that entities adopting the standard for the first time would not have to restate derecognition transactions that occurred before the date of transition to IFRSs.

In addition, first-time adopters would also not have to recalculate 'day 1' differences on initial recognition of financial instruments, where the transaction occurred before the date of transition to IFRSs.

The exposure draft, *Removal of Fixed Dates for First-Time Adopters*, closed for comment on 27 October 2010.

DISCLOSURE

IFRS 1 requires the following disclosures to be made in an entity's financial statements:

- Full reconciliations of the statement of financial position (balance sheet) from previous GAAP to IFRS.
- Full reconciliations of the statement of comprehensive income (income statement) for the comparative period.
- Full explanations of the adjustments to be made in the above reconciliations.

The financial statements must also contain an explicit disclosure that the financial statements comply, in all respects, with IFRS.

Roundup

The aim of IFRS 1 is to ensure that an entity's first IFRS financial statements and interim reports provide high quality and transparent information.

There are five exemptions from fully retrospective application relating to: property, plant and equipment, business combinations, employee benefits, exchange difference reserve and financial instruments.

> The date of transition to IFRS is the start of the earliest period for which comparative information is provided.
>
> Extra disclosures are required in an entity's financial statements where they adopt IFRS for the first-time.

IFRS 2 'SHARE-BASED PAYMENT'

The objective of this standard is to outline the financial reporting requirements that an entity who engages in share-based payment transactions should comply with in their financial statements. It outlines the requirements an entity is to reflect in both its statement of comprehensive income (income statement) and its statement of financial position (balance sheet) that the effects of share-based payments has on the entity's financial statements.

IFRS 2 covers three types of share-based payment transactions:

(a) Equity-settled share-based payment transactions where the entity receives goods or services as consideration for equity instruments of the entity, including shares or share options.
(b) Cash-settled share-based payment transactions where the entity acquires goods or services by incurring liabilities to the supplier of those goods or services for amounts which are based on the price or value of the entity's shares or other equity instruments of the entity.
(c) Transactions in which the entity receives or acquires goods or services and the terms of the arrangement provide either the entity or the supplier of those goods or services with a choice of whether the entity settles the transaction in cash or by issuing equity instruments.

Where an entity has equity-settled share-based payment transactions, an entity should measure the goods or services received together with any corresponding increase in equity, directly at the fair value of the goods or services received. Where the fair value cannot be reliably estimated, the entity is required to measure their value, together with the corresponding increase in equity, indirectly by reference to the fair value of the equity instruments granted.

IFRS 2 also states that:

(a) Transactions with employees and third parties providing similar services should be measured at the fair value of the equity instruments granted at the grant date.
(b) Transactions with parties other than employees have a rebuttable presumption (which is rarely rebutted) that the fair value of the goods or services received can be reliably estimated. The fair value is measured at the date the entity receives the goods or services.
(c) Where goods or services are measured at fair value of the equity instruments granted, IFRS 2 specifies that vesting conditions, other than market conditions, are *not* taken into account when estimating the fair values of the shares or options at the measurement date. Vesting conditions *are* taken into account by adjusting the number of equity instruments included in the measurement of the transaction.

(d)   IFRS 2 requires that fair values are to be based on market prices, where these are available. Where market prices are not available, then fair value is estimated by using a valuation technique to arrive at a valuation that estimates what the value of the equity instruments would be at the measurement date in an arm's length transaction with knowledgeable and willing persons.

Where cash-settled share-based payments are made, these must be measured by the entity at the fair value of the liability. An entity is also required under the provisions of IFRS 2 to re-measure the fair value of the liability at each reporting date until the liability is settled.

Where an entity enters into a share-based payment transaction where the terms of the arrangement allow the entity to settle the transaction in cash or equity instruments, the entity should account for these as a cash-settled share-based payment transaction.

Illustration

Entity A grants two thousand share options to each of its three directors on 1 January 2009. The terms of the option are that the directors must still be in the employment of Entity A on 31 December 2011 when the options vest. The fair value of each option as at 1 January 2009 is $10 and all of the options are expected to vest. The options will only vest if Entity A share price reaches $16 per share. As at 31 December 2009, the share price was only $7 per share and it is not expected to rise in the next two years. Further, it is expected that only two directors will be employed as at 31 December 2011.

The increase in the share price should be ignored for the purposes of calculating the value of the share options as at 31 December 2009. The fact that only two directors will be employed as at 31 December 2011 must, however, be taken into account, therefore:

$$2,000 \text{ options} \times 2 \text{ directors} \times \$10 \times 1 \text{ year} / 3 \text{ years} = \$13,333$$

The entries in the books are:

DR statement of comprehensive income (payroll costs)

CR equity in the statement of financial position

Roundup

IFRS 2 covers three types of share-based payment transaction: 'equity-settled share-based payment', 'cash-settled share-based payment' and 'transactions in which the entity receives or acquires goods or services'.

Equity-settled share-based payment transactions are measured at the fair value of the goods or services received. If fair values cannot be reliably estimated, the entity is required to measure their value, together with corresponding increases in equity, indirectly by reference to the fair value of the equity instruments granted.

Transactions with employees and third parties providing similar services are measured at the fair value of the equity instruments granted at the grant date.

> Transactions with parties other than employees have a rebuttable presumption that the fair value of the goods or services received can be reliably estimated.
>
> Vesting conditions (other than market conditions) are not taken into account where goods or services are measured at fair value of the equity instruments granted.
>
> Fair values are to be based on market prices, where these are available. If market prices are not available, fair value is estimated by using a valuation technique.
>
> Cash-settled share-based payments are measured by the entity at the fair value of the liability.

IFRS 3 'BUSINESS COMBINATIONS'

The objective of this IFRS is to deal with the information that an entity provides within their financial statements about a business combination and the effect that this combination has on the reporting entity's financial statements. IFRS 3 deals with how an acquirer:

(a) Recognises and measures, in its financial statements, the identifiable assets acquired, the liabilities assumed and any non-controlling interest in the acquiree.
(b) Recognises and measures the goodwill acquired in the business combination or a gain from a bargain purchase.
(c) Determines what information to disclose to enable users of the financial statements to evaluate the nature and financial effects of the business combination.

When a business acquires another business, the business combination must be accounted for by applying the acquisition method of accounting. Essentially one party in the transaction is the 'acquirer' and the entity that is being acquired is the 'acquiree'.

All identifiable assets and liabilities of the acquiree are measured at their acquisition-date fair value. Any non-controlling interest in an acquiree is measured at fair value or as the non-controlling interest's proportionate share of the acquiree's net identifiable assets. The non-controlling interest is the interest held in the equity shares of the acquiree by outside investors.

The IFRS requires an acquirer to identify any difference between:

(a) The aggregate of the consideration transferred, any non-controlling interest in the acquiree and, in the case of step acquisitions, the acquisition-date fair value of the acquirer's previously held equity interest in the acquiree.
(b) The net identifiable assets acquired.

The difference between the two will generally be recognised as goodwill. In the situation where there is a bargain purchase, the gain will instead be recognised in the statement of comprehensive income. Any consideration (including contingent consideration) is measured at fair value.

DISCLOSURE REQUIREMENTS

IFRS 3 requires the acquirer to disclose information within the financial statements that enables the user of the financial statements to evaluate the nature and financial effect of the business combination(s) that occurred during the reporting period, or a period after the reporting date but before the financial statements are authorised for issue. After a business combination, the acquirer must also disclose any adjustments recognised in the current reporting period that relate to business combinations that occurred in the current or previous reporting periods.

AMENDMENTS TO IFRS 3

IFRS 3 was amended in January 2008 to converge it more with US GAAP and to place a greater emphasis on control. A summary of the major changes are as follows:

Goodwill

Goodwill can be recognised in full even where control is less than 100%. Before the revisions to IFRS 3, the IFRS stated that, on acquisition, goodwill should only be recognised with respect to the part of the subsidiary undertaking that is attributable to the interest held by the parent. This is still an option in IFRS 3 following the revision but now goodwill can be recognised in full, which now means that the non-controlling interest will be measured at fair value and be included within goodwill.

Illustration

Entity A purchases an 80% equity stake in Entity B for $100. The net assets of Entity B at the date of acquisition were $50.

Using the 'old' method of goodwill recognition, goodwill would be calculated as:

	$
Cost of investment	100
Net assets acquired ($50 × 80%)	(40)
Goodwill	60

Under the 'revised method', the non-controlling interest goodwill is measured at fair value in order to include their share of the goodwill. If we estimate that the fair value of the non-controlling interest's share of goodwill is $10, the calculation is as follows:

	$
Cost of investment	100
Net assets acquired ($50 × 80%)	(40)
	60
Non-controlling interest share of goodwill	10
Goodwill under the revised method	70

The non-controlling interest share of the goodwill is included in Entity A's statement of financial position (balance sheet) as follows:

DR Goodwill (non-current assets)
CR Non-controlling interests (equity)

Acquisition-Related Costs

Prior to the revisions to IFRS 3, transaction costs associated with a business combination (for example, legal fees and accountancy fees for due diligence work) were capitalised along with the cost of the acquisition, thus, forming part of the goodwill calculation. The International Accounting Standards Board concluded that these types of cost must now be expensed as these costs are not part of the fair value exchange between buyer and seller of the business. This means, therefore, that in the year of acquisition the acquirer's statement of comprehensive income will show substantially higher legal and professional fees. However, this reduction in profits should be outweighed in future years because the annual impairment test on the goodwill will be based on a reduced initial balance.

Step Acquisitions

Prior to the revisions of IFRS 3, it was a requirement to measure the assets and liabilities at fair value at every step of the transaction to calculate a portion of goodwill. This requirement was removed during the revision process. Instead an entity should measure goodwill as the difference, at the acquisition date, between the fair value of any interest in the business held before the acquisition, the consideration transferred and the net assets acquired.

Partial Acquisitions

Non-controlling interests are measured as their proportionate interest in the net identifiable assets (as was the case before IFRS 3 was revised). Non-controlling interests can also be measured at fair value.

Recognition of Assets and Liabilities Subject to Contingencies

There were a few (limited) changes to the assets and liabilities recognition criteria under IFRS 3. There is a new requirement to recognise assets and liabilities that are subject to contingencies at fair value at the acquisition date. Any subsequent changes in fair value will be accounted for in accordance with other IFRSs (which will usually be in profit or loss) rather than as an adjustment to goodwill.

Partial Disposal of a Subsidiary Whilst Control is Retained

A partial disposal of an investment in a subsidiary, whilst control is retained, is accounted for as an equity transaction with owners and a gain or loss is not recognised.

A partial disposal of an interest in a subsidiary where the parent loses control but retains an interest and, thus, becomes (for example) an associate, will trigger recognition of a gain or loss on the entire interest. A realised gain or loss is recognised on the portion that has been disposed of; a holding gain is recognised on the interest retained, calculated as the difference between the fair value and book value of the retained interest.

Acquisition of Shares after Control has been Obtained

Where the parent acquires some, or all of the non-controlling interest in a subsidiary, this should be treated as a treasury share-type transaction and therefore should be accounted for as an equity transaction. There is an interpretation summary, IFRIC 11 'IFRS 2: Group and Treasury Share Transactions' which gives guidance in this area.

Roundup

IFRS 3 deals with the information an entity provides in their financial statements concerning a business combination and the effect this combination has on the reporting entity's financial statements.

A business combination is accounted for using the 'acquisition method' of accounting. One party in the transaction is the acquirer and the other party (the party that is being acquired) is the acquiree.

All identifiable assets and liabilities are measured at their acquisition-date fair value.

Non-controlling interests are measured at fair value or as the non-controlling interest's proportionate share of the acquiree's net identifiable assets. This means, therefore, that goodwill can be recognised in full, even if the parent holds less than 100% of the subsidiary.

The revisions to IFRS 3 in 2008 changed the accounting in respect of: acquisition-related costs, step acquisitions, partial acquisitions, recognition of assets and liabilities subject to contingencies, partial disposal of a subsidiary whilst control is retained and acquisition of shares after control has been obtained.

IFRS 4 'INSURANCE CONTRACTS'

The objective of this IFRS is to deal with the financial reporting or insurance contracts by an entity that issue insurance contracts (for example, an insurance company to its policyholders).

An insurance contract is defined as a contract under which one party (the insurer) accepts significant insurance risk from another party (the policyholder) by agreeing to compensate the policyholder if a specific uncertain future event (the insured event) adversely affects the policyholder.

IFRS 4 applies to all insurance contracts that an entity issues and to reinsurance contracts that it holds, except for certain contracts that are dealt with in other IFRSs such as IAS 39 Financial Instruments: Recognition and Measurement.

IFRS 4 also contains the following provisions which entities involved in insurance contracts must comply with. Specifically IFRS 4:

- Prohibits provisions for potential claims under contracts that do not exist at the end of the reporting period.
- Requires a test for the adequacy of recognised insurance liabilities and requires an impairment test to be carried out for reinsurance assets.
- Requires an insurer to keep insurance liabilities in its statement of financial position (balance sheet) until such time that they are discharged, cancelled or expire. It also requires an entity to present insurance liabilities without offsetting them against related reinsurance assets.

An entity that has to report using IFRS 4 can change its accounting policies for insurance contracts but only if, as a result, the financial statements present information that is more relevant and no less reliable, or more reliable and no less relevant. The IFRS also stipulates that an insurer cannot:

- Measure insurance liabilities on an undiscounted basis.
- Measure contractual rights to future investment management fees at an amount that exceeds their fair value by comparison with current fees charged by other market participants for similar services.
- Use non-uniform accounting policies for the insurance liabilities of subsidiaries.

Roundup

IFRS 4 is very industry-specific and deals with the financial reporting for insurance contracts by an entity that issues such contracts.

IFRS 4 also applies to reinsurance contracts, though it does not deal with certain contracts that are dealt with in other IFRSs, such as those dealt with under IAS 39 'Financial Instruments: Recognition and Measurement'.

IFRS 4 prohibits provisions for potential claims under contracts which do not exist at the end of the reporting period. In addition it requires a test for the adequacy of recognised insurance liabilities as well as an impairment test for reinsurance assets. IFRS 4 also requires an insurer to keep insurance liabilities in its statement of financial position (balance sheet) until such time that they are discharged, cancelled or expire. Insurance liabilities cannot be offset against insurance assets.

Accounting policies in respect of insurance contracts can be changed but only if they result in the financial statements presenting information that is more relevant and no less reliable, or more reliable and no less relevant.

IFRS 5 'NON-CURRENT ASSETS HELD FOR SALE AND DISCONTINUED OPERATIONS'

The objective of IFRS 5 is to specify how assets that both qualify for, and are treated as 'held for sale' should be presented and disclosed within a set of financial statements. The standard also deals with discontinued operations.

A non-current asset (or disposal group) that is held for sale must be up for sale in its present condition and the sale must be highly probable. In order for the sale to be classed as 'highly probable', there must be certain characteristics present. These are as follows:

- Management must be committed to a plan to sell the asset.
- There must be an active programme of seeking a buyer.
- The asset (or disposal group) must be available for immediate sale.
- The sale is highly probable.
- The sale is expected to complete within one year of the asset being classified as held for sale.

Where an asset (or disposal group) is classified as held for sale, depreciation of such an asset or disposal group must cease as soon as it is classified as held for sale. The asset or disposal group should be carried in the statement of financial position (balance sheet) at the lower of the carrying amount in the statement of financial position (balance sheet) and fair value less costs to sell. Fair value is essentially how much could be received by knowledgeable and willing persons in exchange for the asset in an arm's length transaction.

DISCONTINUED OPERATIONS

A discontinued operation is a part of an entity that has either been disposed of or is classified as held for sale (for example, a division of a manufacturing plant). A discontinued operation should:

- represent a separate major line of business or geographical area of operations;
- be part of a single co-ordinated plan to dispose of a separate major line of business or geographical area of operation; or
- be a subsidiary acquired exclusively with a view to resale.

Where an entity has a discontinued operation, the revenue, expenses, pre-tax profit or loss and the income tax expense of the discontinued operation should be separately presented on the face of the statement of comprehensive income (income statement) or in the notes to the financial statements.

Roundup

IFRS 5 deals with accounting for assets which both qualify for and are treated as held for sale as well as dealing with discontinued operations.

IFRS 5 requires the sale of a non-current asset or discontinued operation to be 'highly probable'.

To qualify as 'highly probable', IFRS 5 requires: management to be committed to a plan to sell the asset, there must be an active programme of seeking a buyer, the asset (or disposal group) must be available for immediate sale, the sale is highly probable and the sale is expected to complete within one year of the asset being classified as held for sale.

A discontinued operation should: represent a separate major line of business or geographical area of operations, be part of a single co-ordinated plan to dispose of a separate major line of business or geographical area of operation or be a subsidiary acquired exclusively with a view to resale.

An entity is required to disclose revenue, expenses, pre-tax profit or loss and the income tax expense of the discontinued operation separately on the face of the statement of comprehensive income (income statement). Alternatively an entity can make such disclosure within the notes to the financial statements.

IFRS 6 'EXPLORATION FOR AND EVALUATION OF MINERAL RESOURCES'

The objective of this IFRS is to deal with the financial reporting requirements for entities which operate in the mineral extractive industry.

Exploration for and evaluation of mineral resources is the search for mineral resources after the entity has obtained legal rights to explore in a specific area.

In summary, IFRS 6 permits an entity to develop an accounting policy for exploration and evaluation assets without specifically considering the requirements of paragraphs 11 and 12 of IAS 8 'Accounting Policies, Changes in Accounting Estimates and Error'. As a result of this requirement in IFRS 6, an entity can still continue to use the accounting policies it adopted immediately before adopting IFRS (for example, a company who previously reported under UK GAAP).

Where circumstances change which may give rise to the carrying amount of the exploration and evaluation assets being in excess of a recoverable amount, IFRS 6 does require an impairment test to be undertaken. The actual recognition of impairment does vary in IFRS 6 but once impairment has been identified, IFRS 6 requires the entity to measure the impairment in accordance with the provisions laid down in IAS 36 'Impairment of Assets'.

The IFRS also requires that an entity determine an accounting policy for the allocation of exploration and evaluation assets to cash-generating units or groups of cash-generating units for the purposes of impairment testing.

Roundup

IFRS 6 deals with the financial reporting requirements for entities that operate exclusively in the mineral extractive industry.

IFRS 6 permits an entity to develop an accounting policy for exploration and evaluation assets without specifically considering the requirements in IAS 8 'Accounting Policies, Changes in Accounting Estimates and Errors'.

IFRS 6 requires impairment tests to be carried out where circumstances give rise to the carrying amount of the exploration and evaluation assets being in excess of a recoverable amount. Where such impairment tests are required the provisions in IAS 36 'Impairment of Assets' must be complied with.

IFRS 6 requires an entity to determine an accounting policy for the allocation of exploration and evaluation assets to cash-generating units or groups of cash-generating units for the purposes of impairment testing.

IFRS 7 'FINANCIAL INSTRUMENTS: DISCLOSURE'

IFRS 7 came into force for annual periods beginning on or after 1 January 2007, with earlier adoption permitted. Its objective is to deal with the disclosures required in an entity's financial statements in connection with financial instruments. Before the issuance of this IFRS, the disclosure requirements were contained in IAS 32 'Financial Instruments: Presentation and Disclosure'. IAS 32 now contains just the presentation requirements of financial instruments and is renamed 'IAS 32: Presentation'.

This IFRS applies to all entities, including entities that have few financial instruments (for example, simply receivables and payables).

In order to enable users to evaluate the effect of financial instruments in an entity's financial statements, IFRS 7 requires the following disclosures to be contained within the financial statements:

- The significance of financial instruments for the entity's financial position and performance.
- The nature and extent of risks arising from financial instruments to which the entity is exposed during the period and at the end of the reporting period and how the entity manages those risks.

IFRS 7 also requires qualitative and quantitative information about the entity's exposure to risk.

QUALITATIVE DISCLOSURES

The qualitative disclosures describe management's objectives, policies and processes for managing those identified risks.

QUANTITATIVE DISCLOSURES

The quantitative disclosures provide the information needed about the extent to which the entity is exposed to risk based on information provided internally to the entity's key management personnel.

In addition, IFRS 7 requires specific minimum disclosures about credit risk, liquidity risk and market risk.

Roundup

IFRS 7 is a relatively new standard which deals with the disclosures required in an entity's financial statements in connection with financial instruments.

IFRS 7 requires an entity to disclose the significance of its financial instruments for the entity's financial position and performance and the nature and extent of risks arising from financial instruments to which the entity is exposed during the period and at the end of the reporting period. It also requires an entity to disclose how it manages those risks.

IFRS 7 requires qualitative and quantitative disclosures concerning an entity's exposure to risk in addition to specific minimum disclosures about credit risk, liquidity risk and market risk.

IFRS 8 'OPERATING SEGMENTS'

The objective of this IFRS is to deal with the information that an entity should disclose in its financial statements to enable users to evaluate the nature and financial effects of the business activities and the economic environment in which the business operates.

The standard itself deals with two segments:

- Reportable segments.
- Operating segments.

A reportable segment is an operating segment or aggregations of operating segments that meet specified criteria.

Operating segments are components of an entity about which separate financial information is available that is evaluated regularly by the chief operating decision maker in deciding how to allocate resources and in assessing performance. The chief operating decision maker could be the chief executive or some other senior official.

IFRS 8 requires a reporting entity to disclose in their financial statements a measure of operating segment profit or loss and of segment assets. The IFRS also requires a reconciliation of total reportable segment revenues, total profit or loss, total assets, liabilities and other amounts disclosed within the financial statements for reportable segments to corresponding amounts in the entity's financial statements.

The IFRS also requires an entity to report information about the revenues it derives from its products or services and disclose information concerning the countries in which it earns revenues. In addition, the IFRS requires descriptive information to be disclosed concerning the way the operating segments were determined as well as the products and services provided by the segments, the differences between the measurements used in reporting segment information and those used in the entity's financial statements as well as changes in the measurement of segment amounts from period to period.

Roundup

IFRS 8 deals with the information an entity should disclose in its financial statements in respect of reportable segments and operating segments.

A reportable segment is an operating segment or aggregations of operating segments that meet specified criteria.

An operating segment is a component of an entity about which separate financial information is available.

IFRS 8 requires an entity to disclose a measure of operating segment profit or loss and of segment assets. In addition, a reconciliation of total reportable segment revenues, total profit or loss, total assets, liabilities and other amounts disclosed within the financial statements are required.

IFRS 8 requires an entity to report information on how it derives its revenues from its products or services as well as requiring disclosure concerning the countries in which it earns revenues.

IFRS 9 'FINANCIAL INSTRUMENTS'

IFRS 9 'Financial Instruments' was released in November 2009 and is intended to completely replace IAS 39 'Financial Instruments: Recognition and Measurement' by the end of 2010.

The new standard is designed to simplify the way entities account for financial instruments and will apply to accounting periods beginning on or after 1 January 2013, though earlier adoption is permitted.

INITIAL RECOGNITION OF FINANCIAL ASSETS

All financial assets are initially measured at fair value plus, in the case of a financial asset not at fair value through profit or loss.

Preparers of financial statements who use IFRS should note that IFRS 9 only deals with the classification and measurement of financial assets. A consistent theme of IFRS 9 is that it requires financial assets to be classified on initial recognition at amortised cost or fair value.

Financial assets are measured at amortised cost dependant on how the entity manages its financial instruments in its business model (see below). If the entity's business model is to hold financial assets in order to collect contractual cash flows, the financial asset can be measured at amortised cost.

However, the contractual terms must give rise (on specified dates), to cash flows that are solely payments of capital and interest on the capital amount (principal amount) outstanding. The financial asset concerned cannot be recognised at amortised cost if the entity intends to sell it to realise its fair value changes. IFRS 9 does contain several examples to illustrate this condition.

Any other financial asset that does not meet these criteria is measured at fair value.

THE BUSINESS MODEL FOR RECOGNITION OF FINANCIAL ASSETS

Management and key personnel are responsible for their entity's business model in relation to how it manages its financial instruments. (Management and key personnel are dealt with and defined in IAS 24 'Related Party Disclosures'.) This approach was considered appropriate by the IAS because it aligns the accounting for financial assets with the way the entity deploys the assets in the business.

WITHDRAWAL OF OTHER TYPES OF FINANCIAL ASSET

IAS 39 has the following categories of financial assets:

(a) Held-to-maturity assets.
(b) Available-for-sale assets.

In IFRS 9, the above categories are eliminated in an attempt to simplify the process of accounting for such financial assets.

EMBEDDED DERIVATIVES

Under IAS 39, an embedded derivative is a feature within a contract. It acts as a component part of a 'hybrid' financial instrument which also includes a non-derivative host contract. This means that some of the cash flows of the hybrid instrument vary in a similar way to a stand-alone derivative. A hybrid instrument is a combination of both the host contract and the embedded derivative.

A common embedded derivative is where a company raises finance by issuing convertible debt. The host contract is the loan, but this loan contains an option to convert the debt into shares. The option is the embedded derivative because it is deriving its value from fluctuations in the share price. IAS 39 requires the use of 'split accounting' where the host contract (in this case the loan) is split from the derivative (the option).

Under IFRS 9, embedded derivatives are no longer separated from hybrid contracts that have a financial asset host. Instead, the entire hybrid contract is assessed for classification using the principles above.

OPTION TO RECOGNISE AT FAIR VALUE

IFRS 9 allows entities to designate a financial instrument on initial recognition at fair value through profit or loss, even if it meets the criteria for recognition at amortised cost. However, care must be taken here to apply the option when appropriate because the option to measure at fair value should only be exercised where it eliminates, or significantly reduces a measurement or recognition inconsistency, often referred to as an 'accounting mismatch'.

RECLASSIFICATION

Where an entity changes its business model and the change is significant to the entity's operations and demonstrable to third parties, reclassification of the financial asset from fair value through profit or loss to amortised cost or vice versa should take place. Such situations are considered very rare, but if it is done it should be done prospectively from the date of reclassification. Any gains, losses or interest are not restated.

INVESTMENTS IN EQUITY INSTRUMENTS

Under IFRS, an entity will prepare the statement of comprehensive income, which comprises the usual income statement but with an added statement being the statement of 'other comprehensive income'. Other comprehensive income contains any gains and losses which have been taken in the statement of financial position (balance sheet) which would traditionally be reported in the statement of recognised income and expenses such as gains on property revaluations and actuarial gains and losses on defined benefit pension schemes.

Where an entity has shares in other entities (investments in equity instruments), these should be measured at fair value. Where investments in equity instruments are subsequently remeasured, any gains or losses on remeasurement are recognised in profit or loss. However, under IFRS 9, dividends on investments in equity instruments that are not held for trading are recognised in profit or loss as opposed to other comprehensive income. This is consistent with the requirements laid down in IAS 18 'Revenue', provided that none of the dividend represents recovery of the investment.

For an investment in an equity instrument that is not held for trading, IFRS 9 has an option to allow an entity, on initial recognition, to irrevocably elect to measure it at fair value through other comprehensive income, with only dividend income being recognised in profit or loss.

Users of IFRS 9 should note that no amount recognised in other comprehensive income is ever reclassified to profit or loss at a later date.

MEASUREMENT

Under IAS 39, investments in unquoted equity instruments can be measured at cost where fair value cannot be reliably determined. IFRS 9 eliminates this exception and stipulates that all such instruments are measured at fair value. IFRS 9 does, however, contain comprehensive guidance on when cost may be the best estimate of fair value and when cost is not representative of fair value.

IMPAIRMENT

On the subject of impairment of financial assets, the guidance contained in IAS 39 still applies. In designing this standard, the IASB wanted to simplify the process of accounting for financial assets. For this reason, the numerous impairment methods detailed in IAS 39 have been reduced to one single method of impairment in IFRS 9. The intention here is to improve comparability.

CHANGES IN FAIR VALUE OF FINANCIAL ASSETS

Any changes in the fair value of financial assets that are measured at fair value are recognised in profit or loss. However, equity instruments which exercise the option to recognise such changes in other comprehensive income should not be measured in profit or loss. This also applies to any gains or losses relating to financial assets that are also part of a hedge relationship.

FINANCIAL LIABILITIES

IFRS 9 only deals with financial assets and does not consider financial liabilities. The IASB is in the process of dealing with the issues relating to financial liabilities and is expected to issue final requirements at the end of 2010.

Roundup

IFRS 9 is intended to fully replace IAS 39 'Financial Instruments: Recognition and Measurement'.

IFRS 9 was designed to simplify the way entities account for financial instruments and is effective for accounting periods beginning on or after 1 January 2013, though earlier adoption is permitted.

IFRS 9 only deals with financial assets.

Financial assets are measured at amortised cost dependant on how the entity manages its financial instruments in its business model.

IFRS 9 withdraws the classification of financial assets into 'held-to-maturity' assets and 'available-for-sale' assets.

Embedded derivatives are no longer separated from hybrid contracts that have a financial asset host. In contrast, IAS 39 requires the use of 'split accounting' where the host contract is split from the derivative.

IFRS 9 allows an entity to designate a financial instrument on recognition at fair value through profit or loss even if it meets the criteria for recognition at amortised cost.

Reclassification is permitted from fair value through profit or loss and vice versa, but such situations are considered rare. Such reclassification is done prospectively from the date of reclassification and any gains, losses or interest are not restated.

If an entity has shares in other entities (investments in equity instruments), these are measured at fair value. Dividends on investments in equity instruments that are not held-for-trading are recognised in profit or loss rather than in other comprehensive income, provided that none of the dividend represents recovery of the instrument.

No amount recognised in other comprehensive income is ever reclassified to profit or loss at a later date.

IFRS 9 requires all investments in unquoted entities to be measured at fair value.

IFRS 9 contains only one method of impairment, as opposed to the numerous impairment methods contained in IAS 39.

Changes in the fair value of financial assets are recognised in profit or loss. Equity instruments which exercise the option to recognise such changes in other comprehensive income should not be measured in profit or loss.

IAS 1 'PRESENTATION OF FINANCIAL STATEMENTS'

The objective of IAS 1 is to deal with the basis on which an entity presents its general purpose financial statements and the composition of those financial statements.

A complete set of general purpose financial statements of an entity (prepared at least annually) should comprise the following:

- A statement of financial position as at the end of the period (balance sheet).
- A statement of comprehensive income for the period.
- A statement of changes in equity for the period.
- A statement of cash flows for the period.
- Notes to the financial statements.

Illustration

Entity A Inc Statement of Financial Position as at 31 December 2009

	2009 $	2008 $
ASSETS		
Non-current assets		
Property, plant and equipment	X	X
Goodwill	X	X
Investments	X	X
Available-for-sale investments	X̲	X̲
	X	X
Current assets		
Inventory	X	X
Trade and other receivables	X	X
Other current assets	X	X
Cash and cash equivalents	X̲	X̲
	X	X
Total assets	X	X
Equity and liabilities		
Share capital	X	X
Other reserves	X	X
Retained earnings	X	X
Non-controlling interests	X̲	X̲
	X̲	X̲
Non-current liabilities		
Long term loans	X	X
Deferred tax	X	X
Obligations under finance leases	X̲	X̲
	X	X
Current liabilities		
Trade and other payables	X	X
Short term loans	X	X
Current tax	X̲	X̲
	X	X
Total liabilities	X	X
Total equity and liabilities	X	X

Entity A Inc Statement of Comprehensive Income for the year ended 31 December 2009

	2009 $	2008 $
Revenue	X	X
Cost of sales	(X)	(X)
Gross profit	X	X
Distribution costs	(X)	(X)
Administrative expenses	(X)	(X)
Other expenses	(X)	(X)
Finance costs	(X)	(X)

	2009 $	2008 $
Profit before tax	X	X
Income tax expense	(X)	(X)
Profit for the year from continuing operations	X	X

Other Comprehensive Income:

	2009 $	2008 $
Exchange differences on translation of foreign operations	X	X
Gains on property revaluation	X	X
Actuarial gains (losses) on defined benefit pension scheme	X	X
Other comprehensive income for the year net of tax	X	X
Total comprehensive income for the year net of tax	X	X

Entity A Inc Statement of Changes in Equity for the year ended 31 December 2009

	Share Capital	*Retained Earnings*	*Revaluation*	*Total*
Opening balance 1 January 2009	X	X	X	X
Total comprehensive income for the year	X	X		
Revaluation gain	X	X		
Dividends	(X)	(X)		
Balance at 31 December 2009	X	X	X	X

When an entity prepares financial statements that comply with IFRSs it is required to make an explicit and unreserved disclosure of such within its financial statements. An entity cannot make such an explicit and unreserved disclosure of compliance with IFRS if they do not comply with all the requirements of IFRS.

GOING CONCERN

The concept of going concern is central to the basis of determining whether the financial statements should be prepared on a going concern basis or not. When preparing financial statements, management must make an assessment of the entity's ability to continue as a going concern. If management do not intend to liquidate or cease trading, management should prepare the financial statements on a going concern basis.

However, where management deems it necessary to liquidate or cease trading or has no other alternative but to do so, the financial statements must not be prepared on the going concern basis.

Management must also disclose within the financial statements when they become aware of material uncertainties related to events or conditions that may cast significant doubt on the entity's ability to continue as a going concern.

The strained economic climate has thrust the issue of going concern back into the professional headlines recently and it is a concept that practitioners and clients alike encounter difficulties in applying.

Financial statements are prepared on a going concern basis when it is assumed that the entity will continue to operate for the foreseeable future and there is neither the intention nor the need to either liquidate it or cease trading. Directors of small entities are not relieved of their duty to assess going concern because all financial statements are required to give a true and fair view (or present fairly in all material respects). Some directors consider a going concern review should only be undertaken by entities that fall within the scope of statutory audit — this is not the case, and directors of small entities should consider taking advice to ensure that disclosures and accounting treatment of items within the financial statements conform to the financial reporting framework adopted by it.

In October 2009, the Financial Reporting Council in the United Kingdom issued guidance *Going Concern and Liquidity Risk: Guidance for Directors of UK Companies 2009*. This guidance applies to accounting periods ending on or after 31 December 2009, however, the guidance covers existing requirements set out in Financial Reporting Standards and the Financial Reporting Standard for Smaller Entities (FRSSE) and, as a consequence, earlier accounting periods will be expected to comply with this guidance.

ASSESSING GOING CONCERN

Principle 1 in the guidance states:

> *Directors should make and document a rigorous assessment of whether the company is a going concern when preparing annual and half-yearly financial statements. The process carried out by the directors should be proportionate in nature and depth depending upon the size, level of financial risk and complexity of the company and its operations.*

Smaller entities undoubtedly will undertake lesser work in assessing going concern, whereas larger, more complex companies will undertake more detailed assessment of going concern.

Directors should assess going concern at least annually and it should be considered at an early stage. In assessing going concern, directors should take into consideration key factors such as over-dependence on one customer, the extent of borrowing facilities and the likelihood of these being renewed if they are nearing maturity.

BUDGETS AND FORECASTS

Some entities may prepare forecasts and budgets, and the guidance recognises that these are long-established techniques in business management; and undoubtedly medium and large entities will often have this information to hand. Budgets and forecasts can only be as reliable as the underlying information used in their preparation and so realistic presumptions need to be made by the directors in preparing such budgets and forecasts. In situations where the critical assumptions underlying the forecasts and budgets may be challenged, the forecasts and budgets should be revised so they predict the most likely outcome.

SENSITIVITY ANALYSIS AND 'STRESS-TESTING'

The guidance issue by the FRC suggests an entity, particularly a medium and large entity, prepares a sensitivity analysis in order to understand any critical assumptions on which any budgets and forecasts are prepared. 'Stress testing' is a concept which involves assessing the extent to which budgets and forecasts react to changes in variables such as changes in interest rates and exchange rates.

BORROWING FACILITIES

The lack of finance available to entities during recession, particularly smaller entities, has been well-publicised throughout the world. Indeed, some entities are finding it increasingly more difficult to obtain finance, or even renew existing borrowing facilities, as banks and other financial institutions 'tighten their belt'.

The renewal of borrowing facilities or the application for borrowing can be indicative of an entity's ability to continue as a going concern and the guidance issued by the FRC does make the point that in the absence of confirmation from the lenders this does not, in itself, cast significant doubt upon the entity having the ability to continue as a going concern.

CONTINGENT LIABILITIES

Directors should assess the entity's exposure to contingent liabilities. Where entities have frequent disputes with suppliers, the scope for contingent liabilities, which may result in legal proceedings giving rise to large outflows of cash in the future, is much higher than an entity which does not have many disputes.

PRODUCTS AND SERVICES

It is crucially important that directors obtain information about major aspects of the organisation from which they operate, in particular looking at what competitors are doing, how technically up-to-date their products or services are as well as looking at other factors such as economic and political factors.

TIMING OF CASH FLOWS

In assessing going concern, directors should take account of the timing of cash flows. For example, if the entity has a large outflow of cash due to take place in the year, directors should assess how this outflow of cash can be matched with inflows of cash. This is particularly important if the entity has a large tax liability to be settled or if loan repayments are falling due.

PERIOD OF REVIEW

Principle 2 states:

> *Directors should consider all available information about the future when concluding whether the company is a going concern at the date they approve the financial statements. Their review should usually cover a period of at least twelve months' from the date of approval of annual and half-yearly financial statements.*

This is where some directors often misinterpret this principle. The review period should be twelve months from the date of approval of the financial statements — not twelve months from the reporting date.

The guidance recognises that FRSSE, UK GAAP and IFRS each provide for a minimum period that directors should review when assessing going concern. The guidance also recognises that the extent of the review period is a matter of judgement, which is to be based on facts and circumstances and may mean that obtaining information for longer periods may be required.

Where an entity is audited, the directors' review of going concern is less than twelve months from the date of approval of the financial statements and the directors have failed to make such disclosure in the financial statements, the auditor's report must make reference to the fact that the review period is less than twelve months from the date of approval in their report.

DISCLOSURES

Principle 3 states:

> *Directors should make balanced, proportionate and clear disclosures about going concern for the financial statements to give a true and fair view. Directors should disclose if the period that they have reviewed is less than twelve months from the date of approval of annual and half-yearly financial statements and explain their justification for limiting their review period.*

There are three conclusions which all entities can reach in assessing going concern:

1. The use of the going concern basis of accounting is appropriate because there are no material uncertainties related to events or conditions that may cast significant doubt about the ability of the entity to continue as a going concern.
2. The use of the going concern basis is appropriate but there are material uncertainties related to events or conditions that may cast significant doubt on the ability of the entity to continue as a going concern.
3. The going concern basis of accounting is not appropriate.

NO MATERIAL UNCERTAINTIES

In situations where there are no material uncertainties, the financial statements should be prepared under the going concern basis. Relevant disclosures should be made in the financial statements including disclosures concerning the principal risks and uncertainties facing the entity (the Business Review). Listed entities are required to make further disclosure concerning:

- The main trends and factors which are likely to affect the future development, performance or position of the entity's business.
- Information about persons with whom the entity has contractual or other arrangements that are essential to the business of the entity.

MATERIAL UNCERTAINTIES BUT THE GOING CONCERN BASIS IS APPROPRIATE

The financial statements should be prepared on the going concern basis but disclosure should be made in the financial statements concerning the material uncertainties that give rise to the significant doubts about the going concern principle.

GOING CONCERN BASIS IS INAPPROPRIATE

Where the directors conclude that the going concern basis of accounting is inappropriate in the circumstances, disclosure should be made on the accounting basis adopted (for example, using break up values).

OFFSETTING

An entity must present, separately, each class of similar items and must not offset assets and liabilities, income or expense, unless required or permitted by an IFRS.

Illustration

In the case of a capital-based grant, under IAS 20 'Accounting for Government Grants and Disclosure of Government Assistance' an entity can choose to recognise the grant either as deferred income (debit cash, credit deferred income liability), or they can offset the credit against the cost of the non-current asset (debit cash, credit non-current assets).

This illustration highlights when an IFRS permits offsetting.

ACCOUNTING POLICIES

An entity must disclose information about significant accounting policies. It should also disclose the judgements (except those involving estimations) that management has made in the process of applying the entity's accounting policies and that have the most significant effect on the amounts recognised in the financial statements. Accounting policies should relate to the substance (the commercial reality) of the amounts recognised in the financial statements.

Roundup

IAS 1 deals with the basis on which an entity presents its general purpose financial statements and also specifies the contents which those general purpose financial statements must comprise.

An entity is required to make an explicit and unreserved disclosure of compliance with IFRS within their financial statements. Such a statement cannot be made if they do not comply with all the requirements of IFRS.

Financial statements must be prepared on the going concern basis. Where management deems it necessary to liquidate or cease trading, or has no other realistic alternative but to do so, the financial statements must not be prepared on the going concern basis.

IAS 1 states that an entity must not offset assets and liabilities or income and expenses unless required or permitted by an IFRS.

An entity must disclose information about its significant accounting policies and disclose the judgements that management has made in the process of applying those policies which have the most significant effect on the amounts recognised in the financial statements.

IAS 2 'INVENTORY'

IAS 2 prescribes the accounting treatment for inventories held by the entity at the end of a reporting period.

In summary, IAS 2 says that inventory is to be valued at the *lower* of cost or net realisable value.

COST

IAS 2 states that 'cost' should comprise:

- The cost of purchase (for example, the cost of raw materials).
- The costs of conversion (converting raw materials to finished goods).
- Other costs.

'Other costs' should only be recognised as those costs that have been incurred in bringing the inventories to their present location and condition.

VALUATION

IAS 2 prescribes two possible valuation methods for inventories. An entity can adopt either the first-in first-out (FIFO) basis or the weighted average basis. Entities are not permitted to use the last-in first-out (LIFO) basis of valuation.

NET REALISABLE VALUE

Net realisable value is the estimated selling price in the ordinary course of business, less the estimated costs of completion and the estimated costs necessary to make the sale.

Illustration

Entity A Inc imports chemical products from overseas and the reporting date is 31 December 2009. At that date Entity A undertakes an inventory count where inventory has been valued at the lower of cost or net realisable value in accordance with IAS 2 provisions. It has extracted details of the following chemical products.

Product Number	Cost $	NRV $	Valuation $
556–009CCV	200.00	450.00	270.00
556–010CCV	150.00	340.00	150.00
556–011CCV	200.00	120.00	200.00

The first product valuation includes an element of administrative salaries because this product is highly valuable and involves a lot of extra administration work.

The second product appears to be fairly stated.

The third product is obsolete and management deem the net realisable value to be $nil.

The revised inventory valuation based on the above should be as follows:

Product Number	Cost $	NRV $	Valuation $
556–009CCV	. 200.00	450.00	200.00 (1)
556–010CCV	150.00	340.00	150.00
556–011CCV	200.00	$nil	$nil (2)

(1) The administrative salary needs to be deducted because IAS 2 specifically states that general administrative overheads should be excluded from the costs of inventory valuation. (2) Management's assessment is that the saleable value of this product is nil and this product needs to be written down to nil in order to accord with IAS 2 'lower of cost or net realisable value' principles.

Roundup

IAS 2 requires inventory to be valued at the lower of cost or net realisable value.

Cost comprises: purchase cost, costs of conversion and other directly attributable costs.

Net realisable value is the estimated selling price in the ordinary course of business, less the estimated costs of completion and the estimated costs necessary to make the sale.

There are only two acceptable methods of inventory valuation under IAS 2: first-in first-out and average cost method. The last-in first-out method of inventory valuation is specifically prohibited in IAS 2.

IAS 7 'STATEMENT OF CASH FLOWS'

IAS 7 prescribes the provision of information that an entity should disclose about historical changes in cash and cash equivalents of an entity by means of a primary statement of cash flows. *Cash* is cash on hand and 'on demand' deposits. *Cash equivalents* are short-term, highly-liquid investments that are readily convertible to known amounts of cash and which are subject to insignificant risks of changes in value.

The statement of cash flows is a primary statement and as such needs to be given equal prominence as that of the statement of financial position (the balance sheet), the statement of comprehensive income (the income statement) and the statement of changes in equity.

DIRECT AND INDIRECT METHOD

An entity can apply either the direct or the indirect method of preparing its cash flow statements. IFRS does prefer the direct method, though the indirect method is a valid one.

The direct method involves major classes of gross receipts and gross cash payments being disclosed (take 'direct' from the cash book), whilst the indirect method involves profit or loss being adjusted for the effects of transactions of a non-cash nature, any deferrals or accruals of past or future operating receipts or payments and items of income or expense associated with investing or financing cash flows.

Illustration

Direct Method

This method shows each major class of gross cash receipts and gross cash payments and could appear as follows:

Cash receipts from customers	X
Cash paid to suppliers	(X)
Cash paid to employees	(X)
Cash paid for other operating expenses	(X)
Interest paid	(X)
Income taxes paid	(X)
Net cash from operating activities	**X**

Illustration

Indirect Method

The indirect method adjusts the profit or loss (prepared under the accruals basis) for the effects of non-cash transactions and could appear as follows:

Operating profit	X
Adjustments for:	
Depreciation	X
Amortisation	X
(Increase)/decrease in receivables	X
(Increase)/decrease in inventories	X
Increase/(decrease) in payables	X
Interest paid	(X)
Income tax paid	(X)
Net cash from operating activities	**X**

BASIS OF PREPARATION

An entity needs to prepare the statement of cash flows using three standard headings:

- Operating activities.
- Investing activities.
- Financing activities.

Operating activities are the principal day-to-day revenue-producing activities of the entity that are not investing or financing activities.

Investing activities are the acquisition and disposal of long-term assets and other investments not included in cash equivalents.

Financing activities are activities that result in the change and size of the contributed equity and borrowings of the entity.

Illustration

Using the Indirect Method

Entity A Statement of Cash Flows for the year ended 31 December 2009

	$, 000	$, 000
Profit from operations	5,630	
Adjustments for:		
Depreciation	2,172	
Loss on disposal of property, plant and equipment	183	
Operating cash flows before movements in working capital		7,985
Increase in inventories	(335)	
Increase in trade receivables	(266)	
Increase in trade payables	84	
Cash generated by operations		7,468
Income taxes paid	(854)	
Interest paid	(800)	
Net cash from operating activities		5,814
Investing activities		
Proceeds from disposal of property, plant and equipment	509	
Purchases of property, plant and equipment	(13,646)	
Net cash used in investing activities		(13,137)
Financing activities		
New bank loans raised	3,000	
Proceeds of share issue	4,500	
Dividends paid	(700)	
Net cash used in/from financing activities		6,800
Net increase/(decrease) in cash and cash equivalents		(523)
Cash and cash equivalents at beginning of year		587
Cash and cash equivalents at end of year		64

Roundup

The statement of cash flows is a primary financial statement and must be given the same prominence as that of the statement of financial position (balance sheet), the statement of comprehensive income (income statement) and the statement of changes in equity.

Cash is cash on hand and on demand deposits. *Cash equivalents* are short-term, highly-liquid investments that are readily convertible to known amounts of cash and which are subject to insignificant
risks of changes in value.

The statement of cash flows can be prepared using the 'direct' or 'indirect' method of preparation.

The *direct* method involves disclosing major classes of gross receipts and gross cash payments. The
indirect method involves adjusting profit or loss for the reporting period for the effects of non-cash
transactions.

The statement of cash flows is presented under three heading: operating activities, investing activities
and financing activities.

IAS 8 'ACCOUNTING POLICIES, CHANGES IN ACCOUNTING ESTIMATES AND ERRORS'

The objective of this standard is to deal with how an entity should select its accounting policies,
how it deals with changes within these accounting policies (and estimation techniques) and
what to do when an error is discovered within the financial statements.

ACCOUNTING POLICIES

Accounting policies are the specific principles, bases, conventions, rules and practices applied
by an entity in preparing and presenting its financial statements. In selecting their accounting
policies, an entity must ensure that the policies used result in the financial statements providing
reliable and relevant information about the effects of transactions or other events or conditions
concerning the entity's financial position, performance and cash flows. In other words, they
should reflect the 'substance' of transactions.

CHANGES IN ACCOUNTING POLICY

IFRS allows management to change an accounting policy where the change will result in
presenting more relevant and reliable information within the financial statements. Where an
entity changes an accounting policy then the change must be applied retrospectively (as if
the revised policy had always been adopted). This means doing a prior-period adjustment so
the comparative year is consistent. It would be inappropriate to have amounts stated in the
current year using one accounting policy but stated in the comparative year using a different
accounting policy.

Examples of changes in accounting policy are:

- Changing from depreciated historic cost to revaluation in respect of non-current assets.
- Changing from translating the results of foreign subsidiaries at closing rates to translating them at average rates for the year.
- Changing revenue recognition policies in respect of the sale of goods and provisions
  of services.
- Changing from recognising depreciation charges within administrative expenses to
  recognising them in cost of sales.

CHANGES IN ESTIMATION TECHNIQUES

A change in estimation technique is not a change in accounting policy. Changes in estimation techniques result from new information or new developments. The effects of a change in estimation technique is recognised prospectively by way of inclusion in profit or loss in the period of the change where the change affects that period only, or the period of change and future period if the change affects both.

Examples of changes in estimation techniques are:

- Changing depreciation rates from reducing balance to straight-line.
- Changing statistical methods in respect of provisions.
- Changes in after-tax revenue recognition methods for finance leases (such as actuarial after-tax and investment period methods).
- Changes in the methods used to estimate turnover and profits attributable to the stage of completion in respect of construction contracts.
- Changes in the methods used to calculate provisions for slow-moving inventory provisions or bad debt provisions.
- Changes in the basis used to calculate sales returns provisions.

ERROR

Prior period errors are omissions from, and misstatements in, the entity's financial statements for one or more prior periods which have occurred as a result of failure to use or misuse of reliable information that was available when the financial statements were prepared and could reasonably have been expected to have been obtained and taken into account in the preparation and presentation of those financial statements.

To correct an error in the prior period will result in a prior-period adjustment by restating the comparative amounts for the prior period(s) presented in which the error occurred or, if the error occurred before the earliest period presented, by restating the opening balances of assets, liabilities and equity for the earlier prior period presented.

Illustration

Entity A prepares its financial statements to 31 December each year. The following information has been decided upon before the preparation of the financial statements begins:

Entity A will value its inventory on a weighted average basis this year as opposed to LIFO as the weighted average will result in more relevant and reliable being presented.

The revised inventory valuation is a change in accounting policy because the basis of valuation will be different in the current year. Entity A should, therefore, restate the comparative year's inventory valuation and adjust its opening retained earnings in order that the financial statements are comparable and consistent.

Illustration

The depreciation rates for property, plant and equipment will be changed from 20% straight line to 15% reducing balance as this represents a more relevant method of the entity's consumption of the assets.

The change in depreciation rates is a change of estimation technique. The entity is still consuming the asset, though at a slower rate than originally estimated. The initial recognition of the asset has not changed in amount and, therefore, this change should be recognised prospectively with no prior-period adjustment.

Illustration

Depreciation amounts are to be recognised in cost of sales as opposed to administrative expenses.

The change of classification of depreciation rates from expenses to cost of sales is a change in presentation; therefore, a change in accounting policy. This adjustment is required to be made retrospectively.

Roundup

IAS 8 requires an entity to select appropriate accounting policies relevant to the entity's individual circumstances. It also requires an entity to deal with changes in those policies as well as outlining the requirements an entity should adopt in terms of changes in accounting estimates and outlining the requirements an entity is to follow in respect of prior period errors.

Accounting policies are the specific principles, bases, conventions and practices applied by an entity in preparing and presenting its financial statements.

A change in accounting policy must be applied retrospectively to the earliest period reported in the financial statements.

Changes in accounting estimates are applied prospectively.

A prior-period adjustment will be required in the case of error.

IAS 10 'EVENTS AFTER THE REPORTING PERIOD'

The objective of this standard is to prescribe the accounting treatment and disclosure requirements for those events that are adjusting or non-adjusting events.

Events after the reporting period are those events, both favourable and unfavourable, that occur between the end of the reporting period and the date on which the financial statements are approved.

ADJUSTING EVENT

An adjusting event is an event which occurs between the reporting date and the date on which the financial statements are authorised for issue and which provides evidence of conditions that existed at the reporting date which need to be taken into account in the financial statements.

NON-ADJUSTING EVENT

A non-adjusting event refers to conditions that arose after the reporting period but did not exist at the reporting date.

An adjusting event should be taken into account within the financial statements of the reporting entity. A non-adjusting event is disclosed within the notes to the financial statements.

Illustration

Entity A Inc supplies component parts to the vehicle manufacturing industry. At the year-end an inventory count was undertaken and a significant amount of components for a particular vehicle model were held in inventory. The value of these components was significantly high. After the reporting date the vehicle manufacturer announced that the particular vehicle model was being withdrawn from sale immediately and that these components would no longer be required. There is no alternative market for these components.

The above illustration indicates a situation where the entity should write down the value of the components to net realisable value (it is an adjusting event).

Illustration

Entity A has a financial asset which is carried at fair value through profit or loss. The reporting date is 31 December. On 25 January, the value of the share price in respect of the financial asset reduced considerably.

The above illustration indicates a situation where the entity should not write down the value of the investment because it can be demonstrated that the decline occurred after the reporting date.

Roundup

Events after the reporting period can be classified between 'adjusting' and 'non-adjusting' events and can be either favourable or adverse.

An *adjusting event* is an event which occurs between the reporting date and the date on which the financial statements are authorised for issue (i.e. approved). Such events need to be adjusted for within the financial statements.

A *non-adjusting* event is an event that arose after the reporting date but did not exist at the reporting date. A non-adjusting event is not adjusted for in the financial statements but instead may be disclosed within the financial statements.

IAS 11 'CONSTRUCTION CONTRACTS'

The objective of this standard is to deal with the accounting treatment of revenue and costs associated with construction contracts. A standard was needed in this area because of the nature of construction contracts.

It is widely understood that some construction contracts can last for years and, thus, fall into different accounting periods. The problem is knowing how to recognise revenue and costs that fall into different accounting periods.

IAS 11 defines a construction contract as a contract specifically negotiated for the construction of an asset or a combination of assets that are closely interrelated or interdependent in terms of their design, technology and function or their ultimate purpose or use.

REVENUE

Contract revenue is measured at the fair value of the consideration received or receivable.

CONTRACT COST

Contract cost shall comprise:

- Costs that relate directly to specific contracts.
- Costs that are attributable to contract activity in general and can be allocated to the contract.
- Such other costs as are specifically chargeable to the customer under the terms of the contract.

PROFIT-MAKING CONTRACTS

Where a contract is estimated to be profitable then revenue is recognised by reference to the stage of completion. Costs incurred in reaching the stage of completion are taken to the statement of comprehensive income as cost of sales. This is achieved by applying the percentage of completion to the total costs that are expected to occur over the life of the contract.

LOSS-MAKING CONTRACTS

Revenue is recognised by reference to the stage of completion. Cost of sales is essentially the balancing figure to interact with the revenue that has been recognised to generate the required loss. For example, a contract that is expected to make a loss of $100 and the contract revenue to be recognised is $80; cost of sales is $180 to generate a loss of $100.

UNCERTAIN CONTRACTS

Where the outcome of a contract is uncertain, no profit and no loss are recognised. Revenue to be recognised is the same as cost.

PERCENTAGE OF COMPLETION METHOD

The percentage of completion method is a method of accounting that recognises income on a contract as work progresses by matching contract revenue with contract costs incurred, based on the proportion of work completed.

The problem when dealing with the percentage of completion method lies in accurately deciphering the extent to which the projects are being finished and to assess the ability of the entity to actually bill and collect for the work done.

The percentage of completion method uses the contract account to accumulate costs and to recognise income. Under the provisions of IAS 11, income is not based on advances (cash collections) or progress billings. Any advances and progress billings are based on contract terms that do not necessarily measure contract performance.

Where costs and estimated earnings in excess of billings occur, the excess is classified as an asset. If billings exceed costs and estimated earnings, the difference is treated as a liability.

DOUBLE ENTRY

When costs are incurred on the contract:

    DR contract account
    CR cash/accruals/expenses

When amounts are billed:

    DR receivables
    CR contract account

To recognise revenue:

    DR contact account
    CR statement of comprehensive income

To recognise costs:

    DR statement of comprehensive income
    CR contract account

RECTIFICATION COSTS

When mistakes occur during the course of the contract, these are referred to as 'rectification costs'. Such costs are written off to the statement of comprehensive income as they occur.

Roundup

IAS 11 deals with the accounting treatment of revenue and costs associated with construction contracts.

IAS 11 defines a construction contract as

> *a contract specifically negotiated for the construction of an asset or a combination of assets that are closely inter-related or inter-dependent in terms of their design, technology and function or their ultimate purpose or use.*

Contract revenue is measured at the fair value of the consideration received or receivable.

Costs include: costs that are directly attributable to specific contracts and can be allocated to specific contracts and other costs which are specifically chargeable to the customer under the terms of the contract.

The stage of completion method is used to recognise revenue and costs in respect of profit-making contracts. Contract losses are recognised as soon as they are foreseen.

No profit or loss is recognised in respect of uncertain contracts. Revenue recognised is the same as cost.

Rectification costs are written off to profit or loss immediately as they occur.

IAS 12 'INCOME TAXES'

The objective of this standard is to deal with how an entity accounts for income tax (current and deferred tax). However, it also deals with all other taxes such as domestic and foreign taxes which are based on taxable profits. Income taxes also include withholding taxes.

CURRENT TAX

Current tax expense should be estimated by an entity and recognised as a liability to the extent the current tax remains unpaid. Where the amount of current tax paid is in excess of the current tax expense, the excess should be recognised as an asset. All current tax liabilities and assets must be measured at the amount expected to be paid (or recovered) from the tax authorities using tax rates and laws that have been enacted or substantively enacted by the end of the reporting period.

Accounting for current tax is fairly straight forward. The problems arise when we come to look at deferred tax.

DEFERRED TAX

Deferred tax is essentially the differences inherent between accounting profit and taxable profit. Deferred tax is the future tax consequences based on the current period transactions.

DEFERRED TAX ASSETS

Deferred tax assets should be measured at the tax rates that are expected to apply to the period when the asset is realised. Deferred tax assets should only be recognised when it is deemed probable that there will be sufficient taxable profit in future periods to allow the benefit, or part, or all, of that deferred tax asset to be used.

DEFERRED TAX LIABILITIES

Deferred tax liabilities should be measured at the tax rates that are expected to apply to the period when the liability is settled, based on tax rates and laws that have been enacted or substantively enacted at the end of the reporting period.

DISCOUNTING TO PRESENT DAY VALUES

The discounting of deferred tax to present day values is prohibited in IAS 12.

Illustration

Entity A Inc has invested in an item of plant that cost $40,000 and is being depreciated over 5 years. The net book value of the item of plant at the end of year 1 is ($40,000 − $8,000) = $32,000. Entity A operates in a jurisdiction where the taxation authority grants an 'Annual Investment Allowance' of up to $50,000 in a tax year and Entity A has taken advantage of this allowance. Entity A pays tax at 30%.

The accounting value of the item of plant is $32,000 but as Entity A has taken advantage of the tax authority's Annual Investment Allowance, the written down value for tax purposes of the same item of plant is actually $nil. A provision for deferred tax should be made in Entity A's financial statements to represent the fact that Entity A will pay more tax in future periods in order to refund a temporary cash flow advantage by claiming the tax authority's Annual Investment Allowance. The deferred tax liability to be recognised in the financial statements is calculated as:

Net book value	$32,000
Tax written down value	$nil
Difference	$32,000
Deferred tax liability	

$32,000 × 30% = $9,600
DR income tax expense (statement of comprehensive income)
CR deferred tax (statement of financial position)

DEFERRED TAX IN UK GAAP

FRS 19 'Deferred Tax' refers to 'timing differences' which recognise the mismatch between the accounting periods in which gains and losses are reported in the financial statements compared to when the tax effects arise. IAS 12 'Income Taxes' refers to 'temporary differences' which are concerned with the carrying amount of assets and liabilities in the financial statements compared to the effect on taxable profit if the associated assets or liabilities had been sold or settled at the reporting date. This approach is inherently more complex than UK GAAP at FRS 19 and will give rise to many more deferred tax provisions being made.

FRS 19 defines timing differences as:

Differences between an entity's taxable profits and its results as stated in the financial statements that arise from the inclusion of gains and losses in tax assessments in periods different from those in which they are recognised in the financial statements. Timing differences originate in one period and are capable of reversal in one or more subsequent periods.

An example of the above could be where an entity accrues income in 2010 which is subsequently taxable in 2011 on receipt. Conversely, an entity could make a provision for restructuring costs in 2010 which will attract tax relief when the expenditure has been incurred in 2011.

It therefore follows that a timing difference originates when a transaction is accounted for in the financial statements of an entity, but has not yet been accounted for in the tax computation. Timing differences reverse when the transaction is accounted for in the tax computation or the financial statements, whichever the case may be.

There are instances where timing differences arise and then reverse, but are never reflected in the tax computation. Such an example could be a provision for a bad debt done in 2010 and written back in 2011, as the provision has been deemed unnecessary. Other examples of timing differences are:

- Accelerated capital allowances in respect of non-current assets.
- Accrued pension liabilities in the financial statements which are subsequently granted tax relief when they are paid at a later date.
- Assets subject to revaluation, where the revaluation gain only crystallises for tax purposes when the asset is sold.
- Intra-group profits in inventory, which are unrealised at group level, but are reversed on consolidation.

DEFERRED TAX ASSETS

In the UK, the most common transaction giving rise to a deferred tax asset is unutilised tax losses. In times of economic difficulty, these are particularly common. A deferred tax asset is recognised in respect of unutilised tax losses because less tax will be payable in the future as the losses can be offset against future profits.

Care must be taken in recognising a deferred tax asset. A deferred tax asset should only be recognised when it is expected to be recoverable. Therefore, it can only be recognised as a deferred tax asset when it is more likely than not that there will be sufficient taxable profits generated by the entity in future periods from which the future reversal of the underlying timing differences can be deducted.

The term 'more likely than not' is not defined in FRS 19, but FRS 12 at paragraph 23 suggests that it should be taken to mean 'the probability that the event will occur is greater than the probability that it will not'. US GAAP at SFAS 109 'Income Taxes' suggests that something is 'more likely than not' if its likelihood of occurring is more than 50%.

For example, if an entity has tax losses in 2010, but the directors consider that 2011 will yield profits because they have won a lucrative contract, the directors can recognise a deferred tax asset.

In contrast, if an entity is producing losses year-on-year, then not only will doubt be cast on the entity's ability to continue as a going concern, but the chances are that there will not be suitable taxable profits generated in the future. As a consequence, a deferred tax asset should not be recognised. However, the mere existence of unrelieved tax losses should be taken as evidence that there will not be suitable future profits generated to offset the deferred tax asset and evidence to the contrary would normally be identifying the cause of the unrelieved tax losses and the fact that the entity has previously been profitable and past losses have also been able to be utilised against future profits.

DEFERRED TAX LIABILITIES

The most frequent transaction giving rise to a deferred tax liability in the financial statements is accelerated capital allowances.

Illustration

Entity A purchases an item of plant for £45,000. The entity's year-end is 31 July 2010 and it has been trading for a full twelve months. The entity's accounting policy in respect of plant and machinery is to write the cost of the asset off over the useful economic life of the plant using depreciated historic cost with a full year's depreciation charge in the year of acquisition and no depreciation in the year of disposal. In respect of the new item purchased, this machine is deemed to have a useful economic life of five years with no residual value. The entity has also taken advantage of HM Revenue and Custom's 'Annual Investment Allowance' and pays tax at 21%.

In Entity A's financial statements, the new item of plant will have a carrying value of (£45,000 − (£45,000 ÷ 5) £9,000) = £36,000. The entity has taken advantage of HMRC's annual investment allowance and has chosen to write off the whole of this cost in the 2010 tax computation. This results in the item of plant having a nil value for tax purposes.

The fact that HMRC has granted AIA against the full cost of the asset in 2010 has resulted in a disparity between the value of the asset for tax purposes and the value of the same asset for accounting purposes. As a result, the entity will pay more tax in future periods, representing an obligation for the entity to refund a temporary cash flow advantage by claiming the annual investment allowance. The deferred tax liability is calculated as follows:

Net book value of plant and machinery	£36,000
Tax written down value	£0
Difference	£36,000
Deferred tax liability (£36,000 × 21%)	£7,560

UK INDUSTRIAL BUILDINGS ALLOWANCE

Prior to the chancellor's announcement to change the Industrial Buildings Allowance (IBA) regime, the original rules on factories, warehouses, hotels and commercial buildings in enterprise zones meant that IBAs did not need to be repaid if they were retained in the business for a qualifying holding period of twenty-five years following the date of purchase. After the twenty-five-year period had elapsed, no balancing charge arose even if an industrial building was subsequently sold for more than its tax written down value.

Under the old rules, deferred tax which was attributable to capital allowances of this type would be recognised until the conditions for retaining IBAs had been met. Once the conditions were met and there was no possibility that HM Revenue and Customs could claw back the allowances, the differences became permanent and any deferred tax liability previously recognised was reversed — usually at the end of year 25.

In the chancellor's 2007 Budget, he announced two fundamental changes:

- Balancing adjustment provisions and those that recalculate writing-down allowances for purchasers were withdrawn for balancing events occurring on or after 21 March 2007.

- IBAs were to be phased out gradually from 2008/9 onwards by reducing the allowances from 4% to 3% to 2% to 1% with allowances being eliminated thereafter.

The measures introduced in the 2007 Budget meant that balancing adjustments would no longer arise and as a result, any deferred tax liability would never be reclaimed by HM Revenue and Customs. The removal of the balancing adjustment (and the qualifying period for retaining allowances) means that allowances received prior to the removal will become a permanent difference. As a consequence, no deferred tax liability should be made and any such deferred tax should be released. During the phasing out of IBAs, the allowance should be treated as a permanent difference as it arises.

GOVERNMENT GRANTS IN THE UK

Accounting for government grants is dealt with under the provisions laid down in SSAP 4 'Accounting for Government Grants'.

Non-taxable revenue-based grants do not have any deferred tax issues attached to them because the amortised credit to the profit and loss account is a permanent difference. This also applies to non-taxable capital-based grants, except to the extent that accelerated capital allowances apply.

Taxable revenue-based grants that are taxed when the company receives the grant (but recognised in the profit and loss account over a period of time for financial reporting purposes) will give rise to a timing difference on which a deferred tax asset may be required to be recognised on the unamortised balance carried forward to future periods. This is because the deferred tax asset will be recoverable in future accounting periods when the deferred credit unwinds.

Where the grant is received in respect of a non-current asset, the nature of the deferred tax will depend on both the accounting treatment and tax treatment of the grant. SSAP 4 allows the grant to be deducted from the cost of the non-current asset in the same way IAS 20 allows. It is worth mentioning at this point that incorporated entities in the UK are prohibited from deducting government grants from the purchase/production price of assets under the Companies Act 2006 paragraphs 17 and 27 Schedule 1 (SI 2008/410) and under the Financial Reporting Standard for Smaller Entities (FRSSE) at paragraph 6.4 despite SSAP 4 deeming this treatment acceptable. The standard refers only to incorporated entities that are governed by the accounting and financial reporting requirements of UK Companies' Legislation. However, this suggests that an unincorporated entity can deduct the grant from the cost of the asset.

If the grant is deducted from the cost of the asset, the deferred tax implications are simply accelerated capital allowances. If the grant is treated as deferred income for financial reporting purposes but deducted from the cost of the asset for tax calculation purposes, a deferred tax asset will arise on the unamortised grant which will then be offset against the deferred tax liability arising on the capital allowances.

DISCOUNTING DEFERRED TAX

The discounting of deferred tax assets and liabilities in the UK is quite rare. FRS 19 does allow deferred tax balances to be discounted to present day values. In contrast, IAS 12 specifically prohibits the discounting of deferred tax.

CURRENT DEVELOPMENTS

The IASB are planning to replace IAS 12 because the IASB has received many requests to clarify the various aspects of IAS 12.

The proposal is to withdraw the 'temporary difference' approach in IAS 12, which will result in simpler requirements based on principle. In addition, the definition of 'tax basis' is to be changed to be defined as:

The measurement under applicable substantively enacted tax law of an asset, liability or other item.

Other changes include:

- An additional specification that the tax basis of an asset is determined by the tax deductions that would be available if the entity recovered the carrying amount of the asset by sale [ED Para IN8 (b)].
- Introducing an initial step in determining deferred tax assets and liabilities so that no deferred tax arises in respect of an asset or liability if there will be no effect on taxable profit when the entity recovers or settles its carrying amount [ED Para IN8(c)].
- Introducing definitions of *tax credit* and *investment tax credit*.
- Removal of the initial recognition exception in IAS 12. The draft introduces a proposal for the initial measurement of assets and liabilities that have tax bases different from their initial carrying amount. An entity would recognise and measure the former in accordance with IFRSs and recognise a deferred tax asset or liability for any resulting temporary difference between the carrying amount and the tax basis. Where the consideration paid or received differs from the total recognised amounts of the acquired assets and liabilities (including deferred tax), an entity recognises the difference as an allowance against, or premium on, the deferred tax asset or liability [ED Para IN8(e)].

Changes to the exception in IAS 12 from the temporary difference approach relating to a deferred tax asset or liability in respect of subsidiaries, branches, associates and joint ventures. The proposal here is to restrict this to investments in foreign subsidiaries, joint ventures or branches that are essentially permanent in duration with no exception being proposed for associates [ED Para IN8 (f)].

- A proposal to recognise deferred tax assets in full less a valuation allowance to reduce the net carrying amount to the highest amount that is more likely than not to be realisable against taxable profit [ED Para IN8 (g)].
- The ED proposes additional guidance in respect of deferred tax assets, including the treatment of significant expenses for any relevant tax planning strategies [ED Para IN8 (h)].
- Currently IAS 12 is silent on the treatment of uncertain tax amounts. The proposal suggests current and deferred tax assets and liabilities be measured using the probability-weighted average amounts of possible outcomes [ED Para IN8 (i)].
- A proposal to clarify the meaning of 'substantively enacted'. The proposal is to define substantively enacted as future events required by the enactment process that have not historically affected the outcome and are unlikely to do so [ED Para IN8 (j)].
- IAS 12 currently uses the 'undistributed rate' in respect of the tax effects of distributions to shareholders. The proposal is for an entity to measure current and deferred tax assets and liabilities using the rate expected to apply when the tax asset or liability is realised

or settled, including the effect of the entity's expectations of future distributions [ED Para IN8 (k)].

- Adopting SFAS 109 requirements in respect of the allocation of income tax expense to the components of comprehensive income and equity [EED Para IN8 (l)].
- Classification of deferred tax assets and liabilities as either current or non-current. Currently IAS 1 requires all deferred tax to be classified as non-current [ED Para IN8 (m)].
- Clarification that the classification of interest and penalties is an accounting policy option and hence must be applied consistently and the introduction of a requirement to disclose the chosen policy [ED Para IN8 (n)].

Roundup

IAS 12 deals with the accounting for current and deferred income taxes.

Accounting for current tax is very straight forward; the difficulties arise through the accounting for deferred taxation.

IAS 12 uses the 'temporary difference' approach to accounting for deferred tax balances, whereas the UK's version (FRS 19) uses the 'timing difference' approach.

Deferred tax is essentially the differences inherent between accounting and taxable profit. Deferred tax is the future tax consequences based on the current period transactions.

There are plans to replace IAS 12 and an exposure draft was issued by the International Accounting Standards Board in March 2009 outlining their proposals in this area.

Accounting for deferred taxation in the United Kingdom under FRS 19 has notable differences compared to its international counterpart, IAS 12.

Deferred tax assets can only be recognised if it is deemed probable that there will be sufficient taxable profits in future periods to allow the benefit to be utilised.

IAS 12 prohibits the practice of discounting deferred tax balances.

IAS 16 'PROPERTY, PLANT AND EQUIPMENT'

The objective of this standard is to prescribe the accounting treatment for an entity for their property, plant and equipment. It defines 'cost' and deals with how an entity should write off the cost of their property, plant and equipment. It also deals with when an entity should recognise 'subsequent expenditure' on existing property, plant and equipment in the statement of financial position and when to write the subsequent expenditure off to the statement of comprehensive income.

INITIAL MEASUREMENT

An entity is required to measure its property, plant and equipment at cost. Cost comprises:

- Purchase price.
- Import duties.

- Non-refundable purchase taxes.
- Costs directly attributable in bringing the asset to the location and condition necessary for it to be capable of operating in the manner intended.
- Initial estimate of the costs of dismantling and removing the item and restoring the site on which it is located.

Cost should also be net of trade discounts and rebates.

SUBSEQUENT MEASUREMENT

After initial recognition an entity can choose between the cost model and revaluation model for its accounting policy.

Cost Model

This is the most frequently used model. After initial recognition, the asset is simply carried at its original cost less accumulated depreciation and less any amounts recognised in respect of impairment.

Revaluation Model

After initial recognition, the asset is carried at its fair value with any increases or decreases in the fair value being recognised in other comprehensive income and accumulated in equity under the heading of 'revaluation surplus'. Any increases in fair value shall only be recognised in profit or loss to the extent that it reverses a revaluation decrease of the same asset previously recognised in profit or loss.

Where an entity adopts the revaluation model then it must apply this model to all the assets in the same class.

DEPRECIATION

Depreciation is the systematic allocation of the depreciable amount of an asset over its useful life. Depreciable amount is calculated as the cost of the asset, less its residual value. The residual value of an asset is the estimated amount that an entity would currently obtain from disposal of the asset after deducting the estimated costs of disposal.

IMPAIRMENT

Impairments are dealt with under the provisions of IAS 36.

Illustration

An entity purchases a new building for $200,000. Legal costs have been incurred amounting to $3,000 and the building is estimated to have a useful economic life of fifty years when the residual value is estimated to be $100,000.

On initial recognition, IAS 16 states that 'cost' is the purchase price plus any costs directly attributable in bringing the asset to its location and condition necessary for it to be capable of operating in the manner intended by management. On initial recognition, cost will comprise initial purchase price of

---

$200,000 plus the legal fees of $3,000. Depreciable amount will be calculated as cost less residual value over the useful economic life, so:

$$\$203,000 - \$100,000 \div 50 \text{ years} = \$2,060 \text{ depreciation charge per annum}$$

SUBSEQUENT EXPENDITURE

Subsequent expenditure refers to expenditure incurred on an existing asset. Under IAS 16, an entity should capitalise subsequent expenditure where the expenditure enhances an asset beyond its previously assessed state.

Illustration

An entity purchases a machine in 2006 for $100,000 at which time it produced 40 units of output per hour. The entity can purchase a newer model for $150,000 which will produce 100 units per hour. The cost of a new machine is outside the budget of the entity but for $50,000 a component can be fitted to the existing machine which will enable the machine to produce 80 units of output per hour.

The $50,000 should be capitalised because it enhances the machine beyond its previously assessed state. It should also be depreciated over the remainder of the asset's useful economic life.

Illustration

An entity spends $10,000 on a replacement roof for its building. For the purposes of this illustration, the replacement roof is simply a standard roof.

This expenditure is maintenance expenditure and should not be capitalised. It has not enhanced the building in any way beyond its previously assessed state.

Roundup

IAS 16 prescribes the accounting treatment for property, plant and equipment and requires an entity to measure its property, plant and equipment using either depreciated historic cost or revaluation subsequent to initial recognition at cost.

Cost includes: purchase price, import duties, non-refundable purchase taxes, other costs directly attributable to bringing the asset to its location and condition and an initial estimate of costs of dismantling, removal items and restoring the site on which it is located.

Depreciation should be calculated as the cost of the asset, less residual value and apportioned over the expected useful economic life of the asset.

Subsequent expenditure should be capitalised if it enhances an item of property, plant and equipment beyond its previously assessed state. If it does not, the subsequent expenditure should be written off to the income statement as it is incurred.

IAS 17 'LEASES'

The objective of this standard is to prescribe the accounting treatment for reporting entities for their operating and finance leases. It prescribes the situations when leases should be included in the statement of financial position and when they should be included in the statement of comprehensive income.

OPERATING LEASES

An operating lease is a lease that is not a finance lease. Payments of such under an operating lease are charged to the statement of comprehensive income on a straight-line basis over the lease term unless another systematic basis is more appropriate.

FINANCE LEASES

The IASB stipulate that an entity's financial statements should report the economic substance of transactions as opposed to their legal form. IAS 17 perfectly illustrates this requirement.

At the commencement of the lease term, lessees shall recognise finance leases as assets and liabilities in the statement of financial position (balance sheet) at amounts equal to the fair value of the leased property or, if lower, the present value of the minimum lease payments determined at the inception of the lease.

Minimum lease payments are split between that of capital and that of interest (finance costs).

All finance leases give rise to assets which are to be subject to depreciation as per the requirements laid down in IAS 16 'Property, Plant and Equipment' and IAS 38 'Intangible Assets'.

IAS 17 stipulates guidance that substantially all of the risks and rewards of ownership are passed to the lessee if any *one* of the following criteria is met:

- The lease transfers ownership to the lessee at the end of the lease term.
- The lease contains a bargain purchase option at the end of the lease term.
- The lease is for the major part of the asset's useful economic life.
- The present value, at the inception of the lease, of the minimum lease payments is at least equal to substantially all of the fair value of the lease asset, net of grants and tax credits to the lessor at that time (title may or may not eventually pass to the lessee).
- The leased assets are of such a specialised nature that only the lessee can use them without modifications being made.

There are a further three indicators within IAS 17 which may suggest that a lease might be properly considered as a finance lease:

- If the lessee can cancel the lease, the lessor's associated costs with the cancellation are to be borne by the lessee.
- Gains or losses arising from the fluctuation of the fair value of the residual amount will accrue to the lessee.
- The lessee has the ability to continue the lease for a supplemental term at a rent that is substantially lower than market rent (known as a 'peppercorn' rent).

LESSOR ACCOUNTING

Operating Leases

Lessors are required to present assets that are subject to operating leases in the statement of financial position (balance sheet) according to the nature of the asset. Depreciation policies shall also be consistent with the normal depreciation for similar assets and calculated in accordance with the provisions contained in IAS 16 'Property, Plant and Equipment' and IAS 38 'Intangible Assets' where applicable. Lease income shall be recognised in income on a straight-line basis over the terms of the lease.

Finance Leases

Lessors should account for finance leases in their statement of financial position as a receivable at an amount equal to the net investment in the lease. Finance income is reflected at a constant periodic rate of return on the lessor's net investment in the finance lease.

Future Proposals

Lease accounting has always presented problems within the accountancy profession because of the way certain leases are accounted for in an entity's profit and loss account (income statement) and/or balance sheet (statement of financial position). The main problem is the ability to manipulate the financial statements by incorrectly classifying 'finance' leases as 'operating' leases, resulting in off-balance sheet finance.

The introduction of accounting standards in the area of lease accounting was brought in with the intention of mitigating the concept of off-balance sheet finance. However, the *World Leasing Year Book 2009* cited an amount of $760 billion in leases in 2007. The problem of off-balance sheet finance is still prevalent because many leased assets and associated liabilities cannot be found on entities' statements of financial position (balance sheet).

The IASB and the US standard-setters, the Financial Accounting Standards Board (FASB) have joined together to develop a revised standard that will deal with lease accounting. The project has identified a number of problems with current standards, including:

> *Users complain that the financial statements do not depict clearly the effects of operating leases.*
>
> *Similar transactions can be accounted for very differently (due to the split between finance and operating leases).*
>
> *The standards provide opportunities to structure transactions in such a way as to achieve a particular lease classification.*
>
> Source: (IASB Proposal Document)

In analysing lease contracts, the IASB and FASB have concluded that, regardless of whether a lease is classified as an operating lease, lease contracts will always create rights and obligations that meet the IASB and FASB definition of assets and liabilities. As such, the proposal is that all leases will be treated and accounted for as finance leases. The fact that substantially all risks and rewards might remain with the lessor is essentially redundant by virtue of the fact that an obligation is created on the part of the lessee to pay rentals for the rights to use the asset which is subject to the lease.

The IASB's discussion paper also cites the board's proposals for those leases which are more complex than traditional leases, such as those which contain options to renew or terminate the lease contract, options to purchase the leased item, contingent rental arrangements or residual value guarantees.

The discussion paper confirms that the board will not require lessees to recognise the renewal, termination or purchase options separately. Instead, the lessee should determine whether the option will be exercised. If exercising the option is the most likely outcome, then the lessee will account for it accordingly. The board has also confirmed that obligations to pay rentals should include amounts payable under contingent rental arrangements and residual value guarantees.

An exposure draft was issued suggesting improvements to the current regulations on lease accounting. A final standard is due to be issued in 2011.

Leases have always been problematic in the profession because of the scope to manipulate the concept of 'off balance sheet finance'. The proposal to treat leases as liabilities together with the corresponding 'right of use' asset is considered a significant change in the profession and one that standard setters in jurisdictions which do not currently adopt IFRS may consider.

EXISTING REQUIREMENTS

Under the current IFRS regime, IAS 17 'Leases' and Topic 840 on leases in US GAAP require the lessee to recognise an asset and associated liability in finance leases. In contrast, the standard requires the lessee to charge lease payments against profit where the lease is classified as an operating lease. Classification as a finance or operating lease all depends on whether the risks and rewards of the asset's ownership have passed to the lessee (finance lease) or remain with the lessor (operating lease).

The UK's SSAP 21 'Accounting for Hire Purchase and Lease Contracts' takes the same stance.

PROPOSED REQUIREMENTS

According to the IASB's exposure draft, the current accounting requirements have been criticised because they do not provide a faithful representation of leasing transactions. Some critics have said the current accounting requirements can be engineered in such a way as to achieve a desired outcome.

When the IASB introduces or amends existing IFRS the changes must adhere to its 'Framework for the Preparation and Presentation of Financial Statements'. According to the IASB's framework document, the definition of an asset and liability is as follows:

An asset is a resource controlled by the entity as a result of past events and from which future economic benefits are expected to flow to the entity.

A liability is a present obligation of the entity arising from past events, the settlement of which is expected to result in an outflow from the entity of resources embodying economic benefits.

In revising the standards on leasing, the IASB and FASB have recognised that all leases, regardless of whether the risks and rewards of ownership have been passed to the lessee or not, will give rise to an asset (a right to use the asset) and a liability (obligations to pay lease rentals for the right to use the asset).

'Right of use' model

The current accounting requirements for leases have been criticised primarily because they allow manipulation of leases to achieve 'off balance sheet finance'.

The exposure draft suggests that lessees and lessors should use a 'right-of-use' model in accounting for all leases. It should be noted that the draft does not deal with:

- Biological and intangible assets.
- Leases to explore for natural resources.
- The lease of some investment properties.

The draft suggests lessees should recognise an asset and an associated liability, regardless of whether (or not) the lease may previously have been recognised as an operating lease.

A lessor will recognise an asset to represent the future lease payments to be received from the lessee. The lessor should assess its exposure to risks or benefits and will then either:

- recognise a liability under a 'performance obligation' approach; or
- derecognise the rights in the underlying asset which it transfers to the lessee. The lessor will then continue to recognise a residual asset which will represent its rights to the underlying asset at the end of the lease term — this is referred to in the draft as the 'derecognition approach'.

The impact of the proposed new leasing standard on the financial statements would be felt less in respect of current leases which are treated as finance leases. However, entities that are reliant on operating leases as a source of finance will feel the effects more. See the illustration below for some practical examples of how these proposed changes would work.

Illustration

Company A operates in the haulage industry and leases a fleet of trucks from Company B. Company B retains the risks and rewards of ownership and therefore in accordance with IAS 17 the payments in respect of the lease are charged to the income statement on a straight line basis over the life of the lease.

Under the proposals in the exposure draft, Company A will no longer charge the payments directly against profit. Instead an asset will be recognised in the balance sheet (statement of financial position) and an associated liability. The income statement (profit and loss account) will instead take the charges in respect of depreciation and finance costs in respect of the lease.

The proposed revisions to accounting for leases could have a detrimental impact on an entity that currently uses operating leases as a significant source of finance, particularly in times of economic difficulty, because the revised approach could result in lower asset turnover ratios, lower return on capital and have a detrimental impact on gearing ratios. For entities that have covenants in bank or other finance loans, this could result in such covenants being breached.

In contrast, earnings before interest, taxes, depreciation and amortisation (EBITDA) would be raised.

MEASUREMENT OF ASSETS AND LIABILITIES

The draft states that assets and liabilities recognised by lessees and lessors should be measured on a basis which:

- Assumes the longest possible lease term, taking into consideration the effects of any options to extend or terminate the lease.
- Uses an 'expected outcome' technique in respect of the lease payments. Consideration must be given to contingent rentals as well as term option penalties and any residual value guarantees which are specified in the lease term.
- Is updated to take account of changes in facts or circumstances when such facts or circumstances indicate that there would be a significant change in those assets or liabilities since the previous reporting period.

Illustration

Company A (which reports under IFRS) leases an item of plant from Company B. The fair value of the item of plant is $140,000 and lease payments are made monthly over a five year lease term. The present value of the minimum lease payments at the inception of the lease is $130,000. The residual value of the item of plant at the end of the lease term has been estimated as $15,000.

Company A will recognise an asset of $130,000, being the present value of the minimum lease payments. Company A will also record a liability at the lower of the fair value of the leased asset and the present value of the minimum lease payments. The difference between the minimum lease payments and the fair value ($10,000) will represent the present value of the residual value of the plant ($15,000).

IMPLEMENTATION

The IASB's exposure draft is currently open for comment (the deadline for submission of comments was 15 December 2010). The final standard is expected to be issued in 2011, although implementation before 1 January 2013 is unlikely.

Roundup

The objective of IAS 17 is to outline the accounting treatment in respect of operating and finance leases.

Payments in respect of an operating lease are charged to the statement of comprehensive income (income statement) on a straight-line basis over the lease term unless another systematic basis is more appropriate. Lessors are required to present such assets in their statement of financial position (balance sheet) according to the nature of the asset. Depreciation policies shall also be consistent with the normal depreciation for similar assets and calculated in accordance with IAS 16 and IAS 38 requirements.

At the commencement of a finance lease, lessees must recognise an asset at an amount equal to the fair value of the leased property or, if lower, the present value of the minimum lease payments determined at the inception of the lease, together with a corresponding liability. Lessors are required to account for finance leases in their statement of financial position (balance sheet) as a receivable at an amount equal to the net investment in the lease. Finance income is reflected at a constant periodic rate of return on the lessor's net investment in the finance lease.

IAS 17 looks at the substance of the transaction to determine whether substantially all of the risks and rewards of ownership of the leased asset have passed to the lessee. IAS 17 also contains guidance when substantially all of the risks and rewards of ownership have essentially been passed to the lessee.

There is an exposure draft relating to the IASB and FASB intention to overhaul the existing IAS 17 requirements which will essentially require all operating leases to be on an entity's statement of financial position (balance sheet).

IAS 18 'REVENUE'

This standard deals with how a reporting entity reports revenue in its financial statements and at which point revenue should be recognised within the financial statements. The standard deals with the following revenue streams and prescribes the situations when revenue should be recognised in respect of each:

- Sale of goods.
- Rendering of services.
- Interest.
- Royalties.
- Dividends.

Sale of Goods

Revenue in respect of sales of goods should be recognised when the following criteria are met:

- The enterprise has transferred to the buyer the significant risks and rewards of ownership to the goods.
- The enterprise retains neither continuing managerial involvement to the degree normally associated with ownership nor effective control over the goods sold.
- The amount of revenue can be reliably measured.
- It is probable that the economic benefits associated with the transaction will flow to the entity.
- The costs incurred or to be incurred in respect of the transaction can be measured reliably.

Rendering of Services

Revenue in respect of rendering of services should be recognised when the following criteria are met:

- The amount of revenue can be reliably measured.
- It is probable that the economic benefits associated with the transaction will flow to the entity.

- The stage of completion of the transaction at the reporting period can be measured reliably.
- The costs incurred for the transaction and the costs to complete the transaction can be measured reliably.

Interest

Revenue from interest should be recognised on a time-apportioned basis which reflects the effective yield on the asset.

Royalties

Royalty revenue should be recognised on an accruals basis.

Dividends

Revenue from dividends should be recognised when the right to receive payment has arisen.

Roundup

IAS 18 deals with revenue from: sale of goods, rendering of services, interest, royalties and dividends.

Five criteria exist to recognise revenue in respect of the sale of goods. Four criteria are required to be met in respect of rendering of services.

Revenue from interest is recognised on a time-apportioned basis which reflects the effective yield on interest.

Royalty revenue should be recognised on an accruals basis.

Dividend revenue should be recognised when the right to receive payment has arisen.

Correct recognition of revenue is critical to ensure that an entity's financial statements present fairly, in all material respects.

The concept of 'substance over form' is particularly prevalent within IAS 18.

IAS 19 'EMPLOYEE BENEFITS'

IAS 19 deals with how an entity should record transactions that fall under the scope of 'employee benefits'.

Employee benefits are all forms of consideration given by a reporting entity in exchange for the services rendered by its employees. The standard essentially deals with:

- Short-term employee benefits.
- Post-employment benefits.
- Other long-term employee benefits.
- Termination benefits.

SHORT-TERM EMPLOYEE BENEFITS

Short-term employee benefits are employee benefits which fall due within twelve months after the reporting period in which the employees render the related services.

In these respects, a reporting entity must recognise the undiscounted amount of short-term employee benefits for that service as a liability as at that date and as an expense unless another standard requires or permits the inclusion of the benefits in the cost of an asset (for example, IAS 16 'Property, Plant and Equipment'). Where the amount already paid exceeds the undiscounted amount of benefits, the excess if classed as an asset (a prepayment).

POST-EMPLOYMENT BENEFITS

These are sub-divided into two further classifications:

- Defined contribution pension scheme.
- Defined benefit pension scheme.

Defined contribution pension schemes are post-employment benefit plans under which an entity pays fixed amounts of contributions into a separate fund. The employer has no further legal or constructive obligation to pay further contributions – even if the fund does not have sufficient assets to pay all the employee benefits.

The payments are simply charged to the statement of comprehensive income as and when they arise.

Defined benefit pension schemes, however, are more complicated to account for. Defined benefit pension plans are post-employment plans other than defined contribution plans.

These sorts of plans differ substantially from defined contribution plans because under the defined benefit plans an entity is obliged to provide the agreed benefits to current and former employees, even if the plan does not have sufficient assets.

In consequence, therefore, actuarial risk (i.e. that the benefits will cost more than ex-pected) and investment risk fall, in substance, on the reporting entity. This complies with the IASBs requirement to report the economic substance of transactions as opposed to their legal form.

Accounting for defined benefit pension schemes is complicated. Actuarial information is needed to make a reliable estimate of the amount of benefit that employees have earned in return for their services. This benefit is then discounted using the Projected Unit Credit Method in order to determine the present value of the defined benefit obligation and the current service cost.

The charges to the statement of comprehensive income in respect of a defined benefit pension scheme will normally comprise:

Current service cost which is the increase in the present value of the scheme's liabilities expected to arise from employees' service in the current period.

Interest cost is the imputed cost caused by the unwinding of discount because scheme liabilities are closer to settlement.

Past service cost is the increase in the present value of the scheme liabilities relating to employee service in prior periods as a result of either new retirement benefits or improvements to the existing retirement benefits.

Expected return on plans assets is the increase in the market value of the plan assets.

Actuarial gains or losses are changes in actuaries' assumptions and can be recognised in the statement of comprehensive income if they exceed the 10% corridor.

Costs of settlement or curtailment are settlement transactions that relieve the employer, or the plan, of the responsibility for a pension benefit obligation or eliminate the risks to the employer or the plan. A curtailment is an event which significantly reduces the expected years of future service of present employees or eradicates (for a substantial number of employees) the accrual of defined benefits for some or all of their future services, for example, the termination of contracts for services.

Illustration

Entity A Inc reports under IFRS and operates a Defined Benefit Pension Scheme for its employees. The scheme is reviewed on an annual basis and the actuaries have provided the following information:

	31 March 2009 $, 000	31 March 2010 $, 000
Present value of obligation	1,500	1,750
Fair value of plan assets	1,500	1,650
Current service cost to 31 March 2010	160	
Contributions paid to 31 March 2010	85	
Benefits paid to employees as at 31 March 2010	125	
Unrecognised gains as at 1 April 2009	200	
Expected return on plan assets at 1 April 2009	12%	
Discount rate for plan assets at 1 April 2009	10%	

Entity A's statement of comprehensive income will show the following

	$, 000
Current service cost	160
Interest cost (10% × $1,500)	150
Expected return on plan assets (12% × $1,500)	(180)
Recognised actuarial gain in the year (see [3] below)	(5)
Costs per statement of comprehensive income	125

Extracts from Entity A's statement of financial position will show:

	$, 000
Fair value of obligation	1,750
Fair value of plan assets	(1,650)
	100
Unrecognised actuarial gains (see [1] below)	140
Liability per statement of financial position	240

[1] *Movement in Unrecognised Actuarial Gain*

	$, 000
Unrecognised actuarial gain as at 1 April 2009	200
Actuarial gain on plan assets (see [2])	10
Actuarial loss on plan liability (see [2])	(65)
Gain recognised (see [3])	(5)
Unrecognised actuarial gain at 31 March 2010	140

[2] *Plan Assets and Plan Liabilities*

	Assets $, 000	Liabilities $, 000
Balance at 1 April 2009	1,500	1,500
Current service cost	160	
Interest	150	
Expected return	180	
Contributions paid	85	
Benefits paid to employees	(125)	(125)
Actuarial gain β	10	
Actuarial loss β	65	
	1,650	1,750

β = balancing figure

[3] *Gains to be Recognised*

Net unrecognised actuarial gains at 1 April 2009	200
10% corridor (10% × $1,500)	(150)
	50 ÷ 10 years
	= $5,000 gains to be recognised

OTHER LONG-TERM EMPLOYEE BENEFITS

Other long-term employee benefits are any other employee benefits which do not fall due within twelve months after the end of the reporting period in which the employees render the related service.

Under these types of employee benefits, an entity can recognise actuarial gains and losses and past service cost immediately.

TERMINATION BENEFITS

Termination benefits are recognised as a liability and as an expense when, and only when, the entity is demonstrably committed to either:

- terminate the employment of an employee or a group of employees before the normal retirement date; or
- provide termination benefits as a result of an offer made in order to encourage voluntary redundancy.

Any termination benefits which fall due more than 12 months after the end of the reporting period must be discounted to present day values.

Roundup

IAS 19 considers all employee benefits in respect of consideration given by an entity in exchange for the services rendered by its employees.

IAS 19 considers post-employment benefits, in particular defined benefit pension schemes and defined contribution pension schemes.

Defined contribution pension schemes are schemes under which an entity pays a fixed amount of contributions into a separate fund. The employer has no further legal or constructive obligation to pay further contributions even if the fund does not have sufficient assets to pay all the employee benefits.

Defined benefit pension schemes differ substantially from defined contribution schemes because an entity is obliged to provide the agreed benefits to current and former employees, regardless of whether the plan does not have sufficient assets.

Accounting for defined benefit pension schemes is more complicated than accounting for defined contribution schemes because actuarial information is needed to make a reliable estimate of the amount of benefit that employees have earned in return for their services.

Benefits under a defined benefit pension scheme are discounted to present day values using the Projected Unit Credit Method.

Charges to the statement of comprehensive income will comprise: current service cost, interest cost, past service cost, expected return on plan assets and costs of settlement or curtailment.

Actuarial gains and losses are recognised in the statement of comprehensive income where they exceed the 10% corridor.

Termination benefits are only recognised when, and only when, the entity is demonstrably committed to terminating the employment of an employee or group of employees before the normal retirement date or to providing termination benefits as a result of an offer made in order to encourage voluntary redundancy.

IAS 20 'ACCOUNTING FOR GOVERNMENT GRANTS AND DISCLOSURE OF GOVERNMENT ASSISTANCE'

The objective of this standard is to prescribe the accounting treatment and the disclosure requirements of an entity who has received government grants and/or government assistance. Government grants could be given to entities, for example, for setting up a business in a deprived area to provide employment.

GOVERNMENT GRANTS

Government grants are assistance by government in the form of transfers of resources (usually in the form of economic benefits) to an entity in return for past or future compliance with stipulated terms relating to the operating activities of the entity.

GOVERNMENT ASSISTANCE

Government assistance is action by the government designed to provide an economic benefit specific to an entity or range of entities qualifying under certain criteria.

GOVERNMENT GRANTS: RECOGNITION

Government grants must not be recognised within the entity's financial statements until there is reasonable assurance that:

(a)   The entity will comply with the terms and conditions attached to the grant(s).
(b)   The grant will be received by the entity.

There are generally two forms of government grant:

- Capital based.
- Repayable.

Capital-based grants are grants from the government whose primary condition is that an entity qualifying to receive the grant should purchase, construct or otherwise acquire a long-term asset.

Capital-based grants can be treated in two ways:

- DR cash.
- CR deferred income.

In this example, the grant will be released to the statement of comprehensive income (income statement) over the life of the grant.

- DR cash.
- CR non-current asset.

In this example, the grant is deducted in arriving at the carrying value of the asset to be recognised. The grant is recognised in the statement of comprehensive income (income statement) via reduced depreciation charges.

Repayable grants are where repayment of a grant related to income shall be applied first against any unamortised deferred income in the statement of financial position (balance sheet). Where there is no unamortised deferred income, then it shall be recognised immediately as an expense.

Where capital-based grants are concerned, repayment of a grant related to an asset shall be recorded by increasing the carrying amount of the asset or reducing the amount of deferred income balance by the amount payable.

Roundup

IAS 20 deals with the accounting in respect of government grants and disclosure of government assistance and the standard defines the two.

Government grants can only be recognised when there is reasonable assurance that the entity will comply with the terms and conditions attached to the grant(s) and the grant will be receivable by the entity.

Grants can take the form of capital-based grants or revenue-based grants.

Grants received in respect of capital-based grants can be offset against the cost of the asset to which the grant relates or a liability can be set up in respect of the unamortised grant balance.

Repayable grants will first be applied to any unamortised deferred income. Where there is no unamortised deferred income, the repayment will be recognised immediately in the statement of comprehensive income as an expense.

Repayments of capital-based grants will be applied by either increasing the cost of the asset to which the grant related or reducing the amount of deferred income by the amount payable.

IAS 21 'THE EFFECTS OF CHANGES IN FOREIGN EXCHANGE RATES'

The objective of this standard is to prescribe how an entity who carries on foreign activities will account for the effects of changes in foreign exchange rates.

The first thing an entity is required to do is to determine the functional currency of the entity. The functional currency is the currency of the primary economic environment in which it operates (for example, US Dollars). In determining the functional currency, an entity is required to consider the following factors:

- The currency that mainly influences sales prices for goods and services (this will often be the currency in which sales prices for its goods and services are denominated and settled).
- The currency of the country whose competitive forces and regulations mainly determine the sales prices of its goods and services.

In addition, an entity will normally consider the currency that mainly influences labour, materials and other costs of providing goods or services.

FOREIGN CURRENCY TRANSACTIONS

Foreign currency transactions should be recorded initially in the functional currency by using the exchange rate at the date of the transaction.

At the end of the reporting period, an entity should translate foreign currency monetary items of assets and liabilities using the closing rate at the reporting date. Non-monetary items shall be translated using the exchange rate at the date of the transaction.

Non-monetary items that are measured using fair values in a foreign currency should be translated using the exchange rates at the date when the fair value was determined.

Any exchange differences on translation are recognised in profit or loss in the period in which they arise.

Exchange differences that arise on a monetary item that forms part of a reporting entity's net investment in a foreign operation must be recognised in profit or loss in the separate financial statements of the reporting entity or the individual financial statements of the foreign operation, as appropriate. In the consolidated financial statements, exchange differences are recognised initially in other comprehensive income and reclassified from equity to profit or loss on disposal of the net investment.

Presentation of Information Where the Functional Currency is Different from the Presentational Currency

Where an entity's presentational currency differs from its functional currency it should translate its results and financial position into the presentational currency.

Roundup

IAS 21 deals with the accounting required by an entity which carries on foreign activities.

The initial stage is establishing the functional currency of the entity. The functional currency is the currency of the primary economic environment in which it operates.

Transactions should be translated at the exchange rate prevailing at the date of the transaction.

At the end of a reporting period, an entity will translate monetary items of assets and liabilities using the closing rate at the reporting date. Non-monetary items will be translated using the exchange rate at the date of the transaction.

Exchange differences on translation are recognised immediately in the statement of comprehensive income.

Exchange differences which arise on monetary items which form part of a reporting entity's net investment in a foreign subsidiary must be recognised in profit or loss in the separate financial statements of the reporting entity or the individual financial statements of the foreign enterprise as appropriate. In the consolidated financial statements, exchange differences are recognised initially in other comprehensive income and reclassified from equity to profit or loss on disposal of the foreign enterprise.

IAS 23 'BORROWING COSTS'

The objective of this standard is to prescribe the accounting treatment that an entity should follow in dealing with borrowing costs associated with the acquisition, construction or production of a qualifying asset. The fundamental aspect to this standard is determining what constitutes a 'qualifying' asset.

Borrowing costs are interest and other costs that an entity incurs in connection with the borrowing of funds.

The standard requires that an entity should capitalise borrowing costs that are directly attributable to the acquisition, construction or production of a qualifying asset. A qualifying asset is an asset that takes a substantial period of time to get ready for its intended use or sale. The term 'substantial period' is fundamental to this standard. If the asset does not take a substantial period of time, the associated borrowing costs would not qualify for capitalisation.

Examples of qualifying assets include:

- Manufacturing plant.
- Investment properties.
- Intangible assets.

CAPITALISATION RATE

The capitalisation rate at which borrowings are capitalised must be the weighted average of the borrowing costs applicable to the borrowings of the entity that are outstanding during the period, other than borrowings made specifically for the purpose of obtaining a qualifying asset. The amount of borrowing costs that an entity capitalises in a period cannot exceed the amount of borrowing costs it incurred during that period.

The capitalisation of borrowing costs commences when the following conditions are met:

- The entity incurs expenditure for the asset.
- It incurs borrowing costs.
- It undertakes activities that are necessary to prepare the asset for its intended use or sale.

When an entity suspends active development of a qualifying asset, it must suspend capitalisation of borrowing costs.

Illustration

Entity A has three sources of borrowing in the reporting period, shown as follows:

	Outstanding Liability $, 000	Interest Charge $, 000
5 year loan	9,000	1,500
30 year loan	14,000	2,000
Bank overdraft	6,000	750

If all of the above borrowings are used to finance the production of a qualifying asset, the capitalisation rate will be calculated as:

$$\frac{1,500,000 + 2,000,000 + 750,000 \times 100}{9,000,000 + 14,000,000 + 6,000,000} = 14.66\%$$

If the 5 year loan is used to finance a specific qualifying asset, then the capitalisation rate which should be used on the other qualifying assets will be:

$$\frac{2,000,000 + 750,000 \times 100}{14,000,000 + 6,000,000} = 13.75\%$$

Roundup

Borrowing costs are interest and other costs that an entity incurs in connection with the borrowing of funds.

An entity applying IAS 23 is required to capitalise borrowing costs which are directly attributable to the acquisition, construction or production of a qualifying asset.

A qualifying asset is an asset which takes a substantial period of time to construct.

Borrowing costs are capitalised at the weighted average of the borrowing costs applicable to the borrowings of the entity that are outstanding during the period.

The amount of borrowing costs that an entity capitalises in a period cannot exceed the amount of borrowing costs it incurs during that reporting period.

IAS 24 'RELATED PARTY DISCLOSURES'

This standard ensures that transactions with related parties are adequately disclosed within an entity's financial statement. IAS 24 is a wholly disclosure standard.

RELATED PARTIES

A party is related to an entity if:

(a) Directly, or indirectly through one or more intermediaries, the party:

   (i) controls, is controlled by, or is under common control with the entity (this includes parents, subsidiaries and fellow subsidiaries);
   (ii) has an interest in the entity that gives it significant influence over the entity; or
   (iii) has joint control over the entity.

(b) The party is an associate (as defined in IAS 28 'Investments in Associates') of the entity.

(c) The party is a joint venture in which the entity is a venture (IAS 31 'Interests in Joint Ventures').

(d) The party is a member of the key management personnel of the entity or its parent.

(e)   The party is a close member of the family of any individual referred to in (a) or (d).
(f)   The party is an entity that is controlled, jointly-controlled or significantly influenced by, or for which significant voting power in such an entity resides with, directly or indirectly, any individual referred to in (d) or (e).
(g)   The party is a post-employment benefit plan for the benefit of employees of the entity, or of any entity that is a related party of the entity.

IAS 24 is purely a disclosure standard and it requires an entity to disclose the following information if there have been any transactions between related parties:

(a)   The amount of the transactions.
(b)   The amount of outstanding balances and:

   (i)   their terms and conditions, including whether they are secured, and the nature of the consideration to be provided in settlement; and
   (ii)   details of any guarantees given or received.

(c)   Provisions for doubtful debts related to the amount of outstanding balances.
(d)   The expense recognised during the period in respect of bad or doubtful debts due from related parties.

WHO IS A RELATED PARTY?

A related party can be an individual or a corporate entity, whether incorporated or otherwise. A related party can also be a group of individuals, for example, where a group of directors act 'in concert'. For the purposes of financial reporting, there are four criteria for ascertaining whether two or more parties are related parties:

• One party has direct or indirect control of the other party.
• The parties are subject to common control from the same source.
• One party has influence over the other party.
• The parties are subject to influence from the same source.

The above points could, therefore, be headed up as:

• Control.
• Common control.
• Influence.
• Common Influence.

Control

Control is the ability to influence the financial reporting and operating policies of an entity. The controlling party will have a view to gaining economic benefit from such control. More often than not control is obtained when more than 50% of the voting rights in the entity are obtained.

For example, where a director holds 75% of the shares in Entity A, by virtue of his/her shareholding that director has control of Entity A. This 'ultimate control' should be disclosed within the financial statements.

Common Control

Common control can arise, for example, where two entities are subject to common control by the same individual.

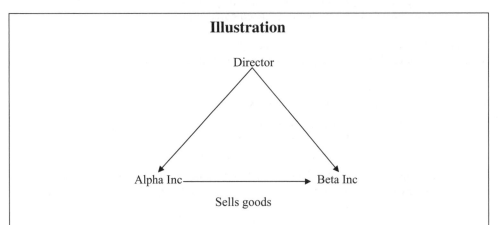

Illustration

In this illustration, Entity A is a related party of Entity B. Entity A is also a related party of Entity C. Both Entity B and Entity C are also related parties because they are subject to common control.

Influence

Influence is essentially where one party has influence over another entity's financial and operating policies to such an extent that the other party could be inhibited from pursuing, at all times, its own separate interests. To some extent it can be unclear whether or not one party influences another party to the extent that it inhibits the subjecting party from pursuing its own interests at all times. This is a 'grey' area and open to interpretation. However, the fact that one party has the ability to influence the other party and, thus, has the power to prevent it from pursuing its separate interests at all times, is generally a trigger for all transactions between the two parties to be disclosed within the financial statements.

Common Influence

Common influence is where parties essentially enter into a transaction and are subject to influence from the same source.

In the illustration above, if Entity A merely had influence over Entities B and C, then both B and C could be inhibited from pursuing their own separate interests at all times because Entity A would have influence over B and C's financial and operating policies.

Transactions require disclosure where influence is actually exerted, that is, one party has placed its own interest after the other's in entering into a transaction. Therefore, it is necessary to look at the facts of the transaction to establish whether (or not) influence has been exerted. If either party has put its own interests after the other party (or parties), in entering into that transaction, disclosure is required of that transaction and all other transactions undertaken in the year.

ONE DIRECTOR IN COMMON

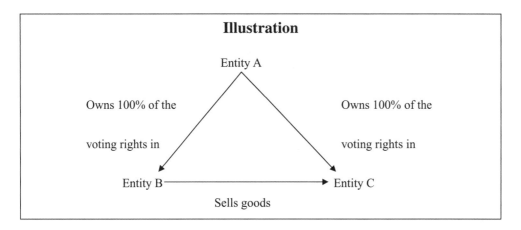

Illustration

Entity A

Owns 100% of the

voting rights in

Owns 100% of the

voting rights in

Entity B → Entity C

Sells goods

In the previous illustration, assume that the director does not control Alpha Inc or Beta Inc. The question in this case is 'are Alpha and Beta related parties?'

Two entities are not related parties just because they have a director in common. More often than not, a director can have influence over the running of the entity but this does not necessarily give rise to Alpha and Beta becoming related parties as Alpha and Beta would be expected to go about their business for the benefit of their respective shareholders.

However, consider a scenario where Alpha had pledged security for Beta's borrowings. This would mean that Alpha has put Beta's interests before its own. In this case Alpha and Beta would be related parties for the entire accounting period in question.

Another example would be if Alpha and Beta had a controlling nucleus of six directors each, five of whom were directors of both entities. In this case, Alpha and Beta would be related parties because they would be under common control.

PERSONS ACTING 'IN CONCERT'

The term 'acting in concert' is referred to when directors of an entity actively co-operate to exercise control or influence over an entity. Where this occurs, control is obtained and disclosure of related party transactions is required. A typical disclosure in the full financial statements of a reporting entity is:

The Directors are regarded as controlling parties by virtue of their ability to act in concert in respect of the operations of the entity.

The term 'key management' includes people who are not on the board of directors but whose duties include directing and controlling an entity's activities.

Illustration

Entity A Inc is a plant hire company that has two divisions, one in the North of England and one in the South. Each division has a branch manager who is not a director. The branch managers would be considered key management because they are responsible for directing and controlling half of the entity's principal activities.

Related parties are renowned for causing a lot of confusion because of their subjective nature. Auditors of entities who could have material related party transactions should comply with the requirements laid down in ISA 550 (revised and redrafted) 'Related Parties'.

Roundup

Related party transactions require disclosure because of the fact that many transactions involving relating parties might not have been entered into on an 'arms-length' basis.

IAS 24 defines when a party is related to an entity.

Control is the ability to influence the financial and operating policies of an entity.

Common control occurs where two entities are subject to common control by the same individual.

Influence is where one party has influence over another entity's financial and operating policies to such an extent that the other party could be inhibited from pursuing, at all times, its own separate interests.

Common influence occurs where parties essentially enter into a transaction and are subject to influence from the same source.

Key management includes people who are not on the board of directors but whose directors include directing and controlling an entity's activities.

IAS 26 'ACCOUNTING AND REPORTING BY RETIREMENT BENEFIT PLANS'

This standard deals with the accounting and reporting by an entity who is involved in Retirement Benefit Plans.

A retirement benefit plan is an arrangement whereby an entity provides benefits for employees on or after termination of employment in the form of annual income or as a lump sum.

In the financial statements of an entity providing such a plan, they must contain a statement of net assets available for benefits and a description of the funding policy.

The financial statements should also contain either:

   (a)   a statement that shows:

       (i)   the net assets available for benefits,

       (ii)   the actuarial present value of promised retirement benefits, distinguishing between vested benefits and non-vested benefits, and

       (iii)   the resulting excess or deficit; or

   (b)   a statement of net assets available for benefits including either:

       (i)   a note disclosing the actuarial present value of promised retirement benefits, distinguishing between vested benefits and non-vested benefits, or

       (ii)   a reference to this information in an accompanying actuarial report.

The financial statements of an entity providing retirement benefits must also explain the relationship between the actuarial present value of promised retirement benefits and the net assets available for the assets.

Retirement benefits must be carried at fair value. Marketable securities are carried at market value.

The financial statements of retirement benefit plans (whether defined benefit or defined contribution) must also contain:

- A statement of changes in net assets available for benefits.
- A summary of significant accounting policies.
- A description of the plan and the effect of any changes in the plan during the period.

Roundup

IAS 26 is very much 'industry-specific' and relates to entities who are involved in retirement benefit plans.

IAS 26 contains the definition of a retirement benefit plan and also contains the requirements that financial statements need to disclose in respect of a retirement benefit plan.

The financial statements of an entity providing retirement benefit plans must also explain the relationship between the actuarial present value of promised retirement benefits and the net assets available for those assets.

Retirement benefits must be carried at fair value — marketable securities are carried at market value.

IAS 26 also requires financial statements of retirement benefit plans to contain: a statement of changes in net assets available for benefits, a summary of significant accounting policies and a description of the plan and the effect of any changes in the plan during the period.

IAS 27 'CONSOLIDATED AND SEPARATE FINANCIAL STATEMENTS'

The objective of this standard is to enhance the relevance, reliability and comparability of a parent company in preparing their individual financial statements and consolidated financial statements.

CONSOLIDATED FINANCIAL STATEMENTS

A parent must consolidate its investment in subsidiaries. A subsidiary is an entity in which the parent has obtained control either through its holding in the subsidiary's equity share capital or by virtue of the parent's ability to influence the financial reporting and operating policies of the subsidiary.

CONSOLIDATION PROCEDURE

All intra-group transactions must be eliminated from the consolidated financial statements. The consolidated financial statements must show the results of the group as a single economic entity.

Consolidated financial statements are prepared by combining the financial statements of parent and subsidiary line by line by adding together like items of assets, liabilities, equity, income and expenses.

The investment by the parent in the subsidiary is eliminated and accounted for in accordance with IFRS 3 'Business Combinations'.

Non-controlling interests in the subsidiary's profit or loss are identified.

Non-controlling interests in the net assets of consolidated subsidiaries are identified separately from the parent's ownership in them and are presented in the consolidated statements of financial position (balance sheet) within equity, separately from equity of the owners of the parent. In addition, total comprehensive income must be attributed to the owners of the parent and the non-controlling interests.

SEPARATE FINANCIAL STATEMENTS

Where an entity elects, or is required by regulation, to present separate financial statements, any investment in subsidiaries must be accounted for in accordance with IAS 39: Financial Instruments: Recognition and Measurement. It is to be noted that IAS 39 is being replaced by IFRS 9: Financial Instruments which will apply for accounting periods starting on or after 1 January 2013; but earlier adoption is permitted.

Roundup

IAS 27 requires a parent to consolidate its investments in subsidiaries. The objective of this process is to show the results of the group as a single reporting entity.

IAS 27 states that a subsidiary is an entity in which the parent has obtained control either through its holding in the subsidiary's equity share capital or by virtue of the parent's ability to influence the financial reporting and operational policies of the subsidiary.

The consolidation process involves combining the financial statements of the parent and subsidiary line by line by adding together like items of assets, liabilities, equity income and expenses.

The cost of the investment in the subsidiary is eliminated and accounted for in accordance with IFRS 3 'Business Combinations'.

IAS 28 'INVESTMENTS IN ASSOCIATES'

The objective of this standard is to prescribe the accounting treatment that an entity who has investments in associates should adopt.

Where an investing company holds 20% or more of the voting power of an investee, this means that they hold 'significant influence'. Significant influence is the power to participate in the financial and operating policy decisions of the investee. If, however, they own more than 50% of the voting rights, this gives rise to a subsidiary which requires consolidation in accordance with IFRS 3 'Business Combinations' and IAS 27 'Consolidated and Separate Financial Statements'.

EQUITY METHOD

Investments in associates are accounted for using the equity method of accounting. This method states that the investment in the associate is initially recognised at cost and the carrying amount of the investment is increased or decreased in order to recognise the investor's share of the profit or loss of the investee after the associate has been acquired.

Where the associate pays dividends to the investor, then these reduce the carrying value of the investment.

Where the associate revalues their property or has a foreign exchange translation difference, these will also give rise to an adjustment to the carrying value of the investment for the investor's proportionate interest — such changes being recognised in the investee's other comprehensive income.

The investor's financial statements must also follow uniform accounting policies for like transactions and events of its investee.

Under the provisions of IAS 28, the standard says that the value of an investment in an associate should be:

Cost + share of associate's post acquisition profit or loss

Cost is the share of the associate's net assets at the date of acquisition plus the associated goodwill.

It follows, therefore, that the carrying value will be equivalent to the share of net assets at the date of acquisition of the associate plus the related goodwill plus the share of post acquisition profit or loss, which can be summarised as:

Share of net assets at the reporting date + goodwill

Roundup

An investor has an associate when they hold 20% or more of the voting rights of an investee, but less than 50%. If they own 51% or more of the voting rights of the investee, the investee is a subsidiary and is accounted for under IAS 27 'Consolidated and Separate Financial Statements'.

IAS 28 requires associates to be accounted for using the equity method of accounting.

Dividends paid to the investor will reduce the carrying amount of that investment.

If an associate revalues their property, or has foreign exchange translation differences, this gives rise to an adjustment to the carrying value of the investment for the investor's proportionate interest and such changes will be recorded in the investee's other comprehensive income.

IAS 29 'FINANCIAL REPORTING IN HYPERINFLATIONARY ECONOMIES'

This standard deals with the accounting requirements for those entities whose functional currency is the currency of a hyperinflationary economy.

Hyperinflation is inflation that is out of control. The financial statements of an entity whose functional currency is the currency of a hyperinflationary economy must be stated in terms of the measuring unit currency at the end of the reporting period. If the financial statements are not restated and are reported in a hyperinflationary economy, clearly they will be unreliable.

Financial statements need to be restated with the use of a general price index that reflects changes in general purchasing power.

Restatement of the financial statements should be as follows:

Non-monetary items carried at cost or cost less depreciation (also referred to as 'depreciated historic cost') should be restated by applying the change in general price index from the date of acquisition to the reporting date to the historical cost and accumulated depreciation.

Non-monetary items carried at revaluation should be restated by applying the change in general price index to their revalued amount from the date of revaluation to the reporting date.

Monetary items do not need to be restated because, by definition, they are already expressed in the monetary unit current at the reporting date.

When an economy ceases to be hyperinflationary and an entity ceases to use the provisions in IAS 29, then it shall treat the amounts expressed in the measuring unit current at the end of the previous reporting period as the basis for the carrying amount in the subsequent financial statements. This is because such an event (the entity ceasing to be in a hyperinflationary economy) is a change in circumstances so should be applied prospectively.

Illustration

An entity operates in a country which is subject to hyperinflation. Data concerning the country's inflation is as follows:

	2007	*2008*	*2009*	*2010*
Inflation rate	40%	33%	41%	
General price level	130	164	261	343

The cumulative inflation rate is $(40 + 33 + 41) = 114\%$ and the cumulative inflation for 2008–2010 is $(343 - 130) \div 130 = 164\%$ and so the three-year inflation rate should be compounded as this basis provides a measure of inflation for the three years taken as a whole.

Roundup

Hyperinflation is inflation which is out of control.

Entities whose functional currency is the currency of a hyperinflationary economy must restate their financial statements in terms of the measuring unit current at the end of a reporting period to ensure they present relevant and reliable information.

Restatement is done by way of use of a general price index that reflects changes in general purchasing power.

When an entity ceases to be in a hyperinflationary economy it will cease to use the provisions in this IAS and treat the amounts expressed in the measuring unit current at the end of the previous reporting period as the basis for the carrying amount in the next financial statements.

IAS 31 'INTERESTS IN JOINT VENTURES'

This standard deals with those entities that have interests in joint ventures and prescribes the accounting for such interests.

JOINT VENTURE

A joint venture is a contractual arrangement where two or more parties are involved in an undertaking that is subject to joint control. Joint control is contractually agreed and involves the sharing of control over an entity. A joint venture can only be classified as such if the financial and operating decisions relating to the activity require the unanimous consent of the parties sharing the control.

There are three types of joint venture that are dealt with in the provisions of IAS 31:

- Jointly-controlled operations.
- Jointly-controlled assets.
- Jointly-controlled entities.

Jointly-controlled Operations

In these joint ventures, each venture uses its own property, plant and equipment and carries its own inventories. It incurs its own expenses and liabilities and raises its own finance. The financial statements of a venture will include:

- The assets that it controls and the liabilities that it incurs.
- The expenses that it incurs and its share of the income that it earns from the sale of goods or rendering of services by the joint venture.

Jointly-controlled Assets

In respect of jointly-controlled assets, a venture must recognise in its financial statements:

- Its share of the jointly-controlled assets, classified according to the nature of the assets.
- Any liabilities that it has incurred.
- Its share of any liabilities incurred jointly with the other venturers in relation to the joint venture.
- Any income from the sale or use of its share of the output of the joint venture, together with its share of any expenses incurred by the joint venture.
- Any expenses that it has incurred in respect of its interest in the joint venture.

Jointly-controlled Entities

This type of entity involves the establishment of a separate entity in which each venture has an interest. IAS 31 allows two possible methods of recognition of jointly-controlled entities in a venturer's financial statements:

- proportionate consolidation; and
- equity method.

Proportionate Consolidation   This involves a venturer's share of each of the assets, liabilities, income and expenses of a jointly-controlled entity is combined on a line by line basis with like items in the venturer's financial statements, or reported as separate line items in the venturer's financial statements.

Equity Method   This involves the venture initially recording the jointly-controlled entity at cost and then adjusting for the post-acquisition change in the venturer's share of net assets of the jointly-controlled entity.

Roundup

IAS 31 deals with the accounting for interests in joint ventures.

Three types of joint venture are dealt with in IAS 31: jointly-controlled operations, jointly-controlled assets and jointly-controlled entities.

There are two possible methods of recognition of jointly-controlled entities: proportionate consolidation and the equity method.

IAS 32 'FINANCIAL INSTRUMENTS: PRESENTATION'

The objective of this standard is to prescribe the presentation of financial instruments as either debt or equity transactions. Disclosure requirements in respect of financial instruments are found in IFRS 7 'Financial Instruments: Disclosure'.

FINANCIAL INSTRUMENT

A financial instrument is any contract that gives rise to a financial asset of one entity and a financial liability in another entity. They can be financial assets, financial liabilities or equity instruments.

Financial Assets

A financial asset is any asset that is:

   (a)   Cash.
   (b)   An equity instrument of another entity.
   (c)   A contractual right:

        (i)   to receive cash or another financial asset from another entity; or
        (ii)   to exchange financial assets or financial liabilities with another entity under conditions that are potentially favourable to the entity.

   (d)   A contract that will or may be settled in an entity's own equity instruments and is:

        (i)   a non-derivative for which the entity is or may be obliged to receive a variable number of the entity's own equity instruments; or
        (ii)   a derivative that will or may be settled other than by the exchange of a fixed amount of cash or another financial asset for a fixed number of the entity's own equity instruments. For this purpose the entity's own equity instruments do not include instruments that are themselves contracts for the future receipt or delivery of the entity's own equity instruments.

Financial assets are also dealt with in IAS 39: 'Financial Instruments: Recognition and Measurement' and in IFRS 9 'Financial Instruments'.

Financial Liabilities

A financial liability is any liability that is:

   (a)   A contractual obligation:

        (i)   to deliver cash or another financial asset to another entity; or
        (ii)   to exchange financial assets or financial liabilities with another entity under conditions which are potentially favourable to the entity.

   (b)   A contract that will or may be settled in the entity's own equity instruments and is:

        (i)   a non-derivative for which the entity is or may be obliged to deliver a variable number of the entity's own equity instruments; or
        (ii)   a derivative that will or may be settled other than by the exchange of a fixed amount of cash or another financial asset for a fixed number of the entity's own equity instruments. For this purpose the entity's own equity instruments do not include instruments that are themselves contracts for the future receipt or delivery of the entity's own equity instruments.

Financial liabilities are also dealt with in IAS 39: 'Financial Instruments: Recognition and Measurement'.

Equity Instruments

An equity instrument is any contract that evidences a residual interest in the assets of an entity after deducting all of its liabilities.

Where a financial instrument has a redemption feature or requires an entity to deliver cash or another financial asset, this is a financial liability and should be recognised as such within the financial statements.

Where financial instruments do not have a redemption feature or the entity does not have an obligation to deliver cash (either to redeem the instrument or in the form of interest or dividends) they are recognised as equity.

Where an entity reacquires its own equity instruments, those instruments are deducted from equity. No gain or loss is recognised in profit or loss on the purchase, sale or cancellation of an entity's own equity instruments. Any consideration paid or received must be recognised directly in equity.

Any interest payments, dividends, losses and gains relating to financial instruments or a component of a financial instrument that has been recognised as a financial liability must be recognised as income or expense in profit or loss.

Distributions (dividends) to holders of an equity instrument must be debited directly to equity net of any related income tax benefit.

Illustration

An entity issues preference shares to shareholders that pay 10% dividends on an annual basis.

The preference shares contain an obligation to pay cash to the preference shareholders and they should be classified as a financial liability. The 10% dividends should be recognised as a finance cost (interest) in the entity's statement of comprehensive income.

Roundup

IAS 32 prescribes the presentation of financial statements as either 'debt' instruments or 'equity' instruments.

A financial instrument can either be a financial asset or a financial liability and IAS 32 stipulates what constitutes a financial asset or financial liability.

If a financial liability contains any form of redemption feature it must be classified as a financial liability. If there is no form of redemption feature, the financial instrument should be classified as equity.

Interest payments, dividends, gains and losses in respect of financial instruments, or a component of a financial instrument, that have been recognised as a financial liability must be recognised as income or expense in profit or loss.

IAS 33 'EARNINGS PER SHARE'

The objective of IAS 33 is to prescribe the calculation and disclosure of an entity's earnings per share.

The scope of this standard applies to the separate financial statements whose debt or equity instruments are publicly traded (or are in the process of being issued in a public market). It also applies to the consolidated financial statements of a group whose parent is required to apply this standard to its own separate financial statements.

BASIC EARNINGS PER SHARE

The calculation of basic earnings per share is straight forward. It is arrived at by dividing the profit (or loss) relating to the ordinary shareholders by the weighted average number of ordinary shares outstanding in the period.

Illustration

An entity has 1,000,000 shares in issue. The profit for the year ended 31 December 2010 (adjusted for the post-tax effect of preference dividends and non-controlling interests) was $200,000.

$$\text{Earnings per Share} = \text{Profit} \div \text{Ordinary Shares}$$

So, $200,000 $\div$ 1,000,000 = 20c per share

PREFERENCE DIVIDENDS

There are generally two types of preference dividend[1]:

- A cumulative preference dividend.
- A non-cumulative preference dividend.

Cumulative Preference Dividends

If no dividend is declared in respect of a reporting period, the holders accumulate their rights.

Non-Cumulative Preference Dividends

If no dividend is declared then the holder(s) of the preference shares lose the right to the dividend.

PARTICIPATING PREFERENCE SHARES

Entities may issue 'participating preference shares' which will ordinarily rank for a dividend which can be split into two parts: the 'fixed' part and the 'variable' part. The fixed element will normally be a stated percentage of the par value of the shares and is accounted for in exactly the same way as an ordinary preference dividend.

If the variable element is limited, an entity will only recognise the full amount in the calculation of earnings per share if the conditions under which the shares participate in profits have been met. If the variable element is unlimited, a separate calculation should be per-

---

[1] Profit or loss will only be adjusted for preference dividends declared in the reporting period.

formed to determine the extent to which the profits generated are attributable to the preference shareholders.

Illustration

Entity A Inc makes a profit of $100,000,000 in the year to 31 December 2010. Entity A has 100,000 $1 preference shares in issue which are subject to the following conditions:

(a)   There is a 5% fixed dividend.
(b)   There is also an additional dividend of 7% of any profits earned by the entity in any year in excess of $500,000.

Fixed Dividend	$
100,000 × 5%	5,000
Variable Dividend	
(1,000,000 – 500,000) × 7%	35,000
	40,000

This $40,000 is deducted from the earnings in order to arrive at the earnings attributable to ordinary shareholders.

WEIGHTED AVERAGE NUMBER OF SHARES

The basic rule in IAS 33 is that the number of ordinary shares is the weighted average number of ordinary shares outstanding for the period. It follows, therefore, that the number of shares in existence at the beginning of the reporting period be adjusted for shares that have been issued for cash or other forms of consideration during the period.

Illustration

An entity's financial reporting period is 1 January 2010–31 December 2010. On 1 January 2010 it had a hundred ordinary shares in issue. On 31 March 2010 it issued a further fifty shares.

The weighted average number of shares is calculated as:

Before the issue	
100 ordinary shares × 3 months / 12 months	25
After the issue	
150 ordinary shares × 9 months / 12 months	113
Weighted average	138

There are occasions when shares are issued but no consideration is received. Such circumstances can arise due to:

- Bonus issues.
- Rights issues.
- Share splits.
- Share consolidations.

Bonus Issues

A bonus issue is always treated as if the shares issued in the bonus issue had been in issue for the whole of the reporting period.

Illustration

An entity issues a bonus share issue of one share for every ten. The bonus fraction becomes:

$$10 + \frac{1}{10} = \frac{11}{10}$$

Rights Issue

A rights issue gives the shareholder the right to buy further shares from the company at a price which is set below that of market value. A rights issue has two inherent advantages:

- The company will receive a consideration which will boost earnings.
- The shareholder receives part of the consideration for no consideration due to the fact that it is deliberately set below market value for the shares in the rights issue.

Because of this, a bonus fraction is applied to the number of shares in issue before the date of the rights issue. The new shares issued are pro-rated as for issues for consideration.

The bonus fraction is:

> the cumulative-rights (cum-rights) price per share
> ÷ the theoretical ex-rights price per share

Illustration

An entity has 1,000 shares in issue on 1 January 2009. On 31 March 2009 it issues a rights issue for one share for every five held at 90c. The market value of the shares as at 31 March 2009 was $1 (cum-rights).

Rights Issue Bonus Fraction

	Shares	$	$
	5	1	5.0
	$\frac{1}{6}$	0.90	$\frac{0.9}{5.9}$

Theoretical Ex-Rights Price

$$5.9 \div 6 = 0.9833$$

		Bonus Fraction	
		Cum-rights price per share	1
		Theoretical ex-rights price	0.9833

Therefore:

	Number
1 January to 31 March $1,000,000 \times 3/12 \times 1/0.9833$	254,237
1 April to 31 December $1,200,000 \times 9/12$	900,000
	1,154,237

Where bonus issues are issued in a reporting period, then an entity must restate the comparative year to account for the bonus issue in order to ensure that the financial statements achieve consistency.

Share Splits

Where an entity splits shares into shares of small par value an entity will account for them in the same way as they do in respect of bonus issues. The two treatments are the same because the number of issued shares has increased but there is no effect on the entity's earning capacity.

Share Consolidation

A consolidation of shares is where the number of shares in issue is reduced by being converted into fewer shares of higher denomination. A share consolidation is similar to a share split or a bonus issue because it alters the number of shares but does not alter the earning capacity of the entity. When an entity undertakes a share consolidation it is treated as affecting all the periods presented in the financial statements.

Illustration

Entity A has 1,200,000 50p shares in issue at the start of its accounting period, which ends on 31 March 2010.

On 30 June 2009 it undertakes a share consolidation and replaces every six shares in issue with five new shares.

The number of shares in issue in the year to 31 March 2010 will be calculated as:

$$1,200,000 \times 3/12 = \quad 300,000$$
$$1,000,000^* \times 9/12 = \quad 750,000$$
$$\overline{1,050,000}$$

* (1,200,000 shares in issue prior to share consolidation $\times$ 5 shares for every / 6 shares) = 1,000,000.

MULTIPLE CHANGES IN CAPITAL DURING A REPORTING PERIOD

Sometimes an entity could issue a mixture of bonus and rights issue or even issue further shares at full market price.

To deal with these, apply the following method:

- Make a note of the number of shares in issue at the start of the year.
- Look forward during the year and note the total number of shares after each capital change.
- Multiply each number by the fraction of the year that it was in existence.
- Where the entity issues a bonus issue, multiply all previous slices by the bonus fraction.

DILUTED EARNINGS PER SHARE

A diluted earnings per share is calculated to inform existing shareholders that earnings per share could be diluted. It acts to give notice to the shareholders that there may be potential ordinary shareholders who may become actual shareholders in the future. This could occur, for example, where an entity has convertible debt (a loan that has the option of being able to be converted into shares in the future).

The new number of ordinary shares should be the weighted average number of shares used in the basic earnings per share calculation plus the weighted average number of ordinary shares which would be issued on the conversion of all the dilutive potential ordinary shares into ordinary shares.

Illustration

Using the numbers in the first illustration to this standard, assume that on 31 March 2010, an entity issues $200,000 6% convertible debt. The terms of the conversion are:

1. 100 shares/$100 if within 5 years.
2. 110 shares/$100 if after 5 years.

The entity pays tax at 30%.

	Number of shares	Profit $
Basic	1,000,000	
Dilution:		
Shares: $\dfrac{200,000}{100} \times 110 \times \dfrac{9}{12}$	165,000	
Interest:		
$200,000 \times 6\% \times 9 \times 0.70$		6,300
1,165,000	206,300	

The earnings per share is calculated as:

$$\$206,300 \div 1,165,000 = \textbf{17.71c per share}$$

DISCLOSURE

Basic and diluted earnings per share should be presented on the face of the statement of comprehensive income for:

- The profit or loss from continuing operations.
- The profit or loss for the period.
- Each class of ordinary shares that has a different right to share in the net profit for the period.

Roundup

IAS 33 is applicable to those entities whose debt or equity instruments are publicly traded (or are in the process of being issued in a public market).

Basic earnings per share is calculated as profit (or loss) divided by the weighted average number of ordinary shares in the period.

Preference dividends can take the form of 'cumulative' preference dividends and 'non-cumulative' preference dividends.

Shares can be issued but no consideration received in instances such as: bonus issues, rights issues, share splits and share consolidations.

Where bonus shares are issued in a period, an entity must restate the comparative year to account for the bonus issue in order to ensure the financial statements achieve consistency.

Diluted earnings per share act as a warning to shareholders that earnings per share may become diluted in the event that other liabilities become shares (for example, with convertible debt).

Earnings per share should be presented on the face of the statement of comprehensive income for: the profit or loss from continuing operations, the profit or loss for the period and each class of ordinary share that has a different right to share in the net profit for the period.

IAS 34 'INTERIM FINANCIAL REPORTING'

The objective of this standard is to deal with the minimum content of a set of interim financial reports as well as outline the principles for recognition and measurement in a complete set of financial statements for an interim period.

INTERIM FINANCIAL REPORTS

Interim financial reports are reports that contain either a complete set of financial statements or a condensed set of financial statements for an interim period. An interim period for the purposes of this IAS is a financial reporting period which is shorter than a full financial year.

MINIMUM CONTENT REQUIREMENTS

As a minimum, an interim financial report must include the following:

(a) A condensed statement of financial position (balance sheet).
(b) A condensed statement of comprehensive income, presented as either:

    (i) a condensed single statement; or
    (ii) a condensed separate income statement and a condensed statement of comprehensive income.

(c) A condensed statement of changes in equity.
(d) A condensed statement of cash flows.
(e) Selected explanatory notes.

Where an entity publishes a set of condensed financial statements the condensed financial statements must include each of the headings and subtotals that were included in its most recent annual financial statements. Additional line items or notes must be included if their omission would render the interim financial statements misleading.

Materiality must be assessed in deciding how to recognise, measure and classify, or disclose, an item for interim financial reporting purposes.

In terms of accounting policies, an entity who prepares interim financial statements must apply the same accounting policies that were applied in its annual financial statements, except for policy changes made after the date of the most recent annual financial statements that are to be reflected in the next annual financial statements.

Practical Insight

BT Group PLC — Auditor's Statement on Summary Financial Statements

Independent Auditors' Statement to the Members of BT Group PLC We have examined the Summary financial statement which comprises the Summary group income statement, Summary group cash flow statement and Summary group balance sheet as set out on pages 6 to 7 and the Summary report on directors' remuneration as set out on pages 8 to 9.

Respective Responsibilities of Directors and Auditors The directors are responsible for preparing the BT Group plc Summary financial statement and notice of meeting in accordance with applicable United Kingdom law. Our responsibility is to report to you our opinion on the consistency of the Summary financial statement within the BT Group plc Summary financial statement and notice of meeting with the full annual financial statements, the Report of the directors and the Report on directors' remuneration and its compliance with the relevant requirements of section 428 of the Companies Act 2006 and the regulations made thereunder. We also read the other information contained in the BT Group plc Summary financial statement and notice of meeting and consider the implications for our statement if we become aware of any apparent misstatements or material inconsistencies with the Summary financial statement. The other information comprises only the financial summary, the Chairman's message and the other items listed on the contents page. This statement, including the opinion, has been prepared for and only for the company's members as a body in accordance with section 428 of the Companies Act 2006 and for no other purpose. We do not, in giving this opinion, accept or assume responsibility for any other purpose or to any other person to whom this statement is shown or into whose hands it may come save where expressly agreed by our prior consent in writing.

Basis of Opinion   We conducted our work in accordance with Bulletin 2008/3 issued by the Auditing Practices Board. Our reports on the company's full annual financial statements describe the basis of our audit opinions on those financial statements, the Report of the directors and the Report on directors' remuneration.

Opinion   In our opinion the Summary financial statement is consistent with the full annual financial statements, the Report of the directors and the Report on the remuneration of BT Group plc for the year ended 31 March 2010 and complies with the applicable requirements of section 428 of the Companies Act 2006, and the regulations made thereunder.

PricewaterhouseCoopers LLP, Chartered Accountants and Statutory Auditors, London, United Kingdom.

12 May 2010

Roundup

IAS 34 deals with the minimum content a set of interim financial reports must contain. It also deals with the principles for recognition and measurement in a complete or reduced set of financial statements for an interim period.

The condensed financial statements must include each of the headings and subtotals that were included in its most recent annual financial statements.

Materiality is assessed in terms of recognition, measurement and classification of items for interim financial reporting purposes.

IAS 36 'IMPAIRMENT OF ASSETS'

This standard prescribes the requirement to ensure that a reporting entity ensures its assets are carried at no more than their recoverable amount.

IMPAIRMENT

An asset is impaired if its carrying amount in the financial statements exceeds the amount to be recovered through use or sale of the asset (its 'recoverable' amount).

Recoverable amount is the *higher* of:

- fair value less costs to sell; and
- value in use.

Fair value less costs to sell is the amount obtaining from the sale of an asset or cash-generating unit in an arm's length transaction between knowledgeable, willing parties, less the costs involved in the disposal.

Value in use is the present value of the future cash flows expected to be derived from an asset or cash-generating unit.

A *cash-generating unit* is the smallest identified group of assets that generates cash flows that are largely independent of the cash inflows from the other assets or group of assets.

INDICATORS OF IMPAIRMENT

Examples of when there are indicators of impairment are as follows:

- A significant decline in the asset's market value during the period.
- Evidence of obsolescence or physical damage to the asset.
- A current period operating loss in the business in which the asset is involved.
- Adverse changes in the business or the market in which the asset or goodwill is involved (for example, a major competitor).
- Changes in the statutory or regulatory environment in which the business operates.
- Indicators of value.
- Major loss of key employees.
- Increase in market interest rates that are likely to affect the asset's recoverable amount.

INTANGIBLE ASSETS

Intangible assets such as goodwill, intangible assets with indefinite useful lives and those intangible assets that are not yet available for use must be tested annually for impairment.

RECOGNITION OF AN IMPAIRMENT LOSS

An impairment loss must be recognised for a cash-generating unit in the following order:

- first to goodwill in the group; then
- to the other assets of the unit on the basis of the carrying amount of each asset in the unit on a pro-rata basis according to their carrying value.

Illustration

An entity has the following net assets in its statement of financial position (balance sheet) as at 31 December 2009:

Statement of Financial Position (extract)

Non-current assets

Property	60
Plant	90
Goodwill	30
	180

In the board meeting, the directors have decided that the recoverable amount of the above net assets amount to $135.

The impairment amounts to ($180 − $135) $45 and must be allocated to goodwill, then to the rest of the assets in the cash-generating unit on a pro-rata basis.

$30 of the impairment loss is allocated to the goodwill, reducing the carrying value of the goodwill to $nil. $6 is allocated to the property with the remaining $9 being allocated to the plant.

Statement of Financial Position (extract)

Post Impairment

Non-current assets

Property	54
Plant	81
Goodwill	—
	135

Illustration

An entity has a manufacturing division who manufacture roller-shutter doors and associated components which are sold on to contractors. The manufacturing division consists of a large group of heavy industrial machines which manufacture the curtains, bottom-rails, guides, angles, barrels and canopies. The reporting date of the entity is 31 December 2009 and, at that date, these machines have a book value amounting to $140,000. The directors of the entity consider that this group of machines constitutes a cash-generating unit under IAS 36 provisions.

The directors have undertaken an exercise relating to the expected cash inflows and outflows which have been based on reduced productivity levels due to the age and condition of the machinery. The analysis is shown below:

Year	Revenues $	Costs $
2010	70,000	27,000
2011	75,000	45,000
2012	85,000	65,000
2013	30,000	20,000

The original manufacturer of the plant has been approached to give a reliable estimate of the net realisable value of the machinery in the cash-generating unit. The manufacturer has informed the directors that the net selling price that an informed, unconnected third party should expect to pay for the equipment is $82,150.

The directors have based their value in use calculations having reference to the above cash flows and have discounted the above cash flows at a rate of 5%, which is the entity's cost of capital. Using this discount rate produces a present value of $93,656 which is calculated as follows:

Year	Cash Flows $	P V Factor $	Present Value
2010			40,936
2011	30,000	0.907	27,210
2012	20,000	0.864	17,280
2013	10,000	0.823	8,230
Value in use			**93,656**

As value in use exceeds the manufacturer's net selling price, then value in use is selected to represent the recoverable amount. This is lower than the current carrying value of the group of assets as at 31 December 2009 and, therefore, an impairment loss of ($140,000 – $93,6556) $46,344 is recognised.

The impairment loss is recognised as an operating expense as either depreciation or a separate heading in the statement of comprehensive income.

Roundup

IAS 36 primary objective is to ensure that assets are not carried in an entity's statement of financial position (balance sheet) at any more than their recoverable amount.

An asset is impaired if its carrying amount in the financial statements exceeds the amount to be recovered through use or sale of that asset.

Recoverable amount is the higher of 'fair value less costs to sell' and 'value in use'.

Intangible assets and intangible assets with indefinite useful lives are tested for impairment at least annually.

Impairment losses in respect of cash-generating units must be charged against goodwill in the group first and then to the other assets of the unit on the basis of the carrying amount of each asset in the unit on a pro-rata basis having regard to their carrying value.

IAS 37 'PROVISIONS, CONTINGENT LIABILITIES AND CONTINGENT ASSETS'

The objective of this standard is to ensure that appropriate recognition criteria are met before a reporting entity recognises a provision and to ensure sufficient disclosure is made to enable users to understand the nature, timing and amount of a provision.

PROVISION

A provision is a liability of an uncertain timing or amount.

Recognition of a Provision

A reporting entity can only recognise a provision within the financial statements if all three of the following criteria are met:

(1) The entity has a present obligation (legal or constructive) as a result of a past event.
(2) It is probable that an outflow of resource embodying economic benefits will be required to settle the obligation.
(3) A reliable estimate can be made of the amount of the obligation.

CONTINGENT LIABILITIES

A contingent liability is not recognised in the financial statements. Instead a contingent liability is disclosed within the notes to the financial statements. A contingent liability is:

(a) A possible obligation that arises from past events and whose existence will be confirmed only by the occurrence or non-occurrence of one or more uncertain future events not wholly within the control of the entity.

(b)   A present obligation that arises from past events but is not recognised because:

   (i)   it is not probable that an outflow of resources embodying economic benefits will be required to settle the obligation; or

   (ii)   the amount of the obligation cannot be measured with sufficient reliability.

CONTINGENT ASSETS

Only if the realisation of the asset is virtually certain will entities recognise a contingent asset.

Illustration

An entity has decided to close down its maintenance department. It puts out a full announcement to the maintenance department on 20 November 2009. It has calculated the redundancy provisions and has included the cost of redundancies in the financial statements for the year ended 31 December 2009.

The entity has an obligation as a result of a past event: the announcement on 20 November 2009.

It is probable (i.e. more likely than not) that an outflow of economic benefits will be required to settle the obligation: the redundancy payments.

It can reliably estimate the redundancy provisions.

Therefore, the entity can recognise a provision in the financial statements as at 31 December 2009.

Illustration

An entity is in the process of litigation and the entity's legal advisers have advised that it is more likely than not that the entity will not be successful in defending the case. The legal advisers have provided a reliable estimate of costs and damages which the entity would be required to pay and a provision has been made in the financial statements for this amount. Negotiations have taken place with the entity's insurers who have agreed that if the entity is unsuccessful in defending their case, they will reimburse the amounts to be paid out in the legal case.

A contingent asset should be recognised in the financial statements representing the amounts to be reimbursed by the entity's insurers, provided that it is virtually certain at the reporting date that reimbursement will actually be made if the entity settles the obligation.

Illustration

An entity is preparing its financial statements for the year ended 31 December 2009. During the year an employee has sustained an injury for which the employee is pursuing damages for an ongoing skin complaint. Investigations into the cause of the accident have been undertaken by the Health and Safety inspectorate and it was found that the entity had not provided the employee with the appropriate safety gloves which the employee should have worn during the course of his work. At the year end the entity's legal advisers have informed the directors that it is unlikely that the entity will be able to successfully defend the case, and it is likely that they will be required to pay damages to the employee but the amount of damages cannot be measured with reliance.

In the above illustration, all three criteria laid down in IAS 37 have not been met as a reliable estimation cannot be made of the obligation. Therefore, a provision cannot be made in the financial statements but a disclosure should be made within the financial statements as a contingent liability.

Roundup

IAS 37 recognises that provisions can only be made in the financial statements of a reporting entity where the entity has met all three specified criteria within the standard.

If an entity cannot meet all three specified criteria within IAS 37 to recognise a provision, the entity will not make a provision; instead they will make disclosure as a contingent liability.

IAS 37 contains the definition of a provision and a contingent liability.

Contingent assets can only be recognised when it is virtually certain that the asset will be realised.

IAS 38 'INTANGIBLE ASSETS'

The objective of this standard is to deal with the accounting treatment for intangible assets that are not dealt with in other accounting standards. IAS 38 does not deal with goodwill; this is dealt with in IFRS 3 'Business Combinations'.

RECOGNITION OF AN INTANGIBLE ASSET

An entity can only recognise an intangible asset when certain criteria are met.

An intangible asset must be recognised if, and only if:

- It is probable that the expected future economic benefits that are attributable to the asset will flow to the entity.
- The cost of the asset can be measured reliably.

Intangible assets are recognised initially at cost and cost comprises:

- Cost of purchase.
- Import duties.
- Irrecoverable taxes.
- Directly attributable costs of preparing the asset for its intended use.
- Any trade discounts or rebates deducted.

INTERNALLY GENERATED INTANGIBLE ASSETS

An entity must not recognise any internally generated goodwill. Similarly, internally generated brands such as mastheads, publishing titles, customer lists and similar items in substance must also not be recognised as intangible assets. They should be treated as either research or development costs.

RESEARCH EXPENDITURE

Any expenditure incurred during the research phase of a project must be recognised as an expense as and when it is incurred.

DEVELOPMENT EXPENDITURE

Once the research phase has been completed and the development phase commences, then any costs incurred during the development stage of a project must be capitalised if, and only if, an entity can demonstrate the following:

(a) The technical feasibility of completing the intangible asset so it will be available for use or sale.
(b) Its intention to complete the intangible asset to either use it or sell it.
(c) The entity's ability to sell the intangible asset.
(d) How the entity can demonstrate that it will generate probable future economic benefits.
(e) The availability of resources in order to complete the intangible asset (resources include those of a technical and financial nature as well as other applicable resources to complete the intangible asset).
(f) The entity's ability to measure the cost reliably.

Practical Insight

Notes to the Financial Statements (extract)

Accounting Policies (extract)

Research and Development   Research and development expenditure, net of the relevant proportion of grants receivable, is charged to the statement of comprehensive income in the year in which it is incurred, unless it is recoverable under a customer contract when it is carried forward as work in progress at the lower of cost and net realisable value.

SUBSEQUENT MEASUREMENT

After initial recognition, an entity can choose either the cost model or revaluation model for subsequent measurement.

Where an entity adopts the revaluation model then all the other intangible assets in its class must also be revalued unless there is no active market for those assets. An active market is where:

• The items traded in the market are homogenous.
• Willing buyers and sellers can normally be found at any time.
• Prices are available to the public.

Illustration

Disclosures in Respect of Intangible Assets

Accounting Policies (extract)

Research and Development Expenditure   Expenditure on research and development is charged to the statement of comprehensive income in the year in which it is incurred with the exception of expenditure on the development of certain major new products where the outcome of those projects is assessed as being reasonably certain as regards viability and technical feasibility. Such expenditure is capitalised and amortised over a period not longer than five years commencing in the year sales of the product are first made.

Notes to the Financial Statements (extract)

	2010 $, 000	2009 $, 000
Profit on ordinary activities before taxation is stated after charging (crediting):		
Depreciation of tangible fixed assets	3,721	4,120
Amortisation of intangible fixed assets	370	—
Research and development expenditure	5,002	4,125
Auditors' remuneration (including expenses)	8,000	7,500
Other fees paid to the auditors	2,700	3,150
Operating lease rentals – plant and machinery	1,221	1,110

Intangible Assets

	Group $,000
Cost as at 1 January 2010	1,500
Additions	1,000
Cost as at 31 December 2010	2,500
Amortisation as at 1 January 2010	1,500
Charge in the year	370
Amortisation as at 31 December 2010	1,870
Net book value as at 31 December 2010	630
Net book value as at 31 December 2009	—

INTANGIBLE ASSETS WITH INDEFINITE USEFUL LIVES

These are not amortised, they are reviewed for impairment in accordance with the provisions laid down in IAS 36 'Impairment of Assets'.

INTANGIBLE ASSETS WITH FINITE USEFUL LIVES

These are amortised on a systematic basis over their useful lives. The amortisation period and the amortisation method for an intangible asset with a finite useful life must be reviewed annually. If there is a change in the expected consumption of the intangible asset, then the amortisation method must be changed accordingly and accounted for as a change in accounting estimate as per IAS 8 'Accounting Policies, Changes in Accounting Estimate and Errors'.

Roundup

IAS 38 prescribes the recognition and measurement criteria in respect of intangible assets.

Goodwill is not dealt with in IAS 38; this is dealt with in IFRS 3 'Business Combinations'.

An intangible asset can only be recognised if it is probable that economic benefits will flow to the entity and the cost of the asset can be measured reliably.

The components of cost include: purchase cost, import duties, irrecoverable taxes, other directly attributable costs and net of any trade discounts and/or rebates.

Internally generated intangible assets cannot be recognised. Such costs are treated as research or development costs.

Research costs are written off to the statement of comprehensive income as incurred. Development costs are capitalised only if the entity can demonstrate compliance with the six capitalisation criteria in IAS 38.

After initial recognition, an entity can choose either the historic cost model or revaluation model for subsequent measurement.

Intangible assets with indefinite useful lives are tested annually for impairment. Intangible assets with finite useful lives are amortised on a systematic basis over their economic useful lives.

IAS 39 'FINANCIAL INSTRUMENTS: RECOGNITION AND MEASUREMENT'

The objective of this standard is to deal with the recognition and measurement of a financial asset, financial liability or other contracts to buy or sell non-financial items. It should be noted that IFRS 9 'Financial Instruments' intends to replace IAS 39 insofar as financial assets are concerned. IFRS 9 is applicable for accounting periods commencing on or after 1 January 2013; but earlier adoption is permitted and early-adopters should, therefore, refer to the provisions in IFRS 9.

IAS 39 is a companion standard to IAS 32 'Financial Instruments: Presentation' and IFRS 7 'Financial Instruments: Disclosure'.

FINANCIAL ASSETS

Financial assets contain four possible classifications within a set of financial statements, they can be:

- Financial assets at fair value through profit or loss.
- Held-to-maturity investments.
- Loans and receivables.
- Available-for-sale financial assets.

It is worth noting that IFRS 9 removes classification of financial assets as:

- financial assets at fair value through profit or loss; and
- loans and receivables.

It follows, therefore, that the only possible classification of financial assets under the new IFRS 9 is held-to-maturity investments and available-for-sale financial assets.

Financial assets at fair value through profit or loss are classified as such if the financial asset is:

- held-for-trading; or
- was designated on initial recognition as one to be measured at fair value through profit or loss.

Held-to-maturity investments are non-derivative financial assets with fixed or determinable payments that an entity intends and is able to hold to maturity and which do not meet the definition of loans or receivables and upon initial recognition are not classified as assets at fair value through profit or loss, or as available-for-sale.

Loans and receivables are non-derivative financial assets with fixed or determinable payments which are not quoted in an active market, not held for trading and not designated on initial recognition as assets at fair value through profit or loss, or as available-for-sale.

Available-for-sale assets are non-derivative financial assets that do not meet any of the above criteria.

FINANCIAL LIABILITIES

Financial liabilities can be classified as:

- Financial liabilities at fair value through profit or loss.
- Other financial liabilities measured at amortised cost using the effective interest method.

EFFECTIVE INTEREST METHOD

The effective interest method is a method of calculating the actual interest rate in a period based on the book value of the financial instrument at the beginning of the period. It works on the basis that if the book value of the financial instrument decreases, so does the amount of interest. Conversely, if the book value of the financial instrument increases, the amount of interest will increase.

In some instances, an entity may buy or sell a financial instrument for an amount other than its par value. In such situations, this would mean that the actual interest rate which is being earned or paid on the investment is different from the stated interest paid on the financial instrument.

Illustration

Entity A buys a financial instrument for $100,000 and the same financial instrument has a par value of $105,000. The interest paid is $5,000 but the actual rate of interest being earned on the investment is:

$$\$5,000 \div \$100,000 = 5\%$$

This illustration shows how the effective interest rate exactly discounts estimated future cash payments or receipts over the expected life of the financial instrument.

Illustration

Entity B acquires a financial instrument with a par value of $100,000, which the issuer will repay in three years and attracts an annual amount of interest of 5% payable at the end of each year. Entity B acquires the debt for $90,000 (obtaining a discount of $10,000). The financial instrument is to be classified as held-to-maturity.

The entries in the books of Entity B on initial recognition are:

Debit held-to-maturity investments	$90,000
Credit cash	$90,000

Entity B can calculate an effective interest rate of 8.95% based on an initial cash outflow of $90,000, three interest payments at $5,000 each and a principal of $100,000 upon maturity. The effective interest calculation can now be completed as follows:

	A	B	C	D	E
		Interest and			Closing
	Opening	*Principal*		*Discount*	*Amortised*
Year	*Amortised Cost*	*Payment*	*Interest Income*	*Amortisation*	*cost*
			(A × 8.95%)	(C − B)	(A + D)
1	90,000	5,000	8,055	3,055	93,055
2	93,055	5,000	8,328	3,328	96,383
3	96,383	8,617	3,617	100,000	105,000

The book entries in Entity B's books at the end of each year are as follows:

Year 1

Debit cash	5,000
Debit held-to-maturity investment	3,055
Credit interest income	(8,055)

Year 2

Debit cash	5,000
Debit held-to-maturity investment	3,328
Credit interest income	(8,328)

Year 3

Debit cash	105,000
Credit held to maturity investment	(96,383)
Credit interest income	(8,617)

INITIAL MEASUREMENT

Financial assets and liabilities should be measured at fair value. Fair value is the amount for which an asset could be exchanged, or a liability settled, between knowledgeable, willing parties in an arm's length transaction.

Illustration

On 1 April 2006 an 8% convertible loan note with nominal value of $600,000 was issued at par. It is redeemable on 31 March 2010 also at par. Alternatively it may be converted into equity shares of the entity on the basis of a hundred new shares for each $200 worth of loan note.

An equivalent loan note without the conversion option would have carried interest at 10%. Interest of $48,000 has already been paid and included as a finance cost within the entity's statement of comprehensive income.

Present value rates are as follows:

	End of Year	Present Values
	8%	10%
1	0.83	0.91
2	0.86	0.83
3	0.79	0.75
4	0.73	0.68

The entity is preparing its financial statements for the year ended 31 March 2007.

In the above illustration we can see that there is an option to convert the shares into equity (the loan note holders do not have to accept the equity shares; they could demand repayment in the form of cash). The provisions in IAS 32 'Financial Instruments: Presentation' prescribe the correct treatment because IAS 32 states that where there is an obligation to transfer economic benefits, there should be a liability recognised. On the other hand, where there is not an obligation to transfer economic benefits, a financial instrument should be recognised in equity.

In the facts above, we have both 'equity' and 'debt' which is commonly referred to as a 'compound' financial instrument. There is an obligation to pay cash: interest at 8% per annum and a redemption amount: the debt element. The equity part of the transaction is the option to convert the loan note into shares.

The facts have disclosed the present value rates, and these need to be used to calculate the debt element of the financial instrument in order to recognise the liability at its present value. The question lies in deciphering which interest rate to use.

The facts inform us that an equivalent loan without the conversion option would have carried interest at a rate of 10%, despite the fact that the entity has paid interest to the loan note holders at a rate of 8%. However, for the purposes of calculating the liability to be recognised in the statement of financial position (balance sheet), we should use the equivalent rate of interest.

We can now calculate the amount to be recognised as a liability and the amount to be recognised as equity as follows:

	8% Interest ($600,000 × 8%) $	Factor at a rate of 10% $	Present Value
Year 1 2007	48,000	0.91	43,600
Year 2 2008	48,000	0.83	39,800
Year 3 2009	48,000	0.75	36,000
			119,400
Year 4* 2010	648,000	0.68	440,600
Amount to be recognised as a liability	**560,000**		
Initial proceeds	**(600,000)**		
Amount to be recognised as equity	**40,000**		

* In year 4, the loan note is redeemed therefore ($600,000 + $48,000) $648,000.

The next thing to incorporate is the adjustments required to the interest charge. The facts inform us that $48,000 has been recognised in the statement of comprehensive income ($600,000 × 8%).

However, the 8% loan note interest is simply the interest the loan note holders receive annually. We have to recognise that an equivalent loan without the conversion option would carry interest at a higher rate (10%) so it is therefore necessary to reflect this in the financial statements.

The present value of the debt which has been calculated above is $560,000. The finance cost at 10% is ($560,000 × 10%) $56,000. $48,000 has already been charged to finance costs in the statement of comprehensive income so a further ($56,000 − $48,000) $8,000 needs to be added to the financial instrument as follows:

DR statement of comprehensive income (finance costs) $8,000
CR liability $8,000

DERIVATIVES

A derivative is a financial instrument:

- Whose value changes in response to a change in underlying variables (for example, a change in interest rates).
- That requires no initial investment, or one that is smaller than would ordinarily be required for a contract with a similar response to changes in market factors.
- Is settled at a future date.

Examples of derivatives are:

- Forward contracts.
- Swaps.
- Forward rate agreements.
- Options.
- Caps and floors.

EMBEDDED DERIVATIVES

An embedded derivative is a feature within a contract. It acts as a component part of a 'hybrid' financial instrument which also includes a non-derivative host contract with the effect that some of the cash flows of the hybrid instrument vary in a similar way to a stand-alone derivative. A 'hybrid' instrument is a combination of both the host contract and the embedded derivative.

Embedded derivatives can arise from deliberate financial engineering (for example, to make a low interest rate debt more attractive by including an equity-linked return). This situation is not absolute and they can arise through market prices and other contractual arrangements; for example, leases and insurance contracts. In fact they can occur in all sorts of contracts and instruments with the objective being to change the nature of cash flows that would otherwise be required by the host contract and effectively shift financial risk between parties.

Illustration

An entity raises finance by issuing convertible debt. The host contract is the loan, but this loan contains an 'option' to convert the debt into shares. The 'option' is the embedded derivative because it is deriving its value from fluctuations in the share price.

DERECOGNITION OF A FINANCIAL INSTRUMENT

Financial Liabilities

A financial liability should be removed from the statement of financial position (balance sheet) when, and only when, the obligation specified within the contract is discharged, cancelled or expired. A gain or loss arising on the derecognition of a financial liability is recognised in the statement of comprehensive income.

Financial Assets

Financial assets require a bit more analysis. An entity needs to consider whether the asset under consideration is:

- An asset in its entirety.
- Specifically identified cash flows from an asset.
- A full proportionate share of the cash flows from an asset.
- A fully proportionate share of specifically identified cash flows from a financial asset.

Once this has been undertaken, consideration is then given to whether the asset has been transferred and, if so, whether the transfer of the asset is eligible for derecognition. An asset is transferred if either the entity has transferred the contractual rights to receive cash flows, or the entity has retained the contractual rights to receive the cash flows from the asset, but has assumed a contractual obligation to pass those cash flows on under an arrangement which meets three conditions:

(1) The entity does not pay the amounts over until it collects an equivalent amount on the original asset.
(2) The entity is prohibited from selling or pledging the original asset other than to the recipient.
(3) The entity has an obligation to remit those funds to the recipient without delay.

The key factor is looking at whether all the risks and rewards have been transferred. If substantially all the risks and rewards of ownership have been passed, the entity can derecognise the asset. If substantially all of the risks and rewards have not been passed over, the entity is prohibited from derecognising the asset.

SUBSEQUENT MEASUREMENT OF FINANCIAL ASSETS AND FINANCIAL LIABILITIES

	In Statement of Financial Position	Gains or Losses
Fair value through profit or loss	Fair value	Statement of comprehensive income
Available-for-sale	Fair value	In equity until derecognition, then recycled via the statement of comprehensive income
Held-to-maturity	Amortised cost	Not applicable
Loans and receivables	Amortised cost	Not applicable

HEDGE ACCOUNTING

In order to qualify for hedge accounting at the inception of a hedge and at each reporting date, the changes in the fair value or cash flows of the hedged item attributable to the hedged risk must be expected to be highly effective in offsetting the changes in the fair value or the cash flows of the hedging instrument on a prospective basis and on a retrospective basis where the actual results are within a range of 80%–125% when offset by an opposite gain or loss.

CATEGORIES

There are three types of hedge:

- Fair value hedge.
- Cash flow hedge.
- Hedge of a net investment in a foreign operation.

For hedge accounting to be applied, certain criteria must be met:

- Formal documentation put in place at the inception of the hedge.
- The designation between the item that is hedged and the hedging instrument itself is formally documented.
- Hedge effectiveness can be measured.
- Where cash flow hedges are concerned, the transaction must be highly probable (in other words, more likely than not).
- Assessment takes place on an on-going basis and is effective throughout the period.

Fair Value Hedge

A fair value hedge is a hedge of the exposure to changes in the fair value of a recognised asset or liability or a firm commitment that is attributable to a particular risk which could affect profit or loss.

The gain or loss from remeasuring the hedging instrument at fair value (for a derivative hedging instrument) or foreign currency component measured in accordance with IAS 21 'The Effects of Changes in Foreign Exchange Rates' is recognised in profit or loss.

The gain or loss on the hedged item attributable to the hedged risk will adjust the carrying amount of the hedged item and should be recognised in profit or loss even if the hedged item is measured at cost. Recognition in profit or loss also applies if the hedged item is an available-for-sale financial asset.

Cash Flow Hedge

A cash flow hedge is a hedge against the exposure to variability in cash flows associated with a recognised asset or liability which could affect profit or loss.

The portion of the gain or loss on the hedging instrument that is determined to be an effective hedge is recognised in other comprehensive income.

The ineffective portion of the gain or loss on the hedging instrument is recognised in profit or loss.

Hedge of a Net Investment in a Foreign Operation

This is linked to IAS 21 'The Effects of Changes in Foreign Exchange Rates' and is a foreign operation (a subsidiary). The portion of the gain or loss on the hedging instrument that is determined to be an effective hedge is recognised in other comprehensive income.

The ineffective portion is recognised in profit or loss.

Roundup

IAS 39 deals with the recognition and measurement of a financial instrument. IAS 32 deals with the presentation issues insofar as classification of the financial as either debt or equity.

IFRS 9 will eventually replace IAS 39 insofar as financial assets are concerned. The IASB are currently dealing with financial liabilities.

Under IAS 39 provisions, there are four possible classifications in respect of financial assets: financial assets at fair value through profit or loss, held-to-maturity investments, loans and receivables and available-for-sale assets.

Financial liabilities can be classified as: financial liabilities at fair value through profit or loss, or other financial liabilities measured at amortised cost using the effective interest method.

The effective interest method calculates the actual interest in a period based on the book value of the financial instrument at the beginning of the period.

Financial assets and liabilities should be measured at fair value.

Fair value is the amount for which an asset could be exchanged, or a liability settled, between knowledgeable, willing parties in an arm's length transaction.

A derivative is a financial instrument whose: value changes in response to underlying variables, requires very little, or no, initial investment and is settled at a future date.

Embedded derivatives in IAS 39 contain a host contract and a non-derivative host contract.

Strict rules exist where the derecognition of financial assets and liabilities are concerned.

There are three types of hedge: fair value hedge, cash flow hedge and hedge of a net investment in a foreign operation. In order to qualify for hedge accounting, certain criteria must be met.

IAS 40 'INVESTMENT PROPERTY'

The objective of this standard is to prescribe the accounting treatment that an entity should apply in dealing with its investment property.

INVESTMENT PROPERTY

Investment property is property that is held for its investment potential. Investment property is not property for use in the production or supply of goods or services, or for administrative purpose. Investment property is also not property that is for sale in the ordinary course of business.

RECOGNITION

Investment property must be recognised as an asset when, and only when:

- It is probable that future economic benefits associated with the investment property will flow to the entity.
- The cost of the investment property can be measured reliably.

An investment property should initially be recorded at its cost.

SUBSEQUENT MEASUREMENT

IAS 40 allows investment property to be subsequently measured using either the cost model or the revaluation model.

The cost model is that used in IAS 16 'Property, Plant and Equipment' and requires an investment property to be measured at depreciated historic cost after initial recognition. Where an entity chooses the revaluation model for subsequent measurement it must disclose the fair value of its investment property within the financial statements.

Illustration

An entity occupies a large factory in the normal course of its business and rents out part of this factory to a third party.

The entity cannot classify the factory (or the part it lets out) as investment property because IAS 40 specifically prohibits property used in the production of supply of goods or services, or for administrative purposes, to be classified as investment property. The factory must be accounted for under the provisions in IAS 16.

Roundup

IAS 40 prescribes the accounting treatment in respect of investment property.

Property that is used in the normal course of business, or for sale in the normal course of business cannot be classified as investment property.

Investment property can only be recognised if it is probable that future economic benefits which are associated with the investment property will flow to the entity and the cost of the investment property can be measured reliably.

An entity will recognise investment property initially at cost and can subsequently measure the investment property using either the depreciated historic cost model or the fair value model.

IAS 41 'AGRICULTURE'

The objective of this standard is to prescribe the accounting treatment related to agricultural activity.

AGRICULTURAL ACTIVITY

Agricultural activity is the management by an entity of the biological transformation of biological assets for sale into agricultural produce or additional biological assets.

BIOLOGICAL ASSET

A biological asset is a living animal or plant.

AGRICULTURAL PRODUCE

Agricultural produce is the harvested product of an entity's biological asset.

Illustration

Biological Asset	Agricultural Produce	Harvested Product
Cattle	Milk	Cheese
Bushes	Leaf	Tea, tobacco
Vines	Grape	Wine
Plants	Cotton	Thread, clothing
Sheep	Wool	Yarn

INITIAL MEASUREMENT

Biological assets should be measured initially, and at each reporting date, at fair value less estimated point-of-sale costs.

Agricultural produce is measured at the point of harvest at fair value less estimated point-of-sale costs.

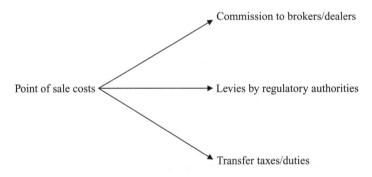

Point of sale costs → Commission to brokers/dealers

Point of sale costs → Levies by regulatory authorities

Point of sale costs → Transfer taxes/duties

Point-of-sale costs do not include costs such as transport or other such costs incurred to get the asset to market.

FAIR VALUE

There is a rebuttable presumption within IAS 41 that says the presumption can be rebutted on initial recognition when market prices are not available and alternative estimates of fair value are clearly unreliable. Where this occurs, an entity should value its biological assets at cost less accumulated depreciation and any impairment losses.

IAS 41 requires that a change in fair value less estimated point-of-sale costs of a biological asset be included in net profit or loss for the period in which it arises. In agricultural activity, a change in physical attributes of a living plant or animal directly enhances or diminishes economic benefits to the entity.

GOVERNMENT GRANTS

If a government grant relates to a biological asset measured at its fair value less estimated point-of-sale costs is conditional, including where a government grant requires an enterprise not to engage in specific agricultural activity, an enterprise should recognise the government grant as income when, and only when, the conditions attaching to the grant are met.

If a government grant relates to a biological asset measured at cost less depreciation and impairment, then the provisions in IAS 20 'Accounting for Government Grants and Disclosure of Government Assistance' apply.

Illustration

On 1 January 2009, a farming entity held a herd of ten two year old animals. The entity purchased an animal aged two and a half years on 1 July 2009 for $108 and one animal was born on 1 July 2009. No animals were sold or disposed of during the period. Per-unit fair values less estimated point-of-sale costs were as follows:

	$	
2 year old animal at 1 January 2009	100	
Newborn animal at 1 July 2009	70	
2.5 year old animal at 1 July 2009	108	
Newborn animal at 31 December 2009	72	
0.5 year old animal at 31 December 2009	80	
2 year old animal at 31 December 2009	105	
2.5 year old animal at 31 December 2009	111	
3 year old animal at 31 December 2009	120	
Fair value less estimate point-of-sale costs of herd		
At 1 January 2009	(10 × $100)	1,000
Purchase 1 July 2009	(1 × $108)	108
Increase in fair value less estimated point-of-sale costs due to price change		
10 × ($105 − $100)	50	
1 × ($111 − $108)	3	
1 × ($72 − $70)	2	55
Increase in fair value less estimated point-of-sale costs due to physical change		
10 × ($120 − $105)	150	
1 × ($120 − $111)	9	
1 × ($80 − $72)	8	
1 × $70	70	237
Fair value less estimated point-of-sale costs of herd		
at 31 December 2009	1,320	
1 × $80	80	1,400

Roundup

IAS 41 applies to the accounting treatment in respect of agricultural and biological assets.

A biological asset is a living animal or plant.

Agricultural produce is the harvested product of an entity's biological asset.

Biological assets are measured at fair value less estimated point-of-sale costs.

Agricultural produce is measured at the point of harvest at fair value less estimated point-of-sale costs.

Point-of-sale costs do not include costs such as transport or other costs needed to get the asset to market.

APPENDIX 2: ILLUSTRATIVE AUDIT TESTS

This Appendix looks at some typical tests that can be undertaken on the key audit areas when using an audit approach which focuses primarily on the statement of financial position (balance sheet). This appendix will look at some typical tests to be performed on the following areas:

- Capital and reserves.
- Related parties.
- Intangible fixed assets.
- Tangible fixed assets.
- Investments.
- Inventories.
- Receivables.
- Bank and cash.
- Creditors.
- Leasing.
- Provisions and contingencies.
- Payroll.
- Value Added Tax (UK).
- Consolidated financial statements.

SHARE CAPITAL AND RESERVES

Objectives

- To confirm that share capital is correctly recorded within the financial statements.
- To confirm that reserves are correctly recorded within the financial statements.
- To confirm that the financial statements agree to any statutory records (such as records held with the Registrar of Companies in the UK).

Tests

- Agree details of the share capital to the statutory records and agree to the financial statements.
- Ensure any amendments to the share capital have been properly notified to any regulatory authority (such as the Registrar of Companies in the UK).
- Obtain or prepare a reconciliation of the movement in all the types of equity in the statement of financial position (balance sheet). Agree that all transfers have been made correctly and agree all transfers to the financial statements.
- Ensure that any dividends paid or proposed are done so with regard to the sufficiency reserves available. Where dividends have been declared in excess of available reserves, then, consider the impact this will have on the audit opinion.
- Ensure where dividends have been declared after the reporting period that they are not included in the financial statements but instead disclosed.
- Ensure all statutory records are up to date and that the relevant regulatory authority has been promptly notified of any changes to the statutory records.

- Review minutes of meetings to ascertain any matter which may affect the financial statements and agree any resolutions made that are relevant to the year under review to the financial statements.

TRANSACTIONS WITH DIRECTORS AND RELATED PARTIES

Objectives

- To identify any directors' loan accounts and transactions which involve directors and related parties.
- To confirm that all details of directors' loans and transactions with related parties have been identified and recorded.
- To identify any ultimate controlling party that may require disclosure under FRS 8 or IAS 24.

Tests

- Obtain reconciliations of all directors' loan accounts in subsistence during the year.
- Review the transactions in the directors' loan accounts and consider their relevance in the context of any money laundering legislation.
- Review accounting records, being alert for evidence of any undisclosed related party transactions.
- Review the bank audit letter (where these have been obtained) and note any potential undisclosed related parties (such as personal guarantees given by management).
- Review receivables and payables listings at the reporting date for any related party transactions/balances outstanding at the year end.
- Consider whether the entity has an ultimate controlling party, either by virtue of majority shareholding or various management having the ability to act in concert in respect of the operations and financial affairs of the entity.
- Review correspondence files (in particular correspondence from lawyers), being alert for evidence of any related parties.
- Obtain details of directors' other activities from external records, such as the records held on any public files (for example, the Registrar of Companies) and ensure adequate related party disclosures have been made where applicable.
- Hold discussions with management/directors and, where applicable, those charged with governance to identify any potential undisclosed related party transactions.

INTANGIBLE NON-CURRENT ASSETS

Audit Objectives

- To ensure that consideration is given to appropriate rates of amortisation and that carrying values of intangible non-current assets remain appropriate.
- To consider any impairment of intangible assets and to ensure that intangible assets are not carried in the statement of financial position (balance sheet) at any more than their recoverable amount.
- To ensure all additions and disposals of intangible assets are properly authorised and included within the financial statements.
- To ensure that entity has appropriate title to intangible assets.

Tests

- Ensure that the amortisation policy is appropriate and is in line with relevant accounting standards (FRS 10, IAS 38 and IFRS 3).
- Where there are indicators of impairment then carry out a review of the valuations placed on goodwill to ensure that it is not recorded at any more than its recoverable amount.
- Where additions and disposals have taken place of intangible assets during the year, obtain documentary evidence to support the additions and disposal proceeds.
- Trace intangible assets to their documents of title, for example, patents and licences and details of any goodwill additions in contracts.
- Undertake proof-in-total calculations on the amortisation charges for the year to ensure that they have been calculated correctly.

TANGIBLE NON-CURRENT ASSETS

Audit Objectives

- To confirm that opening values of cost and accumulated depreciation charges have been correctly brought forward into the current year from the previous reporting period.
- To confirm that non-current assets are included in the financial statements at a cost or valuation that is acceptable.
- To confirm that purchases of non-current assets have been authorised and have been appropriately capitalised in the statement of financial position.
- To confirm that depreciation rates are appropriate and have been correctly calculated in the financial statements.
- To confirm that non-current assets are still in use and that no item of property, plant and equipment is carried in the statement of financial position (balance sheet) at any more than its recoverable amount.
- To confirm ownership of items of property, plant and equipment.
- To confirm that any future commitments in relation to capital expenditure have been sufficiently disclosed within the financial statements.
- To confirm correct treatment of items of property, plant and equipment which have been obtained through leasing arrangements (such as hire purchase contracts).
- To confirm that items of leasehold improvements are correctly valued in the financial statements.

Tests

- Obtain or prepare the reconciliation of non-current assets and agree all opening cost values and all opening depreciation values and ensure they have been properly brought forward into the financial year under audit.
- Obtain details of all additions during the year and perform testing on a representative sample of additions, tracing the items in the sample to source documentation and confirming that:
  - the item that has been capitalised is of a capital nature;
  - any purchase taxes (such as VAT) have been correctly accounted for and that any irrecoverable taxes have been included in the cost price of the item; and
  - the item of capital expenditure has been appropriately authorised.

- Review minutes of meetings and cross reference any major items of capital expenditure to resolutions in the minutes of the meetings.
- Ensure that all items in the year which have been capitalised are appropriate and that they meet the definition of an asset in accordance with IASB 'Framework Document' or other such equivalent.
- Ensure that where any 'subsequent expenditure' has been capitalised, that it is accounted for correctly under the relevant accounting standard (FRS 15/IAS 16).
- Obtain reconciliations of repairs and renewals, computer costs, office stationery and other appropriate revenue expense accounts and ensure that all items within these nominal accounts are revenue and no capital items have been inappropriately written off to the statement of comprehensive income (profit and loss account).
- Obtain details of disposals in the year and trace sales proceeds to source documentation and ensure that disposals have been correctly accounted for in the accounting period.
- Ensure that where an entity receives capital-based grants they have been correctly accounted for in accordance with domestic legislation and accounting standards (SSAP 4/IAS 20).
- Where there are indicators of impairment ensure that non-current assets are not carried at any more than their recoverable amount in the statement of financial position.
- Where an entity adopts the revaluation model, ensure that the model is consistently applied to all assets within the same class and that the value is appropriate at the reporting date.
- Where an entity holds investment properties, ensure that these are accounted for in accordance with relevant accounting standards (SSAP 19 and IAS 40).
- Review depreciation rates and consider their appropriateness.
- Test check depreciation rates to ensure they have been calculated correctly (proof-in-total calculations may be appropriate in this respect).
- Devise a sample of non-current assets and conduct physical verification to make sure that they are in regular use. Where an entity maintains a non-current asset register, trace these items in the sample to the register.
- Discuss with senior officials the possibility of any assets which still have a carrying value, but which may be scrapped.
- In respect of properties, check ownership of properties by reference to documents of title. In addition, check for any charges over the property by financiers and ensure adequate disclosure has been made of these 'secured debts' in the financial statements of the entity.
- Where an entity obtains non-current assets under finance leases, ensure that the capitalisation method is appropriate (finance leases are capitalised, operating leases are not capitalised).
- In respect of leasehold improvements, obtain a copy of the leases and ensure that any improvement works are being depreciated appropriately having regard to the provisions in the lease.

INVESTMENTS

Objectives

- To confirm that recorded investments actually exist and are beneficially owned by the entity.
- To confirm that the investments are appropriately valued and to confirm that appropriate provisions have been made for diminution in values.

- To ensure that all incomes from investments have been correctly recorded in the financial statements.

Tests

- Obtain or prepare a schedule of investments and show all movements in investments during the year.
- Obtain details from the investment register and agree the entries in the investment register to the financial statements.
- Agree additions during the year to source documentation such as agreements, contracts and meeting minutes.
- Where disposals have been made during the year, agree the proceeds to the source documentation and ensure that the disposal has been correctly accounted for in the financial statements.
- Obtain details of share certificates and agree the share certificates to the investments.
- Where there is evidence of impairment, ensure sufficient provision has been made against the investment to ensure that it is carried at no more than its recoverable amount.
- Test the value of listed investments at the reporting date for disclosure within the financial statements.
- For unlisted investments, review the value by reference to the latest financial statements.
- Where the entity has long-term investments, ensure we have sufficient appropriate evidence on file to support the long-term investment.
- Check income has been received on all income-yielding investments on a consistent basis and ensure that it has been correctly accounted for within the financial statements.

INVENTORY

Objectives

- To ensure that any significant adverse variances between the current period and the previous year's inventory movement has been adequately investigated and sufficient explanations received.
- To confirm the existence of inventory.
- To confirm that inventory and work-in-progress are valued correctly.
- To confirm where the entity has any long-term work-in-progress that the valuations placed on this long-term work-in-progress are appropriate and in accordance with relevant accounting standards.
- To confirm that adequate provisions have been made, where applicable, to ensure that inventory is reduced from cost to net realisable value where appropriate.
- To confirm correct recognition of inventory.
- To confirm any inventory held by third parties.
- To confirm the existence of inventory which is not physically verified at the year-end inventory count.

Tests

- Perform analytical review procedures on the inventory valuation, investigating any reasons for any unexpected fluctuations in inventory valuation between the previous and the current year's results.

- Calculate the number of days' sales held in inventory and consider its reasonableness.
- Where inventory and work-in-progress are considered significant, then attendance at the inventory count should have taken place (see below).
- Check sample quantifies taken at the inventory count and agree these counts to the final inventory valuation.
- Agree the casts and cross casts on the inventory sheets and ensure that all inventory sheets are intact with no obvious omissions or errors.
- Test a sample of inventory to its source documentation (purchase invoice).
- Where an entity has work-in-progress, ensure that an appropriate test is undertaken to agree WIP and finished goods to suppliers' invoices, material usage, labour rates and overhead absorption rates.
- Ensure that the valuation of the inventory accords with relevant accounting standards (note IAS 2 does not permit the use of last-in first-out as a method of valuation).
- Review long-term work-in-progress and ensure that costs have been properly recorded and that profit is taken on the basis of work carried out, costs to date, expected costs to complete and total contract value (this is particularly relevant to construction contracts).
- Where losses are foreseen on contracts, ensure that adequate provisions are made as soon as the loss is foreseen.
- Undertake a net realisable value test on a sample of inventory ensuring that the entity is selling the product at more than cost.
- Review items of slow-moving or obsolete inventory and ensure the valuations placed on these items are appropriate (in many cases, cost should be reduced to net realisable value).
- Discuss the level of inventory provisions with management.
- Undertake cut-off tests to ensure that inventory is recognised in the correct accounting period.
- Where an entity has material amounts of inventory which are held by third parties, obtain independent confirmation as to the value of these inventories.

ATTENDANCE AT INVENTORY COUNT

Objective

- The objective of attendance at inventory count is for the auditor to gain an understanding of the procedures adopted by management, whether these procedures will enable an efficient and accurate inventory count to be carried out and whether they would minimise the risk of material misstatement within the inventory valuation.

Tests

- Obtain a list of instructions given by management to individuals involved in the inventory count and ensure that these instructions are adhered to at all times.
- Tour the areas to be covered and establish the nature, locations and size of inventory to be counted.
- During test counts ensure that no items of inventory are omitted from the count.
- Establish the procedures to ensure that no items of inventory can be 'double-counted' and establish how effective the procedures are (usually as inventory is counted it is marked as counted to avoid duplicate counting).
- Identify any inventory that is held by third parties.

- Ensure that all inventory sheets are controlled and signed.
- Select items of inventory in a two-way direction (floor to sheets and sheets to floor) and check the counts.
- Mark the items which have been sampled on the inventory sheets which will enable further audit tests to be carried out to ensure these have been correctly carried through to the final inventory valuation.
- Record the number of rough inventory sheets used and ensure that only appropriate inventory sheets are included.
- Note details of any obvious omissions or errors.
- Note details of any inventory which is slow-moving or obsolete and establish the valuations placed on these items of inventory.
- Ensure that cut-off procedures are adequate to make sure that only inventory which has been purchased at the end of the reporting period is included in the count and exclude those items of inventory which have been sold at the year/period end.
- Obtain details of the last goods inwards note.

TRADE AND OTHER RECEIVABLES

Audit Objectives

- To confirm that receivables are fairly stated and that any significant variances from the previous reporting period have been adequately investigated and explained.
- To confirm that receivables represent amounts which are properly due to the entity at the reporting date and that appropriate provision has been made to ensure that receivables are not over-stated.
- To confirm that amounts in respect of receivables at the reporting date have been realised after the reporting date.
- To confirm that goods or services supplied by the entity are not under-stated and that they are properly accounted for.
- Where the entity has significant cash sales, to ensure that these are complete and correctly recorded in the financial statements.
- To confirm that adequate disclosure in respect of receivables has been made.

Tests

- Obtain a schedule of receivables due at the reporting date and undertake analytical procedures and obtain sufficient explanations in terms of any significant variances from the previous period to the current reporting period.
- Review receivables days for reasonableness.
- Obtain the list of receivables at the reporting date and trace a sample of balance (ensuring the sample is representative of the population) and agree:
  - The ageing of the receivables to the invoices.
  - Receivables balances have been properly cleared after the reporting date by undertaking after-date cash tests.
  - Review any credit balances and establish how these credit balances have been derived.

- Obtain material after date credit notes and ensure that they do not relate to sales made during the period under audit. If they do relate to the period under audit, ensure that adequate provision has been made in the financial statements.
- Consider the need to undertake a receivables circularisation to obtain confirmation of balances owed at the period end from the receivable. Chase up any non-replies and, where non-replies are still outstanding, consider alternative audit procedures, such as after-date cash testing.
- Undertake cut-off tests to ensure that goods or services sold either side of the reporting date are correctly accounted for.
- Confirm completeness of income by selecting a sample of source documents (customer orders or other forms of documentation which initiate a sale) and check:

  - Details to the customer order.
  - Sales invoice agrees to the customer order.
  - Prices recorded on the sales invoice agree to price lists or the customer's order.
  - Casts on the invoice.
  - Posting to relevant VAT accounts.
  - Posting to the receivables ledger account.
  - Posting of the sales invoice to the nominal ledger.

- Trace material other receivables and prepayments to source documentation.
- If the entity deals with cash sales and these are considered significant, then agree the cash takings to source documentation such as receipt books or till rolls. Ensure that receipt books are numerically sequential.
- Ensure that where the entity is required to adopt the use of IFRS 8 'Segment Reporting' that they have made adequate disclosure in accordance with IFRS 8.
- Ensure that where an entity is required to disclose its sales between those of its host country and those of overseas countries, that it does so sufficiently.
- Ensure that where any receivable is due after more than twelve months of the reporting date that it is appropriately classified.

CASH AT BANK AND IN HAND

Audit Objectives

- To confirm that bank balances belonged to the entity and existed at the reporting date.
- To confirm that payments are correctly recorded.
- To identify any large and unusual items.
- To confirm that petty cash is correctly accounted for.

Tests

- Obtain the bank reconciliation statements and agree the statements to the financial statements.
- Agree the balance per the statement on the bank reconciliation to the bank statement at the end of the reporting period and to the bank audit letter (where obtained).
- Check the casts in the bank reconciliation.
- Ensure that outstanding payments and lodgements detailed on the bank reconciliation have properly cleared after the reporting date.

- Review the bank audit letter for details of any securities and cross reference the contents of the bank audit letter to the appropriate sections of the current audit file.
- Select a sample of payments from the cash book and check to paid cheques. Consider the need to obtain copies of paid cheques direct from the bank (where applicable).
- Trace a sample of payments and receipts from the cash book to the nominal ledger.
- Review the cash book for large and unusual items and agree these to source documentation.
- Trace a sample of petty cash from source documentation and agree to the postings in the nominal ledger.
- Ensure that where an entity operates a petty cash system on an 'imprest' basis, that it is correctly applied throughout the year.
- Consider the need to attend cash counts at the reporting date where cash is considered material.

PAYABLES

Audit Objectives

- The overall objective is to confirm that payables represent amounts which are properly due by the entity at the reporting date, properly accounted for and appropriately disclosed. The objective is also to confirm that appropriate costs are recorded completely, properly accounted for and sufficiently disclosed.
- To confirm that liabilities incurred are completely and accurately recorded.
- To confirm that the correct amount for trade payables is disclosed.
- To confirm that there are no incomplete recordings of costs.
- To confirm the correct recording of purchases.
- To confirm that payables and accruals are recorded at their full amount and are recognised in the correct period and on a consistent basis.
- To confirm the correct accounting treatment for accruals and other payables is reasonable.
- To ensure that liabilities are properly classified and details of any security is disclosed within the financial statements.
- To ensure that loans are properly classified and adequate disclosure is made of any security given.

Tests

- Review trade payables days for consistency and investigate the reasons for any large disparity between the current period and the previous reporting period.
- Obtain a sample of statements from trade payables and reconcile these to the payables ledger. Where there are few supplier statements, then consider circularisation of balances.
- Select a sample of purchase orders or goods received notes and agree the details of these to supplier invoices checking for authorisation, casts, calculation of amounts on the invoice (for example VAT, where applicable) and posting into the payables ledger and nominal ledger.
- Undertake cut-off tests to ensure that goods or services received either side of the reporting date have been accounted for in the correct accounting periods.

- Ensure that the balance on the aged payables listing agrees to the control account at the reporting date.
- Review the aged payables listing and ascertain the reasons for any major debit balances.
- Review payments made after the reporting date to check for any unprovided payables or accruals.
- Review supplier invoices received after the reporting date for any undisclosed payables or accruals.
- Review any goods received notes which have not been matched to supplier invoices to ensure that any goods or services received before the reporting date have been accrued for in the financial statements.
- Where the entity has material non-trade payables, trace these to underlying source documentation.
- Ensure that where liabilities are due after more than twelve months from the reporting date that these are appropriately classified within the financial statements.
- Where liabilities are secured, ensure that appropriate disclosure has been made within the financial statements.
- Ensure that bank loans have been classified between those amounts falling due within one year, years two through to five and after more than five years.

HIRE PURCHASE AND LEASING

Audit Objectives

- There are two types of lease: operating leases and finance leases.
- The audit objective is to ensure that the financial statements correctly reflect all hire purchase contracts and finance leases entered into by the entity that capital repayments and interest are correctly treated and that future obligations are sufficiently disclosed.

Tests

- Obtain copies of agreements and confirm that they are either operating or finance leases in accordance with relevant accounting standards (for example, IAS 17 'Leases').
- Ensure that finance leases are appropriately capitalised in the financial statements.
- Ensure that where finance leases are capitalised that adequate disclosure is made in respect of assets obtained under finance leases showing the total net book value and the depreciation charges in the year.
- Check that the interest is calculated using either the rate of interest implicit in the lease or another acceptable method (for example, the 'level spread' method).
- Ensure future obligations in respect of operating leases are correctly allocated and disclosed within the financial statements.

PROVISIONS AND CONTINGENCIES

Audit Objectives

- The general objective is to ensure that all provisions have been correctly recognised in accordance with prescribed accounting standards.
- Ensure that compliance with relevant accounting standards in respect of provisions has been made, for example, under IAS 37 'Provisions, Contingent Liabilities and

Contingent Assets' a reporting entity can only recognise a provision within the financial statements if all three of the following criteria are met:

- the entity has a present obligation (legal or constructive) as a result of a past event;
- it is probable that an outflow of resources embodying economic benefits will be required to settle the obligation; and
- a reliable estimate can be made of the amount of the obligation.

- Ensure that provisions are made by reference to correspondence, after date events and any available minutes from meetings.
- Ensure that any contingent assets have been recognised in accordance with relevant accounting standards. IAS 37 'Provisions, Contingent Liabilities and Contingent Assets' states that a contingent asset can only be recognised if the realisation of the asset is virtually certain.
- Hold discussions with management and, where applicable, those charged with governance to discuss the existence of contingencies, impending litigation and any potential capital commitments.
- Consider the need to liaise directly with the entity's legal advisers in respect of any litigation claims or legal cases.

EMPLOYEE WAGES AND SALARIES

Audit Objectives

- To confirm that expenditure on wages and salaries represents genuine payments to employees at authorised rates.
- To confirm that there is no underpayment of taxes associated with employee costs (such as PAYE and National Insurance Contributions).
- To confirm that payroll costs are disclosed correctly in the statement of comprehensive income.
- To confirm any taxation liabilities in connection with wages and salaries are complete.
- To confirm that all required disclosures are correctly made within the financial statements.
- To confirm that correct and timely returns have been made to taxation authorities in respect of wages and salaries.

Tests

- Confirm a sample of payroll deductions and ensure that these have been correctly calculated.
- Check that a sample of employees physically exist by way of physical verification or reviewing correspondence from the taxation authorities.
- Verify rates of pay are authorised by an appropriate individual within the entity.
- Check that contracts of employments are issued.
- Check that adequate segregation of duties is in existence in respect of payroll preparation (for example, one person prepares the payroll and another person checks the payroll for errors/omissions).
- Check the payroll amounts to the cash book in respect of net wages and any taxation liabilities.

- Review the amounts in the cash book and be alert for any amounts which have been paid to employees or contractors which have not been processed through the payroll and consider any underpaid taxation liabilities.
- Where employees are given benefits, ensure that the appropriate taxation authorities have been properly notified of such benefits in accordance with local taxation legislation.
- Reconcile the payroll charge in the statement of comprehensive income.
- Where there are a large number of employees and reconciliation of the payroll charge in the statement of comprehensive income is time-consuming, check a sample of employees and check the postings from the payroll summaries to the wages costs in the statement of comprehensive income and the associated tax liability accounts.
- Agree the tax liability in respect of payroll at the reporting date to the payroll reports and the cash book.
- Ensure sufficient disclosure is made in respect of directors' remuneration which includes benefits in kind and pension contributions.
- Ensure that sufficient disclosure is made in respect of staff costs.
- Review copies of year-end returns submitted to the taxation authorities and check a sample of these for completeness and accuracy.
- Check a sample of returns and payments and ensure these have been made to the taxation authorities on a timely basis.

TAXATION

Audit Objectives

- To confirm that the liability to taxation on an entity's profits has been disclosed correctly.
- To confirm that tax returns have been submitted for all previous periods by the specified dates.
- To confirm that all amounts in respect of taxation have been paid to the taxation authorities by the normal due date. Where this has not occurred, then consideration should be made to accrue for interest where these amounts are considered material.
- To ensure that any amounts in respect of deferred taxation have been calculated and disclosed correctly within the financial statements.

Tests

- Obtain the tax computation for the current period and consider the need to have this reviewed by a specialist, where applicable.
- Ensure the tax charge in the financial statements has been correctly allocated and the taxation liability is sufficient disclosed.
- Ensure that any movement on the deferred taxation account has been correctly calculated and that disclosure is made in the financial statements of the major components of the deferred taxation provision.
- Undertake a reconciliation of the taxation charge in the statement of comprehensive income.
- Ensure that any provisions for interest have been correctly calculated.

APPENDIX 3: ILLUSTRATIVE FINANCIAL STATEMENTS

The following illustrative financial statements are based on fictitious entities. The illustrative financial statements are intended to illustrate the respective disclosures concerning a published set of financial statements, and it is important that readers use reputable disclosure checklists and not rely wholly on these illustrative financial statements as legislation and accounting standards in various jurisdictions frequently change.

The following illustrative financial statements relate to a small entity reporting under IFRS.

LUCAS INC

Chairman's Statement for the Year Ended 31 May 2009

In the twelve months to 31 May 2009, the company has achieved a number of strategic and operating milestones although this was against the background of a severe global recession and a sustained reduction of our output within the industry as a whole. The key milestones were:

- The award of a multi-year contract with Gabriella Enterprises Inc, a leading supplier of high performance tyres within the European aftermarket, which is forecast to yield revenues of $300,000–$450,000 per annum in future years.
- Accreditation under ISA 9001.
- Completion of the Lucas Inc manufacturing project which provides the capability of carbon infiltration of discs in-house and contributes to the reduction in manufacturing costs of approximately 20% for an automotive brake disc.
- A further $100,000 contract from Alicia Enterprises Inc, the European leader in engineering technology.

There were disappointments as well and these resulted from the very sharp decline in business confidence during the final months of 2008 and the first quarter of 2009. In February 2009, we signalled that the company's revenues for the full year would fall short of the market expectations that were set in August 2008 and that the principal cause of the revenue reduction was a prospective fall in orders from our automotive customers. The company has now met its revised expectations for revenues and operating losses for the full year. Business in the year was considerably higher than budget from the engineering sectors and this provides the company with a platform for growth despite the continued low levels of business expected from the engineering sector during the remainder of 2009 and most of 2010.

Financial Review   In the twelve months to 31 May 2009, revenue was $679,284 (2008: $508,111). This represents an increase of 34% over the prior year.

At 31 May 2009, the order book, representing confirmed orders, was $166,370 (2008: $302,124). The reduction in the order book level over the period is mainly due to the reduction in business from the engineering sector; however, the order book has grown to $308,108 by 5 August 2009. The order book does not reflect orders not yet placed with regards to the annual, multi-year supply contracts the company has signed during 2008 with Alicia Enterprises for engineering components, for carbon-ceramic brake automotive discs with Gabriella Enterprises Inc or the supply of carbon brake discs with a leading European brake systems group.

Losses after taxation for the twelve month period were $840,740 (2008: $594,065). These include a non-cash charge of $94,424 (2008: $56,609) relating to share based payments under IFRS 2.

Earnings per share for the year were a loss of 4.42p (2008: 3.33p).

Capital expenditure for the year was $71,428 (2008: $142,599).

The company had a cash balance of $404,725 (2008: $1,112,719) at 31 May 2009 and it has no borrowings.

Shareholder funds as at 31 May 2009 were $1,026,523 (2008: $1,722,839).

Future Developments   The company has progressed sufficiently far in the application of its technology that it now has a number of globally based customers operating in each of its main end user markets. A number of these clients are either evaluating the company's technology for license or are purchasing brake discs or engineering components for their development programmes or for commercial use.

To facilitate the management of the operation the company has created four wholly-owned operating subsidiaries. The new Group structure commenced on 1 June 2009.

The Group is focussed on achieving new business wins in the engineering sector whilst it recognises that business from other markets will remain subdued until well into the second half of 2010. The Chief Executive's report describes the opportunities in each of the main user markets and there is good reason to be confident that we shall report improved results in the 2010 financial year.

Management has reduced the overhead base by an estimated $200,000 per annum going forward and the company has received initial notice that it has been awarded another multi-year development grant which will reduce overheads further and improve cash flows.

The company secured a fundraising of $410,000 net of expenses during July 2009. The issue of 4,516,580 new ordinary shares at 10p per share will take place on 13 August 2009. This will be used to assist with working capital needs over the next twenty-four months.

Whilst forecasting accurately can be difficult in challenging economic climates, the board is cautiously optimistic that it can increase business revenues and reduce losses in the 2010 financial year and work towards breaking even in cash terms.

Stella Whitaker

Chairman

August 2009

Chief Executive's Report

Following the sharp economic decline within the engineering market, income from the engineering market has remained steady year on year with growth in overall turnover being achieved in other areas as described below. As a result, sales to engineering customers represented 65% of total turnover compared to 84% in 2008.

The company has three main engineering contracts:

- Supply of engineering components to Alicia Enterprises Inc, a leading European after-market component supplier.
- Supply of brake discs to a global automatic brake discs supplier.
- Supply of engineering consultancy services to a supplier of high performance super cars.

Sales to Alicia Enterprises Inc have remained strong; however, revenue from the two other contracts, both with forecast annual revenues of $300,000 to $450,000, has been significantly below the company's initial expectations in July 2008.

The company recognises that trading conditions for the company's current engineering contracts will remain difficult well into 2010.

In addition to the company's existing contracts, the company continues to work to bring in new business, receiving new orders from a US engineering components supplier which has won the contract to supply approximately fifty prototype vehicles for the next generation of UK military transport vehicles.

The company continues to work on development programmes with two brake systems suppliers.

Byrne Enterprises Inc has been, and remains, a key partner of the $1.34 million, three year collaborative R&D project funded by a national charitable organisation. This project is being led by Lucas Inc.

The second development is with a US brake system supplier that supplies both commercial and military aircraft principally in US markets. The company and the customer are pleased with both the pace of developments and the technical advances made during the last twelve months, with the company progressing through a number of key technical milestones.

It is always difficult to predict the adoption of new technologies and the engineering sector is not different. The company expects the development programme with the US supplier to continue to progress, with the focus on the development and commercialisation of the company's proprietary technology.

Lucas Inc is uniquely positioned to deliver affordable, high performance (in terms of extended life and reduced mass) engineering components.

During the last twelve months, the company has seen the level of interest increase significantly, with the engineering sector providing more than 25% of the group's revenues during the financial year.

We have successfully completed year one of a three year development programme with Alicia Enterprises Inc. The $150,000 contract of over three years generated some positive results and led to additional revenues from Alicia Enterprises Inc, including an additional contract in excess of $100,000 to further investigate and accelerate the development. We are also pleased that the company has been officially awarded the year two contract with Alicia Enterprises Inc and continues to work closely with Alicia Enterprises Inc, who recognise the potential for the engineering technology and are focussed on the development of the material for use in its range of products.

The company has signed a new contract for $75,000 over three years with a new customer. The programme, although small, is strategically important to the customer with Lucas Inc technology offering the potential of affordable, high performing components for the future.

In addition the award of a $200,000, two year development contract with a local customer for the development of carbon components further recognises the potential for the use of the material in demanding environments which require affordable solutions.

The company expects the engineering sector to continue to make a significant contribution to the group revenues going forward.

Operations   Affordability is a key requirement for all of our chosen markets, particularly with the current economic pressures the world has been facing. The development and commissioning of a new engineering component filtration system has been completed and has reduced the cost to manufacture an engineering component by 20%.

The operations team successfully achieved ISO 9001 accreditation in September 2008: an important milestone for the business in terms of continuous improvements and a prerequisite to truly operating in our chosen market.

In the autumn of 2008, the management recognised the change in trading conditions in the engineering sector and took steps to reduce its operational cost base by $200,000. The savings came from two areas. Some non-recurring costs associated with achieving ISO accreditation and bringing the new engineering component filtration systems online as well as a reduction in production resources to reflect the reduced demand in two of our main engineering contracts.

The company has a strong senior management team who have shown tremendous commitment and maturity during the last twelve months.

The blend of skills, experience and determination within the teams means that we are well placed to continue the good progress made to date.

I would like to thank all my colleagues for their dedication over the past year.

Leyla Westhead

Chief Executive

August 2009

Directors' Report

The directors present their annual report and the audited financial statements for the year ended 31 May 2009.

Principal Activity The principal activity of the company during the year was the development and manufacture of engineering components.

Business Review A review of the company's activities during the year is dealt with in the financial review section of the chairman's statement.

Key Risks and Uncertainties As in previous years the principal risk faced by the company is considered to be the speed at which our customers and potential customers adopt the new engineering components technology. Indications in the automotive areas are that the technology continues to be well received and is being adopted over an increasing number of vehicles. The risk is constantly assessed by monitoring the level of enquiries and orders for both the company and industry wide. In addition, the company faces the continuing uncertainty created by the current economic climate, particularly within the engineering sector.

Key Performance Indicators The directors continue to monitor the business internally with a number of performance indicators: order intake, sales output, profitability and manufacturing cost of engineering components. The company has met its revised performance targets in each of these areas — please see chairman's report for more details.

- Turnover $679,284 (2008; $508,111).
- Losses after taxation $840,740 (2008: $594,065).
- Order book of $166,730 (as at 31 May 2009).
- Completion of the new engineering technology programme so reducing the cost of an engineering component by 20%.

The company produces an annual business plan and full monthly forecasts detailing sales, profitability and cash flow to help monitor business performance going forward.

Future Developments The board aims to continue with its corporate strategy, which is to exploit its technologies in engineering components by:

- establishing contract development opportunities and collaborations with national and multi-national customers in the engineering sector; and
- expanding commercial sales of engineering products and components.

Research and Development The majority of the company's staff is employed in researching activities which are concentrated on the identification of new products and applications for engineering components and non-friction materials.

Proposed Dividend and Transfer to Reserves The loss for the year after taxation amounted to $840,740 (2008: $594,065). The directors do not recommend the payment of a dividend.

Policy and Practice on Payment of Payables It is the company's policy that payments to suppliers are made in accordance with the terms and conditions agreed between the company and its suppliers, providing that all trading terms and conditions have been complied with. The company does not follow any code or standard on payment practice.

At the year end, there were 27 days' (2008: 53 days) purchases in trade payables.

Political and Charitable Donations   The company made no political or charitable donations during the year (2008: $nil).

Directors and Directors' Interests   The directors who held office during the year were as follows:

> S Whitaker
> L Westhead
> J Heaton*
> N Hall
> A Smythe
> C Reese*

*denotes non-executive director.

A Smythe resigned as director on 3 December 2008.

The directors retiring by rotation are J Heaton and N Hall who, being eligible, offer themselves for re-election.

The directors who held office at the end of the financial year had the following interests in the ordinary shares of the company according to the register of directors' interests:

Number of $0.01 ordinary shares

	% of issued share capital at end of year	*Interest at end of year*	*Interest at start of year*
S Whitaker	5.15	979,661	979,661
L Westhead	1.35	256,986	256,986
J Heaton	0.42	79,750	79,750
N Hall	0.47	90,000	90,000
A Smythe	0.02	4,350	4,350

According to the register of directors' interests, no rights to subscribe for shares in or debentures of the company were granted to any of the directors or their immediate families, or exercised by them during the financial year, except as disclosed in the report of the directors' remuneration.

The directors benefited from qualifying third party indemnity provisions in place during the financial year and at the date of this report.

Corporate Governance   Lucas Inc is committed to maintaining high standards of corporate governance. The company complies with the Combined Code as modified by the recommendations of the respective Government department, to the extent that the directors consider appropriate, given the size of the company, its current stage of development and the constitution of the board.

The board has appointed an audit committee whose primary role is to review the company's interim and annual financial statements before submission to the board for approval. The board has also appointed a remuneration committee, which is responsible for reviewing executive remuneration and performance. The remuneration and audit committees are made up of three non-executive directors. Details of the remuneration committee are disclosed in the Report on Directors' Remuneration.

Disclosure of Information to Auditors   The directors who held office at the date of approval of this directors' report confirm that, so far as they are each aware, there is no relevant audit information of which the company's auditors are unaware; and each director has taken all the steps that he/she ought to have taken as director to make him/herself aware of any relevant audit information and to establish that the company's auditors are aware of that information.

Auditors   In accordance with section 489 of the Companies Act 2006, a resolution for the re-appointment of Ethan Bury & Co as auditors of the company is to be proposed at the forthcoming Annual General Meeting.

Fund Raising   The company secured a fundraising of \$410,000 net of expenses during July 2009 by the issue of new ordinary shares at 10p per share. This will be completed on 13 August 2009 and used to assist with working capital needs over the period of the next twenty-four months.

Post Balance Sheet Events   To facilitate the management of the operations, the company has created four wholly-owned operating subsidiaries.

By Order of the Board

S Whitaker

Chairman

August 2009

Report on Directors' Remuneration

Policy on Executive Directors' Remuneration   The remuneration committee comprises of J Heaton and C Reese.

The remuneration committee is responsible for reviewing and determining the company's policy on executive remuneration (including the grant of options under the Share Options

Scheme) and ensuring compliance with and implementation by the company, as far as reasonably practicable, of the recommendations and guidelines of the Combined Code. Executive remuneration packages are designed to ensure the company's executive directors and senior executives are fairly rewarded for their individual contributions to the company.

Fees for Non-Executive Directors   The fees for non-executive directors are determined by the board. The non-executive directors are not involved in the decisions about their own remuneration.

Directors' Remuneration   Set out below is a summary of the fees and remuneration received by all directors for the year or, where applicable, period out of office:

	2009	*2008*
	$	*$*
Executive Directors		
S Whitaker	115,912	84,399
L Westhead	–	30,049
J Heaton	44,282	53,943
	160,194	168,391
Non-Executive Directors		
J Heaton	55,004	45,253
C Reese	18,000	18,000
	73,004	63,253
	233,198	231,644

With the exception of S Whitaker, none of the directors received pension contributions in respect of their office. In addition to the remuneration received, as stated above, S Whitaker received $4,667 (2008: $3,898) in respect of pension contributions.

Directors' Interests   Details of any contracts in which a director has a material interest are disclosed in note 17.

None of the directors received any remuneration or benefits under long-term incentive schemes.

Share Options   The company operates a share incentive scheme. All options are granted at the discretion of the board. The options granted, date of grant, exercise price and exercise periods under the scheme are set out below.

None of the directors exercised options during the year. S Whitaker and L Westhead surrendered options during the year. Directors' options outstanding and the options which were granted, surrendered and expired during the year are as follows:

Enterprise Management Incentive Scheme

No. of option

Director	Date of grant	Holding at 1/06/08	Granted in year	Expired, waived or lapsed	Holding at 31/05/09	Exercise price	Exercise period	Exercise date
S Whitaker	19/12/02	64,286	–	64,286	–	$0.7000	2005–12	19/12/12
L Westhead	18/04/07	64,286	–	64,286	–	$0.7000	2007–14	18/03/14
J Heaton	14/09/05	133,091	–	–	133,091	$0.2100	2010–17	18.4.2017
J Heaton	18/04/07	330,000	107,219	230,000	207,219	$0.1850	2011–18	22/09/18
C Reese	18/04/07	80,000			766,616	$0.2100	2010–17	18/04/17
		671,663			1,106,926			

The market price of the shares as at 31 May 2009 was $0.115 and during the year varied from $0.195 to $0.075.

By Order of the Board

S Whitaker

Chairman

August 2009

Statement of Directors' Responsibilities in Respect of the Annual Report and the Financial Statements

The directors are responsible for preparing the Directors' Report and the Annual Report in accordance with applicable law and regulations.

Company law requires the directors to prepare financial statements for each financial year. Under that law they have elected to prepare the financial statements in accordance with IFRSs as adopted by the EU and applicable law.

Under company law the directors must not approve the financial statements unless they are satisfied that they give a true and fair view of the state of affairs of the company and of the profit or loss of the company for that period. In preparing these financial statements, the directors are required to:

- Select suitable accounting policies and apply them consistently.
- Make judgements and estimates that are reasonable and prudent.
- State whether they have been prepared in accordance with IFRSs as adopted by the EU.
- Prepare the financial statements on the going concern basis unless it is inappropriate to presume that the company will continue in business.

The directors are responsible for keeping adequate accounting records that are sufficient to show and explain the company's transactions and disclose with reasonable accuracy at any time the financial position of the company and enable them to ensure that the financial statements comply with the Companies Act 2006. They have general responsibility for taking such steps as are reasonably open to them to safeguard the assets of the company and to prevent and detect fraud and other irregularities.

The directors are responsible for the maintenance and integrity of the corporate and financial information included in the company's website. Legislation in the UK governing the preparation and dissemination of financial statements may differ from legislation in other jurisdictions.

Independent Auditors' Report to the Members of Lucas Inc

We have audited the financial statements of Lucas Inc for the year ended 31 May 2009 set out on pages 455–474. The financial reporting framework that has been applied in their preparation is applicable law and International Financial Reporting Standards (IFRSs) as adopted by the EU.

This report is made solely to the company's members, as a body, in accordance with section 495 and 496 of the Companies Act 2006. Our audit work has been undertaken so that we might state to the company's members those matters we are required to state to them in an auditor's report and for no other purpose. To the fullest extent permitted by law, we do not accept or assume responsibility to anyone other than the company and the company's members, as a body, for our audit work, for this report or for the opinions we have formed.

Respective Responsibilities of Directors and Auditors   As explained more fully in the Directors' Responsibilities Statement set out on page 453, the directors are responsible for the preparation of the financial statements and for being satisfied that they give a true and fair view. Our responsibility is to audit the financial statements in accordance with applicable law and International Standards on Auditing (UK and Ireland). Those standards require us to comply with the Auditing Practices Board's (APB's) Ethical Standards for Auditors.

Scope of the Audit of the Financial Statements   We conducted our audit in accordance with International Standards on Auditing (UK and Ireland) issued by the Auditing Practices Board. An audit includes examination, on a test basis, of evidence relevant to the amounts and disclosures in the financial statements. It also includes an assessment of the significant estimates and judgements made by the director in the preparation of the financial statement, and of whether the accounting policies are appropriate to the company's circumstances, consistently applied and adequately disclosed.

We planned and performed our audit so as to obtain all the information and explanations which we considered necessary in order to provide us with sufficient evidence to give reasonable assurance that the financial statements are free from material misstatement, whether caused by fraud or other irregularity or error. In forming our opinion, we also evaluated the overall adequacy of the presentation of information in the financial statements.

Opinion on Financial Statements   In our opinion the financial statements:

- Give a true and fair view of the state of the company's affairs as at 31 May 2009 and of its loss for the year then ended.
- Have been properly prepared in accordance with IFRSs as adopted by the EU.
- Have been prepared in accordance with the requirements of the Companies Act 2006.

Opinion on Other Matter Prescribed by the Companies Act 2006 In our opinion the information given in the Directors' Report for the financial year for which the financial statements are prepared is consistent with the financial statements.

Matters on which we are Required to Report by Exception We have nothing to report in respect of the following matters where the Companies Act 2006 requires us to report to you if, in our opinion:

- Adequate accounting records have not been kept, or returns adequate for our audit have not been received from branches not visited by us.
- The financial statements are not in agreement with the accounting records and returns.
- Certain disclosures of directors' remuneration specified by law are not made.
- We have not received all the information and explanations we require for our audit.

Susan Breary (Senior Statutory Auditor)

For and on behalf of Ethan Bury & Co Chartered Certified Accountants and Registered Auditors

Any Street

Any Town

Any County

14 August 2009

Lucas Inc: Statement of Comprehensive Income for the year ended 31 May 2009

	Note	2009 $	2008 $
Revenue	2	679,284	508,111
Cost of sales		(282,487)	(252,874)
Gross profit		396,797	255,237
Administrative expenses:			
Before research costs		(733,700)	(615,617)
Research costs		(839,509)	(678,078)
Total administrative expenses		(1,573,209)	(1,293,695)
Other operating income	3	166,035	220,652
Operating loss		(1,010,377)	(817,806)
Financial income	6	20,646	67,347
Financial expenses	6	(1,854)	–
Loss before taxation		(991,585)	(750,459)

	Note	2009 $	2008 $
Taxation	7	150,845	156,394
Loss for the year	15	(840,740)	(594,065)
Loss per ordinary share Basic and diluted	18	(4.42p)	(3.33p)

All amounts relate to continuing activities.

Lucas Inc: Statement of Changes in Equity as at 31 May 2009

2008	Share Capital Account $	Share Premium $	Capital Reserve $	Profit and loss $	Total $
Loss for the year	–	–	–	(594,065)	(594,065)
Total recognised income and expenses	–	–	–	(594,065)	(594,065)
Credit in relation to share based payments	–	–	–	56,909	56,909
Issue of new shares	50,000	847,237	–	–	897,237
Opening shareholders funds at 1 June 2007	140,308	4,902,715	463,885	(4,093,850)	1,413,058
Closing shareholders' funds at 31 May 2009	190,308	5,749,952	463,885	(4,631,306)	1,772,839

2009	Share Capital Account $	Share Premium $	Capital Reserve $	Profit and loss $	Total $
Loss for the year	–	–	–	(840,740)	(840,740)
Total recognised income and expense	–	–	–	(840,740)	(840,740)
Credit in relation to share based payments	–	–	–	94,424	94,424
Opening shareholders funds at 1 June 2007	190,308	5,749,952	463,885	(4,631,306)	1,772,839
Closing shareholders funds at 31 May 2009	190,308	5,749,952	463,885	(5,377,622)	1,026,523

Lucas Inc: Statement of Financial Position as at 31 May 2009

	Note	2009 $	2008 $
Non-current assets			
Property, plant and equipment	8	382,448	382,975
Total non-current assets		382,448	382,975
Current assets			
Inventories	9	228,251	258,874
Trade and other receivables	10	212,851	292,923
Cash and cash equivalents		404,275	1,112,719
Total current assets		845,377	1,664,516
Total assets		1,227,825	2,047,491
Current liabilities			
Other interest bearing loans and borrowings	11	(14,438)	–
Trade and other payables	12	(168,669)	(274,652)
Total current liabilities		(183,107)	(274,652)
Non-current liabilities			
Other interest bearing loans and borrowings	11	(18,195)	–
Total liabilities		(201,302)	(274,652)
NET ASSETS		1,026,523	1,772,839
Equity			
Share capital	14	190,308	190,308
Share premium	15	5,749,952	5,749,952
Capital reserve	15	463,885	463,885
Retained earnings	15	(5,377,622)	(4,631,306)
Total equity attributable to equity			
Shareholders of the company		1,026,523	1,772,839

These financial statements were approved by the board of directors on 12 August 2009 and were signed on its behalf by:

S Whitaker

Director

L Westhead

Director

Lucas Inc: Statement of Cash Flows for the Year Ended 31 May 2009

	2009 *$*	*2008* *$*
Cash flows from operating activities		
Loss for the year adjusted for:	(840,740)	(594,065)
Depreciation charge	71,282	49,079
Amortisation charge	—	1,886
Profit on disposal of plant	(4,402)	–
Equity-settled share-based payment		
Costs	94,424	56,609
Financial income	(20,646)	(67,347)
Financial expense	1,854	–
Taxation	(150,845)	(156,394)
	(849,073)	(710,232)
Changes in working capital		
Decrease/ (increase) in inventories	30,623	(46,693)
Decrease/ (increase) in trade and other receivables	80,272	(3,447)
Decrease/ (increase) in trade and other payables	(105,983)	15,641
	844,361	(744,631)
Finance income received	20,646	67,347
Financial expense paid	(1,854)	–
Taxation received	150,845	156,394
Net cash used in operating activities	(674,724)	(520,890)
Cash flows from investing activities		
Acquisition of property, plant and equipment	(22,150)	(142,599)
Proceeds from sale of property, plant and equipment	–	5,075
Net cash used in investing activities	(17,075)	(142,599)
Cash flows from financing activities		
Proceeds from issue of share capital	—	897,237
Payment of finance lease liabilities	(16,645)	–
Net cash from financing activities	(16,645)	897,237
Net decrease/ (increase) in cash and cash equivalents	(708,444)	233,748
Cash and cash equivalents at the beginning of the period	1,112,719	878,971
Cash and cash equivalents at the end of the period	404,725	1,112,719

Lucas Inc: Notes Forming Part of the Financial Statements

1. Accounting Policies   Lucas Inc (the 'company') is a company incorporated and domiciled in the United Kingdom.

The financial statements have been prepared in accordance with International Financial Reporting Standards ('IFRSs') as adopted by the EU.

The financial statements were approved by the board on 12 August 2009.

Basis of Preparation   The financial statements have been prepared in accordance with applicable accounting standards and under the historical cost convention, as modified for financial assets and liabilities at fair value through the statement of comprehensive income.

The accounting policies set out below have, unless otherwise stated, been applied consistently to all periods presented in these financial statements.

Going Concern   The financial statements have been prepared on a going concern basis which the directors believe to be appropriate. The company incurred a net loss of $840,740 during the year; however, the directors are satisfied, based on detailed cash flow projections, that sufficient cash is available to meet the company's needs as they fall due for at least twelve months from the date of signing the financial statements. Revenues are expected to continue to increase in the coming years resulting in the company becoming profitable in due course. In addition, the company has secured a fundraising of $410,000 net of expenses during July 2009. The issue of new ordinary shares at 10p per share will take place on 13 August 2009.

The company's business activities, together with the factors likely to affect future development, performance and position are set out in the Chairman's statement on pages 4–5 and the Directors' Report on pages 8–10. In addition, note 19 to the financial statements includes the group's objectives, policies and processes for managing its capital; its financial risk management objectives; details of its financial instruments and its exposures to credit risk and liquidity risk.

The directors believe that the group is well placed to manage its business risks successfully despite the current uncertain economic outlook. After making enquiries, the directors have a reasonable expectation that the company has adequate resources to continue in operational existence for the foreseeable future. Accordingly, they continue to adopt the going concern basis in preparing the annual report and the financial statements.

Share-Based Payments   The share option programme allows employees to acquire shares of the company. The fair value is measured at the grant date and spread over the period during which the employees become unconditionally entitled to the options. The fair value of the options granted is measured using an option pricing model, taking into account the terms and conditions upon which the options were granted. The amount recognised as an expense is adjusted to reflect the actual number of share options that vest except where forfeiture is only due to share prices not achieving the threshold for vesting.

Intangible Assets and Amortisation   Expenditure on patents is capitalised and amortised to nil by equal annual instalments over the useful economic life of seven and a half years.

Property, Plant and Equipment   Property, plant and equipment are stated at cost less accumulated depreciation and accumulated impairment losses.

Where parts of an item of property, plant and equipment have different useful lives, they are accounted for as a separate item of property, plant and equipment.

Leases in which the company assumes substantially all the risks and rewards of ownership of the leased asset are classified as finance leases. Leased assets acquired by way of finance lease are stated at an amount equal to the lower of their fair value and the present value of the minimum lease payments at inception of the lease, less accumulated depreciation and less accumulated impairment losses. Lease payments are accounted for as described below.

Depreciation is charged to the statement of comprehensive income on a straight-line basis over the estimated useful lives of each part of an item of property, plant and equipment. Land is not depreciated. The estimated useful lives are as follows:

- Plant and machinery   —   12.5% to 20% per annum.
- Fixtures and fittings   —   1% per annum.
- Motor vehicles   —   25% per annum.
- Leasehold improvements   —   over life of the lease.

Depreciation methods, useful lives and residual values are reviewed at each reporting date.

Foreign Currencies   Transactions in foreign currencies are recorded using the rate of exchange ruling at the date of the transaction. Monetary assets and liabilities denominated in foreign currencies are translated to the functional currency at the foreign exchange rate ruling at the reporting date and the gains or losses on translation are included in the statement of comprehensive income.

Leases   Operating Lease Payments

Payments made under operating leases are recognised in the statement of comprehensive income on a straight-line basis over the term of the lease. Lease incentives are recognised in the statement of comprehensive income as an integral part of the total lease expense.

Finance Lease Payments

Minimum lease payments are apportioned between the finance charge and the reduction of the outstanding liability. The finance charge is allocated to each period during the lease term so as to produce a constant periodic rate of interest on the remaining balance of the liability.

Government Grants   Revenue grants are credited to the statement of comprehensive income, and included within other operating income, so as to match them with the expenditure to which they relate.

Post-Retirement Benefits   The company does not operate a pension scheme, but does contribute to specific employees' personal pension schemes. The amount charged to the statement of comprehensive income represents the contributions payable to employees' personal pension schemes during the financial year.

Research and Development Expenditure   Expenditure on research activities is recognised in the statement of comprehensive income as an expense as incurred.

Expenditure on development activities is capitalised if the product or process is technically and commercially feasible and the company intends and has the technical ability and sufficient resources to complete development, future economic benefits are probable and if the company can measure reliably the expenditure attributable to the intangible asset during its development. No research costs met the criteria for capitalisation in the current or preceding years.

Inventories Inventories are stated at the lower of cost and net realisable value. In determining the cost of raw materials and consumables the purchase price is used. For work-in-progress, cost is taken as production cost, which includes an appropriate proportion of attributable overheads.

Taxation The charge for taxation is based on the loss for the year and takes into account taxation deferred or accelerated arising from temporary differences between the carrying amounts of certain items for taxation and for accounting purposes.

Deferred taxation is provide for in full at the tax rate which is expected to apply to the period when the deferred taxation is expected to be realised, including on tax losses carried forward.

Deferred taxation assets are recognised only to the extent that it is probable that future taxable profits will be available against which the temporary differences can be utilised.

Research and development tax credits are recognised on a cash received basis as a reduction in the current tax payable as this is when the tax credit is considered recoverable.

Cash and Cash Equivalents Cash and cash equivalents, for the purposes of the statement of cash flows, comprises cash in hand and deposits repayable on demand.

Revenue Revenue comprises income derived from the supply of engineering components and consultancy work. Revenue is recognised on transfer to the customer of significant risks and rewards of ownership, generally this will be when the goods are despatched to the customer. Turnover excludes value added taxes.

Contractual arrangements exist with specific customers which set selling prices and target volumes for future periods. The revenue derived from specific purchase orders raised against these contracts is recognised in a consistent manner to that described above.

Non-Derivative Financial Instruments Non-derivative financial instruments comprise investments in equity and debt securities, trade and other receivables, cash and cash equivalents, loans and borrowings and trade and other payables.

Trade and Other Receivables Trade and other receivables are recognised initially at fair value. Subsequent to initial recognition they are measured at amortised cost using the effective interest method, less any impairment losses.

Trade and Other Payables Trade and other payables are recognised initially at fair value. Subsequent to initial recognition, they are measured at amortised cost using the effective interest method.

Interest Rate Risk   The Company finances its operations through cash. Cash resources are invested to attract the highest rates for periods that do not limit access to these resources.

Critical Accounting Estimates and Judgements   The preparation of financial statements in conformity with adopted IFRSs requires management to make judgements, estimates and assumptions that affect the application of policies and reported amounts of assets and liabilities, income and expenses. The estimates and associated assumptions are based on historical experience and various other factors that are believed to be reasonable under the circumstances, the results of which form the basis of making the judgements about varying values of assets and liabilities that are not already apparent from other sources. Actual results may differ from these estimates. The estimates and assumptions which have a significant risk of causing a material adjustment to carrying amounts of assets and liabilities within the next financial year are discussed below:

Impairment of Property, Plant and Equipment

Property, plant and equipment are reviewed for impairment if events or changes in circumstances indicate that the carrying amount of an asset is not recoverable.

Provision to Write Inventories Down to Net Realisable Value

The Company makes provisions for obsolescence based on historical experiences and management estimates of future events. Actual outcome could vary significantly from these estimates.

Research and Development Expenditure

The board considers the definitions of research and development costs as outlined in IAS 38 'Intangible Assets' when determining the correct treatment of costs incurred. Where such expenditure is technically and commercially feasible, the company intends and has the technical ability and sufficient resources to complete development, future economic benefits are probable and if the company can measure reliably the expenditure attributable to the intangible asset it is treated as development expenditure and capitalised on the statement of financial position.

In considering whether an item of expenditure meets these criteria, the board applies judgement. During the year all such expenditure has been expensed to the statement of comprehensive income on the grounds that it relates to feasibility studies to identify new applications for the technology or methods of improving the production process. As the technical feasibility of this work is unknown at the time the costs are incurred, none meet the criteria for capitalisation during the current or previous year.

2. Analysis of Revenue   Revenue and loss on ordinary activities before taxation is wholly attributable to the principal activity of the company. As all products are similar in nature and are manufactured using a single production facility, the board have assessed the segmental breakdown of the business during the year and consider that all revenue falls under a single business segment for the purposes of IFRS 8 'Operating Segments'.

The following additional information is presented solely to assist the reader in understanding the performance of the company in the year.

Revenue by type of end user is analysed as follows:

	2009 $	2008 $
Engineering components	241,157	345,464
Consultancy	236,279	83,798
Parts	201,848	78,850
	679,284	508,111

All sales are served by a single production facility. As such, net assets, liabilities, additions to property, plant and equipment, loss before taxation and depreciation cannot be attributed to specific categories.

	2009 $	2008 $
By Geographical Market		
United Kingdom	296,821	138,074
Rest of Europe	375,265	353,964
United States of America	7,098	16,073
	679,284	508,111

Revenue by origin, net assets and profit before interest and tax all relate to the US.

3. Expenses and Auditors' Remuneration

	2009 $	2008 $
Operating loss before taxation is stated		
After charging		
Depreciation of owned tangible non-current assets	71,282	49,079
Research and development expensed as incurred	678,078	839,509
Amortisation of patents and licences	–	1,886
Rents payable under operating leases	53,577	50,251
Loss on exchange	5,609	2,294
After crediting		
Exchange gains	3,831	2,164
Government grants	166,035	220,652

Audit of these financial statements Amounts receivable by auditors and their associates in respect of:

Audit of financial statements pursuant to legislation	17,450	17,450

Government Grants   Grants received comprise revenue grants from the local government.

These are subject to making expenditure as stipulated in the grant application and to audit of the claims. There are no unfulfilled conditions or contingencies associated with government assistance received.

4. Remuneration of Directors   The company considers key management personnel as defined in IAS 24 'Related Party Disclosures' to be the directors of the company. The aggregate amounts of remuneration paid to directors in respect of qualifying services during the year were $233,198 (2008: $231,644). Of this, $115,912 (2008: $84,399) was made to the highest paid director and company pension contributions of $4,667 (2008: $3,898) were made to a money purchase scheme on her behalf.

Full disclosure of directors' emoluments, share options and directors' pension entitlements which form part of the package as well as remuneration and transactions is given in the Report of the Directors' remuneration on pages 451 and 452.

5. Staff Numbers and Costs   The average number of persons employed by the company (including directors) during the year, analysed by category, was as follows:

	2009	2008
Directors	6	6
Other employees	17	14
	23	20

The aggregate payroll costs of these persons were as follows:

	2009 $	2008 $
Wages and salaries	609,510	624,013
Social security costs	72,308	61,685
Other pension costs (see note 16)	29,429	19,497
	711,247	705,195

6. Financial Income and Expenses

Financial Income	2009 $	2008 $
Bank interest receivable	20,646	67,347

Financial Expenses

Interest expense on financial liabilities at amortised cost	1,854

7. Taxation   Analysis of credit in the year:

	2009 $	2008 $
UK corporation tax		
Research and development tax repayment	(150,845)	(156,394)
Income tax credit	(150,845)	(156,394)

Details of the unrecognised deferred tax asset are included in note 13.

Factors affecting the tax credit for the current period   The current tax credit for the year is lower (2008: lower) than the standard rate of corporation tax of 28% (2008: 28%). The differences are explained below:

	2009 $	2008 $
Loss for the year	(840,740)	(594,065)
Total income tax credit	(150,844)	(156,394)
Loss excluding income tax	(991,584)	(750,459)
Current tax at average rate of 28% (2008: 29.67%)	(277,644)	(222,661)
Effects of:		
Non-deductible expenses	359	632
Reduction in tax rate	—	38,681
Change in unrecognised timing differences	42,036	4,976
Current year losses for which no deferred tax recognised	234,979	178,192
Tax incentives	(150,845)	(156,394)
Income tax credit (see above)	150,845	156,394

Factors that may affect future tax charges   The effective tax rate in future years is expected to be below the standard rate of corporation tax due principally to historical losses which have been carried forward.

8. Property, Plant and Equipment

	Asset under construction $	Leasehold improvements $	Plant and machinery $	Fixtures and fittings $	Motor vehicles $	Total $
Cost at						
1/06/08	44,216	63,768	363,455	29,569	28,660	529,668
Additions	–	10,852	45,873	14,703	–	71,428
Disposals	–	–	–	–	28,660	(28,660)
Cost at						
31/05/09	44,216	74,620	409,328	44,272	–	572,436
Depreciation						
1/06/08	44,216	7,011	61,876	9,942	23,648	146,693
Disposals	–	–	–	–	27,985	(27,985)
Charge	–	7,068	50,826	9,051	4,337	71,282
31/05/09	44,216	14,079	112,702	18,993	–	189,990
Net book value						
31/05/08	–	56,757	301,576	19,627	5,012	382,975
31/05/09	–	60,541	296,626	25,279	–	382,446

As at 31 May 2009, the net carrying amount of leased plant and machinery was $44,298 (2008: $nil).

9. Inventories

	2009 $	2008 $
Raw materials and consumables	29,249	28,059
Work-in-progress	201,002	230,815
	228,251	258,874

Raw materials, consumables and changes in finished goods and work-in-progress recognised as cost of sales in the year amounted to $282,487 (2008: $252,874).

10. Trade and Other Receivables

	2009 $	2008 $
Trade receivables	68,626	160,954
Other receivables	83,695	86,475
Prepayments and accrued income	60,530	45,494
	212,851	292,923

All receivables fall due within one year.

11. Other Interest-Bearing Loans and Borrowings   This note provides information about the contractual terms of the company's interest-bearing loans and borrowings, which are measured at amortised cost. For more information about the company's exposure to interest rate and foreign currency risk, see note 19.

	2009 $	2008 $
Current Liabilities		
Current portion of finance lease liabilities	14,438	–
Non-current Liabilities		
Finance lease liabilities	18,195	–

Finance lease liabilities are payable as follows:

	Future minimum lease payments	*Present value of interest*	*Minimum lease payments*
	2009 $	2009 $	2009 $
Less than 1 year	16,684	2,246	14,438
Between 1 and 5 years	19,208	1,013	18,195
More than 5 years	35,892	3,259	32,633

12. Trade and Other Payables: Amounts Falling Due Within One Year

	2009 $	2008 $
Trade payables	77,634	171,620
Taxation and social security	30,209	19,723
Accruals and deferred income	60,826	83,309
	168,669	274,652

13. Deferred Taxation   The elements of deferred taxation are as follows:

	2009 $	2008 $
Difference between accumulated depreciation and amortisation and capital allowances	34,441	17,810
Other short-term timing differences	(1,738)	(2,572)
Tax losses	(625,883)	(566,180)
Unrecognised deferred tax asset	(593,180)	(550,942)

The company has an unrecognised deferred tax asset at 31 May 2009 of $593,180 (2008: $550,942) relating principally to tax losses which the company can offset against future taxable profits from the same trade.

The deferred tax asset has not been recognised in the financial statements because it is not possible to assess whether there will be suitable taxable profits from which the future reversal of the underlying temporary differences can be deducted.

14. Called-Up Share Capital

	2009 $	2008 $
Allotted, called-up and fully paid 19,030,748 shares of $0.01 each	190,308	190,308

Enterprise Management Incentive Scheme   The company operates a share incentive scheme for the benefit of the directors and certain employees. All options are granted at the discretion of the board. The scheme grants options to purchase ordinary shares of $0.01 each. No options were exercised in the period.

The options granted to directors, date of grant and exercise price and exercise periods under the scheme are set out in the Report on Directors' Remuneration on pages 451 and 452. In addition to the directors' share options, certain employees have been granted the following share options:

Date of grant	*Number of unexpired share options at year end*	Exercise price	Exercise period
18/04/2007	170,000	$0.21	18/04/10–18/04/17
30/06/2008	151,200	$0.1825	30/06/11–30/06/18
22/09/2008	575,839	$0.1850	22/09/11–22/09/18

There are a total of 897,039 unexpired options held by employees and a total of 1,106,926 unexpired options held by directors.

15. Share Premium and Reserves

	Share premium account $	*Capital reserve account* $	*Profit and loss account* $
At 31/05/08	5,749,952	463,885	(4,631,306)
Retained loss for the year	–	–	(840,740)
Reversal of charge in relation to share-based payments	–	–	94,424
At 31/05/09	5,749,952	463,885	(5,377,622)

16. Pension Scheme   The company contributes to specific employees' personal pension schemes. The pension cost charge for the year represents contributions payable by the company to the scheme and amounted to $29,429 (2008: $19,497).

There were outstanding contributions of $nil (2008: $nil) at the end of the financial year.

17. Related Party Disclosures   The results of the company include no material transactions with related parties in the current or preceding year.

18. Loss on Ordinary Shares   The calculation of basic loss per ordinary share is based on the loss for the financial year divided by the weighted average number of shares in issue during the year.

Losses and number of shares used in the calculations of loss per ordinary share are set out below:

	2008 *$*	*2009* *$*
Loss after tax	(840,740)	(594,065)
Weighted average number of shares	19,030,748	17,828,562
Loss per share	(4.42p)	(3.33p)

The calculation of diluted loss per ordinary share is identical to that used for the basic loss per ordinary share. This is because the exercise of options would have the effect of reducing the loss per ordinary share from continuing operations and is, therefore, not dilutive under the terms of IAS 33.

19. Derivatives and Other Financial Instruments   The company's policies with regard to financial instruments are set out within the accounting policies note. The risks arising from the company's financial assets and liabilities are set out below with the policies for their respective management.

Currency Risk   The company transacts business in foreign currencies and, therefore, incurs some transaction risk.

The company had no open foreign exchange contracts at the reporting date.

The company's exposure to foreign currency risk was as follows, this is based on the carrying amount for monetary financial instruments:

	31/05/09			31/05/08		
	US $ $	Euro $	Sterling $	US $ $	Euro $	Sterling $
Cash and cash equivalents	–	–	404,725	–	–	1,112,719
Trade receivables	43,267	25,359	–		56,803	104,151
Trade payables	(1,987)	(924)	(74,723)	(19,531)	–	(152,809)
Finance leases	–	–	(32,633)	–	–	–
Net exposure	(1,987)	42,343	322,278	(19,531)	56,803	1,064,781

	Average rate		Reporting date spot rate	
	2009	2008	2009	2008
Sterling	1.643	2.006	1.619	1.976
Euro	1.182	1.385	1.145	1.273

Sensitivity Analysis   A 10% strengthening of the GB Pound against the US Dollar and the Euro as at 31 May 2009 would have (decreased)/increased profit by the amounts below. This analysis assumes that all other variables, in particular interest rates, remain constant. The analysis is performed on the same basis for 2008.

	US Dollar £	Euro £
31/05/09	(180)	3,850
31/05/08	(1,780)	5,160

A 10% weakening of the GB Pound against the US Dollar and the Euro as at 31 May 2009 would have an equal and opposite effect to the amounts shown above, on the basis that all other variables remain constant.

Price Risk   The company aims to minimise its exposure to supplier price increases and customer price decreases by offsetting reciprocal supplier and customer arrangements.

Credit Risk   The company operates a closely monitored collection policy.

The ageing of trade receivables at the reporting date was:

	31/05/09			*31/05/08*		
	Gross £	*Impairment* £	*Net* £	*Gross* £	*Impairment* £	*Net* £
Not past due	21,787	–	21,787	151,381	–	151,381
30 days	–	–	–	9,264	–	9,264
31–90 days	46,389	–	46,389	5,105	(4,796)	309
	68,626	–	68,626	165,750	(4,796)	160,954

The majority of the debt falling in 31–90 days as at 31 May 2009 relates to one customer for whom trading terms have been re-negotiated. This customer has adhered to these revised terms since re-negotiation and as such no impairment of this receivable is deemed necessary.

The movement in the allowance for impairment in respect of trade receivables was as follows:

	Impairment Allowance £
Balance 1/06/07	9,499
Impairment loss recognised	(4,703)
Balance at 31/05/08	4,796
Impairment loss recognised	(4,796)
Balance at 31/05/09	–

Liquidity Risk   The company's objective is to maintain a balance between continuity and flexibility of funding through the use of short-term deposits.

The contractual maturity of all cash and cash equivalents, trade and other receivables at the current and preceding reporting dates is within one year.

The contractual maturity of trade and other payables at the current and preceding reporting dates is within three months.

The contractual maturity of finance lease liabilities can be found in note 11.

Interest Rate Risk   At the reporting date, the interest rate profile of the company's interest-bearing financial instruments was:

	2009 $	*2008* $
Fixed rate instruments		
Finance lease liabilities	32,633	–

The company has cash deposits of £398,780 (2008: £1,039,603). These funds are placed on premium rate deposit at a rate which tracks bank base rate. These deposits are reviewed at least every thirty days. These funds are available on demand. At the year end, the weighted average interest rate for the floating rate cash deposits with the company's bankers base rate of 0.50% (2008: 4.35%).

Fair Values of the Company's Financial Assets and Liabilities

Trade and Other Receivables   The fair value of trade and other receivables is estimated as the present value of future cash flows, discounted at the market rate of interest at the reporting date if the effect is material.

Trade and Other Payables   The fair value of trade and other payables is estimated as the present value of future cash flows, discounted at the market rate of interest at the reporting date if the effect is material.

Cash and Cash Equivalents   The fair value of cash and cash equivalents is estimated as its carrying amount, all cash and cash equivalents are repayable on demand.

Interest-Bearing Borrowings   Fair value, which after initial recognition is determined for disclosure purposes only, is calculated based on the present value of future principal and interest cash flows, discounted at the market rate of interest at the reporting date if the effect is material.

The fair value of financial assets and liabilities, together with carrying amounts shown in the statement of financial position are as follows:

| | 2008 | | 2009 | |
	Carrying value $	Fair value $	Carrying value $	Fair value $
Financial assets				
Cash and cash equivalents	404,275	404,275	1,112,719	1,112,719
Loans and receivables				
Trade and receivables	68,626	68,626	160,954	160,954
Total financial assets	472,901	472,901	1,273,673	1,273,673
Financial liabilities at amortised cost				
Trade payables	(77,634)	(77,634)	(171,620)	(171,620)
Finance lease liabilities	(32,633)	(32,633)	–	–
Total financial liabilities	(110,267)	(110,267)	(171,620)	(171,620)

20. Commitments   Total future commitments under non-cancellable operating leases are as follows:

	Land and buildings $	Motor vehicles $	Land and buildings $	Motor vehicles $
Within 1 year	–	–	–	–
2–5 years	174,103	28,635	183,509	–

21. Share-Based Payments

Share Options The number of options outstanding under the company's share option scheme is as follows:

Number of Share Options — Ordinary Shares at 1p

Note	At 31/05/08	Granted	Surrendered	Lapsed	At 31/05/09	Exercise price	Date from which exercisable	Expiry date
(a)	158,373	—	(78,858)	(80,015)	—	70p	19/12/05	19/12/12
(a)	34,091	—	(34,091)	—	—	88p	08/12/06	08/12/13
(a)	60,000	—	(40,000)	(20,000)	—	66.5p	08/03/07	08/03/14
(a)	85,000	—	(70,000)	(15,000)	—	50p	04/04/08	04/04/15
(a)	424,000	—	(424,000)	—	—	40p	14/09/08	14/09/15
(a)	314,125	—	—	(25,000)	289,125	21p	18/04/10	18/04/17
(b)	110,875	—	—	—	110,875	21p	18/04/10	18/04/17
(a)	—	479,200	—	(17,000)	462,200	18.25p	30/06/11	30/06/18
(b)	—	63,000	—	—	63,000	18.25p	22/09/11	22/09/18
(a)	—	865,327	—	—	865,327	18.5p	30/06/11	30/06/18
(b)	—	213,438	—	—	213,438	18.5p	22/09/11	22/09/18
	1,186,964	1,620,965	(646,949)	2,003,965				

(a) These options have been granted under the EMI approved scheme. There have been no variations to the terms and conditions or performance criteria attached to these share options during the financial year. There are no performance conditions attached to these shares other than continued employment by the company.

(b) These options have been granted under the unapproved scheme. There have been no variations to the terms and conditions or performance attached to these share options during the financial year. There are no performance conditions attached to these shares other than continued employment by the company.

There was no cost payable by the employees on the grant of any of the above options.

The option holder may only exercise his options during employment with the company.

The movement of the EMI and unapproved share options outstanding are shown overleaf.

	EMI scheme		Unapproved scheme	
	Number of awards	Weighted average exercise price $	Number of awards	Weighted average exercise price $
As at 01/06/07	1,148,232	0.43	110,875	0.21
Forfeited	(72,143)	0.47	—	—
As at 31/05/08	1,076,089	0.41	110,875	0.21
Granted	1,344,527	0.18	276,438	0.18
Forfeited and surrendered	(803,964)	0.50	—	—
Outstanding at 31/05/09	1,616,652	0.41	387,313	0.21
Exercisable at 31/05/09	—	—	—	—
Range of exercise prices		18.25–21p		18.25–219p
Weighted average contractual life		9 years 0 months		8 years 11 months

There were no share options exercised during the year (2008: nil).

A charge of £94,424 (2008: £56,609) has been made in the statement of comprehensive income to spread the fair value of the options over the three year service obligations of those incentives.

Assumptions Used in the Valuation of Share-Based Payments   In calculating the fair value of the share-based payment arrangements, the company has used the Black Scholes method. The fair value of the share options granted in 2009 and the assumptions used of their fair value on the date of grant were as follows:

	2009	*2008*
Weighted average assumptions		
Fair value per share option	14.83p	N/A
Share price on date of grant	18.42p	N/A
Exercise price	18.42p	N/A
Share options granted in the year EMI	1,344,527	N/A
Share options granted in the year Unapproved	276,438	N/A
Expected volatility	100%	N/A
Exercise pattern (years)	3–10 years uniformly	N/A
Expected dividend yields	0%	N/A
Risk free rate of return	5%	N/A

The fair value of the share options is applied to the number of options that are expected to vest, which takes into account the expected and actual forfeitures over the vesting period as a result of cessation of employment.

Expected volatility was determined by assessing the company's historic data and the market the company operates in.

22. Capital Management   The board's policy is to maintain a strong capital base so as to maintain investor, creditor and market confidence and to sustain future development of the business. The board of directors monitors the return on capital, defined as net operating income divided by total shareholders' equity.

At present employees and directors would hold 18% of the share capital, following the exercise of all outstanding share options.

23. Events after the Reporting Date   To facilitate the management of the operations and to ensure its competitive advantage is maintained to the highest capacity possible, the company has created four wholly owned operating subsidiaries.

The following illustrative financial statements are for a UK medium-sized entity reporting under UK GAAP.

PARBRALLI ENGINEERING LIMITED

Report of the Directors for the Year Ended 30 April 2009

The directors present their report with the financial statements of the company for the year ended 30 April 2009.

Principal Activity   The principal activity of the company in the year under review was that of manufacturers of engineering components.

Review of Business   Parbralli Engineering Limited has managed to show strong growth and profits, in spite of challenging global trading conditions. By continuing to improve the ranges of components and investing resources into new territories and strengthening existing markets, Parbralli Engineering have been able to mitigate against weaker trading conditions in some of the more developed markets. The sales team has been strengthened with several new appointments, which have already proven to be successful on finding and retaining new business and at the core of our values is a commitment to providing a top quality service to all customers on an ongoing basis.

Parbralli Engineering Limited finished building our new offices and Distribution Centre in 2009 and moved into the building late in 2009. This has been an exciting move and has provided greater efficiencies and room for expansion.

During the year, the previously occupied building suffered an impairment loss amounting to £78,311. This is due to circumstances beyond the control of the company and is attributable to the decline in commercial property valuations during the year. The effect of this is a reduction in our operating profit.

Risks and Uncertainties   Some of the greatest challenges facing the company in this financial year have been currency fluctuations and withdrawal of insurance for some debtors. Global currencies seem to have now stabilised and whilst during the turbulence, Parbralli Engineering Ltd bought well, we are pleased that this is providing less of a distraction to the day-to-day running of the business. Parbralli Engineering are working with the insurers to maintain existing levels of credit for customers and have been delighted to note that this insurance has not been drawn upon in that the company have not incurred any significant bad debt losses for this financial year.

Future Developments   Parbralli Engineering Limited move into the next financial year with a continued strong appetite for growth, which will be achieved by offering unique expertise and service and high-quality products for its customer base. The private-label customer base for Parbralli Engineering is growing and is the focus of much of our efforts. In the next year, we expect to see a large percentage increase in consumer and medical related sales as well as continued growth in the industrial sector.

Dividends   No dividends will be distributed for the year ended 30 April 2009.

Directors   The directors shown below have held office during the whole of the period from 1 May 2008 to the date of this report:

A Smith
B Smith

C Smith
D Smith

Financial Instruments   The company always operates within its agreed overdraft facility with the bank. Sales are made to both UK and overseas customers and purchases are made from suppliers based both in the UK and overseas. The company seeks to minimise its risk in respect of overseas trade debtors and creditors by using hedging arrangements. The company also insures overseas debtors to protect against loss.

The company is exposed to interest rate risk on its borrowings with the bank; and which are subject to bank base rate changes.

The bank is currently very satisfied with the company's financial performance and the directors do not think there is any risk of facilities being withdrawn.

Political and Charitable Donations   During the year the company made the following donations:

Name of charity 1	£1,500
Name of charity 2	£1,500

The purposes of the above were in respect of Charitable Donations.

Statement of Directors' Responsibilities   The directors are responsible for preparing the Report of the Directors and the financial statements in accordance with applicable law and regulations.

Company law requires the directors to prepare financial statements for each financial year. Under that law the directors have elected to prepare the financial statements in accordance with United Kingdom Generally Accepted Accounting Practice (United Kingdom Accounting Standards and applicable law). Under company law the directors must not approve the financial statements unless they are satisfied that they give a true and fair view of the state of affairs of the company and of the profit or loss of the company for that period. In preparing these financial statements, the directors are required to:

- Select suitable accounting policies and then apply them consistently.
- Make judgements and accounting estimates that are reasonable and prudent.
- Prepare the financial statements on the going concern basis unless it is inappropriate to presume that the company will continue in business.

The directors are responsible for keeping adequate accounting records that are sufficient to show and explain the company's transactions and disclose with reasonable accuracy at any time the financial position of the company and enable them to ensure that the financial statements comply with the Companies Act 2006. They are also responsible for safeguarding the assets of the company and hence for taking reasonable steps for the prevention and detection of fraud and other irregularities.

Statement as to Disclosure of Information to Auditors   So far as the directors are aware, there is no relevant audit information (as defined by Section 418 of the Companies Act 2006) of which the company's auditors are unaware, and each director has taken all the steps that he or she ought to have taken as a director in order to make himself or herself aware of any relevant audit information and to establish that the company's auditors are aware of that information.

Auditors The auditors, Auditor & Co Limited, will be proposed for re-appointment at the forthcoming Annual General Meeting.

On Behalf of the Board

A Smith – Director

Date:

Report of the Independent Auditors to the Shareholders of Parbralli Engineering Limited

We have audited the financial statements of Parbralli Engineering Limited for the year ended 30 April 2009 on pages 6–22. The financial reporting framework that has been applied in their preparation is applicable law and United Kingdom Accounting Standards (United Kingdom Generally Accepted Accounting Practice).

This report is made solely to the company's members, as a body, in accordance with Sections 495 and 496 of the Companies Act 2006. Our audit work has been undertaken so that we might state to the company's members those matters which we are required to state to them in a Report of the Auditors and for no other purpose. To the fullest extent permitted by law, we do not accept or assume responsibility to anyone other than the company and the company's members as a body, for our audit work, for this report or for the opinions we have formed.

Respective Responsibilities of Directors and Auditors As explained more fully in the Statement of Directors' Responsibilities set out on page 3, the directors are responsible for the preparation of the financial statements and for being satisfied that they give a true and fair view. Our responsibility is to audit the financial statements in accordance with applicable law and International Standards on Auditing (UK and Ireland). Those standards require us to comply with the Auditing Practices Board's Ethical Standards for Auditors.

Scope of the Audit of the Financial Statements An audit involves obtaining evidence about the amounts and disclosures in the financial statements sufficient to give reasonable assurance that the financial statements are free from material misstatement, whether caused by fraud or error. This includes an assessment of: whether the accounting policies are appropriate to the company's circumstances and have been consistently applied and adequately disclosed; the reasonableness of significant accounting estimates made by the directors; and the overall presentation of the financial statements.

Opinion on Financial Statements In our opinion the financial statements:

- Give a true and fair view of the state of the company's affairs as at 30 April 2009 and of its profit for the year then ended.
- Have been properly prepared in accordance with United Kingdom Generally Accepted Accounting Practice.
- Have been prepared in accordance with the requirements of the Companies Act 2006.

Opinion on Other Matters Prescribed by the Companies Act 2006   In our opinion the information given in the Report of the Directors for the financial year for which the financial statements are prepared is consistent with the financial statements.

Matters on which we are Required to Report by Exception   We have nothing to report in respect of the following matters where the Companies Act 2006 requires us to report to you if, in our opinion:

- Adequate accounting records have not been kept, or returns adequate for audit have not been received from branches not visited by us.
- The financial statements are not in agreement with the accounting records and returns.
- Certain disclosures of directors' remuneration specified by law are not made.
- We have not received all the information and explanations we require for our audit.

B Brown (Senior Statutory Auditor)

For and on behalf of Auditor & Co Ltd

Chartered Certified Accountants and Registered Auditors

123 Any Street

Any County

Any Country

Date: 18 September 2009

Parbralli Engineering Limited: Profit and Loss Account for the Year Ended 30 April 2009

	Notes	2009 £	2008 £
Turnover	2	8,223,189	7,145,548
Cost of sales		5,438,588	4,639,440
Gross Profit		2,784,601	2,506,108
Administrative expenses		2,200,156	1,696,616
Operating profit	4	584,445	809,492
Interest receivable and similar income		3,344	4,575
		587,789	814,067
Interest payable and similar charges	5	226,552	114,578
Profit on ordinary activities before taxation		361,237	699,489
Tax on profit on ordinary activities	6	165,617	216,553
Profit for the financial year after taxation		195,620	482,936

Continuing Operations   None of the company's activities were acquired or discontinued during the current or previous year.

Parbralli Engineering Limited: Statement of Total Recognised Gains and Losses for the Year Ended 30 April 2009

	2009 £	2008 £
Profit for the financial year	195,620	482,936
Revaluation gain on building	232,053	—
Total recognised gains and losses relating to the year	427,673	482,936

Note of Historical Cost Profits and Losses   The difference between the results as disclosed in the profit and loss account and the results on an unmodified historical cost basis is not material.

Parbralli Engineering Limited: Balance Sheet as at 30 April 2009

	Notes	2009 £	2008 £
Fixed assets			
Intangible assets	8	38,686	16,667
Tangible assets	9	3,371,070	1,007,680
		3,409,756	1,024,347
Current assets			
Stocks	10	1,542,865	1,400,801
Debtors	11	1,791,847	1,996,539
Cash at bank and in hand		1,025,082	855,950
		4,359,794	4,253,290
Creditors			
Amounts falling due within 1 year	12	3,444,788	3,192,883
Net current assets		915,006	1,060,407
Total assets less current liabilities		4,327,762	2,084,754
Creditors			
Amounts falling due after 1 year	13	2,300,500	469,751
Net Assets		2,024,262	1,615,003
Capital and reserves			
Called up share capital	17	20,000	20,000
Revaluation reserve	18	232,053	18,414
Profit and loss account	18	1,772,209	1,576,589
Shareholders' funds		2,024,262	1,615,003

The financial statements were approved by the board of directors on 18 September 2009 and were signed on its behalf by:

A Smith — Director B Smith — Director

Parbralli Engineering Limited: Cash Flow Statement for the Year Ended 30 April 2009

	Notes	2009 £	2008 £
Net cash inflow from operating activities	1	852,601	392,760
Returns on investments and servicing of finance	2	(223,208)	(110,003)
Taxation		(140,000)	(185,421)
Capital expenditure	2	(2,327,153)	(651,420)
Equity Dividends Paid		–	(133,000)
		(1,837,760)	(687,084)
Financing	2	2,140,576	176,077
Increase/(decrease) in cash in the period		302,816	(511,007)
Reconciliation of net cash flow to movement in net debt	3		
Increase/(decrease) in cash in the period		302,816	(511,007)
Cash inflow from increase in debt and lease financing		(2,135,236)	(272,660)
Changes in net debt resulting from cash flows		(1,832,420)	(783,667)
Movement in net debt in the period		(1,832,420)	(783,667)
Net debt as at 1 May		(1,492,704)	(709,037)
Net debt as at 30 April		(3,325,124)	(1,492,704)

Parbralli Engineering Limited: Notes to the Cash Flow Statement for the Year Ended 30 April 2009

1. Reconciliation of Operating Profit to Net Cash Inflow from Operating Activities

	2009 £	2008 £
Operating profit	584,445	809,492
Depreciation charges	77,073	73,454
Loss on disposal of fixed assets	–	550
Impairment of tangible fixed assets	96,724	–
Revaluation surplus written off	(18,414)	–
(Increase)/Decrease in stocks	(142,064)	44,701
Decrease/(increase) in debtors	200,951	(504,157)
Increase/(decrease) in creditors	53,886	(31,280)
Net cash inflow from operating activities	852,601	392,760

2. Analysis of Cash Flows for Heading Netted in the Cash Flow Statement

	2009 £	2008 £
Returns on investments and servicing of finance		
Interest received	3,344	4,575
Interest paid	(195,505)	(107,022)
Interest element of hire purchase payments	(6,070)	(7,556)
Loan written off	(24,977)	–
Net cash outflow for returns on investments and servicing of finance	(223,208)	(110,003)
Capital expenditure		
Purchase of intangible fixed assets	(23,183)	(8,757)
Purchase of tangible fixed assets	(2,023,970)	(660,159)
Sale of tangible fixed assets	–	17,496
Net cash outflow for capital expenditure	(2,327,153)	(651,420)

	2009 £	2008 £
Financing		
New loans in year	2,655,185	350,000
Loan repayments in year	(464,646)	(7,294)
Capital repayments in year	(55,303)	(70,046)
Amount withdrawn by directors	5,340	(96,583)
Net cash inflow from financing	2,140,576	176,077

3. Analysis of Changes in Net Debt

	At 1/05/08	Cash flow	At 30/4/09
Net cash:			
At bank and in hand	855,950	169,132	1,025,082
Bank overdrafts	(1,808,986)	133,684	(1,675,302)
	(953,036)	302,816	(650,220)

	At 01/05/08 £	Cash flow	At 30/04/09 £
Debt:			
Hire purchase	(75,022)	55,303	(19,719)
Debts falling due within 1 year	(14,611)	(340,074)	(354,685)
Debts falling due after 1 year	(450,035)	(1,850,465)	(2,300,500)
	(539,668)	(2,135,326)	(2,674,904)
Total	(1,492,704)	(1,832,420)	(3,325,124)

Parbralli Engineering Limited: Notes to the Financial Statements for the Year Ended 30 April 2009

1. Accounting Policies

Accounting Convention   The financial statements have been prepared under the historical cost convention as modified by the revaluation of certain assets.

Turnover   Turnover represents sales of goods, net of trade discounts and exclusive of VAT. The company recognises a sale when goods are despatched.

Patents and Licences   Patents and licences are stated at their original purchase price less accumulated amortisation charges to date.

Patents and licences are amortised at 4% on a straight-line basis as the directors consider this to be a reasonable estimate of their useful economic life.

Tangible Fixed Assets   Depreciation is provided at the following annual rates in order to write off each asset over its estimated useful life or, if held under a finance lease, over the lease term, whichever is the shorter.

Short leasehold	—	2% on cost
Land and buildings	—	2% on cost
Plant and machinery	—	25% on reducing balance and 15% on reducing balance
Fixtures and fittings	—	15% on reducing balance
Motor vehicles	—	25% on reducing balance
Computer equipment	—	33% on cost

Tangible fixed assets are stated at their cost price less accumulated depreciation. In respect of assets that have been subject to the revaluation model, the assets are stated at their latest revalued amount less accumulated depreciation charges to date.

Impairment losses are recognised in the revaluation reserve to the extent that they reverse any previous revaluation gains in respect of the revalued asset. Any excess impairment losses are then recognised in the profit and loss account.

Stocks   Stocks are valued at the lower of cost and net realisable value, after making due allowance for obsolete and slow moving items.

Stocks are valued on an average cost (AVCO) basis.

Foreign Currencies   Assets and liabilities in foreign currencies are translated into sterling at the rates of exchange ruling at the balance sheet date. Transactions in foreign currencies are translated into sterling at the rate of exchange ruling at the date of the transaction. Exchange differences are taken into account in arriving at the operating result.

Hire Purchase and Leasing Commitments   Assets obtained under hire purchase contracts or finance leases are capitalised in the balance sheet. Those held under hire purchase contracts are depreciated over their estimated useful lives. Those held under finance leases are depreciated over their estimated useful lives or the lease term, whichever is the shorter.

The interest element of these obligations is charged to the profit and loss account over the relevant period. The capital element of the future payments is treated as a liability.

Rentals paid under operating leases are charged to the profit and loss account on a straight line basis over the period of the lease.

Pension Costs and Other Post-Retirement Benefits The company operates a defined contribution pension scheme. Contributions payable to the company's pension scheme are charged to the profit and loss account in the period to which they relate.

Financial Instruments Financial instruments are classified and accounted for according to the substance of the contractual arrangement, as either financial assets, liabilities or equity instruments. An equity instrument is any contract that evidences a residual interest in the assets of the company after deducting all liabilities.

2. Turnover The turnover and profit before taxation are attributable to the one principal activity of the company.

An analysis of turnover by geographical market is given below:

	2009 £	2008 £
United Kingdom	3,535,971	3,001,130
Europe	3,683,989	3,787,140
Asia	1,003,229	357,278
	8,223,189	7,145,548

3. Staff Costs

	2008 £	2009 £
Wages and salaries	1,198,998	829,281
Social security costs	65,701	36,956
Other pension costs	47,951	51,554
	1,312,650	917,791

The average monthly number of employees during the year was as follows:

	2009	2008
Directors	4	4
Administration	23	21
Warehouse	4	4
	31	29

4. Operating Profit   The operating profit is stated after charging.

	2008 £	2009 £
Hire of plant and machinery	14,902	10,772
Other operating leases	18,560	17,363
Depreciation — owned assets	61,424	40,011
Depreciation — assets on hire purchase contracts	14,484	32,937
Loss on disposal of fixed assets	–	550
Patents and licences amortisation	1,164	506
Auditors' remuneration	7,500	6,000
Impairment of tangible fixed assets	96,725	–
Directors' remuneration	574,351	308,051
Directors' pension contributions to money purchase schemes	36,000	48,000

The number of directors to whom retirement benefits were accruing was as follows:

Money purchase schemes	4	4

Information regarding the highest paid director is as follows:

	2009 £	2008 £
Directors remuneration etc.	183,363	125,337

5. Interest Payable and Similar Charges

	2009 £	2008 £
Bank interest	105,259	92,125
Bank loan interest	67,594	14,897
Loan written off	47,269	–
Hire purchase	6,070	7,556
	226,552	114,578

6. Taxation

Analysis of the tax charge   The tax charge on the profit on ordinary activities for the year was as follows:

	2009 £	2008 £
Current tax:		
UK corporation tax	165,617	216,553
Tax on profit on ordinary activities	165,617	216,553

Factors affecting the tax charge   The tax assessed for the year is higher than the standard rate of corporation tax in the UK. The difference is explained below:

	2009 £	2008 £
Profit on ordinary activities before tax	361,237	699,489
Profit on ordinary activities multiplied by the standard rate of corporation tax in the UK of 28% (2008: 28%)	101,146	195,857
Effects of:		
Expenses not deductible for tax purposes	13,525	15,670
Depreciation for the period in excess of capital allowances	3,009	3,847
Adjustments in respect of prior years	47,937	1,179
Current tax charge	165,617	216,553

If the building had been sold at its carrying amount stated in the balance sheet, the amount of corporation tax payable would be £43,938 (2008: £13,672).

7. Dividends

	2009 £	2008 £
Ordinary A shares of £1 each	–	76,000
Ordinary B shares of £1 each	–	57,000
	–	133,000

8. Intangible Fixed Assets

Patents and Licences	£
Cost at 01/05/08	17,524
Additions	23,183
Cost at 30/04/09	40,707

Amortisation	
At 01/05/08	857
Amortisation for the year	1,164
	2,021

Net Book Value	
At 30 April 2009	38,686
At 30 April 2008	16,667

9. Tangible Fixed Assets

	Asset under construction	Short L/hold	Land and buildings	Improvements to property
Cost	£	£	£	£
01/05/08	216,828	603,252	–	13,601
Additions	–	1,296	2,179,250	–
Revaluation	–	(96,725)	217,498	–
Reclassification	(603,252)	13,601	603,252	(13,601)
	–	135,000	3,000,000	–
Depreciation				
01/05/08	–	7,137	–	7,418
Charge for year	–	2,700	15,000	–
Revaluation	–	(14,555)	–	–
Reclassification	–	7,418	–	(7,418)
	–	2,700	15,000	–
Net book value				
30/04/09	–	132,300	2,985,000	–
30/04/08	603,252	209,061	–	6,183

	Plant and machinery	Fixtures and fittings	Vehicles	Computers	Totals
Cost	£	£	£	£	£
01/05/08	107,392	102,103	134,597	89,476	1,267,249
Additions	2,738	94,385	12,820	13,481	2,303,970
Revaluations	–	–	–	–	120,773
30/04/09	110,130	196,488	147,417	102,957	3,691,992
Depreciation					
01/05/08	60,147	65,672	44,808	74,387	259,569
Charge in year	7,290	9,264	24,123	17,531	75,908
Revaluations	–	–	–	–	(14,555)
30/04/09	67,437	74,396	68,931	91,918	320,922
Net book value					
30/04/09	42,693	121,522	78,486	11,039	3,371,070
30/04/08	47,245	36,431	89,789	15,089	1,007,680

If leasehold buildings had not been revalued they would have been included at the following historical cost:

	2009	2008
	£	£
Cost	198,414	198,414
Aggregate depreciation	22,976	19,008
Value of land in freehold land and buildings	40,000	40,000

Leasehold buildings were valued on an open market basis on 16 June 2009 by Brown & Son Surveyors.

Fixed assets, included in the above, which are held under hire purchase contracts, are as follows:

	Plant and machinery £	*Motor vehicles* £	*Totals*
Cost			
At 01/05/08	80,917	89,695	170,612
Transfer to ownership	–	(26,300)	(26,300)
At 30/04/09	80,917	63,935	144,312
Depreciation			
At 01/05/08	43,798	42,937	86,735
Charge for year	5,568	8,916	14,484
Transfer to ownership	–	(15,205)	(15,205)
At 30/04/09	49,366	36,648	86,014
Net book value			
At 30 April 2009	31,551	26,747	58,298
At 30 April 2008	37,119	46,758	83,877

10. Stocks

	2009 £	2008 £
Stocks	1,542,865	1,400,801

11. Debtors: Amounts Falling Due Within One Year

	2009 £	2008 £
Trade debtors	1,723,932	1,776,242
Other debtors	12,188	55,227
Tax	–	3,741
Prepayments	45,072	54,478
	1,791,847	1,996,539

12. Creditors: Amounts Falling Due Within One Year

	2009 £	*2008* £
Bank loans and overdrafts (see note 14)	2,029,987	1,823,597
Hire purchase contracts (see note 15)	19,719	55,306
Trade creditors	730,264	874,285
Tax	238,429	216,553
Social security and other taxes	147,394	26,013
Other creditors	42,458	6,916
Directors' current accounts	83,794	78,454
Accrued expenses	152,743	111,759
	3,444,788	3,192,883

13. Creditors: Amounts Falling Due After More than One Year

	2009 £	*2008* £
Bank loans (see note 14)	2,300,500	450,035
Hire purchase contracts (see note 15)	—	19,716
	2,300,500	469,751

14. Loans   An analysis of the maturity of loans is given below:

	2009 £	*2008* £
Amounts falling due within one year and on demand:		
Bank overdrafts	1,675,302	1,808,986
Bank loans	354,685	14,611
	2,029,987	1,823,597
Amounts falling due between one and two years:		
Bank loans 1–2 years	177,424	381,878
Amounts falling due between two and five years:		
Bank loans 2–5 years	707,696	63,757
Amounts falling due in more than five years:		
Bank loans more than 5 years by instalments	1,415,380	4,400

The bank overdraft is repayable on demand whilst the treasury loan is payable in equal instalments of £51,964 and matures on 23 April 2024. The construction loan is payable in one instalment due on 11 March 2010. The interest rates applicable to the loans are set at the Anybank PLC base rate.

15. Obligations Under Hire Purchase Contracts and Leases

Hire Purchase Contracts	2009 £	2008 £
Net obligations repayable:		
Within 1 year	19,719	55,306
Between 1 and 5 years	–	19,716
	19,719	75,022

The following lease payments are committed to be paid within one year:

Land and Buildings	2009 £	2008 £
Within 1 year	50,500	50,500
Between 1 and 5 years	252,500	252,500
In more than 5 years	151,500	202,000
	454,500	505,000

16. Secured Debts   The following secured debts are included within creditors:

	2009 £	2008 £
Bank overdrafts	1,675,302	1,808,986
Bank loans	2,655,185	464,646
Hire purchase contracts	19,719	75,022
	4,530,206	2,348,654

The bank loans and bank overdraft are secured by a first charge over the buildings which are occupied by Parbralli Engineering Limited and also a first charge over the old building.

The bank loans and bank overdrafts are also secured by a first charge over the directors personal homes.

There is a debenture asset in place dated 13 May 1998 given by Parbralli Engineering Limited. This debenture ranks after and is subject to the debenture dated 22 January 1995 in favour of Anybank PLC.

17. Called Up Share Capital

Allotted, issued and fully paid:			*2009* £	*2008* £
Number:	*Class:*	*Nominal Value:*		
8,800	Ordinary A	£1	8,800	8,800
11,200	Ordinary B	£1	11,200	11,200
			20,000	20,000

18. Reserves

	Profit and loss account £	*Revaluation reserve* £	*Total* £
At 01/05/08	1,576,589	18,414	1,595,003
Profit for the year	195,620	–	195,620
Revaluation reserve	–	232,053	232,053
Movement on revaluation b/f	–	(18,414)	(18,414)
	1,772,209	232,053	2,004,262

19. Contingent Liabilities   The company has received a legal claim in respect of the lease of one of its units. The claim arose after the balance sheet date and is still in its infancy and the financial effects of this claim are unable to be quantified. The company is disputing the claim.

20. Transactions with Directors   Mr and Mrs B Smith have made personal guarantees dated 27 July 2006. The personal guarantees are limited to the amount of £20,000.

Included within creditors: amounts falling due within one year are the directors' loan accounts amounting to £83,794 (2008: £78,454). The maximum overdrawn balances during the year were as follows:

B Smith	£21,429
C Smith	£25,347
D Smith	£10,202

These overdrawn balances were cleared by the year end.

21. Related Party Disclosures   During the year, C Smith held a 99% shareholding in Smith Enterprises Limited, a company incorporated in England and Wales under company number 123456 which was dissolved in March 2009. During the year the company paid an amount of

£10,000 (2008: £nil) in respect of Smith Enterprises Limited's bank overdraft. This amount of money was irrecoverable and has been written off to the profit and loss account.

The company did not trade with Smith Enterprises Limited during the year (2008: £nil) and at the balance sheet date no amounts were due to or from Smith Enterprises Limited (2008: £nil).

During the year the company wrote off a loan made to Smith Clothing Limited amounting to £23,977. Smith Clothing Limited is a company incorporated in England and Wales under company number 123456. Mr and Mrs B Smith have an interest in Smith Clothing Limited.

During the year the company recharged Smith Clothing Limited for goods and services incurred on the company's behalf. The company were also recharged from Smith Clothing Limited for similar goods and services. The value of the recharges to Smith Clothing Limited was £11,463 (2008: £19,432). The value of the recharges from Smith Clothing Limited was £7,684 (2008: £24,882). At the balance sheet date an amount of £59 was owed to the company by Smith Clothing Limited (2008: £nil) and an amount of £1,351 was owed by the company to Smith Clothing Limited (2008: £2,144). All trade was entered into under normal commercial terms.

During the year the company occupied premises which are 80% owned by the trustees of the Parbralli Engineering Limited Pension Scheme. The annual rental amounts to £50,500 (2008: £50,500) in accordance with the terms of the lease. The value of the rents paid in the year amounted to £27,696 (2008: £34,462).

22. Ultimate Controlling Party   The directors are regarded as controlling parties by virtue of having the ability to act in concert in respect of the operations of the company.

23. Reconciliation of Movements in Shareholders' Funds

	2009	*2008*
	£	*£*
Profit for the year	195,620	482,936
Dividends	–	(133,000)
	195,620	349,936
Other recognised gains and losses (net)	232,053	–
Revaluation surplus written off	(18,414)	–
Net addition to shareholders' funds	409,259	349,936
Opening shareholders' funds	1,615,003	1,265,067
Closing shareholders' funds	2,024,262	1,615,003

The following financial statements illustrate an entity that is subject to audit and reports under the small companies' regime in the United Kingdom under UK GAAP and the Companies Act 2006.

Small Entity Ltd: Report of the Directors for the Year Ended 31 December 2009

The directors present their report with the financial statements of the company for the year ended 31 December 2009.

Principal Activity   The principal activity of the company in the year under review was that of the manufacture and sale of widgets.

Directors   The directors shown below have held office during the whole of the period from 1 January 2009 to the date of this report.

A Jones
B Jones
C Jones
D Jones

Statement of Directors' Responsibilities   The directors are responsible for preparing the Report of the directors and the financial statements in accordance with applicable law and regulations.

Company law requires the directors to prepare financial statements for each financial year. Under that law the directors have elected to prepare the financial statements in accordance with United Kingdom Generally Accepted Accounting Practice (United Kingdom Accounting Standards and applicable law). Under company law the directors must not approve the financial statements unless they are satisfied that they give a true and fair view of the state of the affairs of the company and of the profit or loss of the company for that period. In preparing these financial statements, the directors are required to:

- Select suitable accounting policies and then apply them consistently.
- Make judgements and accounting estimates that are reasonable and prudent.
- Prepare the financial statements on the going concern basis unless it is inappropriate to presume that the company will continue in business.

The directors are responsible for keeping adequate accounting records that are sufficient to show and explain the company's transactions and disclose with reasonable accuracy at any time the financial position of the company and enable them to ensure that the financial statements comply with the Companies Act 2006. They are also responsible for safeguarding the assets of the company and hence for taking reasonable steps for the prevention and detection of fraud and other irregularities.

Statement as to Disclosure of Information to Auditors   So far as the directors are aware, there is no relevant audit information (as defined by Section 418 of the Companies Act 2006) of which the company's auditors are unaware, and each director has taken all the steps that he or she ought to have taken as a director in order to make himself or herself aware of any relevant audit information and to establish that the company's auditors are aware of that information.

Auditors   The auditors, Auditor & Co LLP, will be proposed for re-appointment at the forthcoming Annual General Meeting.

This report has been prepared in accordance with the special provisions of Part 15 of the Companies Act 2006 relating to small companies.

On behalf of the Board

....

A Jones — Secretary

Date: ....

Report of the Independent Auditors to the Shareholders of Small Entity Limited

We have audited the financial statements of Small Entity Limited for the year ended 31 December 2009 on pages 5–13. The financial reporting framework that has been applied in their preparation is applicable law and the Financial Reporting Standard for Smaller Entities (effective April 2008) (United Kingdom Generally Accepted Accounting Practice applicable to Smaller Entities).

This report is made solely to the company's members, as a body, in accordance with Chapter 3 of Part 16 of the Companies Act 2006. Our audit work has been undertaken so that we might state to the company's members those matters we are required to state to them in a Report of the Auditors and for no other purpose. To the fullest extent permitted by law, we do not accept or assume responsibility to anyone other than the company and the company's members as a body, for our audit work, for this report or for the opinions we have formed.

Respective Responsibilities of Directors and Auditors As explained more fully in the Statement of Directors' Responsibilities set out in the Report of the Directors, the directors are responsible for the preparation of the financial statements and for being satisfied that they give a true and fair view. Our responsibility is to audit the financial statements in accordance with applicable law and International Standards on Auditing (UK and Ireland). Those standards require us to comply with the Auditing Practices Board's Ethical Standards for Auditors.

Scope of the Audit of the Financial Statements An audit involves obtaining evidence about the amounts and disclosures in the financial statements sufficient to give reasonable assurance that the financial statements are free from material misstatement, whether caused by fraud or error. This includes an assessment of: whether the accounting policies are appropriate to the company's circumstances and have been consistently applied and adequately disclosed; the reasonableness of significant accounting estimates made by the directors; and the overall presentation of the financial statements.

Opinion on Financial Statements In our opinion the financial statements:

- Give a true and fair view of the state of the company's affairs as at 31 December 2009 and of its profit for the year then ended.
- Have been properly prepared in accordance with United Kingdom Generally Accepted Accounting Practice.
- Have been prepared in accordance with the requirements of the Companies Act 2006.

Opinion on Other Matter Prescribed by the Companies Act 2006 In our opinion the information given in the Report of the Directors for the financial year for which the financial statements are prepared is consistent with the financial statements.

Matters on which we are Required to Report by Exception We have nothing to report in respect of the following matters where the Companies Act 2006 requires us to report to you if, in our opinion:

- Adequate accounting records have not been kept, or returns adequate for our audit have not been received from branches not visited by us.
- The financial statements are not in agreement with the accounting records and returns.
- Certain disclosures of directors' remuneration specified by law are not made.
- We have not received all the information and explanations we require for our audit.
- The directors were not entitled to prepare the financial statements and the Report of the Directors in accordance with the small companies' regime.

Mr A Auditor (Senior Statutory Auditor)

For and on behalf of Auditor & Co LLP

Chartered Certified Accountants and Registered Auditors

123 Any Street

Any town

Any Country

Date: ....

Small Entity Limited: Profit and Loss Account for the Year Ended 31 December 2009

	Notes	31/12/09 £	31/12/08 £
Turnover	2	6,081,603	5,792,866
Cost of sales		4,897,018	4,643,779
Gross profit		1,184,585	1,149,087
Distribution costs		60,094	81,913
Administrative expenses		820,166	770,224
		304,325	296,950
Other operating income		17,133	21,729
Operating profit	3	321,458	318,679
Interest receivable and similar income		7,400	24,788
		328,858	343,467
Interest payable and similar charges		3,713	14,334
Profit on ordinary activities before taxation		325,145	329,133
Tax on profit on ordinary activities	4	55,260	53,219
Profit for the financial year after taxation		269,885	275,914

Small Entity Limited: Balance Sheet 31 December 2009

	Notes	*31.12.09* £	*31.12.08* £
Fixed assets			
Tangible assets	5	129,409	163,070
Investments	6	121,177	121,177
		250,586	284,247
Current assets			
Stocks		434,763	517,319
Debtors	7	1,214,802	1,214,093
Cash at bank		337,668	317,090
		1,987,233	2,048,502
Creditors			
Amounts due within one year	8	928,292	974,942
Net current assets		1,058,941	1,073,560
Total assets less current liabilities		1,309,527	1,357,807
Provisions for liabilities and charges	10	7,589	16,370
Net assets		1,301,398	1,341,437
Capital and reserves			
Called up share capital	11	194,000	194,000
Profit and loss account	12	1,107,938	1,147,437
Shareholders' funds		1,301,398	1,341,437

The financial statements have been prepared in accordance with the special provisions of Part 15 of the Companies Act 2006 relating to small companies and with the Financial Reporting Standard for Smaller Entities (effective April 2008).

The financial statements were approved by the Board of Directors on . . . . and were signed on its behalf by:

. . . .

A Jones — Director   B Jones — Director

. . . .

C Jones — Director   D Jones — Director

Small Entity Limited: Notes to the Financial Statements for the Year Ended 31 December 2009

1. Accounting policies

Accounting Convention   The financial statements have been prepared under the historical cost convention and in accordance with the Financial Reporting Standard for Smaller Entities (effective April 2008).

Preparation of Consolidated Financial Statements   The financial statements contain information about Small Entity Limited as an individual company and do not contain consolidated financial information as the parent of a group. The company has taken the option under Section 398 of the Companies Act 2006 not to prepare consolidated financial statements.

Turnover   Turnover represents sales of goods despatched net of VAT and trade discounts. The company's policy of revenue recognition is to recognise a sale on despatch of goods.

Tangible Fixed Assets   Depreciation is provided at the following annual rates in order to write off each asset over its estimated useful life:

Plant and machinery	—	at varying rates on cost
Fixtures and fittings	—	at varying rates on cost
Motor vehicles	—	25% on cost

Fixed assets are stated at their original cost price, less accumulated depreciation to date and adjusted for any amounts recognised in respect of impairment.

Stocks   Stocks are valued at the lower of cost and net realisable value, after making due allowance for obsolete and slow-moving items.

Stocks are valued on a first-in first-out (FIFO) basis.

Deferred Tax   Deferred tax is recognised in respect of all timing differences that have originated, but not reversed, at the balance sheet date.

Deferred tax assets are recognised only to the extent that the directors consider that it is more likely than not that there will be suitable taxable profits from which the future reversal of the underlying timing differences can be deducted.

Deferred tax is measured on an undiscounted basis at the tax rates that are expected to apply in the periods in which timing differences reverse, based on tax rates and laws enacted or substantively enacted at the balance sheet date.

Research and Development   Expenditure on research and development is written off in the year in which it is incurred.

Foreign Currencies   Assets and liabilities in foreign currencies are translated into sterling at the rates of exchange ruling at the balance sheet date. Transactions in foreign currencies are translated into sterling at the rate of exchange ruling at the date of the transaction. Exchange differences are taken into account in arriving at the operating result.

Hire Purchase and Leasing Commitments   Where the company enters into a lease which entails taking substantially all the risks and rewards of ownership of an asset, the lease is treated as a Finance Lease. The asset is recorded in the balance sheet as a tangible fixed asset and is depreciated over its estimated useful life or the term of the lease, whichever is the shorter. Future instalments under such leases, net of finance charges, are included in creditors. Rentals payable are apportioned between the finance element, which is charged to the profit and loss account, and the capital element which reduces the outstanding obligation for future instalments.

All other leases are accounted for as Operating Leases and the rental charges are charged to the profit and loss account on a straight-line basis over the life of the lease.

Pension Costs and Other Post-Retirement Benefits   The company operates a defined contribution pension scheme. Contributions payable for the year are charged in the profit and loss account.

Financial Instruments   Financial instruments are classified and accounted for according to the substance of the contractual arrangement, as financial assets, liabilities or equity instruments. An equity instrument is any contract that evidences a residual interest in the assets of the company after deducting all liabilities.

2. Turnover   The turnover and profit before taxation are attributable to the one principal activity of the company.

An analysis of turnover by geographical market is given below:

	2009	*2008*
United Kingdom	54.92%	52.65%
Europe	45.08%	47.35%
	100.00%	100.00%

3. Operating profit   The operating profit is stated after charging/(crediting):

	2009 £	*2008* £
Depreciation — owned assets	65,337	70,081
Profit on disposal of fixed assets	(11,024)	–
Auditors' remuneration	8,100	7,600
Pension costs	296,226	182,503
Directors' remuneration	276,321	265,726

The number of directors to whom retirement benefits were accruing was as follows:	4	4

4. Taxation

Analysis of the tax charge   The tax charge on the profit on ordinary activities for the year was as follows:

	31/12/09 £	*31/12/08* £
Current tax:		
UK corporation tax	64,041	54,662
Deferred tax	(8,781)	(1,443)
Tax on profit on ordinary activities	55,260	53,219

5. Tangible fixed assets

	Plant and machinery £	*Fixtures and fittings* £	*Motor vehicles* £	*Total* £
Cost				
At 01/01/09	962,539	330,871	36,797	1,330,207
Additions	8,213	9,142	20,945	38,300
Disposals	–	(7,096)	(36,797)	(43,893)
At 31/12/09	970,752	332,917	20,945	1,324,614
Depreciation				
31/01/09	848,930	295,245	22,962	1,167,137
Charge for year	39,835	14,157	11,345	65,337
Eliminated on disposal	(1,102)	(7,096)	(29,071)	(37,269)
At 31/12/09	887,663	302,306	5,236	1,195,205
Net book value				
At 31/12/09	83,089	30,611	15,709	129,409
At 31/12/08	113,609	35,626	13,835	163,070

6. Fixed asset investments

	Unlisted investment £
Cost	
At 1 January 2009 and 31 December 2009	121,177
Net book value	
At 31 December 2009	121,177
At 31 December 2008	121,177

The company's investments at the balance sheet date in the share capital of companies include the following:

Subsidiary

Investment A Limited

Nature of business:	Widgets	
Class of shares:	% holding:	
Equity	100.00	

The aggregate capital and reserves for this company amounted to £nil (2008: £nil).

This company has not been consolidated as it was dormant throughout the period.

Associated Company

Nature of business:	Widgets	
Class of shares:	% holding:	
Ordinary	49.00	

	31/12/09 £	*31/12/08* £
Aggregate capital and reserves	1,190,770	853,145
Profit for the year	277,949	149,530

7. Debtors

	31/12/09 £	*31/12/08* £
Amounts falling due within 1 year:		
Trade debtors	942,203	941,255
Amounts owed by group undertaking	24,834	18,147
Sundry debtors	174,671	113,161
Prepayments	57,394	64,630
	1,199,102	1,137,193
Amounts falling due after more than 1 year:		
Sundry debtors	15,700	76,900
Aggregate amounts	1,214,802	1,214,093

Sundry debtors falling due after more than one year relate to a loan to Entity B Limited which attracts interest of 3% per annum above the base rate of Bank Plc (2008: 3%).

8. Creditors: Amounts falling due within one year

	31/12/09 £	*31/12/08* £
Trade creditors	402,426	445,871
Amounts owed to group undertaking	94,390	126,611
Tax	64,974	55,594
Social security and other taxes	24,989	26,129
VAT	4,720	7,588
Other creditors	279,036	279,549
Accrued expenses	57,757	33,600
	928,292	974,942

9. Operating lease commitments   The following operating lease payments are committed to be paid within one year:

	31/12/09 £	*31/12/08* £
Expiring:		
Within 1 year	54,150	54,150
Between 2 and 5 years	103,788	157,938
	157,938	212,088

10. Provisions for liabilities

	31/12/09 £	*31/12/08* £
Deferred tax	7,589	16,370

	Deferred Tax £
Balance at 01/01/09	16,370
Decelerated capital allowances	(8,781)
Balance at 31/12/09	7,589

11. Called up share capital   Allotted, issued and fully paid:

Number:	*Class*	*Nominal value:*	*31/12/09* £	*31/12/08* £
194,000	Ordinary	£1	194,000	194,000

12. Reserves

	Profit and loss account £
At 01/01/09	1,147,437
Profit for the year	269,885
Dividends	(309,384)
At 31/12/09	1,107,938

13. Related party disclosures

Subsidiary Limited The company owns 100% of the share capital of Subsidiary Limited. There was no trading between Small Entity Limited and Subsidiary Limited during the year (2008: £nil) as Subsidiary Limited was dormant throughout the period under review.

Associated Company Limited The company owns 49% (2008: 49%) of the share capital of Associated Company limited. The value of goods and services supplied to Associated Company Limited amounted to £11,987 (2008: £15,889). The value of goods and services supplied to Small Entity Limited amounted to £164,256 (2008: £161,231).

Associated Company Limited has a loan owed to Small Entity Limited amounting to £184,000 (2008: £184,000), repayments of which were due to commence in June 2008. The loan attracts interest at a rate of 3% per annum about the base rate of Bank plc (2008: 3%) and interest payments have arisen in the year in favour of Small Entity Limited amounting to £6,687 (2008: £14,164). As at the year-end an amount of £nil (2008: £nil) was owed to Associated Company Limited and an amount of £24,834 (2008: £19,057) was owed to Small Entity Limited. All transactions entered into were on normal commercial terms.

14. Ultimate controlling party The company is controlled by Parent Co Limited, its parent undertaking, which is incorporated in England and Wales under company number 123456. The ultimate controlling related party is Mr A Jones by virtue of his controlling shareholding in that company.

15. Post balance sheet events On 2 February 2010, the company acquired the goodwill and net assets of NewSub Co Limited for £20,000 financed by a secured bank loan, repayable over ten years.

The following illustrative financial statements relate to a first year set of consolidated financial statements prepared under UK GAAP.

Groupco Limited: Report of the Director for the Year Ended 31 December 2009

The directors present his report with the financial statements of the company and the group for the year ended 31 December 2010.

Principal Activity The principal activity of the group in the year under review was that of commercial property management.

Review of Business   Overall, the director is satisfied with the results of the group which show healthy profits and a strong balance sheet. The company has seen its operations expand into the whole of the country and is now considering options to expand into overseas markets.

The group continues to see upward trends in terms of profitability and net asset position, which is vital in ensuring that the group remains at the height of its competitive advantage. The director is confident that all members of the group will remain profitable and continue to secure additional contracts to remain competitive into the foreseeable future.

The majority of group revenue is derived from Subsidiary 1 Limited. Group turnover for the year was £39.9m; operating profit was £4.4m and profit before taxation amounted to £4.5m.

The Operating Cash for the period shows the cash conversion of these profit streams to be relatively strong.

Dividends   No dividends will be distributed for the year ended 31 December 2009.

Future Developments   The group strives to ensure that it maintains its competitive advantage and seeks to implement initiatives to enable this strategy. Subsidiary 1 Limited is seeing constant rapid growth throughout the whole of the business with additional contracts being managed by the company on a regular basis. The group seeks to ensure that Subsidiary 1 Limited maintains its professional ethos and standing in the marketplace as well as ensuring that a professional service is delivered to its customers at all times.

Subsidiary 1 Limited has negotiated an extension to a lucrative contract it has with a major customer which will see it remain profitable into 2011 and the company recently successfully obtained Quality Assurance Accreditation. This standard of service will continue into the future to enable the company to remain profitable and to secure further business going forward.

Subsidiary 2 Limited has also seen quite a successful year in terms of securing new contracts and is currently in negotiations with a large retail outlet to manage their commercial properties. The director is confident these talks will enable the company to improve profitability.

The group as a whole is committed to delivering high quality services to enable growth and competitive advantage and the director and his senior management team are committed to ensuring this continues.

Director   Mr A Smith held office during the whole of the period from 1 January 2009 to the date of this report.

The director, being eligible, offers himself for election at the forthcoming Annual General Meeting.

Political and Charitable Donations   During the year the Group made the following donations:

Charity 1	£500
Charity 2	£250
Charity 3	£350
Charity 4	£500
Charity 5	£1,000

The purposes of the above were in respect of charitable donations.

Consolidated Financial Statements   The consolidated financial statements, which are provided for the first time this year, include the results of our individual commercial property management entities. These have been produced in the light of the revised Companies Act 2006 which now requires consolidated financial statements for medium-sized group entities.

Post Balance Sheet Events   On 14 April 2010, Groupco Limited acquired a controlling interest in Subsidiary 3 Limited, a company registered in England and Wales under company number 123456. This acquisition was financed by using a share for share exchange.

Statement of Director's Responsibilities   The director is responsible for preparing the Report of the Director and the financial statements in accordance with applicable law and regulations.

Company law requires the director to prepare financial statements for each financial year. Under that law the director has elected to prepare the financial statements in accordance with United Kingdom Generally Accepted Accounting Practice (United Kingdom Accounting Standards and applicable law). Under company law the director must not approve the financial statements unless he is satisfied that they give a true and fair view of the state of affairs of the company and the group and of the profit or loss of the group for that period. In preparing these financial statements, the director is required to:

- Select suitable accounting policies and apply them consistently.
- Make judgements and accounting estimates that are reasonable and prudent.
- Prepare the financial statements on the going concern basis unless it is inappropriate to presume that the company will continue in business.

The director is responsible for keeping adequate accounting records that are sufficient to show and explain the company's and the group's transactions and disclose with reasonable accuracy at any time the financial position of the company and the group and enable him to ensure that the financial statements comply with the Companies Act 2006. He is also responsible for safeguarding the assets of the company and the group and hence for taking reasonable steps for the prevention and detection of fraud and other irregularities.

Statement as to Disclosure of Information to Auditors   So far as the director is aware, there is no relevant audit information (as defined by Section 418 of the Companies Act 2006) of which the group's auditors are unaware, and he has taken all the steps that he ought to have taken as a director in order to make himself aware of any relevant audit information and to establish that the group's auditors are aware of that information.

Auditors   The auditors, Auditor & Co LLP, will be proposed for re-appointment at the forthcoming Annual General Meeting.

On behalf of the board: . . . .

Mr A Jones — Director

Date: . . . .

Report of the Independent Auditors to the Members of Groupco Limited

We have audited the financial statements of Groupco Limited for the year ended 31 December 2009 which comprise the Consolidated Profit and Loss Account, the Consolidated Balance Sheet, the Company Balance Sheet, the Consolidated Cash Flow Statement and the related notes. The financial reporting framework that has been applied in their preparation is applicable law and United Kingdom Accounting Standards (United Kingdom Generally Accepted Accounting Practice).

This report is made solely to the company's members, as a body, in accordance with Chapter 3 of Part 16 of the Companies Act 2006. Our audit work has been undertaken so that we might state to the company's members those matters we are required to state to them in a Report of the Auditors and for no other purpose. To the fullest extent permitted by law, we do not accept or assume responsibility to anyone other than the company and the company's members as a body, for our audit work, for this report or for the opinions we have formed.

Respective Responsibilities of Director and Auditors   As explained more fully in the Statement of Director's Responsibilities, the director is responsible for the preparation of the financial statements and for being satisfied that they give a true and fair view. Our responsibility is to audit the financial statements in accordance with applicable law and International Standards on Auditing (UK and Ireland). Those standards require us to comply with the Auditing Practices Board's Ethical Standards for Auditors.

Scope of the Audit of the Financial Statements   An audit involves obtaining evidence about the amounts and disclosures in the financial statements sufficient to give reasonable assurance that the financial statements are free from material misstatement, whether caused by fraud or error. This includes an assessment of: whether the accounting policies are appropriate to the group's and the parent company's circumstances and have been consistently applied and adequately disclosed; the reasonableness of significant accounting estimates made by the director; and the overall presentation of the financial statements.

Opinion on Financial Statements   In our opinion:

- The financial statements give a true and fair view of the state of the group's and of the parent company affairs as at 31 December 2009 and of the group's profit for the year then ended.
- The group financial statements have been properly prepared in accordance with United Kingdom Generally Accepted Accounting Practice.
- The financial statements have been prepared in accordance with the requirements of the Companies Act 2006.

Opinion on Other Matter Prescribed by the Companies Act 2006   In our opinion the information given in the Report of the Director for the financial year for which the financial statements are prepared is consistent with the financial statements.

Matters on which we are Required to Report by Exception   We have nothing to report in respect of the following matters where the Companies Act 2006 requires us to report to you if, in our opinion:

Adequate accounting records have not been kept by the parent company, or returns adequate for our audit have not been received from branches not visited by us.

- The parent company financial statements are not in agreement with the accounting records and returns. Certain disclosures of director's remuneration specified by law are not made.
- We have not received all the information and explanations we require for our audit.

Mr A Auditor (Senior Statutory Auditor)

Auditor & Co LLP

123 Any Street

Any town

Date: ....

Groupco Limited: Consolidated Profit and Loss Account for the year ended 31 December 2009

	Notes	£	£
Turnover			39,952,552
Acquisitions	2	39,952,252	
Cost of sales	3		31,393,695
Gross Profit	3		8,558,857
Net operating expenses	3		4,134,571
Operating profit	5		4,424,286
Acquisitions		4,424,286	
Interest receivable and similar income			62,637
Profit on ordinary activities before taxation			4,486,923
Tax on profit on ordinary activities	6		1,282,657
Profit for the financial year after taxation			3,204,266
Minority interest – equity			(17,146)
Retained profit for the year for the Group			3,221,412

Total Recognised Gains and Losses   The group has no recognised gains or losses other than the profit for the current year.

Groupco Limited: Consolidated Balance Sheet 31 December 2009

	Notes	£	£
Fixed assets			
Intangible assets	8		1,007
Tangible assets	9		439,432
Investments	10		–
Current assets			
Stocks	11	11,383	
Debtors: due within 1 year	12	5,014,631	
Debtors: due after 1 year	12	2,600,000	
Cash at bank and in hand		3,244,465	
		10,870,479	
Creditors			
Amounts falling due within 1 year	13	5,066,281	
Net current assets		5,804,198	
Total assets less current liabilities			6,244,637
Provisions for liabilities	16		(12,635)
Minority interests	17		17,218
Net Assets			6,249,130
Capital and Reserves			
Called up share capital	18		179
Profit and loss account	19		6,248,951
Shareholders' Funds	24		6,249,130

The financial statements were approved by the director on .... and were signed by:

A. Jones — Director

Groupco Limited: Company Balance Sheet 31 December 2009

	Notes	£
Fixed assets		
Intangible assets	8	–
Tangible assets	9	–
Investments	10	179
		179
Total assets less current liabilities		179
Capital and reserves		
Called up share capital	18	179
Shareholders' funds	24	179

The financial statements were approved by the director on .... and were signed by:

A. Jones — Director

Groupco Limited: Consolidated Cash Flow Statement for the year ended 31 December 2009

	Notes	£
Net cash inflow from operating activities	1	747,658
Returns on investments and servicing of finance	2	62,637
Taxation	2	(652,825)
Capital expenditure	2	(295,265)
Acquisitions and disposals	2	2,690,575
Financing	2	691,685
Increase in cash in the period		3,244,465
Reconciliation of net cash flow to movement in net debt	3	
Increase in cash in the period		3,244,465
Change in net debt resulting from cash flows		3,244,465
Movement in net debt in the period		3,244,465
Net debt at 1 January		—
Net funds at 31 December		3,244,465

Groupco Limited: Notes to the Consolidated Cash Flow Statement for the year ended 31 December 2009

1. Reconciliation of Operating Profit to Net Cash Inflow from Operating Activities

	£
Operating profit	4,424,286
Depreciation charges	192,425
Profit on disposal of fixed assets	(617)
Increase in stocks	(11,383)
Increase in debtors	(7,614,534)
Increase in creditors	3,757,481
Net cash inflow from operating activities	747,658

2. Analysis of Cash Flows for Headings Netted in the Cash Flow Statement

	£
Returns on investments and servicing of finance	
Interest received	62,637
Capital expenditure	
Purchase of intangible fixed assets	(2,013)
Purchase of tangible fixed assets	(296,753)
Sale of tangible fixed assets	3,501
Net cash outflow for capital expenditure	(295,265)

	£

Acquisitions and disposals

Book value of fixed assets transferred	(336,982)
Reserves at acquisition of subsidiary	3,027,539
Minority interest in subs share capital	18
Net cash inflow for acquisitions and disposals	2,690,575

Financing

Amount withdrawn by directors	691,603
Share issue	82
Net cash inflow from financing	691,685

3. Analysis of Changes in Net Debt

	At 01/01/09 £	Cash flow £	At 31/12/09 £
Net cash:	=	3,244,465	3,244,465
Total	=	3,244,465	3,244,465

4. Acquisition of Business   During the year, Groupco Limited acquired the entire holding in Entity A Limited and a controlling holding in Entity B Limited. The company acquired these subsidiaries by way of a share for share exchange and, therefore, none of the consideration comprised cash.

The Group acquired cash balances held at bank amounting to £4,522,436 and a bank overdraft amounting to £176,014.

Groupco Limited: Notes to the Consolidated Financial Statements for the year ended 31 December 2009

1. Accounting policies

Accounting convention   The financial statements have been prepared under the historical cost convention.

Basis of consolidation — subsidiary undertakings   All companies over which the group is able to exercise a dominant influence are consolidated as subsidiary undertakings. Dominant influence is defined as the right to give directions with respect to operating and financial policies. Unless otherwise stated, the acquisition method of accounting has been adopted. Under this method, the results of subsidiary undertakings acquired or disposed of in the period are included in the consolidated profit and loss account from the date of acquisition or up to the date of disposal.

Under section 408 of the Companies Act 2006, the company is exempt from the requirement to present its own profit and loss account.

Turnover Turnover comprises the invoice value of services, inclusive of VAT, of services provided by the group. Income is recognised in the financial statements when it becomes receivable.

Tangible Fixed Assets Depreciation is provided at the following annual rates in order to write off each asset over its estimated useful life.

Fixtures and fittings	—	33% on cost, 20% on cost and 10% on cost
Motor vehicles	—	25% on reducing balance
Computer equipment	—	33% on cost

Stocks Stocks are valued at the lower of cost and net realisable value, after making due allowance for obsolete and slow moving items.

Deferred tax The charge for taxation takes into account taxation deferred as a result of timing differences between the treatment of certain items for taxation and accounting purposes. In general, deferred taxation is recognised in respect of all timing differences that have originated, but not reversed, at the balance sheet date. However, deferred tax assets are recognised only to the extent that the director considers that it is more likely than not that there will be suitable taxable profits from which the future reversal of the underlying timing differences can be deducted.

In accordance with FRS 19 'Deferred Tax', deferred tax is not recognised on revaluation gains. Deferred taxation is measured on a non-discounted basis at the tax rates that are expected to apply in the periods in which the timing differences reverse, based on tax rates and laws enacted or substantively enacted at the balance sheet date.

Hire purchase and leasing commitments Rentals paid under operating leases are charged to the profit and loss account on a straight line basis over the period of the lease.

Investments Investments held as fixed assets are stated at cost less amounts written off for impairment.

Classification of Financial Instruments Following the adoption of FRS 25 'Financial Instruments: Presentation' financial instruments are treated as equity (i.e. forming part of shareholders' funds) only to the extent that they meet the following two conditions:

- They include no contractual obligations upon the company (or group as the case may be) to deliver cash or other financial assets or to exchange financial assets or financial liabilities with another party under conditions that are potentially unfavourable to the company (or group).
- Where the instrument will or may be settled in the company's own equity instruments, it is either a non-derivative that includes no obligation to deliver a variable number of the company's own equity instruments or is a derivative that will be settled by the company's exchanging a fixed amount of cash or other financial assets for a number of its own equity instruments.

To the extent that this definition is not met, the proceeds of issue are classified as a financial liability. Where the instrument so classified takes the legal form of the company's own shares, the amounts presented in these financial statements for call up share capital exclude amounts in relation to those shares.

2. Turnover   The turnover, pre-tax profit and net assets of the group relate to the following classes of business:

Class of Business	Turnover £	Pre-tax Profit £	Net Assets £
Commercial property management	39,952,252	4,579,961	6,327,158
Private property management	nil	(93,038)	(95,156)

3. Analysis of Operations

	31/12/09		
	Continuing £	Acquisitions £	Total £
Cost of sales	=	31,393,695	31,393,695
Gross profit	=	8,558,857	8,558,857
Net operating expenses:			
Administrative expenses	=	4,136,764	4,136,764
Other operating income	=	(2,193)	(2,193)
	=	4,134,571	4,134,571

4. Staff Costs

	£
Wages and salaries	2,320,965
Social security costs	179,511
	2,500,476

The average monthly number of employees during the year was as follows:

Management	7
Administration	186
	193

The above staff numbers relate to the average number of persons employed by the group (including directors).

5. Operating Profit   The operating profit is stated after charging/(crediting):

	£
Hire of plant and machinery	835
Depreciation — owned assets	191,419
Profit on disposal of fixed assets	(617)
Premises lease amortisation	1,006
Auditors' remuneration	9,100
Other services supplied pursuant to such legislation	20,631
Other services relating to taxation	2,000
Director's remuneration	200,000

6. Taxation

Analysis of the tax charge   The tax charge on the profit on ordinary activities for the year was as follows:

	£
Current tax:	
UK corporation tax	1,270,022
Deferred tax	12,635
Tax on profit on ordinary activities	1,282,657

Factors affecting the tax charge The tax assessed for the year is higher than the standard rate of corporation tax in the UK. The difference is explained below:

	£
Profit on ordinary activities before tax	4,486,923
Profit on ordinary activities multiplied by the standard rate of corporation tax in the UK of 28%	1,256,338
Effects of:	
Depreciation in excess of capital allowances	7,314
Expenses not deductible for tax purposes	6,370
Current tax charge	1,270,022

7. Profit of Parent Company   As permitted by Section 408 of the Companies Act 2006, the profit and loss account of the parent company is not presented as part of these financial statements. The parent company's profit for the financial year was £nil.

8. Intangible Fixed Assets

Group	Premises Lease £
Cost	
Additions	2,013
At 31/12/09	2,013
Amortisation	
Amortisation for the year	1,006
At 31/12/09	1,006
Net book value	
At 31/12/09	1,007

9. Tangible Fixed Assets

Group	Plant and machinery	Fixtures and fittings	Vehicles	Total
Cost	£	£	£	£
At 01/01/09	–	288,693	161,912	450,605
Additions	121,707	20,924	154,752	296,753
Disposals	–	–	(3,741)	(3,741)
At 31/12/09	121,701	308,987	312,923	743,617
Depreciation				
At 01/01/09	–	76,518	37,105	113,623
Charge for year	40,164	82,086	69,169	191,419
Eliminated on disposal	–	–	(857)	(857)
At 31/12/09	40,164	158,604	105,417	304,185
Net book value				
At 31/12/09	81,543	150,383	207,506	439,432
At 0101/09	–	212,175	124,807	336,982

10. Fixed Asset Investments

Company	Shares in group undertakings £
Cost	
Additions	179
At 31/12/09	179
Net book value	
At 31/12/09	179

The group or the company's investments at the balance sheet date in the share capital of companies include the following:

Subsidiaries

Entity 1 Limited

Nature of Business:	Commercial Property Investment
Class of Shares:	% Holding
Ordinary	100.00

	£
Aggregate capital and reserves	6,327,158
Profit for the year	3,299,519

Entity 2 Limited

Nature of Business:	Commercial Property Investment
Class of Shares:	% Holding
Ordinary	81.00

	£
Aggregate capital and reserves	(95,156)
Loss for the year	(95,156)

The results of the subsidiaries have been included in the consolidated financial statements of Groupco Limited.

11. Stocks

	Group £
Stocks	11,383

All stocks are held by subsidiary companies.

12. Debtors

	Group £
Amounts falling due within one year:	
Trade debtors	4,834,569
Other debtors	129,543
VAT	773
Called up share capital note paid	97
Prepayments	49,649
	5,014,631
Amounts falling due after more than one year:	
Other debtors	2,600,000
Aggregate amounts	7,614,631

13. Creditors: Amounts Falling Due Within One Year

	Group £
Trade creditors	1,959,141
Tax	617,197
Social security and other taxes	59,931
Other creditors	95,196
Director's current account	691,603
Accrued expenses	1,642,213
	5,066,281

14. Operating Lease Commitments   The following operating lease payments are committed to be paid within one year by the group:

	land and buildings £	*other operating leases* £
Expiring:		
Within 1 year	292,752	77,543
Between 1 and 5 years	371,130	13,010
	663,882	90,553

15. Secured Debts   Bank overdrafts in Entity 1 Limited are secured by a charge over the company's assets amounting to £77,000 dated 20 July 2008.

16. Provisions for Liabilities

	Group £
Deferred tax	12,635

Group

	Deferred Tax £
Accelerated capital allowances	12,635
Balance at 31/12/09	12,635

At the balance sheet date, Entity 1 Limited had ongoing litigation claims in respect of two properties. Since the balance sheet date this subsidiary has paid two amounts totalling £98,099 in respect of these claims and these amounts relate to conditions that existed at the balance sheet date. These liabilities meet the definition of a provision and have been included within these consolidated financial statements under Creditors: Amounts Falling Due within One Year.

17. Minority Interests   Equity minority interests represent the share of the profits less losses on ordinary activities attributable to the interest of equity shareholders in the subsidiary which are not wholly owned by the group.

18. Called Up Share Capital

Allotted and Issued:

Number:	Class:	Nominal Value:	£
179	Ordinary	£1	179

19. Reserves

Group	*Profit and Loss Account* £
At 01/01/09	3,027,539
Profit for the year	3,221,412
At 31/12/09	6,248,951

Company	*Profit and Loss Account* £
Profit for the year	—
At 31/12/09	—

20. Contingent Liabilities   At the balance sheet date, Entity 1 Limited had two contingent liabilities in respect of legal claims in respect of two properties. The company is currently defending the claim and there is no indication as to the outcome of the case.

There is also no reliable estimate of costs available or the financial effects, if any, in respect of the above cases.

21. Transactions with Director   During the year, Mr A Jones transferred his entire holding in Entity 1 Limited and Entity 2 Limited to Groupco Limited.

Included within Creditors: Amounts Falling Due within One year is the director's current account amounting to £691,603. The current account was not overdrawn at any point during the year.

22. Related Party Disclosures   Included within Debtors: Amounts Falling Due within One Year is an interest-free loan to Unrelated Entity Inc. Unrelated Entity Inc is a company registered in Overseas and is under the control of the Jones family. The terms of this loan is based on a ten-year term and no security has been taken by the group in respect of this loan so as to enable Unrelated Inc to expand operations by obtaining other sources of finance.

As at the balance sheet date, an amount of £2.6m was owed to the group in respect of this loan.

During the year, the group occupied premises owned by the Jones family. A market rental of £82,000 was paid to the Jones family in respect of these premises in accordance with the provisions in the licence agreement. Entity 2 Limited occupied premises owned by the Jones family, but occupied these premises on a rent-free basis.

23. Ultimate Controlling Party   The company is under the ultimate control of Mr A Jones by virtue of his controlling shareholding in the company.

24. Reconciliation of Movements in Shareholders' Funds

Group	£
Profit for the financial year	3,221,412
Reserves in Entity 1 Ltd at acquisition date	3,027,539
Investments in subsidiary companies	179
Net addition to shareholders' funds	6,249,130
Opening shareholders' funds	—
Closing shareholders' funds	6,249,130
Equity interests	6,249,130

Company	£
Profit for the financial year	—
Issue of share capital	179
Net addition to shareholders' funds	179
Opening shareholders' funds	—
Closing shareholders' funds	179
Equity interests	179

25. Going Concern Entity 2 Limited is a subsidiary company of Groupco Limited. During the year this subsidiary made a pre-tax loss of £93,038 and had net current liabilities of £105,616. The director has given his written assurance that this company will continue to receive support from the group in order to finance working capital requirements until such a time it turns profitable. The group does not have an obligation to provide finance which may not be recoverable in respect of losses attributable to minority interests.

On this basis, the subsidiary is deemed to be a going concern.

26. Business Combinations On 1 January 2009, Groupco Limited acquired, by way of a share for share exchange, the entire net assets of Entity 1 Limited and Entity 2 Limited. As described in the accounting policies, this business combination was accounted for using the acquisition method of accounting. The shares acquired were as follows:

Ordinary Shares

Entity 1 Limited	100 £1 shares
Entity 2 Limited	79 £1 shares

The book value of the assets and liabilities acquired in the business combination for each subsidiary were as follows:

Entity 1 Limited

Fixed assets	£336,981
Current assets	£7,815,788
Current liabilities	(£5,125,130)
Equity	£3,027,639

Entity 2 Limited

Equity — excluding reserves	£79
Reserves	£nil

As the company's accounting policies were in line with the group's accounting policies, no fair value adjustments were required and no goodwill on acquisition as the acquisition was accounted for by way of a share for share exchange.

The subsidiaries were acquired by Groupco Limited at the start of their financial year which was 1 January 2009 and, therefore, a summarised profit and loss account from the beginning of their financial year to the date of acquisition is not required.

The profit after tax for Entity 1 Limited for the previous financial year (31 December 2008) was £3,027,539 and the shares were wholly-owned in this company. Entity 2 Limited was dormant in the year to 31 December 2008.

The following is an illustrative set of financial statements for a multinational corporation (Nokia).

Nokia Corporation and Subsidiaries: Consolidated Income Statements

	Notes	*2009* *EURm*	*2008* *EURm*	*2007* *EURm*
Net sales		40,984	50,710	51,058
Cost of sales		(27,720)	(33,337)	(33,781)
Gross profit		13,264	17,373	17,277
Research and development expenses		(5,909)	(5,968)	(5,636)
Selling and marketing expenses		(3,933)	(4,380)	(4,379)
Administrative and general expenses		(1,145)	(1,284)	(1,165)
Impairment of goodwill	7	(908)	–	–
Other income	6	338	20	2,312
Other expenses	6, 7	(510)	(1,195)	(424)
Operating profit	2–9,23	1,197	4,966	7,985
Share of results of associated companies	14,30	30	6	44
Financial income and expenses	10	(265)	(2)	239
Profit before tax		962	4,970	8,268
Tax	11	(702)	(1,081)	(1,522)
Profit		260	3,889	6,746
Profit attributable to equity holders of the parent		891	3,988	7,205
Loss attributable to non-controlling interests		(631)	(99)	(459)
		260	3,889	6,746

	Earnings *per share*	*2009 EUR*	*2008 EUR*	*2007 EUR*
For profit attributable to the equity holders of the parent	27			
Basic		0.24	1.07	1.85
Diluted		0.24	1.05	1.83
Average number of shares (1,000s shares)	27			
Basic		3,705,116	3,743,622	3,885,408
Diluted		3,721,072	3,780,363	3,932,008

See notes to consolidated financial statements.

Nokia Corporation and Subsidiaries: Consolidated statements of Financial Position, IFRs

December 31	Notes	2009 EURm	2008 EURm
Assets			
Non-current assets			
Capitalised development costs	12	143	244
Goodwill	12	5,171	6,257
Other intangible assets	12	2,762	3,913
Property, plant and equipment	13	1,867	2,090
Investments in associated companies	14	69	96
Available-for-sale investments	15	554	512
Deferred tax assets	24	1,507	1,963
Long-term loans receivable	15, 33	46	27
Other non-current assets	15	6	10
		12,125	15,112
Current assets			
Inventories	17, 19	1,865	2,533
Accounts receivable, net of allowances for doubtful accounts (2009: EUR 391 million 2008: EUR 415 million)	15, 19, 33	7,981	9,444
Prepaid expenses and accrued income	18	4,551	4,538
Current portion of long-term loans receivable	15, 33	14	101
Other financial assets	15, 16, 33	329	1,034
Investments at fair value through profit and loss, liquid assets	15, 33	580	–
Available-for-sale investments, liquid assets	15, 33	2,367	1,272
Available-for-sale investments, cash equivalents	15, 33	4,784	3,842
Bank and cash	33	1,142	1,706
Total assets		35,738	39,582

Shareholders' equity and liabilities

Capital and reserves attributable to equity holders of the parent

	Notes	2009 EURm	2008 EURm
Share capital	22	246	246
Share issue premium	–	279	442
Treasury shares, at cost	–	−681	−1,881
Translation differences	21	−127	341
Fair value and other reserves	20	69	62

Shareholders' equity and liabilities

Capital and reserves attributable to equity holders of the parent

	Notes	2009 EURm	2008 EURm
Reserve for invested non-restricted equity		3,170	3,306
Retained earnings		10,132	11,692
		13,088	14,208
Minority interests		1,661	2,302
Total equity		14,749	16,510
Non-current liabilities			
Long-term interest-bearing liabilities	15, 33	4,432	861
Deferred tax liabilities	24	1,303	1,787
Other long-term liabilities		66	69
		5,801	2,717
Current liabilities			
Current portion of long-term loans	15, 33	44	13
Short-term borrowings	15, 33	727	3,578
Other financial liabilities	15, 16, 33	245	924
Accounts payable	15, 33	4,950	5,225
Accrued expenses	25	6,504	7,023
Provisions	26	2,718	3,592
		15,188	20,355
Total shareholders' equity and liabilities		35,738	39,582

Nokia Corporation and Subsidiaries Consolidated statements of Cash Flows, IFRS

Financial year ended *December 31*	Notes	2009 EURm	2008 EURm	2007 EURm
Cash flow from operating activities				
Profit attributable to equity holders of the parent		891	3,598	7,205
Adjustments, total	31	3,390	3,024	1,159
Change to net working capital		140	−2,546	605
Cash generated from operations		4,421	4,466	8,969

Financial year ended December 31	Notes	2009 EURm	2008 EURm	2007 EURm
Interest received		125	416	362
Interest paid		−256	−155	−59
Other financial income and expenses, net received		−128	250	67
Income taxes paid, net received		−915	−1,780	−1,457
Net cash from operating activities		3,247	3,197	7,882
Cash flow from investing activities				
Acquisition of Group companies, net of acquired cash		−29	−5,962	253
Purchase of current available-for-sale investments, liquid assets		−2,800	−669	−4,798
Purchase of investments at fair value through profit and loss, liquid assets		−695	–	–
Purchase of non-current available-for-sale investments		−95	−121	−126
Purchase of shares in associated companies		−30	−24	25
Additions to capitalised costs		−27	−131	157
Long-term loans made to customers		–	–	261
Proceeds from repayment and sale of long-term loans receivable		–	129	163
Proceeds from (+) / payment of (−) other long-term receivables		2	−1	5
Proceeds from (+) / payment of (−) short term loans receivable		2	−15	−119
Capital expenditures		−531	−889	−715
Proceeds from disposal of shares in associated companies		40	3	6
Proceeds from disposal of businesses		61	41	—
Proceeds from maturities and sale of current available-for-sale investments, liquid assets		1,730	4,664	4,930

Financial year ended December 31	Notes	2009 EURm	2008 EURm	2007 EURm
Proceeds from maturities and sale of investments at fair value through profit and loss, liquid assets		108	—	—
Proceeds from sale of non-current available-for-sale investments		14	10	50
Proceeds from sale of fixed assets		100	54	72
Dividends received		2	6	12
Net cash used in investing activities		−2,148	−2,905	−710
Cash flow from financing activities				
Proceeds from stock options exercises		—	53	987
Purchase of treasury shares		—	−3,121	−3,819
Proceeds from long-term borrowings		3,901	714	115
Repayment of long-term borrowing		−209	−34	−16
Proceeds from (+) / repayment of (−) short term borrowings		−2,842	2,891	661
Dividends paid		−1,546	−2,048	−1,760
Net cash used in financing activities		−696	−1,545	−3,832
Foreign exchange adjustment		−25	−49	−15
Net increase (+0) / decrease (−) in cash and cash equivalents		378	−1,302	3,325
Cash and cash equivalents at beginning of period		5,548	6,850	3,525
Cash and cash equivalents at end of period		5,926	5,548	6,850
Cash and cash equivalents comprise of:				
Bank and cash		1,142	1,706	2,125
Current available-for-sale investments, cash equivalents	15, 33	4,784	3,842	4,725
		5,926	5,548	6,850

EURm	Number of shares (1000s)	Share capital	Share premium	Treasury shares	Translation differences	Fair value and other reserves	Reserve for invested non-restricted enquiry	Retained earnings	Before minority interests	Minority interests	Total
Balance at December 2006	3,965,730	246	2,707	—	2,060	-34	-14	—	11,123	11,968	92,12,060
Translations differences					-167				-167	16	-151
Net investment hedge gains, net of tax					38				38		38
Cash flow hedges, net of tax						-11			-11	6	-5
Available-for-sale investments, net of tax						48			48		48
Other decreases, net								-40	-40	-6	-46
Profit								7,205	7,205	-459	6,746
Total comprehensive income					-129	37		7,165	7,073	-443	6,630
Stock options exercised	57,269		46				932		978		978
Stock options exercised related to acquisitions		-3							-3		-3
Share-based compensation		228							228		228
Excess tax benefit on share-based compensation		128							128		128
Settlement of performance shares	3,138		-104	58			9		-37		-37
Acquisitions of treasury shares	-180,590			-3,884					-3,884		-3,884
Reissuance of treasury shares	403			7					7		7
Cancellation of treasury shares				2,733				2,733	—		—
Share premium reduction and transfer			-2,358				2,358		—		—
Dividend								-1,685	-1,685	-75	-1,760
Minority interest on formation of Nokia Siemens Networks									—	2,991	2,991
Total of other equity movements	—	—	-2,063	-1,086	—	—	3,299	-4,418	-4,268	2,916	-1,352

EURm	Number of shares (1000s)	Share capital	Share premium	Treasury shares	Translation differences	Fair value and other reserves	Reserve for invested non-restricted enquiry	Retained earnings	Before minority interests	Minority interests	Total
Balance at 31/12/07	3,845,950	246	644	−3,146	−163	23	3,299	13,870	14,773	2,565	17,338
Translation differences					595				595		595
Net investment hedge gains, net of tax					−91				−91		−91
Cash flow hedges, net of tax						42			42	−67	−25
Available-for-sale investments, net of tax						−3			−3	−2	−5
Other increase net								46	46	−17	29
Profit								3,988	3,988	−99	3,889
Total comprehensive income					504	39		4,034	4,577	−185	4,392
Stock options exercised	3,547	1					51		51		51
Stock options exercised related to acquisitions		1							1		1
Share-based compensation		74							74		74
Excess tax benefit on share-based compensation		−117							−117	−6	−124
Settlement of performance and restricted shares	5,622	−179	154					−44	−69		−69
Acquisition of treasury shares	−157,390		−3,123						−3,123		−3,123
Reissuance of treasury shares	143		2						2		2
Cancellation of treasury shares			4,232					−4,232			
Dividend								−1,992	−1,992	−35	−2,027
Acquisitions and other change in minority interests										−37	−37
Vested portion of share-based payment awards related to acquisitions			19						19		19
Acquisiton of Symbian							7	12	12		12
Total of other equity movements		—	−202	−1,265				−6,212	−5,142	−78	−5,220

EURm	Number of shares (1000s)	Share capital	Share premium	Treasury shares	Translation differences	Fair value and other reserves	Reserve for invested non-restricted enquiry	Retained earnings	Before minority interests	Minority interests	Total
Balance at 31/12/08	3,697,872	246	442	−1,881	341	62	3,306	−11,692	14,208	2,302	16,510
Translation differences					−552				−552	−9	−561
Net investment hedge gains, net of tax					84				84		84
Cash flow hedges, net of tax						−35			−35	49	14
Available-for-sale investments, net of tax						42			42	2	44
Other decreases, net								−1	−1	−7	−8
Profit								891	891	−631	260
Total comprehensive income						468	7	890	429	−596	−167
Stock options exercised		7									
Stock options exercised related to acquisitions			−1						−1		−1
Share-based compensation			16						16		16
Excess tax benefit on share-based compensation			−12						−12	−1	−13
Settlement of performance and restricted shares	10,352		−166	230		−136			−72		−72
Reissuance of treasury shares	31			1					1		1
Cancellation of treasury shares				969				−969	—		—
Dividend								−1,481	−1,481	−44	−1,525
Total of other equity movements			−163	1,200			136	−2,450	−1549	−45	1,594
Balance at 31/12/09	3,708,262	246	279	−681	−127	69	3,170	10,132	13,088	1,661	14,749

Dividends declared per share were EUR 0.40 for 2009 (EUR 0.40 for 2008 and EUR 0.53 for 2007), subject to shareholders' approval.

Notes to the Consolidated Financial Statements

1. Accounting Policies

Basis of presentation   The consolidated financial statements of Nokia Corporation ('Nokia' or 'the Group'), a Finnish public limited liability company with domicile in Helsinki, in the Republic of Finland, are prepared in accordance with International Financial Reporting Standards as issued by the International Accounting Standards Board (IASB) and in conformity with IFRS as adopted by the European Union ('IFRS'). The consolidated financial statements are presented in millions of Euros ('EURm'), except as noted, and are prepared under the historical cost convention, except as disclosed in the accounting policies below. The notes to the consolidated financial statements also conform to Finnish Accounting legislation. On March 11, 2010, Nokia's Board of Directors authorized the financial statements for 2009 for issuance and filing.

The Group completed the acquisition of all of the outstanding equity of NAVTEQ on July 10, 2008 and a transaction to form Nokia Siemens Networks on April 1, 2007. The NAVTEQ and the Nokia Siemens Network's business combinations have had a material impact on the consolidated financial statements and associated notes. see Note 8.

Adoption of pronouncements under IFRS   In the current year, the Group has adopted all of the new and revised standards, amendments and interpretations to existing standards issued by the IASB that are relevant to its operations and effective for accounting periods on or after January 1, 2009.

- IAS 1 (revised), Presentation of financial statements, prompts entities to aggregate information in the financial statements on the basis of shared characteristics. All non-owner changes in equity (i.e. comprehensive income) should be presented either in one statement of comprehensive income or in a separate income statement and statement of comprehensive income.
- Amendments to IFRS 7 require entities to provide additional disclosures about the fair value measurements. The amendments clarifying the existing requirements for the disclosure of liquidity risk.
- Amendment to IFRS 2, Share-based payment, Group and Treasury Share Transactions, clarifies the definition of different vesting conditions, treatment of all non-vesting conditions and provides further guidance on the accounting treatment of cancellations by parties other than the entity.
- Amendments to IAS 20, Accounting for government grants and disclosure of government assistance, requires that the benefit of a below-market rate government loan is measured as the difference between the carrying amount in accordance with IAS 39 and the proceeds received, with the benefit accounted for in accordance with IAS 20.
- Amendments to IAS 23, Borrowing costs, changes the treatment of borrowing costs that are directly attributable to an acquisition, construction or production of a qualifying asset. These costs will consequently form part of the cost of that asset. Other borrowing costs are recognized as an expense.
- Under the amended IAS 32, Financial instruments: Presentation, the Group must classify puttable financial instruments or instruments or components thereof that impose

an obligation to deliver to another party, a pro-rata share of net assets of the entity only on liquidation, as equity. Previously, these instruments would have been classified as financial liabilities.

- Amendments to IFRIC 9 and IAS 39 clarify the accounting treatment of embedded derivatives when reclassifying financial instruments.
- IFRIC 13, Customer loyalty programs, addresses the accounting surrounding customer loyalty programs and whether some consideration should be allocated to free goods or services provided by a company. Consideration should be allocated to award credits based on their fair value, as they are a separately identifiable component.
- IFRIC 15, Agreements for the Construction of Real Estate, helps entities determine whether a particular construction agreement is within the scope of IAS 11 Construction Contracts, or IAS 18 Revenue. An issue is whether such an agreement constitutes a construction contract under IAS 11. If so, an entity should use the percentage-of-completion method to recognize revenue. If not, the entity should account for the agreement under IAS 18, which requires that revenue be recognized upon delivery of a good or service.
- IFRIC 16, Hedges of a Net Investment in a Foreign Operation clarifies the accounting treatment in respect of net investment hedging. This includes the fact that net investment hedging relates to differences in functional currency not presentation currency, and hedging instruments may be held anywhere in the group.
- IFRIC 18, Transfers of Assets from Customers clarifies the requirements for agreements in which an entity receives an item of property, plant and equipment or cash it is required to construct or acquire an item of property, plant and equipment that must be used to provide access to a supply of goods or services.
- In addition, a number of other amendments that form part of the IASB's annual improvement project were adopted by the Group.

The adoption of each of the above mentioned standards did not have a material impact to the consolidated financial statements.

Principles of consolidation The consolidated financial statements include the accounts of Nokia's parent company ('Parent Company'), and each of those companies over which the Group exercises control. Control over an entity is presumed to exist when the Group owns, directly or indirectly through subsidiaries, over 50% of the voting rights of the entity, the Group has the power to govern the operating and financial policies of the entity through agreement or the Group has the power to appoint or remove the majority of the members of the board of the entity.

The Group's share of profits and losses of associated companies is included in the consolidated income statement in accordance with the equity method of accounting. An associated company is an entity over which the Group exercises significant influence. Significant influence is generally presumed to exist when the Group owns, directly or indirectly through subsidiaries, over 20% of the voting rights of the company.

All inter-company transactions are eliminated as part of the consolidation process. Minority interests are presented separately as a component of net profit and they are shown as a component of shareholders' equity in the consolidated statement of financial position.

Profits realized in connection with the sale of fixed assets between the Group and associated companies are eliminated in proportion to share ownership. Such profits are deducted from the Group's equity and fixed assets and released in the Group accounts over the same period as depreciation is charged.

The companies acquired during the financial periods have been consolidated from the date on which control of the net assets and operations was transferred to the Group. Similarly the result of a Group company divested during an accounting period is included in the Group accounts only to the date of disposal.

Business combinations   The purchase method of accounting is used to account for acquisition of separate entities or businesses by the Group. The cost of an acquisition is measured as the aggregate of the fair values at the date of exchange of the assets given, liabilities incurred, equity instruments issued and costs directly attributable to the acquisition. Identifiable assets, liabilities and contingent liabilities acquired or assumed by the Group are measured separately at their fair value as of the acquisition date. The excess of the cost of the acquisition over the Group's interest in the fair value of the identifiable net assets acquired is recorded as goodwill.

Assessment of the recoverability of long-lived and intangible assets and goodwill   For the purposes of impairment testing, goodwill is allocated to cash-generating units that are expected to benefit from the synergies of the acquisition in which the goodwill arose.

The Group assesses the carrying amount of goodwill annually or more frequently if events or changes in circumstances indicate that such carrying amount may not be recoverable. The Group assesses the carrying amount of identifiable intangible assets and long-lived assets if events or changes in circumstances indicate that such carrying amount may not be recoverable. Factors that trigger an impairment review include underperformance relative to historical or projected future results, significant changes in the manner of the use of the acquired assets or the strategy for the overall business and significant negative industry or economic trends.

The Group conducts its impairment testing by determining the recoverable amount for the asset or cash-generating unit. The recoverable amount of an asset or a cash-generating unit is the higher of its fair value less costs to sell and its value in use. The recoverable amount is then compared to its carrying amount and an impairment loss is recognized if the recoverable amount is less than the carrying amount. Impairment losses are recognised immediately in the profit and loss account.

Foreign Currency Translation

Function and presentation currency   The financial statement[s] of all Group entities are measured using the currency of the primary economic environment in which the entity operates (functional currency). The consolidated financial statements are presented in Euro, which is the functional and presentational currency of the Parent Company.

Transactions in foreign currencies   Transactions in foreign currencies are recorded at the rates of exchange prevailing at the dates of the individual transactions. For practical reasons, a rate that approximates the actual rate at the date of the transaction is often used. At the end of the accounting period, the unsettled balances on foreign currency assets and liabilities are valued at the rates of exchange prevailing at the year-end. Foreign exchange gains and losses arising from statement of financial position items, as well as fair value changes in the related hedging instruments, are reported in financial income and expenses. For non-monetary items, such as shares, the unrealized foreign exchange gains and losses are recognized in the other comprehensive income.

Foreign group companies   In the consolidated accounts all income and expense of foreign subsidiaries are translated into Euro at the average foreign exchange rates for the accounting period. All assets and liabilities of foreign Group companies are translated into Euro at the year-end foreign exchange rates with the exception of goodwill arising on the acquisition of foreign companies prior to the adoption of IAS 21 (revised 2004) on January 1, 2005, which is translated to Euro at historical rates. Differences arising from the translation of income and expenses at the average rate and assets and liabilities at the closing rate are treated as an adjustment affecting consolidated shareholders' equity. On the disposal of all or part of a foreign Group company by sale, liquidation, repayment of share capital or abandonment, the cumulative amount or proportionate share of the translation difference is recognized as income or as expense in the same period in which the gain or loss on disposal is recognized.

Revenue Recognition   Sales from the majority of the Group are recognized when the significant risks and rewards of ownership have transferred to the buyer, continuing managerial involvement usually associated with ownership and effective control have ceased, the amount of revenue can be measured reliably, it is probable that economic benefits associated with the transaction will flow to the Group and the costs incurred or to be incurred in respect of the transaction can be measured reliably. The Group records reductions to revenue for special pricing agreements, price protection and other volume based discounts. Service revenue is generally recognized on a straight-line basis over the service period unless there is evidence that some other method better represents the stage of completion. License fees from usage are recognized in the period when they are reliably measurable which is normally when the customer reports them to the Group.

The Group enters into transactions involving multiple components consisting of any combination of hardware, services and software. The commercial effect of each separately identifiable component of the transaction is evaluated in order to reflect the substance of the transaction. The consideration received from these transactions is allocated to each separately identifiable component based on the relative fair value of each component. The Group determines the fair value of each component by taking into consideration factors such as the price when the component or a similar component is sold separately by the Group or a third party. The consideration allocated to each component is recognized as revenue when the revenue recognition criteria for that component have been met.

In addition, sales and cost of sales from contracts involving solutions achieved through modification of complex telecommunications equipment are recognized using the percentage of completion method when the outcome of the contract can be estimated reliably. A contract's outcome can be estimated reliably when total contract revenue and the costs to complete the contract can be estimated reliably, it is probable that the economic benefits associated with the contract will flow to the Group and the stage of contract completion can be measured reliably. When the Group is not able to meet those conditions, the policy is to recognize revenues only equal to costs incurred to date, to the extent that such costs are expected to be recovered.

Progress towards completion is measured by reference to cost incurred to date as a percentage of estimated total project costs, the cost-to-cost method. The percentage of completion method relies on estimates of total expected contract revenue and costs, as well as dependable measurement of the progress made towards completing a particular project. Recognized revenues and profits are subject to revisions during the project in the event that the assumptions regarding the overall project outcome are revised. The cumulative impact of a revision in estimates is recorded in the period such revisions become likely and estimable. Losses on projects in progress are recognized in the period they become probable and estimable.

Shipping and Handling Costs   The costs of shipping and distribution products are included in cost of sales.

Research and Development   Research and development costs are expensed as they are incurred, except for certain development costs, which are capitalized when it is probable that a development project will generate future economic benefits and certain criteria, including commercial and technological feasibility, have been met. Capitalized development costs, comprising direct labour and related overhead, are amortized on a systematic basis over their expected useful lives between two and five years.

Capitalized development costs are subject to regular assessments of recoverability based on anticipated future revenues, including the impact of changes in technology. Unamortized capitalized development costs determined to be in excess of their recoverable amounts are expensed immediately.

Other Intangible Assets   Acquired patents, trademarks, licences, software licenses for internal use, customer relationships and developed technology are capitalized and amortized using the straight-line method over their useful lives, generally 3 to 6 years, but not exceeding 20 years. Where an indication of impairment exists, the carrying amount of any intangible asset is assessed and written down to its recoverable amount.

Pensions   The Group companies have various pension schemes in accordance with the local conditions and practices in the countries in which they operate. The schemes are generally funded through payments to insurance companies or to trustee-administered funds as determined by periodic actuarial calculations.

In a defined contribution plan, the Group has no legal or constructive obligation to make any additional contributions if the party receiving the contributions is unable to pay the pension obligations in question. The Group's contributions to defined contributions plans, multi-employer and insured plans are recognized in the income statement in the period to which the contributions relate.

All arrangements that do not fulfil these conditions are considered defined benefit plans. If a defined benefit plan is funded through an insurance contract where the Group does not retain any legal or constructive obligations, such a plan is treated as a defined contribution plan.

For defined benefit plans, pension costs are assessed using the projected unit credit method. The pension cost is recognized in the income statement so as to spread the service cost over the service lives of employees. The pension obligation is measured as the present value of the estimated future cash outflows using interest rates on high quality corporate bonds with appropriate maturities. Actuarial gains and losses outside the corridor are recognized over the average remaining service lives of employees. The corridor is defined as ten percent of the greater of the value of the plan assets or defined benefit obligation at the beginning of the respective year.

Past service costs are recognized immediately in income, unless the changes to the pension plan are conditional on the employees remaining in service for a specific period of time (the vesting period). In this case, the past service costs are amortized on a straight-line basis over the vesting period.

The liability (or asset) recognized in the statement of financial position is pension obligation at the closing date less the fair value of plan assets, the share of unrecognized actuarial gains and losses, and past service costs. Any net pension asset is limited to unrecognized actuarial losses, past service cost, the present value of available refunds from the plan and expected reductions in future contributions to the plan.

Property, Plant and Equipment   Property, plant and equipment are stated at cost less accumulated depreciation. Depreciation is recorded on a straight-line basis over the expected useful lives of the assets as follows:

Buildings and constructions	20−33 years
Production machinery, measuring and test equipment	1−3 years
Other machinery and equipment	3−10 years

Land and water areas are not depreciated.

Maintenance, repairs and renewals are generally charged to expense during the financial period in which they are incurred. However, major renovations are capitalized and included in the carrying amount of the asset when it is probable that future economic benefits in excess of the originally assessed standard of performance of the existing asset will flow to the Group. Major renovations are depreciated over the remaining useful life of the related asset. Leasehold improvements are depreciated over the shorter of the lease term or useful life.

Gains and losses on the disposal of fixed assets are included in operating profit/loss.

Leases   The Group has entered into various operating leases, the payments under which are treated as rentals and recognized in the profit and loss account on a straight-line basis over the lease term unless another systematic approach is more representative of the pattern of the user's benefit.

Inventories   Inventories are stated at the lower of cost or net realizable value. Cost is determined using standard cost, which approximates actual cost on a FIFO (First-in First-out) basis. Net realizable value is the amount that can be realized from the sale of the inventory in the normal course of business after allowing for the costs of realization.

In addition to the cost of materials and direct labour, an appropriate proportion of production overhead is included in the inventory values.

An allowance is recorded for excess inventory and obsolescence based on the lower of cost or net realizable value.

Financial Assets   The Group has classified its financial assets as one of the following categories: available-for-sale investments, loans and receivables, financial assets at fair value through profit or loss and bank and cash.

Available-for-sale investments   The Group classifies the following investments as available-for-sale based on the purpose for acquiring the investments as well as ongoing intentions: (1) highly liquid, interest-bearing investments with maturities at acquisition of less than 3 months, which are classified in the balance sheet as current available-for-sale investments, cash equivalents, (2) similar types of investments as in category (1), but with maturities at acquisition of longer than 3 months, classified in the balance sheet as current available-for-sale investments, liquid assets, (3) investments in technology related publicly quoted equity shares, or unlisted private equity shares and unlisted funds, classified in the balance sheet as non-current available-for-sale investments.

Current fixed income and money-market investments are fair valued by using quoted market rates, discounted cash flow analyses and other appropriate valuation models at the balance sheet date. Investments in publicly quoted equity shares are measured at fair value using 3 exchange quoted bid prices. Other available-for-sale investments carried at fair value include holdings in unlisted shares. Fair value is estimated by using various factors, including, but not limited to: (1) the current market value of similar instruments, (2) prices established from a recent arm's length financing transaction of the target companies, (3) analysis of market prospects and operating performance of the target companies taking into consideration the public market of comparable companies in similar industry sectors. The remaining available-for-sale investments are carried at cost less impairment, which are technology related investments in private equity shares and unlisted funds for which the fair value cannot be measured reliably due to non-existence of public markets or reliable valuation methods against which to value these assets. The investment and disposal decisions on these investments are business driven.

All purchases and sales of investments are recorded on the trade date, which is the date that the Group commits to purchase or sell the asset.

The fair value changes of available-for-sale investments are recognized in fair value and other reserves as part of the shareholders' equity, with the exception of interest calculated using effective interest method and foreign exchange gains and losses on monetary assets, which are recognized directly in profit and loss. Dividends on available-for-sale equity instruments are recognized in profit and loss when the Group's right to receive payment is established. When the investment is disposed of, the related accumulated fair value changes are released from shareholders' equity and recognized in the income statement. The weighted average method is used when determining the cost-basis of publicly listed equities being disposed of. FIFO (First-in First-out) method is used to determine the cost basis of fixed income securities being disposed of. An impairment is recorded when the carrying amount of an available-for-sale investment is greater than the estimated fair value and there is objective evidence that the asset is impaired including but not limited to counterparty default and other factors causing a reduction in value that can be considered permanent. The cumulative net loss relating to that investment is removed from equity and recognized in the income statement for the period. If, in a subsequent period, the fair value of the investment in a non-equity instrument increases and the increase can be objectively related to an event occurring after the loss was recognized, the loss is reversed, with the amount of the reversal included in the income statement.

Loans and receivables   Loans and receivables include loans to customers and suppliers and are initially measured at fair value and subsequently at amortised cost using the effective interest method less impairment. Loans are subject to regular and thorough review as to their collectability and as to available collateral; in the event that any loan is deemed not fully recoverable, a provision is made to reflect the shortfall between the carrying amount and the present value of the expected cash flows. Interest income on loans receivable is recognised by applying the effective interest rate. The long-term portion of loans receivable is included on the statement of financial position under long-term loans receivable and the current portion under current portion of long-term loans receivable.

Financial assets at fair value through profit and loss   Financial investments at fair value through profit and loss include highly liquid financial assets designated at fair value through profit or loss at inception. For investments designated as at fair value through profit or loss, the following criteria must be met: (1) the designation eliminates or significantly reduces the inconsistent treatment that would otherwise arise from measuring the assets or recognizing gains or losses on a different basis; or (2) the assets are part of a group of financial assets, which are managed and their performance evaluated on a fair value basis, in accordance with a documented risk management or investment strategy.

These investments are initially recorded at fair value. Subsequent to initial recognition, these investments are re-measured at fair value. Fair value adjustments and realized gain and loss are recognized in the income statement.

Bank and cash   Bank and cash consist of cash at bank and in hand.

Accounts receivable   Accounts receivable are carried at the original amount due from customers, which is considered to be fair value, less allowances for doubtful accounts based on a periodic review of all outstanding amounts including an analysis of historical bad debt, customer concentrations, customer creditworthiness, current economic trends and changes in our customer payment terms. Bad debts are written off when identified as uncollectable, and are included within other operating expenses.

Financial Liabilities

Loans payable   Loans payable are recognized initially at fair value, net of transaction costs incurred. Any difference between the fair value and the proceeds received is recognized in profit and loss at initial recognition. In the subsequent periods, they are stated at amortized cost using the effective interest method. The long-term portion of loans payable is included on the statement of financial position under long-term interest-bearing liabilities and the current portion under current portion of long-term loans.

Accounts payable   Accounts payable are carried at the original invoiced amount, which is considered to be fair value due to the short-term nature.

Derivative financial instruments   All derivatives are initially recognized at fair value on the date a derivative contract is entered into and are subsequently re-measured at their fair value. The method of recognizing the resulting gain or loss varies according to whether the derivatives are designated and qualify under hedge accounting or not. Generally the cash flows of a hedge are classified as cash flows from operating activities in the consolidated statement of cash flows as the underlying hedged items relate to company's operating activities. When a derivative contract is accounted for as a hedge of an identifiable position relating to financing or investing activities, the cash flows of the contract are classified in the same manner as the cash flows of the position being hedged.

Derivatives not designated in hedge accounting relationships carried at fair value through profit and loss Fair values of forward rate agreements, interest rate options, futures contracts and exchange traded options are calculated based on quoted market rates at each balance sheet date. Discounted cash flow analyses are used to value interest rate and currency swaps. Changes in the fair value of these contracts are recognized in the income statement.

Fair values of cash settled equity derivatives are calculated based on quoted market rates at each balance sheet date. Changes in fair value are recognized in the income statement.

Forward foreign exchange contracts are valued at the market forward exchange rates. Changes in fair value are measured by comparing these rates with the original contract forward rate. Currency options are valued at each balance sheet date by using the Garman & Kohlhagen option valuation model. Changes in the fair value on these instruments are recognized in the income statement.

For the derivatives not designated under hedge accounting but hedging identifiable exposures such as anticipated foreign currency denominated sales and purchases, the gains and losses are recognized within other operating income or expenses. The gains and losses on all other hedges not designated under hedge accounting are recognized under financial income and expenses.

Embedded derivatives are identified and monitored by the Group and fair valued as at each balance sheet date. In assessing the fair value of embedded derivatives, the Group employs a variety of methods including option pricing models and discounted cash flow analysis using assumptions that are based on market conditions existing at each balance sheet date. The fair value changes are recognized in the income statement.

Hedge Accounting

Cash flow hedges; Hedging of anticipated foreign currency denominated sales and purchases The Group applies hedge accounting for 'Qualifying Hedges'. Qualifying hedges are those properly documented cash flow hedges of the foreign exchange rate risk of future anticipated foreign currency denominated sales and purchases that meet the requirements set out in IAS 39. The cash flow being hedged must be 'highly probable' and must present an exposure to variations in cash flows that could ultimately affect profit or loss. The hedge must be highly effective both prospectively and retrospectively.

The Group claims hedge accounting in respect of certain forward exchange contracts and options, or option strategies, which have zero net premium or a net premium paid, and where the critical terms of the bought and sold options within a collar or zero premium structure are the same and where the nominal amount of the sold option component is no greater than that of the bought option.

For qualifying foreign exchange forwards the change in fair value that reflects the change in spot exchange rates is deferred in shareholders' equity to the extent that the hedge is effective. For qualifying foreign exchange options, or option strategies, the change in intrinsic value is deferred in shareholders' equity to the extent that the hedge is still effective. In all cases the ineffective portion is recognized immediately in the profit and loss account as financial income and expenses. Hedging costs, expressed either as the change in fair value that reflects the change in forward exchange rates less the change in spot exchange rates for forward foreign exchange contracts, or changes in the time value for options, or options strategies, are recognized within other operating income or expenses.

Accumulated fair value changes from qualifying hedges are released from shareholders' equity into the income statement as adjustments to sales and cost of sales, in the period when the hedged cash flow affects the income statement. If the hedged cash flow is no longer expected to take place, all deferred gains or losses are released immediately into the profit and loss account as adjustments to sales and cost of sales. If the hedged cash flow ceases to be highly probable, but is still expected to take place, accumulated gains and losses remain in equity until the hedged cash flow affects the income statement.

Changes in the fair value of any derivative instruments that do not qualify for hedge accounting under IAS 39 are recognized immediately in the income statement. The fair value changes of derivative instruments that directly relate to normal business operations are recognized within other operating income and expenses. The fair value changes from all other derivative instruments are recognized in financial income and expenses.

Cash flow hedges: Hedging of foreign currency risk of highly probable business acquisitions and other transactions   The Group hedges the cash flow variability due to foreign currency risk inherent in highly probable business acquisitions and other future transactions that result in the recognition of non-financial assets. When those non-financial assets are recognized in the balance sheet the gains and losses previously deferred in equity are transferred from equity and included in the initial acquisition cost of the asset. The deferred amounts are ultimately recognized in the profit and loss as a result of goodwill assessments in case of business acquisitions and through depreciation in cash of other assets. In order to apply for hedge accounting, the forecasted transactions must be highly probable and the hedges must be highly effective prospectively and retrospectively.

The Group claims hedge accounting in respect of forward foreign exchange contracts, foreign currency denominated loans, and options, or option strategies, which have zero net premium or a net premium paid, and where the terms of the bought and sold options within a collar or zero premium structure are the same.

For qualifying foreign exchange forwards, the change in fair value that reflects the change in spot exchange rates is deferred in shareholders' equity. The change in fair value that reflects the change in forward exchange rates less the change in spot exchange rates is recognized in the profit and loss account within financial income and expenses. For qualifying foreign exchange options the change in intrinsic value is deferred in shareholders' equity. Changes in the time value are at all times recognized directly in the profit and loss account as financial income and expenses. In all cases the ineffective portion is recognized immediately in the income statement as financial income and expenses.

Cash flow hedges: Hedging of cash flow variability on variable rate liabilities   The Group applies cash flow hedge accounting for hedging cash flow variability on variable rate liabilities. The effective portion of the gain or loss relating to interest rate swaps hedging variable rate borrowings is deferred in shareholders' equity. The gain or loss relating to the ineffective portion is recognized immediately in the income statement as financial income and expenses.

Fair value hedges   The Group applies fair value hedge accounting with the objective to reduce the exposure to fluctuations in the fair value of interest-bearing liabilities due to changes in interest rates and foreign exchange rates. Changes in the fair value of derivatives designated and qualifying as fair value hedges, together with any changes in the fair value of the hedged liabilities attributable to the hedged risk, are recorded in the income statement within financial income and expenses.

If a hedge no longer meets the criteria for hedge accounting, hedge accounting ceases and any fair value adjustments made to the carrying amount of the hedged item during the periods the hedge was effective are amortized to profit or loss based on the effective interest method.

Hedges of net investments in foreign operations   The Group also applies hedge accounting for its foreign currency hedging on net investments.

Qualifying hedges are those properly documented hedges of the foreign exchange rate risk of foreign currency denominated net investments that meet the requirements set out in IAS 39. The hedge must be effective both prospectively and retrospectively.

The Group claims hedge accounting in respect of foreign exchange contracts, foreign currency denominated loans, and options, or option strategies, which have zero net premiums or a net premium paid, and where the terms of the bought and sold options within a collar or zero premium structure are the same.

For qualifying foreign exchange forwards, the change in fair value that reflects the change in spot exchange rates is deferred in shareholders' equity. The change in fair value that reflects the change in forward exchange rates less the change in spot exchange rates is recognized in the profit and loss account within financial income and expenses. For qualifying foreign exchange options the change in intrinsic value is deferred in the shareholders' equity. Changes in the time value are at all times recognized directly in the profit and loss account as financial income and expenses. If a foreign currency denominated loan is used as a hedge, all foreign exchange gains and losses arising from the transaction are recognized in shareholders' equity. In all cases the ineffective portion is recognized immediately in the income statement as financial income and expenses.

Accumulated fair value changes from qualifying hedges are released from shareholders' equity into the income statement only if the legal entity in the given country is sold, liquidated, repays its share capital or is abandoned.

Income taxes   The tax expense comprises current tax and deferred tax. Current taxes are based on the results of the Group companies and are calculated according to local tax rules. Taxes are recognized in the income statement, except to the extent that it relates to items recognized in the other comprehensive income or directly in equity, in which case the tax is recognized in other comprehensive income or equity, respectively.

Deferred tax assets and liabilities are determined, using the liability method, for all temporary difference arising between the tax bases of assets and liabilities and their carrying amounts in the consolidated financial statements. Deferred tax assets are recognized to the extent that it is probable that future taxable profit will be available against which the unused tax losses or deductible temporary differences can be utilized. When circumstances indicate it is no longer probable that deferred tax assets will be utilized, they are assessed for realizability and adjusted as necessary. Deferred tax liabilities are recognized for temporary differences that arise between the fair value and tax base of identifiable net assets acquired in business combinations. Deferred tax assets and deferred tax liabilities are offset for presentation purposes when there is a legally enforceable right to set off current tax assets against current tax liabilities, and the deferred tax assets and the deferred tax liabilities relate to income taxes levied by the same taxation authority on either the same taxable entity or different taxable entities which intend either to settle current tax liabilities and assets on a net basis, or to realize the assets and settle the liabilities simultaneously, in each future period in which significant amounts of deferred tax liabilities or assets are expected to be settled or recovered.

The enacted or substantially enacted tax rates as of each balance sheet date that are expected to apply in the period when the asset is realized or the liability is settled are used in the measurement of deferred tax assets and liabilities.

Provisions   Provisions are recognized when the Group has a present legal or constructive obligation as a result of past events, it is probable that an outflow of resources will be required to settle the obligation and a reliable estimate of the amount can be made. Where the Group expects a provision to be reimbursed, the reimbursement is recognized as an asset only when the reimbursement is virtually certain. At each balance sheet date, the Group assesses the adequacy of its pre-existing provisions and adjusts the amounts as necessary based on actual experience and changes in future estimates.

Warranty provisions   The Group provides for the estimated liability to repair or replace products under warranty at the time revenue is recognized. The provision is an estimate calculated based on historical experience of the level of repairs and replacements.

Intellectual property rights (IPR) provisions   The Group provides for the estimated future settlements related to asserted and unasserted past alleged IPR infringements based on the probable outcome of potential infringement.

Tax provisions   The Group recognizes a provision for tax contingencies based upon the estimated future settlement amount at each balance sheet date.

Restructuring provisions   The Group provides for the estimated cost to restructure when a detailed formal plan of restructuring has been completed and the restructuring plan has been announced.

Other provisions   The Group recognizes the estimated liability for non-cancellable purchase commitments for inventory in excess of forecasted requirements at each balance sheet date.

The Group provides for onerous contracts based on the lower of the expected cost of fulfilling the contract and the expected cost of terminating the contract.

Share-based compensation   The Group offers three types of global equity settled share-based compensation schemes for employees: stock options, performance shares and restricted shares. Employee services received, and the corresponding increase in equity, are measured by reference to the fair value of the equity instruments as of the date of grant, excluding the impact of any non-market vesting conditions. Non-market vesting conditions attached to the performance shares are included in assumptions about the number of shares that the employee will ultimately receive. On a regular basis, the Group reviews the assumptions made and, where necessary, revises its estimates of the number of performance shares that are expected to be settled. Share-based compensation is recognized as an expense in the income statement over the service period. A separate vesting period is defined for each quarterly lot of the stock options plans. When stock options are exercised, the proceeds received net of any transaction costs are credited to share issue premium and the reserve for invested non-restricted equity.

Treasury shares   The Group recognizes acquired treasury shares as a deduction from equity at their acquisition cost. When cancelled, the acquisition cost of treasury shares is recognized in retained earnings.

Dividends   Dividends proposed by the Board of Directors are not recorded in the financial statements until they have been approved by the shareholders at the Annual General Meeting.

Earnings per share   The Group calculates both basic and diluted earnings per share. Basic earnings per share is computed using the weighted average number of shares outstanding during the period. Diluted earnings per share is computed using the weighted average number of shares outstanding during the period plus the dilutive effect of stock options, restricted shares and performance shares outstanding during the period.

Use of estimates and critical accounting judgements   The preparation of financial statements in conformity with IFRS requires the application of judgement by management in selecting appropriate assumptions for calculating financial estimates, which inherently contain some degree of uncertainty. Management bases its estimates on historical experience and various other assumptions that are believed to be reasonable under the circumstances, the results of which form the basis for making judgements about the reported carrying values of assets and liabilities and the reported amounts of revenues and expenses that may not be readily apparent from other sources. Actual results may differ from these estimates under different assumptions or conditions.

Set forth below are areas requiring significant judgement and estimation that may have an impact on reported results and the financial position.

Revenue recognition   Sales from the majority of the Group are recognized when the significant risks and rewards of ownership have transferred to the buyer, continuing managerial involvement usually associated with ownership and effective control have ceased, the amount of revenue can be measured reliably, it is probable that economic benefits associated with the transaction will flow to the Group and the costs incurred or to be incurred in respect of the transaction can be measured reliably.

Sales may materially change if management's assessment of such criteria was determined to be inaccurate. The Group enters into transactions involving multiple components consisting of any combination of hardware, services and software. The consideration received from these transactions is allocated to each separately identifiable component based on the relative fair value of each component. The consideration allocated to each component is recognized as revenue when the revenue criteria for that component have been met. Determination of the fair value for each component requires the use of estimates and judgement taking into consideration factors such as the price when the component is sold separately by the Group or the price when a similar component is sold separately by the Group or a third party, which may have a significant effect on the timing and amount of revenue recognition.

The Group makes price protection adjustments based on estimates of future price reductions and certain agreed customer inventories at the date of the price adjustment. Possible changes to these estimates could result in revisions to the sales in future periods.

Revenue from contracts involving solutions achieved through modification of complex telecommunications equipment is recognized on the percentage of completion basis when the outcome of the contract can be estimated reliably. Recognized revenues and profits are subject to revisions during the project in the event that the assumptions regarding the overall project outcome are revised. Current sales and profit estimates for projects may materially change due to the early stage of a long-term project, new technology, changes in the project scope, changes in costs, changes in timing, changes in customers' plans, realization of penalties, and other corresponding factors.

Customer financing   The Group has provided a limited number of customer financing arrangements and agreed extended payment terms with selected customers. Should the actual financial position of the customers or general economic conditions differ from assumptions, the ultimate collectability of such financings and trade credits may be required to be re-assessed, which could result in a write-off of these balances and thus negatively impact profit in future periods. The Group endeavours to mitigate this risk through the transfer of its rights to the cash collected from these arrangements to third party financial institutions on a non-recourse basis in exchange for an upfront cash payment.

Allowances for doubtful accounts   The Group maintains allowances for doubtful accounts for estimated losses resulting from the subsequent inability of customers to make required payments. If the financial conditions of customers were to deteriorate, resulting in an impairment of their ability to make payments, additional allowances may be required in future periods.

Inventory-related allowances   The Group periodically reviews inventory for excess amounts, obsolescence and declines in market value below cost and records an allowance against the inventory balance for such declines. These reviews require management to estimate future demand for products. Possible changes in these estimates could result in revisions to the valuation of inventory in future periods.

Warranty provisions   The Group provides for the estimated cost of product warranties at the time revenue is recognized. The Group's warranty provision is established based upon best estimates of the amounts necessary to settle future and existing claims on products sold as of each balance sheet date. As new products incorporating complex technologies are continuously introduced, and as local laws, regulations and practices may change, changes in these estimates could result in additional allowances or changes to recorded allowances being required in future periods.

Provision for intellectual property rights, or IPR, infringements   The Group provides for the estimated future settlements related to asserted and unasserted past alleged IPR infringements based on the probable outcome of potential infringement. IPR infringement claims can last for varying periods of time, resulting in irregular movements in the IPR infringement provision.

The ultimate outcome or actual cost of settling an individual infringement may materially vary from estimates.

Legal contingencies   Legal proceedings covering a wide range of matters are pending or threatened in various jurisdictions against the Group. Provisions are recorded for pending litigation when it is determined that an unfavourable outcome is probable and the amount of loss can be reasonably estimated. Due to the inherent uncertain nature of litigation, the ultimate outcome or actual cost of settlement may materially vary from estimates.

Capitalized development costs   The Group capitalizes certain development costs when it is probable that a development project will generate future economic benefits and certain criteria, including commercial and technological feasibility, have been met. Should a product fail to substantiate its estimated feasibility or life cycle, material development costs may be required to be written-off in future periods.

Business combinations   The Group applies the purchase method of accounting to account for acquisitions of businesses. The cost of an acquisition is measured as the aggregate of the fair values at the date of exchange of the assets given, liabilities incurred, equity instruments issued and costs directly attributable to the acquisition. Identifiable assets, liabilities and contingent liabilities acquired or assumed are measured separately at their fair value as of the acquisition date. The excess of the cost of the acquisition over our interest in the fair value of the identifiable net assets acquired is recorded as goodwill.

The allocation of fair values to the identifiable assets acquired and liabilities assumed is based on various valuation assumptions requiring management judgement. Actual results may differ from the forecasted amounts and the difference could be material. See also Note 8.

Assessment of the recoverability of long-lived assets, intangible assets and goodwill   The recoverable amounts for long-lived assets, intangible assets and goodwill have been determined based on the expected future cash flows attributable to the asset or cash-generating unit discounted to present value. The key assumptions applied in the determination of recoverable amount include the discount rate, length of the explicit forecast period and estimated growth rates, profit margins and level of operational and capital investment. Amounts estimated could differ materially from what will actually occur in the future. See also Note 7.

Fair value of derivatives and other financial instruments   The fair value of financial instruments that are not traded in an active market (for example, unlisted equities, currency options and embedded derivatives) are determined using various valuation techniques. The Group uses judgement to select an appropriate valuation methodology as well as underlying assumptions based on existing market practice and conditions. Changes in these assumptions may cause the Group to recognize impairment or losses in future periods.

Income taxes   Management judgement is required in determining income tax expense, tax provisions, deferred tax assets and liabilities and the extent to which deferred tax assets can be recognized. When circumstances indicate it is no longer probable that deferred tax assets will be utilized they are assessed for realizability and adjusted as necessary. If the final outcome of these matters differs from the amounts initially recorded, differences may impact on the income tax expense in the period in which such determination is made.

Pensions   The determination of pension benefit obligation and expense for defined benefit pension plans is dependent on the selection of certain assumptions used by actuaries in calculating such amounts. Those assumptions include, among others, the discount rate, expected long-term rate of return on plan assets and annual rate of increase in future compensation levels. A portion of plan assets is invested in equity securities which are subject to equity market volatility. Changes in assumptions and actuarial conditions may materially affect the pension obligation and future expense. See also Note 5.

Share-based compensation   The Group operates various types of equity settled share-based compensation schemes for employees. Fair value of stock options is based on certain assumptions, including, among others, expected volatility and expected life of the options. Non-market vesting conditions attached to performance shares are included in assumptions about the number of shares that the employee will ultimately receive relating to projections of net sales and earnings per share. Significant differences in equity market performance, employee option activity and the Group's projected and actual net sales and earnings per share performance, may materially affect future expense. See also Note 23.

New accounting pronouncements under IFRS   The Group will adopt the following new and revised standards, amendments and interpretations to existing standards issued by the IASB that are expected to be relevant to its operations:

IFRS 3 (revised) Business Combinations replace IFRS 3 (as issued in 2004). The main changes brought about by IFRS 3 (revised) include clarification of the definition of a business, immediate recognition of all acquisition-related costs in profit or loss, recognition of subsequent changes in the fair value of contingent consideration in accordance with other IFRSs and measurement of goodwill arising from step-acquisitions at the acquisition date.

IAS 27 (revised) 'Consolidated and Separate Financial Statements' clarifies presentation of changes in parent-subsidiary ownership. Changes in a parent's ownership interest in a subsidiary that do not result in the loss of control must be accounted for exclusively within equity. If a parent loses control of a subsidiary it shall derecognize the consolidated assets and liabilities, and any investment retained in the former subsidiary shall be recognized at fair value at the date when control is lost. Any differences resulting from this shall be recognized in profit or loss. When losses attributed to the minority (non-controlling) interests exceed the minority's interest in the subsidiary's equity, these losses shall be allocated to the non-controlling interests even if this results in a deficit balances.

IFRS 9 will change the classification, measurement and impairment of financial instruments based on our objectives for the related contractual cash flows.

Amendments to IFRS 2 and IFRIC 11 that an entity that receives goods or services in a share-based payment arrangement should account for those goods or services no matter which entity in the group settles the transaction, and no matter whether the transaction is settled in shares or cash.

Amendment to IAS 32 requires that if rights issues offered are issued pro rata to entity's all existing shareholders in the same class for a fixed amount of currency, they should be classified as equity regardless of the currency in which the exercise price is denominated.

Amendments to IFRC 14 and IAS 19 address the circumstances when an entity is subject to minimum funding requirements and makes an early payment of contributions to cover those requirements. The amendment permits such an entity to treat the benefit of such an early payment as an asset.

IFRIC 19 clarifies the requirements when an entity renegotiates the terms of a financial liability with its creditor and the creditor agrees to accept the entity's equity instruments to settle the financial liability fully or partially. The entity's equity instruments issued to a creditor are part of the consideration paid to extinguish the financial liability and the issued instruments should be measured at their fair value.

In addition, there are a number of other amendments that form part of the IASB's annual improvement project which will be adopted by the Group on January 1, 2010.

The Group will adopt IFRS 3 (revised), IAS 27 (revised) and the amendments to IFRS 2 and IFRIC 11, IFRIC 14 and IAS 19 and IAS 32 as well as the additional amendments that form part of the IASB's annual improvement project on January 1, 2011. The Group does not expect that the adoption of these new standards, interpretations and amendments will have a material impact on the financial condition and results of operations.

The Group is required to adopt IFRS 9 by January 1, 2013 with earlier adoption permitted. The Group is currently evaluating the potential impact of this standard on the Group's accounts.

2. Segment Information   Nokia is organized on a worldwide basis into three operating and reportable segments: Devices and Services, NAVTEQ, and Nokia Siemens Networks. Nokia's reportable segments represent the strategic business units for which monthly financial information is provided to the chief operating decision maker.

As of January 1, 2008, the Group's three mobile device business groups and the supporting horizontal groups have been replaced by an integrated business segment, Devices and Services. Commencing with the third quarter 2008, NAVTEQ is also a reportable segment. Prior period results for Nokia and its reportable segments have been regrouped for comparability purposes according to the new reportable segments effective in 2008.

Devices and Services is responsible for developing and managing the Group's portfolio of mobile devices, services and their combinations as well as designing and developing services, applications and content. Devices and Services also manages our supply chains, sales channels, brand and marketing activities, and explores corporate strategic and future growth opportunities for Nokia.

NAVTEQ is a leading provider of comprehensive digital map information and related location-based content and services for automotive navigation systems and mobile navigation devices, internet-based mapping applications, and government and business solutions.

Nokia Siemens Networks provides mobile and fixed network solutions and related services to operators and service providers.

Corporate Common Functions consist of companywide functions.

The accounting policies of the segments are the same as those described in Note 1. Nokia accounts for intersegment revenues and transfers as if the revenues or transfers were to third parties, that is, at current market prices. Nokia evaluates the performance of its segments and allocates resources to them based on operating profit.

No single customer represents 10% or more of Group revenues.

2009 EURm	Devices and services	NAVTEQ	Nokia Siemens Networks	Total reportable segments	Corporate[4,6] common functions and corporate unallocated	Eliminations	Group
Profit and loss information							
Net sales to external customers	27,841	579	12,564	40,984	—		40,984
Net sales to other segments	12	91	10	113	—	−113	—
Depreciation and amortization	432	488	860	1,780	4		1,784
Impairments	56	—	919	975	34		1,009
Operating profit/loss[1]	3,314	−344	−1,639	1,331	−134		1,197
Share of results of associate companies	—	—	32	32	−2		30
Balance sheet information							
Capital expenditure[2]	232	21	278	531	—		531
Segment assets[3] of which:	9,203	6,145	11,015	26,363	12,479	−3,104	35,738
Investments in associate companies	−5	5	26	31	38		69
Segment liabilities[5]	8,268	2,330	7,927	18,525	5,568	−3,104	20,989
2008 EURm profit and loss information							
Net sales to external customers	35,084	318	15,308	50,710	—		50,710
Net sales to other segments	15	43	1	59	—	−59	—
Depreciation and amortization	484	238	889	1,611	6		1,617
Impairment	58	—	47	105	33		138
Operating profit/loss	5,816	−153	−301	5,362	−396		4,966
Share of results of associated companies	—	—	−13	−13	19		6

2009 EURm	Devices and services	NAVTEQ	Nokia Siemens Networks	Total reportable segments	Corporate[4,6] common functions and corporate unallocated	Eliminations	Group
Balance sheet information							
Capital expenditures[2]	578	18	292	888	1		889
Segment assets[3] of which:	10,300	7,177	15,652	33,129	9,641	−3,188	39,582
Investments in associate companies	—	4	62	66	30		96
Segment liabilities[5]	8,425	2,726	10,503	21,654	4,606	−3,188	23,072
2007 EURm profit and loss information							
Net sales to external customers	37,682	—	13,376	51,058	—		51,058
Net sales to other segments	23	—	17	40	41	−81	—
Depreciation and amortization	489	—	714	1,203	3		1,206
Operating profit/loss[1]	7,584	—	1,308	6,276	1,709		7,985
Share of results of associated companies	—	—	4	4	40		44

[1] Nokia Siemens Networks operating loss in 2009 includes a goodwill impairment loss of EUR 908 million. Corporate Common Functions operating profit in 2007 includes a non-taxable gain of EUR 1,879 million related to the formation of Nokia Siemens Networks.

[2] Including goodwill and capitalized development costs, capital expenditures in 2009 amount to EUR 590 million (EUR 502 million in 2008). The goodwill and capitalized development costs consist of EUR 7 million in 2009 (EUR 752 million in 2008) for Devices & Services, EUR 22 million in 2009 (EUR 3,673 million in 2008) for NAVTEQ, EUR 30 million in 2009 (EUR 188 million in 2008) for Nokia Siemens Networks, and EUR 0 million in 2009 (EUR 0 million in 2008) for Corporate Common Functions.

[3] Comprises intangible assets, property plant and equipment, investments, inventories and accounts receivable as well as prepaid expenses and accrued income except those related to interest and taxes for Devices and Services and Corporate Common functions. In addition, NAVTEQ's and Nokia Siemens Networks' assets include cash and other liquid assets, available-for-sale investments, long-term loans receivable and other financial assets as well as interest and tax related prepaid expenses and accrued income. These are directly attributable to NAVTEQ and Nokia Siemens Networks as they are separate legal entities.

[4] Unallocated assets include cash and other liquid assets, available-for-sale investments, long-term loans receivable, and other financial assets as well as interest and tax related prepaid expenses and accrued income for Devices & Services and Corporate Common Functions.

[5] Comprises accounts payable, accrued expenses and provisions except those related to interest and taxes for Devices & Services and Corporate Common Functions. In addition, NAVTEQ's and Nokia Siemens Networks' liabilities include non-current liabilities and short-term borrowings as well as interest and tax related prepaid income and accrued expenses and provisions. These are directly attributable to NAVTEQ and Nokia Siemens Networks as they are separate legal entities.

[6] Unallocated liabilities include non-current liabilities and short-term borrowings as well as interest and tax related prepaid income, accrued expenses and provisions related to Devices & Services and Corporate Common Functions.

Net sales to external customers by geographic area by location of customer

	2009	*2008 EURm*	*2007 EURm*
Finland	390	362	322
China	5,990	5,916	5,898
India	2,809	3,719	3,684
UK	1,916	2,382	2,574
Germany	1,733	2,294	2,641
USA	1,731	1,907	2,124
Russia	1,528	2,083	2,012
Indonesia	1,458	2,046	1,754
Other	23,249	30,001	30,049
Total	40,984	50,710	51,058

Segment non-current assets by geographic area[1]

	2009 EURm	*2008 EURm*
Finland	1,698	1,154
China	358	434
India	180	154
UK	228	668
Germany	243	306
USA	5,859	7,037
Other	1,377	2,751
Total	9,943	12,504

[1] *Comprises intangible and tangible assets and property, plant and equipment.*

3. Percentage of Completion

Contract sales recognized under percentage of completion accounting were EUR 6,868 million in 2009 (EUR 9,220 million in 2008 and EUR 8,329 million in 2007). Service revenue for managed services and network maintenance contracts were EUR 2,607 million in 2009 (EUR 2,530 million in 2008 and EUR 1,842 million in 2007).

Included in accrued expenses were advances received related to construction contracts of EUR 136 million at December 31, 2009 (EUR 261 million in 2008). Included in accounts receivable were contract revenues recorded prior to billings of EUR 1,396 million at December 31, 2009 (EUR 1,423 million in 2008) and billings in excess of costs incurred of EUR 451 million at December 31, 2009 (EUR 677 million in 2008).

The aggregate amount of costs incurred and recognized (net of recognized losses) under open construction contracts in progress since inception (for contracts acquired inception refers to April 1, 2007) was EUR 15,351 million in 2009 (EUR 11,707 million in 2008).

Retentions related to construction contracts, included in accounts receivable, were EUR 265 million at December 31, 2009 (EUR 211 million at December 31, 2008).

4. Personnel Expenses

EURm	2009	2008	2007
Wages and salaries	5,658	5,615	4,664
Share-based compensation expense, total	13	67	236
Pension expenses, net	427	478	420
Other social expenses	649	754	618
Personnel expenses as per profit and loss account	6,747	6,914	5,938

Share-based compensation expense includes pension and other social costs of EUR 3 million in 2009 (EUR 7 million in 2008 and EUR 8 million in 2007) based upon the related employee benefit charge recognized during the year.

Pension expenses, comprised of multi-employer, insured and defined contribution plans were EUR 377 million in 2009 (EUR 394 million in 2008 and EUR 289 million in 2007). Expenses related to defined benefit plans comprise the remainder.

Average Personnel	2009	2008	2007
Devices & Services	56,462	57,443	49,887
NAVTEQ	4,282	3,969	—
Nokia Siemens Networks	62,129	59,965	50,336
Group Common Functions	298	346	311
Nokia Group	123,171	121,723	100,534

5. Pensions

The group operates a number of post-employment plans in various countries. These plans include both defined contribution and defined benefit schemes.

The group's most significant defined benefit pension plans are in Germany and in the UK. The majority of active employees in Germany participate in a pension scheme which is designed according to the Beitragsorientieerte Siemens Altersversorgung (BASV). The funding vehicle for the BSAV is the NSN Pension Trust. In Germany, individual benefits are generally dependent on eligible compensation levels, ranking within the group and years of service.

The majority of active employees in Nokia UK participate in a pension scheme which is designed according to the Scheme Trust Deeds and Rules and is compliant with the Guidelines of the UK Pension Regulator. The funding vehicle for the pension scheme is Nokia Group (UK) Pension Scheme Ltd which is run on a Trust basis. In the UK, individual benefits are generally dependent on eligible compensation levels and years of service for the defined benefit section of the scheme and on individual investment choices for the defined contribution section of the scheme.

In prior years, the Group had a significant pension plan in Finland. Prior to March 1, 2008, the reserved benefits portion of the Finnish state Employees' Pension Act (TyEL) system that was pre-funded through a trustee-administered Nokia Pension Foundation, was accounted for as a defined benefit plan. As of March 1, 2008 the Finnish statutory pension liability and plan related assets of Nokia and Nokia Siemens Networks were transferred to two pension insurance companies. The transfer did not affect the number of employees covered by the plan nor did it affect the current employees' entitlement to pension benefits.

At the transfer date, the Group has not retained any direct or indirect obligation to pay employee benefits relating to employee service in current, prior or future periods. Thus, the Group has treated the transfer of the Finnish statutory pension liability and plan assets as a settlement of the Group's TyEL defined benefit plan as a defined contribution plan. The transfer resulted in [a] EUR 152 million loss consisting of a EUR 217 million loss impacting Common Group Functions and a EUR 65 million gain impacting Nokia Siemens Network operating profit. These are included in the other operating income and expense, see Note 6. Subsequent to the transfer of the Finnish statutory pension liability and plan assets, the Group retains only certain immaterial voluntary defined benefit pension liabilities in Finland.

The following table sets forth the changes in the benefit obligation and fair value of plan assets during the year and the funded status of the significant defined benefit pension plans showing the amounts that are recognized in the Group's consolidated statement of financial position as at December 31:

EURm	*2009*	*2008*
Present value of defined benefit obligations at beginning of year	−1,205	−2,266
Foreign exchange	5	56
Current service cost	−55	−79
Interest cost	−69	−78
Plan participants' contributions	−12	−10
Past service cost	—	−2
Actuarial gain (+)/loss (−)	−139	105
Acquisitions	2	−2
Curtailment	—	10
Settlements	2	1,025
Benefits paid	60	36
Present value of defined benefit obligations at end of year	−1,411	−1,025
Plan assets at fair value at beginning of year	1,197	2,174
Foreign exchange	−7	−58
Expected return on plan assets	70	71
Actuarial gain (+)/loss (−) on plan assets	56	−39
Employer contribution	49	141
Plan participants' contributions	12	10
Benefits paid	−44	−24
Curtailments	—	−5
Settlements	−2	−1,078
Acquisitions	−1	5
Plan assets at fair value at end of year	1,330	1,197

EURm	2009	2008
Surplus (+)/deficit (−)	−81	−8
Unrecognized net actuarial gain (−)/losses (+)	−21	−113
Unrecognized past service cost	1	1
Amount not recognized as an asset in the balance sheet because of limit in IAS 19 paragraph 58(b)	−5	—
Prepaid (+)/accrued (−) pension cost in statement of financial position	−106	−120

Present value of obligations include EUR 822 million (EUR 707 million in 2008) of wholly funded obligations, EUR 516 million of partly funded obligations (EUR 416 million in 2008) and EUR 73 million (EUR 82 million in 2008) of unfunded obligations.

The amounts recognized in the income statements are as follows:

EURm	2009	2008	2007
Current service cost	55	79	125
Interest cost	69	78	104
Expected return on plan assets	−70	−71	−95
Net actuarial (gain) losses recognized in the year	−9	—	10
Impact of paragraph 58(b) limitation	5	—	—
Past service cost gains (−)/losses (+)	—	2	—
Curtailment	—	−12	−1
Settlement	—	152	−12
Total, included in personnel expenses	50	228	131

Movements in prepaid/accrued pension costs recognized in the statement of financial position are as follows:

EURm	2009	2008
Prepaid (+)/accrued (−) pension costs at beginning of year	−120	−36
Net income (expense) recognized in the profit and loss account	−50	−228
Contributions paid	49	141
Benefits paid	16	12
Acquisitions	1	3
Foreign exchange	−2	−12
Prepaid (+)/accrued (−) pension cost at end of year*	−106	−120

included within prepaid expenses and accrued income/accrued expenses.

The prepaid pension cost above is made up of a prepayment of EUR 68 million (EUR 55 million in 2008) and an accrual of EUR 174 million (EUR 175 million in 2008).

EURm	2009	2008	2007	2006	2005
Present value of defined benefit obligation	−1,411	−1,205	−2,266	−1,577	−1,385
Plan assets at fair value	1,330	1,197	2,174	1,409	1,276
Surplus (+)/Deficit (−)	−81	−8	−92	−168	−109

Experience adjustments arising on plan obligations amount to a loss of EUR 12 million in 2009 (gain of EUR 50 million in 2008, a loss of EUR 31 million in 2007 and EUR 25 million in 2006). Experience adjustments arising on plan assets amount to a gain of EUR 54 million in 2009 (a loss of EUR 22 million in 2008, EUR 3 million in 2007 and EUR 11 million in 2006).

The principal actuarial weighted average assumptions used were as follows:

%	2009	2008
Discount rate for determining present values	5.3	5.8
Expected long-term rate of return on plan assets	5.4	5.7
Annual rate of increase in future compensation levels	2.8	2.7
Pension increases	2.0	1.9

The expected long-term rate of return on plan assets is based on the expected return multiplied with the respective percentage weight of the market-related value of plan assets. The expected return is defined on a uniform basis, reflecting long-term historical returns, current market conditions and strategic asset allocation.

The Group's pension plan weighted average asset allocation as a percentage of Plan Assets at December 31, 2009 and 2008 by asset category are as follows:

%	2009	2008
Asset category:		
Equity securities	21	12
Debt securities	65	72
Insurance contracts	8	8
Real estate	1	1
Short-term investments	5	7
Total	100	100

The objective of the investment activities is to maximize the excess of plan assets over projected benefit obligations, within an accepted risk level, taking into account the interest rate and inflation sensitivity of the assets as well as the obligations.

The Pension Committee of the Group, consisting of the Head of Treasury, Head of HR and other HR representatives, approves both the target asset allocation as well as the deviation limit. Derivative instruments can be used to change the portfolio asset allocation and risk characteristics.

The foreign pension plan assets include a self investment through a loan provided to Nokia by the Group's German pension fund of EUR 69 million (EUR 69 million in 2008). See Note 30.

The actuarial return on plan assets was EUR 126 million in 2009 (EUR 31 million in 2008).

In 2010, the Group expects to make contributions of EUR 69 million to its defined benefit pension plans.

6. Other Operating Income and Expenses

Other operating income for 2009 includes a gain on sale of security applicable business of EUR 68 million impacting Devices & Services operating profit and a gain on sale of real estate in Oulu, Finland of EUR 22 million impacting Nokia Siemens Networks operating loss. In 2009, other operating expenses includes EUR 178 million of charges related to restructuring activities in Devices & Services due to measures taken to adjust the business operations and cost base according to market conditions. In conjunction with the decision to refocus its activities around specified core assets, Devices & Services recorded impairment charges totalling EUR 56 million for intangible assets arising from the acquisitions of Enpocket and Intellisync and the asset acquisition of Twango.

In 2008, other operating expenses include EUR 152 million net loss on transfer of Finnish pension liabilities, of which a gain of EUR 65 million is included in Nokia Siemens Networks' operating profit and a loss of EUR 217 million in Corporate Common expenses. Devices & Services recorded EUR 259 million of restructuring charges and EUR 81 million of impairment and other charges related to closure of the Bochum site in Germany. Other operating expenses also include a charge of EUR 52 million related to other restructuring activities in Devices & Services and EUR 49 million charges related to restructuring and other costs in Nokia Siemens Networks.

Other operating income for 2007 includes a non-taxable gain of EUR 1,879 million relating to the formation of Nokia Siemens Networks. Other operating income also includes a gain on sale of real estates in Finland of EUR 128 million of which EUR 75 million is included in Common Functions' operating profit and EUR 53 million in Nokia Siemens Networks' operating profit. In addition, a gain on business transfer of EUR 53 million impacted Common Functions' operating profit. In 2007, other operating expenses include EUR 58 million in charges related to restructuring costs in Nokia Siemens Networks. Devices & Services recorded a charge of EUR 17 million for personnel expenses and other costs as a result of more focused R&D. Devices & Services also recorded restructuring costs of EUR 35 million primarily related to restructuring of a subsidiary company.

In all three years presented, 'Other operating income and expenses' include the costs of hedging highly probable forecasted sales and purchases (forward points of cash flow hedges). As from 2009, on the same line are included also the fair value changes of derivatives hedging identifiable and probable forecasted cash flows.

7. Impairment

EURm	2009	2008	2007
Capitalized development costs	—	—	27
Goodwill	908	—	—
Other intangible assets	56	—	—
Property, plant and equipment	1	77	—
Inventories	—	13	—
Investments in associated companies	19	8	7
Available-for-sale investments	25	43	29
Other non-current assets	—	8	—
Total, net	1,009	149	63

Capitalized Development Costs In 2009 and 2008, the Group did not recognize any impairment charge on capitalized development costs. During 2007, Nokia Siemens Networks recorded an impairment charge on capitalized development costs of EUR 27 million. The impairment loss was determined as the full carrying amount of the capitalized development program costs related to products that will not be included in future product portfolios. This impairment amount is included within research and development expenses in the consolidated income statement.

Goodwill Goodwill is allocated to the Group's cash-generating units (CGU) for the purpose of impairment testing. The allocation is made to those cash-generating units that are expected to benefit from the synergies of the business combination in which the goodwill arose. The Group has allocated goodwill to three cash-generating units, which correspond to the Group's operating and reportable segments: Devices & Services CGU, Nokia Siemens Networks CGU and NAVTEQ CGU.

The recoverable amounts for the Devices & Services CGU and the NAVTEQ CGU are based on value in use calculations. The cash flow projections employed in the value in use calculation are based on financial plans approved by management. These projections are consistent with external sources of information, wherever available. Cash flows beyond the explicit forecast period are extrapolated using an estimated terminal growth rate that does not exceed the long-term average growth rates for the industry and economies in which the CGU operates.

The recoverable amount for the Nokia Siemens Networks CGU is based on fair value less costs to sell. A discounted cash flow calculation was used to estimate the fair value less costs to sell of the Nokia Siemens Networks CGU. The cash flow projections employed in the discounted cash flow calculation have been determined by management based on the best information available to reflect the amount that an entity could obtain from the disposals of the Nokia Siemens Networks CGU in an arm's length transaction between knowledgeable, willing parties, after deducting the estimated costs of disposal.

During 2009, the conditions in the world economy have shown signs of improvement as countries have begun to emerge from the global economic downturn. However, significant uncertainty exists regarding the speed, timing and resiliency of the global economic recovery and this uncertainty is reflected in the impairment testing for each of the Group's CGUs.

Goodwill amounting to EUR 1,227 million was allocated to the Devices & Services CGU. The impairment testing has been carried out based on management's expectation of the stable market share and normalized profit margins in the medium to long-term. The goodwill impairment testing conducted for the Devices & Services CGU for the year ended December 31, 2009 did not result in any impairment charges.

In the third quarter of 2009, the Group recorded an impairment loss of EUR 908 million to reduce the carrying amount of the Nokia Siemens Networks CGU to its recoverable amount. The impairment loss was allocated in its entirety to the carrying amount of goodwill arising from the formation of Nokia Siemens Networks and from subsequent acquisitions completed by Nokia Siemens Networks. This impairment loss is presented as impairment of goodwill in the consolidated income statement. As a result of the impairment loss, the amount of goodwill allocated to the Nokia Siemens Networks CGU has been reduced to zero.

The recoverability of the Nokia Siemens Networks CGY has declined as a result of a decline in forecasted profits and cash flows. The Group evaluated the historical and projected financial performance of the Nokia Siemens Networks CGU taking into consideration the challenging competitive factors and market conditions in the infrastructure and related services business. As a result of this evaluation, the Group lowered its net sales and gross margin projections for the Nokia Siemens Networks CGU. This reduction in the projected scale of the business had a negative impact on the projected profits and cash flows of the Nokia Siemens Networks CGU.

Goodwill amounting to EUR 3,944 million has been allocated to the NAVTEQ CGU. The impairment testing has been carried out based on management's assessment of the financial performance and future strategies of the NAVTEQ CGU in light of current and expected market and economic conditions. The goodwill impairment testing conducted for the NAVTEQ CGU for the year ended December 31, 2009 did not result in any impairment charges. The recoverable amount of the NAVTEQ CGU is between 5–10% higher than its carrying amount. The Group has concluded that a reasonably possible change of 1% in the valuation assumptions for long-term growth rate or discount rate would give rise to an impairment loss.

The key assumptions applied in the impairment testing analysis for each CGU are presented in the table below:

	Cash-Generating Unit		
	Devices & *Services %*	*Nokia Siemens* *networks %*	*NAVTEQ %*
Terminal growth rate	2.00	1.00	5.00
Post-tax discount rate	8.86	9.95	10.00
Pre-tax discount rate	11.46	13.24	12.60

The group has applied consistent valuation methodologies for each of the group's CGUs for the years ended December 31, 2009, 2008 and 2007. The discount rates applied in the impairment testing for each CGU have been determined independently of capital structure reflecting current assessments of the time value of money and relevant market risk premiums. Risk premiums included in the determination of the discount rate reflect risks and uncertainties for which the future cash flow estimates have not been adjusted. Overall, the discount rates applied in the 2009 impairment testing have decreased in line with declining interest rates and narrowing credit spreads.

The goodwill impairment testing conducted for each of the group's CGUs for the years ended December 31, 2008 and 2007 did not result in any impairment charges.

Other intangible assets   In conjunction with the group's decision to refocus its activities around specified core assets, the group recorded impairment charges in 2009 totalling EUR 56 million for intangible assets arising from the acquisitions of Enpocket and Intellisync and the asset acquisition of Twango. The impairment charge was recognized in other operating expense and is included in the Devices & Services segment. In connection with the decline in the group's profit and cash flow projections of the Nokia Siemens Networks CGU, the group conducted an assessment of the carrying amount of the identifiable intangible assets arising from the formation of Nokia Siemens Networks concluding that such carrying amount was recoverable.

Property, plant and equipment and inventories   In 2008, resulting from the Group's decision to discontinue the production of mobile devices in Germany, an impairment loss was recognized amounting to EUR 55 million. The impairment loss related to the closure and sale of production facilities at Bochum, Germany and is included in the Devices & Services segment.

In 2008, Nokia Siemens Networks recognized an impairment loss amounting to EUR 35 million to the sale of its manufacturing site in Durach, Germany. The impairment loss was determined as the excess of the book value of transferring assets over the fair value less costs to sell for the transferring assets. The impairment loss was allocated to property, plant and equipment and inventories.

Investments in associated companies   After application of the equity method, including recognition of the associate's losses, the Group determined that recognition of an impairment loss of EUR 19 million in 2009 (EUR 8 million in 2008, EUR 7 million in 2007) was necessary to adjust the Group's net investment in the associate to its recoverable amount.

Available-for-sale investments   The Group's investment in certain equity securities held as non-current available-for-sale suffered a permanent decline in fair value resulting in an impairment charge of EUR 25 million in 2009 (EUR 43 million in 2008, EUR 29 million in 2007).

8. Acquisitions

Acquisitions completed in 2009   During 2009, the Group completed acquisitions that did not have a material impact on the consolidated financial statements. The purchase consideration paid and the total goodwill arising from these acquisitions amounted to EUR 29 million and EUR 32 million, respectively. The goodwill arising from these acquisitions is attributable to assembled workforce and post acquisition synergies.

- Plum Ventures, Inc, based in Boston, USA, develops and operates a cloud-based social media sharing and message service for private groups. The Group acquired certain assets of Plum on September 11, 2009.

- Dopplr Oy, based in Helsinki, Finland, provides a Social Atlas that enables members to share travel plans and preferences privately with their networks. The Group acquired a 100% ownership interest in Dopplr on September 28, 2009.
- Huano Technology Co., Ltd, based in Changsha, China, is an infrastructure service provider with Nokia Siemens Networks as its primary customer. Nokia Siemens Networks increased its ownership interest in Huano from 49% to 100% on July 22, 2009.
- T-Systems Traffic GmbH is a leading German provider of dynamic mobility services delivering near real-time data about traffic flow and road conditions. NAVTEQ acquired a 100% ownership interest in T-Systems Traffic on January 2, 2009.
- Acuity Mobile, based in Greenbelt, USA, is a leading provider of mobile marketing content delivery solutions. NAVTEQ acquired a 100% ownership interest in Acuity Mobile on September 11, 2009.

Acquisitions completed in 2008

NAVTEQ   On July 10, 2008, the Group completed its acquisition of all of the outstanding common stock of NAVTEQ. Based in Chicago, NAVTEQ is a leading provider of comprehensive digital map information for automotive systems, mobile navigation devices, internet-based mapping applications and government and business solutions. The Group will use NAVTEQ's industry leading maps data to add context-time, place, people to web service optimized for mobility.

The total cost of the acquisition was EUR 5,342 million and consisted of cash paid of EUR 2,772 million, debt issued of EUR 2,539 million, costs directly attributable to the acquisition of EUR 12 million and consideration attributable to the vested portion of replacement share-based payment awards of EUR 19 million.

The following table summarizes the estimated fair values of the assets acquired and liabilities assumed at the date of acquisition:

EURm	Carrying amount	Fair value	Useful lives
Goodwill	114	3,673	
Intangible assets subject to amortization:			
Map database	5	1,389	5 years
Customer relationships	22	388	4 years
Developed technology	8	110	4 years
License to use trade name and trademark	7	57	6 years
Capitalized development costs	22	—	
Other intangible assets	4	7	
	68	1,951	
Property, plant and equipment	84	83	
Deferred tax assets	262	148	
Available-for-sale investments	36	36	
Other non-current assets	6	6	
Non-current assets	456	2,224	

EURm	Carrying amount	Fair value	Useful lives
Inventories	3	3	
Accounts receivable	94	94	
Prepaid expenses and accrued income	36	36	
Available-for-sale investments, liquid assets	140	140	
Available-for-sale investments, cash equivalents	97	97	
Bank and cash	57	57	
Current assets	427	427	
Total assets acquired	**997**	**6,324**	
Deferred tax liabilities	46	786	
Other long-term liabilities	54	39	
Non-current liabilities	100	825	
Accounts payable	29	29	
Accrued expenses	96	120	
Provisions	5	8	
Current liabilities	130	157	
Total liabilities assumed	230	982	
Net assets acquired	767	5,342	

The goodwill of EUR 3,673 million has been allocated to the NAVTEQ segment. The goodwill is attributable to assembled workforce and the synergies expected to arise and subsequent to the acquisition including acceleration of the Group's internet services strategy. None of the goodwill acquired is expected to be deductible for income tax purposes.

Symbian   On December 2, 2008, the Group completed its acquisition of 52.1% of the outstanding common stock of Symbian Ltd. As a result of this acquisition, the Group's total ownership interest has increased from 47.9% to 100% of the outstanding common stock of Symbian. A UK-based software licensing company, Symbian developed and licensed Symbian OS, the market-leading open operating system for mobile phones. The acquisition of Symbian is a fundamental step in the establishment of the Symbian Foundation.

The Group contributed the Symbian OS and S60 software to the Symbian Foundation for the purpose of creating a unified mobile software platform with a common UI framework. The goal of the Symbian Foundation is to extend the appeal of the platform among all partners, including developers, mobile operators, content and service providers and device manufacturers. The unified platform will promote innovation and accelerate the availability of new services and experiences for consumers and business users around the world. A full platform was available for all Foundation members under a royalty-free license from the Foundation's first day of operations.

The acquisition of Symbian was achieved in stages through successive share purchases at various times from the formation of the company. Thus, the amount of goodwill arising from the acquisition has been determined via a step-by-step comparison of the cost of the individual investments in Symbian with the acquired interest in the fair values of Symbian's identifiable net assets at each stage. Revaluation of the Group's previously held interests in Symbian's identifiable net assets is recognized as a revaluation surplus in equity. Application of the equity method has been reversed such that the carrying amount of the Group's previously held interests in Symbian have been adjusted to cost. The Group's share of changes in Symbian's equity balances after each stage is included in equity.

The total cost of the acquisition was EUR 641 million consisting of cash paid of EUR 435 million, costs directly attributable to the acquisition of EUR 6 million and investments in Symbian from previous exchange transactions of EUR 200 million.

The following table summarizes the estimated fair values of the assets acquired and liabilities assumed at the date of acquisition:

EURm	Carrying amount	Fair value
Goodwill	—	470
Intangible assets subject to amortization:		
Developed technology	5	41
Customer relationships	—	11
License to use trade name and trademark	—	3
	5	55
Property, plant and equipment	33	31
Deferred tax assets	7	19
Non-current assets	45	105
Accounts receivable	20	20
Prepaid expenses and accrued income	43	43
Bank and cash	147	147
Current assets	210	210
Total assets acquired	255	785
Deferred tax liabilities	—	17
Financial liabilities	—	20
Accounts payable	5	5
Accrued expenses	48	53
Total liabilities assumed	53	95
Net assets acquired	202	690
Revaluation of previously held interest in Symbian	22	
Nokia share of changes in Symbian's equity after each stage of the acquisition	27	
Cost of the business combination	641	

The goodwill of EUR 470 million has been allocated to the Devices & Services segment. The goodwill is attributable to assembled workforce and the significant benefits that the Group expects to realize from the Symbian Foundation. None of the goodwill acquired is expected to be deductible for income tax purposes.

The contribution of the Symbian OS and S60 software to the Symbian Foundation has been accounted for as a retirement. Thus, the Group has recognized a loss on retirement of EUR

165 million consisting of EUR 55 million book value of Symbian identifiable intangible assets and EUR 110 million book value of capitalized S60 development costs.

For NAVTEQ and Symbian, the Group has included net losses of EUR 155 million and EUR 52 million, respectively, in the consolidated profit and loss. The following table depicts pro-forma net sales and operating profit of the combined entity as though the acquisition of NAVTEQ and Symbian had occurred on January 1, 2008:

Pro forma (unaudited) EURm	*2008*
Net sales	51,063
Net profit	4,080

During 2008, the Group completed five additional acquisitions. The total purchase consideration paid and the total goodwill arising from these acquisitions amounted for EUR 514 million and EUR 339 million respectively. The goodwill arising from these acquisitions is attributable to assembled workforce and post acquisition synergies.

- Trolltech ASA, based in Oslo, Norway, is a recognized software provider with world-class software development platforms and frameworks. The Group acquired a 100% ownership interest in Trolltech ASA on June 6, 2008.
- Oz Communications Inc., headquartered in Montreal, Canada, is a leading consumer mobile messaging solution provider delivering access to popular instant messaging and email services on consumer mobile devices. The Group acquired a 100% ownership interest in Oz Communications Inc., on November 4, 2008.
- Atrica, based in Santa Clara, USA, is one of the leading providers of Carrier Ethernet solutions for Metropolitan Area Networks. Nokia Siemens Networks acquired a 100% ownership interest in Atrica on January 7, 2008.
- Apertio Ltd., based in Bristol, England, is the leading independent provider of subscriber-centric networks for mobile, fixed and converged telecommunications operators. Nokia Siemens acquired a 100% ownership interest in Apertio Ltd. on February 11, 2008.
- On January 1, 2008, Nokia Siemens Networks assumed control of Vivento Technical Services from Deutsche Telekom.

Acquisitions completed in 2007 The Group and Siemens AG (Siemens) completed a transaction to form Nokia Siemens Networks on April 1, 2007. Nokia and Siemens contributed to Nokia Siemens Networks certain tangible and intangible assets and certain business interests that comprised Nokia's networks business and Siemens' carrier-related operations. This transaction combined the worldwide mobile and fixed-line telecommunications network equipment businesses of Nokia and Siemens. Nokia and Siemens each own approximately 50% of Nokia Siemens Networks. Nokia has the ability to appoint key officers and the majority of the members of the Board of Directors. Accordingly, for accounting purposes, Nokia is deemed to have control and thus consolidates the results of Nokia Siemens Networks in its financial statements.

The transfer of Nokia Networks business was treated as a partial sale to the minority shareholders of Nokia Siemens Networks. Accordingly, the Group recognized a non-taxable gain on the partial sale amounting to EUR 1,879 million. The gain was determined as the Group's ownership interest relinquished for the difference between the fair value contributed, representing the consideration received, and book value of the net assets contributed by the Group to Nokia Siemens Networks. Upon closing of the transaction, Nokia and Siemens contributed net assets with book values amounting to EUR 1,742 million and EUR 2,385 million, respectively. The Group's contributed networks business was valued at EUR 5,500 million. In addition, the Group incurred costs directly attributable to the acquisition of EUR 51 million.

The table below presents the reported results of Nokia Networks prior to the formation of Nokia Siemens Networks and the reported results of Nokia Siemens Networks since inception.

	2007			*2006*		
EURm	*Jan–Mar*	*Apr–Dec*	*Total*	*Jan–Mar*	*Apr–Dec*	*Total*
Net sales						
Nokia Networks	1,697	*	1,697	1,699	5,754	7,453
Nokia Siemens Networks	*	11,696	11,696	N/A	N/A	N/A
Total	1,697	11,696	13,393	1,699	5,754	7,453
Operating profit						
Nokia Networks	78	*	78	149	659	808
Nokia Siemens Networks	*	−1,386	−1,386	N/A	N/A	N/A
Total	78	−1,386	−1,308	149	659	808

* No results presented as Nokia Siemens Networks began operations on April 1, 2007.

It is not practicable to determine the results of the Siemens' carrier-related operations for the three month period of January 1, 2007 to March 31, 2007 as Siemens did not report those operations separately. As a result pro forma revenues and operating profit as if the acquisition had occurred as of January 1, 2007 have not been presented.

The following summarizes the estimated fair values of the assets acquired and liabilities assumed at the date of acquisition:

	Carrying amount EURm	*Fair value EURm*	*Useful lives years*
Intangible assets subject to amortization:			
Customer relationships	—	1,290	6
Developed technology	—	710	4
License to use trade name and trademark	—	350	5
Capitalized development costs	143	154	3
Other intangible assets	47	47	3–5
	190	2,551	

	Carrying amount EURm	Fair value EURm	Useful lives years
Property, plant and equipment	371	344	
Deferred tax assets	111	181	
Other non-current assets	153	153	
Non-current assets	825	3,229	
Inventories	1,010	1,138	
Accounts receivable	3,135	3,087	
Prepaid expenses and accrued income	870	846	
Other financial assets	55	55	
Bank and cash	382	382	
Current assets	5,452	5,508	
Total assets acquired	**6,277**	**8,737**	
Deferred tax liabilities	171	997	
Long-term interest-bearing liabilities	34	34	
Non-current liabilities	205	1,031	
Short-term borrowings	231	213	
Accounts payable	1,539	1,491	
Accrued expenses	1,344	1,502	
Provisions	463	397	
Current liabilities	3,577	3,603	
Total liabilities assumed	**3,782**	**4,634**	
Minority interest	**110**	**108**	
Net assets acquired	**2,385**	**3,995**	
Cost of acquisition	5,500		
Goodwill	**1,505**		
Less non-controlling interest in goodwill	753		
Plus costs directly attributable to the acquisition	51		
Goodwill arising on formation of Nokia Siemens Networks	**803**		

The goodwill of EUR 803 million has been allocated to the Nokia Siemens Networks segment. The goodwill is attributable to assembled workforce and the synergies expected to arise subsequent to the acquisition. None of the goodwill acquired is expected to be deductible for income tax purposes.

The amount of the loss specifically attributable to the business acquired from Siemens since the acquisition date included in the Group's profit for the period has not been disclosed as it is not practicable to do so. This is due to the ongoing integration of the acquired Siemens' carrier-related operations and Nokia's networks business, and management's focus on the operations and results of the combined entity, Nokia Siemens Networks.

During 2007, the Group completed the acquisition of the following three companies. The purchase consideration paid and goodwill arising from these acquisitions was not material to the group:

- Enpocket Inc, based in Boston USA, a global leader in mobile advertising providing technology and services that allow brands to plan, create, execute, measure and optimize mobile advertising campaigns around the world. The Group acquired 100% ownership interest in Enpocket Inc. on October 5, 2007.
- Avvenu Inc., based in Palo Alto, USA, provides internet services that allow anyone to use their mobile devices to securely access, use and share personal computer files. The Group acquired 100% ownership interest in Avvenu Inc. on December 5, 2007.
- Twango provides a comprehensive media sharing solution for organizing and sharing photos, videos and other personal media. The Group acquired substantially all assets of Twango on July 25, 2007.

9. Depreciation and Amortization

EURm	2009	2008	2007
Depreciation and amortization by function			
Cost of sales	266	297	303
Research and development[1]	909	778	523
Selling and marketing[2]	424	368	232
Administrative and general	185	174	148
Total	1,784	1,617	1,206

[1] *In 2009, depreciation and amortization allocated to research and development included amortization of acquired intangible assets of EUR 534 million (EUR 351 million in 2008 and EUR 136 million in 2007, respectively).*
[2] *In 2009, depreciation and amortization allocated to selling and marketing included amortization of acquired intangible assets of EUR 401 million (EUR 343 million in 2008 and EUR 215 million in 2007, respectively).*

10. Financial Income and Expenses

EURm	2009	2008	2007
Dividend income on available-for-sale financial investments	3	1	—
Interest income on available-for-sale financial investments	101	357	355
Interest income on loans receivables carried at amortized cost	—	—	1
Interest expense on financial liabilities carried at amortized cost	−243	−185	−43
Net realized gains (or losses) on disposal of fixed income available-for-sale financial investments	2	−4	−17
Net fair value gains (or losses) on investments at fair value through profit or loss	19	—	—

EURm	2009	2008	2007
Interest income on investments at fair value through profit or loss	11	—	—
Net fair value gains (or losses) on hedged items under fair value hedge accounting	−4	—	—
Net fair value gains (or losses) on hedging instruments under fair value hedge accounting	—	—	—
Other financial income	18	17	43
Other financial expenses	−29	−31	−24
Net foreign exchange gains (or losses) from foreign exchange derivatives designated at fair value through profit and loss account	−358	432	37
From balance sheet revaluation	230	−595	−118
Net gains (net losses) on other derivatives designated at fair value through profit and loss account	−15	6	5
Total	−265	−2	239

During 2008, interest expense has increased significantly due to increased interest-bearing liabilities mainly related to NAVTEQ acquisition. Foreign exchange gains (or losses) have increased due to higher cost of hedging and increased volatility on the foreign exchange market. During 2009, interest income has decreased significantly due to lower interest rates and interest expense has increased given higher long-term funding with higher cost.

11. Income Taxes

EURm	2009	2008	2007
Income tax:			
Current tax	−736	−1,514	−2,209
Deferred tax	34	433	687
Total	−702	−1,081	−1,522
Finland	76	−604	−1,323
Other countries	−778	−477	−199
Total	−702	−1,081	1,522

The difference between income tax expense computed at statutory rate (in Finland 26%) and income taxes recognized in the consolidated income statement is reconciled as follows as at December 31, 2009:

EURm	2009	2008	2007
Income tax expense at statutory rate	250	1,292	2,150
Permanent differences	−96	−65	61
Non-taxable gain on the formation of Nokia Siemens Networks[1]	—	—	−489

EURm	2009	2008	2007
Non-taxable deductible impairment of Nokia Siemens Networks' goodwill[2]	236	—	—
Tax for prior years	−17	−128	20
Taxes on foreign subsidiaries' profits in excess of (lower than) income taxes at statutory rates	−145	−181	−138
Changes in losses and temporary differences with no tax effect[3]	577	—	15
Net increase (+)/decrease (−) in tax contingencies[4]	−186	2	50
Change in income tax rates	4	−22	−114
Deferred tax liability on undistributed earnings[5]	111	220	−37
Other	−32	−37	4
Income tax expense	702	1,081	1,522

[1] *See Note 8.*
[2] *See Note 7.*
[3] *In 2009 this item primarily relates to Nokia Siemens Networks' losses and temporary differences for which no deferred tax was recognized.*
[4] *See Note 26.*
[5] *In 2008 and 2007 the change in deferred tax liability on undistributed earnings mainly related to changes to tax rates applicable to profit distributions.*

Certain of the Group companies' income tax returns for the periods ranging from 2003 through 2009 are under examination by tax authorities. The Group does not believe that any significant additional taxes in excess of those already provided for will arise as a result of the examinations.

12. Intangible Assets

EURm	2009	2008
Capitalised development costs		
Acquisition cost 1 January	1,811	1,817
Additions during the period	27	131
Retirements during the period	—	−124
Disposals during the period	−8	−13
Accumulated acquisition cost 31 December	1,830	1,811
Accumulated amortization 1 January	−1,567	−1,439
Retirements during the period	—	14
Disposals during the period	8	11
Amortization for the period	−128	−153
Accumulated amortization 31 December	−1,687	−1,567
Net book value 1 January	244	378
Net book value 31 December	143	244
Goodwill		
Acquisition cost 1 January	6,257	1,384
Translation differences	−207	431

EURm	2009	2008
Acquisitions	32	4,482
Disposals during the period	−3	−35
Impairments during the period	−908	—
Other changes	—	−5
Accumulated acquisition cost 31 December	5,171	6,257
Net book value 1 January	6,257	1,384
Net book value 31 December	5,171	6,257
Other intangible assets		
Acquisition cost 1 January	5,948	3,218
Translation differences	−142	265
Additions during the period	50	95
Acquisitions	3	2,189
Retirements during the period	−26	−55
Impairments during the period	−94	—
Disposals during the period	−2	−214
Accumulated acquisition cost 31 December	5,287	5,498
Accumulated amortization 1 January	−1,585	−860
Translation differences	56	−32
Retirements during the period	17	—
Impairments during the period	38	—
Disposals during the period	2	48
Amortization for the period	−1,053	−741
Accumulated amortization 31 December	−2,525	−1,585
Net book value 1 January	3,913	2,358
Net book value 31 December	2,762	3,913

13. Property, Plant and Equipment

EURm	2009	2008
Land and water areas		
Acquisition costs 1 January	60	73
Translation differences	—	−4
Additions during the period	1	3
Impairments during the period	—	−4
Disposals during the period	−2	−8
Accumulated acquisition cost 31 December	59	60
Net book value 1 January	60	73
Net book value 31 December	59	60
Buildings and constructions		
Acquisition cost 1 January	1,274	1,008
Translation differences	−17	−9
Additions during the period	132	382
Acquisitions	—	28

EURm	2009	2008
Impairments during the period	—	−90
Disposals during the period	−77	−45
Accumulated acquisition cost 31 December	1,312	1,274
Accumulated depreciation 1 January	−350	−239
Translation differences	3	1
Impairments during the period	—	30
Disposals during the period	42	17
Depreciation for the period	−80	−159
Accumulated depreciation 31 December	−385	−350
Net book value 1 January	924	769
Net book value 31 December	927	924
Machinery and equipment		
Acquisition cost 1 January	4,183	4,012
Translation differences	−67	−10
Additions during the period	386	613
Acquisitions	1	68
Impairments during the period	−1	−21
Disposals during the period	−518	−499
Accumulated acquisition cost 31 December	3,984	4,183
Accumulated depreciation 1 January	−3,197	−3,107
Translation differences	50	−8
Impairments during the period	—	8
Disposals during the period	489	466
Depreciation for the period	−510	−556
Accumulated depreciation 31 December	−3,168	−3,197
Net book value 1 January	986	905
Net book value 31 December	816	986
Other tangible assets		
Acquisition cost 1 January	30	20
Translation differences	−2	2
Additions during the period	19	8
Accumulated acquisition cost 31 December	47	30
Accumulated depreciation 1 January	−15	−9
Translation differences	1	
Depreciation for the period	−13	−6
Accumulated depreciation 31 December	−27	−15
Net book value 1 January	15	11
Net book value 31 December	20	15
Advance payments and fixed assets under construction		
Net carrying amount 1 January	105	154
Translation differences	−2	—
Additions	29	67
Acquisitions	—	26

EURm	2009	2008
Diposals	−1	−13
Transfers to:		
Other intangible assets	−3	−12
Buildings and construction	−34	−76
Machinery and equipment	−36	−41
Other intangible assets	−13	—
Net carrying amount 31 December	45	105
Total property, plant and equipment	1,867	2,090

14. Investments in Associated Companies

EURm	2009	2008
Net carrying amount 1 January	96	325
Translation differences	−4	−19
Additions	30	24
Deductions[1]	−50	−239
Impairment	−19	−8
Share of results	30	6
Dividends	—	−6
Other movements	−14	13
Net carrying amount 31 December	69	96

[1] *On December 2, 2008, the Group completed its acquisition of 52.1% of the outstanding common stock of Symbian Ltd, a UK based software licensing company. As a result of this acquisition, the Group's total ownership interest has increased from 47.9% to 100% of the outstanding common stock of Symbian. See Note 7.*

Shareholdings in associated companies are comprised of investments in unlisted companies in all periods presented.

15. Fair Value of Financial Instruments

Carrying amount

	Current available-for-sale financial assets	Non-current available-for-sale financial assets	Financial instruments at fair value through profit or loss	Loans and receivables measured at amortized cost	Financial liabilities measured at amortized cost	Total carrying amount	Fair value
At 31/12/09 EURm							
Long-term loans receivable				46		46	40
Other non-current assets				6		6	6

Carrying amount

	Current available-for-sale financial assets	Non-current available-for-sale financial assets	Financial instruments at fair value through profit or loss	Loans and receivables measured at amortized cost	Financial liabilities measured at amortized cost	Total carrying amount	Fair value
Amounts receivable				7,981		7,981	7,981
Current portion of long-term loans receivable				14		14	14
Derivative assets			316			316	316
Other current financial assets				13		13	13
Fixed income and money-market investments carried at fair value	7,151	31				7,182	7,182
Investments designated at fair value through profit and loss			580			580	580
Total financial assets	7,151	554	896	8,060	—	16,661	16,655
Long-term interest bearing liabilities					4,432	4,432	4,691
Other long-term non-interest bearing financial liabilities					2	2	2
Current portion of long-term loans payable					44	44	44
Short-term borrowings					727	727	727
Derivative liabilities			245			245	245
Accounts payable					4,950	4,950	4,950
Total financial liabilities			245		10,155	10,400	10,659
Available-for-sale investments in publicly quoted equity shares		8				8	8
Other available-for-sale investments carried at fair value		225				225	225

Carrying amount

	Current available-for-sale financial assets	Non-current available-for-sale financial assets	Financial instruments at fair value through profit or loss	Loans and receivables measured at amortized cost	Financial liabilities measured at amortized cost	Total carrying amount	Fair value
Other available-for-sale investments carried at cost less amortization		241				241	241
Long-term loans receivable				27		27	24
Other non-current assets				10		10	10
Accounts receivable				9,444		9,444	9,444
Current portion of long-term loans receivable				101		101	101
Derivative assets			1,014			1,014	1,014
Other current financial assets				20		20	20
Fixed income and money-market investments carried at fair value	5,114	38				5,152	5,152
Total financial assets	5,114	512	1,014	9,602	—	16,242	16,239
Long-term interest-bearing liabilities					861	861	855
Other long-term non-interest-bearing financial liabilities					3	3	3
Current portion of long-term loans payable					13	13	13
Short-term borrowings					3,578	3,578	3,578
Derivative liabilities			924			924	924
Accounts payable					5,225	5,225	5,225
Total financial liabilities			924		9,680	10,604	10,598

The current fixed income and money-market investments include available-for-sale liquid assets of EUR 2,367 (EUR 1,272 million in 2008) and cash equivalents of EUR 4,784 (EUR 3,842 million in 2008). See Note 33, section Financial Credit Risk, for details on fixed income and money-market investments.

For information about the valuation of items measured at fair value see Note 1.

In the tables above, fair value is set to carrying amount for other available-for-sale investments carried at cost less impairment for which no reliable fair value has been possible to estimate.

The fair value of loan receivables and payables is estimated based on the current market values of similar instruments. Fair value is estimated to be equal to the carrying amount for short-term financial assets and financial liabilities due to limited credit risk and short-time to maturity.

The amount of change in the fair value of investments designated at fair value through profit or loss attributable to changes in the credit risk of the assets was deemed inconsequential during 2009. Fair value changes that are attributable to changes in market conditions are calculated based on relevant benchmark interest rates.

Note 16 includes the split of hedge accounted and non-hedge accounted derivatives.

The following table presents the valuation methods used to determine fair values of financial instruments carried at fair value.

At December 31, 2009 EURm	*Instruments with quoted prices in active markets (Level 1)*	*Valuation techniques using observable data (Level 2)*	*Valuation techniques using non-observable data (Level 3)*	*Total*
Fixed income and money-market investments carried at fair value	6,933	249	—	7,182
Investments at fair value through profit and loss	580	—	—	580
Available-for-sale investments in publicly quoted equity shares	8	—	—	8
Other available-for-sale investments carried at fair value	—	15	242	257
Derivative assets	—	316	—	316
Total assets	7,521	580	242	8,343
Derivative liabilities	—	245	—	245
Total liabilities	—	245	—	245

Level 1 category includes financial assets and liabilities that are measured in whole or in significant part by reference to published quotes in an active market. A financial instrument is regarded as quoted in an active market if quoted prices are readily and regularly available from an exchange, dealer, broker, industry group, pricing service or regulatory agency and those prices represent actual and regularly occurring market transactions on an arm's length basis. This category includes listed bonds and other securities, listed shares and exchange traded derivatives.

Level 2 category includes financial assets and liabilities measured using a valuation technique based on assumptions that are supported by prices from observable current market transactions. These include assets and liabilities for which pricing is obtained via pricing services, but where prices have not been determined in an active market, financial assets with fair values based on broker quotes and assets that are valued using the group's own valuation models whereby the material assumptions are market observable. The majority of Group's over-the-counter derivatives and several other instruments not traded in active markets fall within this category.

Level 3 category includes financial assets and liabilities measured using valuation techniques based on non market observable inputs. This means that fair values are determined in whole or in part using a valuation model based on assumptions that are neither supported by prices from observable current market transactions in the same instrument nor are they based on available market data. However, the fair value measurement objective remains the same, that is, to estimate an existing price from the perspective of the Group. The main asset classes in this category are unlisted equity investments as well as unlisted funds.

The following table shows a reconciliation of the opening and closing recorded amount of level 3 financial assets and liabilities which are measured at fair value.

EURm	*Other available-for-sale investments carried at fair value*
Balance at 31/12/08	**214**
Total gains/losses in income statement	−30
Total gains/losses recorded in other comprehensive income	15
Purchases	45
Sales	−2
Transfer from level 1 and 2	—
At 31/12/09	**242**

The gains and losses from Level 3 financial instruments are included in the line other operating expenses of the profit or loss for the period. A net loss of EUR 14 million related to Level 3 financial instruments held at December 31, 2009, was included in the profit and loss during 2009.

16. Derivative Financial Instruments

	Assets		Liabilities	
2009 EURm	*Fair value[1]*	*Notional[1]*	*Fair value[2]*	*Notional[2]*
Hedges of net investment in foreign subsidiaries:				
Forward foreign exchange contracts	12	1,128	−42	2,317
Cash flow hedges:				
Forward foreign exchange contracts	25	8,062	−25	7,027
Interest rate swaps	—	—	−2	330
Fair value hedges:				
Interest rate swaps	117	1,750	−10	68
Cash flow and fair value hedges:[4]				
Cross currency interest rate swaps	—	—	−77	416
Derivatives not designated in hedge accounting relationships carried at fair value through profit and loss:				
Forward exchange contracts	147	5,785	68	6,504
Currency options bought	8	442	—	—
Currency options sold	—	—	−1	102
Interest rate swaps	7	68	−20	499
Cash-settled equity options bought[3]	—	6	—	—
	316	17,241	−245	17,263
2008, EURm Hedges of net investments in foreign subsidiaries:				
Forward exchange contracts	80	1,045	−14	472
Currency options bought	30	724	—	—
Currency options sold	—	—	−44	768
Cash flow hedges:				
Forward foreign exchange contracts	562	14,577	445	11,792
Derivatives not designated in hedge accounting relationships carried at fair value through profit and loss:				
Forward foreign exchange contracts	322	7,817	416	7,370
Currency options bought	6	21	—	—
Currency options sold	—	—	−5	186
Interest rate futures	6	21	—	—
Interest rate swaps	7	618	—	—
Cash-settled equity options bought[3]	1	25	—	—
Cash settled equity options sold[4]				−13
	1,014	25,028	−924	20,575

[1] *The fair value of derivative financial instruments is included on the asset side under heading Other financial assets and on the liability side under Other financial liabilities.*
[2] *Includes the gross amount of all notional values for contracts that have not yet been settled or cancelled. The amount of notional value outstanding is not necessarily a measure or indication of market risk, as the exposure of certain contracts may be offset by that of other contracts.*
[3] *Cash settled equity options are used to hedge risk relating to employee incentive programs and investment activity.*
[4] *These cross-currency interest rate swaps have been designated partly as fair value hedges and partly as cash flow hedges.*

17. Inventories

EURm	2009	2008
Raw materials, supplies and other	409	519
Work in progress	681	744
Finished goods	775	1,270
Total	1,865	2,533

18. Prepaid Expenses and Accrued Income

Prepaid expenses and accrued income totalled EUR 4,551 million (EUR 4,538 million) in 2008.

In 2009, prepaid expenses and accrued income included advance payments to Qualcomm of EUR 1,264 million (1,358 million in 2008). In 2008, Nokia and Qualcomm entered into a new 15-year agreement, under the terms of which Nokia has been granted a license to all Qualcomm's patents for the use in Nokia mobile devices and Nokia Siemens Networks infrastructure equipment. The financial structure of the agreement included an up-front payment of EUR 1.7 billion, which is amortized over the contract period and on-going royalties payable to Qualcomm. As part of the licence agreement, Nokia also assigned ownership of a number of patents to Qualcomm. These patents were valued using the income approach based on projected cash flows, on a discounted basis, over the assigned patents' estimated useful life. Based on the valuation and underlying assumptions Nokia determined that the fair value of these patents were not material.

In addition, prepaid expenses and accrued income primarily consists of VAT and other tax receivables. Prepaid expenses and accrued income also include prepaid pension costs, accrued interest income and other accrued income, but no amounts which are individually significant.

19. Valuation and Qualifying Accounts

EURm	Balance at beginning of year	Charged to costs and expenses	Deductions[1]	Acquisitions	Balance at end of year
Allowances on assets to which they apply:					
2009					
Allowance for doubtful accounts	415	155	−179	—	391
Excess and obsolete inventory	348	192	−179	—	361
2008					
Allowance for doubtful accounts	332	224	−141	—	415

EURm	Balance at beginning of year	Charged to costs and expenses	Deductions[1]	Acquisitions	Balance at end of year
Excess and obsolete inventory	417	151	−221	1	348
2007					
Allowance for doubtful accounts	212	38	−72	154	332
Excess and obsolete inventory	218	145	−202	256	417

[1] Deductions include utilization and releases of the allowances.

20. Fair Value and Other Reserves

	Hedging reserves			Available for sale Investments			Total		
EURm	Gross	Tax	Net	Gross	Tax	Net	Gross	Tax	Net
Balance at 31/12/06	69	−19	50	−66	2	−64	3	−17	−14
Cash flow hedges:									
Net fair value gain (+)/losses(−)	103	−27	76	—	—	—	103	−27	76
Transfer of gains (−)/losses (+) to profit and loss account as adjustment to net sales	−794	214	−580	—	—	—	−794	214	−580
Transfer of gains (−)/losses (_) to profit and loss account as adjustment to cost of sales	684	−185	499	—	—	—	684	−185	499
Available-for-sale investments:									
Net fair value gains (+)/losses (−)	—	—	—	32	−1	31	32	−1	31
Transfer to profit and loss account on impairment	—	—	—	29	—	29	29	—	29
Transfer of net fair value gains (−)/losses to profit and loss account on disposal	—	—	—	−12	—	−12	−12	—	−12

	Hedging reserves			Available for sale Investments			Total		
EURm	Gross	Tax	Net	Gross	Tax	Net	Gross	Tax	Net
Movements attributable to minority interests	−8	2	−6	—	—	—	−8	2	−6
Balance at 31/12/07	54	−15	39	−17	1	−16	37	−14	23
Cash flow hedges:									
Net fair value gain (+)/losses (−)	281	−67	214	—	—	—	281	−67	214
Transfer of gains (−)/losses (+) to profit and loss account as adjustments to net sales	−631	177	−454	—	—	—	−631	177	−454
Transfers of gains (−)/losses (+) to profit and loss account as adjustments to cost of sales	186	−62	124	—	—	—	186	−62	124
Transfer of gains (−)/losses (+) as a basis adjustment to assets and liabilities	124	−32	92	—	—	—	124	−32	92
Available-for-sale investments:									
Net fair value gains (+)/losses (−)	—	—	—	−29	9	−20	−29	9	−20
Transfer to profit and loss account on impairment	—	—	—	1	—	1	1	—	1
Transfer of net fair value gains (−)/losses (+) to profit and loss account on disposal	—	—	—	13	1	14	13	1	14
Movements attributable to minority interests	87	−21	66	3	−1	2	90	−22	68
Balance at 31/12/08	101	−20	81	−29	10	−19	72	−10	62
Cash flow hedges:									
Net fair value gains (+)/losses (−)	−19	6	−13	—	—	—	−19	6	−13
Transfer of gains (−)/losses (+) to profit and loss account as adjustment to net sales	873	−222	651	—	—	—	873	−222	651

EURm	Hedging reserves			Available for sale Investments			Total		
	Gross	*Tax*	*Net*	*Gross*	*Tax*	*Net*	*Gross*	*Tax*	*Net*
Transfer of gains (−)/losses (+) to profit and loss account as adjustment to cost of sales	−829	205	−624	—	—	—	−829	205	−624
Available-for-sale investments:									
Net fair value gains (+)/losses (−)	—	—	—	36	−4	32	36	−4	32
Transfer to profit and loss account on impairment	—	—	—	14	—	14	14	—	14
Transfer of net fair value gains (−)/losses (+) to profit and loss account on disposal	—	—	—	−2	—	−2	−2		−2
Movements attributable to minority interests	65	16	−49	−2	—	−2	−67	16	−51
Balance at 31/12/09	61	−15	46	17	6	23	78	−9	69

The presentation of the 'fair value and other reserves' footnote has been changed to correspond with the presentation of the statement of comprehensive income.

In order to ensure that amounts deferred in the cash flow hedging reserve represent only the effective portion of gains and losses on properly designated hedges of future transactions that remain highly probable at the balance sheet date, Nokia has adopted a process under which all derivative gains and losses are initially recognized in the profit and loss account. The appropriate reserve balance is calculated at the end of each period and posted to the fair value and other reserves.

The Group continuously reviews the underlying cash flows and the hedges allocated thereto, to ensure that the amounts transferred to the fair value reserves during the years ended December 31, 2009, 2008 and 2007 do not include gains/losses on forward exchange contracts that have been designated to hedge forecasted sales or purchases that are no longer expected to occur.

All of the net fair value gains or losses recorded in the fair value and other reserve at December 31, 2009 on open forward foreign exchange contracts which hedge anticipated future foreign currency sales or purchases are transferred from the Hedging Reserve to the profit and loss account when the forecasted foreign currency cash flows occur, at various dates up to approximately 1 year from the balance sheet date.

21. Translation Differences

EURm	Translation differences			Net investment hedging			Total		
	Gross	Tax	Net	Gross	Tax	Net	Gross	Tax	Net
Balance at 31/12/06	−37	—	−37	41	−38	3	4	−38	−34
Translation differences:									
Currency translation differences	−151	—	−151	—	—	—	−151	—	−151
Transfer to profit and loss (financial income and expense)	—	—	—	—	—	—	—	—	—
Net investment hedging:									
Net investment hedging gains (+)/losses (−)	—	—	—	51	−13	38	51	−13	38
Transfer to profit and loss (financial income and expense)	—	—	—	—	—	—	—	—	—
Movement attributable to minority interests	−16	—	−16	—	—	—	−16	—	−16
Balance at 31/12/07	−204	—	−204	92	−51	41	−112	−51	−163
Translation differences:									
Currency translation differences	595	—	595	—	—	—	595	—	595
Transfer to profit and loss (financial income and expense)	—	—	—	—	—	—	—	—	—
Net investment hedging:									
Net investment hedging gains (+)/losses (−)	—	—	—	−123	32	−91	−123	32	−91
Transfer to profit and loss (financial income and expense)	—	—	—	—	—	—	—	—	—
Movements attributable to minority interests	—	—	—	—	—	—	—	—	—
Balance at 31/12/08	391	—	391	−31	−19	−50	360	−19	341
Translation differences:									
Currency translation differences	556	2	−554	—	—	—	556	2	−554
Transfer to profit and loss (financial income and expense)	−7	—	−7	—	—	—	−7	—	−7
Net investment hedging:									
Net investment hedging gains(+)/losses (−)	—	—	—	114	−31	83	114	−31	83

EURm	Translation differences			Net investment hedging			Total		
	Gross	Tax	Net	Gross	Tax	Net	Gross	Tax	Net
Transfer to profit and loss (financial income and expense)	1	—	1	—	—	—	1	—	1
Movement attributable to minority interests	8	1	9	—	—	—	8	1	9
Balance at 31/12/09	−164	3	−161	84	−50	34	−80	−47	−127

22. The Shares of the Parent Company

Nokia shares and shareholders

Shares and share capital   Nokia has one class of shares. Each Nokia share entitles the holder to one vote at General Meetings of Nokia.

On December 31, 2009, the share capital of Nokia Corporation was EUR 245,896,461.96 and the total number of shares issued was 3,744,956,052.

On December 31, 2009, the total number of shares included 36,693,564 shares owned by the Group companies representing approximately 1.0% of the share capital and the total voting rights.

Under the Articles of Association of Nokia, Nokia Corporation does not have minimum or maximum share capital or a par value of a share.

Authorizations

Authorization to increase the share capital   At the Annual General Meeting held on May 3, 2007, Nokia shareholders authorized the Board of Directors to issue a maximum of 800 million new shares through one or more issues of shares or special rights entitling to shares, including stock options. The Board of Directors may issue either new shares or shares held by the Company. The authorization includes the right for the Board to resolve on all the terms and conditions of such issuances of shares and special rights, including to whom the shares and the special rights may be issued. The authorization is effective until June 30, 2010.

At the end of 2009, the Board of Directors had no other authorizations to issue shares, convertible bonds, warrants or stock options.

Other authorizations   At the Annual General Meeting on May 8, 2008, Nokia shareholders authorized the Board of Directors to repurchase a maximum of 370 million Nokia shares by using funds in the unrestricted shareholders' equity. Nokia repurchased 71,090,000 shares under this authorization in 2008. In 2009, Nokia did not repurchase any shares on the basis of this authorization. This authorization was effective until June 30, 2009 as per the resolution of the Annual General Meeting on May 8, 2008, but it was terminated by the resolution of the Annual General Meeting on April 23, 2009.

At the Annual General Meeting held on April 23, 2009, Nokia shareholders authorized the Board of Directors to repurchase a maximum of 360 million Nokia shares by using funds in the unrestricted shareholders' equity. The amount of shares corresponds to less than 10% of all shares of the company. The shares may be repurchased under the buy-back authorization in order to develop the capital structure of the company. In addition, shares may be repurchased in order to finance or carry out acquisitions or other arrangements, to settle the company's equity-based incentive plans, to be transferred for other purposes, or to be cancelled. Nokia has not purchased any shares based on this authorization. The authorization is effective until June 30, 2010 and the authorization terminated the authorization for repurchasing of the company's shares resolved at the Annual General Meeting on May 8, 2008.

Authorizations proposed to the Annual General Meeting 2010   The Board of Directors will propose to the Annual General Meeting to be held on May 6, 2010, that the Annual General Meeting authorize the Board to resolve to repurchase a maximum of 360 million Nokia shares by using funds in the unrestricted shareholders' equity. The proposed maximum number of shares represents less than 10% of all the shares of the company. The shares may be repurchased in order to develop the capital structure of the company, finance or carry out acquisitions or other arrangements, settle the company's equity-based incentive plans, be transferred for other purposes, or be cancelled. The authorization would be effective until June 30, 2011 and terminate the current authorization granted by the Annual General Meeting on April 23, 2009.

The Board of Directors will also propose to the Annual General Meeting to be held on May 6, 2010, that the Annual General Meeting authorize the Board to resolve to issue a maximum of 740 million shares through issuance of shares or special rights entitling to shares (including stock options) in one or more issues. The Board proposes that the authorization may be used to develop the company's capital structure, diversify the shareholder base, finance or carry out acquisitions or other arrangements, settle the company's equity-based incentive plans, or for other purposes resolved by the Board. The proposed authorization includes the right for the Board to resolve on all the terms and conditions of the issuance of shares and special rights entitling to shares, including issuance in deviation from the shareholders' pre-emptive rights. The authorization would be effective until June 30, 2013 and terminate the current authorization granted by the Annual General Meeting on May 3, 2007.

23. Share-Based Payment

The Group has several equity-based incentive programs for employees. The programs include performance share plans, stock options plans and restricted share plans. Both executives and employees participate in these programs.

The equity-based incentive grants are generally conditional upon continued employment as well as fulfilment of such performance, service and other conditions, as determined in the relevant plan rules.

The share-based compensation expense for all equity-based incentive awards amounted to EUR 16 million in 2009 (EUR 74 million in 2008 and EUR 228 million in 2007).

Stock options   Nokia's global stock option plans in effect for 2009, including their terms and conditions, were approved by the Annual General Meeting in the year when each plan was launched, i.e. in 2003, 2005 and 2007.

Each stock option entitles the holder to subscribe for one new Nokia share. The stock options are non-transferable. All of the stock options have a vesting schedule with 25% of the options vesting one year after grant and 6.25% each quarter thereafter. The stock options granted under the plans generally have a term of five years.

The exercise price of the stock options is determined at the time of grant on a quarterly basis. The exercise prices are determined in accordance with a pre-agreed schedule quarterly after the release of Nokia's periodic financial results and are based on the trade volume weighted average price of a Nokia share on NASDAQ OMX Helsinki during the trading days of the first whole week of the second month of the respective calendar quarter (i.e. February, May, August or November). Exercise prices are determined on a one-week weighted average to mitigate any short-term fluctuations in Nokia's share price. The determination of exercise price is defined in the terms and conditions of the stock option plan, which are approved by the shareholders at the respective Annual General Meeting. The Board of Directors does not have the right to amend the above-described determination of the exercise price.

The stock option exercises are settled with newly issued Nokia shares which entitle the holder to a dividend for the financial year in which the subscription occurs. Other shareholders' rights commence on the date on which the shares subscribed for are registered with the Finnish Trade Register.

Pursuant to the stock options issued under the global stock option plans, an aggregate maximum number of 22,755,509 new Nokia shares may be subscribed for, representing 0.6% of the total number of votes at December 31, 2009. During 2009, the exercise of stock options resulted in an increase of Nokia's share capital prior to May 3, 2007. After that date the exercises of stock options have no longer resulted in an increase of the share capital as thereafter all share subscription prices are recorded in the fund for invested non-restricted equity as per a resolution by the Annual General Meeting.

There were no stock options outstanding as of December 31, 2009, which upon exercise would result in an increase of the share capital of the parent company.

The table below sets forth certain information relating to the stock options outstanding at December 31, 2009.

Plan (year of launch)	Stock options outstanding 2009	Number of participants (approx)	Option (sub) category	Vesting status (as % of total number of stock options outstanding	First vest date	Last vest date	Expiry date	Exercise price/ share EUR
2003[1]	0	0	2004 2Q	Expired	July 1 2005	July 1, 2008	December 31, 2009	11.79
			2004 3Q	Expired	October 3, 2005	October 1, 2008	December 31, 2009	9.44
			2004 4Q	Expired	January 2, 2006	January 2, 2009	December 31, 2009	12.35
2005[1]	12,120,029	7,000	2005 2Q	100.00	July 1, 2006	July 1, 2009	December 31, 2010	12.79
			2005 3Q	100.00	October 1, 2006	October 1, 2009	December 31, 2010	13.09
			2006 4Q	93.75	January 1, 2007	January 1, 2010	December 31, 2010	14.48
			2006 1Q	87.50	April 1, 2007	April 1, 2010	December 31, 2011	14.99
			2006 2Q	81.25	July 1, 2007	July 1, 2010	December 31, 2011	18.02
			2006 3Q	75.00	October 1, 2007	October 1, 2010	December 31, 2011	15.37
			2006 4Q	68.75	January 1, 2008	January 1, 2011	December 31, 2011	15.38
			2007 1Q	62.50	April 1, 2008	April 1, 2011	December 31, 2011	17.00
2007[1]	10,635,480	9,000	2007 2Q	56.25	July 1, 2008	July 1, 2011	December 31, 2012	18.39
			2007 3Q	50.00	October 1, 2008	October 1, 2011	December 31, 2012	21.86
			2007 4Q	43.75	January 1, 2009	January 1, 2012	December 31, 2012	27.53
			2008 1Q	37.50	April 1, 2009	April 2, 2012	December 31, 2013	24.15
			2008 2Q	31.25	July 1, 2009	July 1, 2012	December 31, 2013	19.16
			2008 3Q	25.00	October 1, 2009	October 1, 22012	December 31, 2013	17.80
			2008 4Q	—	January 1, 2010	January 1, 2013	December 31, 2013	12.43
			2009 1Q	—	April 1, 2010	April 1, 2013	December 31, 2014	9.82
			2009 2Q	—	July 1, 2010	July 1, 2013	December 31, 2014	11.18
			2009 3Q	—	October 1, 2010	October 1, 2013	December 31, 2014	9.28
			2009 4Q	—	January 1, 2011	January 1, 2014	December 31, 2014	8.76

[1] *The Group's current global stock option plans have a vesting schedule with a 25% vesting one year after grant, and quarterly vesting thereafter, each of the quarterly lots representing 6.25% of the total grant. The grants vest fully in four years.*

Total stock options outstanding as at December 31, 2009[1]

	Number of shares	Weighted average exercise price, EUR[2]	Weighted average share price, EUR[2]
Shares under option at 01/01/07	**93,285,229**	**16.28**	
Granted	3,211,965	18.48	
Exercised	57.776,205	16.99	21.75
Forfeited	1,992,666	15.13	
Expired	1,161,096	17.83	
Shares under option at 31/12/07	**35,567,227**	**15.28**	
Granted	3,767,163	17.44	
Exercised	3,657,985	14.21	22.15
Forfeited	783,557	16.31	
Expired	11,078,983	14.96	
Shares under option at 31/12/08	**23,813,865**	**15.89**	
Granted	4,791,232	11.15	
Exercised	104,172	6.18	9.52
Forfeited	893,943	17.01	
Expired	4,567,020	13.55	
Shares under option at 31/12/09	**23,039,962**	**15.39**	
Options exercisable at 31/12/06 (shares)	69,721,916	16.65	
Options exercisable at 31/12/07 (shares)	21,535,000	14.66	
Options exercisable at 31/12/08 (shares)	12,895,057	14.77	
Options exercisable at 31/12/09 (shares)	**13,124,925**	**16.09**	

[1] *Includes also stock options granted under other than global equity plans. For further information see 'Other equity plans for employees' below.*
[2] *The weighted average exercise price and the weighted average share price do not incorporate the effects of transferable stock option exercises during 2007 by option holders not employed by the Group.*

The weighted average grant date fair value of stock options granted was EUR 2.34 in 2009, EUR 3.92 in 2008 and EUR 3.24 in 2007.

The options outstanding by range of exercise price at December 31, 2009 are as follows:

Exercise price, EUR	Number of shares	Weighted average remaining contractual life in years	Weighted average exercise price, EUR
0.81–9.93	215,987	4.27	6.07
10.26–14.99	10,498,214	3.06	12.10
15.37–19.86	12,202,542	2.61	18.28
21.86–37.37	123,219	2.03	26.63
	23,039,962		

Nokia calculates the fair value of stock options using the Black-Schole's model. The fair value of the stock options is estimated at the grant date using the following assumptions:

	2009	*2008*	*2007*
Weighted average expected dividend yield	3.63%	3.20%	2.30%
Weighted average expected volatility	43.46%	39.92%	25.24%
Risk-free interest rate	1.97–2.94%	3.14–4.58%	3.79–4.19%
Weighted average risk-free interest rate	2.23%	3.65%	4.09%
Expected life (years)	3.60	3.55	3.59
Weighted average share price, EUR	10.82	16.97	18.49

Expected term of stock options is estimated by observing general option holder behaviour and actual historical terms of Nokia stock options plans.

Expected volatility has been set by reference to the implied volatility of options available on Nokia shares in the open market and in light of historical patterns of volatility.

Performance Shares   The Group has granted performance shares under the global 2005, 2006, 2007, 2008 and 2009 plans, each of which, including its terms and conditions, has been approved by the Board of Directors. A valid authorization from the Annual General Meeting is required when the plans are to be settled by using the Nokia newly issued shares or treasury shares. The Group may also settle the plans by using cash instead of shares.

The performance shares represent a commitment by the Group to deliver Nokia shares to employees at a future point in time, subject to Nokia's fulfilment of pre-defined performance criteria. No performance shares will vest unless the Group's performance reaches at least one of the threshold levels measured by two independent, pre-defined performance criteria: the Group's average annual net sales, growth for the performance period of the plan and earnings per share ('EPS') at the end of the performance period.

The 2005 plan had a four-year performance period with a two-year interim measurement period. The 2006, 2007, 2008 and 2009 plans have a three-year performance period with no interim payout. The shares vest after the respecting interim measurement period and/or the performance period. The shares will be delivered to the participants as soon as practicable after they best. Until the Nokia shares are delivered, the participants will not have any shareholders rights, such as voting or dividend rights associated with the performance shares.

The following table summarizes our global performance share plans.

Plan	Performance shares outstanding at threshold[1,2]	Number of participants (approx)	Interim measurement period	Performance period	1st (interim) settlement	2nd (final) settlement
2005	0	11,000	2005–2006	2005–2008	2007	2009
2006	0	12,000	N/A	2006–2008	N/A	2009
2007	0	5,000	N/A	2007–2009	N/A	2010
2008	2,178,538	6,000	N/A	2008–2010	N/A	2011
2009	2,892,063	6,000	N/A	2009–2011	N/A	2012

[1] Shares under performance share plan 2007 vested on 31 December 2009 and are, therefore, not included in the outstanding numbers.
[2] Does not include 23,359 outstanding performance shares with deferred delivery due to leave of absence.

		Threshold Performance		Maximum Performance	
Plan		EPS[1,2] EUR	Average annual net sales growth[1]	EPS[1,2] EUR	Average annual net sales growth[1]
2005	Interim measurement	0.75	3%	0.96	12%
	Performance period	0.82	8%	1.33	17%
2006	Performance period	0.96	11%	1.41	26%
2007	Performance period	1.26	9.5%	1.86	20%
2008	Performance period	1.72	4%	2.76	16%
2009	Performance period	1.01	−5%	1.53	10%

[1] Both the EPS and average annual net sales growth criteria have an equal weight of 50%.
[2] The EPS for 2005, 2006 and 2007 plans: basic reported. The EPS for 2008 plan: diluted excluding special items. The EPS for 2009 plan: diluted non-IFRS.

Performance shares outstanding as at 31/12/09[1]

	Number of performance shares at threshold	Weighted average grant date fair value EUR[2]
Performance shares at 01/01/07[3]	12,614,389	
Granted	2,163,901	19.96
Forfeited	1,001,332	
Vested[4]	222,400	

Performance shares outstanding as at 31/12/09[1]

	Number of performance shares at threshold	Weighted average grant date fair value EUR[2]
Performance shares at 31/12/07[5]	13,554,558	
Granted	2,463,033	13.35
Forfeited	690,909	
Vested[3,4,6]	7,291,463	
Performance shares at 31/12/08	**8,035,219**	
Granted	2,960,110	9.57
Forfeited	691,325	
Vested[5,7]	5,210,044	
Performance shares at 31/12/09	**5,093,960**	

[1] Includes also performance shares granted under other than global equity plans. For further information see 'Other equity plans for employees' below.

[2] The fair value of performance shares is estimated based on the grant date market price of the Company's share less the present value of dividends expected to be paid during the vesting period.

[3] Based on the performance of the Group during the Interim Measurement Period 2004–2005, under the 2004 Performance Shares Plan, both performance criteria were met. Hence, 3,595,339 Nokia shares equalling the threshold number were delivered in 2006. The performance shares related to the interim settlement of the 2004 Performance Share Plan are included in the number of performance shares outstanding at January 1, 2007 as these performance shares were outstanding until the final settlement in 2008. The final payout, in 2008, was adjusted by the shares delivered based on the Interim Measurement Period.

[4] Includes also performance shares vested under other than global equity plans.

[5] Based on the performance of the Group during the Interim Measurement Period 2005–2006, under the 2005 Performance Share Plan, both performance criteria were met. Hence, 3,980,571 Nokia shares equalling the threshold number were delivered in 2007. The performance shares related to the interim settlement of the 2005 Performance Share Plan are included in the number of performance shares outstanding between December 31, 2007 as these performance shares were outstanding until the final settlement in 2009. The final payout in 2009, was adjusted by the shares delivered based on the Interim Measurement Period.

[6] Includes performance shares under Performance Share Plan 2006 that vested on December 31, 2008.

[7] Includes performance shares under Performance Share Plan 2007 that vested on December 31, 2009.

Restricted shares   The Group has granted restricted shares under global plans to recruit, retain, reward and motivate selected high potential employees, who are critical to the future success of Nokia. It is Nokia's philosophy that restricted shares will be used only for key management position and other critical talent. The outstanding global restricted share plans, including their terms and conditions, have been properly approved by the Board of Directors. A valid authorization from the Annual General Meeting is required when the plans are to be settled by using Nokia newly issued shares or treasury shares. The Group may also settle the plans by using cash instead of shares.

All of our restricted share plans have a restriction period of three years after grant, after which period the granted shares will vest. Once the shares vest, they will be delivered to the participants. Until the Nokia shares are delivered, the participants will not have any shareholder rights, such as voting or dividend rights, associated with the restricted shares.

Restricted shares outstanding as at December 31, 2009[1]
Weighted average grant

	Number of restricted shares	Date fair value EUR[2]
Restricted shares at 01/01/07	**6,064,876**	
Granted	1,749,433	24.37
Forfeited	297,900	
Vested	1,521,080	
Restricted shares at 31/12/07	**5,995,329**	
Granted[3]	4,799,543	13.89
Forfeited	358,747	
Vested	2,386,728	
Restricted shares at 31/12/08	**8,049,397**	
Granted	4,288,600	
Forfeited	446,695	
Vested	2,510,300	
Restricted shares at 31/12/09	**9,381,002**	

[1] *Includes also restricted shares granted under other than global equity plans. For further information see 'Other equity plans for employees' below.*
[2] *The fair value of restricted shares is estimated based on the grant date market price of the company's shares less the present value of dividends, if any, expected to be paid during the vesting period.*
[3] *Includes grants assumed under 'NAVTEQ' (as defined below).*

Other equity plans for employees   In addition to the global equity plans described above, the Group sponsors immaterial equity plans for Nokia-acquired businesses or employees in the United States or Canada that do not result in an increase in the share capital of Nokia. These plans are settled by using Nokia shares or ADSs acquired from the market. When treasury shares are issued on exercise of stock options any gain or loss is recognized in share issue premium.

On basis of these plans the Group had 0.3 million stock options outstanding on December 31, 2009. The weighted average exercise price is USD 16.13.

In connection with our July 10, 2008 acquisition of NAVTEQ, the Group assumed NAVTEQ's 2001 Stock Incentive Plan ('NAVTEQ Plan'). All unvested NAVTEQ restricted stock units under the NAVTEQ Plan were converted to an equivalent number of restricted stock units entitling their holders to Nokia shares. The maximum number of Nokia shares to be delivered to NAVTEQ employees during the years 2008–2012 is approximately 3 million, of which approximately 1 million shares have already been delivered by December 31, 2009. The Group does not intend to make further awards under the NAVTEQ Plan.

24. Deferred Taxes

EURm	*2009*	*2009*
Deferred tax assets:		
Intercompany profit in inventory	77	144
Tax losses carried forward	263	293
Warranty provision	73	117
Other provisions	315	371
Depreciation differences and untaxed reserves	796	1,059
Share-based compensation	15	68
Other temporary differences	320	282
Reclassification due to netting of deferred taxes	−352	−371
Total deferred tax assets	1,507	1,963
Deferred tax liabilities:		
Depreciation differences and untaxed reserves	−469	−654
Fair value gains/losses	−67	−62
Undistributed earnings	−345	−242
Other temporary differences[1]	−774	−1,200
Reclassification due to netting of deferred taxes	352	371
Total deferred tax liabilities	1,303	1,787
Net deferred tax asset	204	176
Tax charge to equity	−13	−128

[1] *In 2009 other temporary differences include a deferred tax liability of EUR 744 million (EUR 1,140 million in 2008) arising from the purchase price allocation related to Nokia Siemens Networks and NAVTEQ.*

At December 31, 2009, the Group had loss carry forward, primarily attributable to foreign subsidiaries of EUR 1,150 million (EUR 1,013 million in 2008), most of which will expire within 20 years.

At December 31, 2009 the Group had loss carry forwards and temporary differences of EUR 2,532 million (EUR 102 million in 2008) for which no deferred tax asset was recognized due to uncertainty of utilization of these items. Most of these items do not have an expiry date.

At December 31, 2009 the Group had undistributed earnings of EUR 322 million (EUR 274 million in 2008) for which no deferred tax liability was recognized as these earnings are considered to be permanently invested.

25. Accrued Expenses

EURm	*2009*	*2008*
Social security, VAT and other taxes	1,808	1,700
Wages and salaries	474	665
Advance payments	546	532
Other	3,676	4,126
Total	6,504	7,023

Other operating expense accruals include deferred service revenue, accrued discounts, royalties and marketing expenses as well as various amounts which are individually insignificant.

26. Provisions

EURm	Warranty	Restructuring	IPR infringements	Project losses	Tax	Other	Total
At 01/01/08	1,489	617	545	116	452	498	3,717
Exchange differences	−16	—	—	—	—	—	−16
Acquisitions	1	—	3	—	6	2	12
Additional provisions	1,211	533	266	389	47	747	3,193
Change in fair value	—	—	—	—	—	−7	−7
Changes in estimates	−240	−211	−92	−42	−45	−143	−773
Charged to profit and loss	**971**	**322**	**174**	**347**	**2**	**597**	**2,413**
Utilized during year	−1,070	−583	−379	−218	—	−284	−2,534
At December 31/12/08	**1,375**	**356**	**343**	**245**	**460**	**813**	**3,592**
At 01/01/09	1,375	356	343	245	460	813	3,592
Exchange differences	−13	—	—	—	—	—	−13
Additional provisions	793	268	73	269	139	344	1,886
Change in fair value	—	—	—	—	—	−1	−1
Changes in estimates	−178	−62	−9	−63	−325	−174	−811
Charged to profit and loss account	**615**	**206**	**64**	**206**	**−186**	**169**	**1,074**
Utilized during year	−1,006	−378	−17	−254	—	−280	−1,935
At 31/12/09	**971**	**184**	**390**	**197**	**274**	**702**	**2,718**

EURm	2009	2008
Analysis of total provisions at 31/12/09:		
Non-current	841	978
Current	1,877	2,614

Outflows for the warranty provisions are generally expected to occur within the next 18 months. In 2009, warranty provision decreased compared to 2008 primarily due to lower sales volumes in Devices & Services. Timing of outflows related to tax provisions is inherently uncertain. In 2009, tax provisions decreased due to the positive development and outcome of various prior year items.

The restructuring provision is mainly related to restructuring activities in Devices & Services and Nokia Siemens Networks segments. The majority of outflows related to the restructuring are expected to occur in 2010.

In 2009, Devices & Services recognized restructuring provisions of EUR 208 million mainly related to measures taken to adjust our business operations and cost base according to market conditions. In 2008, resulting from the Group's decision to discontinue the production of mobile devices in Germany, a restructuring provision of EUR 259 million was recognized. Devices & Services also recognized EUR 52 million related to other restructuring activities.

Restructuring and other associated expenses incurred in Nokia Siemens Networks in 2009 totalled EUR 310 million (EUR 64 million in 2008) including mainly personnel related expenses as well as expenses arising from the elimination of overlapping functions, and the realignment of production portfolio and related replacement of discontinued products in customer sites. These expenses included EUR 151 million (EUR 402 million in 2008) impacting gross profit, EUR 30 million (EUR 46 million in 2008) administrative expenses and EUR 14 million (EUR 49 million in 2008) other operating expenses. EUR 514 million was paid during 2009 (EUR 790 million during 2008).

Provisions for losses on projects in progress and related to Nokia Siemens Networks' onerous contracts.

The IPR provision is based on estimated future settlements for asserted and unasserted past IPR infringements. Final resolution of IPR claims generally occurs over several periods. In 2008, EUR 379 million usage of the provisions mainly relates to the settlements with Qualcomm, Eastman Kodak, Intertrust Technologies and ContentGuard.

Other provisions include provisions for non-cancellable purchase commitments, product portfolio provisions for the alignment of the product portfolio and related replacement of discontinued products in customer sites and provision for pension and other social security costs on share-based awards.

27. Earnings per Share

	2009	*2008*	*2007*
Numerator/EURm			
Basic/diluted:			
Profit attributable to equity holders of the parent	891	3,988	7,205
Denominator/1,000 shares			
Basic:			
Weighted average shares	3,705,116	3,743,622	3,885,408
Effect of dilutive securities:			
Performance shares	9,614	25,997	26,304

	2009	2008	2007
Restricted shares	6,341	6,543	3,693
Stock options	1	4,201	16,603
	15,956	36,741	46,600
Diluted:			
Adjusted weighted average shares and assumed conversions	3,721,072	3,780,363	3,932,008

Under IAS 33, basic earnings per share is computed using the weighted average number of shares outstanding during the period. Diluted earnings per share is computed using the weighted average number of shares outstanding during the period plus the dilutive effect of stock options, restricted shares and performance shares outstanding during the period.

In 2009, stock options equivalent to 12 million shares (11 million in 2008) were excluded from the calculation of diluted earnings per share because they were determined to be anti-dilutive.

28. Commitments and Contingencies

EURm	2009	2008
Collateral for our own commitments		
Property under mortgages	18	18
Assets pledged	13	11
Contingent liabilities on behalf of group companies		
Other guarantees	1,350	2,896
Contingent liabilities on behalf of other companies		
Financial guarantees on behalf of third parties[1]	—	2
Other guarantees	3	1
Financing commitments		
Customer finance commitments[1]	99	197
Venture fund commitments[2]	293	467

[1] *See also note 33 (b).*
[2] *See also note 33 (a).*

The amounts above represent the maximum principal amount of commitments and contingencies.

Property under mortgages given as collateral for our own commitments include mortgages given to the Finnish National Board of Customs as a general indemnity of EUR 18 million in 2009 (EUR 10 million of available-for-sale investments in 2008).

Other guarantees include guarantees of EUR 1,012 million in 2009 (EUR 2,682 million in 2008) provided to certain Nokia Siemens Networks' customers in the form of bank guarantees or corporate guarantees issued by Nokia Siemens Networks' Group entity. These instruments entitle the customer to claim payment as compensation for non-performance by Nokia of its obligations under network infrastructure supply agreements. Depending on the nature of the guarantees, compensation is payable on demand or subject to verification of non-performance. Volume of Other guarantees has decreased due to release of certain commercial guarantees and due to exclusion of those guarantees where possibility for claim is considered as remote.

Contingent liabilities on behalf of other companies were EUR 3 million in 2009 (EUR 3 million in 2008).

Financing commitments of EUR 99 million in 2009 (EUR 197 million in 2008) are available under loan facilities negotiated mainly with Nokia Siemens Networks' customers. Availability of the amounts is dependent upon the borrower's continuing compliance with stated financial and operations covenants and compliance with other administrative terms of the facility. The loan facilities are primarily available to fund capital expenditure relating to purchases of network infrastructure equipment and services.

The Group is party of routine litigation incidental to the normal conduct of business, including, but not limited to, several claims, suits and actions both initiated by third parties and initiated by Nokia relating to infringements of patents, violations of licensing arrangements and other intellectual property related matters, as well as actions with respect to products, contracts and securities. In the opinion of the management outcome of and liabilities in excess of what has been provided for related to these or other proceedings, in the aggregate, are not likely to be material to the financial conditions, or result of operations.

Nokia's payment obligations under the subscriber unit cross-license agreements signed in 2002 and 2001 with Qualcomm Incorporated ('Qualcomm') expired on April 9, 2007. The parties entered into negotiations for a new license agreement with the intention of reaching a mutually acceptable agreement on a timely basis. Prior to the commencement of negotiations and as negotiations proceeded, Nokia and Qualcomm were engaged in numerous legal disputes in the United States, Europe and China. On July 24, 2008 Nokia and Qualcomm entered into a new license agreement covering various current and future standards and other technologies. Nokia has been granted a license under all Qualcomm's patents for use in Nokia's mobile devices and Nokia Siemens Networks' infrastructure equipment, and Nokia has agreed not to use any of its patents directly against Qualcomm. The financial terms included a one-time lump-sum cash payment of EUR 1.7 billion made by Nokia to Qualcomm in the fourth quarter of 2008 and on-going royalty payments to Qualcomm. The lump-sum payment made to Qualcomm will be expensed over the term of the agreement. Nokia also agreed to assign ownership of a number of patents to Qualcomm.

As of December 31, 2009, the Group had purchase commitments of EUR 2,765 million (EUR 2,351 million in 2008) relating to inventory purchase obligations, service agreements and outsourcing arrangements, primarily for purchases in 2010.

29. Leasing Contracts

The Group leases office, manufacturing and warehouse space under various non-cancellable operating leases. Certain contracts contain renewal options for various periods of time.

The future costs for non-cancellable leasing contracts are as follows:

Leasing payments, EURm	*Operating leases*
2010	348
2011	254
2012	180
2013	131
2014	99
Thereafter	210
Total	1,222

Rental expense amounted to EUR 436 million in 2009 (EUR 418 million in 2008 and EUR 328 million in 2007).

30. Related Party Transactions

At December 31, 2009, the Group had borrowings amounting to EUR 69 million (EUR 69 million in 2008 and EUR 69 million in 2007) from Nokia Unterstutzungskasse GmbH, the Group's German pension fund, which is a separate legal entity. The loan bears interest at 6% per annum and its duration is pending until further notice by the loan counterparts who have the right to terminate the loan with a 90 day notice period.

There were no loans made to the members of the Group Executive Board and Board of Directors at December 31, 2009, 2008 or 2007.

EURm	*2009*	*2008*	*2007*
Transactions with associated companies			
Share of results of associated companies	30	6	44
Dividend income	—	6	12
Share of shareholders' equity of associated companies	35	21	158
Sales to associated companies	8	59	82
Purchases from associated companies	211	162	125
Receivables from associated companies	2	29	61
Liabilities to associated companies	31	8	69

Management compensation   The following table sets forth the salary and cash incentive information awarded and paid or payable by the company to the Chief Executive Officer and President of Nokia for fiscal years 2007–2009 as well as the share-based compensation expense relating to equity-based awards, expensed by the company.

EUR	2009			2008			2007		
	Base salary	*Cash incentive payments*	*Share-based compensation expense*	*Base salary*	*Cash incentive payments*	*Share-based compensation expense*	*Base salary*	*Cash incentive payments*	*Share-based compensation expense*
Olli-Pekka Kallasvuo President & CEO	1,176,000	1,288,144	2,840,777	1,144,800	721,733	1,286,370	1,037,619	2,348,877	4,805,722

Total remuneration of the Group Executive Board warded for the fiscal years 2007–2009 was EUR 10,723,777 in 2009 (EUR 8,859,567 in 2008 and EUR 13,634,791 in 2007), which consisted of base salaries and cash incentive payments. Total share-based compensation expense relating to equity-based awards expensed by the company was EUR 9,668,484 in 2009 (EUR 4,850,204 in 2008 and EUR 19,837,583 in 2007).

Board of directors The following table depicts the annual remuneration paid to the members of our Board of Directors, as resolved by the Annual General Meetings in the respective years.

Board of Directors	2009		2008		2007	
	Gross annual fee EUR[1]	*Shares received*	*Gross annual fee EUR[1]*	*Shares received*	*Gross annual fee EUR[1]*	*Shares received*
Jorma Ollila, Chairman[2]	440,000	16,575	440,000	9,499	375,000	8,110
Dame Marjorie Scardino, Vice chairman[3]	150,000	5,649	150,000	3,238	150,000	3,245
Georg Ehrnrooth[4]	155,000	5,838	155,000	3,346	155,000	3,351
Lalita D Gupte[5]	140,000	5,273	140,000	3,022	140,000	3,027
Bengt Holmstrom	130,000	4,896	130,000	2,806	130,000	2,810
Henning Kagermann	130,000	4,896	130,000	2,806	130,000	2,810
Olli-Pekka Kallasvuo[6]	130,000	4,896	130,000	2,806	130,000	2,810
Per Karlsson[7]	155,000	5,838	155,000	3,346	155,000	3,351

Board of Directors	2009 Gross annual fee EUR[1]	2009 Shares received	2008 Gross annual fee EUR[1]	2008 Shares received	2007 Gross annual fee EUR[1]	2007 Shares received
Isabel Marey-Semper[8]	140,000	5,273	—	—	—	—
Risto Siilasmaa[9]	140,000	5,273	140,000	3,022	—	—
Keijo Suila[10]	130,000	4,896	140,000	3,022	140,000	3,027
Vesa Vainio[11]	—	—	—	—	140,000	3,027

[1] *Approximately 60% of the gross annual fee is paid in cash and the remaining 40% in Nokia shares purchased from the market and included in the table under 'Shares Received'. Further, it is Nokia policy that the directors retain all company stock received as director compensation until the end of their board membership, subject to the need to finance any costs including taxes relating to the acquisition of the shares.*

[2] *This table includes fees paid to Mr Ollila, Chairman, for his services as Chairman of the Board only.*

[3] *The 2009, 2008 and 2007 fees of Ms Scardino amounted to EUR 150,000 for services as Vice Chairman.*

[4] *The 2009, 2008 and 2007 fees of Mr Ehrnrooth amounted to a total of EUR 155,000, consisting of a fee of EUR 130,000 for services as a member of the Board and EUR 25,000 for services as Chairman of the Audit Committee.*

[5] *The 2009, 2008 and 2007 fees of Ms Gupte amounted to a total of EUR 140,000, consisting of a fee of 130,000 for services as a member of the Board and EUR 10,000 for services as a member of the Audit Committee.*

[6] *This table includes fees paid to Mr Kallasvuo, President and CEO, for his services as a member of the Board only.*

[7] *The 2009, 2008 and 2007 fees of Mr Karlsson amounted to a total of EUR 155,000, consisting of a fee of EUR 130,000 for services as a member of the Board and EUR 25,000 for services as Chairman of the Personnel Committee.*

[8] *The 2009 fee paid to Ms Marey-Semper amounted to a total of EUR 140,000, consisting of a fee of EUR 130,000 for services as a member of the Board and EUR 10,000 for services as a member of the Audit Committee.*

[9] *The 2009 and 2008 fee of Mr Sillasmaa amounted to a total of EUR 140,000, consisting of a fee of EUR 130,000 for services as a member of the Board and EUR 10,000 for services as a member of the Audit committee.*

[10] *The 2008 and 2007 fees of Mr Suila amounted to a total of EUR 140,000, consisting of a fee of EUR 130,000 for services as a member of the Board and EUR 10,000 for services as a member of the Audit Committee.*

[11] *Mr Vainio was a member of the Board of Directors and the Audit Committee until the end of the Annual General Meeting on May 8, 2008. Mr Vainio received his fees for services as a member of the Board and as a member of the Audit Committee, as resolved by the shareholders at the Annual General Meeting on May 3, 2007, already in 2007 and thus no fees were paid to him for the services rendered during 2008. The 2007 fee of Mr Vainio amounted to a total of EUR 140,000, consisting of a fee of EUR 130,000 for services as a member of the Board and EUR 10,000 for services as a member of the Audit Committee.*

Pension arrangements for certain Group Executive Board Members Olli-Pekka Kallasvuo can, as part of his service contract, retire at the age of 60 with full retirement benefit should he be employed by Nokia at the time. The full retirement benefit is calculated as if Mr Kallasvuo had continued his service with Nokia through retirement age of 65. Hallstein Moerk, following his arrangement with a previous employer, and continuing in his current position at Nokia, has a retirement benefit of 65% of his pensionable salary beginning at the age of 62 and early retirement is possible at the age of 55 with reduced benefits. Mr Moerk will retire at the end of September 2010 at the age of 57.

31. Notes to Cash Flow Statements

EURm	2009	2008	2007
Adjustments for:			
Depreciation and amortization (note 9)	1,784	1,617	1,206
Plant and equipment and available-for-sale			
investments	−111	−11	−1,864
Income taxes (note 11)	702	1,081	1,522
Share of results of associated companies (Note 14)	−30	−6	−44
Minority interest	−631	−99	−459
Financial income and expenses (Note 10)	265	2	−239
Transfer from hedging reserve to sales and cost of			
sales (Note 20)	44	−445	−110
Impairment charge (Note 7)	1,009	149	63
Asset retirements (Notes 8, 12)	35	186	—
Share-based compensation (Note 23)	16	74	228
Restructuring charges	307	448	856
Finnish pension settlement (Note 5)	—	152	—
Other income and expenses	—	−124	—
Adjustments Total	**3,390**	**3,024**	**1,159**
Change in net working capital			
Decrease (+)/increase (−) in short term receivables	1,145	−534	−2,146
Decrease (+)/increase (−) in inventories	640	321	−245
Decrease (−)/increase (+) in interest-free			
short-term borrowings	−1,698	−2,333	2,996
Loans made to customers	53	—	—
Change in net working capital	**140**	**−2,546**	**605**

The transfer from hedging reserve to sales and cost of sales for 2008 and 2007 have been reclassified for comparability purposes from Other financial income and expenses to Adjustments to profit attributable to equity holders of the parent within Net cash from operating activities on the Consolidated Statement of Cash Flows.

The Group did not engage in any material non-cash investing activities in 2009 and 2008. In 2007 the formation of Nokia Siemens Networks was completed through the contribution of certain tangible and intangible assets and certain business interests that comprised Nokia's networks business and Siemens' carrier-related operations. See Note 8.

32. Principal Nokia Group Companies at December 31, 2009

		Parent holding %	*Group Majority %*
US	Nokia Inc	—	100.0
DE	Nokia GmbH	100.0	100.0
GB	Nokia UK Limited	—	100.0
KR	Nokia TMC Limited	100.0	100.0
CN	Nokia Telecommunications Ltd	4.5	63.9
NL	Nokia Finance International BV	100.0	100.0
HU	Nokia Komarom Kft	100.0	100.0
IN	Nokia India Pvt Ltd	99.9	100.0
IT	Nokia Italia SpA	100.0	100.0
ES	Nokia Spain SSAU	100.0	100.0
RO	Nokia Romania SRL	100.0	100.0
BR	Nokia do Brazil Technologia Ltda	99.9	100.0
RU	ODO Nokia	100.0	100.0
US	NACTEQ Corp	—	100.0
NL	Nokia Siemens Networks BV	—	50.0[1]
FI	Nokia Siemens Networks Oy	—	50.0
DE	Nokia Siemens Networks GmbH & Co KG	—	50.0
IN	Nokia Siemens Networks Pvt Ltd	—	50.0

[1] *Nokia Siemens Networks BV, the ultimate parent of the Nokia Siemens Network Group, is owned approximately 50% by each of Nokia and Siemens and consolidated by Nokia. Nokia effectively controls Nokia Siemens Networks as it has the ability to appoint key officers and the majority of the members of its Board of Directors, and accordingly, Nokia consolidated Nokia Siemens Networks.*

33. Risk Management

General risk management principles   Nokia has a common and systematic approach to risk management across business operations and processes. Material risks and opportunities are identified, analyzed, managed and monitored as part of business performance management. Relevant key risks are identified against business targets either in business operations or as an integral part of long and short term planning. Nokia's overall risk management concept is based on visibility of the key risks preventing Nokia from reaching its business objectives rather than solely focussing on eliminating risks.

The principles documented in Nokia's Risk Policy and accepted by the Audit Committee of the Board of Directors require risk management and its elements to be integrated into business processes. One of the main principles is that the business, function or category owner is also the risk owner, but it is everyone's responsibility at Nokia to identify risks, which prevent Nokia to reach the objectives. Risk management covers strategic, operations, financial and hazard risks.

Key risks are reported to the Group level management to create assurance on business risks as well as to enable prioritization of risk management activities at Nokia. In addition to general principles there are specific risk management policies covering, for example, treasury and customer related credit risks.

Financial risks   The objective for Treasury activities in Nokia is twofold: to guarantee cost-efficient funding for the Group at all times, and to identify, evaluate and hedge financial risks. There is a strong focus in Nokia on creating shareholder value. Treasury activities support this aim by (i) mitigating the adverse effects caused by fluctuations in the financial markets on the profitability of the underlying businesses; and (ii) managing the capital structure of the Group by prudently balancing the levels of liquid assets and financial borrowings.

Treasury activities are governed by policies approved by the CEO, Treasury Policy provides principles for overall financial risk management and determines the allocation of responsibilities for financial risk management in Nokia. Operating Procedures cover specific areas such as foreign exchange risk, interest rate risk, use of derivative financial instruments, as well as liquidity and credit risk. Nokia is risk averse in its Treasury activities.

(a) Market risk

Foreign exchange risk   Nokia operates globally and is thus exposed to foreign exchange risk arising from various currencies. Foreign currency denominated assets and liabilities together with expected cash flows from highly probable purchases and sales contribute to foreign exchange exposure. These transactions exposures are managed against various local currencies because of Nokia's substantial production and sales outside the Euro zone.

According to the foreign exchange policy guidelines of the Group, which remain the same as in the previous year, material transaction foreign exchange exposures are hedged unless hedging would be uneconomical due to market liquidity and/or hedging cost. Exposures are mainly hedged with derivative financial instruments such as forward exchange contracts and foreign exchange options. The majority of financial instruments hedging foreign exchange risk have duration of less than a year. The Group does not hedge forecasted foreign currency cash flows beyond two years.

Since Nokia has subsidiaries outside the Euro zone, the Euro-denominated value of the shareholders' equity of Nokia is also exposed to fluctuations in exchange rates. Equity changes resulting from movements in foreign exchange rates are shown as a translation difference in the Group consolidation.

Nokia uses, from time to time, foreign exchange contracts and foreign currency denominated loans to hedge its equity exposure arising from foreign net investments.

At the end of year 2009 and 2008, the following currencies represent significant portion of the currency mix in the outstanding financial instruments:

2009 EURm	USD	JPY	CNY	INR
FX derivatives used as Cash flow hedges (net amount)[1]	−1,767	663	—	−78
FX derivatives used as net investment hedges (net amount)[2]	−969	−6	−983	−208
FX exposure from balance sheet items (net amount)[3]	−464	−421	−1,358	80
FX derivatives not designated in a hedge relationship and carried at fair value through profit and loss (net amount)[3]	−328	578	1,633	−164
Cross currency/interest rate hedges	375			

2008 EURm	USD	JPY	GBP	INR
FX derivatives used as cash flow hedges (net amount)[1]	−3,359	2,674	—	−122
FX derivatives used as net investment hedges (net amount)[2]	−232	—	−699	−179
FX exposure from balance sheet items (net amount)[3]	729	−494	−579	236
FX derivatives designated in a hedge relationship and carried at fair value through profit and loss (net amount)[3]	−615	480	527	−443

[1] *The FX derivatives are used to hedge the foreign exchange risk from forecasted highly probable cash flows related to sales, purchases and business acquisition activities. In some of the currencies, especially in US Dollar, Nokia has substantial foreign exchange risks in both estimated cash inflows and outflows, which have been netted in the table. See Note 20 for more details on hedge accounting. The underlying exposures for which these hedges are entered into are not presented in the table, as they are not financial instruments as defined under IFRS 7.*
[2] *The FX derivatives are used to hedge the Group's net investment exposure. The underlying exposures for which these hedges are entered into are not presented in the table, as they are not financial instruments as defined under IFRS 7.*
[3] *The balance sheet items which are denominated in the foreign currencies are hedged by a portion of FX derivatives not designated in a hedge relationship and carried at fair value through profit and loss resulting in offsetting FX gains or losses in the financial income and expenses.*

Interest rate risk   The Group is exposed to interest rate risk either through market value fluctuations of balance sheet items (i.e. price risk) or through changes in interest income or expenses (i.e. re-financing or re-investment risk). Interest rate risk mainly arises through interest bearing liabilities and assets. Estimated future changes in cash flows and balance sheet structure also expose the Group to interest rate risk.

The objective of interest rate risk management is to optimize the balance between minimizing uncertainty caused by fluctuations in interest rates and maximizing the consolidated net interest income and expenses.

The interest rate exposure of the Group is monitored and managed centrally. Nokia uses the Value-at-Risk (VaR) methodology to assess and measure the interest rate risk of the net investments (cash and investments less outstanding debt) and related derivatives.

As at the reporting date, the interest rate profile of the Group's interest-bearing assets and liabilities is presented in the table below:

EURm	Fixed rate	Floating rate	Fixed rate	Floating rate
Assets	5,712	3,241	2,946	4,007
Liabilities	−3,771	−1,403	−3,604	−785
Assets and liabilities before derivatives	1,941	1,838	−658	3,222
Interest rate derivatives	1,628	−1,693	—	—
Assets and liabilities after derivatives	3,569	145	−658	3,222

Equity price risk   Nokia is exposed to equity price risk as the result of market price fluctuations in the listed equity instruments held mainly for strategic business reasons.

Nokia has certain strategic minority investments in public listed equity shares. The fair value of the equity investments which are subject to equity price risk at December 31, 2009 was EUR 8 million (EUR 8 million in 2008). In addition, Nokia invests in private equity through venture funds, which, from time to time, may have holdings in equity instruments which are listed in stock exchanges. These investments are classified as available-for-sale carried at fair value. See Note 15 for more details on available-for-sale investments.

Due to the insignificant amount of exposure to equity price risk, there are currently no outstanding derivative financial instruments designated as hedges for these equity investments.

Nokia is exposed to equity price risk on social security costs relating to its equity compensation plans. Nokia mitigates this risk by entering into cash settled equity option contracts.

Value-at-Risk   Nokia uses the Value-at-Risk (VaR) methodology to assess the Group exposures to foreign exchange (FX), interest rate, and equity risks. The VaR gives estimates of potential fair value losses in market risk sensitive instruments as a result of adverse changes in specified market factors, at a specified confidence level over a defined holding period.

In Nokia the FX VaR is calculated with the Monte Carlo method which simulates random values for exchange rates in which the Group has exposures and takes the non-linear price function of certain FX derivative instruments into account. The variance-covariance methodology is used to assess and measure the interest rate risk and equity price risk.

The VaR is determined by using volatilities and correlations of rates and prices estimated from a one-year sample of historical market data, at 95% confidence level, using a one-month holding period. To put more weight on recent market conditions, an exponentially weighted moving average is performed on the data with an appropriate decay factor.

Table A.1   Foreign exchange positions Value at Risk

	Var from financial instruments	
EURm	*2009*	*2008*
At December 31	190	442
Average for the year	291	337
Range for the year	160–520	191–730

This model implies that within a one-month period, the potential loss will not exceed the VaR estimate in 95% of possible outcomes. In the remaining 5% of possible outcomes, the potential loss will be at minimum equal to the VaR figure, and on average substantially higher.

The VaR methodology relies on a number of assumptions, such as, (a) risks are measured under average market conditions, assuming that market risk factors follow normal distributions; (b) future movements in market risk factors allow estimated historical movements; (c) the assessed exposures do not change during the holing period. Thus it is possible that, for any given month, the potential losses at 95% confidence level are difference and could be substantially higher than the estimated VaR.

FX risk   The VaR figures for the Group's financial instruments which are sensitive to foreign exchange risks are presented in Table A.1 above. As defined under IFRS 7, the financial instruments included in the VaR calculation are:

- FX exposures from outstanding balance sheet items and other FX derivatives carried at fair value through profit and loss which are not in a hedge relationship and are mostly used for hedging balance sheet FX exposure.
- FX derivates designated as forecasted cash flow hedges and net investment hedges. Most of the VaR is caused by these derivatives as forecasted cash flow and net investment exposures are not financial instruments as defined under IFRS 7 and thus not included in the VaR calculation.

Interest rate risk   The VaR for the Group interest rate exposure in the net investment and debt portfolios is presented in Table A.2 below. Sensitivities to credit spreads are not reflected in the below numbers.

The sizeable difference between the 2009 and 2008 numbers is mainly due to the fact that Nokia issued bonds with long maturities during the first half of 2009 which resulted in a significant increase in the Group's exposure to long-term interest rates.

Equity price risk   The VaR for the Group equity instruments in publicly traded companies is insignificant.

Table A.2   Treasury investment and debt portfolios Value-at-Risk

EURm	*2009*	*2008*
At December 31	41	6
Average for the year	33	10
Range for the year	4–52	4–25

(b) Credit risk   Credit risk refers to the risk that a counterparty will default on its contractual obligations resulting in financial loss to the Group. Credit risk arises from bank and cash, fixed income and money-market investments, derivative financial instruments, loans and receivables as well as credit exposures to customers, including outstanding receivables, financial guarantees and committed transactions. Credit risk is managed separately for business related and financial-credit exposures.

Except as detailed in the following table, the maximum exposure to credit risk is limited to the book value of the financial assets as included in the Group's balance sheet:

EURm	*2009*	*2008*
Financial guarantees given on behalf of customers and other third parties	—	2
Loan commitments given but not used	99	197
	99	199

Business related credit risk   The Company aims to ensure highest possible quality in accounts receivable and loans due from customers and other third parties. The Group Credit Policy, approved by Group Executive Board, lays out the framework for the management of the business related credit risks in all Nokia group companies.

Credit exposure is measured as the total of accounts receivable and loans outstanding due from customers and other third parties, and committed credits.

Group Credit Policy provides that credit decisions are based on credit evaluation including credit rating for larger exposures. Nokia and Nokia Siemens Networks Rating Policy defines the rating principles. Ratings are approved by Nokia and Nokia Siemens Networks Rating Committee. Credit risks are approved and monitored according to the credit policy of each business entity. These policies are based on the Group Credit Policy. Concentrations of customer or country risks are monitored at the Nokia Group level. When appropriate, assumed credit risks are mitigated with the use of approved instruments, such as collateral or insurance and sale of selected receivables.

The Group has provided impairment allowances as needed including on accounts receivable and loans due from customers and other third parties not past due, based on the analysis of debtors' credit quality and credit history. The Group establishes an allowance for impairment that represents an estimate of incurred losses. All receivables and loans due from customers and other third parties are considered on an individual basis for impairment testing.

Top three customers account for approximately 2.2%, 2.2% and 1.9% (2008: 4.0%, 3.8% and 3.5%) of Group accounts receivable and loans due from customers and other third parties as at December 31, 2009, while the top three credit exposures by country amounted to 7.2%, 6.5% and 5.6% (2008: 8.5%, 7.2% and 7.2%), respectively.

As at December 31, 2009, the carrying amount before deducting any impairment allowance of accounts receivable relating to customers for which an impairment was provided amounted to EUR 2,528 million (2008: EUR 3,042 million). The amount of provision taken against that portion of these receivables considered to be impaired was EUR 391 million (2008: EUR 415 million) (see also Note 19 Valuation and qualifying accounts).

An amount of EUR 679 million (208: EUR 729 million) relates to past due receivables from customers for which no impairment loss was recognized. The ageing of these receivables is as follows:

EURm	2009	2008
Past due 1–30 days	393	453
Past due 31–180 days	170	240
More than 180 days	116	36
	679	729

The carrying amount of accounts receivable that would otherwise be past due or impaired but whose terms have been renegotiated was EUR 36 million (EUR 0 million in 2008).

As at December 31, 2009, the carrying amount before deducting any impairment allowance of loans due from customers and other third parties for which impairment was provided amounted to EUR 4 million (2008: EUR 4 million). The amount of provisions taken for these loans was EUR 4 million (2008: EUR 4 million).

There was no past due loans from customers and other third parties.

Financial credit risk   Financial instruments contain an element of risk of loss resulting from counterparties being unable to meet their obligations. This risk is measured and monitored centrally by Treasury. Nokia manages financial credit risk actively by limiting its counterparties to a sufficient number of major banks and financial institutions and monitoring the credit worthiness and exposure sizes continuously as well as through entering into netting arrangements (which gives Nokia the right to offset in the event that the counterparty would not be able to fulfil the obligations) with all major counterparties and collateral agreements (which require counterparties to post collateral against derivative receivables), with certain counterparties.

Nokia's investment decisions are based on strict creditworthiness and maturity criteria as defined in the Treasury Policy and Operating Procedure. Due to global banking crisis and the freezing of the credit markets in 2008, Nokia applied an even more defensive approach than usual within Treasury policy towards investments and counterparty quality and maturities, focusing on capital preservation and liquidity. As a result of this investment policy approach and active management of outstanding investment exposures, Nokia has not been subject to any material credit losses in its financial statements.

(c) Liquidity Risk Liquidity risk is defined as financial distress or extraordinary high financing costs arising due to a shortage of liquid funds in a situation where business conditions unexpectedly deteriorate and require financing. Transactional liquidity risk is defined as the risk of executing a financial transaction below fair market value, or not being able to execute the transaction at all, within a specific period of time.

The objective of liquidity risk management is to maintain sufficient liquidity and to ensure that it is available fast enough without endangering its value, in order to avoid uncertainty related to financial distress at all times.

Nokia guarantees a sufficient liquidity at all times by efficient cash management and by investing in liquid interest bearing securities. The transactional liquidity risk is minimized by only entering transaction where proper two-way quotes can be obtained from the market.

Due to the dynamic nature of the underlying business, Nokia and Nokia Siemens Networks aim at maintaining flexibility in funding by keeping committed and uncommitted credit lines available. Nokia and Nokia Siemens Networks manage their respective credit facilities independently and facilities do not include cross-default clauses between Nokia and Nokia Siemens Networks or any forms of guarantees from either party. At the end of December 31, 2009 the committed facilities totalled EUR 4,113 million.

The most significant existing Committed Facilities include:
Borrower(s):

Nokia Corporation: USD 1,923 million Revolving Credit Facility maturing 2012.
Nokia Siemens Networks Finance BV and Nokia Siemens Networks OY: EUR 2,000 million Revolving Credit Facility maturing 2012.
Nokia Siemens Networks Finance BV: EUR 750 million Credit Facility, maturing 2013.

USD 1,923 million Revolving Credit Facility of Nokia Corporation is used primarily for US and Euro Commercial Paper Programs back up purposes. As at year end 2009, this facility was fully withdrawn.

EUR 2,000 million Revolving Credit Facility of Nokia Siemens Networks Finance BV and Nokia Siemens Networks OY is used for general corporate purposes. The Facility includes financial covenants to gearing test, leverage test and interest coverage test of Nokia Siemens Networks. As of December 31, 2009 EUR 49 million of the facility was utilized and all financial covenants were satisfied. The EUR 750 million Credit Facility of Nokia Siemens Networks Finance BV was fully utilized for general funding purposes.

As of December 31, 2009, the weighted average commitment fee on the committed credit facilities was 0.70% per annum.

The most significant existing funding programs include:

Issuer(s):

Nokia Corporation:	Medium Term Note (EMTN) program, totalling EUR 5,000 million.
Nokia Corporation:	Shelf registration statement on file with US Securities and Exchange Commission.
Nokia Corporation:	Local commercial paper program in Finland, totalling EUR 750 million.
Nokia Corporation:	US Commercial Paper (USCP) program, totalling USD 4,000 million.
Nokia Corporation and Nokia International Finance BV:	Euro Commercial Paper (ECP) program, totalling USD 4,000 million.

Of the above funding programs, EMTN, Shelf registration and US Commercial Paper program have been utilized in 2009. On December 31, 2009 a total of EUR 1,750 million, USD 1,500 million and USD 693 million were outstanding under these programs, respectively. Local commercial paper program and ECP program have not been used to a material degree in 2009.

Nokia's international creditworthiness facilitates the efficient use of international capital and loan markets. The ratings as of December 31, 2009 were:

Short-term:	Standard & Poor's	A-1
	Moody's	P-1
Long-term:	Standard & Poor's	A
	Moody's	A2

The following table below is an undiscounted cash flow analysis for both financial liabilities and financial assets that are presented on the balance sheet, and off-balance sheet instruments such as loan commitments according to their remaining contractual maturity. Line-by-line reconciliation with the balance sheet is not possible.

At December 31, 2009 EURm	Due within 3 months	Due between 3 and 12 months	Due between 1 and 3 years	Due between 3 and 5 years	Due beyond 5 years
Non-current financial assets					
Long-term loans receivable	—	—	36	6	4
Other non-current assets	—	—	3	1	1
Current financial assets					
Current portion of long-term loans receivable	4	11	—	—	—

At December 31, 2009 EURm	*Due within 3 months*	*Due between 3 and 12 months*	*Due between 1 and 3 years*	*Due between 3 and 5 years*	*Due beyond 5 years*
Short-term loans receivable	1	1	—	—	—
Investments at fair value through profit and loss	3	22	29	515	139
Available-for-sale investment	6,417	322	290	110	116
Cash	1,142	—	—	—	—
Cash flows related to financial assets net settled:					
Derivative contracts-receipts	88	−47	80	110	27
Cash flows related to derivative financial assets gross settled:					
Derivative contracts-receipts	14,350	1,067	—	—	—
Derivative contracts – payments	−14,201	−1,037	—	—	—
Accounts receivable[1, 2]	5,903	1,002	73	—	—
Non-current financial liabilities					
Long-term liabilities	−124	−96	−594	−2,973	−2,596
Current financial liabilities					
Current portion of long-term loans	−3	−41	—	—	—
Short-term liabilities	−628	−100	—	—	—
Cash flows related to derivative financial liabilities net settled:					
Derivative contracts – payments	−6	6	−2	10	52
Cash flows related to derivative financial liabilities gross settled:					
Derivative contracts – receipts	14,528	1,422	—	—	—
Derivative contracts – payments	−14,646	−1,443	—	—	—
Accounts payable	−4,873	−74	−3	—	—

At December 31, 2009 EURm	Due within 3 months	Due between 3 and 12 months	Due between 1 and 3 years	Due between 3 and 5 years	Due beyond 5 years
Contingent financial assets and liabilities					
Loan commitments given undrawn[2]	−59	−40	—	—	—
Loan commitments obtained undrawn[3]	—	—	2,841	—	—

At December 31, 2008	Due within 3 months	Due between 3 and 12 months	Due between 1 and 3 years	Due between 3 and 5 years	Due beyond 5 years
Non-current financial assets					
Long-term loans receivable	—	—	19	6	8
Other non-current assets	1	1	3	—	1
Current financial assets					
Current portion of long-term loans receivable	5	101	—	—	—
Short-term loans receivable	8	2	—	—	—
Available-for-sale investment	3,932	483	583	120	254
Cash	1,706	—	—	—	—
Cash flows related to derivative financial assets net settled:					
Derivative contracts – receipts	5	3	1	—	—
Cash flows related to derivative financial assets gross settled:					
Derivative contracts – receipts	19,180	5,184	—	—	—
Derivative contracts – payments	−18,322	−5,090	—	—	—
Accounts receivable[1]	6,702	1,144	70	—	—

At December 31, 2008	Due within 3 months	Due between 3 and 12 months	Due between 1 and 3 years	Due between 3 and 5 years	Due beyond 5 years
Non-current financial liabilities					
Long-term liabilities	−1	−46	−741	−64	−159
Current financial liabilities					
Current portion of long-term loans	—	−14	—	—	—
Short-term liabilities	−3,207	−388	—	—	—
Cash flows related to derivative financial liabilities gross settled:					
Derivative contracts – receipts	15,729	4,859	—	—	—
Derivative contracts – payments	−16,599	−4,931	—	—	—
Accounts payable	−5,152	−67	−5	—	—
Contingent financial assets and liabilities					
Loan commitments given undrawn[2]	−197	—	—	—	—
Financial guarantee given uncalled[2]	−2	—	—	—	—
Loan commitments obtained undrawn[3]	—	—	50	362	—

[1] *Accounts receivable maturity analysis does not include accrued receivables and receivables accounted based on the percentage of completion method of EUR 1,004 million (2008: EUR 1,528 million).*
[2] *Loan commitments given undrawn and financial guarantees given uncalled have been included in the earliest period in which they could be drawn or called.*
[3] *Loan commitments obtained undrawn have been included based on the period in which they expire.*

Hazard risk   Nokia strives to ensure that all financial, reputation and other losses to the Group and our customers are minimized through preventive risk management measures. Insurance is purchased for risks, which cannot be efficiently internally managed and where insurance markets offer acceptable terms and conditions. The objective is to ensure that hazard risks, whether related to physical assets (e.g. buildings) or intellectual assets (e.g. Nokia) or potential liabilities (e.g. product liability) are optimally insured taking into account both cost and retention levels.

Nokia purchases both annual insurance policies for specific risks as well as multi-line and/or multi-year insurance policies, where available.

APPENDIX 4: ILLUSTRATIVE AUDITOR REPORT (UK AND IRELAND)

The following illustrative auditors' reports are based on the requirements in ISA 700 (revised) 'The Independent Auditor's Report on a Complete Set of General Purpose Financial Statements', ISA 705 'Modifications to the Opinion in the Independent Auditor's Report' and ISA 706 'Emphasis of Matter Paragraphs and Other Matter Paragraphs in the Independent Auditor's Report'. Each jurisdiction may have their own wording in certain areas of the auditor's report and, therefore, it is advisable to consult the recommended practice issued by regulatory authorities in each jurisdiction.

ILLUSTRATION 1 — UNQUALIFIED OPINION

Report of the Independent Auditor to the Shareholders of Audit Client Limited

We have audited the financial statements of Audit Client Limited for the year ended 31 July 2010 on pages five to seventeen. The financial reporting framework that has been applied in their preparation is applicable law and United Kingdom Accounting Standards (United Kingdom Generally Accepted Accounting Practice).

This report is made solely to the company's members, as a body, in accordance with Chapter 3 of Part 16 of the Companies Act 2006. Our audit work has been undertaken so that we might state to the company's members those matters we are required to state to them in a Report of the Auditors and for no other purpose. To the fullest extent permitted by law, we do not accept or assume responsibility to anyone other than the company and the company's members as a body, for our audit work, for this report, or for the opinions we have formed.

Respective Responsibilities of Directors and Auditors As explained more fully in the Statement of Directors' Responsibilities set out on page three, the directors are responsible for the preparation of the financial statements and for being satisfied that they give a true and fair view. Our responsibility is to audit the financial statements in accordance with applicable law and International Standards on Auditing (UK and Ireland). Those standards require us to comply with the Auditing Practices Board's Ethical Standards for Auditors.

Scope of the Audit of the Financial Statements An audit involves obtaining evidence about the amounts and disclosures in the financial statements sufficient to give reasonable assurance that the financial statements are free from material misstatement, whether caused by fraud or error. This includes an assessment of: whether the accounting policies are appropriate to the company's circumstances and have been consistently applied and adequately disclosed; the reasonableness of significant accounting estimates made by the directors; and the overall presentation of the financial statements.

Opinion on Financial Statements In our opinion the financial statements:

- Give a true and fair view of the state of the company's affairs as at 31 July 2010 and of its profit for the year then ended.
- Have been properly prepared in accordance with United Kingdom Generally Accepted Accounting Practice.
- Have been prepared in accordance with the requirements of the Companies Act 2006.

Opinion on Other Matter Prescribed by the Companies Act 2006   In our opinion the information given in the Report of the Directors for the financial year for which the financial statements are prepared is consistent with the financial statements.

Matters on which We are Required to Report by Exception   We have nothing to report in respect of the following matters where the Companies Act 2006 requires us to report to you if, in our opinion:

- adequate accounting records have not been kept, or returns adequate for our audit have not been received by branches not visited by us;
- the financial statements are not in agreement with the accounting records and returns;
- certain disclosures of directors' remuneration specified by law are not made; or
- we have not received all the information and explanations we require for our audit.

Mr A Auditor (Senior Statutory Auditor)

Auditor & Co LLP

123 Any Street

Anytown

Any Country

Date: ....

The following illustrates the use of an 'emphasis of matter' paragraph in accordance with ISA 706 'Emphasis of Matter Paragraphs and Other Matter Paragraphs in the Independent Auditor's Report'.

Report of the Independent Auditors to the Shareholders of Audit Client Limited

We have audited the financial statements of Audit Client Limited for the year ended 31 July 2010 on pages five to seventeen. The financial reporting framework that has been applied in their preparation is applicable law and United Kingdom Accounting Standards (United Kingdom Generally Accepted Accounting Practice).

This report is made solely to the company's members, as a body, in accordance with Chapter 3 of Part 16 of the Companies Act 2006. Our audit work has been undertaken so that we might state to the company's members those matters we are required to state to them in a Report of the Auditors and for no other purpose. To the fullest extent permitted by law, we do not accept or assume responsibility to anyone other than the company and the company's members as a body, for our audit work, for this report, or for the opinions we have formed.

Respective Responsibilities of Directors and Auditors   As explained more fully in the Statement of Directors' Responsibilities set out on page three, the directors are responsible for the preparation of the financial statements and for being satisfied that they give a true and fair view. Our responsibility is to audit the financial statements in accordance with applicable law and International Standards on Auditing (UK and Ireland). Those standards require us to comply with the Auditing Practices Board's Ethical Standards for Auditors.

Scope of the Audit of the Financial Statements   An audit involves obtaining evidence about the amounts and disclosures in the financial statements sufficient to give you reasonable assurance that the financial statements are free from material misstatement, whether caused by fraud or error. This includes an assessment of: whether the accounting policies are appropriate to the company's circumstances and have been consistently applied and adequately disclosed; the reasonableness of significant accounting estimates made by the directors; and the overall presentation of the financial statements.

Opinion on Financial Statements   In our opinion the financial statements:

- Give a true and fair view of the state of the company's affairs as at 31 July 2010 and of its profit for the year then ended.
- Have been properly prepared in accordance with United Kingdom Generally Accepted Accounting Practice.
- Have been prepared in accordance with the requirements of the Companies Act 2006.

Emphasis of Matter   Without qualifying our opinion we draw attention to Note 21 in the financial statements. The company is the defendant in a lawsuit alleging infringement of certain patent rights and claiming royalties and punitive damages. The company has filed a counter action, and preliminary hearings and discovery proceedings on both actions are in progress. The ultimate outcome of the matter cannot presently be determined, and no provision for any liability that may result has been made in the financial statements.

Opinion on Other Matter Prescribed by the Companies Act 2006   In our opinion the information given in the Report of the Directors for the financial year for which the financial statements are prepared is consistent with the financial statements.

Matters on which We are Required to Report by Exception   We have nothing to report in respect of the following matters where the Companies Act 2006 requires us to report to you if, in our opinion:

- adequate accounting records have not been kept, or returns adequate for our audit have not been received from branches not visited by us;
- the financial statements are not in agreement with the accounting records and returns;
- certain disclosures of directors' remuneration specified by law are not made; or
- we have not received all the information and explanations we require for our audit.

Mr A Auditor (Senior Statutory Auditor)

For and on behalf of Auditor & Co LLP

123 Any Street

Anytown

Any Country

Date: ....

The following illustrates circumstances where the auditor's opinion is qualified 'except for' in respect of a limitation on audit scope concerning attendance at inventory count.

Report of the Independent Auditors to the Shareholders of Audit Client Limited

We have audited the financial statements of Audit Client Limited for the year ended 31 July 2010 on pages five to seventeen. The financial reporting framework that has been applied in their preparation is applicable law and United Kingdom Accounting Standards (United Kingdom Generally Accepted Accounting Practice).

This report is made solely to the company's members, as a body, in accordance with Chapter 3 of Part 16 of the Companies Act 2006. Our audit work has been undertaken so that we might state to the company's members those matters we are required to state to them in a Report of the Auditors and for no other purpose. To the fullest extent permitted by law, we do not accept or assume responsibility to anyone other than the company and the company's members as a body, for our audit work, for this report, or for the opinions we have formed.

Respective Responsibilities of Directors and Auditors   As explained more fully in the Statement of Directors' Responsibilities set out on page three, the directors are responsible for the preparation of the financial statements and for being satisfied that they give a true and fair view. Our responsibility is to audit the financial statements in accordance with applicable law and International Standards on Auditing (UK and Ireland). Those standards require us to comply with the Auditing Practices Board's Ethical Standards for Auditors.

Scope of the Audit of the Financial Statements   An audit involves obtaining evidence about the amounts and disclosures in the financial statements sufficient to give reasonable assurance that the financial statements are free from material misstatement, whether caused by fraud or error. This includes an assessment of: whether the accounting policies are appropriate to the company's circumstances and have been consistently applied and adequately disclosed: the reasonableness of the significant accounting estimates made by the directors; and the overall presentation of the financial statements.

Qualified Opinion on Financial Statements Arising From Limitation on Scope   We did not observe the counting of the physical inventories as of 31 July 2010, since that date was prior to the time we were initially engaged as auditors for the company. Owing to the nature of the company's records, we were unable to satisfy ourselves as to the inventory quantities by other procedures.

In our opinion, except for the effects of such adjustments, if any, as might have been determined to be necessary had we been able to satisfy ourselves as to the physical inventory quantities, the financial statements:

- Give a true and fair view of the state of the company's affairs as at 31 July 2010 and of its profit for the year then ended.
- Have been properly prepared in accordance with United Kingdom Generally Accepted Accounting Practice.
- Have been prepared in accordance with the requirements of the Companies Act 2006.

Opinion on Other Matter Prescribed by the Companies Act 206   In our opinion the information given in the Report of the Directors for the financial year for which the financial statements are prepared is consistent with the financial statements.

Matters on which We are Required to Report by Exception   We have nothing to report in respect of the following matters where the Companies Act 2006 requires us to report to you if, in our opinion:

- adequate accounting records have not been kept, or returns adequate for our audit have not been received from branches not visited by us;
- the financial statements are not in agreement with the accounting records and returns;
- certain disclosures of directors' remuneration specified by law are not made; or
- we have not received all the information and explanations we require for our audit.

Mr A Auditor (Senior Statutory Auditor)

For and on behalf of Auditor & Co LLP

123 Any Street

Any Town

Any Country

Date: ....

The following illustrates an adverse audit opinion due to non-compliance with the Financial Reporting Standard for Smaller Entities (effective April 2008) in respect of non-disclosure of, and failing to account for, a defined benefit pension scheme.

Report of the Independent Auditors to the Shareholders of Audit Client Limited

We have audited the financial statements of Audit Client Limited for the year ended 31 July 2010 on pages five to seventeen. The financial reporting framework that has been applied in their preparation is applicable law and the Financial Reporting Standard for Smaller Entities (effective April 2008) (United Kingdom Generally Accepted Accounting Practice applicable to Smaller Entities).

This report is made solely to the company's members, as a body, in accordance with Chapter 3 of Part 16 of the Companies Act 2006. Our audit work has been undertaken so that we might state to the company's members those matters we are required to state to them in a Report of the Auditors and for no other purpose. To the fullest extent permitted by law, we do not accept or assume responsibility to anyone other than the company and the company's members as a body, for our audit work, for this report, or for the opinions we have formed.

Respective Responsibilities of Directors and Auditors   As explained more fully in the Statement of Directors' Responsibilities set out on page three, the directors are responsible for the preparation of the financial statements and for being satisfied that they give a true and fair view. Our responsibility is to audit the financial statements in accordance with applicable law and International Standards on Auditing (UK and Ireland). Those standards require us to comply with the Auditing Practices Board's Ethical Standards for Auditors.

Scope of the Audit of the Financial Statements   An audit involves obtaining evidence about the amounts and disclosures in the financial statements sufficient to give reasonable assurance that the financial statements are free from material misstatement, whether caused by fraud or error. This includes an assessment of: whether the accounting policies are appropriate to the company's circumstances and have been consistently applied and adequately disclosed: the reasonableness of the significant accounting estimates made by the directors; and the overall presentation of the financial statements.

Adverse Opinion   As more fully explained in Note 21 of the financial statements, the company has not complied with the requirements of paragraph 10.4 and Appendix II of the Financial Reporting Standard for Smaller Entities (effective April 2008) 'Accounting for Retirement Benefits: Defined Benefit Schemes' as the directors consider that the costs involved in obtaining the information cannot be justified. In our opinion the company's accounting policy with respect to the pension scheme should comply with the requirements of paragraph 10.4 Appendix II 'Accounting for Retirement Benefits: Defined Benefit Pension Schemes'. If the company's accounting policy had complied with these requirements, the financial statements would reflect, at fair value, the assets and liabilities arising from the pension scheme, the changes in these fair values and other disclosures relating to the scheme as required under the Financial Reporting Standard for Smaller Entities (effective April 2008). In view of the effect of the failure of the company to comply with the requirements of paragraph 10.4 and Appendix II 'Accounting for Retirement Benefits: Defined Benefit Schemes', as referred to above, in our opinion the financial statements do not give a true and fair view, in accordance with United Kingdom Generally Accepted Accounting Practice, of the state of the company's affairs as at 31 July 2010 and of its profit for the year then ended. In all other respects, in our opinion the financial statements have been properly prepared in accordance with the Companies Act 2006.

Opinion on Other Matter Prescribed by the Companies Act 2006   In our opinion the information given in the Report of the Directors for the financial year for which the financial statements are prepared is consistent with the financial statements.

Matters on which We are Required to Report by Exception   We have nothing to report in respect of the following matters where the Companies Act 2006 requires us to report to you if, in our opinion:

- adequate accounting records have not been kept, or returns adequate for our audit have not been received from branches visited by us;
- the financial statements are not in agreement with the accounting records and returns;
- certain disclosures of directors' remuneration specified by law are not made;
- we have not received all the information and explanations we require for our audit; or
- the directors were not entitled to prepare the financial statements and the Report of the Directors in accordance with the small companies regime.

Mr A Auditor (Senior Statutory Auditor)

Audit & Co LLP

123 Any Street

Any Town

Any Country

Date: . . . .

The following illustrates an auditor's report for a company who has prepared consolidated and parent company financial statements, where a group member's going concern is brought into question.

Report of the Independent Auditors to the Members of Medium Group Co Limited

We have audited the financial statements of Medium Group Co Limited for the year ended 30 April 2009 which comprise the Consolidated Profit and Loss Account, the Consolidated Balance Sheet, the Company Balance Sheet, the Consolidated Cash Flow Statement and the related notes. The financial reporting framework that has been applied in their preparation is applicable law and United Kingdom Accounting Standards (United Kingdom Generally Accepted Accounting Practice).

This report is made solely to the company's members, as a body, in accordance with Chapter 3 of Part 16 of the Companies Act 2006. Our audit work has been undertaken so that we might state to the company's members those matters we are required to state to them in a Report of the Auditors and for no other purpose. To the fullest extent permitted by law, we do not accept or assume responsibility to anyone other than the company and the company's members as a body, for our audit work, for this report, or for the opinions we have formed.

Respective Responsibilities of Director and Auditors As explained more fully in the Statement of Directors' Responsibilities, the director is responsible for the preparation of the financial statements and for being satisfied that they give a true and fair view. Our responsibility is to audit the financial statements in accordance with applicable law and International Standards on Auditing (UK and Ireland). Those standards require us to comply with the Auditing Practices Board's Ethical Standards for Auditors.

Scope of the Audit of the Financial Statements An audit involves obtaining evidence about the amounts and disclosures in the financial statements sufficient to give reasonable assurance that the financial statements are free from material misstatement, whether caused by fraud or error. This includes an assessment of: whether the accounting policies are appropriate to the group's and parent company's circumstances and have been consistently applied and adequately disclosed; the reasonableness of significant accounting estimates made by the director; and the overall presentation of the financial statements.

Opinion on Financial Statements In our opinion:

The financial statements give a true and fair view of the state of the group's and of the parent company's affairs as at 30 April 2009 and of the group's profit for the year then ended.

- The group financial statements have been properly prepared in accordance with United Kingdom Generally Accepted Accounting Practice;
- Have been prepared in accordance with the requirements of the Companies Act 2006.

Emphasis of Matter Without qualifying our opinion, we draw attention to Note 21 of the Consolidated Financial Statements which indicates that a subsidiary company, Subsidiary Limited, incurred a net loss of £95,000 during the year ended 30 April 2009 and, as at that date, the company's current liabilities exceeded its total assets by £93,000. Reference is made to the company's ability to continue as a going concern in Note 22 of the Consolidated Financial Statements.

These conditions indicate the existence of a material uncertainty which may cast significant doubt about the ability of the company to continue as a going concern.

Opinion on Other Matter Prescribed by the Companies Act 2006 In our opinion the information given in the Report of the Director for the financial year for which the financial statements are prepared is consistent with the financial statements.

Matters on which We are Required to Report by Exception We have nothing to report in respect of the following matters where the Companies Act 2006 requires us to report to you if, in our opinion:

- adequate accounting records have not been kept by the parent company, or returns adequate for our audit have not been received from branches not visited by us;
- the parent company financial statements are not in agreement with the accounting records and returns;
- certain disclosures of directors' remuneration specified by law are not made; or
- we have not received all the information and explanations we require for our audit.

Mr A Auditor (Senior Statutory Auditor)

Audit & Co LLP

123 Any Street

Any Town

Any Country

Date: ....

The following illustrates the auditor's report for an entity preparing financial statements under International Financial Reporting Standards (IFRS).

Independent Auditor's Report [Insert appropriate addressee]
Report on Financial Statements

We have audited the accompanying financial statements of Entity A Inc, which comprise the statement of financial position as at December, 31 2010, and the statement of comprehensive income, statement of changes in equity and statement of cash flows for the year then ended, and a summary of significant accounting policies and other explanatory information.

Management's Responsibility for the Financial Statements Management is responsible for the preparation and fair presentation of these financial statements in accordance with International Financial Reporting Standards, and for such internal control as management determines is necessary to enable the preparation of financial statements that are free from material misstatement, whether due to fraud or error.

Auditor's Responsibility   Our responsibility is to express an opinion on these financial statements based on our audit. We conducted our audit in accordance with International Standards on Auditing. Those standards require that we comply with ethical requirements and plan and perform the audit to obtain reasonable assurance about whether the financial statements are free from material misstatement.

An audit involves performing procedures to obtain audit evidence about the amounts and disclosures in the financial statements. The procedures selected depend on the auditor's judgement, including the assessment of the risks of material misstatement of the financial statements, whether due to fraud or error. In making those risk assessments, the auditor considers internal control relevant to the entity's preparation and fair presentation of the financial statements in order to design audit procedures that are appropriate in the circumstances, but not for the purpose of expressing an opinion on the effectiveness of the entity's internal control. An audit also includes evaluating the appropriateness of accounting policies used and the reasonableness of accounting estimates made by management, as well as evaluating the overall presentation of the financial statements.

We believe that the audit evidence we have obtained is sufficient and appropriate to provide a basis for our audit opinion.

Opinion   In our opinion, the financial statements present fairly, in all material respects [or give a true and fair view of] the financial position of Entity Inc as at 31 December 2010, and [of] its financial performance and its cash flows for the year then ended in accordance with International Financial Reporting Standards.

Report on Other Legal and Regulatory Requirements   [The form and content of this section of the auditor's report will vary depending on each respective jurisdiction's reporting requirements].

[Auditor's signature]

[Date of the auditor's report]

[Auditor's address]

INDEX

ACCA 19
accepting an audit client, Code of Ethics
for Professional Accountants 19–21,
321–33
accounting policies 37–8, 73–8, 96–7,
109, 116–19, 200–1, 266–7, 316,
345, 357–8, 362–4, 418, 453–4,
458–62, 476, 482–3, 495–7,
526–45
changes 362–4
definition 96–7
IAS 1 'Presentation of Financial
Statements' 221–2, 357–8, 526–42
IAS 8 'Accounting Policies, Changes
in Accounting Estimates and Errors'
345, 362–4, 538–42
illustrative financial statements 453–4,
458–62, 482–3, 495–7, 526–42
Nokia Corporation 526–45
SMEs 316
accounting records 27–8, 35–8, 133–4,
139, 455, 492, 494, 503
adequacy assessments 27–8, 133–4,
455, 492, 494, 503
evidence generation requirements
27–8
third party service organisations
139
accruals basis of accounting
concepts 301–5
definition 301
accrued expenses
concepts 191, 585–6
Nokia Corporation 585–6
acquisitions 118–19, 314–15, 318–19,
339–42, 392–7, 505, 507–8,
510–17, 521–63
see also business combinations
fair value 339–42, 558–60
FRS 6 'Acquisitions and Mergers'
314–15
Nokia Corporation 521–63
'acting in concert' persons, IAS 24
'Related Party Disclosures' 203,
395–6
actuarial gains/losses 152, 384–7,
547–50
Acute Mobile 554
addressee paragraph, auditors' reports
257–63
adjusting events
see also subsequent . . .
definition 216, 364, 365
IAS 10 'Events After the Reporting
Period' 27, 213, 216–19, 364–5
types 216
adverse auditors' opinions 65–6, 68,
210–11, 229–30, 258–63, 265–8,
289, 295, 611–12
definition 261–2, 267
illustrative auditors' reports 229, 267,
289, 611–12

advocacy threats, concepts 17–19
after-date cash testing 440
agent sellers, revenue recognition
58–9
agricultural activities 316, 428–31
Aidan Inc. 101
AIM 94–5
Alex Inc. 309
Alicia Enterprises 208
alternative accounting rules 73
alternative GAAP, groups 244
AMG Inc. 239
amortisation/depreciation, estimation
techniques 191, 193–201
analytical procedures 10, 52, 54–5,
59–61, 92, 106–7, 146–7, 170–2,
173–9
see also evidence . . . ; 'proof in
total' . . . ; ratio analysis; reviews;
substantive . . .
audit planning 173–4, 176–7
concepts 173–9
definition 173–4
illustrations 177–8
income statement expenditure reviews
175–6
ISA 520 (redrafted) 'Analytical
Procedures' 10, 173–9
prior-period financial information
175
reliance factors 174
suggested tests 176–9
techniques 175–9
timing factors 131–2, 174–5,
177–8
ANG 55
annual reports
see also financial statements
directors' responsibilities 259–60,
411–12, 453–4, 476, 477, 492–3,
503, 504, 607, 608–9, 610, 611,
613, 614–15
anomalous errors, concepts 142–4
Apertio Ltd 557
appendices
IASs/IFRSs 335–431
illustrative audit tests 433–44
illustrative auditors' reports 607–15
illustrative financial statements
445–605
application controls, information systems
105–6
applied criteria, summary financial
statements 291–8
appointments
auditors 19–21, 35–8, 85, 169–70,
321–33, 492, 503
auditors' experts 254
appropriateness evaluations, evidence
generation requirements 27–8,
133–4, 145–55, 225–6
Arbold Enterprises 112–19

Articles of Association, requirements 3
assertion level 28–9, 33, 108–9, 127–34,
147–55, 173–9
categories 108–9, 147
material misstatements 28–9, 33,
108–9, 127–34
assets
see also contingent . . . ; current . . . ;
intangible . . . ; non-current . . .
definitions 177, 303–4, 379
IAS 1 'Presentation of Financial
Statements' 352–8
IAS 17 'Leases' 314, 377–82, 442
IFRS 1 'First-Time Adoption of IFRS'
310–12, 335–7
IFRS 5 'Non-Current assets Held for
Sale and Discontinued Operations'
307, 343–4
IFRS 9 'Financial Instruments'
348–51
impairment of assets 375, 412–15,
419, 460, 462, 471, 480, 482–4,
509, 518, 528–45, 551–3, 563
associates 203–11, 239–48, 315, 318,
392, 399–400, 499, 501, 526,
542–605
see also related parties
definition 399
FRS 9 'Associates and Joint Ventures'
315, 316
IAS 24 'Related Party Disclosures' 75,
203, 392–6
IAS 28 'Investments in Associates'
392, 399–400, 553, 565
subsidiaries contrast 399
assurance engagements, definition 3
Atrica 557
Audit Client Limited, illustrative
auditors' reports 607–9
audit committees 71–8, 250–2, 594
communications 71–8
Nokia Corporation 594
audit documentation 10, 45–8, 61, 70–8,
89–90, 110–11, 124–5, 134, 144,
154–5, 170–2, 234–7, 245–8,
323–33
audit planning 89–90, 245–8, 327
communications 70–8, 234–7
evidence generation requirements 134,
154–5, 170–2, 328–33
groups 245–8
internal auditors 251–2
ISA 230 (redrafted) 'Audit
Documentation' 10, 45–8, 110–11,
134, 155
materiality 124–6, 144, 235
quality controls 323–33
reviews 154–5, 329–33
risk assessments 110–11, 134
significant matters 47–8, 61, 110–11
uncorrected misstatements 144
written representations 233–7

audit engagements 3, 10–11, 19–21,
  35–8, 85–90, 169–72, 274–7,
  284–5, 291–8
  see also opening balances; 'reasonable
    assurance' reference
  concepts 3, 21–2, 35–8, 85–90,
    169–72, 274–7, 284–5, 291–8
  definition 3, 35–6, 169–70
  ISA 210 (redrafted) 'Agreeing the
    Terms of Audit Engagements' 10,
    35–8, 85, 284
  ISA 510 (redrafted) Initial Audit
    Engagements–Opening Balances'
    10, 86, 169–72, 274–7
  ISA 810 'Engagements to Report on
    Summary Financial Statements' 11,
    291–8
  letters of engagement 21–2, 36–8,
    331–2
  preconditions 35–6, 38, 292
  summary financial statements 11,
    291–8
audit fieldwork, quality controls
  328
audit files *see* audit documentation
audit planning 4–6, 10, 23, 30, 32–3,
  50–1, 76, 85–90, 117–19, 121–6,
  132–4, 173–4, 192–3, 241–2,
  245–8, 288–90, 327–33
  activities 85, 86, 327
  analytical procedures 173–4,
    176–7
  audit documentation 89–90, 245–8,
    327
  audit procedures 132–3
  changes 88
  communications 89–90
  definition 87–8, 327
  direction/supervision/review aspects
    88–90, 322–33
  estimation techniques 192–3
  groups 245–8
  ISA 300 (redrafted) 'Planning an
    Audit of Financial Statements' 4–5,
    10, 85–90, 91, 241–2
  ISA 320 (revised and redrafted)
    'Materiality in Planning and
    Performing an Audit' 10, 121–6,
    141–2
  reviews 88–90
audit procedures
  audit planning 132–3
  definition 132
  estimation techniques 195,
    198–201
  evidence considerations 131–4,
    145–55
  going concern principle 226–30
  related parties 205–6
  subsequent events 213–19
  summary financial statements
    292–3
audit sampling *see* sampling
audit strategy, ISA 300 (redrafted)
  'Planning an Audit of Financial
  Statements' 4–5, 10, 85–90, 91,
  241–2

audit tests 54–61, 157–63, 165–7, 181–9,
  192–201, 328–33, 433–44, 609
  see also evidence . . .
  attendance at inventory counts 158–60,
    171–2, 438–9
  cash at bank and in hand 165–7, 440–1
  contingent assets 442–3
  contingent liabilities 148, 150, 160–2,
    442–3
  deferred taxes 444
  definition 54–5
  directors' transactions 434
  employee wages and salaries 443–4
  estimation techniques 192–201
  illustrative audit tests 433–44
  intangible assets 434–5, 609
  inventories 157–63, 437–9, 610–11
  investments 436–7
  leases 54, 442
  non-current assets 434–6
  payables 441–2
  provisions 442–3
  receivables 165–7, 181–9, 439–40
  related parties 434
  share capital and reserves 433–4
  taxes 444
  trade payables 441–2
  trade receivables 165–7, 181–9,
    439–40
  types 54–5
auditing
  see also audits; ISA . . .
  in accordance with ISAs 31
  assurance engagements 3
  completion procedures 329–30
  definition 1–6, 26–7, 454–5, 607
  exemptions 273
  historical background 1–6
  internal/external contrasts 2–3, 249–50
  limitations 2–3, 30, 123–4, 145,
    170–2, 191–2, 265–8
  risk-based auditing 2, 4–6, 8–13,
    107–8, 112
  stakeholders 2–3, 5–6, 70–8
  thresholds' table 2–3
  timing factors 329
Auditing Practices Board (APB) 259–60,
  281, 454, 493, 504, 607, 608, 611,
  613, 615
  see also Ethical Standards;
    International Standards on Auditing
auditor association, summary financial
  statements 297
auditors 1–6, 7–13, 15–23, 37–8, 39–43,
  48, 239–48, 321–33, 411–12,
  454–5, 463–4, 476–8, 484, 492–4,
  497, 503–5, 511, 607–15
  appointments 19–21, 35–8, 85,
    169–70, 321–33, 492, 503
  Code of Ethics for Professional
    Accountants 15–23, 39–43, 321–33
  complaints 332–3
  component auditors 7–8, 10, 48,
    239–48
  confidentiality requirements 15,
    16–17, 40–3, 76, 324–33
  conflicts of interest 16, 21, 22–3

ethics 15–23, 39–43, 85, 170, 244–5,
  321–33, 454, 493, 504, 607, 608,
  611, 613, 615
  family/close relationships 22–3
  fees 2, 6, 21–2, 37–8, 76–7, 463–4,
    484, 497, 511
  gifts/hospitality problems 22
  groups 239–48
  historical background 1–6
  independence requirements 4–6,
    15–23, 76–7, 85, 322–33
  integrity requirements 15–16, 40–3,
    85, 322–33
  ISA 200 (revised and redrafted)
    'Overall Objective of the
    Independent Auditor, and the
    Conduct of an Audit in Accordance
    with ISAs' 10, 26–33, 123–4, 287–8
  ISQC 1 (redrafted) 'Quality Control
    for Firms that Perform Audits and
    Reviews of Financial Statements,
    and Other Assurance and Related
    Service Engagements' 7, 11, 39–43,
    48, 321–33
  leadership responsibilities within audit
    firms 321–33
  non-audit services 23, 42–3
  objectives 1–6, 26–33, 79, 121–2, 127,
    221–3, 231–2, 249–50, 287–8,
    321–33, 454–5, 607
  objectivity requirements 15, 16, 40–3,
    322–33
  professional competence and due care
    requirements 15, 16, 17, 19–20,
    39–43, 240–2, 249–52, 321–33
  qualifications 2, 16, 17, 20, 242,
    322–33
  quality controls 7, 10, 11, 19, 39–43,
    45–8, 85–90, 154–5, 251–2, 321–33
  'reasonable skill, care and caution'
    duties 1–2, 16, 40–3
  resignations 325, 327
  responsibilities 1–6, 10–13, 26–33,
    35–8, 39–40, 49–61, 63–8, 69–78,
    80–2, 97–8, 171, 195–6, 222,
    249–50, 259–60, 261–3, 279–82,
    321–33, 411–12, 454–5, 477, 493,
    504, 607, 608–9, 610, 611, 613, 615
  rights/duties to report regulatory
    non-compliance 67–8, 83–4,
    139–40, 210–11
  sceptical attitudes 30, 54–5, 60–1,
    101–2
  threats and safeguards to ethical
    standards 6, 17–23, 325–33
  training and development activities
    18–19, 323–4, 332
auditors' experts 10, 32, 41–3, 88–9,
  146, 150–2, 158, 198, 253–5
  appointments 254
  communications 255
  definitions 253
  evidence generation requirements
    150–2, 198
  ISA 620 (revised and redrafted) 'Using
    the Work of an Auditor's Expert' 10,
    32, 88–9, 146, 151, 158, 198, 253–5

auditors' opinions 1–6, 10, 11, 16, 26–33, 41–3, 47, 65–6, 125–6, 139–40, 145–6, 170–2, 210–11, 257–63, 265–8, 284–5, 289, 330–3, 411–12, 454–5, 477–8, 493–4, 504–5, 607–15
see also adverse . . . ; disclaimed . . . ; qualified . . . ; unqualified . . .
communications 72–8, 143–4, 267–8, 330–3
definition 4, 260–3
disclaimed auditor opinions 139, 171–2, 226–30, 258–63, 2620–3
going concern principle 226–30
historical background 1–6
illustrative auditors' reports 607–15
illustrative financial statements 454–5, 477–8, 493–4, 504–5
ISA 700 (redrafted) 'The Independent Auditor's Report on a Complete Set of General Purpose Financial Statements' 10, 11, 47, 125–6, 257–63, 284–5, 288, 607
ISA 705 'Modifications to the Opinion in the Independent Auditor's Report' 139, 159, 162, 263, 265–8, 607
non-compliance with regulations 65–6, 83–4, 139–40, 210–11
related parties 210–11
special purpose frameworks 284–5, 295–6
summary financial statements 293–5
third party service organisations 139–40
types 260–3, 330–1
auditors' reports 1–6, 7–13, 43, 75–6, 213–19, 257–63, 321–33, 454–5, 477–8, 492–4, 503–5, 607–15
see also ISA . . . ; 'reasonable assurance' reference
contents 257–63, 284–5, 293–4
dates 258
definition 257–8, 454, 607
historical background 1–6
illustrative auditors' reports 607–15
illustrative financial statements 454–5, 477–8, 492–4, 503–5
ISA 700 (redrafted) 'The Independent Auditor's Report on a Complete Set of General Purpose Financial Statements' 10, 11, 47, 125–6, 257–63, 284–5, 288, 607
ISA 705 (revised and redrafted) 'Modifications to the Opinion in the Independent Auditor's Report' 139, 159, 162, 263, 265–8, 607
ISA 706 (revised and redrafted) 'Emphasis of Matter Paragraphs and Other Matter(s) Paragraphs in the Independent Auditor's Report' 10, 11, 228, 263, 269–71, 607, 608–9
modifications 75–6, 77, 139, 159, 162–3, 172, 210–11, 215–19, 265–8, 607
quality controls 321–33

'reasonable assurance' reference 3, 123–6, 145–55
related parties 210–11
scope 8, 21–2, 32, 36–8, 66, 68, 166, 170, 236–7, 257–63, 265–8, 324–33, 607, 609, 610, 611–12, 613
signing processes 43, 213–15, 257–63
subsequent events 213–19
summary financial statements 293–5
users 3, 5–6
audits
see also auditing; ISA . . .
budgets 4–5
concepts 1–6, 7–13, 454–5, 607
definition 1–6, 26–7, 454–5, 607
features 4–5, 26–33
historical background 1–6
authorisation procedures, control environment 103–4
available-for-sale assets 308, 348, 351, 420–7, 524–6, 531–42, 553–60, 565–9, 572–4
AVCO inventory valuations 482
Avvenu Inc. 560
Azlan Group PLC 217
Azure Inc. 204

bad debts 191, 213–14, 370, 519, 533–42, 571–2, 586–7
balance sheets
see also assets; liabilities
auditing thresholds' table 3
Framework for the Preparation and Presentation of Financial Statements (IASB) 300–5
IAS 1 'Presentation of Financial Statements' 221–2, 351–8
IAS 34 'Interim Financial Reporting' 411–12
IAS 36 'Impairment of Assets' 413–14
IFRS 1 'First-Time Adoption of IFRS' 310–12, 335–7
IFRS 2 'Share-Based Payment' 337–9, 446, 541–2
IFRS 5 'Non-Current assets Held for Sale and Discontinued Operations' 343–4
illustrative audit tests 433–44
illustrative financial statements 457, 479, 485–91, 495–501, 506, 516–17, 543–605
Nokia Corporation 519–605
risk assessments 106–7, 112
bank audit letters 132, 146, 148, 165–7, 206
see also external confirmations
bank reconciliation statements, audit tests 53, 106, 165–7, 440–1
biases, estimation techniques 194
bill and hold arrangements, revenue recognition 57–8
biological assets, IAS 41 'Agriculture' 429–31
Black–Scholes options' pricing method 474, 581
block-selection non-statistical sampling, concepts 183–5

bonds 530–42, 569–70
bonus issues
definition 407
IAS 33 'Earnings Per Share' 406–10
borrowing costs 312–13, 391–2, 467, 472, 488–91, 520–605
definition 391
IAS 23 'Borrowing Costs' 391–2, 526–42
borrowing facilities, going concern considerations 221–30, 355
Brahm, Euan 204
break-up values 357
BT Group PLC 411–12
budgets, going concern considerations 221–30, 354–5
Bury Enterprises Inc. 159–60
business combinations 311–12, 314–15, 318–19, 335, 339–42, 397–8, 517, 526–605
see also acquisitions; groups
IFRS 3 'Business Combinations' 96, 339–42, 398, 399, 541–2
business related credit risk 599–600
see also credit risk
business risks, concepts 97–103, 113–19
Byrne Enterprises Inc. 228, 304

CAATs *see* computer assisted audit techniques
Cahill Chemicals Inc. 209
Canada, Nokia Corporation 557, 584, 594
capital allowances, deferred tax liabilities 371, 511, 515
capital concepts 304–5
capital maintenance, concepts 304–5
capital-based grants, IAS 20 'Accounting for Government Grants and Disclosure of Government Assistance' 388–9, 526–42
capitalised borrowing costs 391–2, 436, 442, 459, 519, 521–2, 540–2, 551–60
caps 424–7
cash, definition 359
cash at bank and in hand 165–7, 440–1, 461, 470, 472, 479, 495, 522–6, 531–42, 555–60, 565–70
audit tests 165–7, 440–1
cash books, audit tests 148, 440–1, 444
cash equivalents, definition 359
cash flow hedge 426–7, 524, 534–6, 550, 570
definition 426–7, 534–5
cash flow statements *see* statements of cash flow . . .
cash generating units (CGUs) 412–15, 551–3
definition 413, 551
IAS 36 'Impairment of Assets' 412–15
cash-flow timings, going concern considerations 221–30, 355
cash-settled share-based payments, concepts 337–9, 570
CGUs *see* cash generating units

chairman's statements, illustrative
  financial statements 445–6, 459
Charlotte Inc. 102
chief executive's reports, illustrative
  financial statements 446–8
China 159, 239, 545, 554
'Chinese walls' 21, 23
circularisation of receivables
  see also external confirmations;
  receivables
  concepts 27–8, 165–7
  definition 165
Clarified ISAs 7–13, 31–3, 79, 83, 195
  effective dates 13, 31
  'should'/'shall' changes 12, 13, 31–3
  structural changes 11–13, 31
client assets, Code of Ethics for
  Professional Accountants 22
clients
  see also directors
  Code of Ethics for Professional
    Accountants 15–23, 39–43, 85, 170,
    244–5, 321–33
  communications 5, 7, 8–9, 10, 13, 32,
    50, 51, 61, 69–78, 79–84, 111–12,
    124–6, 143–4, 148–50, 210–11,
    227–30, 231–7, 244–5, 247–8,
    267–8, 327–33
  ISA 265 'Communicating Deficiencies
    in Internal Control to those Charged
    with Governance and Management'
    5, 7, 8–9, 10, 13, 32, 77, 79–84,
    111–12, 210–11, 331
  ISQC 1 (redrafted) 'Quality Control
    for Firms that Perform Audits and
    Reviews of Financial Statements,
    and Other Assurance and Related
    Service Engagements' 7, 11, 39–43,
    48, 321–33
  written representations 10, 74–6, 144,
    148–50, 208–11, 224–6, 231–7
closing balances, ISA 510 (redrafted)
  Initial Audit Engagements —
    Opening Balances' 10, 77, 86,
    169–72, 274–7
Code of Ethics for Professional
  Accountants 15–23, 39–43, 85, 170,
  244–5, 321–33
  see also quality controls
  accepting an audit client 19–23,
    321–33
  client assets 22
  conflicts of interest 16, 21, 22–3
  family/close relationships 22–3
  fees 21–2
  fundamental principles 15–17, 20,
    321–33
  gifts/hospitality problems 22
  non-audit services 23
  parts A/B/C 15
  safeguards 17–23, 325–33
  threats 6, 17–23, 325–33
codes of conduct 5–6, 67, 100–1
'cold' file reviews 19, 43, 154–5,
  331–2
Combined Code for Corporate
  Governance 451

'comfort letters' 227
commercial paper 602–5
common control/influence aspects, IAS
  24 'Related Party Disclosures' 203,
  392–6, 434, 527
communications 5–10, 13, 32, 50, 51,
  60–1, 69–78, 79–84, 111–12,
  124–6, 143–4, 148–50, 210–11,
  227–30, 231–7, 244–5, 247–8,
  267–8, 327–33
  audit planning 89–90
  auditors' experts 255
  auditors' opinions 72–8, 143–4,
    267–8, 330–3
  forms 70, 80–4, 233–5, 237
  fraud matters 60–1, 150, 235
  groups 244–5, 247–8
  internal auditors 249, 251–2
  internal control systems 5, 7, 8–9, 10,
    13, 32, 76, 77, 79–84, 111–12
  ISA 260 (revised and redrafted)
    'Significant Difficulties' 9, 10,
    69–78, 111–12, 126, 247, 330–1
  ISA 265 'Communicating Deficiencies
    in Internal Control to those Charged
    with Governance and Management'
    5, 7, 8–9, 10, 13, 32, 77, 79–84,
    111–12, 210–11, 331
  ISAs requiring communications
    77–8
  listed clients 76–8, 83–4
  material misstatements 126, 143–4,
    276–7, 329–33
  matters prior to the audit 72
  oral communications with the client
    70–8, 233–5, 237
  qualitative aspects of accounting
    practices 73, 74
  regulators 67–8, 83–4, 143–4,
    325–33
  risk assessments 111–12
  significant difficulties 9, 10, 69–78,
    210–11
  two-way communications 69–70
  written representations 10, 74–6, 144,
    148–50, 208–11, 224–6, 231–7
Companies Act 2006 2–3, 26, 39, 60,
  63–8, 139, 197–8, 258, 260, 261,
  281, 314, 316, 318, 372, 454–5,
  476–8, 491–501, 503–5, 509, 511,
  607–15
Companies House 206, 277, 433–4
company law 2–6, 26–33, 39, 60, 63–8,
  139, 197–8, 258, 260, 281, 314,
  316, 318, 372, 453–5, 476–8,
  491–501, 503–5, 509, 511,
  607–15
comparability qualitative characteristic
  of financial statements 301–5
comparative information
  definitions 273
  ISA 710 (redrafted) 'Comparative
    Information, Corresponding Figures
    and Comparative Financial
    Statements' 11, 237, 270, 273–7,
    296
complaints about auditors 332–3

compliance tests *see* tests of controls
component auditors, ISA 600 (revised
  and redrafted) 'The Audit of Group
  Financial Statements' 7–8, 10, 48,
  239–48
computer assisted audit techniques
  (CAATs) 55
Conceptual Framework Approach to
  Independence 5–6
condensed financial statements, IAS 34
  'Interim Financial Reporting'
  411–12
confidentiality requirements, auditors 15,
  16–17, 40–3, 76, 324–33
conflicts of interest
  see also objectivity requirements
  Code of Ethics for Professional
    Accountants 16, 21, 22–3
consolidated financial statements 2, 193,
  239–48, 310–11, 315, 397–9,
  405–10, 496, 503, 504–17,
  518–605, 613–14
  see also financial statements; groups
  IAS 27 'Consolidated and Separate
    Financial Statements' 2, 193, 240,
    310–11, 397–9, 541–2
construction contracts 56–7, 95, 161,
  191, 365–8, 527–42, 545–6, 564
  definition 161, 366, 367
  IAS 11 'Construction Contracts' 56–7,
    95, 365–8, 527–42
  Nokia Corporation 545–6, 564
contingent assets
  audit tests 442–3
  definition 416–17
  FRS 12 'Provisions, Contingent
    Liabilities and Contingent Assets'
    133, 370
  IAS 37 'Provisions, Contingent
    Liabilities and Contingent Assets'
    26–7, 133, 150, 161, 216–17, 303,
    415–17, 442–3
contingent liabilities
  audit tests 148, 150, 160–2, 442–3
  definition 415–16
  FRS 12 'Provisions, Contingent
    Liabilities and Contingent Assets'
    133, 370
  IAS 1 'Presentation of Financial
    Statements' 355
  IAS 37 'Provisions, Contingent
    Liabilities and Contingent Assets'
    26–7, 133, 150, 161, 216–17, 303,
    415–17, 442–3
  IFRS 3 'Business Combinations'
    341–2, 541–2
  illustrative audit tests 442–3
  illustrative financial statements 490,
    515–16, 540–2, 586–7, 588–9
  Nokia Corporation 588–9, 604–5
continuing audits, quality controls 40,
  321–33
Continuing Professional Development
  (CPD) 18–19, 323–4
control aspects, IAS 24 'Related Party
  Disclosures' 203, 392–6, 434, 491,
  501, 516, 527

control environment 100–1, 103–6,
114–19, 128–34, 158–60
monitoring needs 106
responsible persons 106
control risk 29–30, 100–1, 108–9, 112,
128–34, 179, 183, 188–9
see also internal control systems
definition 29, 108, 128
controlling parties, related parties
208–11
convertible debt 115, 349–51, 409–10,
424–7
Cordonisos Inc. 159
corporate governance 8–9, 10, 18–19,
35–8, 60–1, 63–8, 69–78, 79–84,
89–90, 210–11, 232–3, 280–2,
331–3, 451
Corporate Governance Code *see*
Combined Code for Corporate
Governance
corporation tax
see also taxes
illustrative financial statements 465,
484–5, 498, 511
corresponding figures
definition 273
ISA 710 (redrafted) 'Comparative
Information, Corresponding Figures
and Comparative Financial
Statements' 11, 77, 237, 270, 273–7
costs 53–4, 178, 303–5, 358–9, 366–8,
374–7, 399, 417, 436, 438, 463–4,
498–501, 505–17, 518–605
definitions 358, 374–5, 376, 399, 417
IAS 2 'Inventory' 358–9, 438
IAS 11 'Construction Contracts' 56–7,
366–8, 527–42
IAS 16 'Property, Plant and
Equipment' 303–4, 318, 374–7,
436
CPD *see* Continuing Professional
Development
credit notes 439–40
credit rating agencies 99, 602–5
credit risk 99, 346, 470–1, 568, 595,
599–600, 602–5
see also business related . . . ;
financial . . .
concepts 599–600
creditors *see* trade payables
creditworthiness assessments 599–600,
602–5
cumulative preference dividends
405–10
cumulative-rights (cum-rights) price per
share, rights issues 407–10
current assets 277, 303–4, 352–8, 457,
479, 495, 506–17, 519–605
IAS 1 'Presentation of Financial
Statements' 352–8
opening balances 277
current liabilities 277, 304, 457, 479,
495, 506–17, 519–605
current taxes 368–74, 561–2
customer financing arrangements
539–42
customer loyalty programs 527–42

Daniels Inc 98–9
dates
see also timing . . .
auditors' reports 258
debentures 489
debtors *see* trade receivables
deferred tax assets, concepts 368, 370–1,
585
deferred tax liabilities, concepts 368,
371–2, 444, 585
deferred taxes 116–19, 191, 301, 315,
368–74, 444, 461, 467–8, 496, 498,
509, 511, 515, 519–20, 536–42,
554–60, 561–2, 585
audit tests 444
capital allowances 371, 511, 515
definition 368
discounting 369, 372–3
estimation techniques 191
FRS 19 'Deferred Tax' 315, 369–70,
374, 509
IAS 12 'Income Taxes' 368–74
illustrative financial statements 461,
467–8, 496, 498, 509, 511, 515,
519–20, 536–42
Nokia Corporation 519–20, 536–42,
554–60, 585
defined benefit pension schemes 151–2,
191–2, 315, 384–7, 530–42,
546–50, 611–12
IAS 19 'Employee Benefits' 384–7
Projected Unit Credit Method 384–6,
387
defined contribution pension schemes
116–19, 384–7, 530–42, 546–50
IAS 19 'Employee Benefits' 384–7
depreciation 58, 118–19, 153, 191,
343–4, 362–4, 375–7, 381, 435,
459–60, 466, 480–91, 496,
497–501, 507–17, 531–42, 543–5,
564–5
see also non-current assets
definition 375
estimation techniques 191, 193–201
IAS 8 'Accounting Policies, Changes
in Accounting Estimates and Errors'
362–4
IAS 16 'Property, Plant and
Equipment' 318, 375–7, 381,
531–42
IAS 38 'Intangible Assets' 381,
435
IFRS 5 'Non-Current assets Held for
Sale and Discontinued Operations'
343–4
intangible assets 381, 434–5, 512
methods 363, 460, 482–3, 496, 509,
531–42
derecognition, financial instruments
310–11, 317, 425–7
derivatives 317, 349–51, 403–4, 424–7,
469, 509–10, 527–42, 561, 566–70,
574, 595–605
see also caps; financial instruments;
floors; forward . . . ; futures . . . ;
options; swaps
definition 424

embedded derivatives 349, 424–7,
527–42
Nokia Corporation 527–42, 561,
566–70, 574, 595–605
despatch notes 131–4
detection risk 28–30, 33, 50–61, 107–8,
112, 179, 182–3, 188–9
see also non-sampling . . .
definition 29, 107, 183, 188
Deutsche Telekom 557
development costs, intangible assets 313
difference error-projection method,
concepts 186–7
diluted earnings per share 409–10, 469,
518, 538–42, 587–8
definition 409
IAS 33 'Earnings Per Share' 409–10,
469
direct/indirect controls, internal control
systems 130
direct/indirect methods, statements of
cash flow for the period 360–2
directional testing, concepts 157–60
directors 1–6, 26–33, 35–8, 50–61, 70–8,
231–7, 392–6, 411–12, 434,
449–53, 455, 459, 464, 468, 475–7,
483–4, 490–1, 492–3, 501–4, 516,
576–86, 590–2, 607–15
see also clients; management . . . ;
written representations
loans 434
Nokia Corporation 576–86, 590–4
related parties 203–11, 392–6, 434,
464, 516, 590–2
remuneration 26, 177–8, 216–17,
450–3, 455, 464, 468, 483–4, 494,
497, 591–2, 611
responsibilities 1, 36–8, 50–1, 98, 171,
192, 196, 221–2, 232–7, 259–60,
261–3, 280, 411–12, 453–4, 476,
477, 492–3, 503, 504, 607, 608–9,
610, 611, 613, 614–15
directors' reports 280–2, 449–51, 455,
459, 475–7, 492–3, 501–3, 609
directors' transactions 434, 450–3,
490–1
disagreements
see also adverse . . . ; disclaimed . . . ;
qualified . . .
concepts 266–8
disclaimed auditor opinions 139, 171–2,
226–30, 258–63, 265–8, 289, 295
definition 262, 267
illustration 267, 289
disclosures
accounting policies 357–8, 526–42
fair value 200–1
going concern principle 221–30,
356–8
IAS 24 'Related Party Disclosures' 75,
203, 233, 302, 392–6, 434, 464,
469, 490–1, 501, 516
IAS 32 'Financial Instruments:
Presentation and Disclosure' 336,
345, 402–4, 423, 427, 526–42
IFRS 1 'First-Time Adoption of IFRS'
310–12, 336–7

disclosures (*cont.*)
  IFRS 3 'Business Combinations'
    339–40, 399, 541–2
  IFRS 7 'Financial Instruments:
    Disclosure' 345–6, 402, 420,
    526–42, 598
  illustrative financial statements
    445–605
  intangible assets 418–19
  ISA 501 (redrafted) 'Audit Evidence
    Regarding Specific Financial
    Statement Account Balances and
    Disclosures' 10, 157–63
  ISA 540 (revised and redrafted)
    'Auditing Accounting Estimates,
    Including Fair Value Accounting
    Estimates, and Related Disclosures'
    7, 8, 10, 30, 161, 191–201
  related parties 75, 150, 203, 207–11,
    233, 302, 392–6, 434, 464, 469,
    490–1, 501, 516
discontinued operations
  definition 344
  IFRS 5 'Non-Current assets Held for
    Sale and Discontinued Operations'
    343–4
discounting
  deferred taxes 369, 372–3
  impairment of assets 551–3
  measurement of shares 319
discussions 50, 51, 61, 93–4, 111
disposals, non-current assets 56, 511,
  521–6, 563–5, 572–4
dividends 98–9, 207, 218, 318, 349–51,
  382–3, 399–400, 404, 405–10,
  449–50, 475–6, 485, 491, 501, 502,
  522–6, 532–42, 560–1, 590–3
  audit tests 433–4
  revenue recognition 382–3, 529–42
Dodgy Inc. 161
Dopplr Oy 554
dormant entities 209

earnings management, concepts 49–50,
  53–4
earnings per share 404–10, 446, 469,
  518, 538–42, 587–8
  concepts 404–10
  definition 404–5
  diluted earnings per share 409–10,
    469, 518, 538–42, 587–8
  IAS 33 'Earnings Per Share' 307,
    404–10, 469
  multiple changes in capital during a
    reporting period 409
  Nokia Corporation 518, 538–42,
    587–8
EBITDA 381
effective interest method, concepts
  421–7
electronic audit documentation 46,
  166
elements, financial statements 11,
  287–90, 303–5
embedded derivatives
  concepts 349, 424–7, 527–42
  definition 424

'emphasis of matter' paragraphs 10, 11,
  215, 228, 269–71, 285, 288, 330–1,
  607, 608–9, 613–14
  definition 269
  illustrative auditors' reports 228, 270,
    607, 608–9, 613–14
  ISA 706 (revised and redrafted)
    'Emphasis of Matter Paragraphs and
    Other Matter(s) Paragraphs in the
    Independent Auditor's Report' 10,
    11, 228, 263, 269–71, 607, 608–9
employee benefits 312, 335, 337–9,
  383–7, 396–7, 452–3, 459, 460–1,
  468, 473–4, 483–4, 497, 530–42,
  546–50, 577–86, 592
  see also pension schemes; retirement
    benefits
  IAS 19 'Employee Benefits' 262,
    383–7
  IAS 26 'Accounting and Reporting
    by Retirement Benefit Plans'
    396–7
  types 383–7, 396–7, 452–3
employee fraud
  see also fraud
  concepts 49–61, 100
  definition 49–50
employee wages and salaries 178, 443–4,
  464, 483–4, 510–11
  see also human resources
  audit tests 443–4
  Nokia Corporation 546
engagement partners
  see also auditors
  concepts 39–43, 240–8, 321–33
engagement performance, quality
  controls 321–33
engagement teams, quality controls
  40–1, 88–90, 93–4, 321–33
Enpocket Inc. 560
the entity
  ISA 315 (redrafted) 'Obtaining an
    Understanding of the Entity and its
    Environment and Assessing the
    Risk of Material Misstatements'
    4–5, 10, 28–32, 47, 51–2, 64, 80–1,
    86, 87–8, 91–119, 127, 135–6, 192,
    196–7, 204, 240–1, 251
  nature 95–6, 136–7
the environment
  groups 241–3
  ISA 315 (redrafted) 'Obtaining an
    Understanding of the Entity and its
    Environment and Assessing the
    Risk of Material Misstatements'
    4–5, 10, 28–32, 47, 51–2, 64, 80–1,
    86, 87–8, 91–119, 127, 135–6, 192,
    196–7, 204, 240–1, 251
environmental pollution regulations 65
equity
  see also shareholders' funds
  definition 304
  statements of changes in equity for the
    period 351–8, 411–12, 456
equity instruments, IAS 32 'Financial
  Instruments: Presentation and
  Disclosure' 402–4, 497, 526–42

equity method of accounting 315,
  399–400, 402, 553
equity price risk 470–1, 597–8
equity-settled share-based payments,
  concepts 337–9
Ernst and Young 28
errors 1, 37, 49–61, 105, 121–6, 186–9,
  302–3, 363–4, 538–42
  see also material misstatements
  definition 1, 49
  difference error-projection method
    186–7
  IAS 8 'Accounting Policies, Changes
    in Accounting Estimates and Errors'
    363–4, 538–42
  projections 125, 186–9
  ratio error-projection method 186–7
estimation techniques 7, 10, 30, 161,
  191–201, 363–4, 462, 476–7,
  538–42
  audit planning 192–3
  audit procedures 195, 198–201
  biases 194
  definition 192
  depreciation/amortisation 191,
    193–201
  evidence generation requirements
    191–201
  fair value 191–201
  IAS 8 'Accounting Policies, Changes
    in Accounting Estimates and Errors'
    363–4, 538–42
  illustrations 193, 196–8
  ISA 540 (revised and redrafted)
    'Auditing Accounting Estimates,
    Including Fair Value Accounting
    Estimates, and Related Disclosures'
    7, 8, 10, 30, 161, 191–201
  litigation and claims 191, 194–5
  reviews 192–3
  subsequent events 194–5, 200–1
  testing 192–201
  types 191–2, 193–4
Ethical Standards 15–23, 40–3, 170,
  244–5, 321–33, 454, 493, 504, 607,
  608, 611, 613, 615
  see also Auditing Practices Board
ethics
  see also independence requirements
    for auditors
  Code of Ethics for Professional
    Accountants 15–23, 39–43, 85, 170,
    244–5, 321–33
EU 453–4, 459, 526
events after the reporting period 27,
  213–19, 364–5, 474, 501, 503
evidence generation requirements 5–6,
  10, 16–23, 27–9, 32, 35–6, 37–8,
  41–2, 45–8, 54–5, 66, 106–8,
  110–11, 127–34, 145–55, 157–67,
  181–9, 191–2, 225–6, 232–7,
  267–8, 328–33
  see also external confirmations;
    inquiry; inspection . . . ;
    observance . . . ; recalculations;
    reperformed . . . ; substantive
    procedures; tests of controls

audit documentation 134, 154–5, 170–2, 328–33
audit procedures 131–4, 145–55
audit tests 54–61, 157–63, 165–7, 433–44, 609
auditors' experts 150–2, 158, 198
definition 132, 145–6
directional testing 157–60
estimation techniques 191–201
external confirmations 10, 77, 165–7, 198–9, 227–30
inventories 157–63
ISA 500 (redrafted) 'Considering the Relevance and Reliability of Audit Evidence' 10, 27–8, 47, 145–55
ISA 501 (redrafted) 'Audit Evidence Regarding Specific Financial Statement Account Balances and Disclosures' 10, 157–63
ISA 505 (revised and redrafted) 'External Confirmations' 10, 77, 165–7, 198–9
ISA 510 (redrafted) Initial Audit Engagements — Opening Balances' 10, 77, 86, 169–72, 274–7
litigation and claims 157, 160–2
opening balances 10, 77, 86, 169–72, 274–7
recurring audits 128–9, 148, 274–7
related parties 203–11
segment information 157, 162–3
sources 5, 27–8, 35–6, 41–2, 54–5, 66, 110–11, 127–34, 146–55, 173–4, 181–9
substantive procedures 110–11, 127–34, 173–9
sufficiency/appropriateness evaluations 27–8, 133–4, 145–55, 225–6
written representations 232–3
year-end inventory counts 104–5, 158–60, 437–9, 610–11
'except for' auditors' opinions, illustrative auditors' reports 610–11
exchange difference reserve 335–6
exemptions
    auditing 273
    IFRS 1 'First-Time Adoption of IFRS' 310–12, 335–6
expenses
    see also costs
    concepts 191, 304, 585–6
    definition 304
expertise, definition 254
experts, definitions 253–4
extended warranties, revenue recognition 58, 191
external auditing 2–6, 71–8, 249–50
    see also auditing
    definition 2
    internal auditing 249–50
external confirmations 10, 27–8, 59, 132–4, 146–55, 198–9, 227–30
    see also evidence . . .
    audit evidence 132–4, 146–55, 198–9, 227–30

evaluations 166–7, 198–9
ISA 505 (revised and redrafted) 'External Confirmations' 10, 77, 165–7, 198–9
refusals by management 166–7
external reviews, Code of Ethics for Professional Accountants 18–19

factoring agreements 98–9
factual misstatements, concepts 142–4, 185–6, 279–82
fair value 7, 8, 10, 191–201, 308, 312, 337–42, 343–4, 348–51, 366–8, 397, 412–15, 420–7, 429–31, 459, 472, 474, 519–20, 522–42, 551–61, 565–9, 572–4
    acquisitions 339–42, 558–60
    definition 195–6
    disclosures 200–1
    estimation techniques 191–201
    evaluations 197–8
    financial instruments 197–8, 308, 316
    IAS 36 'Impairment of Assets' 412–15, 551–3
    IAS 41 'Agriculture' 429–31
    IFRS 5 'Non-Current assets Held for Sale and Discontinued Operations' 343–4
    IFRS 9 'Financial Instruments' 348–51, 420, 565–9
    illustrative financial statements 459, 472
    ISA 540 (revised and redrafted) 'Auditing Accounting Estimates, Including Fair Value Accounting Estimates, and Related Disclosures' 7, 8, 10, 30, 161, 191–201
    models 200
    share-based payments 337–9
fair value hedge 426–7, 570
familiarity threats, concepts 18–19, 327
family/close relationships, Code of Ethics for Professional Accountants 22–3
FASB *see* Financial Accounting Standards Board
fees
    auditors 2, 6, 21–2, 37–8, 76–7, 463–4, 484, 497, 511
    Code of Ethics for Professional Accountants 21–2
    'lowballing' fees 21–2
fictitious journal entries, fraud 54
FIFO inventory valuations 496, 531–2
finance leases 54, 118–19, 377–82, 442, 460–1, 467, 470, 482–3, 496–7
    definition 377, 442, 496–7
    IAS 17 'Leases' 303, 314, 377–82, 442
    illustrative financial statements 460–1, 467, 470
Financial Accounting Standards Board (FASB)
    IASB 54, 314, 378–9, 382
    lease accounting 314, 378–9, 382

financial assets 308, 402–4, 420–7, 461, 497, 531–42, 565–9, 604–5
    IAS 32 'Financial Instruments: Presentation and Disclosure' 402–4, 423, 427, 526–42
    IAS 39 'Financial Instruments: Recognition and Measurement' 198, 310–11, 420–7, 565–9
financial concept of capital maintenance 304–5
financial credit risk 599–600
    see also credit risk
financial instruments 191–2, 197–8, 308, 316, 336, 342, 343, 345–6, 348–51, 398, 402–4, 420–7, 461–2, 469, 476, 483–4, 497, 509–10, 526–42, 565–9
    see also derivatives
    definition 316, 402–3, 420–2
    derecognition 310–11, 317, 425–7
    fair value 197–8, 308, 316
    FRS 25 'Financial Instruments' 509–10
    FRS 26 'Financial Instruments: Measurement' 316, 318
    IAS 32 'Financial Instruments: Presentation and Disclosure' 336, 345, 402–4, 423, 427, 526–42
    IAS 39 'Financial Instruments: Recognition and Measurement' 198, 303, 308, 310–11, 336, 342, 343, 348–51, 398, 420–7, 526–42, 565–9
    IFRS 7 'Financial Instruments: Disclosure' 345–6, 402, 420, 526–42, 598
    IFRS 9 'Financial Instruments' 348–51, 398, 420–1, 427, 541–2
    Nokia Corporation 509–10, 526–42, 565–70
    types 197–8, 308, 402–3, 461, 509–10
financial issues, going concern principle 221–2, 354–5
financial liabilities 308, 402–4, 421–7, 461–2, 497, 533–42, 565–9
    IAS 32 'Financial Instruments: Presentation and Disclosure' 402–4, 526–42
    IAS 39 'Financial Instruments: Recognition and Measurement' 310–11, 421–7
financial performance, measurement and review 98–9
financial ratios 175, 178–9, 186–7, 280
Financial Reporting Council in the United Kingdom. *Going Concern and Liquidity Risk: Guidance for Directors of UK Companies 2009* 354
Financial Reporting Standard for Smaller Entities (FRSSE) 308–19, 354, 356, 372, 493–501, 611–12
financial reviews, illustrative financial statements 445
financial statement risk, concepts 28–30, 107–8, 112, 113–14

financial statements 11, 207, 221–2,
    229–305, 310–12, 351–8, 445–605
see also balance sheets; IAS . . . ;
    IFRS . . . ; income statements;
    interim reports; ISA . . . ; notes . . . ;
    statements of . . .
accruals basis of accounting 301–5
audit features 4–5, 26–33
contents 207, 299–305, 351–8
elements 11, 287–90, 303–5
Framework for the Preparation and
    Presentation of Financial
    Statements (IASB) 299–305
going concern principle 28, 65, 109,
    118–19, 150, 221–30, 301–5,
    353–8, 453–4, 459, 476, 503, 517,
    613–14
IAS 1 'Presentation of Financial
    Statements' 221–2, 351–8, 526–42
IFRS 1 'First-Time Adoption of IFRS'
    310–12, 335–7
IFRS for SMEs 307–19
illustrative audit tests 433–44
illustrative financial statements 300–5,
    445–605
Nokia Corporation 518–605
objectives 299–301
presentation 221–2, 299–305, 351–8,
    526–42
qualitative characteristics 301–5
related party disclosures 75, 150, 203,
    207–11, 392–6, 464, 469, 490–1
special purpose financial statements
    11, 283–5
subsequent events 10, 147–8, 150,
    194–5, 200–1, 213–19, 243–4,
    364–5, 474, 501, 503
underlying assumptions 301–5
financing activities, statements of cash
    flow for the period 360–2, 458, 480,
    481, 507–8, 520–6, 593–4
financing sources 115
finite useful lives, intangible assets
    419–20
Finnish accounting legislation 526
fire regulations 65
floors 424–7
Folicent Manufacturing Inc. 214
forecasts 354–5, 363–4
    see also estimation . . .
foreign exchange options 570
foreign exchange rates 389–90, 400,
    426–7, 460, 463–4, 469–70, 482–3,
    496, 522–42, 561, 575–6, 595–6
foreign exchange risk 469–70, 595–8
forward contracts 424–7, 534–6, 570
forward rate agreements 424–7, 534
Framework for the Preparation and
    Presentation of Financial
    Statements (IASB) 299–305
fraud 1–6, 10, 28–30, 37, 49–61, 76, 80,
    93–4, 100, 104–5, 123–4, 139–40,
    150, 166–7, 235–7, 454, 492, 493,
    503, 615
    see also material misstatements
characteristics 52–4
communication matters 60–1, 150, 235

concepts 1–6, 28–30, 49–61, 76, 80,
    100, 139–40, 150, 166
definition 1, 30, 49
discussions 50, 51, 61, 111
employee fraud 49–61, 100
ISA 240 (redrafted) 'The Auditor's
    Responsibility to Consider Fraud in
    an Audit of Financial Statements'
    10, 49–61, 93–4, 110, 166, 237
management fraud 49–61
misappropriation of assets 52–61
revenue recognition 53–4, 55–61
risk assessments 50–61, 166–7
third party service organisations
    139–40
types 49–50, 52–4
written representations 235–7
fraudulent financial reporting
concepts 52–61
definition 53–4
FRS 2 'Accounting for Subsidiary
    Undertakings' 316
FRS 5 'Reporting the Substance of
    Transactions' 55–6, 317
FRS 6 'Acquisitions and Mergers'
    314–15
FRS 8 'Related Party Disclosures'
    434
FRS 9 'Associates and Joint Ventures'
    315, 316
FRS 10 'Goodwill and Intangible Assets'
    193, 313–14, 435
FRS 12 'Provisions, Contingent
    Liabilities and Contingent Assets'
    133, 370
FRS 15 'Tangible Fixed Assets' 312–13,
    318, 436
FRS 19 'Deferred Tax' 315, 369–70,
    374, 509
FRS 25 'Financial Instruments' 316,
    509–10
FRS 26 'Financial Instruments:
    Measurement' 316, 318
FRSSE *see* Financial Reporting Standard
    for Smaller Entities
functional currency, IAS 21 'The Effects
    of Changes in Foreign Exchange
    Rates' 390, 529–42
fundamental principles, Code of Ethics
    for Professional Accountants 15–17,
    20, 321–33
futures contracts 534, 570
FX . . . *see* foreign exchange . . .

GAAP 86, 193–4, 197–8, 244, 270, 281,
    309, 310–19, 335–6, 345, 356,
    369–70, 474–517, 607–15
    see also FRS . . .
alternative GAAP 244
IFRS for SMEs 312–19
Gabriella Industries Inc. 233, 302
general controls, information systems
    105–6
Germany, Nokia Corporation 545, 546,
    554, 594
gifts/hospitality problems, Code of Ethics
    for Professional Accountants 22

going concern principle 28, 65, 109,
    118–19, 150, 221–30, 301–5,
    353–8, 453–4, 459, 476, 503, 517,
    613–14
assessment considerations 65, 221–30,
    354–6
audit procedures 226–30
auditors' opinions 226–30
definition 221–2, 301
disclosures 221–30, 356–8
evaluations of management
    assessments 225
external factors 221–2, 354–5
financial issues 221–2, 354–5
groups 244
IAS 1 'Presentation of Financial
    Statements' 221–2, 353–8
illustrations 224, 228–30
inappropriate basis 228–9
information systems 227
ISA 570 (redrafted) 'Going Concern'
    9, 10, 28, 221–30, 357
managerial/operational issues 221–2,
    354–5
material uncertainties 227–30, 356–8
period of review 223, 355–6
preliminary assessments 223–5
refusals by management 229–30
written representations 224–6, 235
goods or services, share-based payments
    337–9, 541–2
goodwill 96, 193, 313–14, 318–19, 335,
    339–42, 352–8, 399–400, 413–15,
    417, 419–20, 435, 518, 519,
    528–42, 551–60, 562–3
estimation techniques 193–4
FRS 10 'Goodwill and Intangible
    Assets' 193, 313–14, 435
negative goodwill 318–19
governance contrasts, management
    73–4
government grants/assistance 357,
    372–3, 388–9, 430–1, 460–1, 463–4
definitions 388
IAS 20 'Accounting for Government
    Grants and Disclosure of
    Government Assistance' 357,
    388–9, 430, 526–42
IAS 41 'Agriculture' 430–1
SSAP 4 'Accounting for Government
    Grants' 372–3
'gross' concept, auditing thresholds'
    table 2–3
Groupco Limited, illustrative financial
    statements 501–17
groups 2–3, 7–8, 10, 48, 203–11,
    239–48, 314–15, 339–42, 392–6,
    501–17, 526–605, 613–14
    see also business combinations; parent
    companies; subsidiaries
alternative GAAP 244
audit completion procedures 247–8
audit planning 245–8
communications 244–5, 247–8
concepts 239–48
the environment 241–3
going concern principle 244

IAS 27 'Consolidated and Separate Financial Statements' 2, 193, 240, 310–11, 397–9, 541–2
ISA 600 (revised and redrafted) 'The Audit of Group Financial Statements' 7–8, 10, 48, 239–48
materiality 243–8
subsequent events 243–4

haphazard non-statistical sampling, concepts 183–5
harvested products, IAS 41 'Agriculture' 429–31
hazard risks, Nokia Corporation 605
Health and Safety at Work Act 63, 65, 67–8
hedge accounting 310–11, 317–18, 426–7, 524, 527–42, 550, 561, 570, 595–605
    definition 317–18, 424, 534–6
    IAS 39 'Financial Instruments: Recognition and Measurement' 310–11, 426–7, 534–42
    types 426–7, 534–6, 570
hedge of a net investment in a foreign operation, definition 427, 536
held-to-maturity assets 197–8, 308, 348, 351, 420–7
hire purchase 314, 379, 442, 481, 482–4, 487–91, 496–7, 509, 511–17
    see also leases
historic cost basis 200, 316, 362–4, 376, 459, 479, 486–7, 495–6, 526
history of auditing 1–6
Holandos Inc. 216–17
'hot' file reviews 19, 43, 154–5, 327, 332
Huano Technology Co., Ltd 554
human resources 100–5, 114–15, 321–33
    see also employee...
    quality controls 321–33
    segregation of duties 100–5, 114–15
hybrid contracts 349–51, 424–7
    definition 424
    IFRS 9 'Financial Instruments' 349–51
hyperinflationary economies
    definition 400
    IAS 29 'Financial Reporting in Hyperinflationary Economies' 400–1

IAASB *see* International Auditing and Assurance Standards Board
IAS 1 'Presentation of Financial Statements' 221–2, 351–8, 526–42
IAS 2 'Inventory' 358–9, 438
IAS 7 'Statement of Cash Flows' 359–62
IAS 8 'Accounting Policies, Changes in Accounting Estimates and Errors' 345, 362–4, 538–42
IAS 10 'Events After the Reporting Period' 27, 213, 216–19, 364–5, 501
IAS 11 'Construction Contracts' 56–7, 95, 365–8, 527–42
IAS 12 'Income Taxes'
    concepts 368–74
    proposed changes 373–4

IAS 16 'Property, Plant and Equipment' 303–4, 374–7, 381, 384, 436
IAS 17 'Leases' 303, 314, 377–82, 442
    existing requirements 379
    proposed requirements 379–82
IAS 18 'Revenue' 55–6, 303, 350, 382–3, 527–42
IAS 19 'Employee Benefits' 262, 383–7, 541–2
IAS 20 'Accounting for Government Grants and Disclosure of Government Assistance' 357, 388–9, 430, 526–42
IAS 21 'The Effects of Changes in Foreign Exchange Rates' 389–90, 426–7, 529–42
IAS 23 'Borrowing Costs' 391–2, 526–42
IAS 24 'Related Party Disclosures' 75, 119, 150, 203, 233, 302, 392–6, 434, 464, 469, 516
IAS 26 'Accounting and Reporting by Retirement Benefit Plans' 396–7
IAS 27 'Consolidated and Separate Financial Statements' 2, 193, 240, 310–11, 397–9, 541–2
IAS 28 'Investments in Associates' 392, 399–400, 553, 565
IAS 29 'Financial Reporting in Hyperinflationary Economies' 400–1
IAS 31 'Interests in Joint Ventures' 392, 401–2
IAS 32 'Financial Instruments: Presentation and Disclosure' 336, 345, 402–4, 423, 427, 526–42
    see also IAS 39...; IFRS 7...
    overview 402–4
IAS 33 'Earnings Per Share' 307, 404–10, 469
IAS 34 'Interim Financial Reporting' 307, 410–12
IAS 36 'Impairment of Assets' 375, 412–15, 419, 551–3
IAS 37 'Provisions, Contingent Liabilities and Contingent Assets' 26–7, 133, 150, 161, 216–17, 303, 415–17, 442–3
IAS 38 'Intangible Assets' 377, 381, 417–20, 462
IAS 39 'Financial Instruments: Recognition and Measurement' 198, 303, 308, 310–11, 336, 342, 343, 348–51, 398, 420–7, 526–42, 565–9
    see also IAS 32...; IFRS 9...
    overview 420–7
IAS 40 'Investment Property' 427–8, 436
IAS 41 'Agriculture' 428–31
IASB *see* International Accounting Standards Board
IASs 335–431
    see also IFRS...
IBA *see* Industrial Buildings Allowance
IFAC *see* International Federation of Accountants
IFRIC 4 'Determining Whether an Arrangement Contains a Lease' 311

IFRIC 9 'Reassessment of Embedded Derivatives' 527
IFRIC 11 'IFRS 2 Group and Treasury Share Transactions' 342, 541–2
IFRIC 13 'Customer Loyalty Programs' 527–42
IFRIC 14 'Minimum Funding Requirements' 541–2
IFRIC 15 'Agreements for the Construction of Real Estate' 527–42
IFRIC 16 'Hedges of a Net Investment in a Foreign Operation' 527–42
IFRIC 19 'Extinguishing Financial Liabilities with Equity Instruments' 542
IFRS 1 'First-Time Adoption of IFRS' 310–12, 335–7
    disclosures 310–12, 336–7
    exemptions 310–12, 335–6
IFRS 2 'Share-Based Payment' 337–9, 446, 526–42
IFRS 3 'Business Combinations' 96, 193, 339–42, 398, 399, 417, 419, 435, 541–2
    amendments 340–2, 541
    disclosures 339–40, 541–2
    overview 339–42
IFRS 4 'Insurance Contracts' 307, 342–3
IFRS 5 'Non-Current assets Held for Sale and Discontinued Operations' 307, 343–4
IFRS 6 'Exploration for and Evaluation of Mineral Resources' 344–5
IFRS 7 'Financial Instruments: Disclosure' 345–6, 402, 420, 526–42, 598
    see also IAS 32...; IAS 39...
    overview 345–6
IFRS 8 'Operating Segments' 162–3, 307, 346–7, 440, 462–3
IFRS 9 'Financial Instruments' 348–51, 398, 403–4, 420–1, 427, 541–2
    see also IAS 39...
IFRSs 4, 26, 36, 76, 94–5, 97, 161, 192, 198, 204, 299–305, 307–19, 335–431, 445–605, 614–15
    see also IAS...
    overview 335–431
    for SMEs 307–19
illustrative audit tests 433–44
illustrative auditors' reports 607–15
illustrative financial statements 300–5, 445–605
impairment of assets 375, 412–15, 419, 460, 462, 471, 480, 482–4, 509, 518, 528–45, 551–3, 563
    see also recoverable amount
    definition 412–13
    discount rates 551–3
    IAS 36 'Impairment of Assets' 375, 412–15, 419
    indicators 413
    intangible assets 413–15, 551–3, 563
    Nokia Corporation 518, 528–45, 551–3, 563–4
    recognition 413–15

impairment of financial assets, IAS 39
'Financial Instruments: Recognition
and Measurement' 310–11, 350–1,
551–3
imprest system, petty cash 441
income, definition 304
income statements
analytical procedures 175–6
Framework for the Preparation and
Presentation of Financial
Statements (IASB) 300–5
IAS 1 'Presentation of Financial
Statements' 221–2, 351–8
IAS 33 'Earnings Per Share' 410
IAS 34 'Interim Financial Reporting'
411–12
IFRS 1 'First-Time Adoption of IFRS'
310–12, 335–7
IFRS 2 'Share-Based Payment' 337–9,
446, 541–2
IFRS 5 'Non-Current assets Held for
Sale and Discontinued Operations'
343–4
IFRS 9 'Financial Instruments'
349–51
illustrative financial statements 455–6,
460, 478, 494, 505, 511, 517,
543–605
Nokia Corporation 518–605
income taxes 368–74, 465, 536–42,
561–2
inconsistency, definition 279
indefinite/finite useful lives, intangible
assets 419–20
independence in appearance, definition
5–6
independence of mind, definition 5
independence requirements for auditors
see also ethics
concepts 4–6, 15–23, 76–7, 85,
322–33
definition 5–6, 326–7
threats 6, 17–19, 23, 326–7
indirect controls, internal control systems
130
indirect method, statements of cash flow
for the period 360–2
Industrial Buildings Allowance (IBA),
concepts 371–2
inflation
estimation techniques 195
IAS 29 'Financial Reporting in
Hyperinflationary Economies'
400–1
influence aspects, IAS 24 'Related Party
Disclosures' 203, 392–6, 434,
527–8
information systems 103–6, 109, 129,
136, 197, 227
application controls 105–6
control environment 103–6
general controls 105–6
going concern principle 227
ISA 402 (revised and redrafted) 'Audit
Considerations Relating to an Entity
Using a Third Party Service
Organisation' 10, 135–40, 197

inherent risk
concepts 29–30, 107–8, 112, 179, 183,
188
definition 29, 107–8
input data, application controls 105
inquiry, evidence sources 146–8
insignificant deficiencies, internal control
systems 82–3, 248
inspection procedures 92–3, 146–7, 199
see also evidence . . .
insurance contracts 307, 312, 342–3
definition 342
IFRS 4 'Insurance Contracts' 307,
342–3
risk management 605
intangible assets 313–14, 377, 381,
413–15, 417–20, 434–5, 459, 463,
479, 481, 484–5, 506–17, 519,
528–42, 551–60, 562–5
see also goodwill; licences; patents
audit tests 434–5, 609
definition 417
depreciation 381, 434–5, 512
development costs 313
disclosures 418–19
estimation techniques 193–4
FRS 10 'Goodwill and Intangible
Assets' 193–4, 313–14, 435
IAS 38 'Intangible Assets' 377, 381,
417–20, 462
illustrative audit tests 434–5
impairment of assets 413–15, 551–3,
563
indefinite/finite useful lives 419–20
Nokia Corporation 519, 528–42,
551–60, 562–5
notes to the financial statements
418–19, 459, 463, 551–60
revaluations 314
integrity requirements, Code of Ethics
for Professional Accountants 15–16,
40–3, 85, 322–33
intellectual property rights (IPRs) 537,
539–42, 586–7
interest payments 382–3, 444, 462,
464–5, 467, 471–2, 478, 481,
484–5, 494, 501, 521, 529–42
interest rate risk 462, 471, 596–8
interest rate swaps 534, 570
interim reports
see also financial statements
definition 410–11
IAS 34 'Interim Financial Reporting'
307, 410–12
IFRS 1 'First-Time Adoption of IFRS'
310–12, 336–7
minimum content requirements 411
internal auditing 2–3, 10, 249–52, 288
definition 2, 249
external auditing 249–50
ISA 610 (redrafted) 'The Auditor's
Consideration of the Internal Audit
Function' 10, 249–52, 288
internal auditors 249–52
audit documentation 251–2
communications 249, 251–2
definition 249

internal control systems 5–6, 8, 29–30,
37–8, 49–51, 76, 79–84, 94–5,
99–105, 127–34, 137–40, 249–52
see also control risk; internal audit . . . ;
tests of controls
communications 5, 7, 8–9, 10, 13, 32,
76, 77, 79–84, 111–12
concepts 5–6, 8, 29–30, 37–8, 76,
94–5, 99–105, 127–34, 137–40
deficiencies 5, 7, 8–9, 10, 13, 32, 76,
77, 79–84, 99–105
definition 99–100
direct/indirect controls 130
insignificant deficiencies 82–3, 248
ISA 265 'Communicating Deficiencies
in Internal Control to those Charged
with Governance and Management'
5, 7, 8–9, 10, 13, 32, 77, 79–84,
111–12, 210–11, 331
limitations 100, 123–4
material weaknesses 76, 79–84,
99–105, 329–33
operational effectiveness 127–34,
137–40, 249–52
responsible persons 80–1, 106
International Accounting Standards
Board (IASB) 54, 177, 205,
299–305, 307–19, 336, 378–9, 382,
436, 526–7, 542
see also IAS . . . ; IFRS . . .
FASB 314, 378–9, 382
Framework for the Preparation and
Presentation of Financial
Statements 299–305
IAS 12 proposals 373
IFRS adopters 336
lease accounting 314, 378–9, 382
International Auditing and Assurance
Standards Board (IAASB) 7, 11–13,
79, 83, 124, 195, 332
International Federation of Accountants
(IFAC)
Code of Conduct 5–6
Code of Ethics for Professional
Accountants 15–23, 326
International Standards on Auditing
(ISAs) 1–6, 7–13, 31–3, 37–8,
321–3, 328–33, 454, 504, 607,
608–9
see also Auditing Practices Board;
ISA . . .
auditing in accordance with ISAs 31
Clarified ISAs 7–13, 31–3, 79, 83, 195
communication-requirements list of
ISAs 77–8
concepts 1–6, 7–13, 31–3, 37–8, 321–3
departures 48
effective dates 13, 31
redrafted/revised versions' overview
7–13
'should'/'shall' changes 12, 13, 31–3
intimidation threats, concepts 18–19
inventories 56–7, 104–5, 118–19, 150,
157–63, 170–2, 191, 235–7,
315–16, 358–9, 365, 437–9, 457,
461–2, 466, 479–80, 482–3, 487,
495, 496, 506–17, 519–605, 610–11

attendance at inventory counts 158–60, 171–2, 438–9
audit tests 157–63, 437–9, 610–11
AVCO inventory valuations 482
control environment 104–5
directional testing 157–60
evidence generation requirements 157–63
FIFO inventory valuations 496, 531–2
IAS 2 'Inventory' 358–9, 438
illustrative audit tests 437–9
ISA 501 (redrafted) 'Audit Evidence Regarding Specific Financial Statement Account Balances and Disclosures' 157–63
LIFO inventory valuations 315–16, 438
net realisable value 358–9, 365, 461–2, 531–42
Nokia Corporation 571
opening balances 170–2
third party service organisations 159
valuations 150, 157–63, 170–2, 235, 315–16, 358–9, 365, 438, 461–2, 482–3, 496, 509, 531–42, 571–2
year-end counts 104–5, 158–60, 437–9, 610–11
investing activities, statements of cash flow for the period 360–2, 458, 480, 481, 507–8, 521–6, 593–4
investment properties
definition 427
IAS 40 'Investment Property' 427–8, 436
investment tax credits 373
investments 392, 399–400, 427–8, 436–7, 498–501, 506–17, 553, 560–1
audit tests 436–7
illustrative audit tests 436–7
investments in associates 392, 399–400, 553, 565
invoices 55–61, 82–3, 98–102, 129–34, 439–40, 441–2
ISA 200 (revised and redrafted) 'Overall Objective of the Independent Auditor, and the Conduct of an Audit in Accordance with ISAs' 10, 26–33, 287–8
auditing in accordance with ISAs 31
concepts 26–33, 123–4, 287–8
ISA 210 (redrafted) 'Agreeing the Terms of Audit Engagements' 10, 35–8, 85, 284
ISA 220 (redrafted) 'Quality Control for an Audit of Financial Statements' 10, 39–43, 85, 240, 247
ISA 230 (redrafted) 'Audit Documentation' 10, 45–8, 110–11, 134, 155
ISA 240 (redrafted) 'The Auditor's Responsibility to Consider Fraud in an Audit of Financial Statements' 10, 49–61, 77, 93–4, 110, 166, 237
ISA 250 (redrafted) 'The Auditor's Responsibilities Related to Laws

and Regulations in an Audit of Financial Statements' 10, 63–8, 77, 237
ISA 260 (revised and redrafted) 'Significant Difficulties' 9, 10, 69–78, 111–12, 126, 247, 330–1
ISA 265 'Communicating Deficiencies in Internal Control to those Charged with Governance and Management' 5, 7, 8–9, 10, 13, 32, 77, 79–84, 111–12, 210–11, 331
ISA 300 (redrafted) 'Planning an Audit of Financial Statements' 4–5, 10, 85–90, 91, 241–2
ISA 315 (redrafted) 'Obtaining an Understanding of the Entity and its Environment and Assessing the Risk of Material Misstatements'
concepts 4–5, 10, 28–32, 47, 51–2, 64, 80–1, 86, 87–8, 91–119, 127, 135–6, 192, 196–7, 204, 240–1, 251
planning notes 111–19
ISA 320 (revised and redrafted) 'Materiality in Planning and Performing an Audit' 10, 121–6, 141–2
see also ISA 450 . . .
ISA 330 (redrafted) 'The Auditor's Procedures in Response to Assessed Risks' 10, 32, 88, 101–2, 110, 127–34, 138, 193–4
ISA 402 (revised and redrafted) 'Audit Considerations Relating to an Entity Using a Third Party Service Organisation' 10, 135–40, 197
ISA 450 'Evaluation of Misstatements Identified During the Audit' 7, 9, 10, 32–3, 77, 121–6, 141–4, 237
see also ISA 320 . . .
ISA 500 (redrafted) 'Considering the Relevance and Reliability of Audit Evidence' 10, 27–8, 47, 145–55
ISA 501 (redrafted) 'Audit Evidence Regarding Specific Financial Statement Account Balances and Disclosures' 10, 157–63, 237
ISA 505 (revised and redrafted) 'External Confirmations' 10, 77, 165–7, 198–9
ISA 510 (redrafted) Initial Audit Engagements — Opening Balances' 10, 77, 86, 169–72, 274–7
ISA 520 (redrafted) 'Analytical Procedures' 10, 173–9
ISA 530 (redrafted) 'Audit Sampling' 9, 10, 181–9
ISA 540 (revised and redrafted) 'Auditing Accounting Estimates, Including Fair Value Accounting Estimates, and Related Disclosures' 7, 8, 10, 30, 161, 191–201
ISA 550 (revised and redrafted) 'Related Parties' 8, 10, 77, 96, 203–11, 237
ISA 560 (redrafted) 'Subsequent Events' 10, 77, 200, 213–19, 237, 270, 296
ISA 570 (redrafted) 'Going Concern' 9, 10, 28, 77, 221–30, 237

ISA 580 (revised and redrafted) 'Written Representations' 10, 231–7
ISA 600 (revised and redrafted) 'The Audit of Group Financial Statements' 7–8, 10, 48, 70, 239–48, 288
ISA 610 (redrafted) 'The Auditor's Consideration of the Internal Audit Function' 10, 249–52, 288
ISA 620 (revised and redrafted) 'Using the Work of an Auditor's Expert' 10, 32, 88–9, 146, 151, 158, 198, 253–5
ISA 700 (redrafted) 'The Independent Auditor's Report on a Complete Set of General Purpose Financial Statements' 10, 11, 47, 125–6, 257–63, 284–5, 288, 607
ISA 705 (revised and redrafted) 'Modifications to the Opinion in the Independent Auditor's Report' 77, 139, 159, 162, 263, 265–8, 607
ISA 706 (revised and redrafted) 'Emphasis of Matter Paragraphs and Other Matter(s) Paragraphs in the Independent Auditor's Report' 10, 11, 77, 228, 263, 269–71, 607, 608–9
ISA 710 (redrafted) 'Comparative Information, Corresponding Figures and Comparative Financial Statements' 11, 77, 237, 270, 273–7, 296
ISA 720 (redrafted) 'The Auditor's Responsibility in Relation to Other Financial Information in Documents Containing Audited Financial Statements' 11, 77, 270, 279–82
ISA 800 (revised and redrafted) 'Special Considerations — Audits of Financial Statements Prepared in Accordance with Special Purpose Frameworks' 11, 283–5
ISA 805 (revised and redrafted) 'Special Considerations — Audits of Single Financial Statements and Specific Financial Statements, Accounts or Items of a Financial Statement' 11, 287–90
ISA 810 'Engagements to Report on Summary Financial Statements' 11, 291–8
ISAs *see* International Standards on Auditing
ISO 9001 106, 445, 448
ISQC 1 (redrafted) 'Quality Control for Firms that Perform Audits and Reviews of Financial Statements, and Other Assurance and Related Service Engagements' 7, 11, 39–43, 48, 321–33
see also quality controls

joint ventures 203–11, 239–48, 312, 315, 318, 392–6, 401–2
definition 401
FRS 9 'Associates and Joint Ventures' 315, 316

joint ventures (*cont.*)
  IAS 24 'Related Party Disclosures'
    203, 392–6
  IAS 31 'Interests in Joint Ventures'
    392, 401–2
  types 401–2
journal, the 54, 148
judgement-selection non-statistical
    sampling, concepts 183–5
judgemental misstatements, concepts
    142–4, 185–6

key performance indicators 280–2, 449
Kingston Cotton Mill case (1896) 1
KPMG 217

Lakeside Clothing Inc. 129
Lakeside Engineering Inc. 36–8, 64–5
leadership responsibilities within audit
    firms, quality controls 321–33
leases 54, 118–19, 303, 311–12, 314,
    377–82, 442, 460–1, 463–4, 466–7,
    470, 472, 482–91, 496–7, 500,
    509–17, 531–42, 589–90
  see also finance . . . ; hire purchase;
    operating . . .
  audit tests 54, 442
  IAS 17 'Leases' 303, 314, 377–82, 442
  illustrative audit tests 442
  illustrative financial statements 463–4,
    466–7, 470, 482–91
  Nokia Corporation 531–42, 589–90
  'right of use' model 380–2
  types 377, 460, 496–7
legal contingencies, Nokia Corporation
    540
letters of engagement 21–2, 36–8, 331–2
letters of representation
  see also written representations
  concepts 74–6
liabilities
  see also contingent . . . ; current . . .
  definition 304, 379
  IAS 1 'Presentation of Financial
    Statements' 352–8
  IAS 12 'Income Taxes' 368–74
  IAS 17 'Leases' 303, 314, 377–82, 442
  IFRS 1 'First-Time Adoption of IFRS'
    310–12, 335–7
  IFRS 4 'Insurance Contracts' 307,
    342–3
licences 435, 463, 482, 484–5, 530–42,
    554–60
LIFO inventory valuations 315–16, 438
limitations, auditing 2–3, 30, 123–4, 145,
    170–2, 191–2, 265–8
liquidity risk 109, 346, 354, 471, 601–5
listed clients
  AIM 94–5
  communications 76–8, 83–4
litigation and claims
  estimation techniques 191, 194–5
  ISA 501 (redrafted) 'Audit Evidence
    Regarding Specific Financial
    Statement Account Balances and
    Disclosures' 157, 160–2

loans 118–19, 308, 420–7, 434, 467, 481,
    484–5, 488–91, 499–501, 520–605
  directors 434
  IAS 39 'Financial Instruments:
    Recognition and Measurement'
    420–7
Lopez, Lord Justice 1
loss-making contracts, IAS 11
    'Construction Contracts'
    366–8
'lowballing' fees 21–2
Lucas Inc., illustrative financial
    statements 445–74

management
  see also directors
  experts 254
  going concern principle 221–2,
    354–8
  governance contrasts 73–4
management fraud
  see also fraud
  concepts 49–61
  definition 49–50
management representation letters *see*
    letters of representation
manipulation of financial statements *see*
    earnings management
Marchant Home Products 229
market risk 346, 595–8
material misstatements 1–13, 16–23,
    26–32, 37–8, 47, 49–53, 64, 75–6,
    80–4, 86, 87–8, 91–119, 121–6,
    127–34, 141–4, 160–3, 169–72,
    174–9, 185–9, 193–4, 203–11, 245,
    329–33
  see also errors; fraud
  assertion level 28–9, 33, 108–9,
    127–34
  communications 126, 143–4, 276–7,
    329–33
  definition 141, 142–3
  detection risk 28–30, 33, 50–61,
    107–8, 112, 179, 182–3, 188–9
  effects 124–5
  ISA 315 (redrafted) 'Obtaining an
    Understanding of the Entity and its
    Environment and Assessing the
    Risk of Material Misstatements'
    4–5, 10, 28–32, 47, 51–2, 64, 80–1,
    86, 87–8, 91–119, 127, 135–6, 204,
    240–1
  ISA 320 (revised and redrafted)
    'Materiality in Planning and
    Performing an Audit' 10, 121–6,
    141–2
  ISA 450 'Evaluation of Misstatements
    Identified During the Audit' 7, 9,
    10, 32–3, 121–6, 141–4, 237
  prior-period uncorrected
    misstatements 143–4
  related parties 203–11
  risk assessments 4–5, 10, 28–32, 37–8,
    47, 51–2, 64, 80–1, 86, 87–8,
    91–119, 125–6, 127–34, 160–3,
    169–72, 174–9, 185–9, 193–4,
    203–11

risk conditions/events 109
third party service organisations
    138–40
material uncertainties, going concern
    principle 227–30, 356–8
materiality 26–7, 121–6, 141–4, 188,
    215–19, 227–30, 235, 243–8,
    266–8, 280–2
  audit documentation 124–6, 144, 235
  definition 26–7, 121–2, 141–2
  groups 243–8
  ISA 320 (revised and redrafted)
    'Materiality in Planning and
    Performing an Audit' 10, 121–6,
    141–2
  revisions 124
  sample sizes 188–9
matter paragraphs 10, 11, 215, 228, 263,
    269–71, 285, 288, 330–1, 607,
    608–9, 613–14
  illustrative auditors' reports 607–15
  ISA 706 (revised and redrafted)
    'Emphasis of Matter Paragraphs and
    Other Matter(s) Paragraphs in the
    Independent Auditor's Report' 10,
    11, 228, 263, 269–71, 607, 608–9
medium term notes (MTNs) 602–5
medium-sized companies
  see also small . . .
  auditing thresholds' table 3
medium-sized groups, auditing
    thresholds' table 3
mergers
  see also acquisitions
  FRS 6 'Acquisitions and Mergers'
    314–15
mineral extractive industry, IFRS 6
    'Exploration for and Evaluation of
    Mineral Resources' 344–5
minority interests 505, 506, 515, 520,
    527–8, 559–60, 573–6, 593–4
misappropriation of assets 52–61
  see also fraud
misstatements
  see also factual . . . ; judgemental . . . ;
    material . . . ; projected . . .
  communications 143–4
  definitions 141, 279
  evaluations 7, 9, 10, 32–3, 121–6,
    141–4, 185–6
  ISA 450 'Evaluation of Misstatements
    Identified During the Audit' 7, 9,
    10, 32–3, 121–6, 141–4, 237
  types 141–2, 185–6, 235, 279–82
models, fair value 200
modifications to auditors' reports 75–6,
    77, 139, 159, 162–3, 172, 210–11,
    215–19, 265–8, 274–7, 295, 607
  see also adverse . . . ; disclaimed . . . ;
    qualified . . .
Money Laundering Regulations 22, 60,
    324–5
monitoring needs
  control environment 106, 128–34
  quality controls 321–33
Monte Carlo simulations 597–8
Moody's 602

NASDAQ OMX Helsinki 578
National Insurance Contributions (NICs)
    443
NAVTEQ 526, 542–605
    see also Nokia . . .
negative assurance
    see also review engagements
    definition 3
negative goodwill, IFRS for SMEs
    318–19
'net' concept, auditing thresholds' table
    2–3
net investment hedging, Nokia
    Corporation 527–42
net realisable value 358–9, 365, 461–2,
    509, 531–42, 560–1
    definition 358
    IAS 2 'Inventory' 358–9
Nokia Corporation 518–605
    see also NAVTEQ; Symbian Ltd
    accounting policies 526–45
    accrued expenses 585–6
    acquisitions 521–63
    audit committee 594
    commitments 588–9
    construction contracts 545–6, 564
    contingent liabilities 588–9, 604–5
    credit risk 568, 595, 599–600
    deferred taxes 519–20, 536–42,
        554–60, 585
    depreciation and amortisation 560,
        564–5
    derivatives 527–42, 561, 566–70, 574,
        595–605
    directors 576–86, 590–4
    earnings per share 518, 538–42,
        587–8
    employee wages and salaries 546
    fair value of financial instruments
        565–9
    financial income and expenses 560–1
    financial instruments 509–10, 526–42,
        565–70
    hazard risks 605
    impairment of assets 518, 528–45,
        551–3, 563–4
    income taxes 536–42, 561–2
    intangible assets 519, 528–42, 551–60,
        562–5
    inventories 571
    investments in associates 553, 565
    leases 531–42, 589–90
    liquidity risk 601–5
    market risk 595–8
    other operating income and expenses
        550
    pension schemes 546–50, 592
    performance shares 581–3, 587–8
    principal group companies 594
    property, plant and equipment 519,
        531–42, 553, 554–60, 563–5
    provisions 533–42, 571–2, 586–7
    related party transactions 590–3
    reserves 572–4
    restricted shares 583–4
    risk management 594–605
    segment information 542–5

share capital 576–7
share-based payments 522–42, 577–88
shares of the parent company 576–7
statements of cash flow for the period
    520–6, 593–4
translation differences 575–6
Nokia Siemens Networks 526, 542–605
non-adjusting events
    see also subsequent . . .
    definition 218, 365
    IAS 10 'Events After the Reporting
        Period' 27, 216–19, 364–5
    types 218
non-audit services
    Code of Ethics for Professional
        Accountants 23
    concepts 23, 42–3
non-compliance
    definition 63–4
    regulations 63–8, 83–4, 107, 139–40,
        210–11
non-controlling interests 310–11, 398,
    518, 541–2
    IAS 27 'Consolidated and Separate
        Financial Statements' 310–11, 398,
        541–2
non-cumulative preference dividends
    405–10
non-current assets 56, 276–7, 303–5,
    312–13, 434–6, 457, 459–60,
    463–4, 466, 479, 481–91, 495–501,
    506–17, 519–605
    see also depreciation; property, plant
        and equipment
    audit tests 434–6
    disposals 56, 511, 521–6, 563–5,
        572–4
    FRS 15 'Tangible Fixed Assets'
        312–13, 318, 436
    IAS 1 'Presentation of Financial
        Statements' 352–8
    IAS 16 'Property, Plant and
        Equipment' 303–4, 374–7, 436
    IFRS 5 'Non-Current assets Held for
        Sale and Discontinued Operations'
        343–4
    illustrative audit tests 434–6
    opening balances 276–7
non-current liabilities 304, 457, 479,
    506–17, 519–605
non-executive directors 450–2
non-sampling risk
    see also detection risk
    concepts 179, 182–9
    definition 179
Norway, Nokia Corporation 557
notes to the financial statements 344, 351,
    364–5, 411–12, 418–19, 458–74,
    480–91, 495–501, 507–17, 526–605
    discontinued operations 344
    IAS 10 'Events After the Reporting
        Period' 27, 216–19, 364–5, 501
    illustrative financial statements
        458–74, 480–91, 495–501, 507–17,
        526–605
    intangible assets 418–19, 459, 463,
        551–60

objectives
    auditors 1–6, 26–33, 79, 121–2, 127,
        221–3, 231–2, 249–50, 287–8,
        321–33, 454–5, 607
    financial statements 299–301
    quality controls 323
objectivity requirements
    see also conflicts of interest
    auditors 15, 16, 40–3, 322–33
observance procedures
    see also evidence . . .
    concepts 59, 92–3, 146–7
off-balance sheet transactions 54,
    378–82, 602–5
offsetting, concepts 357
oil and gas assets, IFRS for SMEs 311
omissions 16–23, 26–33, 121–6
opening balances 10, 86, 169–72, 274–7,
    309–10
    ISA 510 (redrafted) Initial Audit
        Engagements — Opening Balances'
        10, 86, 169–72, 274–7
    lack of supporting evidence 170–2,
        274–7
opening paragraphs, auditors' reports
    257–63
operating activities, statements of cash
    flow for the period 360–2, 458, 480,
    507–8, 520–6, 593–4
operating leases 54, 118–19, 377–82,
    442, 460, 463–4, 466, 472, 484,
    497, 500, 509–17, 589–90
    definition 377, 442, 497
    IAS 17 'Leases' 303, 314, 377–82, 442
operating segments 162–3, 346–7,
    462–3, 542–5
    see also segment information
    definition 162, 347
    IFRS 8 'Operating Segments' 162–3,
        307, 346–7, 462–3
operational effectiveness, internal control
    systems 127–34, 137–40, 249–52
operational risk, concepts 107–8
options 349–51, 424–7, 474, 522–42,
    570, 578–86
    see also derivatives
    Black–Scholes pricing method 474,
        581
    IFRS 9 'Financial Instruments'
        349–51
oral communications with the client
    70–8, 233–5, 237
other information
    definition 279–80
    ISA 720 (redrafted) 'The Auditor's
        Responsibility in Relation to Other
        Financial Information in Documents
        Containing Audited Financial
        Statements' 11, 77, 270, 279–82
'other matter' paragraphs 10, 11, 215,
    262, 269–71, 295, 607–15
    illustrative auditors' reports 607–15
    ISA 706 (revised and redrafted)
        'Emphasis of Matter Paragraphs and
        Other Matter(s) Paragraphs in the
        Independent Auditor's Report' 10,
        11, 263, 269–71, 607, 608–9

outsourced functions
  concepts 135–40, 197, 251–2
  ISA 402 (revised and redrafted) 'Audit
    Considerations Relating to an Entity
    Using a Third Party Service
    Organisation' 135–40, 197
over-the-counter (OTC) derivatives
  569
overrider provisions 117–18
Oz Communications Inc. 557

Palbarro Inc. 193–4
Parbralli Engineering Limited,
  illustrative financial statements
  475–91
parent companies 2, 193, 203–11, 240,
  310–11, 397–9, 405–10, 511–12,
  518–605, 613–14
  see also related parties; subsidiaries
partial acquisitions, IFRS 3 'Business
  Combinations' 341–2
participating preference shares 405–10
passwords 104–5
patents 435, 463, 482, 484–5, 530–42,
  554–60, 571, 609
payables 441–2, 449–50, 457, 461–2,
  467, 470, 472, 478, 479–80,
  488–91, 495–501, 506–17, 519–605
  audit tests 441–2
  illustrative financial statements 457,
    461–2, 467, 470, 472, 479–80,
    488–91, 495–501, 506–17, 519–605
PAYE 443
payments in advance, revenue
  recognition 57
payroll *see* employee wages and salaries
pension schemes 116–19, 151–2, 191–2,
  315, 384–7, 396–7, 460–1, 464,
  469, 483–4, 497, 530–42, 546–50,
  592
  see also defined benefit . . . ; defined
    contribution . . . ; employee benefits;
    retirement benefits
  IAS 19 'Employee Benefits' 262,
    384–7
  Nokia Corporation 546–50, 592
  types 384–6, 460, 469, 546
percentage of completion method 366–8,
  527–42, 545–6
performance issues, quality controls
  321–33
performance materiality, concepts
  122–6
performance reviews, control
  environment 103–4
performance shares, Nokia Corporation
  581–3, 587–8
period of review, going concern
  consideration 223, 355–6
'pervasive', concepts 266, 316
PEST analysis 97–8
petty cash, audit tests 440–1
physical concept of capital 304–5
physical controls environment 104–5,
  158–60
Placebo Chemicals Inc. 66
Plum Ventures Inc. 553–4

political/charitable donations 450, 476,
  502–3
post-date events *see* subsequent events
post-employment benefits
  definition 384
  IAS 19 'Employee Benefits' 383–7
preconditions, audit engagements 35–6,
  38, 292
preference shares 404, 405–10
prepayments 466, 487, 499, 514, 519,
  555–60
'present fairly' IFRS requirements
  concepts 4, 16, 32, 172, 267–8, 614–15
  definition 4, 614–15
present values 422–3, 467, 547–8
presentation of financial statements
  221–2, 299–305, 351–8, 526
  Framework for the Preparation and
    Presentation of Financial
    Statements (IASB) 299–305
  IAS 1 'Presentation of Financial
    Statements' 221–2, 351–8, 526–42
presentational currency, IAS 21 'The
  Effects of Changes in Foreign
  Exchange Rates' 390, 529–42
price quotations, fair value 198–9
price risk 470–1, 597–8
principal auditors
  concepts 239–48
  definition 239
principal/agent sellers, revenue
  recognition 58–9
prior-period financial information
  analytical procedures 175, 176–7
  comparative information 273–7
  errors 363–4
products and services, going concern
  considerations 221–30, 355
professional accountants, Code of Ethics
  for Professional Accountants 15–23,
  39–43, 321–33
professional competence and due care
  requirements, auditors 15, 16, 17,
  19–20, 39–43, 240–2, 249–52,
  321–33
profit and loss accounts *see* income
  statements
profit-making contracts, IAS 11
  'Construction Contracts' 366–8
projected misstatements, concepts
  142–4, 185–9
Projected Unit Credit Method, defined
  benefit pension schemes 384–6, 387
'proof in total' analytical procedures,
  concepts 152–3, 175–6, 179
property, plant and equipment 231, 318,
  374–7, 436, 457, 459–60, 462, 466,
  482–3, 486–91, 496–501, 519,
  531–42, 553, 554–60, 563–5
  see also depreciation; non-current
    assets
  cost/revaluation models 73, 231, 312,
    318, 375, 376, 482–3, 555–7
  IAS 16 'Property, Plant and
    Equipment' 303–4, 374–7, 436
  Nokia Corporation 519, 531–42, 553,
    554–60, 563–5

provisions 26–7, 133, 191, 213–14, 370,
  415–17, 442–3, 462, 495, 500–1,
  506–17, 519, 533–42, 571–2, 586–7
  audit tests 442–3
  bad debts 191, 213–14, 370, 519,
    533–42, 571–2, 586–7
  definition 415
  IAS 37 'Provisions, Contingent
    Liabilities and Contingent Assets'
    26–7, 133, 150, 161, 216–17, 303,
    415–17, 442–3
  illustrative audit tests 442–3
  Nokia Corporation 533–42, 571–2,
    586–7
prudence concept 303
public accountability, definition 307–8
public interest entities 82
purchase day books 148
put options 526–7

Qualcomm 571, 587, 589
qualifications, auditors 2, 16, 17, 20, 242,
  322–33
qualified opinions 27–33, 65–6, 68, 139,
  170–2, 210–11, 226–30, 231,
  236–7, 258–63, 265–8, 275–7, 295,
  330–3, 610–15
  definition 261, 266
  illustrative auditors' reports 275–6,
    610–15
qualitative characteristics of financial
  statements 301–5
quality controls 7, 10, 11, 19, 39–43,
  45–8, 85–90, 154–5, 251–2,
  321–33
  see also Code of Ethics for
    Professional Accountants
  'cold' file reviews 19, 43, 154–5,
    331–2
  complaints about auditors 332–3
  concepts 39–43, 45–8, 85, 321–33
  continuing audits 40, 321–33
  engagement performance 321–33
  engagement teams 40–1, 88–90, 93–4,
    321–33
  ethics 15–23, 39–43, 85, 170, 244–5,
    321–33, 454, 493, 504, 607, 608,
    611, 613, 615
  'hot' file reviews 19, 43, 154–5, 327,
    332
  human resources 321–33
  illustration 323–33
  ISA 220 (redrafted) 'Quality Control
    for an Audit of Financial
    Statements' 10, 39–43, 85, 240, 247
  ISQC 1 (redrafted) 'Quality Control
    for Firms that Perform Audits and
    Reviews of Financial Statements,
    and Other Assurance and Related
    Service Engagements' 7, 11, 39–43,
    48, 321–33
  leadership responsibilities within audit
    firms 321–33
  monitoring needs 321–33
  objectives 323
  performance issues 321–33
  reviews 19, 41, 42–3, 322–33

random statistical sampling, concepts 183–5
ratio analysis 175, 178–9, 186–7, 280
ratio error-projection method, concepts 186–7
'reasonable assurance' reference
see also audit engagements; auditors' reports
concepts 3, 123–6, 145–55
definition 3, 123
'reasonable skill, care and caution' duties 1–2, 16, 40–3
reasonableness tests *see* 'proof in total' analytical procedures
recalculations
see also 'proof in total' analytical procedures
evidence sources 146–7, 175–6
receivables 55–61, 98–9, 131–4, 165–7, 181–9, 308, 420–7, 439–40, 457, 461–2, 466, 470–2, 475, 478–80, 487–91, 494–501, 505–17, 519–605
see also circularisation . . . ; trade receivables
audit tests 165–7, 181–9, 439–40
factoring agreements 98–9
IAS 39 'Financial Instruments: Recognition and Measurement' 310–11, 420–7, 565–9
illustrative audit tests 439–40
illustrative financial statements 457, 461–2, 466, 470–2, 478–80, 487–91, 494–501, 505–17, 519–605
opening balances 170–2
schedules 439–40, 470–1
reclassifications, IFRS 9 'Financial Instruments' 349–51
recoverable amount 375, 412–15, 528–42, 551–3
see also impairment of assets
definition 412–13
IAS 36 'Impairment of Assets' 375, 412–15
rectification costs, IAS 11 'Construction Contracts' 367–8
recurring audits 128–9, 148, 274–7, 321–33
evidence generation requirements 128–9, 148, 274–7
tests of controls 128–9
redrafted/revised versions' overview, ISAs 7–13
reducing balance depreciation method 363, 482, 509
refusals by management
amended financial statements 280–1
external confirmations 166–7
going concern principle 229–30
summary financial statements 292
written representations 236–7
Registrar of Companies 206, 277, 433–4
regulations 2–6, 10–11, 18–23, 26–33, 39–43, 63–8, 82, 83–4, 103, 106, 116–19, 129, 139, 150, 215–19, 235, 260, 279–82, 325–33, 372, 453–5, 476–8, 491–501, 503–5, 509, 511, 607–15

see also company law
characteristics of non-compliance 67
communications 67–8, 83–4, 325–33
ISA 250 (redrafted) 'The Auditor's Responsibilities Related to Laws and Regulations in an Audit of Financial Statements' 10, 63–8, 237
non-compliance 63–8, 83–4, 107, 139–40, 210–11
rights/duties to report non-compliance 67–8, 83–4, 139–40, 210–11
types 63–5
regulators, communications 67–8, 83–4, 143–4
related parties 8, 10, 96, 119, 150, 203–11, 233, 235–7, 315, 392–6, 434, 464, 469, 490–1, 501, 516, 542–605
see also associates; groups; joint ventures; subsidiaries
audit procedures 205–6
audit tests 434
auditors' opinions 210–11
auditors' reports 210–11
concepts 203–11, 233, 235–7, 315, 392–3
controlling parties 208–11
definition 392–3
directors 203–11, 392–6, 434, 464, 516, 590–2
disclosures 75, 150, 203, 207–11, 233, 302, 392–6, 434, 464, 469, 490–1, 501, 516
evidence generation requirements 203–11
FRS 8 'Related Party Disclosures' 434
IAS 24 'Related Party Disclosures' 75, 119, 150, 203, 233, 302, 392–6, 464, 490–1, 501
illustrations 204–5, 434
ISA 550 (revised and redrafted) 'Related Parties' 8, 10, 96, 203–11, 237
material misstatements 203–11
types 392–3, 501
written representations 208–11, 233, 235–7
relevance qualitative characteristic of financial statements 301–5
reliability qualitative characteristic of financial statements 301–5
remuneration committees 26, 451–3, 455, 468
rendering of services, revenue recognition 382–3, 529–42
rents 177–8, 207
repayable grants, IAS 20 'Accounting for Government Grants and Disclosure of Government Assistance' 388–9
reperformed reconciliations
see also evidence . . .
evidence sources 146–7
reportable segments
definition 162–3, 347
IFRS 8 'Operating Segments' 162–3, 307, 347, 462–3

reporting the substance of transactions 55–6, 317
research and development costs 95, 313, 417–18, 449, 460–2, 465, 496, 518, 530–42, 560
IAS 38 'Intangible Assets' 417–18, 462
SSAP 13 'Accounting for Research and Development' 313
reserves 433–4, 449–50, 456–7, 468–9, 473–4, 479, 485, 490, 495–501, 505–17, 519–605
audit tests 433–4
Nokia Corporation 572–4
resignations, auditors 325, 327
restricted shares, Nokia Corporation 583–4
restructuring costs 103, 537, 550, 586–7
retained earnings 121, 520
retirement benefits 396–7, 460–1, 483–4, 497, 530–42, 592, 612
see also employee benefits; pension schemes
IAS 26 'Accounting and Reporting by Retirement Benefit Plans' 396–7
retrospective application of IFRSs, IFRS for SMEs 310–11
return on capital, definition 474
revaluations 73, 231, 312, 314, 318, 335, 353–8, 362–4, 375, 376, 418–20, 479, 480, 482–3, 486–91, 509, 555–7
revenue 26–7, 49–50, 53–4, 55–61, 98–102, 131–4, 350, 362–4, 366–8, 382–3, 461, 462–3, 478, 483–4, 494, 496, 497, 502, 505, 509–17, 518, 527–605
analysis illustration 462–3, 483
earnings management 49–50
IAS 18 'Revenue' 55–6, 303, 350, 382–3, 527–42
revenue recognition 53–4, 55–61, 315, 350, 362–4, 366–8, 382–3, 461, 462–3, 496, 527–605
bill and hold arrangements 57–8
extended warranties 58, 191
fraud 53–4, 55–61
IAS 8 'Accounting Policies, Changes in Accounting Estimates and Errors' 362–4, 538–42
IAS 11 'Construction Contracts' 56–7, 366–8, 527–42
IAS 18 'Revenue' 55–6, 303, 350, 382–3, 527–42
payments in advance 57
principal/agent sellers 58–9
procedures 59–61
'right to consideration' (critical events) 56–7, 315
rights of return 58
UITF Abstract 40 56–7, 315
review engagements
see also negative assurance
definition 3
reviews
analytical procedures 175–9
audit documentation 154–5, 329–33

reviews (*cont.*)
  audit planning 88–90
  estimation techniques 192–3
  financial performance 98–9
  quality controls 19, 41, 42–3,
    322–33
revisions, risk assessments 110–11
Revolving Credit Facility, Nokia
  Corporation 601–2
'right to consideration' (critical events),
  revenue recognition 56–7, 315
'right of use' model, leases 380–2
rights issues 217–18, 406–10
rights of return, revenue recognition 58
risk 2, 4–6, 8–13, 28–33, 37–8, 47,
    50–61, 64, 80–1, 86, 87–8, 91–119,
    346, 354, 449, 462, 470–1, 475,
    496–7, 552–3, 594–605
  see also credit . . . ; hazard . . . ; interest
    rate . . . ; liquidity . . . ; market . . . ;
    price . . .
  attitudes 114–15
  business risks 97–103, 113–19
  change of circumstances 103
  control risk 29–30, 100–1, 108–9, 112,
    128–34, 179, 183, 188–9
  detection risk 28–30, 33, 50–61,
    107–8, 112, 179, 182–3, 188–9
  inherent risk 29–30, 107–8, 112, 179,
    183, 188
  Nokia Corporation 594–605
  types 29–30, 97–103, 107–8, 113–19,
    470–2, 594–605
risk assessments 4–6, 8–13, 28–33, 37–8,
    47, 50–61, 64, 80–1, 86, 87–8,
    91–119, 125–6, 127–34, 160–3,
    169–72, 174–9, 185–9, 193–4,
    198–9, 203–11, 594–605
  approaches 106–8
  audit documentation 110–11, 134
  balance sheets 106–7, 112
  communications 111–12
  concepts 4–6, 28–33, 50–61, 91–119,
    125–6, 127–34, 198–9
  fraud 50–61, 166–7
  human resources 101–2
  inquiry considerations 91–2
  ISA 315 (redrafted) 'Obtaining an
    Understanding of the Entity and its
    Environment and Assessing the
    Risk of Material Misstatements'
    4–5, 10, 28–32, 47, 51–2, 64, 80–1,
    86, 87–8, 91–119, 127, 135–6, 192,
    196–7, 204
  ISA 330 (redrafted) 'The Auditor's
    Procedures in Response to Assessed
    Risks' 10, 32, 88, 101–2, 110,
    127–34, 138, 193–4
  material misstatements 4–5, 10,
    28–32, 37–8, 47, 51–2, 64, 80–1,
    86, 87–8, 91–119, 125–6, 127–34,
    160–3, 169–72, 174–9, 185–9,
    193–4, 203–11
  processes 102–3
  revisions 110–11
  specific consideration factors 95,
    181

systems-based approaches 106–7, 112
third party service organisations
    135–40
risk management 4–6, 32–3, 127–34,
    594–605
  concepts 4–6, 127–34
  insurance policies 605
  Nokia Corporation 594–605
risk policies 594–605
risk-based auditing, concepts 2, 4–6,
    8–13, 107–8, 112
Roche Inc. 96
royalties 382–3, 586, 609

safeguards, Code of Ethics for
    Professional Accountants 17–23,
    325–33
sale of goods 55–61, 98–102, 382–3,
    462–3, 529–42
  see also invoices; revenue recognition
sales day books 148
sales ledgers 131–4
sales order cycle, tests of controls 129–34
sampling 1–6, 9, 10, 123–4, 142–4,
    152–5, 179, 181–9
  definition 1, 153, 181–2
  error projections 125, 186–9
  evaluations 185–9
  illustrations 181–2, 184
  ISA 530 (redrafted) 'Audit Sampling'
    9, 10, 181–9
  materiality factors 188–9
  selection considerations 183–5
  size considerations 182–3, 188–9
  sub-populations 182
  techniques 183–5
sampling risk
  see also detection . . .
  concepts 179, 182–9
  definition 182, 188
sceptical attitudes 30, 54–5, 60–1, 101–2
schedules, receivables 439–40, 470–1
scope of auditors' reports 8, 21–2, 32,
    36–8, 66, 68, 166, 170, 236–7,
    257–63, 265–8, 324–33, 607, 609,
    610, 611–12, 613
secured debts, illustrative financial
    statements 489–90, 514
segment information
  see also operating segments;
    reportable segments
  evidence generation requirements 157,
    162–3
  ISA 501 (redrafted) 'Audit Evidence
    Regarding Specific Financial
    Statement Account Balances and
    Disclosures' 157
  Nokia Corporation 542–5
segregation of duties, control
    environment 100–5, 114–15
self-interest threats, concepts 17–19, 21
self-review threats, concepts 6, 17–19, 23
sensitivity analysis, concepts 355, 470,
    597–8
service organisations *see* third party
    service organisations
SFAS 109 'Income Taxes' 370, 374

share capital and reserves 121–2, 207,
    277, 319, 433–4, 456–7, 468,
    473–4, 479, 485, 490, 495–501,
    506–17, 519–605
  see also capital . . . ; equity . . .
  audit tests 433–4
  IFRS for SMEs 319
  illustrative financial statements 456–7,
    468, 479, 485, 490, 495–501,
    506–17, 519–605
  Nokia Corporation 576–7
share consolidations, IAS 33 'Earnings
    Per Share' 406, 408–10
share options 337–9, 452–3, 459, 468,
    473–4, 522–42, 577–88
share premium and reserves
  IFRS for SMEs 319
  illustrative financial statements 468–9,
    523–6
share splits, IAS 33 'Earnings Per Share'
    406, 408–10
share-based payments 191–2, 311–12,
    337–9, 446, 452–3, 459, 468,
    473–4, 522–42, 577–86
  IFRS 2 'Share-Based Payment' 337–9,
    446, 526–42
  illustrative financial statements 446,
    452–3, 459, 468, 473–4, 522–42,
    577–86
  Nokia Corporation 522–42, 577–88
  types 337
shareholders
  communications 70–8
  pressures 98–9
shareholders' funds, illustrative financial
    statements 457, 479, 485–91,
    506–17, 519–605
short-term employee benefits
  definition 384
  IAS 19 'Employee Benefits' 383–7
'should'/'shall' changes, Clarified ISAs
    12, 13, 31–3
significant difficulties
  communications 9, 10, 69–78, 210–11
  concepts 9, 10, 42, 109–10, 116–19,
    210–11
  definition 73
  ISA 260 (revised and redrafted)
    'Significant Difficulties' 9, 10,
    69–78, 111–12, 126, 247, 330–1
significant findings, definition 70–1
significant influence
  definition 399, 527–8
  IAS 28 'Investments in Associates'
    399–400
significant matters
  audit documentation 47–8, 61, 110–11
  fair value 199–200
significant risks, concepts 109–10,
    116–19
signing processes, auditors' reports 43,
    213–15, 257–63
single financial statements, concepts 11,
    287–90
size considerations
  comparative information 273
  sampling 182–3, 188–9

Small Entity Ltd, illustrative financial statements 492–501
small groups, auditing thresholds' table 3
small and medium-sized entities (SMEs)
auditing thresholds' table 3
concepts 307–19
definition 307
FRSSE 308–19, 354, 356, 372, 493–501, 611–12
IFRS for SMEs 307–19
Smyth Industries Inc. 207–8
solicitors 20
Southern Inc. 224
special purpose frameworks
auditors' opinions 284–5, 295–6
ISA 800 (revised and redrafted) 'Special Considerations — Audits of Financial Statements Prepared in Accordance with Special Purpose Frameworks' 11, 283–5
specific consideration factors 10, 95, 157–63, 181, 236–7, 239–48, 283–5, 321–33
ISA 501 (redrafted) 'Audit Evidence Regarding Specific Financial Statement Account Balances and Disclosures' 10, 157–63, 237
ISA 600 (revised and redrafted) 'The Audit of Group Financial Statements', groups 7–8, 10, 48, 239–48
written representations 236–7
'split accounting', IAS 39 'Financial Instruments: Recognition and Measurement' 349, 351
SSAP 4 'Accounting for Government Grants' 372–3
SSAP 9 'Stocks and Work-in-Progress' 56, 315–16
SSAP 13 'Accounting for Research and Development' 313
SSAP 19 'Accounting for Investment Properties' 312, 436
SSAP 21 'Accounting for Hire Purchase and Lease Contracts' 314, 379
stakeholders, auditing requirements 2–3, 5–6, 70–8
Standard & Poor's 602
statements of cash flow for the period
direct/indirect methods 360–2
Framework for the Preparation and Presentation of Financial Statements (IASB) 300–5
headings 360–2
IAS 1 'Presentation of Financial Statements' 351–8
IAS 7 'Statement of Cash Flows' 359–62
IAS 34 'Interim Financial Reporting' 411–12
illustrative financial statements 300–1, 458, 480, 507, 520–6
Nokia Corporation 520–6, 593–4
statements of changes in equity for the period
IAS 1 'Presentation of Financial Statements' 351–8

IAS 34 'Interim Financial Reporting' 411–12
illustrative financial statements 456
statements of comprehensive income *see* income statements
statements of financial position *see* balance sheets
statements of total recognised gains and losses, illustrative financial statements 479, 491, 505, 534, 572–6
straight-line depreciation method 363, 377, 460–1, 509, 531–42
stratified statistical sampling, concepts 183–5
'stress-testing' concepts 355
structural changes, Clarified ISAs 11–13, 31
sub-populations, sampling 182
subsequent events 10, 147–8, 150, 194–5, 200–1, 213–19, 235, 243–4, 296, 364–5, 474, 501, 503
see also adjusting . . . ; non-adjusting . . .
audit procedures 213–19
definition 213
estimation techniques 194–5, 200–1
groups 243–4
IAS 10 'Events After the Reporting Period' 27, 213, 216–19, 364–5, 501
illustrations 214, 216–18
ISA 560 (redrafted) 'Subsequent Events' 10, 200, 213–19, 237, 270, 296
subsidiaries 203–11, 239–48, 316, 392–6, 397–9, 474, 499, 501–17, 518–605
see also parent companies; related parties
associates contrast 399
definition 316, 398, 399
FRS 2 'Accounting for Subsidiary Undertakings' 316
IAS 24 'Related Party Disclosures' 203, 392–6
IAS 27 'Consolidated and Separate Financial Statements' 2, 193, 240, 310–11, 397–9, 541–2
Nokia Corporation 518–605
substantive procedures 5, 30, 54–5, 106–7, 110–11, 112, 127–34, 173–9, 185–6, 188–9, 327, 329–33
see also analytical . . . ; evidence . . .
categories 131
definition 5, 127, 130–1, 173
evidence generation requirements 110–11, 127–34
timing of tests 131–2, 174–5, 177–8
sufficiency/appropriateness evaluations, evidence generation requirements 27–8, 133–4, 145–55, 225–6
summary financial statements
audit procedures 292–3
auditor association 297
auditors' reports 293–5
definition 291

ISA 810 'Engagements to Report on Summary Financial Statements' 11, 291–8
refusals by management 292
timing factors 296
unaudited information 296
swaps 424–7, 534, 570
SWAT analysis 97–8
Symbian Ltd 524, 555–7
see also Nokia . . .
systemic (interval) statistical sampling, concepts 183–5
systems-based approaches, risk assessments 106–7, 112

T-Systems Traffic GmbH 554
tax credits 373, 465
tax returns 444
taxes 21, 23, 53, 55–6, 300–1, 315, 368–74, 435, 443–4, 456, 461, 465, 467–8, 484–5, 488, 494–5, 496, 498, 500–1, 502, 505–7, 509, 511–17, 518–20, 536–42, 554–60, 561–2, 585
see also corporation . . . ; current . . . ; deferred . . . ; income . . .
audit tests 444
IAS 12 'Income Taxes' 368–74
illustrative financial statements 300–1, 456, 461, 465, 467–8, 478, 484–5, 488, 494–5, 498, 500–1, 502, 505–7, 511–17, 518, 536–42
VAT 119, 173, 433, 435, 440, 441, 461, 496, 500, 509, 514
termination benefits
definition 387
IAS 19 'Employee Benefits' 383–7
tests of controls
see also evidence . . . ; internal control systems
concepts 5, 107, 127–34, 138–40, 185–7, 328–33
definition 5, 107, 127
extent 130
recurring audits 128–9
sales order cycle 129–34
third party service organisations 138–9
theoretical ex-rights price, rights issues 407–10
third party confirmations *see* external confirmations
third party service organisations
accounting records 139
auditors' opinions 139–40
fraud 139–40
inventories 159
ISA 402 (revised and redrafted) 'Audit Considerations Relating to an Entity Using a Third Party Service Organisation' 10, 135–40, 197
material misstatements 138–40
risk assessments 135–40
tests of controls 138–9
type 1 and 2 reports 136, 137–8
types 135–6
threats, Code of Ethics for Professional Accountants 6, 17–23, 325–33

thresholds' table, auditing 2–3
timing differences, deferred taxes 369–70
timing factors
  analytical procedures 131–2, 174–5, 177–8
  auditing 329
  substantive procedures 131–2, 174–5, 177–8
  summary financial statements 296
title paragraph, auditors' reports 257–63
trade payables 441–2, 457, 461–2, 467, 470, 472, 479–80, 488–91, 495–501, 506–17, 519–605
  audit tests 441–2
  illustrative financial statements 457, 461–2, 467, 470, 472, 479–80, 488–91, 495–501, 506–17, 519–605
trade receivables 49–50, 131–4, 165–7, 181–9, 439–40, 457, 461–2, 466, 470–2, 479–80, 487–91, 494–501, 505–17, 519–605
  see also circularisation . . . ; receivables
  audit tests 165–7, 181–9, 439–40
  earnings management 49–50
  illustrative financial statements 457, 461–2, 466, 470–2, 479–80, 487–91, 494–501, 505–17, 519–605
  opening balances 170–2
training and development activities, CPD 18–19, 323–4, 332
translation differences, Nokia Corporation 575–6
treasury risk 595
trivial misstatements, concepts 141–4, 185–6, 235
Trolltech ASA 557
true and fair views 4, 16, 141, 172, 260, 281, 329–33, 453–4, 476, 477–8, 492, 493, 503–4, 607–15
turnover
  see also revenue . . .
  auditing thresholds' table 3
  definition 55

Twango 560
type 1 and 2 reports, third party service organisations 136, 137–8

UITF Abstract 40, revenue recognition 56–7, 315
UK 86, 193–4, 197–8, 244, 259–60, 270, 281, 309, 310–19, 335–6, 345, 354, 356, 369–70, 454, 474–517, 545, 546, 557, 594, 607–15
  Financial Reporting Council 354
  GAAP 86, 193–4, 197–8, 244, 270, 281, 309, 310–19, 335–6, 345, 356, 369–70, 474–517, 607–15
  Nokia Corporation 545, 546, 557, 594
uncorrected misstatements, concepts 142–4
underlying assumptions, financial statements 301–5
understandability qualitative characteristic of financial statements 301–5
unqualified opinions 27–33, 75–6, 258–63, 330–3, 607–15
  definition 20
  illustrative auditors' reports 607–15
unquoted equity instruments, valuations 350–1
unutilised tax losses, deferred tax assets 370–1
USA
  FASB 54, 314, 378–9, 382
  Nokia Corporation 545, 553–4, 557, 560, 584, 594, 601–5

Vadher Inc. 198
valuations
  fair value 337–42, 343–4, 348–51, 366–8, 397, 412–15, 420–7, 429–31, 459, 472, 474, 519–20, 522–42, 551–61, 565–9, 571–2
  inventories 150, 157–63, 170–2, 235, 315–16, 358–9, 365, 438, 461–2, 482–3, 496, 509, 531–42, 571–2

value in use
  definition 412–13
  IAS 36 'Impairment of Assets' 412–15
Value-at-Risk (VaR) 597–8
Vantis PLC 28
variance-covariance methodology 597–8
VAT 119, 173, 433, 435, 440, 441, 461, 496, 500, 509, 514
Vivento Technical Services 557

warehouses, control environment 104–5, 158–60
warranties 58, 191, 537–42, 586–7
weighted average number of shares 405–10, 518
  definition 406–7
  IAS 33 'Earnings Per Share' 405–10
Westhead Enterprises Limited 197–8
work-in-progress (WIP) 56–61, 191, 438–9, 457, 461, 466, 571
working papers *see* audit documentation
written representations
  see also letters of representation
  audit documentation 233–7
  concepts 10, 74–6, 144, 148–50, 208–11, 224–6, 231–7
  definition 232
  evidence generation requirements 232–3
  fraud 235–7
  going concern principle 224–6, 235
  illustrations 231–2, 233–5
  ISA 580 (revised and redrafted) 'Written Representations' 10, 231–7
  limitations 231–2
  refusals by management 236–7
  related parties 208–11, 233, 235–7
  reliability concerns 232, 233, 236–7
  specific consideration factors 236–7
  uncorrected misstatements 144

year-end counts, inventories 104–5, 158–60, 437–9, 610–11

Index compiled by Terry Halliday